POLAND,
WHAT HAVE I TO DO WITH THEE...

RAFAEL F. SCHARF

POLAND,
WHAT HAVE I TO DO WITH THEE...
Essays without Prejudice

FUNDACJA JUDAICA
KRAKÓW

The publication of this book was funded by
The Ministry of Culture and the National Heritage, Warsaw
The Governor's Office, Cracow
The Municipality of Cracow
The American Society for Jewish Heritage in Poland, New York
The Evangelical Church in Rhineland, Düsseldorf
The Stefan Batory Foundation, Warsaw

Wydanie książki było możliwe dzięki pomocy finansowej
Ministerstwa Kultury i Dziedzictwa Narodowego
Wojewody Małopolskiego
Gminy miasta Kraków
Amerykańskiego Towarzystwa na rzecz Żydowskiego Dziedzictwa w Polsce
z Nowego Jorku
Krajowego Kościoła Ewangelickiego w Nadrenii-Westfalii w Düsseldorfie
Fundacji im. S. Batorego w Warszawie

Editor of the English texts Redaktor tekstów angielskich	Michael Jacobs
Editor of the Polish texts Redaktor tekstów polskich	Jerzy Lohman
Technical editor Redakcja techniczna	Wanda Lohman
Cover design Projekt okładki	Anna Gałuszka
Cover dtp Montaż elektroniczny okładki	Piotr Szylkiewicz
Cover printing Druk okładki	Małopolska Poligrafia

ISBN 83-7052-734-5
TAiWPN UNIVERSITAS

Printed by the Jagiellonian University Printing House in Cracow

Contents

Contents

Foreword

Who on earth, today, walking along Dietla Street in Cracow, can still recall any of its former inhabitants? They have virtually all perished, for Dietla Street, with its avenue of trees, was the very heart of the Jewish quarter. The only person, perhaps, who recalls not just one but all of those people, is Rafael Scharf, a pupil of the Hebrew High School, in his youth an ardent Zionist, who on his way from Poland to Palestine paused in London, fell in love, married. The outbreak of war stopped him in his stride... And so he took upon himself the role of guardian of Cracovian and Jewish memory, the role, as it were, of the last witness, who strives to record this Jewish-Cracovian particularity. Like Gebirtig in his songs, Scharf bears live, authentic testimony to the character of that city and its community, which filled those walls to the roof, in a state of more or less peaceful cohabitation with their Polish co-citizens.

It would seem that nothing had predestined Scharf for that role. He grew up in a moderately prosperous family; his father — born in Oswiecim — established himself in Cracow, within the milieu which, like the majority of the population, was observant of religion and tradition. The hero of his youth was the radical Zionist leader, Jabotinsky, an allegiance to whom, if pursued to the extreme, could lead to becoming a "terrorist." "I was not all that far from it," he says today half in jest. He was saved from this fate by common sense and, I think, by an innate good nature. He settled in London, but only, as it were, with a part of his being, and kept on writing articles on Israel and the Diaspora, particularly the Polish part of it. He was among the first who — the moment it became politically practicable — devoted himself to the recovery and preservation of the Jewish-Cracovian past, to bridge-building between Jews and Poles, to finding a language in which rational dialogue between the two peoples could be conducted.

What is so specific about this memory of Cracow? Memoirs, recollections, reminiscences abound. The picture which emerges is diverse, but it seems to me that the Jewish community in Cracow went further than any other in embracing Polish culture. Whilst it retained its religious beliefs and customs, it opened itself up to contemporary currents and participated in the cultural life of the city. Historical memory must have echoed in that process, the memory of Esterka and Kazimierz, the king and the city named after him. Also the ethos of the Habsburg Empire, where ethnic tensions were lessened since the interest of the State was paramount and took precedence over the particularities of its many nationalities.

Yet another mechanism operated here — the search for religious truth, and later the search for all truth; intellectual pursuits enjoyed special status in the Jewish community. The scholar was rated above the priest, who was merely a leader, an activist. "This ethos, in vestigial form, was maintained," writes Scharf. One might note that it was also maintained in the Christian community in Cracow. That city, derided and mocked for its miserly provincialism and its pretentious claims to be "historically superior," had a scale of values on which artists and intellectuals were held in higher esteem than traders and business-people, no matter how prosperous. Was not the moral leadership of Cracow, over the years, in the hands of the aristocracy, the clergy and university teachers? As Scharf reminds us, Cracovians were used to seeing at the head of ceremonial processions, this odd trinity: Archbishop Sapieha supported by the town's Mayor Kapellner-Kaplicki and the commander of the garrison, General Mond, the only Jew of that rank in the Polish army. One could thus surmise that the spirit in the town was not anti-Semitic.

Did this mean, however, that the Jew was accepted and treated as equal, part of the fabric of Polish life? No, that was far from being the case. As Scharf shows and emphasises, the lives of the Polish and the Jewish communities ran on separate tracks.

Scharf's father, in common with the other inhabitants of Dietla Street and that whole district, had virtually no social contacts outside Jewish circles. Even more separate were the Jewish workers, craftsmen, stall-holders, middlemen. But with time they too were not untouched by outside influences. As the communities came closer to each other, so also the tension and mutual resentments grew. Knowledge of the wider culture fuelled bigger aspirations and led to internal conflict — as Scharf illustrates by his own example. He immersed himself in Polish literature, adopted — like so many others — Polish models, patterns of thought and behaviour, even in politics (was not Jabotinsky an admirer of Pilsudski?). At the same time he felt rejected, was pained to see the growing hostility, resented the assumed superiority of his Polish colleagues. He felt that great changes were in the air, a premonition of a catastrophe, perhaps.

He decided, as a matter of principle, to go to Palestine. But it appeared that he was in no great hurry to get there, because he found it so difficult to part from his parents, friends, Cracow, Europe... His reminiscences are full of mixed feelings: the more he loves Cracow and Poland, the more he is baffled by the growing detestation of the Jew. He could not fathom why the fear of the future (also felt by the Poles) should express itself in the growth of anti-Semitism. His personal life presents a perpetual paradox. How is it that this man who "was never inside a truly Polish home" declares that were he to be stripped of his

Polishness he would feel greatly impoverished? Because "the interwar years, despite the growing impoverishment and the rising tide of anti-Semitism, could be seen as a sort of golden age of Polish Jewry," he affirms.

What an interesting, unusual opinion! One is used to hearing from Jews and non-Jews alike quite a different assessment of that era. But Scharf looks further, deeper than a mere politician or economist does.

As the dominant feature of the interwar Jewish community in Poland he perceives "a degree of spirituality," a belief that "man lives not by bread alone," that irrespective of material conditions man must strive for the realisation of some ideal, however defined; that honest daily life and obedience to God's laws will speed up the coming of the Messiah and give rise to an era of universal justice. Fine words, but also strange... I understand them to mean that in those days, probably as the result of the Zionist idea, many Polish Jews were overcome by the desire for some great renewal, regeneration, improvement and justification of their lives — a desire which found expression in the religious, cultural and political sphere and gave new meaning to Jewish identity. I see here a close analogy with the frame of mind and the climate of the seventies and the eighties in Poland.

And all this transformation was happening in the hearts and minds of men, rather than in their external actions, and was not blemished by egoism and self-interest.

Such are the memories — and dreams — of Rafael Scharf. What a pity that we did not hear and were not sensitive to these voices and longings at the time when they were being uttered and might have borne fruit. The opposite was the case: in those days the lunacy of anti-Semitism was engulfing ever-widening circles and the parting of the ways took ever more painful, more cruel forms. Scharf wants us to recognise and acknowledge that this was not through some fault of the Jews. This modest plea moved me deeply when I first heard it from him some years ago. It enables us to understand and to relive those "Cracow years" which Rafael Scharf brings so vividly before our eyes.

Jan Błoński

Poland, what have I to do with Thee...

A few words of explanation concerning the somewhat unusual form of this book: it was written in Polish and in English, in turns. Thus it reflects accurately the individuality of the author, the dual track of his life, the entanglements of roots. In the course of writing I felt that Polish served me better in describing some periods and themes, English seemed to serve better for others. Subsequently, what I wrote in Polish I translated into English and vice versa. These translations were not always literal: on occasion, when I felt it would be better thus, I departed from the "original," most often when some quotations of Polish poetry would have had little meaning for the English reader, or where I felt that a different style of utterance would be closer to the spirit of the language.

This collection is not conceived as a book with a specific beginning, middle or end, to be read in a prescribed sequence. Its fragments were written at different times, on different occasions, as casual comments, reflections, *pensées*, material for discussion.

I haven't got a clear image of my reader. The majority of those who might have formed the natural readership have perished; a great many of those who survived the cataclysm are also no longer with us. Years have flown past, as is their wont, quickly and imperceptibly; former girlfriends, if lucky, have become grandmothers; the snows of yesteryear have melted.

In Jewish folklore there is a myth that when the Angel of Death comes to do his worst and finds the intended victim preoccupied with something important, like writing a book, he relents, for the time being, and fills in the quota with someone else who appears idle — hence the rabbis always pretend to be so busy (perhaps, subconsciously, I act from a similar motive).

When I was very young, I was in the habit, in the company of adults, of speaking out of turn (some of this appears to have survived till old age). My mother used to cool down my excess of zest: "Do not open your mouth till you think what to say." To which I used to reply with iron, childlike logic: "How am I to know what I think until I've said it?" Such a Cartesian thesis: "I speak, therefore I think — *loquor ergo cogito*."

I have given these pages a title: "Poland, what have I to do with Thee?" an echo of St. John (John 2:4), where Jesus rebukes his mother for urging him to perform a miracle. (This passage has always struck me as not ringing true —

a Jewish boy would not have addressed his mother so arrogantly. In fact, looking at the original Greek τι ἐμοι και σοι γύναι, the passus does lend itself to a much milder translation than the commonly used, brash, "What have I to do with thee, Woman?" or "Your concern, Mother, is not mine.")

I have a need to clarify once and for all (no, not once and for all — only to the next, deeper clarification) what sort of a Pole I am, what my connection with Poland is, how I view Polish matters, the old ones and the current ones, from the perspective of a Jewish émigré. What still moves me, to what have I grown indifferent? I am using the personal pronoun "I" here, but the matter is not about me alone — were it so, I would not have cared to put pen to paper.

I attempt to speak of people of a specific formation. There are many of us, spread across the world, whose identity is not easily defined. The spectrum of Polish Jews, or Jews of Polish origin, is wide and not clear-cut, from the strictly Orthodox to those completely assimilated. There are those who have consciously severed their ties with their country of origin, who want to have nothing to do with it. Others, to whom the labels and the definitions mean little, who have merged with their surroundings, have no need of introspection or stating of position. There are also those who have genuine affection for Poland. All of these groups, with their nuances and shadings, have their conscious and subconscious reasons for relating to these matters thus and not otherwise. The fact that I have the need to delve into some of these issues would point to my position in the spectrum. What additional light I shall be able to throw on these complex matters remains to be seen — I can hardly contain my own curiosity.

I hope this will not sound immodest — I feel I have special qualifications in this area. I was an eyewitness to a singular period of Polish and Jewish history, one of the last still surviving. Soon the field will be open to a different, indirect kind of account and analysis. Our children and grandchildren may want to know how it appeared to us, a future historian might reproach us that we did not leave enough evidence, the passage of time will bring a different perspective. I feel free to speak openly and without constraint and whilst I do so I may rethink some of my own views.

The personal pronoun is the most suspect part of speech. How we relate to the "I" defines our personality. For the sake of objectivity its use should be reduced to the minimum. In the English mode of expression, self-depreciation is commonly acceptable. It is not quite so in America. Before one of my lectures at a conference in New York, my friend who knows the local custom warned me against it. It appears that if you declare in front of your audience that you are not the greatest expert in your subject and your utterance is not the definitive word in the matter, they will take you at your word and wonder why you have invited them to listen to you.

This reminds me of a Jewish anecdote — how on the Day of Atonement, as is the habit, the rabbi steps in front of the Ark, beats his breast and says: "God, forgive me my sins, I am a mere nothing." After him, the head of the community does the same — beats his breast and says: "God forgive me — I am a mere nothing." Then the beadle steps out, beats his breast and says: "God forgive me my sins, I am a mere nothing." Whereupon the head of the community nudges the rabbi and whispers: "Look at him. What cheek, he also fancies himself a nothing!"

In that heartrending lament which the great Polish poet Julian Tuwim wrote in exile, when he first heard the news of what was happening to Jews in Poland, a lament to which he gave the title "We, Polish Jews," there is the following statement: "I am a Pole because I like it that way." Some variation on that theme, for example: "I am a Pole even though I don't like it" or "I am a Pole even though they don't like it" or "I am a Pole because I don't know how to cease to be one" might well serve as a motto for these reflections.

These variants show how complicated is the definition of identity of a Jew of Polish origin. In my case, not as dramatic, of course, as that of Tuwim, the problem has an additional twist. Poles have always taken me for a Jew, Jews for an Englishman, the English for a Pole. I myself, in turn, could say that I look upon England as a wife, on Israel as a lover, on Poland as a stepmother.

This is written half in jest to illustrate the depth of these dilemmas but, in fact, personally I have no difficulties with it. I feel no internal split of any sort. I know perfectly well who I am, irrespective of what others might take me for. I am a Jew, *tout court*, completely, openly and naturally. In contradistinction to this, my "Polishness" does require proofs, and if called upon I could produce them aplenty. The great Polish journalist and essayist, Stefan Kisielewski, has written that "Poland is Catholic not only by faith and tradition. A Pole is a Catholic by temperament, by choice, and most importantly — by his perception of the world." That concept, of course, says nothing to me and of me; an unbridgeable gap separates me from it.

Is it possible to "convert" from being Polish? Consciously, by an act of will, by a declaration of intent, to shed it forever? I think it is possible, particularly if one lives abroad, if one has been wounded by the way many Poles have treated Jews, if one remembers what happened to Jews who lived in Poland — it is possible to turn one's back on it, sever all emotional connection, no longer feel any common bond with that country. Many people within my circle of friends have done just that. I see nothing wrong or unworthy in such an attitude; all I want is for them to show similar tolerance to my attitude. I have lived for over half-a-century outside Poland; nobody in my family speaks Polish, not my wife, not my children, not my grandchildren. I have not taken part in the life of the Polish community in exile, have no input into the Polish heirdom — but do not want to "convert" from my "Polishness." Certain thoughts about Poland drive me to distraction, and many things which I see and remember fill me with aversion — but to "convert"? No.

I am thinking what would be left of me if by some ungodly edict I were to be stripped of all that is Polish in me. First, of the language, which — although somewhat rusty and neglected — remains part of the furniture without which the inner space would be empty; of the poems and verses with which I lull myself to sleep; of the recollection of the landscape, its singular sights and smells. (Janusz Korczak remarked, during his stay in Palestine, that the eucalyptus speaks to him differently from the pine.)

Were one to lose the link with that language and landscape, with the good and not-so-good memories of the common past, and with that part of one's personality which reflects the Polish character (for — contrary to appearances — the long, multifaceted relationship of the Poles and their Jewish co-citizens resulted in some remarkable resemblances) — one would feel bereft, impoverished, incomplete. This Polish facet, or its residue — it is not easy to quantify it — gives life an added dimension. Who of us is so richly endowed as to afford the loss of this heritage?

I must be grateful to fate, not altogether blind, which made me live the greater part of my life in England. England has proved, on the whole, a hospitable land to a stranger (particularly if he is white-skinned) with that civilised lack of curiosity about the neighbour, not prying into his private matters (or parts). There used to be a widespread feeling of superiority with regard to foreigners. Slowly, through frequent contacts with people of different nationalities, the influx of tourists, mass tourism abroad, and also due to a manifest lack of commercial success in a global sense, that feeling of superiority has been knocked out of the English; the pendulum has swung the other way. They have become very self-critical, and thereby also more human and *sympathique*.

It has been a life-enhancing experience to find oneself in the orbit of Anglo-Saxon culture and gain direct access to the treasures of the English language and literature, which are amongst the greatest achievements of the human spirit.

There was a time when I would have given my right arm (or some other part of the anatomy) to speak English without a foreign accent and not to be recognised as a "foreigner" the moment I opened my mouth. I now think that that wish was misplaced, not to say pitiful. I have cured myself of that feeling of inferiority and see that the object of my admiration was not essentially better but only different from me. I have recognised that greater value lies in colourful differentiation than in grey uniformity. Today, perhaps to spite myself, when I have very nearly lost the traces of the foreign accent, I purposely cling to its remnants to sound a bit different from the rest.

It seemed to me, at first, that these recollections were somehow too fragmentary and amounted to little, that all of this took place in a very distant past, before the Flood, the other side of the nightmare. But nothing is ever lost in memory, not even that which we push into the subconscious and try to forget. It only requires a trigger — like, for me, a walk through these little streets of Cracow — to bring it all whirling and bubbling to the surface, forming a continuous flow.

However, I shall restrict myself to talking only about such aspects as throw some light on this period of history, on Jewish society, its features and habits, and shall postpone the merely personal to some later date, *sine die*.

We had, in my time, in Cracow, a rabbi by the name of Szmelkes. He gave "religious instruction" to Jewish students from state schools — that was a part of the compulsory curriculum. A story went round that when he was being engaged to deliver an occasional speech at a wedding or some other festive occasion he would say: "I can offer you a speech for which I charge 150 zlotys, I can offer you a speech for which I charge 100 zlotys. I can also offer you a speech for which I only charge 50 zlotys. But I wouldn't advise you to take the one for 50 zlotys." I have the ambition to serve up something for, say, no less than 100 zlotys.

* * *

There was a time when Yiddish was denied even the dignity of being called a "language" — in the eyes, or rather ears, of the Poles, and also many of the so-called "assimilated" Jews, it was a jargon, gibberish, used by those black-bearded, "sidelocked" Jews, who were no doubt plotting something sinister or casting spells. Those harsh, throaty sounds, accompanied by this wild gesticulation, boded no good.

In fact it is a language whose early forms were created and developed by the Ashkenazi Jews (*ashkenaz* in Hebrew means Germany) inhabiting territories in Upper Rhineland, including towns like Mainz, Worms and Regensburg, who, in the course of their wanderings, had settled in Central and Eastern Europe. Here they further developed the language, enriching it with the vocabulary of the local population.

The dictionary *Der groyser Verterbuch fun der yidisher Sprach* contains 180,000 words. The greater part derives from various German dialects, but Yiddish changes their style, structure, pronunciation and grammar. The second part is drawn from Hebrew sources, that is, from the Old Testament, liturgy and medieval literature. Finally, the third part is taken from the languages of the countries where Jews lived, mainly from Polish, Russian, Ukrainian, Byelorussian. It became the lingua franca of the Jews of Europe, from Holland to Poland, Rumania, Hungary and the Balkan Countries, and was carried across the ocean in the immigrants' luggage to North and South America. It is estimated that on the eve of the outbreak of the Second World War eleven million people spoke Yiddish. The figure diminished dramatically as the result of the extermination of the Jews and also through cultural changes.

There was a time, at the dawn of Zionism and the pioneering effort in Palestine, when Yiddish was considered, and for good reason, to be a threat to the revival of the Hebrew language. The rebirth of Hebrew was, as a matter of principle, to go hand in hand with the rebirth of the Nation in its own Land, with the conquest of the desert, with the breaking away from the way and tradition of the Diaspora.

In that conflict the opposing forces were uneven. Almost everybody spoke or at least understood Yiddish — this was so easy. Very few spoke Hebrew — this was so difficult. For two thousand years Hebrew was a dead language — at the time of Jesus it was already not Hebrew but Aramaic which was in daily use in Palestine. The fact that from that battle, against overwhelming odds, Hebrew emerged victorious is one of the miracles of modern times and living proof of the stiff-necked obstinacy of the Jewish people. In that early period in Palestine, whoever ventured to speak Yiddish in public invited contempt. There were no publications of any sort in Yiddish. When in 1927 there was an attempt to introduce Yiddish as a subject at the university, there was an almighty outcry that "pagan gods are being brought into the Temple" and the project had to be withdrawn. It was only in 1951, when there was already a third generation that considered Hebrew to be their mother tongue, that Yiddish was accepted as a legitimate subject at the university. The circle was squared — nostalgia for the past, idealised and irretrievably lost, a recognition of the beauty and value of the treasures of the Yiddish literature, embodied in the works of Isaac Leib Peretz, Shalom Aleichem, Mendele Mocher Seforim, Scholem Asch, the Singer brothers and others, the awareness that this was an integral part of the national heritage, that this was the language on the lips of the people who had perished — all this combined to surround Yiddish with an aura of prestige.

Isaac Bashevis Singer declared in his acceptance speech on receiving the Nobel Prize for Literature that the honour bestowed upon him was really a recognition of the Yiddish language — "a language without land, without frontiers, a language not supported by any government, a language not supported by the rulers and the mighty of this world, a language which is the expression of thousands of years' experience of the Jewish people." So said Bashevis Singer, and nobody knew more about these things than he did.

The language is pithy, colourful, expressive, earthy — and at the same time poetic, full of singular turns of phrase, metaphors, proverbs, wit. It reflects the spirit of the societies that used it — their character, disposition, way of thinking, sense of humour. It is warm, full of diminutives. Martin Buber remarked that when a Jew addresses himself to God with the word "*Gotteniu*" this marks as intimate a relationship to God as man is capable of achieving.

A curiosity: the highest compliment, distinction, homage to another person which can be expressed in Yiddish is the phrase "*Er iz a mensch*" — he is a man, such as a person should be, such as can be relied upon in all circumstances. In one sense Yiddish is unique among languages. It is a language — please consider this — in which it is virtually impossible to make a grammatical error. However you say it, provided it is clear what you mean to say, even if only with the help of the accompanying gesture, it will pass as acceptable, without a censorious comment. If you want an object to be feminine gender, even though it is normally considered to be masculine gender — "*zoll zayn*," let it be so. If you want to alter the sequence of words in a sentence, introduce a neologism known only to you or invented by you — it's fine, it's not the end of the world (and the end of the world, in Yiddish, is also not the end of the world!), nobody will take you on account of this for an ignoramus or simpleton. It will not be "classical" Yiddish, not everybody has aspirations to be a Peretz or a Singer. If you consider how much suffering has been caused to humanity by efforts to master articles, cases, declensions, how people who commit grammatical errors or have the wrong accent are looked down upon by their fellow creatures, you will realise what a marvellous invention this is, this independence, freedom and tolerance, which may be the envy of other languages but which can never be imitated.

*   *
*

We lived in a three-room flat, with balcony, on the third floor, in a tenement house, on the corner of St. Sebastian Street and Berek Joselewicz Street. As in most houses in that district, with the exception of the caretaker who lived with his family in the basement, and one other of whom more later, all the tenants were Jewish — the wealthier ones in the front, the poorer in the back — a microcosm of the Jewish community. On each floor some little world of its own, some human comedy, loving, feuding, intriguing, gossiping — a seething cauldron.

When one talks of those better off and those poorer, one has to bear in mind the Yiddish proverb "*m'kennish shetzen a yiddishe kishke*," which means — if those peculiarities can be translated — that it is hard to guess the contents of a Jewish purse. Indeed, whilst everyone knew what was cooking in one's neighbour's pot (even if nothing was cooking), it was customary to keep one's financial status secret, mainly from the tax inspector but also from a jealous neighbour; showing off one's wealth was deemed to be vulgar and stupid. Many Jews used to invest their savings in bricks and mortar, even property abroad, in

Berlin or Vienna. Hence the disproportionate number of properties in Jewish hands.

To illustrate the point — a small digression. One of the janitors at the Hebrew School in Brzozowa Street was a man called Hamer. He kept a tuck-shop in a niche on the ground floor, open during the breaks and afternoon activities; this was to compensate him for his beggarly wage. His son, not a high-flyer, in fact a bit of a dunce, was accepted after his matriculation for medical studies at the Jagiellonian University. It was obvious that this could only have been achieved by way of a substantial bribe to an official in that department's administration. In fact such a scam came to light in a subsequent investigation — no one was in the least surprised. The surprise was — where did Hamer get the money from?

Bribery, using influence, exploiting connections, was an integral part of daily life, it was accepted as normal (*plus ça change?*), it alleviated, in a way, the full rigour of the law. It was known that most problems could be settled for money, one only had to know the right channel and the current tariff. Mrs. Lustig knew who mattered at the town hall, Mr. Buchholz at the police, Mr. Bader at the courts of law. I remember how one such go-between was relating to my father a conversation he had had with a tax official: "We stood on the corner of Dietla and Starowislna Streets, at the Koerner family's apartment house. I told him — 'Take a good look at this building, it could be yours if you settle this matter we are discussing favourably.' Imagine" — here his voice trembled with indignation — "he refused. Refused! Dirty dog! Now I shall have to find someone else, it will cost more."

Money mattered, as always, as everywhere (it mattered also later, up to a point, in the ghettos). But there is an old Jewish tradition, expressed in a saying from the Talmud, that a learned person takes precedence over the high priest. This ethos, in vestigial form, was maintained. True respect was accorded to Osias Thon, to Rabbi Kornitzer, to Chaim Hilfstein — not to Mr. Wasserberger, the milling magnate, or Mr. Lachs of the Suchard chocolate factory.

On the ground floor, in the courtyard, there was a *cheder*, a Jewish elementary school for boys, where reading the Bible was taught. Boys from the neighbouring houses were brought there by a *belfer*, often by force, against their will. All day long, through the half-closed windows, the courtyard was filled with a rhythmic singsong, children repeating after the teacher, the *melamed*, verses from the Scriptures. Now and again there was a shriek, some kid being beaten by the *melamed* with a belt or a whip — the traditional teaching method.

I went to *cheder* once only; my father considered this to be my (or rather his) duty, although my mother protested. I did not like it — and refused to go again. The few prayers for daily use my father taught me gently — they sufficed for a long time (though not for life). Worse than that — I ended, after one attempt, my piano lessons. I did not like the teacher. He threatened, the imbecile, to box my ears if I didn't practise — again, a teaching method, but in my case the least effective. On such details depends, sometimes, the course of one's life — what would I not have given later for the facility, like my brother, to sit down to the piano and play Chopin's études. I hold it against my parents that they indulged me too much, for a bit more strictness would have produced, perhaps, a better end product. Apparently they saw no cause to be strict: at school I was always top of the class, things appeared to come easily, too easily. My mother used to show off to neighbours my end-of-term reports: "My Felus," she used to say, "has 'tenacious' for application, 'commendable' for behaviour and 'very good' from top to bottom."

The ground-floor flat was occupied by the Einhorn family, a couple with two sons — Oscar, a contemporary of my older brother, and Bruno, slightly my junior. Mr. Einhorn came to Cracow from abroad, probably from Czechoslovakia. He spoke Polish with a funny accent, although that alone would not mark him out; many Jews, if they spoke Polish at all, spoke with a funny accent. The names of the boys — Oscar, Bruno — sounded more "progressive" than those in common usage, derived from the Bible. One could deduce a great deal from the sound of first names. My brother, four years my senior, had in his birth certificate as first names "Jechiel Kalman," inheriting them, as was the custom, from one of his grandfathers. I had in my birth certificate "Rafael" after no one in particular; my mother fancied that it sounded "modern" and yet was within the Jewish tradition — after all an archangel he, (true, only one of four, and the one who guarded "the rear" — as my brother was fond of reminding me). The fact that "Rafael" soon and irreversibly changed into "Felek" is due to the tendency of the Polish language to diminutivise — a suffix makes an object smaller and smaller, a caressing gradation. (The English language lacks this, one has to labour: table, little table, sweet little table.) One cannot call a child "Rafael," it gets softened to "Rafael-ek"; from there it is only a step to "Felek." Between my brother's "Jechiel Kalman" and my "Rafael" there are four years during which my mother, a "modern" woman, enlightened and widely read, waged a battle, step by step, against the tradition of my father's home. Father would voice, now and again, a token protest, but deep down he agreed with her and submitted to the progressive change.

Something must have been known about Mr. Einhorn's past, for my mother was less than delighted when I visited their flat to play with the boys. They had a huge box of building bricks from which we used to erect fortresses and ramparts for our armies of lead soldiers — I brought with me my own contingent. Rumour had it that Mr. Einhorn had gambled away a fortune at cards and had had to flee Prague, for such "debts of honour" could have serious consequences, outside the law.

Cracow had its own quota of such gamesters, of whom it was known that they neglected their families and lost fortunes playing cards (we never heard of those who won, which was puzzling). One of the scenes where these card games were played was the Hotel City at the Wawel Hill end of the Planty promenade. When, occasionally, I would accompany my mother on a walk through that neighbourhood, she would command me to look away from that place of iniquity, which, of course, had just the opposite effect.

The idea that cards were the invention of the devil meant that there was not a pack at home, not even for playing children's games, and to this day I don't distinguish clubs from spades. Later, when the game of bridge reached Cracow and took it by storm, my early aversion prevented me from learning that splendid game and deprived me of a social asset. I was left with an undying passion for chess. If not for that early, puritanical idea that moving little pieces over a chessboard, no matter how clever, is ultimately a waste of time, I felt I could happily have devoted most of my time to the game of chess. Today this passes for a respectable activity, one can earn a living thereby, or even make a fortune. In those days there was absolutely no money in it, great masters played in tournaments for a pittance.

(A little glimpse from the past: A few days after our arrival in this country, in May 1938, my friend Joe and I spotted a notice in the paper: Alexandre Alekhine will be playing a simultaneous game, against all comers, in the National Liberal Club in Northumberland Avenue in London. Wow! There's London for you, we thought excitedly, you can see the legendary Alekhine in person. We rushed there, of course, at the appointed time, and not only did we see him but we bought ourselves a place at a chessboard, one of twenty, to play against him. We paid for it (I swear my memory does not deceive me, unlikely as it sounds) one shilling between us, sixpence each. The play lasted two and a half hours. Joe and I on board twenty were the last to finish the game, we drew (I knew we should not have taken that "poisoned" pawn, but Joe thought otherwise.) This means that Alekhine, one of the greatest masters of all time, played, in the year 1938, for two and a half hours, to earn himself one pound sterling. I know about inflation and all that, but...)

That puritanical streak which coloured our lives extended to alcohol. There was always a bottle of vodka on the sideboard from which Father would pour out a glass to the rare non-Jewish visitor whom he happened to entertain, whilst for himself he would fill a glass with water from an identical bottle. Maybe this was not typical, for in the Jewish tradition alcohol is not condemned — the Hassids, egging themselves on to a state of ecstasy, found a measure of slivovitz helpful. In the Bible, references to the consumption of wine vary.

Total abstinence is regarded as retrograde, and the Book of Proverbs contains warnings but also encouragement. The Talmud says, lightheartedly, that at the Feast of Purim one should drink until the distinction between the blessing of Mordechai and the cursing of Haman becomes blurred. Drunkenness among Jews was unknown. It was unthinkable to find a Jew in one of the drinking dens, even those in Jewish quarters. He might be an innkeeper but would rarely touch vodka himself. Perhaps this was a reaction against the widespread and vulgar drunkenness around. A Jewish song ran something like this: *Shikker is a goy — Shikker is er — trinken miz er — weil er is a goy* (A goy is a drunkard — but drink he must — because he is a goy.)

I revert to the house. On the first floor, on the right, lived the Zuckermans. The father had a timber yard in Podgorze, and also a sawmill somewhere in the Carpathian Mountains. There was a large radio receiver in the flat, allegedly for listening to foreign stock exchange quotations. There were four children in the family, all of whom went to the Hebrew school round the corner. The oldest, Baruch, was in the same form as my brother and was a member of the Communist Party. One day, there pulled up in front of the house a Black Maria; two civilian police agents came out, knocked at Zuckerman's door and conducted a search, that is, they turned the flat upside down looking for illegal publications, arrested Baruch and took him to the local prison, called St. Michael's, whose iron-grilled windows gave on to the Planty promenade. We used to go to "visit" him, gathered in a small group outside. We saw him at the window and waved to him. He would respond, clenching his fist.

The fact that his parents were dying a thousand deaths was less important to him than the advancement of the world revolution. Soon after there was a court case (because in that fascist prewar Poland one could not be kept in custody without trial, and during the trial one could defend oneself and make communist propaganda). The case went under the name of "Henner and associates," against a few students from the university, a few from high schools. The public prosecutor was the notorious Mr. Szypula, who deplored the corruption of the young men, stressing their Jewish origin. They were defended by the able advocate Mr. Bross, eloquently but to no good purpose. They all got sentenced to a few years in prison, the normal tariff. The war opened the gates of the prisons. I met Zuckerman after the war, under a different name; he was some high dignitary — rightly so, who else? A prewar sentence for "subversion" served as unquestionable qualification for office.

On the same floor lived many members of the family Apfelbaum, very Orthodox, three generations, bearded men in kaftans, women in wigs, youngsters in black caps, with shoulder-length sidelocks. I don't know how they made a living. It was noticeable how clean they were, one could say elegant, in a sort of way. I never exchanged a single word with any of them, although I prowled through that staircase ceaselessly and brushed against them, but with some sense of embarrassment, uncertain how to relate to them. They, wrapped up in their own world, walked past, hardly noticing our existence. I remember how one day I passed their door and from behind it I heard loud laughter. A shiver ran down my spine — they are capable of laughter? What were they laughing at?

A floor above lived Mr. Danziger with wife and son. Mr. Danziger was portly, wore pince-nez, had a waxed, turned-up moustache. During the First World War he had been a *Feldwebel*, a sergeant major in the Austrian army. On the sideboard in their dining room, in a glass showcase, there was his photograph in uniform and with an Iron Cross. He was a teacher by profession, at the red brick school in Miodowa Street. His son, Zygmunt, a good-looking youngster, was a student in the St. Jacek High School in Sienna Street. Our housemaid, Emilia, said of him, with a sneer, that he was "spoilt"; presumably he made passes at her, but fruitlessly. She was like a nun and, despite my mother's warnings, ended up in a nunnery.

Zygmunt had more luck with his own housemaid, the comely Wanda. Mrs. Danziger made no secret of it — like a latter-day Mrs. Dulska she explained that she had hired her so that Zygmunt should not have to loiter the streets for pickups. When the housemaid became pregnant Mrs. Danziger grew indignant that Wanda had cheated her, because when questioned about her sex life she had assured her that she was clean, healthy and had three abortions behind her. With these credentials she received a better wage than the usual, and despite that — look what happened... She was, of course, dismissed on the spot. What would follow in a case like that — and it was by no means exceptional — is a matter for speculation. She might return to her village to give birth or to abort or — if she were afraid to show herself on her home ground — she would find the woman in the back street who advertised her services with the notice "Cups, leeches applied" and would, for a small sum, do what was necessary.

There was a sequel to this story. I remember how, one day, Wanda appeared in front of the Danzigers' flat, wrapped in a shawl, with a child at her breast, banged at the door with her fists and screamed: "Take this bastard from me." The doors remained shut, Wanda got hoarse, she sat on the doorstep of the house barring the entrance, no one dared go past her. She was not there next morning; one assumed the Danzigers had bought her off with a hefty ransom. Zygmunt told me later that he had threatened his parents that he would marry Wanda.

On the same floor, at the other end of the corridor, lived the Bertrams. The lady of the house was Salcia Bertram, a corset-maker. That was, in those days, an important and difficult craft. We are not talking of these airy-fairy girdles and bras of today, bought ready-made, but of those artful suits of armour, made to measure, with stays and whalebone, frills, buckles, ribbons and strings to tighten the waist. That part of a lady's wardrobe was no trivial matter, for it required expert craftsmanship to make sure that it fitted here and there, and advice on how to put it on and, more importantly, how to take it off. Mrs. Bertram had a small shop-atelier in Szewska Street, under the sign "Gracja"; she had a select clientele and not every woman could afford a corset from Mrs. Bertram. The trouble was that in the same limited space her husband plied his trade as a watchmaker. When a lady came in for a fitting, Mr. Bertram hid behind a screen and held his breath.

The younger daughter in the Bertram's household was Olga, the most beautiful maiden of her generation in the whole neighbourhood — nobody would dispute that. (Whether she was the most beautiful in the whole of Cracow would have been disputed by some, since the competition for that title was fierce.) Olga learned her trade at her mother's knee and learned it well, which — as it turned out later — was providential. Olga was the childhood sweetheart of my friend Johnny Erteszek from Brzozowa Street No. 13. A year before the outbreak of war Johnny went to the United States, obtained the so-called "first documents" which entitled him to reentry, and in August 1939 arrived in Cracow in order to marry Olga and carry her away to the Golden Land. The outbreak of war thwarted that plan but after some wandering through Russia, through Japan, with some strange adventures and coincidences, the young couple landed in California. Now the story developed a twist worthy of a Hollywood scriptwriter. Olga made up a sample of a new model bra, Johnny offered it to one of the biggest department stores — Macy's or Bloomingdales — and got a substantial order. One has to know how to exploit such opportunities; they built a small factory, then a bigger one, naturally under the trademark "Olga." The firm prospered and grew into a public company with shares on the stock exchange. Every garment produced in the line of "intimate apparel" — corsets, girdles, brassieres — carried a label with Olga's photograph and the slogan "Behind every Olga garment, there is a real Olga." Her face became known in America like that of a film star.

Johnny came from a fairly Orthodox family — they had a shop, a ladies' outfitters in Grodzka Street, closed, of course, on Saturdays. The father would go to the synagogue on important holidays, the kitchen was kosher, Johnny was a pupil at the Hebrew school. When I received the first letter from Johnny and Olga after their arrival in America I was overjoyed to hear that they were alive. Some time later, Johnny mentioned that he and Olga had become members of a church (Episcopalian? Congregational? I did not know the difference). I was a bit startled but assumed that they had had good utilitarian reasons for such a step. I only knew converts of that kind, and although I had a distaste for such a procedure I was not censorious. However, it transpired from further correspondence, and later in personal encounters, that we were facing a different phenomenon. Johnny asserted that he had converted out of conviction, that he had had a revelation of a new, great, blinding Truth.

I do not know why it was, and is, so difficult for me to accept such a statement at face value. Millions of people change their faith and convert from one set of beliefs to another. It would be arrogant to doubt the sincerity of their motives.

But with Johnny, no, I simply could not believe in the authenticity of his revelation. I am naturally sceptical of such phenomena and deeply suspicious of "inner voices." All the more so when this goes, as it did in this case, with an aggressive condemnation of Judaism. After that time our discussions, verbally and in writing, turned solely around this topic; Johnny tried to persuade me of the truth of his new faith. This had just the opposite effect: in search of arguments I delved deeper into the principles and practice of Judaism and blunted somewhat my uncompromising agnosticism. When I begged of Johnny to cease to practise on me his missionary zeal, he used to say: "Do not ask this of me, I do it out of friendship and respect for you, I have seen the light, you remain in darkness, I have the inner compulsion to open your eyes."

There is no denying that this different outlook on basic questions cooled our relationship a little, which saddened me for I have great affection for friends with whom I went to school, to university, and with whom I shared a happy past in Cracow. Only a few of them survived, many have since died the unnatural Jewish death in their own beds — I cherish every one of them.

To revert to the story of the house. On the second floor, overlooking the courtyard, there was a room occupied by a small, portly, middle-aged man who lived alone. His name was Itzie Mann and he was a cantor in one of the synagogues. He had a beautiful, powerful voice. From that room often rose the sounds of Italian operatic arias: *Vesta la giuba* or *La donna e mobile*. One day Mr. Mann disappeared and gossip had it that he was performing in the Metropolitan Opera in New York. A little ditty was composed, making fun of him, reminding him of the days when he was a poor, Jewish cantor.

On the third floor — Scharfs, Fischers, Rehmans. About Fischer the shoemaker, who occupied a tiny flat, one room and kitchen, with his wife, six sons and a daughter ("There is no shortage of space in Mother's home" — he used to quote from the Talmud) I write in another place.

Rehman, except for the janitor the only non-Jew in that house, was a chimney sweep. His mother, by appearance and disposition a witch-like figure, had the concession to sweep chimneys in a prescribed district — that was a source of a small but secure income. Young Rehman had to learn the trade, formal qualifications had to be acquired, exams had to be passed. He went to some school in Austria. Whilst there he learned to speak German and, through close contacts with his Jewish neighbours, Yiddish.

He was a broad-shouldered youth, bright, intelligent, good-humoured. In his free time he would sit on the balcony reading or solving the crossword puzzles which at that time began to feature in newspapers. He was on the best of terms with my family and the other tenants, and best of all — the house was no place for keeping secrets — with Mrs. Glass in the neighbouring house. When she gave birth to a boy, people discerned a resemblance.

I remember him in his full regalia, all in black, soft cap on his head, scoop on one arm, a coil of wire ending with a brush and a heavy metal ball on the other — like a figure in old photographs. (Meeting a chimney sweep was considered to be a good omen.) I saw him climbing on roofs, letting the ball fall through the chimney to displace the soot, then pushing the brush. He used to come home smeared from head to foot, face covered with soot, only the whites of his eyes gleaming.

When Jews were being ordered to move to the ghetto and my mother decided to move to Warsaw where she thought it would be easier for her to hide, she left everything of value, mainly paintings of which there were many, in Rehman's safekeeping, as he was one of the few gentiles she knew. He had her address in Warsaw; from time to time he would sell a painting and send her the money.

He himself did not have an easy time. With a German-sounding name and his knowledge of the language he could have improved his lot by passing himself off as a *Volksdeutsch*, and indeed there was pressure put on him to, but he resisted and damned the consequences. After the war he handed back all that was left — which, perhaps, would not deserve mention if not for the fact that the opposite was the rule. Those poor wretches who came up to claim their possessions were often shown the door or worse. Men such as Rehman were a rarity.

Such was just one, ordinary tenement house, one strand in a patchwork, a tiny stone in a crazy paving. Nothing, nothing remains of it all.

Young women of marriageable age were divided between those of whom it was known that they had a dowry and those who had none. It was understood that the dowry should be in an inverse ratio to the beauty of the bride. That was a theme of interminable chitchat and gossip in the homes and coffeehouses, which seemed to exist for precisely this purpose. Guessing the size, the whereabouts, the form, was fun. Mr. F., for instance, gave his daughter as dowry a tenement house in which, allegedly, many years ago there had been a brothel — that was a long time ago, but such things Cracovians do not forget. This caused much titter and amusement (perhaps prompted by jealousy, for the bride was very beautiful and would have found many a suitor) — it was said that Frederica received as her dowry a brothel. It was known who among the eligible men was a particularly avid "dowry chaser," what the tariff was for professional degrees — doctors, lawyers, engineers. What also counted a little was *yichus*, that is, noble birth of sorts, a good name derived from rabbinical descent, or old established, not newly acquired wealth.

When my parents got married, the match was, of course, "brokered." The story was that my father sought assurance that the bride-to-be was not a redhead — and he went to get a glimpse of her from afar. It was known that the females in the Loewy family were ginger, but they were only half-sisters to my mother.

Marriage-broking in that society was an indispensable institution. How otherwise would a female "from a good home" find a suitable husband? Opportunities to meet, to talk to, to make friends — not to mention other things — with the opposite sex, were very limited outside the family circle. Young maidens in those days (I speak of the turn of the twentieth century — after that, progress, or regress if you will, was rapid) grew up not merely as virgins, but often in ignorance of the facts of life. One of the older aunts would instruct the bride about what to expect on the wedding night, sometimes only when it was no longer prudent to delay. Whether the male would also grow up in such a state of innocence one can only surmise — I suspect that the more gregarious lifestyle in the *cheder* and the yeshiva gave many opportunities to talk these things over; it would not be surprising if, besides the disputations over the holy texts, sex were the main topic under discussion. What, in those conditions, went on in bed on wedding nights is today hard to imagine — it is unlikely that there was a great deal of mutual pleasure. (In some communities the groom's parents were entitled to and did inspect the sheet.)

A marriage-broker would bring together couples who, according to his knowledge of matters human and financial, were likely to get on. He would take into account social standing, education and money, and would negotiate the delicate subject of the dowry.

It was obvious that at the base of this transaction was not "love" — the very notion as we understand it belonged to a different planet — but the acceptance of a working convention. To remain unmarried was considered the worst thing that could happen to a woman. The threat "you will grow a grey-haired tress" had to be taken seriously. The community felt responsible for marrying off those who had no one to take care of them — to whom they were given in such cases is another matter, but even this was better than nothing.

The husband was the one who, above all, was to earn a living and provide for the family: the wife was to look after the home, prepare meals, bear children and bring them up. That was the basic division of labour — life, of course, played variations on the theme. It happened, not all that infrequently, that the burden of earning a living would fall on the wife.

Among the Orthodox there was still another practice. The girl's father, if he could afford it, would travel round the yeshivahs and inspect students of a suitable age to choose his future son-in-law. It was understood that such a young man would be kept, for life, by the father-in-law. He would have no other duties but to study the holy books and produce children in the intervals.

Divorces were rare. The expectation of "happiness" in marriage was low; husbands, as a rule, were not drunkards or wife-beaters; opportunities for infidelity were hard to come by; censure from family and neighbours was severe, concern for the welfare of children deep. Above all — what would a divorcee do with herself, what would her lot be?

All this contributed to the stability of marriages. According to Jewish law it is only the husband who has the power to divorce his wife if he wishes (we know how our forefather Abraham sent away his wife Hagar with the little boy Ishmael — the Arab-Jewish hatred has ancient roots); he may grant or refuse a divorce as he wishes. In Orthodox Jewish circles these laws have caused a lot of misery to women and have been subject to fierce controversy as to how they are to be applied and interpreted.

In that system a woman often married beneath her station: her choices were limited and pressure to marry irresistible. Thus also my mother, who had only a stepmother, could not afford to be unduly fussy and accepted her lot with good grace. She covered up the differences in the level of culture between the spouses. She came from a fairly prosperous home; her father had been a wine merchant. She had a good upbringing, went to a German school, was well-read in German literature (which proved, in the event, a lifesaver) and also, though somewhat less so, in Polish. She exercised a civilising influence on the home and on my father. She had, one has to say, more time than he had. Running a small household was not very time-consuming, there was always a housemaid, time was left for reading books from the lending library and working for charities — she was active in the Orphan's Home, and the Parent-Teacher Committee of the Hebrew High School. She cooked and delivered meals to some old people in the neighbourhood. In the afternoons she often spent an hour or two in a coffeehouse, meeting friends, chatting about children, about housemaids, gossiping.

There were many subjects to dwell on. You've heard about it, haven't you? Yesterday Mrs. N. burst into the coffeehouse across the road where Mr. N. was playing cards and made such a scene that the poor man dare not show himself in the street, she's ruined his life... This could not have happened to Mr. K., who was also there; he would have broken her bones... You know to whom the Nattels want to marry off their daughter, the one with the squint? To Dr. S. from Przemysl; people say he will soon get a chair at the Cracow University. Our maid who is friendly with the one in service with the Nattels told us that he was at a party there last night celebrating the engagement, and on departure he slipped her a large tip and pinched her bottom hard... Mr. B. who lost his wife recently is courting the young actress who lodged with them; he should allow for a decent interval at least, but he cannot wait to get his paws on her, shame... Have you read, it was on the first page of the *Illustrated Courier*, Mr. G., the lawyer, brought home some whore and she bit his tongue. He will no longer be the silver-tongued orator he fancied himself to be... You know the Latin teacher at the Hebrew High School, Bronstein? Pupils adore him. He was dismissed by Dr. Hilfstein who thought he might be a communist. With a name like that, probably a relative of Trotsky... And young Bader, who shot his rival dead, got away with it scot-free, he pleaded it was a duel, no way, it must have cost a small fortune in bribes... Mrs. Lustig's son, a known dumbhead, got accepted to study medicine, that woman knows every back door... And so it went on. Nobody was safe from the wagging tongues.

My father was severe, there was no arguing with him. He thought it was his birthright to have the first and last word on every issue. It was totally inconceivable that he should change nappies when the baby cried or push the pram or carry a shopping basket with provisions. He never looked into the kitchen; he would put his shoes there for cleaning before going to bed and pick them up highly polished next morning. He would come home for lunch from his office which was not far away (in Cracow nothing was far away) and have his afternoon nap; we would then walk on tiptoe and speak in whispers.

He concentrated entirely on the business of making a living and improving his and our material lot, and in this he had a measure of success. He first served as a salesman in a leather store, and soon after, as often was the case with Jewish employees, opened a little store of his own in competition with his former boss. His boss, a Mr. Nebenzahl, had a reputation for shrewdness. It was said that he developed his own method of personnel selection. He watched his employees like a hawk. Whenever a clerk went to the toilet, Mr. N. would look at the watch and count the time of his absence — if the man ran to his desk quickly, buttoning up his fly (that was before the zip-fastener era), it earned him good marks, ahead of his less nimble colleagues. My father clearly was one of those who would take too long over his business and so was quickly dismissed. A few years on and he advanced to be a manufacturer — "The Viennese Factory of Leather Belting," proclaimed the sign over the door. It had nothing to do with Vienna, other than that capital being a symbol of excellence.

Money for housekeeping was dispensed in small doses; Father never lost the feeling of insecurity, the anxiety that there would be a shortfall, that the rainy day could not be far away. In the thirties, the word which was continually on people's lips was "the crisis." The object of awe was the so-called "*Wechsel*," a promissory note; there was a pile of them on Father's desk, the shaky foundation of the family's fortune. If a "promise to pay" embodied in such a document was not honoured, the note — lengthened by a slip of paper with a seal — was added and the note was presented to the first "guarantor" on the list. If he refused to pay, a further slip of paper with a seal was added and the note was presented to the second guarantor, and so on. Sometimes such a *Wechsel* with its "protests" stretched for yards. I remember these rolls of paper as the symbol of "the crisis." Bankruptcies of individuals and firms, genuine and fraudulent, abounded, causing a chain reaction. "A Scharf does not go bankrupt" — my father would pronounce with pride, as if the mere fact that one paid one's debts was, in contrast to others, especially praiseworthy.

Even in a small place like Cracow, where Kazimierz, the Jewish quarter, existed cheek by jowl with the non-Jewish, the lives of those neighbouring communities were, in many important senses, separate. It was possible for a Jew to grow up in a family circle, study, or prepare for a trade yet not cross the border dividing the Polish and Jewish communities. A great many Jews, in the district of Nalewki in Warsaw, in the hundreds of *shtetlach*, besides a sporadic contact with a supplier or a client, lived thus — not together, but next to each other, on parallel lines, in a natural, contented isolation. During my whole life in Cracow, till my departure before the war, I was never inside a truly Polish home, whose smell, caught in passing, was somehow different, strange. I did not miss it, considered this division natural. I also do not remember whether in our home, always full of people, guests, visitors, passers-by, friends of my parents, my brother's and mine, there ever was a non-Jew, except for one neighbour and the caretaker who would come to collect his tips, and, of course, the maid who inhabited the kitchen.

The kitchen was large, more interesting than the drawing room. I spent a lot of my time there, learned a great many things from one or another of the maids, of whom some were in our service for a number of years, sometimes till they got married. They were mainly peasant girls for whom there was no room in their village home — service with a middle-class Jewish family in a town was for them a social advancement and offered shelter from the dangers of city life into which they otherwise might have drifted. They would acquire "manners," would learn to speak "properly." They worked hard — cleaning, scrubbing floors, beating carpets on the stand in the courtyard, carrying coal from the cellar, making fires in the huge tiled stoves, and cleaning out the ashes afterwards. When the washerwoman would come and do the monthly laundry in a giant tub, they would hang up the washing in the attic at the top of the house, then carry it in a wicker basket to a nearby mangle, after which they would do the ironing. They got up early and went to bed after all the members of the family, leaving their shoes for cleaning behind the kitchen door, had retired.

They had their "free" day on Sundays — they would go to church, often bringing back with them devotional broadsheets full of ugly cartoons of Jews and poisonous articles — the Church's calculated antidote to their contacts with Jews, whom they had a chance to observe at close quarters and see that they were not as black as painted. Afterwards, Mary, Catherine or Wanda would meet her swain, usually a soldier (Cracow was a garrison city), and go with him, arm in arm, for long walks through the Planty promenade or along the bank of the River Vistula. Towards evening she would bring him home — they would sit, till late, on the back stairs, where she would feed him with delicacies from the larder, the like of which were not on the menu in the barracks — a reward and a bait for the future.

When I was a small boy my mother would sometimes take me shopping for poultry in the "New Square" in the heart of the Jewish quarter, with its market stalls and the butchers and fishmongers in the round brick building in its centre. I recall the procedure — first the purchase, after a bit of haggling, of a live bird, a chicken or goose, from the country woman by the kerbside (a fraction cheaper than from the butcher's). The bird would be handed over to a ritual slaughterer nearby who would slit its throat with one deft move of the knife — the blood would squirt into the gutter. The desperate screeching and cackling of birds provided musical background to the whole scene. From there, on to the stall of the pluckers — a few women with kerchiefs, on low stools, would pluck the bird, feathers would fly around, and the operation would be over in a few minutes. Payment was in kind — the down and feathers were valuable merchandise in the hands of big exporters. The naked, repulsive corpse, wrapped in newspaper, would be thrown into the capacious shopping bag to reappear on the kitchen table, awaiting further procedures skilfully performed by my mother.

Many memories connect with the sports ground of the Makkabi Club, at the end of Dietla and Koletek Streets, the scene of football matches in summer and an ice rink in winter. To play football for that club was the dream of every aspiring Jewish youngster, the players were famous, I could name the team today. There was also a second Jewish club, Jutrzenka (Morning Star), playing in black-and-white shirts (Makkabi played, of course, in blue-and-white), but that was a workers' club and did not enjoy our fanatical support.

In the wooden fence surrounding the ground there were many cracks and holes, and by pressing one eye to them one could see part of the field ("move away you so-and-so, that was my hole"); during matches the ground was thickly surrounded by such viewers. There were a few houses in an enviable position, from whose windows part of the field was visible. I had access to one such window in a flat in Koletek Street belonging to the family Simanowicz. The father of that family was partially paralysed. Shortly before the outbreak of war the family obtained a "certificate" for entry to Palestine, but it would have been unthinkable to leave the father behind. One day he got himself, somehow, to the window and fell to his death to free the family from the burden.

"The School" — The Hebrew Primary and Secondary School (Gymnasium) to give it its full title — was an educational establishment with the full curriculum in the Polish language, as prescribed by the Ministry of Education. This, after matriculation, gave automatic access to most departments of the universities. Parallel with the instruction in secular subjects there was a programme of studies in Hebrew — the Bible, Jewish history and literature, according to the plan of Hebrew schooling developed and practised in Poland. From its inception till the outbreak of war, this school gave tuition to more than 2,000 pupils of both sexes and left its mark on them. The memory of the teachers, who virtually all perished in the Shoah, is cherished by former pupils to the present day. The school was a sort of oasis where pupils could maintain an illusion that the world was and would remain a benevolent place.

I remember those distant days of my youth and childhood with utter clarity — it is known that with age the long-term memory sharpens (whilst it is increasingly difficult to remember what one had for dinner yesterday). And the patchwork of those recollections does not consist of any great historical events but, more often than not, of trivial details, passing shadows, seemingly insignificant happenings, which for no apparent reason left a lasting trace in the grey matter.

The triangular area between Brzozowa, Berka Joselewicza and Sebastiana Streets was where young urchins romped all day long, playing cops and robbers or a kind of rounders or kicking around a rag-ball — a real football with an inner tube and a leather cover was quite out of their reach. A rag-ball made from an old sock, packed tight with scraps of textiles into a round shape with string — to make such an object fit to be kicked around in the dust and mud — that was a special art. The best artist in this field and the best player in those games was the son of the concierge of our house — barefoot, in tatters, rachitic, but nimble as a monkey. He used to parade in front of the house walking on his hands — I admired him greatly and envied him, but it was unthinkable that I should be permitted to play with him. The basement, at the rear of the courtyard, where the sun never reached, thronged with families of the poor, often riven by disease due to malnutrition.

Only once did I penetrate that territory — during the taking of the national census students like myself were engaged in collecting data. After this experience, whoever did not turn into a revolutionary, at least in his mind, and did not want to abolish the system which tolerated such a state of affairs, lost the respect of his peer group. (It was said that the official publication *The Statistical Yearbook*, which used to appear in red covers, was the best recruiting material for the Communist Party.)

I would like to portray myself as a true child of the district of Kazimierz — this would not have been considered, in its day, as something to be proud of, rather the contrary, but with the passing of time we value things for their rarity.

In fact my Cracow (and I use that pronoun without hesitation) was not just Kazimierz. I would go there occasionally, to visit a friend, to attend a performance in the Yiddish theatre in Bochenska Street, or take part in a protest meeting in the large courtyards in Krakowska Street.

But my daily path from school, situated on the corner of Brzozowa Street and Podbrzezie, led from the family home in Dietla Street (third from the corner of Starowislna Street) in the direction of the town centre, towards the main post office, to the Rynek — the main town square — under the arcades of the Cloth Hall through the Planty promenade, at the side of the university, to the open spaces of the Blonia commons, or directly through Karmelicka Street to the swimming pool in the Cracovian Park.

It might appear from this long register of streets that they stretch over some vast area — in fact, the space we are talking of was quite small, everything was within walking distance, there was nowhere to hide. On occasions when I used to come home in the late evening, after some assignation on the town's periphery, my father already knew whom I had been walking with arm-in-arm and there was some evasive explaining to do.

One could have disappeared in the darkness of a cinema — a tactful projectionist in the Promien picture-house would sound a bell to warn that the show was about to end. Early American films were widely shown. We saw Charlie Chaplin and Jackie Coogan, Harold Lloyd, Buster Keaton, Johnny Weissmuller as Tarzan, the cowboy Tom Mix, Greta Garbo. German films with Martha Eggert-Kiepura, Emil Jannings, Marlene Dietrich, Lilian Harvey, Franciska Gaal; French films with Maurice Chevalier, Charles Boyer, Simone Simon, Danielle Darieux. Also, if one was so inclined — Polish films with Brodzisz, Bodo, Junosza-Stepowski, Smosarska. (Antoni Slonimski, asked by a *Wiadomosci Literackie* journalist which foreign film and which Polish film he considered best, replied: "The best foreign film is Renée Claire's *Vive la Liberté*. I do not go to see Polish films.")

Films generally were a popular form of entertainment. The Slowacki Theatre was another. No performance was missed although I do not recall ever buying an entrance ticket. We had an arrangement with one of the ushers who, for a small tip, would let us in to the "gods." The theatre director in those days was Teofil Trzcinski; after him came Zygmunt Nowakowski (whom I had occasion to meet during the war, in London, as the editor of Grydzewski's *Wiadomosci*); after him, Osterwa. The repertoire was varied, mainly light. I remember seeing there the popular vaudeville *Krakowiacy i Gorale*, an American play *The Artists* with Stefan Jaracz and the adorable Zofia Jaroszewska, and the Hungarian plays of Molnar and Bus-Fekete. Occasionally there were plays by Shakespeare, Bernard Shaw — interestingly enough, some of Shaw's plays had their first showings in Poland, before they appeared in England. (To this day, in productions of *The Applecart*, King Magnus often wears a square hat with a feather, modelled on King Stefan Batory as painted by Jan Matejko.) And, naturally, there was the whole range of the classic Polish repertoire — Slowacki, Mickiewicz, Wyspianski, Zapolska, Fredro — whose statue stands in front of the theatre, and Balucki, whose statue stands at the back. We greatly admired the leading actors — Solski, Adwentowicz, Zelwerowicz, Nowakowski, Osterwa — their art was equal to the finest on the stages of the West.

From the theatres to the cafes. There was the Feniks in the Main Square, Bisanz in Basztowa Street, Secesja in St. Anne Street, Esplenade on the corner of Straszewski Street, Cyganeria in Szpitalna Street. (That was the one where, in 1942, a few Jewish teenagers threw a bomb, knowing that this was the meeting place of German officers.) In that cafe, on the few square feet of polished floor, there was dancing every day at five in the afternoon.

The period of university studies was a happy one. This had little to do with the merits of the university — though it had many — but with the fact that if a youngster between his nineteenth and twenty-third year, who has a good home, many friends of both sexes, good health, curiosity and zest is not happy, then there is something very wrong with him. I chose law for my studies — that was my natural inclination, with a view to practising a "free profession." It is worth noting that in prewar Poland, that backward and undemocratic country, every student who passed his matriculation, irrespective of grades, had automatic access to university — I don't know where else this is or was the case. It is true that there was the so-called *"numerus clausus"* in the Faculty of Medicine, meaning that only a restricted number of Jewish students were accepted — and we made a great deal of fuss about it. If there had been no restrictions of that kind and if admission had been governed strictly by the excellence of grades, Jewish medical students might have greatly outnumbered their non-Jewish colleagues — a situation which, not surprisingly, was not tenable in the prevailing conditions. Considering that sons and daughters of practising doctors of medicine could, if they wished, enter the Faculty outside the quota, that *numerus clausus* rule, in retrospect, does not appear so monstrous.

The Faculty of Law had, at that time, many distinguished professors. Wroblewski and Taubenschlag in Roman law, Krzyzanowski in economics, Kutrzeba, Vetulani, Gwiazdomorski, Zoll — all worthy teachers to learn from. A few of the professors were Jewish; some were baptised, which made it easier for them.

I completed my four-year studies with the master's degree (*Magister Iuris*). I thought that I would write my doctoral thesis, even when my plan to go to England was taking shape. I discussed the choice of subject with Professor Langrod, who suggested that in view of my stay in England I should write "An Outline of Colonial Administration," no less. This, he thought, would be useful and of current interest. In certain political circles in Poland at that time the idea was being propagated that on the international forum Poland should claim for itself colonies in Africa. There was an organisation with branches in various cities called the Maritime and Colonial League — preparing the ground and ready to step in when such plans took shape. Perhaps Professor Langrod saw in me a future governor of Cameroon or Zanzibar. As we know, these plans did not materialise. In any event I did not write that thesis and did not gain such qualifications; other events claimed my attention. When I lecture these days in Poland, in Germany or in the States, I am always addressed as "Professor" or, at least, as "Doctor" — it is wearisome to try to set the record straight each time. I am content with my modest title of *Magister Iuris* and only once did I have a pang of regret. Some years ago I was present in the *Aula* or formal hall of the Jagiellonian University at the ceremony of the "renewal of the doctorate" of Dr. Altschuler from Jerusalem. It was precisely fifty years after my diploma. Had I been, all those years ago, more diligent and written my thesis, I would also have qualified for the "renewal of the doctorate," and the ceremonial robes and hat would have fitted me well and made me look uncommonly distinguished.

I have always been a passionate reader of newspapers. There was no shortage of them in Cracow. There was the staid, conservative *Czas* (Time), the socialist *Naprzod* (Forward), the nationalistic, right-wing *Glos Narodu* (Nation's Voice) and the popular, pro-government, omnipresent *Ilustrowany Kurier Codzienny* (Illustrated Daily Courier). The owner of that paper was Marian Dabrowski, a member of the Polish legislature, a press magnate, who also owned a whole range of other papers and magazines. Considering to what depth the gutter press can sink, fifty years on, in England, the *Ikac*, as it was known for short, does not in retrospect appear so bad. It had to defend itself once in court against the accusation that it was publishing obscene ads. The sample quoted was: "A hundred-percent virgin looks for a macho lover" — small beer by today's standards.

At the other end of town, towards the River Vistula, in Orzeszkowa Street, was situated the *Nowy Dziennik* (New Daily), a Jewish daily newspaper in the Polish language (one of three such newspapers in Poland — the others being *Nasz Przegląd* (Our Review) in Warsaw and *Chwila* (A Moment) in Lwow). That newspaper served the Jews of Cracow as the main source of information, reporting events in the wide world, in Poland, in Palestine. The leading articles were often written by Dr. Osias Thon, the pride of Cracow Jewry, a member of the Polish legislature, the chairman of the Jewish Parliamentary Club, the rabbi of the Progressive (Tempel) Synagogue and an ardent Zionist. The *Nowy Dziennik* was an institution without which the life of Cracow Jewry was unthinkable. I started my journalistic career there and became its foreign correspondent in London.

A small digression: on my last visit to Cracow some months ago, I paid a visit to the reading room of the Jagiellonian Library, locus of many happy memories and — on an impulse — requested to be shown the bound folios of *Nowy Dziennik* from the year 1938. I wanted to cast a glance over those pages, reread the articles which I then wrote to the joy of my father and, perhaps, some other readers. The folio was put on my desk. With trembling hands I started to turn the flimsy pages. I was overcome with memories. Every headline, every name, every advert ("Buy lottery tickets from Safir Brothers — every other ticket wins"), every small ad ("You will speak English like a native Englishman — Karmel, Koletek Street 3") brought forth a flood of images, faces, scenes, events. Immersing myself entirely in that old world, slowed down by the turning of the pages, I did not get to my own articles before closing time. I had paused too long over a notice, one day in January 1938, which read: "On Wednesday, at the premises of the Masada youth group (of which I was then the leader), at 8 p.m., Felek Scharf will give a talk entitled: 'How to get rid of the British in Palestine'."

One day, on another visit, I shall get to see the correspondence "From Our Own Reporter in London." I happen to remember one article, in particular, the last one I wrote in August 1939, wherein there was a passage saying that "I stake my journalistic reputation (*sic*) on the prediction that there will be no war." At the time when this article would have reached the editor's desk — the Germans were already in Cracow.

In retrospect this looks as if I had been blind and naive to a degree — which might well have been true, but the prediction by itself is no proof of this. I was in good company. Many prophets, among them the widely circulated *Daily Express* of Lord Beaverbrook, throughout 1938 and until the last day carried a banner headline: "There will be no war." It is assumed now that everybody knew, that it was obvious to everyone that war was inevitable. This is not how matters looked then, particularly to an observer newly arrived in England, dazzled by the wealth and apparent power of the Empire, with possessions around the globe, where the sun never set. I saw it — would not Hitler see it? He would not dare...

It follows that it is difficult to predict — particularly the future.

One year and a bit before the outbreak of World War II, I left Cracow "voluntarily" (a good deal could be written about those inverted commas). I was conscious that the decision was irreversible and would decide the future course of my life. It matured slowly, during many a sleepless and talked-through night. It meant parting with a safe and cosy home to which I was greatly attached, particularly to my mother. Leaving it made me feel guilty. I saw it as a kind of escape from the battlefield, a shedding of responsibility for a common fate. I had a circle of friends of both sexes, such as I have never had since — it was not easy to part company with them.

On the other hand, life in Poland appeared less and less attractive to me. Anti-Semitism permeated the space around. The professional prospects for a newly qualified student of law were gloomy; first five years of "articles," then practice in an overcrowded profession. One day I returned from the courts of law where I had represented a client whose Semitic features were against him, but whose claim was undoubtedly just, even in such inexperienced hands as mine. I lost the case and it was obvious that the judge was biased. One was used to a measure of discrimination by the authorities, but the dispensation of justice was a different matter — it symbolised a qualitative change.

I returned to the office taking a long, roundabout way. I handed the files to my patron and told him I would not come to the office again. He huffed a bit: "Don't take it so hard, we shall go to appeal and have this decision rescinded. Such things are unpleasant but one must adjust to realities." "Let him" — I thought — "go on adjusting if he wants to, I will not." That was the end of my career as a lawyer.

The incident, on the face of it, was trivial, but the fact that I have not forgotten it shows how deeply it cut. Whilst I try, as far as possible, to recreate my train of thought and the open and the hidden motives for my departure, the heart of the matter was that I felt constrained and wanted out, into the wide world.

The idea which at that time exercised more than any other the minds and hearts of people in my circles was Zionism. At school and at university I was an active Zionist — I wrote articles, spoke at meetings, agitated for emigration to Palestine, to pioneer, to conquer the desert, to create a Jewish State. (There circulated at that time a definition of a Zionist which had a grain of truth in it: it was a Jew who, using the money of another Jew, sends a third Jew to Palestine.) I was determined to go to Palestine, but like St. Augustine who implored God to make him chaste but "not just yet," I was not quite ready "just yet" to sacrifice myself for the great cause, before I had tasted life a bit more, learned a bit more. My contribution, so I argued, would be the more valuable for it. And so the matter got postponed and never realised. There came the war, love, marriage, responsibilities.

Why, when leaving Poland, did I choose England as my port of call? We were persuaded that Great Britain, at that time, was the centre of "civilisation," and it was necessary for all sorts of reasons to get acquainted with it. I had invested time and money in learning the language. I thought that I had learned a good bit, although it transpired soon after arrival that my teacher in Cracow had been only a few pages ahead of me in the Berlitz primer.

I read, passionately, a selection of English novels (in Polish translations) — Galsworthy, Somerset Maugham, all of Kipling — *Stalky and Co.* was one of my favourites; boys at a "public school," that was the life. Thomas Hardy, P. G. Wodehouse, above all Aldous Huxley — that sophisticated, intellectual ambience, that modern society, those discussions of profound ideas — these writers formed my view of the land I was heading for.

The year was 1938. To be let into England was by no means simple. I could show a double cause, to be sure. I had been accepted to do a course of post-graduate studies at the London School of Economics, and I was a foreign correspondent for *Nowy Dziennik*. Indeed, soon after arrival, I started sending short articles, snapshots of everyday life, tittle-tattle about English eccentricities, literary gossip. I do not know what my readers made of it; more importantly for me, my father liked it, was proud to see my name in print, received congratulations for my efforts in the synagogue or the coffeehouses (more often there) and therefore found it easier to send me my monthly allowance. Sterling stood high; the few pounds necessary for a modest upkeep, when translated into Polish zlotys, represented in his view a lot of money and he did not suspect that my mother was sending me some more, saved from her household allowance.

After a long journey by train and boat, I arrived by way of Hook of Holland and Harwich at Liverpool Street Station, then one of the less attractive rail terminals in London. I was laden like a pack-mule with a heavy trunk filled with a carefully planned wardrobe: tailor-made suits (it was habitual for middle-class people to have suits and dresses made to measure) from "Made in England" cloth, according to the latest Cracovian fashion (far ahead, as it appeared, of that prevailing in England). The inevitable *smoking*, that is, dinner jacket, for those receptions in high society which would come my way thick and fast; plus fours, like those of the Prince of Wales in a photograph which I had passed on to my tailor. I proudly carried a portable typewriter — let it be seen that I am a journalist — an Underwood with Polish letters. It weighed 10.5 kilograms (I had the feeling that the decimal point dropped out en route.) A small rucksack filled with cakes my mother gave me for the journey — I ate them all, sitting on the iron steps on a side platform, enveloped in smoke — the last taste of home. Nothing ever again tasted so heavenly. I was a bit frightened, and excited at the same time — England, here I come: Prepare to be conquered!

I travelled by underground to the East End; it was then a Jewish district with its famous Whitechapel High Street. I spent the night in a Salvation Army hostel; next morning I went in search of lodgings. There was dense, yellow fog, which I knew from my Sherlock Holmes, settling in the nose and throat; shirt and undershirt were soon blackened with soot. The sun fought feebly to penetrate the cover. I walked around the streets a bit and was startled to see shop signs with Hebrew letters. But the human landscape was strangely familiar — Jews from Poland, from Russia, trading among themselves and jabbering in their Anglo-Yiddish jargon.

I found a room with a family, dark and poky, unlike the one which I had at home, light-years away from the Forsytes, Kipling and Huxley (but close to Zangwill). As it turned out it had its compensations. The landlady, whose family hailed from Chrzanow, took the trouble to keep one of my appetites satisfied; her pretty daughter, the other.

Round the corner from where I lodged, in Ridley Road, Dalston, I some-times observed, in the afternoons, a public meeting, a speaker on a soapbox addressing a score or so of bystanders, who clapped and shouted approval. Ah, I thought, an example of British democracy in action. One day I came closer to pick up the sense of the tirade. I must mention that I was wearing a black shirt, practical and fashionable. Suddenly, from a nearby housing estate there rushed a group of Jewish youngsters, who with a few kicks, blows and shoves set the speaker and the gathering to flight. I remember this, for as I stood near the speaker, somewhat disoriented, I took a knock on the head. It turned out that the speaker was Oswald Mosley, the founder and leader of the British fascists, Blackshirts as they were called from the colour of their uniforms, and the meeting was a regular provocation of his gang in the heart of the Jewish neighbourhood. Ridley Road became notorious for this. It was somewhat ironical that, wanting to observe British democracy at work, I took a blow meant for a fascist.

Life took such a course that England, which was to be a staging post, became my home, where I have spent my adult life, have children and grandchildren — all of them good, healthy, normal, a veritable God's garden. In the course of that long journey (long according to the calendar though it feels as if it has passed in a flash) I have not become, in any sense, English. I have been spared all ambiguity in this respect by this unflinching and constant awareness that I am, totally, a Polish Jew, and cannot and would not be anything else. I nurture for this, my adopted country, feelings of deep though not uncritical affection, and am concerned for its well-being; I am grateful to fate for having thrown me here and not elsewhere, but despite my family bonds, ties of true friendship, love of the language and the landscape, I remain a stranger in the land and I find that position on the margin comfortable.

This "alienation" bears, in some way, on the relationships in my own home, with my own family, with those whom I love and who are closest to me of all. I do not share with them to the full my internal landscape. Matters which preoccupy me the most — Jewish matters, Israeli matters, are not, cannot be central to their being. I have not transmitted to them a great deal of my past, and therefore a great deal of myself. I did not know perhaps how to do it; maybe I thought this to be some sort of burden which should remain private and not be shifted to other people's shoulders.

I do think, sometimes, that had I found myself in the thirties and forties in Palestine, I would have been more useful, whatever part I played; there — there was a time when a mere Jewish presence was useful.

That was also the time — it did not last long and could not have lasted long — when that small settlement of Jews in Palestine, consisting of idealists, inspired by the vision of a physical and spiritual regeneration of the Jewish people in their own country, represented a model of a society which had no equal and deserved one's unqualified admiration.

But it seems to me that had I been at the time in Palestine, taking into account my former ties with the Revisionist Zionist movement in Poland, with some of my closest friends in Etzel, the fighting group around Begin, I would have perforce become a part of that group, with all the consequences that entailed. Even if their methods were against my conviction that the end cannot justify any means, my loyalty to old comrades and solidarity with friends would have probably proved stronger than other principles. I could easily, all too easily, have become a "terrorist" (but a bad one, *malgré moi*).

The period of German occupation in Poland dominates my internal landscape and casts a shadow over everything that happened to me before or after. From the moment when the trickle of news about the extermination camps began to reach London, I stood close to the sources of information. I was working at that time with Ignacy Schwarzbart who, until the arrival of Szmul Zygielbojm, was the only Jewish representative in the Polish National Council of the émigré government in London, and I was with him when he received the first fateful telegram from the Polish underground and he wrote, with a trembling hand, in his diary: "This is not possible." I was with him when later reports reached him which no longer left room for any doubt, and he wrote in his diary: "It is true nonetheless." Some people may say that all this was a long time ago, but there has not been a day in my life that I have not reverted in my thoughts to those events.

My mother survived the war with the help of false documents, the so-called "Aryan papers," by a series of miracles — without miracles no Jew survived. She had, in the then-current phrase, "good looks," which in that context meant only the lack of Semitic features. She spoke impeccable Polish, and also German, which was her first language. When interrogated by the Gestapo officer into whose hands she was delivered by a blackmailer whom she had ceased paying, knowing that since he knew her address there would have been no end to it, the officer took the view that she did not look or speak like a Jewess; a view influenced perhaps by the fact that during the interrogation my mother played with her golden wedding ring, which she casually let drop on the carpet.

In 1943, when the ghetto was burning, my mother lived in a rented room with a Polish family who of course had no notion of her identity, within sniffing distance of the ghetto walls — the acrid smoke floated through the windows. Her hosts, in whose apartment there were frequent conspiratorial meetings, looked on with chilling indifference. How my mother managed not to give herself away by a twitch of the face or an overflowing tear; how she sharpened her senses to observe and imitate the religious habits during festive meals, visits to church, the kneeling, the crossing oneself, the muttering of prayers, the hundred-and-one little gestures which belong to a culture not her own, will remain a mystery.

Money for board and lodging came from a gradual disposal of pieces of jewellery — a few rings, brooches, earrings, a pearl necklace — birthday presents or anniversary gifts which she used to receive, as was customary among moderately affluent middle-class families. Each sale made it painfully clear that soon there would be nothing more to sell. From time to time she received a small remittance from Cracow — it came from her former neighbour, Rehman, bless him, who occasionally disposed of the paintings which Mother had left in his safekeeping. The paintings were mainly by contemporary Polish artists, the Kossaks — Wojciech and Jerzy, Falat, Wyczolkowski, Malczewski, Wodzinowski, Vlastimil Hofman, Rychter-Janowska. It was the fashion in those days to cover the drawing-room wall with paintings, and I think that the main buyers of paintings were Jews.

To disguise from her hosts the fact that she had some sort of an "income," Mother acquired a large ball of wool from which she was seen through most of her waking hours to be crocheting a garment. When this was ready she used to go out into the street with the avowed purpose of selling it. She would come back with the bundle in her bag, and at night my Penelope would unstitch it, in order next morning to be seen at her labour as usual.

Those who survived and described "life on Aryan papers" conveyed a picture of a haunted, nightmarish existence. The fact that they found themselves in a hostile environment, where a wrong word or gesture was a matter of life or death, meant that many of them who, at enormous cost and risk, had managed to settle on the "Aryan" side, could not endure the continuous fear and strain and returned to the ghetto, to suffer, starve and eventually perish — but amongst their own people.

When I think what my own chances would have been had I been there, I am convinced that I would not have survived. The options were limited. One was flight eastwards from the advancing German army. Many people who took that route did survive, even through gulags and "settlements"; there was in the end the saving grace of General Anders' exodus. My only brother, with his young wife, was not so lucky — they were caught in the German advance and killed. My father, who in his flight had reached Lwow, was soon after deported by the Russians to the tundra in Karelia, in the far north, to fell trees — an occupation which he was not used to and could not do, one of the millions of victims of the noble socialist maxim "who works not eats not" (*kto nie rabotayet' nie kushayet'*). My mother, we all thought, was not fit to embark on an arduous trek eastwards and I would not have left without her.

To cross to the "Aryan side" would not have been a feasible option for me — I had no friends over there and my looks, even though not so strikingly Jewish as to betray me to the Germans, whose discernment in this matter was not great, would undoubtedly have caught the attention of one of the all-too-many eagle-eyed Poles.

Our housemaid, a peasant woman who would have been glad to go through fire for us and who in fact did give shelter to my mother for a while, could not have done the same for me — men were more difficult to hide.

There would have been nothing for me but to go, like the rest of the community, to the ghetto or labour camp and share their fate to the end. It is true that even among those there was a handful of survivors, but that called for enormous endurance and luck (if you could call it that) and above all an iron will to survive which, I am convinced, would not have been at my command, seeing what was happening around me. But one must add this proviso: that no one really knows beforehand what he can endure and what he is capable of in circumstances which defy all imagining.

When I asked my mother what gave her the strength and the will to survive, she maintained that it was the thought that I was somewhere far away, safe, and that one day I would return and take her away with me. The moment the war ended she returned to Cracow, to lodgings in one of the houses which, formally, she owned — and waited. Indeed, not too long, for as in a fairy story, I was soon knocking at her door. Those emotions and the gratitude for my good fortune, one case in a million, I cannot, nor will I try to describe.

I brought my mother to England, she lived with me and my family for another ten years, learned the language, managed the household, saw the birth of grandchildren. It would seem, on the surface, that she had wholly recovered and the nightmare of the past was being forgotten. Till the last, however, when there was a ring at the door and I was getting up from my chair to answer it, she would go pale and grab my sleeve: "Don't go," she would whisper, and then nod her head and smile wanly. For years I sat in the evenings by her bedside, listening, interminably, to her improbable true stories. For her it was a kind of therapy, for me an experience of heartbreaking immediacy. Since then I have read a great deal and even written a little about this subject; nothing has

44

embedded itself so deeply in my consciousness as my mother's recounting of those consummately hideous times.

The greatest pain to which a human being can be exposed is that of a mother or a father looking on the suffering of their child and not being able to help or relieve it. Think of how much of this kind of pain there was at that time, parents helplessly witnessing their child slowly dying of hunger, parents separated from their offspring during a "selection," parents, with their child, being pushed into the gas chamber.

When I think of what my mother went through in those days — thoughts which I have learned to ward off but which haunt me during sleepless nights, I am overcome by a desire to set the world on fire. And that "only" a mother, not a child.

There were many different ways in which a Jew could have perished in Poland in wartime: from disease, from hunger, during an *Aktion*, from a bullet — because a German had a fancy to shoot him; he could have committed suicide when life became too hard to endure; he could have been worked to extinction in a labour camp or tortured to death in a concentration camp. He could also, lost among the Poles, have died as a Pole.

Tracing the fate of members of my family I discovered a Scharf in every one of those categories. How does one cope with that sort of knowledge, that almost everybody one knew — family, friends, teachers, neighbours, shopkeepers, beggars — all died some horrible death and it is only due to some accidental twist of fate that one has not gone the same way. When I want to recall a face I knew, I see it contorted, gasping for breath, in a mass of swirling bodies. (The Germans also had at their disposal Zyklon C — a poison gas swifter in action but somewhat more expensive to produce. Well, let the Jews suffer a bit longer.)

How does one adjust to what, in ordinary life, passes for "normality"? How does this awareness shape one's *Weltanschauung*, one's perception of history, of religion, of morality, of man?

The generation of Jews of the post-Holocaust era, the "survivors" in the broadest sense, are a people apart. Burdened by their memory, walking-wounded, in eternal mourning. I do not think that an outsider can understand this condition.

*   *
*

I would like to recall the following story. At one of the summer camps of the Cracow branch of an organisation of university students known by its acronym ZAKMIK (The Jewish Academic Circle of Lovers of Nature!), in Kuznica on the Baltic Coast, a year before the outbreak of war, I struck up a friendship with Staszek K. from Warsaw. He was, like myself, a dedicated mountaineer. We went together for summer and winter holidays to Zakopane, at the foot of the Tatra Mountains, for the conquest of the lesser peaks — and women (in both respects there was more talk than real achievement). Staszek was a sturdily built, muscular youngster, blond and blue-eyed. After matriculation he took up a university course in physical education. He used to tell me that among his fellow students there was a group of right-wing nationalists who made a habit of taunting him, calling him abusive names, urging him to go to Palestine. This had its own irony, for Staszek came from a very assimilated background: his father was a lawyer, his mother a collector and expert on Sevres china — his Jewish ties were atrophied and only these racist attacks prevented him from forgetting that he was a Jew and, in the end, turned him into an ardent Zionist.

One student in particular, a Silesian by the name of Jurczyga, was always truculent and enjoyed provoking a quarrel, attacking Staszek physically. Since Staszek was not one to give way easily, it often ended in fisticuffs, a black eye or a tooth knocked out — fairly normal side-effects of university life in those days.

When the ghetto was created in Warsaw, Staszek had not for a moment considered the possibility of being locked in. He foresaw, correctly, that he would have felt totally alienated from his fellows there — it is true to say that at the very bottom of that cauldron of degradation which was the ghetto, were the converts and the assimilationists, who felt no bond of kinship with the surrounding multitude, but only dislike and revulsion for them, a feeling which was heartily reciprocated.

Staszek said goodbye (as it turned out — forever) to his parents, bought a certificate of baptism (as luck would have it of a person with the same initials — he did not have to remove the embroidered monograms from his shirts) and made his way to Zakopane — where else? He took up lodgings with a peasant whom he knew from our prewar escapades, on the way to the Koscieliska Valley. He acquired two fierce Alsatian dogs, partly for company, partly for further disguise — nobody could possibly take for a Jew this athletic, blond young man, with Alsatian dogs on a lead, speaking, on occasion, the local argot. In that respect he felt completely safe and preferred not to think what would happen when the money ran out, when the time came to part with the golden cigarette case, the signet ring, the Waterman fountain pen, the Omega watch, and how long the money would last.

One day he went out as usual for a walk in the town's centre. Suddenly, as in a bad dream, he came face-to-face with his persecutor, the Silesian from the physical education course. Fright, panic, too late to avoid the clash — "this is the end," thought Staszek.

Jurczyga took another step forward, fell on Staszek's neck, gave him a warm hug. "My friend," he cried, "for God's sake, are you afraid of me? What do you take me for? I'll lay down my life for you. Here's money, take it, take it all, here's my address. Whenever you're in need, day or night, just knock at the door, count on me."

It so happened that soon after, when Staszek, having been denounced, was running away from the Gestapo, Jurczyga saved his life at the risk of his own.

In every discussion of these themes of the German occupation one has to bear in mind that those were apocalyptic times, that the circumstances in which people lived and acted were unprecedented. The decisions which they were often asked to take were so horrifying that one must beware of jumping to conclusions or passing judgement. A mother faced with the choice of which of her two children to save if there were a chance of saving only one of them — the very thought of having to make such a choice curdles the blood and renders one helpless. Such situations were frequent — who can put oneself in such a place and enter into a rational discussion of rights and wrongs?

In the years after the war, among my Cracovian contemporaries there was frequent mention of one Arthur Loeffler. He was a colleague of mine from school and university; we were very close. At school he was known for playing the first trumpet in the school orchestra: at the school's summer camps the day would begin with Arthur rousing the boys and girls from their sleep with the traditional Cracovian trumpeter's call. After matriculation he turned his musical talent to good use, playing in jazz bands, in cafes, *thes dansants*, society balls. He was not a highflyer, not known for special gifts, but an ordinary, popular, good chap.

During the war Arthur was recruited to serve in the OD, the "Jewish police." How much recruitment to the OD was voluntary and how much compulsory is a moot point. It was clear that the role of the "Jewish police" was solely to serve the Germans and do their dirty work for them — nobody expected to go through that service with their hands clean. Nonetheless there were many cases where the presence and the action of Jewish policemen tempered somewhat the frightfulness of the situation.

We know from the accounts of eyewitnesses that Arthur in the course of his duties behaved badly; that, above all, he traced and delivered to the Gestapo people whom he recognised as Jews, among them some of his former school friends. In the interminable discussions and recollections of those times, the question would crop up again and again: "How could he, how could he?"

That question "How could he?" concerns, of course, not only Arthur Loeffler but thousands of others whose actions and decisions seem to us now incomprehensible and contemptible. There is no need to justify such deeds — there are moral limits which must not be exceeded in any circumstances. But we must bear in mind what physical and mental pressure the German monster could and did exercise to get his way. And when one puts the question of how he could take some of his former friends to the Gestapo, a Waechter or a Schenker, one must remember that before he was sent out on his deadly hunt to fill the quota of victims he was told in no uncertain terms that should he return empty-handed, his father or mother, his sister or his brother would be killed instead. Let those who can pass a moral judgement.

*   *
*

The *Shema*, the key text of the Jewish liturgy, contains a commandment to teach the next generation, ceaselessly, the essence of Judaism. In the Haggadah, the story commemorating the exodus from Egypt, recited during the feast of Passover, there is a demonstration of how to instruct all of them — those who are keen to learn, and those who want no part in it, those who are indifferent, and those who do not even know what questions to ask.

The extermination of Jews in Europe during the last war is the most tragic event in the whole long martyrology of the Jewish people. The recollection of it dominates my internal landscape — everything I think and do, my view of everything around me is filtered through this awareness. And yet, despite these commands and instructions, I do not know how much of this awareness I have passed on to my children.

The motives for this reticence were diverse, not always clear even to myself. They know, of course, that I am a Jew, I have always stressed it. They know of my origin, my connection with Israel, with Poland — such always was and is the climate of my family home. But the extermination of the Jews, of my family, of what this means to me — these matters were seldom raised. I thought, perhaps, that they were growing up free from that trauma, cheerful, carefree, normal — why influence their disposition, cast the shadow which has darkened my life?

Another probable reason was that I found talking about these matters exceedingly difficult and had no language which I thought adequate or appropriate. I feel a bit guilty on this account. I did not appreciate, perhaps, that the past is not only a burden but also a heritage, and that in shielding them from the pain I also deprived them of something of value. A generation which does not know its roots, which is not in dialogue with its past, is, in some way, not whole. And if the awareness of that past is painful, it is, perhaps, a price worth paying.

How to do the "passing on"? There are many professionals in this field, but the majority of us are amateurs who have to find their own way (but I console myself with the thought that the Titanic was built by professionals and the Ark by an amateur). The greatest difficulty, as I see it, is how to present the boundless horror of those events which have no analogy in history and at the same time not to undermine the belief in the sense of creation, in human values, in justice.

Individual testimonies, which are legion, strike deeper than mere statistics, however stark. There are many sources of great value — one must learn how to use them, the timing, the dosage.

I have a friend, a woman writer, who lost her whole family in the Shoah. She told me that many years ago she was on vacation in Spain with her ten-year-old son. In that holiday resort, at that time, there was a veritable plague of insects, which made their stay well-nigh intolerable. One day she shut tight all the doors and windows of their apartment, sprayed every nook and cranny with insecticide and took her son for a long walk. When they returned after some hours and opened the door to the apartment to verify the efficacy of the operation the floor and the walls were covered with insects, dead or twitching in their last throes. At this sight the boy asked her: "Mummy, is this how Jews were poisoned? Is this how they died in the gas chambers?"

What had she told her son once, what picture had entered his little head, that he should come out with a remark like that? What scar did this image leave on him for life? Did she have the right to mark him so? Did she have the right not to?

I read somewhere an aphorism which amused me: "Love is a physiological function which made a career." It could be said that anti-Semitism is a primitive idea which made a career. (Another definition is "a Christian disease of which Jews die.")

The target is well chosen — Jews have this mysterious gift of provoking jealousy and contempt at the same time. They are weak (despite the myth of their power) and dispersed; it is easy to get at them. Anti-Semitism is a light sleeper and it is a very durable product — it survived the destruction of millions of Jews, it appears that it can thrive even in their absence. The Poles did not invent anti-Semitism — it is an ancient phenomenon, religious, social, economic, political — but this last variant, that is, anti-Semitism without Jews, can be called a Polish invention.

In various essays in this small collection, in my discussion with Andrzej Szczypiorski in the Paris *Kultura*, in my utterances at conferences in Oxford and Jerusalem, I have given expression to my thoughts on this subject. In a sense, everything I write revolves around this theme.

I am prompted here to add to this some further thoughts because during my recent visits to Poland I have been struck by the fact that, despite the passage of time, when a new generation has grown up, changes for the better have not been blindingly apparent. There is still a thicket of prejudice, ignorance and ill will. There persists the demonisation of the Jew, the thought that there must be some truth in the accusation that Jews commit ritual murder; that Jews as a race, nation, community, have in them an ineradicable element of evil. There lives a mere handful of Jews in Poland today, a sorry remnant of a three-and-a-half-million-strong presence, and yet many Poles cultivate their grudges against them and are ready to activate their hostility. That phrase which one heard after the war — "For one thing Hitler should be thanked: he did leave Poland free of Jews" — is the most odious expression to which human thought and language can sink. If this in any way reflects the prevailing mentality, then the moral devastation of which it is an example does indeed bode ill for the future of the country.

What have the Jews done, what unpardonable sins have they committed, that such should be their picture in the mind and the subconscious of many Poles? Is this merely an expression of the common, ordinary hatred of "the other," "the alien," the target of the traditional Christian doctrine of deicide, or is it something more, something specifically Polish, the roots of which must be sought not in Jewish characteristics but in the Polish psyche?

Whatever the case, the effect is a psychopathological phenomenon, a neurosis of a sick organism, which obscures a true picture of the world. Were I a "true" Pole (in the definition of President Walesa) I would deplore this national obsession, not on account of the Jews, to whom this no longer matters very much, but because I care for the health of the nation. I would grieve not only because of the misdirected energy and the sheer stupidity of it all, but because of the nagging question: whose side are you on in this matter? On the side of Hitler?

Yet another approach is possible. If Poles (many of them) are so hostile to Jews and hate them so, and the hatred is so deeply rooted and long-lasting, perhaps there are good reasons for such feelings, and if so, what are they and can they be removed?

It seems to me that posing the question thus is based on a false premise. It assumes that Jews are hated because they exhibit such and such failings — remove those failings and Jews will be hated no longer. I do not believe that such a proposition reflects reality. Where Jews are hated, they are hated because they are, because they exist — and the only remedy would be to cease to exist (at times, it has seemed, even that would not suffice). Their great, incurable failing (and they have many) is their Jewishness. Who among them would not wish that they were better? Room for improvement is vast (although it is not quite clear what precisely would constitute improvement and how one would go about achieving it). It is an illusion to think that if they were better they would have avoided their worst fate. To wish that they were different is to wish they ceased to be themselves.

An inviolate dogma of Polish perception is the view that POLAND is without blemish. Nobody in Poland will deny that Poles are capable of committing deeds foul, shameful or treacherous — Poles are prone to self-criticism. But, paradoxically, POLAND, independently of Poles, as it were, remains unsullied, is always the innocent victim, the Christ of Nations, and woe unto those who attempt to tarnish that dogma.

Many Poles will confess openly (some with pride) that Poland was and is the home of many anti-Semites. But the accusation that POLAND was an anti-Semitic country surprises them; they resent it, seem not to understand why their country should have this reputation. They believe it is the Jews who spread this opinion, repaying with ingratitude the good they received, villains that they are. And why, indeed, should Jews be doing this (except that it is in their nature to pervert the truth)? Because they feel guilty about the role some of them played in Poland — Rozanski, Swiatlo, Brystygierowa and their ilk. Moreover, Jews in America and in the West are ashamed that they did nothing to save their fellow Jews during the war. (What, precisely, they could have done and what sin of omission they are supposed to be ashamed of is not clear. One of the then-leaders of American Jewry, Rabbi Stephen Wise, confessed after the war that he regretted not having blockaded the entrance to the White House with his own body. That would have been a gesture but it would have had no effect. Roosevelt had the same answer to all Jewish appeals — Allied victory will bring release to all, including Jews.)

That mental muddle, the *non sequiturs* and ignorance of facts are typical of Polish apologetics in Jewish matters. The awareness that there are real charges to be answered, and the unwillingness to enter into a serious, informed discussion, cause them to sidetrack the issues, to pursue false trails, to settle for arguments *ad personam*.

For many years there was in Poland no possibility of free, honest, open discussion of many issues. There was a rigid frame of official doctrine, misrepresentation and bending of facts, outright, brazen lies. Mental habits engendered by such practice die hard. It is necessary to learn anew, to face the truth, even if Poland does not always emerge from this process unsullied.

I will not, once again, go over the whole range of issues arising from the history of the Jews in Poland, but would like to make it clear to my Polish friends, who often do not know the facts, that in the short interwar period, when the Poles were at last responsible for their own fate and the fate of their ethnic minorities, the Jews were left in no doubt that they were not fully fledged citizens, equal in all respects — that was the basic fact of their existence in the Diaspora. Their formal equality was guaranteed by the Constitution, there was also the greatly resented Minority Treaty for their protection, but a Jew, even one who to all outer appearances was indistinguishable from his Polish neighbour, knew in his heart of hearts that he was considered to be here as a guest and not as of right. Should he want to forget it for a while, reminders of it would meet him at every step — at school, on the street, in the press, in every professional and political walk of life.

Were one to compile an anthology of articles and statements from the newspapers and publications of all sorts, often illustrated by cartoons that could have been copied from Streicher's *Der Stuermer*, it would serve as an antidote to any sentiment which tended to look at the past through rose-tinted glasses.

In the image of Poland engraved in the Jewish consciousness there are also events from postwar history — the pogroms in Cracow and in Kielce, the loathsome campaign of the late sixties which forced the final Jewish exodus from Poland. What would have happened after the war if Jews, many of them, had returned to the places of their birth and habitation and had claimed their property? The reception they got in those rare cases when they did so fills one with a melancholy view of human nature.

It is true that many Jews, after their experiences in this century, conceive the whole world as being set against them and they see no reason for excluding Poles from that picture.

This view is unselective, one-sided and unjust. It is incumbent upon us to remember that Polish anti-Semitism, even in its ugliest and most brutal mani-festations, was a phenomenon of a different order and category from the Nazi doctrine and practice. What the Germans did was outside the mental horizon and imagination of even the most rabid Polish anti-Semite.

*　　*
*

It behooves me to say something about being an émigré, since that notion has formed a significant part of my state and existence.

What marks an immigrant is the fact that he is not greatly concerned or preoccupied with the events in the country around him, while at the same time he has grown a bit cool about what is going on in his country of origin. This means a general drop in emotional temperature. Life is probably, in the material sense, better and safer here, but also emptier. Even though the thought of "return" has long been abandoned; the whole existence here has been, as it were, "temporary," "provisional" — and never had the French saying "*Rien ne dure que le provisoire*" a truer confirmation.

The core of one's personality is memory. What we remember of our past and how we relate to it make us what we are. The interruption of the flow of one's existence is the definition of the fate of an émigré. The mother tongue becomes gradually less vivid, fluent and proficient, an impoverishment of one's personality follows — that is part of the price, a huge one, paid for the new status. To what extent one manages to compensate for that loss with new knowledge, new language, new interests is the measure of the quality of this second life.

It is one of the stark facts of social behaviour that an immigrant is viewed with dislike by the native population — that is how the herd instinct manifests itself. That dislike, paradoxically, is often strongest in an environment which contains a large section of recent immigrants and also not-so-recent immigrants who feel threatened by the new influx. Jews who came to England a long time ago and acquired good protective colouring often viewed with unease and resentment Jews arriving from Russia, or later from Germany. They were a little ashamed of them, afraid of the responsibility for them.

In the early days of our stay in Great Britain our relationship with the native population was marked by a degree of insincerity on our part — it would have been impolite and also imprudent to voice openly what our thoughts of them were. And they were, naturally enough, disparate: we envied them their normal, stable existence, admired some of the traits of character and behaviour, wanted to get included in the stream of their lives, to earn a good opinion in their eyes. We would flatter them if that was going to help. On the other hand we were critical of them; they appeared to be cold and remote, with a feeling of natural superiority; we often felt we were being patronised. The elementary fact escaped us that — as in every nation and society — there were among them all sorts of people — warm and cold, stiff and accessible, wise and stupid, good and bad.

At the time of our arrival Great Britain's rule extended over a large part of the globe. Now it is a small country, struggling with economic and social problems, uncertain of its role in Europe and the world. It would appear that the British, as a nation, as people, have in the light of these changes altered for the better. One could say that the pendulum has swung the other way. Instead of the stereotypical self-confident, somewhat arrogant, superior being, one meets all too often those who are self-disparaging, severely and unjustly critical of their country and their fellow men.

I realised, relatively early, that there was no need for me to feel inferior, to imitate the native, to strive to be like him and in the deepest sense of the word his equal, although he and his parents were born here and this is "his" country and I have only been thrown here by fate.

In the course of the years, on various occasions, a question has come to the fore: how would the British have behaved if the war had been lost and the country occupied by Hitler? After all, it was not such a fanciful thing to imagine. How would the British have behaved towards the German occupier and — what is to me of greater interest still — towards the Jews? Would they have behaved like the Poles, or like the French, or the Italians, or differently from all those? It is a painful speculation, fortunately only theoretical. Were I pressed to express an opinion on this, based on my understanding of the ways of the British and of human nature, I would incline to the view that they, like others, would not have emerged from such a devilish trial with credit (a small object-lesson from the Channel Islands destroys all illusions). There is no doubt that a Quisling or a Petain would quickly have emerged from the ranks of the Mosleys or Halifaxes or Ravensdales to "save" Britain through collaboration with the Nazis and at their bidding would have delivered to them first the "foreign" Jews, those who had come from Germany recently, and then "their own," that is, those who had come somewhat earlier.

I think, however — and this is the measure of my respect for my adopted country — that when it came to private succour, saving individuals, hiding them, helping small groups to escape — the proportion of such people would have been larger, maybe significantly so, than in other countries. (Such a statement is, of course, without proof and throws light not on the British but only on my view of them.)

A Jew, no matter of what origin, makes a different immigrant from a Pole. An émigré Pole looks at such a turn of events as a passing phase, does not on the whole think that this may extend to the second or third generation, to eternity. He does not think about striking root, about assimilation, about "going native" — what purpose would that serve? A Jewish émigré sees it differently. There is no thought in his head of "returning," he accepts immediately that emigration means a new beginning and believes that the new country may be for him, and certainly his children, better than the one he left behind. He also often has in his new abode some community, near or more distant relatives from previous waves of emigration. But even without relatives in the strict sense of the word there would be, everywhere, a "native" Jewish community, towards which he would gravitate and where he would expect support. ("Jews hold together," the Poles would say, reproachfully. In fact this is a fine quality, not to be sneered at.) Even though emigration is not a phenomenon unknown to Polish history, Jews are, one could argue, historically better-equipped to cope with it — until recently the Diaspora, a state of dispersion, was the natural condition of their existence. It follows also that Jews quickly create an input into the host culture, whilst Poles rarely do so, their creativity finding expression in their own language and own culture.

If, after spending some years in a Wellsian time-machine, I had landed now, in the nineties, in Poland, unaware of recent events, I would have looked round and to my indescribable joy have realised that I was in a free and independent country, not threatened by neighbours from the East or from the West. Moreover, that the geopolitical conditions had changed to such an extent that such a threat could be eliminated from any political prognosis. (I nearly said "forever," but

54

"forever" means a very, very long time and we have observed how unimaginable changes can and sometimes do take place unexpectedly and rapidly.)

I would see that Poland is ethnically and religiously united, without the problems with minorities which were her blight before the war and with which she could not cope. She finds herself within physical and political borders more favourable than any in previous history (if we are not to return to the bombastic concept of "from the Baltic to the Black Sea").

Never before have such favourable conditions prevailed for Poland to be master of its own fate and decide its own future.

Seeing all this, assuring myself that I was not dreaming, I would fall to my knees and be in ecstasy. Why do I not see around me Poles jumping for joy?

Is it possible that in their subconscious there lingers a thought that this ethnic and religious homogeneity does not represent a gain, but an awesome, irreparable loss which will lead to a cultural and spiritual impoverishment?

* * *

To stimulate conversation in good company and to give food for thought, I sometimes throw in the following question: Have you ever met, face to face, somebody who is out of the ordinary, exceptional, qualitatively different from the rest of us, unquestionably above the common herd — in one word, great? People seldom come up with a ready example, which only goes to show the fairly obvious point that such persons are rare and that opportunities to brush against them do not often come our way.

I myself have no hesitation in giving a positive answer. A number of times I found myself in the presence of Vladimir Jabotinsky, and I was acutely aware, every time, that I was in the presence of a phenomenon, in the magnetic field of an overpowering personality, whom I admired, respected and owed allegiance to; more — a feeling that I would have been ready to go through fire at his behest.

That was partly due to a kind of brainwashing to which I was submitted in my youth. Jabotinsky was the founder and leader of the Zionist Revisionist Party (whose "fighting arm" was the organisation Brit Trumpeldor or Betar). From early days I was a member of the Masada student organisation within that party. The vigorous, aggressive programme and the fiery rhetoric of Jabotinsky, positing "a Jewish State on both sides of the River Jordan," appealed to my youthful patriotic fervour more than the diplomatic play and the "leftish," too peaceable — as it seemed to me — policy of Chaim Weizmann, Nahum Sokolow or, later, David Ben-Gurion, Shertok or Arlossorof. We sang, enthusiastically, the "Hymn of Betar" composed by Jabotinsky, of the great, courageous generation which would raise the flame of rebellion, conquer the mountain or die — that was the way and the spirit. In the thirties Jabotinsky sent weekly articles to the Jewish newspapers in Poland (first to *Der Hajnt*, then to *Der Moment*). These articles were very influential in forming Jewish public opinion. This was journalism at its best, persuasive and prophetic.

In the late thirties there appeared in Cracow a journal called *Trybuna Narodowa*, the organ of the Zionist Revisionist Party. I was on the editorial board of that paper and one of my functions was to translate from Yiddish into Polish Jabotinsky's articles sent to us from his office in Rue de la Boetie in Paris.

One of our "achievements" was the publication of a "special supplement" to the conservative Polish daily *Czas*; they agreed to print material supplied by us. The main article, on the front page, was written by Jabotinsky (translated by me), entitled "A Favourable Storm." For it he analysed the hopelessness of the Jewish situation in Europe, to which the only remedy, according to him, was a mass evacuation of Jews from Poland and other countries of the Diaspora to Palestine. (How that was to be achieved in practice and how the British were to be persuaded to open the gates of Palestine were questions left aside for the time being.) Such a thesis was, of course, grist to the mill of the Polish nationalists and right-wingers who wanted to be rid of the Jews at any price. They were delighted to claim Jabotinsky as a new ally and quoted him in support of their slogans. He should have foreseen that such abuse of his thesis would follow, and that to enter the public arena with a programme for evacuation in those circumstances was an act of criminal irresponsibility. But Jabotinsky's prediction that Jews in Europe faced a terminal threat of physical extinction proved all-too-tragically accurate.

Jabotinsky visited Cracow from time to time and spoke at public meetings, four hours at a stretch. As an orator he had no equal; he was inspired and coolly calculating at the same time, in the tradition of true people's tribunes.

From Cracow he would make forays into neighbouring towns — that was the way Zionist propaganda was organised. Speakers did their rounds of local meetings, as I did. But a visit from Jabotinsky was an event which was talked about long before and long after. Often, when he arrived at a railway station and got into his droshky, his supporters would unharness the horse and pull the carriage to the hotel. There was a cult of Jabotinsky such as no other Zionist leader enjoyed.

A friend of mine who survived the war in exile in the depths of Russia described to me a little incident which throws some light on what the name of Jabotinsky meant to some people. In the Siberian twilight a long, bedraggled column of deportees moves slowly. On the horizon another one appears, moving towards them. When they come within shouting distance of each other a voice floats across: "*Jabotinsky lebt?*" In that remote, snowy desert, at the extremity of the human condition, someone is concerned with that one thing —

is Jabotinsky alive? If he were, then the world would be redeemed and it was worthwhile trying to survive.

At that time — it must have been in 1941 — these poor wretches in Siberia had no way of knowing that Jabotinsky was no more. He had died in America in 1940, aged sixty.

His place in history remains contentious. He was willful, could not work in harness and gave free rein to his own, grandiose ideas. In 1935 he did great damage to the cause he meant to serve; he broke away from the World Zionist Organisation and founded his own New Zionist Organisation, causing a huge loss of resources and energy through fratricidal quarrels. Rabid partisanship in the community was rife — it persisted even at the most tragic moment in history, the Warsaw Ghetto Uprising. The Revisionist Zionists would not submit to the unified command of the Jewish Fighting Organisation under Anielewicz of Hashomer Hatzair. They fought separately, on their own section of the front. They all perished without trace.

Mutual hatred did not cool down in Palestine, nor even after the creation of the State of Israel — on the contrary. The fight continues to the present day. I am inclined to the view that only Jews can hate each other so. But I remember the Irish. Also the Poles.

Where does this exposition or meditation lead me? It leads me to the conclusion that my Motherland is not territorial, that it does not depend on this or that scrap of territory, on a border, a banner or an emblem. It is not Poland or Cracow where I was born, where the birth certificate was issued and where I spent my childhood and my early youth. It is not England where I have spent my whole adult life, where my naturalisation papers were registered and where I feel more or less at home. It is not Israel and Jerusalem, which I love but where I am only a casual guest, not deserving special consideration. One could surmise from this that I am a "rootless cosmopolitan," an appellation which at certain times and in certain countries was deeply defamatory and dangerous. It was simply a cryptonym replacing the word "Jew," at a time when official doctrine negated anti-Semitism but in fact the system was rabidly anti-Semitic.

I would be ready to rehabilitate this epithet. I place true cosmopolitanism high on the scale of human values, in direct opposition to chauvinism, which I hate — whether in England, in Poland or in Israel. It is an ideal worth striving for. It is not easily achievable, it calls for shedding many prejudices and bad mental habits. The climate for it is, for the time, unfavourable. After the dark night of communism, in many countries there is the deadly ferment of primitive nationalism which has been in the past and could again become the ruin of Europe.

As for the designation "rootless," I answer — following George Steiner — that trees have roots and stand immobile in one spot; humans have legs and can move around this earth where the spirit moves them (and the frontier guard allows passage, a cynic might add, but that's another matter). Life's elixir should be drawn from universal, all-embracing sources. Above all, I would like to be able to say, after Lamartine, *"Ma patrie c'est la verité."* The distance which separates one from being able to say this without some vast distortion is the measure, in my eyes, of one's success or failure in life's long journey.

What shall we tell Miriam?

I have given my little piece a title which might strike you as quaint. I call it "What shall we tell Miriam?" It is thus entitled on the assumption that there must be many Miriams and Sarahs and Shulamiths and Samuels and Josephs and Daniels everywhere in the world where Jews have set foot (which means virtually everywhere) who are or very soon now will be asking their parents and grandparents questions to which hitherto they have seemed strangely indifferent: what was life really like in that country where you were born, in that incredibly distant past, before the Second, before the First World War? What were these people like, the grandparents and the great-grandparents, how did they live, what did they do, what did they think, what did the places look like, what did they smell of... In the words of the historian Ranke: "*Wie es wirklich gewesen.*" Posing such questions is part of a natural cyclical process: indifference — then curiosity.

I think it is important to tell them — for our sake and for their sake. Who will, if we won't? Ours is the last and vanishing generation of living witness. The point arises how to do it, the young have little patience, their concentration span is short. Of course it would be simple enough to use the precept of the Sage Hillel — "*tseh ul'mad*" — go to the library, read and learn, there is no shortage of sources. But that, I fear, is a counsel of perfection, rarely followed.

There is another, more personal way, and I would like to give an example how this might be done, bringing it home through the story of one's own family. I am somewhat reticent about introducing an autobiographical note — the personal pronoun is the most suspect part of speech — but I think in the event it is justified, since my family, in its mainstream and offshoots, serves as a not-untypical illustration of the many aspects of Jewish life in Western Galicia, that is, the "Austrian" part of Poland, in and around Cracow at the end of the nineteenth and the first decades of the twentieth century.

I am descended on my father's side from a long line of rabbis or, the less snobbish would say, *melameds* — religious teachers, who would surely be horrified at what has happened to their issue. My father was the youngest of fifteen children. They did not all have the same mother and, of course, did not all survive to adulthood. To give a thumbnail sketch of the family one would need a very large thumb indeed.

The grandfather, a white-bearded patriarch, by trade an innkeeper, in his youth reputedly an oak of a man, with proof of virility for all the world to see, as I remember him was already a shadow of himself, bent in half, toothless, shrunken with incessant toil, worry and the blows of fortune; he died at a then-good age, certainly less than "threescore years and ten"; and the saying at the time was *"a yingerer zol nysh shtarben"* — let never a man younger than him die — and this tells its own story.

As can easily be calculated, the Scharfs were so thick on the ground in that part of the land, in the villages, townlets like Chrzanow (the headquarters), Kalwaria, Alwernia, Zywiec, Bochnia and the environs of Cracow, that it is a wonder there was room for anybody else. (Incidentally, if you are interested in statistics, the great majority of the Jewish population inhabited localities of less than 20,000 people.)

This vast clan was seething with activity and appeared to be in a state of perpetual motion, travelling with trunks, cases, parcels, by train or horse-drawn carts in feverish pursuit of their affairs big and small, and also to family gatherings — the weddings, the circumcisions, the funerals. I remember the colourful, noisy crowd passing at various times through our house in Cracow, en route to their next port of call, to rest awhile, to exchange family news, to seek advice from my mother or a loan from my father and refreshing themselves with a cup of tea — but no more. My mother's kitchen was suspect to them, rightly so. Even though the meat was kosher and ham was never eaten inside the house, the dessert after goose could well be wild strawberries and cream, in defiance of the ritual command.

The spectrum of religious orthodoxy, belief and practice was wide. There was my oldest uncle, Motl, almost forty years my father's senior, an ascetic and forbidding figure, a follower to distraction of the Rebbe of Belz, and not on speaking terms with his younger brother Saul, who was not — God forbid — an "anti-Hassid" but, ridiculously, a follower of another "wonder rabbi" not nearly as holy. As a boy, I firmly refused to visit him after the day when he pinched my cheek, in a supposed sign of affection, but, as I well knew, in retribution for the fact that, as he discovered to his disgust, I was not wearing *tsitsit* — the four-cornered garment which a Jew is enjoined to wear through the waking hours.

There was Cousin Hymie, a dreamer and a schemer, frantically engaged in projects which, if successful, would shed enormous benefits on the whole family, but in the meantime required continuous injections of cash, a figure modelled to a T, in the way life imitates or rather parodies art, on Shalom Aleichem's Menachem Mendl.

There was Aunt Rachel, an early widow, with as many children as there had been years in her happy marriage, making a living in an otherwise male preserve as a marriage-broker. Since that involved continuous travel in search of information, developing connections, soothing anxieties and supervising *bekucks* (the preview to which the couple was entitled) — a subtle and sophisticated pursuit — she was also a ministering angel to the sick in the family wherever she found them (and she found them aplenty), applying her uncanny knowledge of folk remedies and deep psychological insights. Long before the name was invented she understood the nature of psychosomatic illness, which featured in her sources as *anredinish is arger vi a krenk* — meaning that you can talk yourself into an imaginary illness, worse than a real one.

There was, before my time, deeply secreted in the tribe's common memory, the allegedly beautiful Auntie Rosa, her yellowing photograph buried in my mother's knickknacks drawer, safe — but not from my probing hands — who, I can only piece the story together, eloped with an "Austrian" officer, and after he had had enough of her (as he would) finished up in the gutter as a streetwalker. There is no evidence for this, but it was felt that the story could not have ended otherwise. Her parents, of course, cast her out and went through the ritual of mourning the dead and were till their dying day, which came all the sooner for it, consumed by grief and shame.

This motif, which with slight variations recurs frequently in Yiddish and also Polish literature until it becomes a stereotype, is proof enough that such skeletons rattled in many families' cupboards. Traumas of this kind tore the guts out of the community; no worse thing was conceivable. Yet in the limited interaction of the group with the surrounding world, menacing yet alluring, an occasional crossing of the barrier was inevitable. Revulsion against what was seen as suffocating obscurantism also played its part. But the convert remained in the eyes of his contemporaries an abhorrent and despised figure. No Jew could believe that the change of faith was genuine (a suspicion shared widely, I think, by the receiving side). How *could* it be? It was generally considered that, with minuscule exceptions, the convert — indifferent to the old religion and dissimulating the new — was in it merely for personal advantage of one sort or another.

A case less dramatic than that of Auntie Rosa, but probably no less typical, revolved around my Uncle Joshua. His, and my mother's, stepmother decided that the parental home was no longer the place for him, and he was packed off, just like that, to go to America. This, as we know, was not an uncommon practice in those days, and that migration, as a whole, proved to be the most timely and beneficial of all. But Joshua — what would he have been? fourteen, fifteen years of age? — was not concerned with History, other than his own — a lost, castaway boy. What were the mechanics of these journeys? I presume he had a *Schiffskarte* sewn into his pocket and was supposed to sail from Liverpool; how he was to get there in the first place I do not know. In the event, he didn't make it — first time round. En route, it transpired, he met fellow travellers who knew the family and considered it wicked of them to send the boy away thus, depriving him of his "portion" of the inheritance (of which, no doubt, they had a vastly exaggerated notion). He turned back, and on his return journey, I gather, he must have been spotted by some members of a missionary society, in whose eyes (mistakenly I think) the conversion of the Jews must precede the Coming (Second Coming, if one accepts their reckoning) of the Messiah, and they decided that Joshua's destiny was to speed Him on his way. Anyway, a hot meal and a few kind words could — then as now — do wonders. I can still sense the horror with which my mother related the story — half-a-century on — of how people, neighbours and friends, came rushing into the house, utterly scandalised, to tell his father and stepmother and the other children that Joshua was standing in the central square selling missionary tracts! There was heartbreak, remorse and dread of scandal. In the end — by bribery, persuasion or force — the boy was despatched again, this time effectively, to reach the Other Shore. Virtually nothing was heard of him after that — until shortly before the last war some members of the family started digging for his address to write to him to plead for an "affidavit." It was too late.

My father was an early rebel. Feeling constrained by the life in the *shtetl* he cut his jacket "short" and changed his hat from the round black velvety kind, part of the Orthodox uniform, for one of lighter colour, fashionable but not very. This declaration required probably more courage than we imagine. He arrived in Cracow in search of wife and fortune — and soon succeeded in his first objective beyond his wildest dreams. The second became somehow less important. He retained, of course, a total attachment to Judaism. He knew nothing else, felt not the slightest need for anything else.

I see him on a Saturday afternoon, reaching for a volume of the Talmud, and from the way he handled it, the caress, one knew the book was holy. Bending over an open folio he would slowly turn the pages, as if feeling his way through an embarrassment of riches, and then, with a familiarity that breeds contentment, he would settle down to the study of a chosen passage. He was no scholar — he had the mandatory few years of *cheder* behind him and was quite unable to make his own way through the undergrowth of commentaries, sprinkled with the poppyseed of glosses. But no matter, he was not looking for solutions to problems or rulings of law, but seeking to wash away the triviality and harshness of everyday existence in the waves of the eternal. He believed, simply, that the book contained the truth and that it was good to touch it.

He wished to persuade me to share his outlook but we did not know how to talk to each other, and he realised that an argument with a precocious know-all only led to an aggravation of spirit. Only once, I remember, he exploded when

I asked him: "What is all this for?" "What is this *for*, fool? The whole of life is for *this*!"

He saw his role at home as that of the breadwinner, and even though he genuinely believed that all he had aspired to was for our sake, the bringing up of children would not have been part of his conscious concern. What little modicum of success he had as a merchant and small-time manufacturer was brought about by ceaseless hustle and total immersion in the task at hand. He would provide for all our needs — and be the sole judge of how these were defined. While spending money on books was grudgingly approved, there was much pursing of lips and shaking of the head. Novels, in his eyes, were *narishkeiten*, foolishness and frivolity. How could adult men and women give serious attention to the imaginary misfortunes of nonexistent people! I argued that they nourish the sources of feeling and imagination, open the door to experience beyond one's personal orbit and give a glimpse of the many faces of truth. Where else could knowledge of the ways of the world come from? Were not the scandalous infidelities of Mrs. G. next door made comprehensible through the reading of Madame Bovary?

My father understood perhaps more of these matters than he thought fit to concede. He and I maintained a brittle truce which lasted till just before the outbreak of war, when I left home and hearth for a foreign land. I never saw him again: he died in 1942, felling trees at the Arctic Circle, a task for which he was ill-prepared.

There was, in those days, a yawning, unbridgeable "generation gap" by comparison with which our contemporary conflicts are puny. The rebellion against the old order was gathering momentum. The tribe was bursting at the seams and moving in all directions. It proliferated into a human landscape of great diversity. Some young members of the family became communists, card-carrying members. Now, that was serious business, illegal and dangerous. It could and often did end badly. Police searches at home, to the dreadful distress of parents; arrests, prison sentences. In spite of that, or rather because of that, this attracted some very good people indeed. The idea was irresistible — it was offering a solution not only to the Jewish question, which seemed trivial by comparison, but to all other questions of social injustice and exploitation, in the trail of its historically inevitable victory of the proletariat. The brotherhood of nations would come naturally, as a bonus. This idea deserved sacrifices — and there were many, including the ultimate, and massive, under Stalin's execution wall. My favourite cousin Moishe, later Misha, a brilliant linguist and chess player, perished thus.

Some of the clan gave their allegiance to the Jewish Workers Movement, the Bund, but the large majority was swept by the liberating wind of Zionism, in all its hues. You could say that by the late twenties and early thirties the *shtetl*, the Jewish townlet, had been left behind, and most of the members of the family had migrated to larger towns, mainly Cracow, where they embraced and penetrated and intermingled with other families, to the extent that virtually everybody was or became a relative: the black-bearded Schwarzbarts and the red-bearded Rotbarts, the ubiquitous Landaus, Grosses and Kleins, Schusters and Schneiders, Wolfs and Schaffs, Sperlings and Spatzes, Spiras, Schapiras, Kohns and Kahans and Kohens (here also belong the Loewys), Sonntags, Montags, Freitags and Sonnabends, Zuckers and Pfeffers, Gruens and Brauns, Golds and Silvers, Nussbaums, Gruenbaums, Rosenbaums, all the other -baums, and Aschkenase and Gumplowicz. I have named only those of whom I have direct knowledge of a bond with the Scharfs.

It was an interesting community, of a mixed profile. I was told a story which describes it nicely. A man goes to Cracow and on return tells his friend: "The Jews of Cracow are remarkable people. I saw a Jew who spends all his nights dreaming and all his days planning the revolution. I saw a Jew who spends all his time studying the Talmud. I saw a Jew who chases every skirt he sees. I saw a Jew who didn't want anything to do with women. I saw a Jew who is full of schemes how to get rich quick." The other man says: "I don't know why you are astonished: Cracow is a big city and there are many Jews, all sorts of people." "No," says the first, "it was the same Jew."

But I also want to draw another profile of a Jew of those days. It comes from a little verse called "*Avi*" (My Father) by Itzhak Katzenelson, the author of what is possibly the greatest poem written during and about the Shoah: "The Song of the Murdered Jewish People." He writes: "When did he [my father] learn the Bible by heart? The translations of Onkelos and Martin Luther? The Talmud, Codes, Midrash, Shakespeare and Heine? When did he read Gogol, Thucydides and Plutarch? When did he study the Holy Zohar? When did he sleep?"

If not for the fact that all these people lived, and soon after died, in apocalyptic times, some of that profusion of humanity would have overspilled into other streams, all over the map, and with their diverse talents, energy and purposefulness they would have enriched the world. As it is, from my closest family (and that, as has been said, included hundreds of individuals) — there was not a single survivor except, blissfully, my mother.

When talking about Polish Jewry before the War, before the Wars, it is important to steer a clear course between nostalgia and reality. In mourning the past it would be wrong to idealise it. The literature of that time, the only authentic descriptive record, in Yiddish and Hebrew, is sharply and mercilessly critical, even though the criticism is tempered by compassion, as behooves the prophetic tradition. Mendele, Shalom Aleichem, Peretz, Opatoshu, portray the sordid conditions — the poverty, the powerlessness, the oppression, the obscurantism — and lash out against it; that is the function, or the mission, of literature. If you want to know, for instance, what the position of women was in that society, a short passage from the book *Debora* by Esther Kreitman, the sister of the Singer brothers (and brushed by the talent so prodigiously bestowed on them) will tell you more than a dozen learned tracts.

Once, when she overheard her father saying proudly of Joshua: "One day he will be a brilliant Talmudic scholar" she asked: "And Father, what am *I* going to be one day?" Her father looked as if he didn't quite understand the question. "What are *you* going to be one day? Nothing, of course!" Do you need to know any more?

It is true to say that poverty was dire and widespread. But it is well to remember that it was not a specifically Jewish poverty, which contrasted with non-Jewish well-being. On the contrary, urban squalor knew no boundaries and the gentile unemployed workman suffered the same, if not worse, hardship and degradation. The countryside could be harsher still: the small holder and landless peasant led, in a bad year, a pitiful existence.

On the other hand, the idea that Jewish life in Poland was always one of unredeemed gloom and oppression is ill-founded. There were lights as well as shadows: the rich fabric of Jewish existence is woven of many strands, and some of its brightest and most life-enhancing manifestations took place on Polish soil. When faced with the bleakness of the picture one can well ask the question: if it was so bad, why was it so good?

The structure of what somebody has called "The Jewish Nation in Poland" was diverse. It had its urban proletariat with its industrial workers, tradesmen and craftsmen (mainly tailors and shoemakers), its *Luftmenschen* with no visible means of support, a large and amorphous middle class of shopkeepers and business people of all categories, its free professions — doctors, lawyers, scholars — and its plutocracy of manufacturers, bankers, big industrialists.

The community's religious administration lay in the hands of the *kahal*, with considerable autonomy and a wide range of competence. There were Jewish and Hebrew schools of all grades; yeshivahs and high schools, scholarly institutes — among them the famous YIVO in Vilna and the Institute of Jewish Studies in Warsaw, which had university status. A Jewish press flourished, in Yiddish, Polish and Hebrew (in 1939, according to a recent study, there were thirty Jewish daily newspapers and 130 periodicals of all kinds). There were innumerable trade and professional associations, of writers, journalists, doctors, lawyers, engineers, merchants, homeowners (in the late thirties, forty percent of town property was in Jewish hands).

There was a network of charitable institutions, hospitals, orphanages, provident funds and summer camps to help the disadvantaged. There were sports clubs giving scope to aspiring and actual record-holders in all disciplines. Above all, there were the political parties, with their affiliated youth organisations, with a vision of a better future. Jewish deputies represented the whole spectrum of political life in both chambers of the Polish legislature.

The community was fragmented and torn by internal strife, but there was one unifying factor — a sense of sharing a common fate which transcended social and political differences. There was a marked spirituality, even among the nonreligious, an instinctive allegiance and response to what was felt to be the Jewish ethos: a deeply ingrained, universal conviction that, beyond the mundane, man had to aspire to higher things, however defined.

It is also important to remember that there existed a considerable area where the division between the Polish and the Jewish world was blurred and the long cohabitation resulted in mutual acceptance, tolerance and harmony. This produced a cross-fertilisation with an untold enrichment of both cultures. Polish literature of the time glitters with illustrious names — Lesmian, Tuwim, Slonimski, Wittlin, Bruno Schulz, to name but a few. A civilisation flourished here with its traditions, language, folklore, literature and music, and with roots deeper than Polish civilisation. Did it ever occur to a Pole that, in the neighbouring town or for that matter on the very same street, something was happening that could engage his attention and deserved his interest? With a few notable exceptions, the answer is no. The Jewish population was commonly regarded as a "dark continent," backward and primitive, evoking feelings of aversion and repugnance. The Poles automatically regarded themselves as infinitely superior — each Pole superior to each Jew, be he a rabbi, a writer, a merchant, a shoemaker. The Jews requited it with a shrug of their shoulders: what could you expect of "them"?

To complete the picture, here are three snapshots from memory, which illustrate the pressures of growing up and living as a Jew in a country where Catholicism dominated and filled the atmosphere like ether.

Once, a very long time ago, our housemaid, out of affection for me and genuine concern for my soul, took me with her to church and confronted me with that huge human figure stretched on His Cross, nails piercing hands and legs, droplets of blood oozing from open wounds. She whispered urgently: "This is God Jesus and He loves you, though you are a Jew and your forefathers crucified Him — and you mustn't tell your mother about it!" I was struck with terror and nausea. On coming home I sobbed inconsolably but would not let on why. (Perhaps this experience left me with my lifelong interest in theology. Many years and many learned books later, with the clock ticking ever faster, I remain an unregenerate agnostic, thank God. This serves me reasonably well by day, if not so well by night.)

When the street urchin from next door where we lived wanted to chase me and harm me, it was not with a stick or with a stone (that also, sometimes) but with what he felt was a much more potent weapon: he used to make his index fingers into a sign of the Cross — I was supposed to cower in the face of it and run. I did, too.

I think that in this image alone, in the small example of *Ecclesiae Militans*, there is enough food for thought to make one ponder what happened, no, what was bound to happen in the future to the generation of both boys — the one making the sign of the Cross and the one who was made to run away from it.

On returning to Cracow for the first time after the war, I avoided the street where we used to live. But in time, it seemed, the wounds partly healed and I was overcome by an irrepressible impulse to cast a glance over the place where we lived — was the old furniture there, my bookcase, the paintings on the walls?

The house stood facing the Planty, the park around the old city centre, in a district which was then respectable, reasonably prosperous, and later — like most buildings — fell into neglect, decay, nobody's property.

I entered the familiar entrance hall. I struck a match to discover from the list of tenants the name of the owner of flat 4. As I was gathering courage and composing my thoughts on how to explain my ghostly visit, the doors opened on the ground floor, and a man — menacing, cross and angry, as is the habit of the land — came close to me: "What are you looking for? There is nothing here for you!" Indeed, I thought. How well he put it. There is nothing here for me.

Finally, a scene from my recent visit to Cracow. Usually, as dusk falls, I am in the habit of leaving my favourite seat in the Cafe Noworolski, under the arcades of the Sukiennice, to stroll across the square, the Rynek, into the Church of the Holy Virgin Mary, from whose tower, the taller of the two, there sounds the famous, hourly trumpet call. I spend there a quiet hour or so, contemplating the altarpiece by Wit Stwosz, a magnificent example of religious art. I also listen to the quiet evening service.

On my last visit some months ago, my neighbour in the pew happened to be a youngish man of fine face, who prayed silently with great concentration. At the end of the service, as we were leaving the church together, we got talking, with growing sympathy and openness — two authentic Cracovians, spanning two generations. After complimenting me on my Polish, which oddly has not gone rusty after half-a-century away from the country, he confided in me thus: "I am a believer, as you see, and a practising Catholic. I am also a student of ancient history. I know, and it no longer causes me any difficulty to accept this, that Our Lord Jesus was a Jew. But in no way am I able to accept that Our Holy Virgin Mary, the Queen of the Crown of Poland, as we like to call her, was a Jewess..."

I didn't know what to say. To understand these things, on a level which does justice to the depth and complexity of these predicaments, is too difficult for me, for most of us.

The Jews in Poland
Jagiellonian University, Cracow 1992

Cracow of blessed memory

It does not take much to set an old Cracovian musing, by the waters of the Thames, about his old city: an odd word, somebody's name, an echo of a melody, the taste of a madeleine. The photographs of Stanislaw Markowski open the floodgates of memory. But I have no desire to let the stream flow; on the contrary, my impulse is to get out of its way. It was all a long time ago, before the Flood, the other side of the nightmare. Continuity was suddenly, brutally, irrevocably disrupted. People with whom I shared that past have dispersed all over the world (mainly to the other!). I want to run away — yet something is holding me back.

I have been an eyewitness to that period of history which remains tattooed on my consciousness. There is a duty to bear witness, every piece of evidence counts. There is not a great deal of it left, and it will be all that will remain after we are gone.

For me, Poland of those days meant, almost exclusively, Cracow. I did not go "to Kutno or Sieradz," I did not visit Warsaw; whatever for? After holidays in nearby Zakopane, Zawoja or Rabka, the return to Cracow was always joyful. I presume that those less privileged who lived in Lwow, Lodz or Warsaw had similar local patriotism, but I find it hard to imagine. The town must have had a singular charm which endeared it to its inhabitants, since true old Cracovians, wherever you find them (not all that often in Cracow itself!) speak of it with such warmth and affection (even those who appear quite indifferent to the rest of the country).

It was small and beautiful. Smallness is a quality more and more appreciated. My longest walk (excluding Wolski Forest, Wola Justowska or Sikornik) was from the periphery of the Blonia commons; skirting the park named after Dr. Jordan, the football pitch of the Cracovia Sports Club, along Wolska Street, past the university, then along Szewska Street, the Main Square, Sienna and Starowislna Streets, crossing the "Third Bridge" to Podgorze, to the front door of the house where my girlfriend lived — a daily walk, not long enough to say to each other everything that needed to be said.

Some while ago I met in London an elderly gentleman who now lives in Mexico. It transpired that he was born in Cracow, hence an immediate bond of mutual attraction (as if that alone guaranteed quality). Somehow we had not bumped into each other before the war. Where did you live? In Sebastiana

Street. Isn't that odd, so did I. What number? Thirty-three. Ah, I lived at number six. That was a long way away, no wonder we did not know each other.

Cracow was beautiful. Surrounded by tree-lined paths, in springtime brimming with jasmine and lilac, with enchanting little byways, a "swan lake," statues of Copernicus, Grottger, Balucki. There was Wawel Castle with its cathedral, the great bell of King Sigismund, the "Dragon's Cave," the monument to Thaddeus Kosciuszko, views over the River Vistula.

When you stood under the arcades of the Cloth Hall looking towards the Main Square, the monument of Adam Mickiewicz, the Church of the Virgin Mary, and the little chapel of St. Adalbert, you had in front of your eyes an urban vista beyond compare. (I catch myself using the past tense, but why? All this, blissfully, stands now as it stood then, virtually unchanged, and only for me does it seem to be placed in the very distant past.)

Go down Grodzka Street and Stradom, here is the Warszawa Cinema, where crowds gathered to listen to Vladimir Jabotinsky on his visits to Cracow. Cross Dietla Street, and you find yourself in the heart of what was the Jewish quarter of Kazimierz. Here was the tavern of Mr. Thorn, here the tenement house of Mr. Süsser, whose huge courtyard could well have served as an inspiration to the famous poem "*El Mole Rachamim*" by Wiktor Gomulicki. That courtyard was the habitual scene of public demonstrations. There were no microphones — the speakers, addressing the crowds from the balcony, were shouting their hearts out, rousing the crowds against the injustices of this world; against the British government's White Paper limiting the immigration quota to Palestine, against Mrs. Prystor's proposal to abolish ritual slaughter of animals, against the pogrom in Przytyk — such causes abounded.

Penetrate this labyrinth of lanes, alleyways and cul-de-sacs. Where else in the Diaspora were streets named after figures of the Old Testament — Jacob, Isaac, Joseph, Esther? Here, on the square at Szeroka Street, was a flea-market, you could call it "the mother of all flea-markets." Here also stands the famous Remuh Synagogue, named after the great Cracovian rabbi and scholar Moses Isserles. Nearby is the great Alterschul, the old synagogue.

The corner of Brzozowa and Podbrzezie Streets is the site of the Hebrew school (primary and secondary, the so-called "*Gimnazjum*"). The names of the streets suggest birch trees, but there were none — the prevailing aroma was that of freshly baked bread from the bakery of the aptly named Mr. Beigel. Some years ago it fell to me to unveil two memorial tablets — one in Polish, one in Hebrew — on the facade of that building, to remind the passer-by of the former Jewish presence within those walls.

That school had a state-approved secular curriculum, which entitled those who passed the matriculation exam to enter the university. But over and above that there was a comprehensive syllabus taught in Hebrew — Bible, Jewish history and literature. Pupils came from far and wide, from Debniki, Pradnik, Krowodrza, even from Wieliczka. Fees were modest, most pupils had them reduced, nobody was barred from admission for lack of funds. The school was held in great affection by the pupils. It was a kind of oasis, where one felt free and on home ground, had the illusion that the world was and would remain benevolent. One could also — if one were so inclined — acquire a little learning.

In Miodowa Street stood the Tempel Synagogue of the "Progressive" Jews. Its rabbi and preacher was the estimable Dr. Osias Thon, a member of the national legislature and a Zionist leader. Nearby were other synagogues: Popper's, Kupa, Ajzyk's, Wysoka. At Orzeszkowa Street No. 7 were the editorial offices and printing house of *Nowy Dziennik*, a Jewish daily newspaper in Polish. That was, for many readers, the main and irreplaceable source of information about events in Poland, in Palestine, around the world. Its circulation grew when there was something which gave cause for particular concern. In 1924/25, for example, there was, in Lwow, a court case against a Jew by the name of Steiger, for an alleged attempt on the life of the President of the Republic. He was defended by many eminent advocates, among them Natan Lewenstein and Lejb Landau (also Szurlej and Grek, non-Jews). Their arguments, cross-examinations and speeches kept readers in a state of feverish excitement. In the event — despite the plotting of the authorities — Steiger was acquitted, to the great relief of the Jewish community, which had felt slandered and threatened by the whole affair.

On Bochenska Street there was the Jewish Theatre at which repertory companies from all over Poland, including the famous Vilna Troupe of Jonas Turkow, performed the classic Yiddish repertoire: plays by Peretz, Shalom Aleichem, Goldfaden, Anski. Around the corner, on Skawinska Street, was the seat of the Kahal — the Council of the Jewish Community.

One of the centres of Jewish life in Cracow was the stadium of the Makkabi Sports Club — a football field in summer, a skating rink in winter. (One glorious year the soccer team beat the champions, Cracovia, 1:0. That happened only once, a long time ago — but who would ever forget it!) Women in the field events notched up some remarkable records and the water polo team were the national champions of Poland. On state holidays and the Jewish feast of Lag b'Omer the orchestra of the Hebrew school (my elder brother was its first drum major and I, playing the euphonium, basked in his reflected glory), with its blue-and-white flag, led the entire school to the stadium, where there were exhibitions of gymnastics and other sport events for boys and girls.

Not far from the stadium were the premises of the youth organisation Hashomer Hatzair — on the far left, close (some thought too close) to communism. Other rooms in various parts of Kazimierz housed a variety of youth organisations — Hashachar, Akiba, Gordonia, Masada, Betar.

While some youngsters were engaged in high-minded, ideological pursuits, others spent their time in bars and cafes (I recall finding time for both). My favourite cafe was the famous Jama Michalika, at one time the seat of the Zielony Balonik (Green Balloon) cabaret, immortalised by Boy-Zelenski in his incomparable *Slowka*. I misspent there many an hour in the days of yore. Even now, when I happen to recline there on the old sofa, I have the impression that the velvet is still moist from the tears of my then-girlfriend (I was unkind to her, I regret it).

It behooves me to mention Szpitalna Street which, although outside the perimeter of Kazimierz, was, in a way, a Jewish street. Not only because it had a synagogue, but because it was the scene of a second-hand book market. Familiar names, Taffets, Seidens, carried on a long family tradition in that trade, which — like shoemaking and watch repairing — was almost entirely in Jewish hands. At the beginning of each school year that street provided a background to a veritable carnival — crowds of students of all ages milled around the pavements and shops, buying, selling and bartering old books for new, having a great deal of fun on the way.

Dietla Street, with its hundred houses, ran from the Vistula to the railway viaduct in the Grzegorzki district. These houses were inhabited mainly by Jewish families, in their thousands (my own lived there for a time). When I walk down that street now, I seem to remember them all, their faces, their names — Einhorns, Johaneses, Luftglasses, Lipschitzes, Bloeders, Sonntags, Fallmanns, Ohrensteins, Rakowers, Weisbrods, Holzers, not forgetting the Schneiders, a family of nine brothers, mighty sportsmen and soda-water manufacturers.

At a certain time my family lived in a house on the corner of Saint Sebastian and Berek Joselewicz (a Jewish colonel during the Kosciuszko Uprising), so close to the school that when I heard the bell at home it was enough for me to quicken my pace and reach the classroom ahead of the teacher. The street named after Berek Joselewicz is referred to, obliquely, by Boy-Zelenski, as one "having, in Cracow, a peculiar destination." He pokes gentle fun at Professor Wilhelm Feldman, his origin and accent, who might one day also have a street named after him, where gentlemen might arrive in hansom cabs to visit a bordello. (A social historian could deduce from this that Cracow was not well endowed with houses of ill-repute if gentlemen had to be driven, in search of pleasure, as far as Jewish Kazimierz.)

For me the association with Berek Joselewicz Street was of a different nature. At number 5 there lived Mordechai Gebirtig, a carpenter. I remember his slight, inconspicuous figure. Nobody paid much attention to him, no one would have predicted that he would achieve, posthumously, international fame. Gebirtig was an authentic folk singer, the bard of the Jewish street. He set his own words to music and these Yiddish songs gained wide popularity. One of his best-known songs is the one written in 1936 after the pogrom in Przytyk, "*Dos shtetl brent*" (Our Town's on Fire), calling for action — in later years often sung in the ghettoes. In another of his poems, as he is forced to leave his home, he says: "Farewell, Cracow, farewell — A horse-drawn cart is waiting for me out in the street — I'm driven out of here like a dog — Will I ever see you again? — This place is so close to me — I've wept my heart out on my mother's grave and shed my last tear on my father's tombstone — this hallowed ground..." Another poem written in 1940, entitled "*S'tut vey*" (This Hurts), Gebirtig addresses to "those Polish sons and daughters who bring shame on their country," who sneer at the suffering of the Jews inflicted on them by their common foe. Anna Kamienska wrote a beautiful ballad about the "Jewish carpenter and poet from Cracow."

Gebirtig had two lovely daughters. He wrote a song about one of them: a boy stands on the pavement opposite and whistles, a signal for her to come down. Her mother warns her — "don't go, this must be some non-Jewish good-for-nothing, Jewish boys don't behave like that." She was wrong — that boy might well have been me. Many a time did I stand there waiting for Reisele to come down.

Gebirtig was murdered, with his daughters, by the Germans in 1942. After the war his songs were collected, published and recorded; they are widely performed — a part of the Jewish, Cracovian heritage.

We had a neighbour, a shoemaker, by the name of Fischer. He had his workshop on the ground floor, giving on to the street; one could see him, bent over his last, till the early hours. He lived with his family in a tiny flat, one room and kitchen, at the back of the house, on top of a spiral staircase. He proclaimed that he would continue to father children until he was blessed with a daughter, so first came Jankiel, then Hesiek, Josek, Berek, Shmulik, Mojshe and only then, blissfully, Sabcia.

Of them all there was one survivor — the wily Shmulik, my contemporary. When I met him in Cracow soon after the liberation, he told me his story. He had played a squeeze-box on the steps of St. Catherine's Church, humming Hassidic tunes, the only ones he knew. He was in rags, had a dirty face, kept his eyes shut, feigning blindness (but what he did see would fill volumes). He slept in some cellar, in a cardboard box stuffed with old newspapers, plagued by rats. Throughout that time he never opened his mouth to speak to anybody. Good people would throw him a coin, a crust of bread. At night he would search dust bins for scraps, would steal food when he could. At the first opportunity after the war he went to Palestine. He fell in the War of Independence, in 1948, from an Egyptian bullet. A child of our times, you might say, a Jewish child of our times.

A snapshot from memory: I remember the last stage of Marshal Pilsudski's funeral, in May 1935 — the hearse driven through the town to the cathedral on Wawel Hill. I watched the procession from the windows of an office in the centre of town belonging to "Brothers Safir, Agents for the National Lottery" (trading under the slogan: "Looking for luck? — Just drop in for a moment").

In the cortege behind the hearse, among the dignitaries from all over Europe, marched Marshal Herman Goering, resplendent in his uniform, dripping with medals. The local contingent was represented by the town's president, Kapellner-Kaplicki, a former fighter in Pilsudski's Brigade (reaping, as was the custom, his dividend for loyalty to his old leader) and the garrison commander, General Bernard Mond (the only Jew of that rank). Cracovians were used to seeing, on state occasions, an odd trinity: Archbishop Sapieha supported by the two Jews — Kaplicki and Mond.

The country was gripped by mourning — sincere and feigned. It would have been foolhardy to belittle the tragic loss, and not display sorrow. The praises and eulogies in the press and from the public platform knew no bounds. But there was, undoubtedly, a widespread and genuine grief — "Grandad," the real one and the mythical one, was greatly loved. Many people felt that the fate of the nation had rested in safe hands.

I remember that my father, usually wrapped up completely in his daily cares, cried on hearing the news of the Marshal's death. I was startled by this reaction; I was not used to seeing my father moved to tears by matters of that sort. He must have shared a perception common among Jews in Poland that Pilsudski, a sworn adversary of Dmowski, would protect them against the wilder excesses of the "Endeks" and that with his passing away history would take a more threatening, dangerous course. That premonition proved accurate all too soon.

Cracovians were proud of their town, boasted of its culture and tradition. The citizens of Warsaw, Lodz or Lwow looked down on us, provincial and miserly, with gentle mockery. It was true that by 10 p.m. the town would be deserted, its burghers scurrying home before the house gates were shut — the concierge would demand twenty groszy for letting them in after ten. It was said that a typical Cracovian invitation was: "Come and visit us after supper — there will be tea freshly brewed this morning."

Society, Polish as well as Jewish, was sharply stratified; one was supposed to adhere to one's place on the social ladder. The pecking order was well established and ideas above one's station were discouraged.

The following picture springs to mind. On the corner of Starowislna and Dietla Streets used to sit a beggar. I use the word "sit" but that is an exaggeration. He had no legs, only stumps wrapped in rags. He moved along the pavement by raising his trunk, yard by yard, with some wooden handgrips. It is not easy to visualise that mode of locomotion. When there was mud on the street (as there frequently was, and of a quality seldom found these days) the rags splashed about, leaving a smudge of dirt in the beggar's wake. It was a gruesome sight, but familiarity bred composure — one used to throw, in passing, a coin into a cup dangling from his neck.

One day it came to my knowledge that this beggar had offspring. I was startled out of my wits — how does he do it? I found out about this because he applied for his son to be admitted to our school — my father was on the committee adjudicating exemptions from fees. This became the subject of a heated argument over the dinner table. My father thought such ambition arrogant and presumptuous, whereas my brother and I argued that the beggar's son had an entitlement equal to ours, if not better. "Better?!" — my father nearly had an apoplectic fit, fearing that he had fathered a couple of imbeciles.

* *
*

"There is a multitude of them — nowhere" says Jerzy Ficowski. That crowded, eternal absence is far more tangible here than anywhere else in the world. How is one to settle down to the normal business of living when one knows that all the people whom one then knew — family, friends, neighbours, teachers, shopkeepers, beggars — have perished, from hunger, by the bullet, from gas, in torment; and that oneself, just through some odd twist of fortune, did not perish with them? I find it difficult to express this in words. I think such words do not exist.

That human landscape which Markowski records in his photographs did not, at that time, appear to us to be attractive. On the contrary — I am ashamed to admit — many of us looked on these people with a sense of embarrassment. Those beards, sidelocks, crooked noses, misty eyes, what do our non-Jewish fellow citizens make of this?

It is now clear that those faces, lined with care and wisdom, glowing with some inner light, as if they had stepped down from portraits by Rembrandt, were beautiful. We realise that now, when they are no more.

Cum ira et studio

P ress reports, letters and conversations demonstrate that the Oxford Conference gained the approval of the participants and also of those whom news of it reached. As was the intention of the organisers, an opportunity was given for an exchange of views and for a study into what life was really like for Jews in Poland. It is hoped that further serious discussion will follow and will serve, also, as a sort of therapy.

The theme is wide, complicated and — in most of its aspects — unpleasant; both sides approach it with a heavy heart. I believe that Poles who want to talk and think about these matters (maybe only a handful of them) feel somewhat ill at ease with the subject, as if expecting that something will come up that they will find difficult to cope with. No one likes to be censured, least of all justly.

Amongst the Jews themselves there are many who have no wish to return to these matters, nor open up old wounds; they want to forget about the past in Poland, turn their backs on it forever. They regard conferences, symposia, discourses on these matters as drawing-room games. "Who needs this now?" they ask.

The extermination of the Jews in Poland (I purposely avoid the term "Holocaust," because it is ill-chosen and remote, even in those languages where its constant use has made it into a household word, and in Polish it is certainly totally artificial) has left scars on the psyche of the survivors so deep and crippling that their reactions are not always finely balanced. One must bear in mind that we will not talk about the subject "objectively" — objectivity, that is, distance, calm, equilibrium, would be out of place here.

The fabric of Polish-Jewish cohabitation on Polish soil has been irreversibly destroyed. No one is under any illusion that the few thousand Jews remaining in Poland who openly consider themselves to be such and who, as it were, apologise for being alive, are not physically and spiritually a community in terminal decline. They have no schools, no synagogues, no rabbis, no contact with Israel, no leadership, no future. It has to be admitted, albeit regrettably, that world Jewry has ceased to care for them, they have been written off as lost. Therefore, from the Jewish point of view, we are talking not about current affairs but exclusively about history.

For the Poles, however, it is, I believe, a subject of primary importance. A millennium of the Jewish presence on Polish lands and their sudden and final absence, are facts without which Poles are not able to understand their past and, therefore, their present. The history of Poland in the version taught and presented to the nation is full of falsehoods, as happens everywhere where an official version has a monopoly fitting the current dogma and where the researcher is hampered by censorship and lack of access to sources. Moral regeneration calls for an authentic dialogue with the past. The way other people see us must serve as a corrective to the way we see ourselves in the mirror. In the case of Poles gaining self-knowledge, the Jews appear as a witness who must be listened to carefully and who can, of course, be questioned.

If a means has been found for Poles and Jews to meet on neutral ground, it is important that they should tell each other what most concerns them, not for the sake of recrimination and rhetoric, but in order to come closer to the truth. There was a time when the Poles could say publicly what they liked (or more usually what they did not like) about the Jews. The Jews had to swallow it or resort, in debate, to codes or euphemisms. It is a relief to be able to talk about it all openly and frankly. All too often, Poles, among themselves, speak of Jews differently from the way they speak in public (especially as, for the time being, anti-Semitism is not deemed respectable), and so do Jews with regard to Poles. It is time we freed ourselves of this double-think and double-talk and abandoned the stereotypes.

The Jewish stereotype in Polish eyes was radically transformed after Israel's Six Day War (but immediately a new one took its place, equally distorted). Jews, in turn, commonly take it for granted that a Pole is an anti-Semite, and call for special proof when it is claimed that one or another of them is not — he is then seen as an exception.

Thus the augury for an honest and productive discussion is not all that propitious. One ought to begin by agreeing some historical facts, but what constitutes a historical fact is also subject to question.

Take this vast, if now somewhat enveloped in mist, subject of Polish-Jewish relations in interwar Poland. If the question were asked whether Poland was a country where anti-Semitism grew and was rampant, the answer for every Polish Jew, every eyewitness, would be so obvious and unequivocal that he would be angered and resentful of anybody doubting it. As soon as Poland regained independence after World War I, the framework of an anti-Jewish movement began to take shape. It grew in strength and came to be for us an ever-present force, filling the atmosphere like ether. The fact that the Poles were and are not aware of this — at least this is what many claim — is for us hard to believe and understand. They have either forgotten how it was or have

76

been seeing life from an altogether different perspective. The young have been told nothing and have nowhere where they can find out.

Is it undue prickliness which makes us remember the "Endecja" (National Democratic Party), the "Chadecja" (Christian Democratic Party), the ONR (National Radical Camp) — political parties whose main programme was a more or less brutal battle against their fellow Jewish citizens? Was it a figment of our imagination that there was an officially approved boycott, discrimination in all areas of state service, daily incitement in the press, the programmatic and primitive anti-Judaism of the Church, sporadic pogroms. In the universities, in some faculties, there was a *numerus clausus* and often "ghetto benches." (Maria Dabrowska called it "the annual shame" — it is good to remember her for this.)

At the end of the thirties the dominant party was OZON (National Unity Camp), which vied with other parties in their anti-Semitism, and it is very probable that, but for the outbreak of war, a variant of the Nuremberg Laws would have been presented to the lower house of the Polish legislature, the Sejm (draft legislation was ready). These were the political realities of interwar Poland — some kind of anti-Jewish obsession, one might say, which diverted attention from other problems, infinitely more important.

It behooves us, however, to give due weight also to the other side of the picture. Someone asked very pertinently: if it was so bad, why was it so good? Because despite the fact that the climate was severe (and maybe thanks to it, who knows?) on these lands there blossomed a full, rich, varied and creative Jewish life. There was total freedom of worship, autonomy in religious matters, rabbis of all types from the ultra-Orthodox to the so-called "Progressives" (and like today, everywhere, in perpetual strife); there were many Hassidim with their "courts" of faithful; there were schools where instruction was held in Hebrew, and yeshivahs for Talmudic studies; there were newspapers printed in Polish, Yiddish and Hebrew (according to Marian Fuchs of the Jewish Historical Institute in Warsaw, there were thirty dailies and 130 periodicals in Poland in 1939). There were political parties — Zionist, religious, workers, assimilationist; there were Jewish members of the Sejm and Senate; there were men of science and men of letters. There were theatres, charitable and educational associations, sports clubs. A specific civilisation flourished.

Painful and difficult though it is for both sides, we must face up to the time of the occupation. Here is the source of the most acute friction in Polish-Jewish relations — I am not sure that much can be done about this. The problem has been bitterly aggravated by the fact that this has never been openly discussed and written about in Poland. The whole subject of the extermination of the Jews has been treated grudgingly and half-heartedly, and only in accordance with the official line. This was, that a large majority of Poles sympathised with the Jews, and helped and saved them where they could, and that the sporadic incidents (about which so much noise is made in the world) of blackmail and informing and of Jews being handed over to the Germans, were isolated cases perpetrated by "the scum of society" whom the underground was sentencing to death. It is held that the Polish community as a whole came through this unprecedented trial with moral credit and with their honour unstained.

I well understand that the Poles want to, that they *must* believe this. Wladyslaw Bartoszewski, an eyewitness, and one of the organisers of help for the Jews, therefore well qualified to express an opinion worthy of a hearing, believes this. I myself would give a great deal to be able to believe this.

Unfortunately — and this is the heart of the whole matter — the opinion of Jews, that is, those who know best, those who lived through it or who were given firsthand evidence, is overwhelmingly that this thesis is contrary to their experience; that the Poles, with a few exceptions — for them great and eternal praise — did not show any sympathy, did not help or save, that a Jew in hiding or in disguise lived in fear not so much of the Germans but of his neighbours or passers-by, with their acute Polish sensitivity for Jewish features, manner of speaking or fear in their eyes. If the Jews could have depended not on active help, which called for heroism, but neutrality, causing the Pole to look the other way — the chances of survival would have increased a hundredfold. And if they could have joined partisan units, how many could have been saved (it cost many who thought this was their chance, their lives).

Let us consider an interesting document — the report of Jan Karski, daredevil and hero, who has gone down in history as an eyewitness to the extermination of the Jews at the Belzec death camp. He was the first person to bring out to the West an authentic account of the gas chambers and crematoria. Previously, Karski, as one of the first couriers from occupied Poland, had arrived in Angers in France, the seat of the Polish government-in-exile, in February 1940.

Karski was, as he was to prove, very well acquainted with all aspects of the situation in Poland. The Minister of Home Affairs, Stanislaw Kot, avid for every minute detail of all that was happening in Poland, asked Karski to write, among other things, a report on the situation of the Jews.

Karski gives an acute and farsighted account, full of pertinent observations. He declares in it that many Poles are openly hostile to the Jews and in principle sympathise with the objective of the Germans to "solve" the Jewish question in the occupied territories. Here are a few excerpts:

> The solution of the "Jewish Question" by the Germans — I must state this with a full sense of responsibility for what I am saying — represents a very dangerous tool in the

hands of the Germans, leading toward the "moral pacification" of a broad section of Polish society... Although the nation loathes them [the Germans] mortally, this question creates a kind of a narrow bridge, upon which the Germans and a large part of Polish society find themselves in agreement... This situation threatens to demoralise broad segments of the populace and this, in turn, may present many problems to the future authorities endeavouring to reconstruct the Polish State... Hitler's lesson is well taken... Might it not be possible in some way, taking the existence of three adversaries (if, of course, one should currently regard the Jews as an adversary), for the two weaker partners to form something of a common front against the third more powerful and deadly enemy, leaving the accounts between the other two to be settled later?... The establishment of such common front would be beset with very many difficulties, for a wide segment of the Polish population remains as anti-Semitic as ever...[1]

There is a good deal more of it. This is not just Jewish invective and slander — this is Karski's report.

And a further turn of the screw: members of the government (it is clear from the annotations that the report was available only to a selected few), Mikolaj-czyk, Stronski, Kot, realised that this was dynamite. If the extent and persistence of anti-Semitism among the Polish population, even during the war against Hitler, became public knowledge, Poland's cause would have been discredited in the eyes of her Allies. What was to be done? Another version of the report was prepared, in which the whole Polish population was portrayed as being united to a man in their condemnation of German anti-Jewish activities: *Sapienti sat*.

A few years ago, in a discussion with Andrzej Szczypiorski in the Paris monthly *Kultura*, I wrote that, when the crematoria were being stoked, when the trains were rolling night and day to Chelmno, Sobibor, Belzec, Treblinka, Majdanek and Auschwitz, and for months smoke bellowed from the chimneys, if it had been known that it was not the Jews who were being incinerated but Polish fathers, husbands, mothers, wives and children, the explosion of wrath and revenge would have been uncontrollable, even if it came to — I used the expression — "tearing up the rails with bare teeth."

Szczypiorski argued fiercely with me at the time, emphasising the impotence of the Poles in the face of such actions as the "pacification" of the Zamosc region, street roundups and transports to concentration camps, public executions, the systematic decimation of the Polish intelligentsia, and later the crushing of Warsaw, whose victims were Polish flesh and blood. Even then —

---

[1] The original documents are in the Hoover Institution Archives, Stanford, California: "Polish Government Documents Collection" set 921; a second copy is in the Stanisław Mikołajczyk file, labelled "Jews in occupied Poland." I am indebted for this information to David Engel; viz. his article in *Jewish Social Studies*, vol. XLV, no. l.

Szczypiorski pointed out — no one "tore up rails with their teeth." Therefore my objections on that point were ill-founded and unjust.

Thinking further about these things, as I do always, I fear that I am unable to alter my judgement. The fact that the gassing and burning of Jews, which went on for years, was never interrupted by a single external act of blind rage, has strengthened my conviction that the Poles, although they may have observed it all with compassion, did not feel sufficiently moved and enraged to intervene individually or collectively, with their bare teeth or by whatever means, regardless of consequences. What the Germans did in the death camps could only have been done to the Jews.

It is true that in their bitterness Jews often were and are insensitive to the predicament and misery of the Poles. They do not remember that attempts to help a Jew threatened death; they tend to think that the attitude to Jewry is the only important matter, to the exclusion of all other matters; they brood over the dark side of things, because, as the poet says, "wrong is engraved in stone, and kindness in sand." As long as Polish apologetics stick unwaveringly to the official version and Jewish opinion on this matter is considered libellous, we shall be engaged in a "dialogue of the deaf." It is the tragedy of the Poles that in the midst of the cruel visitations of fate, they were exposed to an unprecedented moral trial. They did not come through it victorious. It can be argued that nobody would have come through it any better, but that is little comfort for the Jews.

A few words about the role of the Church. Bartoszewski absolves the Polish Church too lightly, methinks. In any honest balance sheet the debit will look differently. If at some stage the Church has the inner need and the courage to carry out a self-examination, it will see with horror and contrition what role its immemorial and relentless anti-Judaism played in the extermination of the Jews — *in capite* and *in membris*. The record of the Polish Church with regard to the Jews is disgraceful — the sowing of hate does not yield a harvest of mercy. Michal Borwicz has discussed the attitude of clergy with regard to pogroms and murders of Jews after the war. One sentence from the statement of Bishop Wyszynski (as he then was) haunts me and undermines my faith in the effectiveness of dialogue: "At the trial of Beilis many old and contemporary books were brought forth, but the question of the use of blood by the Jews was not determined decisively." If the question of whether the Jews use blood for matzah is not clear to Wyszynski, what do his priests believe and what does the flock believe? And if so, with whom are we to engage in a dialogue, and on what subject?

There is yet another ironical thread: Poland's newest saint, Father Kolbe, was in theory and practice an ardent anti-Semite, and although his heroic martyr's death calls for admiration and respect, it cannot alter the assessment of his anti-Jewish activities over many years, which, to put it mildly, were no qualification for sainthood.

In his heart-rending lament *My, Żydzi polscy* (We, Polish Jews) which Julian Tuwim wrote in America, where he learnt of the death camps, there is the following passage:

> ...On the armbands worn in the ghettoes, the Star of David was painted. I believe in a future Poland, in which that star, the one from the armband, will be one of the highest decorations awarded to the most gallant Polish soldiers and officers. They will wear it proudly on their breasts, next to the Virtuti Militari. There will also be a Cross of the Ghetto, a deeply symbolic title. There will be the Order of the Yellow Patch, more honourable than many a previous trinket... With pride, mournful pride we shall count ourselves of that glorious rank which will outshine all others, the rank of the Polish Jew, we, who by a miracle or by chance remained alive...

Sancta simplicitas. Poor Tuwim — endowed with genius (which deserted him in postwar Poland), naive and "not of this world," lived long enough to see that the yellow patch remained a yellow patch. It was decided to turn one's back on all matters Jewish, as if nothing of any consequence had happened. A shroud of forgetfulness was thrown over this awesome breach in society's fabric. People tried hard not to notice this great absence (although the Jews recruited for the Department of Security were scrupulously counted). Even in Auschwitz, for years, the Jews were passed over in silence. "Babi Yar"-style. Information on the Jewish section could only be obtained by persistent questioning, and then the key had to be searched for. All this was supposedly in line with the principle that although only Jews were gassed and incinerated and many more of them died than all the others put together, no distinction should be made among the victims according to nationality.

There was a widespread feeling of relief among the Poles, that the "Jewish problem" had been "solved" in a manner for which they could not be blamed, and that Poland could now be rebuilt without the Jews — and all the better for it. The Jewish survivors who came out of the camps and hiding places often heard the opinion that, like it or not, Hitler had done a good job on the Jews. Hitler's lesson — as Karski foresaw — found adept pupils.

The majority of the few who survived due to "Aryan documents" realised that in the existing climate it was safer to continue the masquerade, often not betraying their real identity, not even to their own children. Those returning from Russia soon took note of the climate and, whenever possible, assumed some sort of protective cover. It appeared that these latter-day Marranos would somehow get by, but — as it turned out — their ugly origin had been duly marked in their files, for future use. And the future, as is its wont, was not long in coming.

In the baneful period of 1967 and the following years, when the authorities again unleashed a wave of anti-Semitism (trusting that this would always be well received), the former Jewish names, to the surprise of their owners, were recalled and heralded, as a stigma which automatically disqualified (thus, dear Tuwim, goes your "rank which outshines all others"). This infamy needs separate discussion, but whatever interpretation one puts on it, it was the final signal for the Jews that Poland had no place for them.

In the consciousness of the Jews who left Poland and settled in various parts of the world, there is a deeply embedded feeling of wrong suffered — during the prewar years, during the occupation and during the postwar period. Let Poles who complain that Jews damage Poland's reputation in the world ask themselves to what extent this distant and recent past could breed ambassadors of goodwill.

And finally, let it be mentioned, the trauma of unreciprocated love. Many Jews of this last generation, nearing its close, cannot erase from their hearts this country where "they were born and grew up," where — as Tuwim wrote — "in Polish they confessed the disquiet of their first love and in Polish they stammered of its rapture and tempests"; where they loved the landscape, the language, the poetry; where they were ready to shed their blood for Poland and be her true sons. That this was, evidently, not enough leaves them broken-hearted.

The paths of "two of the saddest nations on this earth" have parted forever. I wonder how far the Poles are aware of the fact that with the Jews an authentic part of *their* Poland was obliterated. The question begs to be asked: Will that Poland one day be better, richer in spiritual and material goods, without the Jews?

Lecture at the International Conference
in Oxford, 1984

Let us talk...

I am limited by time, by the Chairman's tolerance and, what is more important, the audience's patience — those are narrow boundaries. I have, therefore, prepared only loose pages, which can easily be shuffled and, if necessary, omitted. I shall raise, at random, a few problems which I consider to be fundamental. Perhaps these fragments will join up, in some way, to form a more coherent account.

When I was thinking what title to give to my talk, various ideas came to mind. At one time, I thought to call it "To My Polish Friends," but this echo of Mickiewicz ("*Do Przyjaciół-Moskali*") could have sounded, in my mouth, a bit pretentious. I played with the title "At the Crossroads," imitating the famous "*Al Parashat Derakhim*" of Achad Ha'am, an excellent heading, universally applicable (are we not eternally at some sort of crossroads?) — I discarded it as too general. I thought of calling it "Very Difficult Accounts" — but that would give the impression of a contest and it is my intention to get away from the "settling" of accounts. I tried to call it "Not All is Black and White," which does define my approach, but in the end I brought it down to the simple, "Let Us Talk — With Whom and About What?"

With whom, then? If there is to be a dialogue, one must have a clear profile of one's interlocutor. I take here a model which one might define as elitist. I want to sit down to the table with the best and not the worst. Not with those who hated the Jews before the war, who were betraying them to the Germans during the war and who drove them out of Poland after the war. Not with the Poland of "Grunwald," the Poland of the Moczars, not with those who sell copies of the *Protocols of the Elders of Zion*, nor with those who at every opportunity spout virulent rubbish about Israel or write that Korczak ill-treated Christian children, and not with those who, like that journalist in the paper *Ład* in Warsaw, declare that "if the Jews don't change their ways the time will come when we shall have to hide them again in cellars" (it is easy to guess how many he would hide). Nor yet with those whom I often overhear in London, declaring "No matter what we say, the Jews shout us down anyway." There is no shortage of dimwits, cranks and bigots anywhere, sadly also amongst us, the Jews. I quite understand that a Pole cannot enter into a dialogue with those who hold that every Pole is an anti-Semite; who have seen and continue to see in Poland nothing but anti-Semitism; who maintain that the extermination camps were located in Poland because the Germans could count on the passivity of the Poles and that there is no point in discussing these things any further.

I want to speak with Poles about a Poland which gave birth to Kochanowski, Mickiewicz, and Norwid, Konopnicka, Prus, Orzeszkowa, Gomulicki, Dabrowska, Nalkowska, and also Turowicz, Blonski, Bartoszewski, Kolakowski, Anna Kamienska, Wislawa Szymborska, Milosz, Ficowski. About a Poland where there flourished, and died, a Jewish civilisation, unique and unrepeatable.

In one of my earlier addresses I remarked that the culture which existed cheek by jowl, nay, right in the middle of the Polish community, remained totally unknown and uninteresting to the Poles; indeed, they would have been staggered to be told that something was taking place here which deserved to be called culture.

It is worth considering here how the Poles, generally, saw their Jewish fellow citizens, as that view, after all, would have formed their opinions and attitudes. In the first place, then, they saw the dark, motley crowd, Jews in their traditional garb, with beards and sidelocks, in kaftans, in skullcaps, in black hats, in the small towns, in market places, jabbering, noisy, uncouth, poor, though their poverty was somehow different from the Polish poverty. They saw the petty merchants, the small shopkeepers with whom they traded and from whom they bought, often on credit, in spite of the slogans "Buy from Your Own" and the officially sponsored boycott. The Jewish shopkeepers were competitive, the more so as Poles very often regarded trade as being beneath their dignity. The Poles saw the artisans, watchmakers, cobblers, tailors, unsurpassed in their skills. They saw the middle classes in the larger towns, who in their dress and behaviour differed little from the Poles, although their lifestyle was somewhat different. They saw "landlords," owners of tenement houses — bricks and mortar being the preferred Jewish investment — the proportion of Jewish owners was substantial. They saw, at school, fellow students who, if they differed at all, differed by their diligence and ability. They saw colleagues at university who often (let it be said — not always and not everywhere) were forced to sit on separate benches. They saw the Jewish professional classes, the doctors and lawyers, amongst them doubtless some of the best. They saw a few (and even those seemed too many) Jews in high positions, probably converts. On the literary scene they saw great luminaries of contemporary literature — Lesmian, Tuwim, Slonimski, Wittlin, writing often for that excellent paper *Wiadomości Literackie*, owned and edited by Grycendler-Grydzewski (and Borman). This illustrated a process of osmosis at the boundaries between the two communities, and it comprised that part of the Jewish community which identified with Polish national aspirations to a degree only possible under the regime of Pilsudski. The process of assimilation became increasingly difficult and unrewarding, and this, it so happens, was in keeping with the instinctive stance of the overwhelming majority of the Jewish community. That majority was separated from the Polish community, and all the more effectively as both sides favoured separation. To give you a small example: at the time when I lived in Poland in the interwar years, not once did I go into a Polish house or flat, unless you count a peasant's cottage rented for the holidays in Zakopane or Zawoja. What is more, I did not look upon this as a deprivation, I took it to be the most natural thing in the world. I had many non-Jewish friends at university, we also had many such clients in our legal practice, but as a rule there were no social contacts.

The reasons for this were many, but the main one was that the Poles did not consider the Jews to be their equals as human beings. They looked down on us from a position of natural superiority. Regardless of their social position, Poles, as a rule, considered themselves to be better and superior to Jews, any Pole to any Jew; superior, as it were, by definition. This lack of a feeling of any common bond, the result of existing conditions, comes closest to explaining the fact that the greater part of the Polish community was insensitive to the fate of the Jews under the occupation. Quite apart from "the scum on the periphery of society" (the term commonly used in Poland); apart, also, from that section of the political and moral spectrum which openly welcomed the destruction of the Jews by foreign hands, granting also that there must have been vast numbers of good, ordinary people who were deeply shocked by the monstrous spectacle enacted in front of their own eyes and who had genuine compassion for its victims, it is an undeniable fact that the majority of the Poles remained indifferent.

We know that active help was risky and demanded courage and altruism. It was simply not to be expected that general attitudes, developed over the generations, would change overnight. Teresa Prekierowa, from the data available to her, estimated that 1–2½% percent of the population actively participated in helping the Jews. (This includes a considerable number who did this for money, but that is a mere detail.)

One can argue the accuracy of statistics and round off a percentage here and there (I do not decry the value of work done in this field, I value it highly), but the Jews have no need of statistics, *they know how it was*. Poles, generally, do not know, they cannot know, perhaps they do not want to know. The Jews are bitterly resentful, but no one would claim that they were expecting it to be different — and that alone provides a tragic commentary. The rancour, which they are not slow to express, sometimes noisily, is not only against the Poles, but against the world in which such things were possible and tolerated. And in the last instance, against the Almighty who, also, did not cover Himself in glory (but this is a separate theme).

A question occurs: are we to judge human behaviour by the absolute standards of ethics and morality, or are we to deem these concepts utopian and unattainable and resign ourselves soberly, not to say cynically, to the fact that dark and primitive instincts effectively dominate human nature and cause humans to be base and cruel?

And further: if, in our weakness or understandable concern for our own lives and the lives of those close to us, we are unable to behave morally and measure up to those high principles which we know from religion and philosophy and which we approve in theory, do we in such a situation consider our behaviour blameless and justified by rational requirements; or rather, are we left with a sense of shame that we did not live up to the call of conscience, shame increased by the knowledge that someone else — true, not many, but somebody, somewhere — did live up to it? I am putting these thoughts for consideration to those who sleep peacefully since, as they say, "nothing could be done."

Blonski's example, the moral tone of his utterance, prompts me to raise the discussion above a mere settling of scores, recrimination, verbal squabbles and rhetorical victories. That sort of contest might have been in order in the past, nay, it has been unavoidable; blunt speaking helped to clear the air of accumulated poison. At that stage I was myself an active participant in that debate. We are nearing a time when there will not be a single eyewitness, none who themselves went through that inferno, there will no longer be survivors from the camps and from the bunkers, those who owe their life to "Aryan papers," those whose salvation proved to be exile in Siberia. There will be no one from Gomulka's Fifth Column, no Jews from the security apparatus and none from the expellees of 1968; gone will be those who have never recovered from their love of Poland, those who on the banks of the River Thames dream of their Vistula, and those who, like myself — and forgive me if it sounds precious — after fifty years away from Poland put themselves to sleep with lines from *Crimean Sonnets* or "The Grave of Agamemnon." I believe that then the historical perspective and the parameters of these issues will change. With the passage of time it will become clear that the agenda is not about us alone, that our debate and controversy is merely incidental to something bigger and more comprehensive. What is at issue here is a great, common cause of universal significance. The extermination of the Jews on Polish territory was a crucial event in history, marking the crisis of Christianity and the crisis of our civilisation (some people regard those concepts as synonymous, but fortunately that is not so). Those events cannot be forgotten or ignored, they will weigh upon future generations for all time.

86

What lessons will human beings draw from this? How will they face up to it, conscious of the enormity of evil which they are capable of perpetrating? How will they renew their faith in the basic moral values in a world of which, in Adorno's words, "we cannot be too much afraid" and where there exist instruments of destruction which put even the gas chambers in shadow? On answers to these questions hang all our tomorrows.

I revert to my title: what shall we talk about? Someone might say that there is nothing to be added to what has already been said in the context of Polish-Jewish discourse. Let me answer with the sentence from the Haggadah which begins "*Af im kulanu hakhamim*" (Even if we were all wise...), which in free translation might be taken to mean that although we have learned from many sources and have absorbed a great deal of wisdom, nonetheless it is incumbent upon us to tell this story...

I know not everybody will agree with me that there is plenty to talk about. Many of my friends both in Israel and in England say, "Why bother yourself, and us, with these matters, what good will it do? Everything connected with that time is so sad and painful, why rub salt into open wounds?" I take the point but am not persuaded by it. To turn one's mind away from these topics would be, in my view, an impoverishment, and I suspect that those who want to distance themselves from them would distance themselves from other serious topics as well.

I believe that the more things concern us the better. Surely there is plenty to talk about: about our history — the part that is common and the part that is separate; about how things really went between us, at close quarters and at a distance; about the climate that nurtured us, the conditions that formed us; about mutual influences, good and bad; about the wrongs endured and the benefits received; about that which united and that which divided us; about all of that, as long as it is not superficial but serious and with concern for the truth. This does not mean that we shall see the truth in the same way, because the truth is complicated and has many dimensions; we are sensitive to some of its aspects, blind to others; only some segments of it are accessible to each of us. The sheer awareness that this is so seems to be a step in the right direction.

We who form a link in the chain of the thousand years of the Jewish presence on Polish soil, does it not behoove us to remember that part of our heritage is to cultivate it and pass it on? Every brick, every stone, every graveyard, every footprint, each document, each scrap of paper, each trace in whatever form, is valuable beyond measure for a nation whose roots give sense to its history and whose memory of the past vouchsafes the continuity of its existence. The history of the Jews did not begin in 1948 with the creation of the State of Israel. A large part of the history was enacted on Polish lands. Should one, could one, turn one's back on it, bury it, forget it? Surely not, surely the very opposite must be the case.

I learn from the papers and friends in Poland that there is, mainly among the young, a growing and lively interest in things Jewish: history, literature, monuments, and relics. One of them wrote to me thus: "Are we, the Poles, not a strange nation? For forty years all these matters were hidden under a shroud of forgetfulness, a shamefaced silence, a programmatic taboo — as if the Jews had never existed. And now, suddenly, this seemingly spontaneous outburst of interest, curiosity, desire to know. Is this salutary? Where will this lead to?" What shall I answer him? Better late than never? If such interest has been awakened and if it is genuine and not merely morbid or psychopathic, then I applaud it and I think that there is a helpful role for us to play in this pursuit. I am not afraid, as my correspondent seems to be, of the possible undesirable consequences, that the pendulum will once again swing in the opposite direction — we are by now beyond reach of any malevolence threatening from that side.

I think that when this new generation become acquainted with that part of their history and discover how it was with the Jews in Poland and what sort of community it was, this will not only open their eyes but will be good for their souls. They will need to ponder about the past and face up to it squarely. I want to believe that a generation of Poles is coming into its own, which is not poisoned by the virus of anti-Semitism and anti-Judaism. That is, however, not our problem but theirs, because we shall never again, as a community, find ourselves physically in close proximity.

I read Blonski's article, for the first time, with growing excitement and quickened pulse. At one point he makes reference to one of the speakers at the conference in Oxford in 1984, whose words, he said, inspired him to ponder these matters. From the words quoted by him it was clear that he was referring to me. I was startled and also moved to see how one word, a sentence, a thought can strike another man's mind, can germinate there and bear fruit beyond expectation. I was talking then, at least that is how Blonski understood it, to the effect that we Jews no longer expected anything from the Poles but the admission that they have been, in some way, at fault. For many years we listened, waited for a sign — but we heard no voices. In the end, I had thought we would be straining our ears in vain. But now, at last — we hear the voice of Blonski.

Many people in Poland say that Blonski is fouling his own nest and that even if what he has to say is true he should not be saying it in public, as this brings succour to Poland's enemies. That is an old argument — "Do not rock the boat." We know it particularly well in Israel where there is a widespread tendency to merciless self-criticism, but also great concern that this should remain in the family — a slippery path.

More than a year has passed since Blonski's voice sounded. I would like to assure all those who feared that it would have a harmful effect on Poland, that quite the opposite has occurred. His article is seen, in itself, as a certain rehabilitation of sorts. When, paradoxically and undeservedly, I am put in the role of an *advocatus Poloniae*, I myself, in many instances, recall this article and those which followed. I maintain that one can no longer speak loosely about the Poles' opinion on the subject without taking into consideration these new voices, which save the reputation of Poland.

That reputation is a source of considerable difficulty. It rebounds on every Pole abroad, particularly in America, where in a foreign forum he has continually to explain — and not always knowing the facts — that not every Pole is and was an anti-Semite. That "foreign forum" is very often not well informed in the matter, but always knows one thing and that is enough: that in Poland life for the Jews was bad.

Poles often complain that it is the Jews who influence this unflattering opinion, by spreading falsehoods, greatly exaggerating their past misfortunes and generally blackening the good name of the country of their birth.

If that were true, the question arises, why should these Jews (I am talking of those at whom the reproaches are directed) want to do such things? Is it pure malice, is it because they are naturally nasty people? Does this ring true? Or is it perhaps, if such is their perception, that it is the result of their experience, their ordeals, their feelings of injury? I am putting it thus in order to illustrate how quickly, if we are not careful, we can find ourselves back to square one: seeing one's own side of the picture alone.

All the more, it seems to me, that the public reckoning of Blonski offers a different model and calls for a new climate of relationship. It deserves an adequate response. It behooves us to remember that anti-Semitism is not a peculiarly Polish invention. It is an age-old sociological, theological, and political phenomenon which, to a greater or lesser degree, is always with us, which defines us and in the absence of which (but there is no danger of that) we would feel strange. We would certainly be a different nation, a different community, different people — it is doubtful that we would be better. That does not mean that one should accept anti-Semitism complacently and turn the other cheek. Quite the opposite, one must fight it by all possible means — I think that our meeting here in Jerusalem, the capital of the Jewish state, is a significant act in that struggle.

At the source of Blonski's discourse are poems of Czeslaw Milosz. This is understandable. Poetry touches the essence of our being, our thoughts and feelings, and brings forth resources which we ourselves are often not aware of. Joseph Brodsky, in his Nobel Prize acceptance speech, said: "It is more difficult to break a man who reads poetry than one who does not." I am thinking at this moment of Max Boruchowicz — Michal Borwicz, who, sadly, is no longer with us, missed as no other. In his book *Literatura w obozie* (Literature in the

Camp, Krakow, 1946) he describes how fragments of poetry known by heart were a kind of life-belt, which in the most atrocious conditions of human degradation helped him, and others, to survive. I am thinking of that scene in the Janowski camp when a "selection" was taking place, when his comrade, on the point of collapse, begged him with his eyes for a word of solace, and how Borwicz then spoke aloud a couple of lines of poetry (some banal verses of his own, he says) and how these words, somehow, renewed his friend's failing strength and will to live.

My Polish of fifty years ago is no match for Blonski's. But in order to remain in stylistic harmony with him I seek recourse to someone else's words and want to end these remarks with an excerpt from a poem by my friend Jerzy Ficowski, entitled fittingly "The Way to Yerushalaim":

> through woodlands rivers
> through an autumn of bowed candlesticks
> through gas chambers
> graveyards of air
> they went to Yerushalaim
> both the dead and the living
> into their returning olden time
> and that far they smuggled
> a handful of willow pears
> and for a keepsake
> a herring bone
> that sticks to this day

Lecture delivered at the International Conference
in Jerusalem, February 1988

As in a dream

Some of you may wonder why it has fallen to me of all people to speak on this important occasion — in truth, I am wondering myself. I confess that I consider this to be no mean honour and that I am moved by it. It is due not to any special merit — I am not conscious of any — but to the accident of birth which makes me appear in this context a sort of museum specimen: an authentic, prewar *Homo Cracoviensis* — and a Jew, to boot. A Cracovian Jew who is ready to rush to Cracow, in weather fair or foul, to respond to every call from there.

I dreamt one night, a short while ago, that I saw on a television screen the Prime Minister of Israel, Itzhak Rabin, shaking the hand of Yasser Arafat, and those two creased their faces in a semblance of a smile. All this, it seemed, was taking place on the steps of the White House in Washington and, as happens in dreams, there were some familiar faces in the background: President Carter, Bush, Clinton, Kissinger... Voices were coming at me from all sides, that we were witnessing the dawn of a new era, that there would be peace in the Middle East, in Israel... It is a pity to wake up from such a dream.

Another night I dreamt that in Cracow, in Kazimierz, there arose a beautiful building which called itself the Center for Jewish Culture, that the privilege of opening that Institution fell to me, and that I stood in front of a big and distinguished audience and — which does not happen to me often — I was at a loss for words.

It seems to me that this ceremony marks for me a long and tortuous journey. I left my Cracow, family and friends more than fifty years ago, before the outbreak of World War II. Why I left Cracow — on that theme one could write a tract about Polish-Jewish relations in the thirties; now is not the time to mull over this.

But it would be insincere and not in the spirit in which we want to lead this Center, not to call things by their name. Suffice it to say that I, and many like me, could not find our place in Poland at that time. I got offended, turned my back on it, wanted to forget it, to "convert" from my Polishness — but the vaccine, as it were, did not take. I realised that were I, in some way, to shed my Polishness, be stripped of it — I would be damaged, impoverished, incomplete. Moreover, when I am thinking of those times, as I often do, the idea occurs to me — when it was so bad, why was it so good?

And so I come back here, after "years stormy and turbulent," to cast an eye over the landscape of my youth and my childhood, where every stone is laden with sweet memories, to walk through the streets where our fates intermingled, where the Street of Corpus Christi crossed with the Street of Rabbi Meisels, and the Street of Saint Sebastian with that of Berek Joselewicz; to tramp through the alleyways named after Esther, Jacob and Isaac — where else in the Diaspora were streets named after the biblical patriarchs? To walk again down Koletek Street towards the sports ground of the Makkabi Club, Orzeszkowa Street to *Nowy Dziennik*, Miodowa Street to the Tempel prayer-house, Brzozowa Street to the Hebrew school. To pause in front of the synagogues — the Alterschul, Popper's, Kupa, Remuh — one could deduce from the number of synagogues that the Jews of Cracow were singularly pious. Well — many were; but there were also those who — as described by Isaac Deutscher, the son of a Cracow printer and a famous biographer of Lenin, Stalin and Trotsky — there were those who, like himself, on Yom Kippur, the Day of Atonement, went to the grave of the holy Rabbi Isserles and ate a ham sandwich — to spite him and their parents.

One could say that Cracow was wonderfully overflowing with Jews. This was a community whose tone was set by Dr. Osias Thon, the preacher in the liberal synagogue and a member of the national legislature; Dr. Ignacy Schwarzbart, a Zionist leader (during the war a member of the National Council of the Polish government-in-exile); Dr. Chaim Hilfstein, after whom the Hebrew school was named; teachers of that school — Scherer, Haber, Mifelew, Rapaport, Katz, Szmulewicz, Feldhorn, Stendig, Waldman, Metalman, Mrs. Goldwasser — many others, each of them deserving an epitaph of their own; lawyers — Susskind, Hoffman, Feldblum, Goldblat, Bader, Schechter; the Orthodox Rabbi Kornitzer; the assimilated chairman of the Kahal Dr. Landau; Wilhelm Berkelhammer, Moses Kanfer, David Lazer of the *Nowy Dziennik*; Rywek Wolf from the students' home; Rosa Rock of the orphanage. Here were active the Przedświt-Hashachar youth organisation, Hashomer Hatzair, Gordonia, Akiba, Masada; the Makkabi and Jutrzenka sports clubs; here flourished the worthy middle-class families of Tigner, Einhorn, Fallman, Lipschutz, Leser, Selinger, Bester, Rosthal, Stoeger, Freiwald, Herzig, Aleksandrowicz, Karmel, Freilich, Monderer, Ehrlich...

This sounds like a grey list of tenants, but for me it is anything but grey — every single name evokes, with poignant clarity, a distinctive face, movements, gestures, expressions, as if it were yesterday. I think of them with unfading affection. I could find my way to their dwellings with my eyes shut, touching, to be sure, the cavity on the side of the door where there used to be the mezuzah.

That human landscape is etched in my heart, my memory. I cannot forget for a single moment that the majority of them, family, friends, acquaintances —

none of them was a stranger to me — were hounded to death in the ghettoes, in the labour camps, the death factories, the gas chambers. We have got used to talking about this, using words derived from ordinary, everyday discourse, but nobody is able to take in the real meaning of that loss.

I love that Jewish Poland which is no more. I love it with a love which is different from the one I nurture for the State of Israel. I know that my feeling is filtered through the memories of my youth and my childhood and smacks of a Proustian "remembrance of things past." But there is more to it. I see and feel that it was a world of authentic, uniquely Jewish experience — in a sense in which this is not recreated in a normal country like Israel. Zionism, which brought about the State of Israel, was, in its basic assumptions, a protest against the life in the Diaspora, and one must be eternally grateful to its Founding Fathers that their vision was realised at the time of Jewry's greatest catastrophe and despair. Due to this alone the Jewish Nation lived on to be reborn.

But the result of these events, its side-effects, intended and accidental, was the irrevocable loss of those forms and values which were the essence of Jewish life in the Diaspora. One of its hallmarks was the conviction that — irrespective of the poor living conditions and the daily struggle — man must aspire to things above the mundane, strive for a realisation of some high ideal, however defined. There was a deeply ingrained perception that decent behaviour towards fellow human beings, religious practice, the observance of ethical norms, respect for the scholar, pursuit of learning, would speed the Messiah on his way and would initiate an era of universal justice.

We are witnessing today an astonishing event. In the year 1993, and the year 5754 according to the Jewish calendar, in the heart of old Kazimierz, like the phoenix from the ashes, there arises a structure calling itself the Center for Jewish Culture. That such a thing can happen in Cracow today, at this juncture of this country's history, is little short of miraculous.

Like all miracles, this would not and could not have come about without human aid. It is, in truth, due to the vision, enthusiasm and hard work of a few dedicated people whom I hestitate to single out, but it is no secret that the merit lies mainly (not to say solely) with our devoted friend Mark Talisman from Washington, Professor Gierowski and Joachim Russek. I congratulate them on this realisation of their vision and express to them our gratitude.

I see in this enterprise a sort of new beginning. Maybe it will be seen — a future historian will utter a verdict — to mark a turning point on our way to reconciliation and alliance in the common cause: the point at which Poland emerges at last from the sickness of anti-Semitism which had addled her brain and done so much harm; the point at which we begin to see in each other the best and not the worst; the point at which old wounds start to heal and a new generation grows up free from bigotry and prejudice. It may be that Poland and the State of Israel, which to a large extent was fashioned by Polish Jews, will now enter into the best of relations and serve, perhaps, on the international forum as an example of civilised behaviour. There is a saying in Yiddish expressing a pious wish: *"Fun dein moyl ins Gotts oyren"* — let this go from your mouth into God's ears.

The creation of this Center is deeply symbolic. But it would not accord with our wishes and it would not deserve the enormous effort and money that has gone into it if it were to remain a symbol only. A symbol on the one hand — but solid, daily labour on the other.

The walls, the roof over our heads — this is something tangible. It is a frame, a shell which will be filled with rich and vibrant contents. It is an address which was lacking until today, an address to which visitors from near and far will direct their steps on arrival in Cracow, where they will find a friendly face behind the desk, books and information of every kind, where they will rest awhile and lose themselves in thought, where they will meet like-minded people, where they will feel at home.

It is here, in this place, that we shall cherish and cultivate the memory of Polish Jews. We shall be proclaiming the truth of their existence. In this quarrelsome world of ours, riven by fratricidal wars, in Yugoslavia, Ireland, in Russia and South Africa, we will be able to point out that here, for centuries, despite everything, there existed a model of co-existence, of a common life, of a symbiosis of two cultures resulting in mutual enrichment.

There is an expression in Hebrew: *"ir va'em beyisroel"* — "city and mother in Israel." Not many places on earth are graced with this epithet, but Cracow, our Cracow of blessed memory, is one of them. Let me finish with the prayer of thanksgiving that we have lived to see this day — *"Shehecheyanu vekiyemanu lazman hazeh."*

Opening speech at the inauguration of the Center for Jewish Culture in Cracow
24th November 1993

From the abyss

My theme is "Literature from the ghetto in the Polish language" — I give it the title "*Z otchłani*" (From the Abyss), for such was the title of a collection of poems published in the Warsaw ghetto in 1944. Considering the circumstances in which these poems were written and came to light, I have no hesitation in calling that little volume an event unique in the history of literature.

The volume was smuggled to London and then to New York, where it appeared in print in 1945, with an introduction by Jacob Appenszlak. The poems were reprinted and their story told for the first time after the war in a volume edited and prefaced by Michal Borwicz, otherwise known as Max Boruchowicz, my colleague from the Hebrew High School in Cracow, himself a survivor (of whom more later). In 1947, it appeared under the imprint of the Central Jewish Committee in Poland, entitled *Pieśń ujdzie cało* (The Song Will Survive). (This phrase, as every reader of Polish poetry will know, comes from a poem by Adam Mickiewicz, wherein he predicts that when all other monuments lie in ruins, the song, the poetry will continue to be heard; he likens it to a nightingale which escapes from a burning building, rests for a while on the roof, and when the building collapses flies away to the forest to continue to sing its mournful song.)

I cannot speak on the subject without referring, in the first place, to the book by Frieda Aaron, *Bearing the Unbearable*, published in 1990 by the State of New York Press. Frieda Aaron has analysed some of the most significant poems written in the ghetto. She was there at the time and her personal memoir in that book is one of the most moving I have ever read. I myself am not a survivor *sensu stricto* but only one of the millions of the walking-wounded who lost members of their families and friends in the Shoah.

A debt is also owed to Irena Maciejewska, who edited a comprehensive anthology of writing in the Polish language on the subject of Jewish martyrdom and destruction under the title *Męczeństwo i Zagłada Żydów w zapisach literatury polskiej*. I confess that I am having a number of difficulties in addressing this subject here — whether and how I shall overcome them I myself am waiting to see.

The first is that I must assume that Polish is not the language of the majority of my audience and so I am unable to quote the poems in the original and thus convey their full power and meaning (Robert Frost said that poetry is what gets left out in a translation). I can only talk about them, around them, show through a glass darkly, as it were.

The second difficulty is that the texts I am to speak of should, like a dangerous potion, carry a health warning. Through continuous reading — and for the purpose of this paper rereading of them — I have become a casualty; I have abused and damaged, not irreversibly I hope, my literary sensibility. I do not want to sound like that proverbial nurse who was known to complain that she had a terrible night because her patient tossed and turned and would not let her sleep, but the truth is that a total immersion in this material makes one unfit for reading other literature.

What is facing us here makes other matters appear trivial and artificial. Kochanowski grieving in his "Threnody" over the loss of his Ursula; Slowacki's "Ojciec Zadżumionych," a father losing through pestilence members of his family one by one; Dante's Ugolino gnawing at the head of his son who died from hunger; Jeremiah lamenting the Fall of Jerusalem; Job tested by Satan to the limits of endurance and beyond — superb works of literature one and all — what are they in the face of the gradual murder of a whole people and real suffering on a scale which defies comprehension? When the true human condition is, for all the world to see, manifested in the ghettoes, the camps, the death factories, isn't literature which brings catharsis and solace a cruel mockery? And writing, which is an act of faith in man, an impermissible self-indulgence? It is that which made Adorno say that writing poetry after Auschwitz is barbarous. By normal standards many of these poems would appear crude, amateurish, some outright bad.

The trite phrase that they were verses "written in blood" acquires here a fresh, literal meaning. They were written by people on the edge of an open mass grave, in haste, before the bullet. They are like messages scratched on the walls of the death cells. Despair dictates phrases which are cruel, accusations which may be unjust, curses on the perpetrators, bystanders, the world.

They are voices of men and women outside the law — man's law and God's law; they speak of suffering, of pain, of hope and the loss thereof, of loneliness and helplessness, of utter darkness of the soul. They bear witness to courage, tenacity, a will to live in conditions of terminal agony, of death, one's own and that of everyone one loved.

They are also the instrument of resistance. They proved one's humanity — against all the efforts of the Germans to reduce Jews to a subhuman level. Writing or merely listening to poetry offered a breath of air, a momentary escape from the reality around. It was a kind of healing magic.

Borwicz describes a moment when, in the Janowski camp in Lwow, one of the more advanced places of slow torture and murder, his companion in the ranks of prisoners on the *Appelplatz* is at the end of his endurance, visibly sinking, and how he, Borwicz, recites to him two lines of poetry which came to his head. His companion somehow felt reinvigorated and seemed to regain his strength and the will to live. Examples like that abound. Joseph Brodsky says that it is harder to break a man who reads poetry than one who does not.

For a small illustration of how such poetry came to be written I go again to Borwicz. Remembering that writing of any kind was forbidden in the camps on pain of death, it was done between one beating and another, between one execution and the next one.

"An icy January in 1943," writes Borwicz in an essay called "The Baccillus of Literature." "For sixteen hours every day, without respite, exposure to piercing frost, turning a man into an icicle. We hack ice and clear snow in Zamarstynowska Street in Lwow. During this activity I feel, ever more clearly, the pressure of words, unprompted, forming in my mind a poem. Having become conscious of it, without interrupting the physical work, I try to smooth out and improve certain lines. When the first stanza appears to be ready, I begin to think of noting it down. Pushing the wheelbarrow with ice towards the canal I find on the rubbish heap a dirty sheet of paper. With a pencil stub which I had secreted, at a suitable moment, using the dust-cart as my desk, with fingers numb with cold, I scribble the lines on paper and put it in my pocket. The next line begins to sprout in my mind..." Where is the room here for comparison with "writing" as we know it?

In one respect at least the Germans were unlucky in their choice of victim. "The People of the Book" were literate and had faith in the written word. The compulsion to record, to leave a trace in writing, was widespread and over-whelming. The fear that the incredible events of which they were the witness and victim might not become known or would not be believed was greater than concern for their own survival. The last words in one of the most searing documents of that time, the diary of Chaim Kaplan, before his deportation to Treblinka, were: "If I die, what will happen to my diary?"

In the Warsaw ghetto alone, between June 1940 and July 1942 there appeared 56 different publications — 26 in Yiddish, twenty in Polish, ten in Hebrew. What has reached us, by a chain of miracles, is merely the tip of the iceberg — but even that makes the Shoah the best documented period in history. I think, therefore, that the so-called "revisionists," both those who are evil and those who are merely demented, are irritating but not really dangerous.

One of the most desolate and heartrending scenes imaginable was the sight of the ghettoes after an *Aktion* — the empty flats from which people were dragged away, feathers flying from bedding ripped open to disclose hidden treasures, odd articles of clothing lost or abandoned, the corpses of those who were not able to keep pace, and papers, single sheets or sheaves of pages, copybooks strewn over staircases or flying in the wind — the writing, choked halfway. What flowering of human thought and feeling, what possible master-pieces...

From the general to the particular. Undoubtedly the most significant poet writing in the ghetto in the Polish language was Wladyslaw Szlengel, who was born in 1914 in Warsaw and died in 1943 in a bunker, during the Warsaw Ghetto Uprising. He lived in the ghetto from its formation till the end. He was little known before the war, although he had some lighthearted satirical texts published in *Nasz Przegląd* — the Jewish paper in the Polish language appearing in Warsaw, also in the famous humorous journal *Szpilki*.

In the ghetto he grew in stature and had, as it were, greatness thrust upon him. He observed and recorded the life in the ghetto in all its aspects. The facts are well known and have been described many times. Hunger was rampant, typhus took its daily toll, at times too fast for the corpses to be cleared from the streets. Nobody knew when he would be awakened by the sound of the *Aktion*, whether he would be murdered in his bed, or whether he would return from the street to the quarters which had to pass for home.

Every night Szlengel appeared in a sort of cabaret in the Cafe Sztuka in the Leszno district. He was the moving spirit, the announcer, the main provider of texts, which varied from the merely amusing, to divert the audience for a short moment from the grim reality around, to poems tugging at the heartstrings by bringing back memories of life before the nightmare. Then there were those dealing with daily life in the ghetto with its new, sinister vocabulary, bitter tirades against the oppressors, sallies against his own brethren and co-victims and those beyond the wall, those free spirits in the faraway wide world, who didn't know or didn't want to know how tragic human fate can be. He had forebodings of the approaching end — forebodings all-too-soon fulfilled.

After the so-called *"Grossaktion"* of July to September 1942, when 300,000 Jews were murdered by bullet or gas, Szlengel, astonishingly, reaches the peak of his creativity, expressed in some of his most potent poems. He himself described them as "pages written in a U-boat which will not surface." Like the entries in the diary of Czerniakow or Janusz Korczak, or the notes of Ringelblum, these verse-documents recorded the history of people condemned to death.

These verses, those that survived — we have knowledge of other poems of his that have not reached us and never will — were published after the war in a collection called *Co czytałem umarłym* (What I Read to the Dead), Szlengel's own title.

I must restrict myself to only a brief summary of some of these poems.

In the early verse *"Klucz u stróża"* (Key with the Concierge) he makes light of the fact that his former doorman now parades in his, Szlengel's, fur coat which he looted, and is clearly content with the new social order which has been created.

Szlengel's flat happens to have "an impudent Jewish window" ("*Okno na tamtą stronę*") through which he takes a forbidden look over the sleeping city beyond the wall, now totally unattainable, paradise lost.

In the verse "*Telefon*" (the same in all languages) he has a sudden impulse to phone somebody outside the wall (remarkably, this was for a while possible) and realises, with a shock, that there is no one there to receive his call, that in 1939 there was a parting of the ways, lifelong friendships were severed, there is no one, no one to speak to... He dials a familiar number — the time clock; and now every stanza in which he recollects the golden times of yore, the cafes, the cinemas, ends with the sound: "ten fifty three..." "ten fifty six..."

Szlengel had contact with Janusz Korczak. He wrote the invitation for the performance in the orphanage of Rabindranath Tagore's play *The Post* in which an Indian boy is shown on his deathbed — Korczak's idea of familiarising the children with death. The sight of Korczak's march through the ghetto with the children to the *Umschlagplatz* in August 1942 during the *Grossaktion* has entered the folk memory as one of the symbolic images of that time, contrasting mindless German barbarism with the children and the noblest human spirit. Szlengel was a witness of that scene and he was the first to describe it in a poem "*Kartka z dziennika 'akcji'*" (A Page from the Diary of the *Aktion*) where he stresses the spiritual significance of Korczak's unswerving devotion to his children, unto death.

In another poem entitled "*Pomnik*" (A Monument) he reverts to mundane, everyday things. He describes an ordinary woman, a very ordinary woman, a wife and mother, who by her mere presence spread comfort around her. One day she was taken away, while she was cooking supper. Her husband, her son, will come home, will find it empty, no fire in the hearth. A cold pot staring at them — her monument...

One of the most original and artful poems is called "*Rzeczy*" (Things). It traces the path Jews were forced to take from the streets where there was still room to breathe, stage by stage, to the ever-more-constricted space until all life is extinguished. In Szlengel's imagination it is not people who walk that path but the inanimate Jewish possessions of which their owners were gradually stripped: tables, chairs, trunks, bundles, suitcases and bedding, dresses and pictures, pots, pans and carpets, jars and kettles, books and knickknacks. As they are driven from place to place the possessions get fewer and fewer and fewer, until all that remains is a little poison-pill. In later days, slowly, order is resumed in the empty, abandoned houses, things are put where they stood before, new, non-Jewish inhabitants lead their normal, ordinary lives. But, one day, when all has seemingly been forgotten, Szlengel has a surrealist vision:

all the former Jewish possessions, the things, the tables and chairs, trunks and bundles, the suits and kettles, everything will jump out of the windows and will march down the streets and will gather on the highways, along the black railway tracks, and will disappear, and no one will know what the meaning of all this is — only the little poison-pill will bear evidence.

During the first days of armed resistance in the ghetto in January 1943 Szlengel wrote a poem entitled *"Dwie śmierci"* (Two Deaths), where he compares the way it is given to a Pole to die in battle with the way the Jew is killed like a dog. The first death, face to face with the enemy, in a great cause, praised and honoured; the second in an attic or a cellar, wholesale, anonymous, meaningless — an ugly death, fit for a dustheap. When those two deaths meet each other — they bicker, as Life, the same Life, mean, cunning and evil looks on, mockingly...

On learning about the gas chambers in Treblinka — and from the factual details he cites there is no doubt he knew by then the unspeakable truth — Szlengel bursts into full-blooded blasphemy. I hesitated to include it in my selection here, but the picture would remain incomplete without it. Besides, sitting in judgement upon God's inscrutable ways is well within the Hassidic and kabbalistic tradition, like that group of rabbis in the Vilna ghetto who reportedly put God on trial, adjudged Him guilty and — minding the time of day — adjourned to say the evening prayers. Szlengel in his terrifying poem entitled *"Już Czas"* (It Is High Time) is more rational, severe and unforgiving. God's guilt is clear and calls for revenge. He has delivered us into the hands of the killers. Through the millennia we have been His loyal children, dying with His name on our lips, on the crosses of the Romans, on the pyres of Spain, at the hands of the Cossacks and now in Treblinka — we shall pay Him back for all this. We shall bring Him to that place of torture to die a Jewish death. The poem ends with this stanza:

> And when the executioner will chase and force You
> Drive and push You onto the steam floor,
> And seal behind You the hermetic door,
> Hot vapours will choke You...
> And You will scream and weep and want to flee —
> And when Your death agony comes to an end,
> You'll be dragged, and in a monstrous pit land,
> Then they will tear out Your stars — the gold teeth from your
> jaws —
> Then they will burn You.
>   And You'll be ash.

(Translation by Frieda W. Aaron)

Echoes of puzzlement with the ways of God are frequent enough in the poetry of the ghetto. "God, have you ever been hungry?" asks Joseph Bau. Izabela Gelbard-Czajka tells of Abram Gepner, a merchant, Czerniakow's deputy in the Judenrat and a man above reproach, who is greatly troubled that the balance sheet of God's justice seems grossly deficient. Stefania Ney tells of a little boy, Herszek, in a poem of that name, who prays to God to let him return safely from yet another smuggling escapade, but "God has at that time other weighty matters on His mind anyway, it is difficult to reach Him all the way from the ghetto" and Herszek is killed. The theme of the boy smuggler is taken up also by Henryka Lazowert. Born in 1910, died in 1942 in the ghetto, Henryka Lazowert was established and respected as a poetess before the war. In the poem left to us she speaks of the cunning little boy who knows that each escapade may be his last and has only one worry — if I don't make it, who, Mother dear, will bring you bread tomorrow?

A few words about some poets who wrote outside the ghetto, on "Aryan papers." Zuzanna Ginczanka, a beautiful Jewish girl, of legendary charm, had many prewar admirers in the literary milieu. She was discovered in her hiding place in Cracow, was imprisoned and killed in autumn 1944. The poem which reached us entitled "*Non omnis moriar*," on which her fame rests, is a paraphrase of one of the best known poems by Juliusz Slowacki, "*Testament mój*." She invites her friends to gather around and drink to her memory, whilst her enemies share out her worldly goods. In a memorable image she visualises how the feathers from the bedding which they ripped open in search of hidden gold and diamonds cling to their outstretched arms, stuck together by her blood, and form the wings of angels, giving shape to Slowacki's vision of turning ordinary men, by the force of his poetry, into angels.

Mieczyslaw Jastrun, who survived the war and continued his literary activity in Poland, was born in 1903; his real name was Agatstein. He already had a considerable reputation before the war. He wrote poetry on the "Aryan side" in Warsaw, published immediately after the liberation in the small collection "*Godzina Strzeżona*" (The Guarded Hour). One of the most moving of his poems, which appeared during the war in the volume *From the Abyss*, is one called "*Tu także jak w Jeruzalem*" (Here Too as in Jerusalem), where he dwells on the motif of the abandonment and isolation of those dying: "No one cast the good earth — onto that mass grave — greeted by silence, free of treacherous words — When with mouths like wounds — parched, you called for water — No one brought water — to the sealed trains."

Like Jastrun, Stanislaw Jerzy Lec was writing poetry outside the ghetto walls and he speaks openly of his Jewishness. The situation of those on "Ayran papers" has been described many times and took many forms, the common feature being a sense of terrible isolation and omnipresent, marrow-chilling fear. We know of many cases of people who risked their all to find a hiding place outside the walls and, unable to take the strain, returned to the ghetto to share the fate of their own people. Lec speaks of feeling like a hunted beast, of fearing that he will be unable to disguise his pain in front of the shopkeeper, the neighbour, his companion, nay, himself — the death of his people is writ large, indelibly, on his face.

One cannot speak of poetry arising from and concerning the ghetto without referring to that Righteous Gentile Czeslaw Milosz, whose poem "Campo di Fiori," written during the Warsaw Ghetto Uprising and printed for the first time in the volume *From the Abyss*, is one of the finest in all his opus — and that is saying a great deal.

The tragedy which Milosz describes acquires a historical perspective and is universal: a man, Giordano Bruno, is burnt at the stake for his convictions — people remain indifferent to what goes on under their very eyes, the passing crowd is paying little attention, is laughing, trading, playing. Before the ash of the pyre cools down — the man is already forgotten. Milosz likens this scene to the famous carousel and swings near the wall of the ghetto, which on a bright Sunday morning attracted merry crowds. Hot wind from the burning ghetto was billowing girl's skirts, the playful melody drowned the salvoes from behind the wall. Those consumed by flames, dying their lonely death, were already sinking into oblivion...

Milosz's poem is passionate, but it is written from the outside; it is controlled, polished and balanced, as behooves a mature thinker and poet. It is a far cry from the cries of anguish from the heart of the ghetto.

I have restricted myself — as was my brief — to some of the more important poems of that time and place, which have reached us by various routes. Since then, of course, writings in the Polish language on that subject have been massive. Slonimski, Tuwim, Wittlin, Broniewski, Wierzynski, Borowski, Kamienska, Szymborska, Ficowski, Nalkowska, Newerly, Rudnicki, Wygodzki, Wojdowski, Grynberg — their work forms a lasting testimony to this most tragic period of our times and leaves an indelible trace, as only artists can, on the consciousness of mankind. Whether all this writing will feed our hope or deepen our despair is quite beyond me, beyond any of us to judge.

I would like to finish with a few simple words — and they could not be simpler — not my own. They are the words of some children, overheard by somebody who, later, put them down on paper.

"Daddy," says a Jewish boy, "Daddy, when I grow up, I want to be a German."

A child's voice heard in Belzec: "Mummy, I have tried to be good — it is so dark here, so dark..."

Another: "Mummy, when they kill us, will it hurt?" "No, my dearest, it will not hurt. It will only take a minute."

It only took a minute — but it is enough to keep us awake till the end of time.

Lecture delivered at a conference
at the Yeshiva University, New York, 1993

The lesson of Auschwitz

I am humbled by the task thrust upon me — who wouldn't be? — of addressing this distinguished audience, at this solemn time, when people in all parts of the world gather together in assembly halls and houses of prayer, to mourn the dead and ponder the meaning of Auschwitz, on the 50th anniversary of its liberation. It is particularly poignant for us here, in the physical proximity of the camp site, within its sinister shadow.

I must explain why this heavy duty falls on me, even though I am not a survivor *sensu stricto*, but only one of the millions of walking-wounded who lost their families and friends in the Shoah.

My father's family came from that innocent *shtetl* called Oswiecim, which had its name forcibly changed and gained posthumous fame as Auschwitz — the most accursed sound in the language. My father was one of fifteen children, so you can reckon that in Oswiecim, there were, literally, hundreds of Scharfs, of all ages, shapes and sizes, from the ninety-year-old patriarch Elias to the four-year-old Chanele. There were no survivors. They did not have far to go.

But I have yet another title. We are assembled here, in the heart of Kazimierz, the former Jewish quarter of Cracow, the city of my birth, which makes me a true Cracovian, and the city which I love — which makes me even more so. I am familiar with every street, every house, every nook and cranny — its doorways seem to be haunted, the windows stare at me like empty eye-sockets. I want to cry out with Jeremiah: "How lonely sits the city that was full of people — How like a widow has she become — She that was great among the nations…"

Cracow, and within it Kazimierz ("*ir va'em beyisroel*"), was the place where, for generations, Jewish life thrived and Jewish culture flourished. Singular, authentic Jewish life and culture — which was brought to an abrupt, violent end and the like of which will not be seen again. Cracow stands for the life that was. When we think of the numbing statistics of Auschwitz, Cracow, as it were, gives a face to those who perished there, makes us think of what it was that we mourn.

Paradoxically, the interwar years, despite the growing impoverishment and the rising tide of anti-Semitism, could be seen as a sort of golden age of Polish Jewry. Jews were born, grew up, had families, studied, earned their livelihood through craft and trade and the practice of professions, maintained *cheders* and yeshivahs, secular schools and institutions of higher learning, built synagogues and theaters, played and danced and enjoyed themselves, wrote books sacred and profane, pursued their manifold and diverse interests and — above all — (and therefore I call it the golden age) died in their own beds and were buried in ordinary cemeteries.

They lived, on the whole peaceably, among their Polish neighbours, separately yet together, and made an enormous contribution to industry and commerce, to Polish literature and culture. The nations among whom Jews dwelt have always greatly benefitted by their presence.

Were one to specify a single dominant feature in this rich and diverse tapestry of Jewish life, one could say that it was a degree of spirituality. No matter how poor, humble or oppressed, or — conversely — how prosperous and successful, Jews, in their majority, knew that "man lives not by bread alone," that he has to rise above the mundane and has to strive for the fulfilment of some ideal, however defined.

It is well-nigh impossible to sustain a rational discourse about Auschwitz. The very word lacerates a raw nerve. It means many things. It is not only a physical place in Poland. It is also an abstract notion which fills us with awe and profound unease. It is a symbol — holding different meanings for different people.

To Jews, Auschwitz is the symbol of the Holocaust. They are surprised and outraged at any attempt to invest it with a different meaning. But for Poles it is a symbol of the German rape of their country and the persecution of their nation — and they have their very good reasons for perceiving it thus.

Similarly, to Christians, the Cross is a sign of love and hope: how are they to be made to understand that to most Jews it symbolises oppression, persecution, the Church's triumphalism, the intention to convert "the stray brothers"? Can they see that the Cross, in what is perceived as the greatest Jewish cemetery of all times, offends the deepest Jewish sensibilities?

I am going to say something which may be resented by my non-Jewish friends, but this is no time for equivocation. What prompted this thought was my first visit to Auschwitz. I am sorry to admit that, through the years, I could not bring myself to go there, but some two years ago I participated in an international conference in Cracow, with speakers from many countries and many denominations, and a visit to the site could not be avoided. On return, when we all sat together, huddled deep in thought, I felt impelled to say that a Jewish perception and response to Auschwitz is different from that of a non-Jew, no matter how sensitive, compassionate and well-intentioned. One of my Polish friends, a man for whom I have the highest regard, told me afterwards that he was hurt and offended by my remark: "Does my pulse beat in a different rhythm to yours?" he asked. "My feelings, my emotions, my reason — are they essentially different from yours, somehow less human? Am I less capable than you of grasping the magnitude and the universality of the tragedy?" No, I certainly did not mean to give offence or to exclude. On the contrary, I think that our thoughts and our concern about Auschwitz bring us together and in the face of Auschwitz we are all, in the most profound way, equal. But Jews have been marked as people apart, selected to die, and die they did by the million. Others would get over it (sometimes all too quickly). Jews have not, nor will they. The sense of loss and the pain are always present. In my journeys in all parts of the world I have not come across a single family that did not have near or more distant relatives perish in the Shoah. The Jewish national psyche has been shaped by this experience. Every Jewish reflex, individual, communal or national, is conditioned by the memory of Auschwitz. Am I wrong to hold that for Jews Auschwitz means something more and something different than for non-Jews?

When we want to talk about Auschwitz, we face an intractable dilemma. We are only capable of comprehending the world through words, of communicating through language. Yet in this instance we feel that words are not adequate. By talking about it we trivialise. Adorno said: "Poetry after Auschwitz is an act of barbarity," meaning that what Auschwitz was and what it truly means should not, in all decency, be used as raw material for literature. When the true human condition is, for all the world to see, manifested in the ghettoes, the camps, the death factories, is not literature which brings catharsis and solace a cruel mockery? And writing, which is an act of faith, an impermissible self-indulgence? By the same token it should not be used for rhetoric, for speechifying, for effect.

Yet this view would set limits on our deepest needs — to share, to instruct, to warn, to transmit. By talking we trivialise and thus falsify, yet by keeping silent we betray.

We have not kept silent. A massive literature exists — memoirs, reports, histories, documents, analyses — considering and illuminating every aspect and detail, and the end is not in sight. (Therefore the efforts of the "revisionists" and those who deny that it all happened are not dangerous but merely ridiculous.)

The problems are so baffling — we read and study and write and discuss and have come no nearer to understanding the basic questions.

How did a seemingly civilised nation, in the twentieth century, in the heart of Europe, allow itself to be seduced by a gang of perverts and in the course of a few years to be brought down to a state of barbarity? How was it possible to conceive and carry out a plan to build gas chambers and crematoria and, in cold blood, exterminate human beings, by the million? It took so many "ordinary" people to do it and so many more to allow it to be done — the bystanders, both individual and nations; the accepted order was so easily and so totally subverted.

How did it happen that a great and ancient civilisation could be extirpated and wiped out in the course of four years, so that we have to scrape around for its traces in the land where it flourished? And, most importantly, how are we, the survivors of Polish Jewry, to carry on with our daily lives, burdened with the memory of what happened to our people and how it happened?

What are we to do? How do we conceive our duty towards the new generation, towards the world? What are we to transmit and how?

In the Jewish tradition there is a strong command to teach the young about the past ("*ve shinantam le 'vanecha*").

I want to share with you a little instructive tale told me by a woman who knows a great deal about these things and who, like myself, gives them serious thought.

Some years ago — she tells me — she went with her son, then a precocious ten-year-old, on holidays to Spain. It so happened that in the place she rented there was a severe plague of flies and insects, which became intolerable, tending to spoil the holidays. One day she undertook a radical measure: she shut tightly all doors and windows and sprayed the space and every corner with a strong insecticide, whereupon she went with her son for a long walk. When she came back and opened the door, she was taken aback by a macabre sight. The walls and the floor were covered by layers of dead and half-dead insects, some still crawling heavily. The boy, looking at this for a while, asked her: "Mummy, is that how Jews were dying in the gas chambers?"

What must she have told her son once, that such an image got stuck in his little head? Did she have the right to tell him such a thing? Did she have the right not to tell him? Are we telling our children and grandchildren enough? At the right time?

Surely there are lessons to be drawn from Auschwitz. How corruptible the creature *homo-so-called-sapiens* is, how thin the veneer of civilisation. Fifty years on, as I speak, a hundred different wars are being fought around the world, some in distant places of which we know nothing, some in nearby places of which we want to know nothing. The most terrifying lesson of Auschwitz seems to be that it will be easier next time round.

One must try not to give way to despair. Excessive mourning is discouraged in Orthodox Jewish teaching (as it is supposed to imply that "the mourner is possessed of more compassion than the Almighty"). Surely, life must go on (in some ways it has gone on as if nothing happened). The spiritual resources have not dried up, there is rebirth, renewal, the march of generations. Above all, for us, there is the State of Israel, a source of strength and pride and fulfilment.

For sanity's sake we must cling to the notion that somehow, ultimately, there is on this earth a balance of justice (though not easily seen with the naked eye), that our philosophical, theological assumptions are not without foundation.

The Holocaust throws into relief both the worst that human beings can do to each other and the best of which the human spirit is capable. This brings us to the crucial conviction that there is always a choice between the best and the worst; and that there may be times in a person's life when he or she is called upon to make that choice, perhaps at great risk — "all that is necessary for evil to flourish is that good men do nothing."

Custom and good manners require one not to end an utterance like this on an entirely bleak note. Not much optimism, as you will have gathered, can be expected of me. I am too far gone, have spent too much time wandering in that ungodly territory. Nonetheless — Hope Dies Last.

Speech on the 50th Anniversary of the camp's liberation,
at the Center for Jewish Culture in Cracow, 1995

On the 50th anniversary of the Warsaw Ghetto Uprising

I take pleasure in the fact that Polish circles in London have taken the initiative in commemorating the anniversary of the Warsaw Ghetto Uprising, and although I am not sure why I of all people have been asked to say a few words on this occasion, I confess I feel honoured.

Perhaps my title to speak out on this subject, should someone question it, lies in this — that the majority of my family on my father's side came from Oswiecim, an innocent townlet, which later under its accursed pseudonym entered history and covered itself in sinister, posthumous fame. Jews formed the great majority in that townlet and among them the Scharf family was thick on the ground.

Polish-Jewish dialogue has often been, somehow, half-hearted, not open and sincere. One has the impression that many Poles, when speaking about Jews among themselves in private, express views different from those they utter in public — and Jews do the same (I try to fight this — on both fronts). Often when Poles touch upon these Jewish themes, the war, the occupation, they show some disquiet, as if they fear that they will be put on the defensive, will be asked about things difficult to explain, will find themselves, generally, on unfamiliar ground. Few Poles had real knowledge of Jewish life, their writing, internal politics, views and concerns, what made them tick — these matters were simply of no interest to the average Pole. In England we would often recriminate and argue until we were blue in the face. Our views on Polish-Jewish relations in the interwar years and, above all, under the German occupation, differ.

The anniversary which we now commemorate serves as a good example. When Jews speak of "The Uprising" they refer to the uprising in the Warsaw ghetto; when Poles speak of "The Uprising" they mean, naturally, the Warsaw Uprising, that memorable and tragic episode in Polish history.

In Poland the Ghetto Uprising used to be commemorated at regular intervals. On occasion I observed these ceremonies at close quarters. One invariably had the impression that their true purpose was not to pay sincere homage to the heroes and their memory but to prove some official thesis, to demonstrate, for instance, how the powers-that-be cared for their Jews or how wrong it was to accuse the regime of anti-Semitism (which no longer existed in Poland). On other occasions the stress was on the help which the People's Army brought to the ghetto fighters — a list of arms and ammunition to the last bullet (it amounted to precious little even by their own reckoning). At other times the so-called "commemoration" gave a chance to declaim about the German-Zionist conspiracy threatening Polish independence — of which the sole true protector was Soviet Russia.

The Warsaw Ghetto Uprising was a hopeless, desperate, suicidal gesture, the outcome of which could only spell death to the heroes. Such a typical Polish gesture — I use this adjective advisedly, for Poles and Jews, seemingly so different, in many ways resemble each other (particularly in their tendencies to internal discord). In the history of underground resistance it occupies a unique place. It has become a symbol, on a world scale.

The Ghetto Uprising is sometimes regarded as some partial rehabilitation of a Jewish community often accused of passivity, of going like sheep to the slaughter, without resistance. I disagree with the view that Jews could have shown more will to fight. One must bear in mind the total disproportion of forces: on the one side a population exhausted by disease and hunger, terrorised and defenceless — on the other a mighty, victorious army and the whole apparatus of a police state. In Auschwitz, for instance, there was a group of 13,000 Russian prisoners of war, young, strong, disciplined. When Auschwitz was liberated there were only 92 of them left alive. If they could not offer any resistance, what could be expected of the rest?

Moreover, the Germans conducted their policy of extermination with extreme perfidy and cunning. The prisoners were isolated from the outside world, unaware of what was in store for them, always with a flicker of hope of survival. The slightest sign of resistance was instantaneously and brutally suppressed, including measures of collective punishment. Despite that, there were attempts at armed uprising in the ghettoes in Czestochowa and Bialystok and in the death camps of Treblinka and Sobibor.

It is well to bear in mind that resistance means not only a desperate shot from a pistol, the throwing of a hand grenade or petrol bomb. Resistance is also the underground teaching of adults and children; resistance means a network of charitable organisations; resistance means collecting reports and documents (the Ringelblum Archives are our main source of knowledge about those days); resistance is artistic activity, concerts, satirical songs, verses written on scraps of paper; resistance is the underground press, bulletins, the spreading of information from received broadcasts. Resistance is Janusz Korczak, a model of human dignity, staying with his children to the last.

Resistance means, above all, every good deed which restores faith in man, a sign that in that flood of barbarity all is not irretrievably lost.

In retrospect, no one other than those who fought and strove in the ghetto emerges from the story with credit. Not the Allied governments who turned a deaf ear to the heartrending appeals from the ghetto, including the personal appeal of that audacious hero Jan Karski, or the suicide of Szmul Zygielbojm.

Roosevelt held on to the thesis that "the defeat of Germany will bring with it the rescue of Jews." The vast majority of Europe's Jews did not live to see the defeat of Germany.

Little credit attaches to the Polish underground. The Home Army, which reflected accurately the profile of the Polish nation, was — with few exceptions — indifferent to the fate of the Jews and in many cases was downright hostile. The commander-in-chief, General Grot-Rowecki, in a radio-telegram to the Polish government-in-exile, reports thus: "Various Jewish groupings, including communists, have turned to us lately requesting arms, as if we had plenty. As an experiment I gave them a few pistols. I am not sure they will make use of them. I shall not give them any more, you know that we have not a great deal ourselves..."

Also one must not overlook the part played by the so-called "Narodowe Siły Zbrojne" — the National Armed Forces. Contemporary historians are not always honest when dealing with this subject but it remains an incontrovertible fact that in collaboration with the Germans and in accordance with their programme these groups themselves murdered thousands of Jews.

During the Warsaw Ghetto Uprising the Polish government-in-exile was suddenly confronted with the revelations of Katyn and the rupture of relations with Russia — these matters left little time for anything else.

Among those who did not cover themselves with glory were the leaders and activists of American Jewry. The spokesmen for the Uprising called upon them to lie down on the steps of the White House, if necessary, and not budge until the American government promised to undertake some moves towards rescue or retaliation. It is possible that Nahum Goldman or Stephen Wise approached Roosevelt by the back door, but no one lay down on the steps of the White House, no one stirred public opinion, no one achieved anything to any effect. The inhabitants of the ghetto — and that was the most painful aspect of their existence — felt abandoned by God and men.

The possibility of rendering help, and the nature and extent of it, differed of course, enormously. One thing could be expected from Roosevelt, another from Churchill, yet another from Nahum Goldman. No one, no one beside the fighters themselves, emerged from this with credit; some with eternal shame.

Whoever wants to form a view on these matters must remember that those were truly apocalyptic times, without precedent in history, when all basic concepts, mental habits, normal reflexes, ceased to function. There were situations so monstrous, so — literally — inhuman, that passing judgement on them in retrospect, applying ordinary standards, would be totally misleading. How do you divide your bread ration among members of your family when there is not enough to go round? How does a mother decide which of her two children to save when there is a chance to save only one? What do you do when a Jew pursued by the Gestapo knocks at your door, when you know that offering him shelter can result in your own and your family's death? You might have heard of the case of one Adina Szwajger, who died not long ago in Lodz and whose obituary notices appeared in *The Times* and *The Independent*.

She was a doctor in the children's hospital in the ghetto. When the hospital was being evacuated for transport to Treblinka, Adina Szwajger, to save the children the torment of that journey to the gas chamber, went from bed to bed and gave the children a lethal injection. By what categories can you judge such an action? Read the following extract from a diary written in the ghetto by one Jan Mawult:

"Think of this, a handful of people decide to defend themselves. They have no arms, they cannot erect barricades, they cannot collect ammunition, every pistol has to be bought, smuggled in with great effort. They've decided to die, one and all. Fine. But what to do with the old people, their mothers and fathers, the children? Wives will fight with their menfolk, shoulder to shoulder, but what about the rest? Leave them to their fate? Their fate by now would mean to be burnt alive, not even being poisoned by gas. To leave them to that fate? Impossible. So what is there to be done? It would seem that we have to kill them ourselves. But even that is not simple. The few bullets we possess are precious, must not be wasted, each is destined for a German. To poison them then, but how? The gas is cut off. Cyanide is not available in sufficient quantities. And when, at what precise moment, is this to be done?"

Since it is difficult to talk about these things I thought to escape the inadequacy of common words and resort to poetry, for poetry sometimes manages to deal with the otherwise inexpressible. I am thinking, for instance, of that famous poem by Czeslaw Milosz, "Campo di Fiori," which Milosz wrote in Warsaw, at Easter 1943. He speaks there of the loneliness of those who die, like Giordano Bruno, at the stake, and how the crowd passes by, indifferent, how people "trade, play, love" and "forget before the ashes have cooled down." He likens it to the famous fairground near the Warsaw ghetto walls which, when the ghetto was burning, was attracting local citizenry. I quote some stanzas:

> The bright melody drowned
> the salvos from the ghetto wall
> and couples were flying
> high in the blue sky.
>
> At times wind from the burning
> would drift dark kites along
> and riders on the carousel
> caught petals in midair.

blew open the skirts of the girls
and the crowds were laughing
on the beautiful Warsaw Sunday.

Those dying here, the lonely
forgotten by the world,
our tongue becomes for them
the language of an ancient planet...

The uprising in the Warsaw ghetto is undoubtedly the last chapter in the history of the Jews on Polish soil. The Warsaw ghetto was razed to the ground and became not only the grave of that last group of fighters but also a symbolic tombstone of Jewish civilisation in Eastern Europe. It was there, on Polish soil, in that raw climate, that there flourished the most creative, resilient, life-enhancing branch of the Jewish nation in the Diaspora.

One third of the Jewish people perished, were gassed, extirpated, turned into ashes. In those ashes how many potential Einsteins and Freuds, Heines and Mendelssohns, Gottliebs and Chagalls, Tuwims and Korczaks — people burdened with that genetic endowment which gives rise to genius.

A thousand years of Jewish civilisation in Poland, that which was shared and that which was separate, were destroyed in the course of four years of Teutonic barbarism. This is a fact which the mind cannot encompass and from the enormity of which thought and imagination recoil.

The Jewish people have emerged from this war not only physically truncated but also mentally damaged, in the sense that all other evil in the world appears, by comparison with what happened to us, trivial. Our sensitivity to other people's suffering has been diminished.

It is customary on occasions like this for the speaker to end on an uplifting note, with an accent on hope and optimism, as if to say that despite it all — and so on... You must forgive me — I cannot rise to that. I stand helpless, orphaned, with a sense of an enormous, irreparable wrong.

There is not a day in my life but that I think of this. I cannot forget, must not forget, don't want to forget. The world should also be made to remember.

Speech at the Polish Cultural Center in London
19th April 1995

Rumkowski of the Lodz ghetto

Chaim Mordechai Rumkowski is one of those figures — complex, grotesque, tragicomic — worthy of the pen of Balzac or Dostoyevsky —
a figure which could come into existence only in demented circumstances when time was out of joint.

To begin with he was an ordinary *Lodzermensch*, an individual of limited
education but great native intelligence and iron will, who had once made
a fortune and then lost it, a not-uncommon case of the rise and fall of that type
in the "Promised Land" which was Lodz at the turn of the century. He took an
active part in the life of the community, was a philanthropist. In the interwar
years he built, from funds he raised himself, a great orphanage in Helenowek,
which was named "Little Palestine," as the wards were taught agriculture in
preparation for their emigration to the Holy Land.

When the Germans occupied Lodz, they called together the Jewish coun-
cillors, in order to set up the Judenrat. They nominated Rumkowski as chairman
(*der Alteste der Juden*); it is not clear why — probably merely because he had
bushy white hair and stood out — after all it was all the same to them who was
to carry out their orders, one little worm passing orders to other little worms.

The Germans could not have foreseen how lucky they were in their choice.
In Rumkowski they found a functionary of demonic energy and outstanding
organisational talent. It looked as if his whole life so far had been a preparation
for this role, to become, in the full flowering of his sixty years, to the joy of his
masters, "the King of the Ghetto."

Behind the barbed wire, in the district of Baluty, without a sewage system,
six people to a room, Rumkowski created a self-governing territory, a mini-state,
with its own administration, courts, currency — the notes carried his portrait —
and, of course, its own police and prisons.

Food rations, principally bread, were a visible instrument of absolute power
and a sufficient sanction to enforce obedience.

Rumkowski organised factories, workshops, hospitals, soup kitchens, schools
— there was a time when people still gave thought to the education of children.
From his office Rumkowski directed the whole network of enterprises. He was
the sole link with the Germans, the only conduit of their orders.

It is clear, in retrospect, that he was not evil, like some who collaborated
with the Germans for their own gain and did their dirty work for them to save

their own skins. He was undoubtedly a man of good intentions, convinced that he was acting in the interest of the community. He surrounded himself with a number of able people whose hands remained clean. He carried one idea in his head which guided him like a lodestar: if the Jews proved useful, if they worked, worked, worked till they wore themselves to the bone — they would justify their existence and survive.

It is easy to see today how utterly senseless this idea was. Neither Rumkowski nor anyone else could have then known nor foreseen in their darkest nightmares that the Germans were planning the total extermination of the Jewish people, and that this plan took priority over all other commitments. Nothing, but nothing that Rumkowski did or omitted to do, could have had any influence on the fate of the Jews.

Although he was no more than a puppet in Germans' hands, the role he played turned him into a megalomaniac. He used to speak of "my factories, my hospitals, my doctors, my Jews," addressed "his" population, haranguing them continually in the manner of Goebbels. In exchange he expected, and received, paeans of praise: "Our great Chairman, our wise Chairman…" How little real power he had and how his German masters did not even pretend that they owed him anything for his sterling services was shown when one day he went courageously to the Gestapo to intervene on behalf of his arrested colleague from the Judenrat. He was beaten and thrown out like any other Jew.

Whether Rumkowski was deceiving himself or whether he was striking attitudes in order to impress his fellow creatures is hard to know. He acquired the manners of a despot and this semblance of power turned his head.

Czerniakow, the chairman of the Judenrat in Warsaw, who in similarly tragic circumstances also played an ambiguous role carrying out German orders, when it came to signing the edict about "resettlement" at the time when he knew already that the terminal stations of "resettlement" were the death camps, refused to sign and committed suicide. This act also, of course, had no influence on the fate of the Jews, but Czerniakow did thus rehabilitate himself in the eyes of posterity. Not so Rumkowski — till the last he countersigned the orders put in front of him, until he himself, with his young wife (whom he married in the ghetto), his adopted son and other members of his family, was dispatched to Auschwitz. It is said that the true ruler of the ghetto, Max Biebow, the merchant from Bremen for whom Rumkowski was ceaselessly amassing a fortune, on 23rd August 1944 despatched Rumkowski to Auschwitz not in a cattle truck, like other Jews, but in a first-class carriage.

Was Rumkowski a monster, a benefactor, a fool, a leader? It is impossible to form a balanced view. It is worthwhile to quote his speech to the population on 4th September 1942, after he received an order to deliver for "resettlement" 20,000 people from among the children and the old:

"Terrible tragedy has befallen the ghetto. We are asked to give up what is most precious to us — our children and our old people. I have not been fortunate enough to have children of my own, therefore I gave the best years of my life to other people's children. I never thought that it would be my lot to have to sacrifice children. It has fallen to me to stretch my arms out to you and implore you: brothers and sisters, fathers and mothers — give up your children to me" [sobbing then convulsed the crowd].

Rumkowski went on: "I had a foreboding of some terrible threat. I was awaiting some blow, I kept vigil, day and night, in case it were in my power to avert it.

"I failed to do so, I did not know what was in store for us. I did not foresee that they would even carry out the sick from the hospitals — but of this you have the best proof, my nearest and dearest were among them and I could do nothing for them. I thought after that that we shall have peace for a while. And now a new threat emerges. Such is the Jewish fate — ever new and more dire suffering.

"Yesterday afternoon we received an order to deport 20,000 people from the ghetto. 'If you do not do it' — we were told — 'we shall do it ourselves.' We were given the choice: to do it or let them do it. With that in mind — not how many will die but how many we shall be able to save — I and my closest aides have taken the decision that, however ghastly the task is for us, we must take the responsibility for carrying out this decree. I cannot escape from having to carry out this bloody operation. I must sunder the limbs in order to save the body. I must take the children from you, else others will die with them.

"I have not come to bring you solace, I have not come to lighten your hearts — I am here to share the awesome burden of your grief. I come like a thief to steal what is most precious to you. I have not spared myself to have this decree annulled. When that proved impossible, I tried to blunt its severity. I made a register of the children of nine years and older, to get at least those reprieved — they would not have it. I succeeded in one respect — those ten years old and above will not fall victim to the decree. Let this be some consolation.

"We have in the ghetto a great number of people infected with TB, who have only a few days, maybe a few weeks to live. I do not know, maybe this idea is diabolical, but I am asking you: should we not give up those sick people in order to save the healthy? I know that every family takes particular care of their sick. But in the face of this threat we must weigh this up and decide: who can, who should be saved? Common sense dictates that we try to save those who have a chance of survival and not those who will die anyway. We exist in circumstances where there is not enough food to sustain those in good health, let alone the sick. Every one of us keeps a sick person going at the cost of our own health, giving them our own crust of bread, our own lump of sugar, our own mouthful of meat — but this is not enough to save them and we ourselves fall ill. I understand that such sacrifices are noble. But if I am faced with the choice whether to save the sick ones or the healthy ones I cannot hesitate for long. I ordered the doctors to give up all those incurably sick, to save in their place those who can live [wailing and weeping shakes the crowd].

"I do understand you, mothers, I see your tears. I feel for you, fathers, who, tomorrow, when your children will have been taken away, will have to go to work as usual. I know all this and my heart breaks.

"Since four o'clock yesterday afternoon, when the decree was brought to my knowledge, I have been a broken man, I share your pain with you, I don't know how to gather strength to continue living. I tell you one thing — the demand was for 24,000 deportees, 3000 per day for eight days, I managed to bring it down to 20,000, but only on condition that all children under ten must go. Because these children and the old people add up to only 13,000, we must make up the quota by giving up the sick. I appeal to you, help me to carry out this task. I shudder to think that, God forbid, it will be left to others to carry it out.

"You have in front of you a wreck of a man. This is the most terrible moment of my life. I stretch my arms to you and implore you: make this sacrifice to spare us from having to make even greater sacrifices, in order to protect the remaining Jewish community of 100,000..."

It seems to me that nobody who was not there has the right to form a judgement on Rumkowski and on those who found themselves in a similar situation.

Jehoshuah Sobol, an Israeli playwright, wrote a play about the Vilna ghetto, where one of the protagonists is Jakub Gens, the chief of the Jewish police, and later — like Rumkowski — the chairman of the Judenrat. Gens is faced with the same dilemmas — he is "serving" the Germans, supplies the work force, prepares lists of those to be transported to the death camps — always with the thought that he might be able to save somebody. Sobol puts into Gens' mouth the following speech:

"Many of you consider me a traitor. And wonder how I still exist among you, the pure, the innocent, the incorruptible ones. I, Jakub Gens, who uncovers your hideouts, who delivers you to the Germans, am the same Jakub Gens who is plotting day and night how to save Jewish lives. I weigh up Jewish blood, not Jewish dignity. When they ask of me one thousand Jews, I deliver to them one thousand Jews, otherwise they will come to fetch not one but ten thousand. You and your tender consciences! Where there is villainy and filth you avert your eyes. If any of you survives, he will have clean hands, whereas mine are dripping from slime, soaked in blood. I shall appear in front of Jewish judges, shall submit to their verdict. I shall say to them — whatever I did, I did to save Jews, as many as possible, to lead them to freedom. In order to do so I had to lead others to death, yes, with my own hands. So that you should keep your conscience clean, I had to sink in filth. I could not afford the luxury of a good conscience..."

I don't know whether it serves any good purpose talking about this further. What is there left to say? How much can human sensitivity endure and reason grasp? I confess that even though I have spent the greater part of my life thinking about these things, I am no nearer to understanding how this could have happened, no nearer to grasping the dimensions of the catastrophe and the extent of its consequences. The mind refuses to act — it is better thus, not to look into the very bottom of the pit.

But of this one must be constantly aware: that the extermination of Jews on Polish soil is a critical event in history, concerning not only Germans, Poles and Jews, but the whole of humanity. It marks the crisis of Christianity and the crisis of our civilisation (there are those who would consider those two notions synonymous, but fortunately this is not so).

What lesson humanity will draw from that cataclysm; how it will cope with the awareness of the depth to which man showed himself capable of sinking; how man will renew belief in basic moral values, in a world possessing means of destruction, by comparison with which even the gas chambers pale into insignificance: on answers to these questions depends the future of humankind.

Janusz Korczak and his time

The folk memory works in mysterious ways. From the huge mass of events, words and images which leave their imprint on the common consciousness, it selects and fastens onto some quintessential image or figure or a set of words which iron out the complexities and symbolise the whole epoch. Thousands perished at Inquisitional stakes to affirm freedom of thought — it is Giordano Bruno burning in Campo di Fiori who illuminates the age. The self-immolating torch of Jan Palach glows over Prague. Yevtushenko's *Babi Yar* has an impact stronger than all the efforts to drain the event of its true meaning. The prolonged *Shema* of Rabbi Akiba reverberates with all the voices of Jewish saints. Of the countless photographs of Nazi brutality, in and outside the camps — the one that haunts us through sleepless nights is of the boy in the Warsaw ghetto, in the oversize peaked cap, with raised arms, the big eyes looking at us, knowing too much.

Thus also Janusz Korczak is a legend of our time. The story which makes him so is simple — but it stands at the heart of the Holocaust and it illustrates perhaps more than any other the horror and the pity of it. On the 5th of August 1942, as part of the liquidation of the Warsaw ghetto, the Germans ordered Korczak's orphanage to be emptied and the children transported to their death in Treblinka. Korczak arranged his 200 wards in orderly ranks and marched quietly ahead of the column to the *Umschlagplatz* on the corner of Stawki and Dzika Streets, where he and his children were packed into the trucks and despatched to the ovens.

This march through the streets of the ghetto, seen at the time by a mere few hundred people, has cast a long shadow ahead, and the small figure of Korczak, on his road to Calvary, unconscious of heroics, wretched with grief, doing what was natural to him, has captured man's imagination. The news of it spread like a bushfire, stories began to be told, filling out the details. How Korczak carried two little ones in his arms — improbably, since he was so sick that he could hardly drag himself along; how — due to the last-moment intervention of the Judenrat — a messenger caught up with the column with a German warrant to set Korczak free and how he, disdainfully, pushed the messenger aside; how the guard in charge of the trucks, just before sealing the door, offered to leave Korczak out — and how Korczak mounted the steps without a backward glance. How to spare the children anxiety he told them that they were going for a joyride in the countryside and how they trustingly followed him without a tear or murmur. The story in its stark outline wants no embellishment and nothing need be added to make it more telling. The antithesis of spirit and force or, if you like, of the Jew and the Nazi, is pinpointed and fixed. The learned, selfless, caring, man *in excelsis* against the mindless, malevolent barbarian, here at his fiendish worst.

Among the million anonymous deaths, Korczak's death acquired a meaning. As the news spread through the camps and the ghettoes, it provided an inspiration at the time when the greatest single help to survival was the stubborn residual belief, in the teeth of all the evidence to the contrary, that human dignity could still have its triumph.

The underground literature in the camps and on the "other side" bears witness to the comfort and pride which Korczak's finest hour gave to his contemporaries. Since then his fame has spread and a cult has developed. The world was not slow to recognise the moral symbolism of Korczak. Articles, books and plays are written about him, stamps are issued, statues are erected, institutions are given his name, prizes are given to commemorate him.

It behooves us to see to it that the manner of his death does not overshadow the manner of his life. Henryk Goldschmit, to use for once his real name — Janusz Korczak being a pseudonym which he picked from an obscure novel — was born in Warsaw a hundred years ago, into a well-to-do family. The fact that his father was a fashionable lawyer and his grandfather a doctor illustrates the degree to which this particular milieu was assimilated. He had a sheltered and solitary childhood and grew up hardly conscious of his Jewish origin or what that meant. When still a schoolboy he lost his father, who fell prey to a mental illness, as a result of which the family fell from relative affluence to utter penury. As soon as he was able he took it upon himself to support his mother and sister, and he knew years of near-starvation and of hard struggle while he studied medicine. Only when he became a doctor did success begin to smile upon him, partly due to his growing reputation as a writer — but then, moved by some inner compulsion, he took deliberate steps to alter the course of his life.

From the moment when at the age of 34 he abandoned his career as a practising doctor and took up residence at "Nasz dom" (Our Home), the orphanage which till the end remained connected with his name, he was like a man possessed of a magnificent monomania — to live his life in the service of the child. He was no starry-eyed idealist but he was endowed with an uncanny empathy with children and had a sober and steely concern for children's rights in a world ruled by adults. He had a mistrust of the adult world but, like every true reformer, he believed that it is better to light a candle than to deplore the darkness. His insights were unclouded by sentimentality, but were based on continuous clinical observation and meticulous listing and shifting of data. He was wise, loving and utterly single-minded, without a thought for such needs as affect other mortals — money, fame, home or family.

The orphanage, an institution built and supported entirely by private charity, was at the service of the most deprived, the children of the poorest quarters of Warsaw. The raising of money for good causes, then as now, has its vulgar side which tends to irk those depending on it. Korczak shook his head over "the cost of the wax to polish the dance floor for the charity ball" and begrudged the time spent showing visitors round the home. However, by the force of his personality he established a proper respect for his work, and donors came to understand the privilege of supporting it.

He was an original and pragmatic thinker in the field of child psychology and education, and he pioneered concepts which became models of their kind. He continually sought to perfect a system which was based on understanding of the child's deepest needs. Korczak exercised his influence through his close presence and also through his writing for the house newspaper, which was produced for and by the children and the communal reading of which was an important weekly event. It is said that in thirty years of pressing activity Korczak never failed to deliver his weekly contribution. Part of the system of self-government was the administration of justice, according to a Code, with its dreaded Paragraph 1000 — the ultimate sanction of expulsion from the home. Every child with a grievance had the right to summon the offender to face the court of his peers — Korczak himself had to appear when called upon and had to submit to its judgement. At the end of his day, after the last inspection of the dormitories, Korczak would retire to his small room in the attic, the only "home" he had all his adult life, to compile his notes and to write his books.

He was a prolific writer in his professional field, but above all of stories for and about children. Deceptively simple in form and content, with a blend of melancholy and humour which reflected his own inner disposition, often sharply satirical of society, always heartwarming and perceptive — they left an indelible trace in the memory of readers young and old.

In the mid-thirties Korczak visited Palestine twice, staying in the Kibbutz Ein Harod. He felt spiritually refreshed and moved by what he saw. Prompted and encouraged by his many friends and former pupils, he began to think seriously about moving to Palestine for good. The obstacles he saw were many. It troubled him greatly that he could not find a suitable successor to fill his place and carry on his work in Warsaw. The thought of tearing up his roots from his native soil was unendurable. In letters to friends explaining the delay he speaks movingly of "my Vistula," "my beloved Warsaw," the parting from which, he knew, would leave him disconsolate. Also — he was penniless and feared that he might become a burden.

But the rising tide of anti-Semitism in Poland was sweeping the essential decencies aside and Korczak could stand it no more. He was ousted from the radio, he had to resign from the non-Jewish orphanage of which he was the founder. The year was 1939. He decided to pack and go.

Stefa Wilczynska, a woman of great heart and shining courage, who over many years was Korczak's close colleague and twin pillar of the venture, had already gone to Palestine a year or two before. Knowing Korczak's helplessness in worldly matters, she now returned to help him wind up his affairs and make the journey. The outbreak of war caught her in the trap. She naturally took up again her post in the orphanage, at Korczak's side.

When the Germans ordered the Jews of Warsaw to move into the ghetto, the orphanage lost its home in Krochmalna Street, which was on the "Aryan" side, and had to move to makeshift accommodations within the walls. By then Korczak saw more clearly than most people that the screw would continue to be turned pitilessly till all life expired. But he would not give up his inalienable right to relieve suffering. Himself in deepest despair and ailing, he gathered his remaining strength, day after desperate day, in an effort to replenish the essential stock of food and medicine. He steadfastly went on his begging missions for stores and money, at times quite futile, often yielding only a pittance. He felt no constraints in appealing, begging, shaming people into support of this best of all causes. On days when nothing else availed he would go to plead with the execrable ringleaders of the Jewish gang of smugglers and extortionists.

While hunger was growing and disease spreading, he tried to maintain inside the home the pretence of normalcy — teaching, playing, caring, as ever. Into the woefully congested quarters he frequently brought in a new boy or girl, whom he picked up from the street with life ebbing away and for whom being taken, for the moment, under Korczak's wing was the only salvation.

In this extremity of the human condition, such as in saner times is beyond imagining, we have in Korczak, in his daily round, a witness to what a single true man can do out of love.

His was an exemplary life — and it is tempting to see in him, in the frail figure in a janitor's apron, which was his habitual uniform and which is how most people remember him — an epitome of the whole generation, the archetypal "Child of Our Time." His greatness, which lay in the pursuit of his worldly task, was of a kind potentially within everybody's grasp, and even the high drama of his death became ordinary where martyrdom was commonplace. Insofar as a single individual, through the strands which make up the pattern of his life, expresses the authentic pitch of history at a particular junction, it would be hard to find a figure who more pertinently than Korczak embodies what was significant and particular of his time and place.

Korczak grew up feeling Polish to the core. In his attachment to Polish soil, history, literature and language nobody could be more so. In this he was typical of a segment of Jewish society in love with the *idea of Poland*. It was only by a gradual and painful process, in the cooling moral climate, that he was forced to recognise that his case was one of love unrequited, and no matter how pure and worthy his devotion he would stay condemned by the sheer fact of his origin. The unhealed wound of this rejection never ceased to plague him.

To understand this fully one must look at the issues in the context of Jewish life as it was, the world of yesterday which came to an abrupt end.

It has been observed, acutely, that Poland has always been a country with a great deal of history but little geography. Constantly imperilled, frequently occupied and ruled by its big and rapacious neighbours, it had few opportunities to develop into an independent, balanced entity. The heavy and ubiquitous hand of the Catholic Church, the ethnic fragmentation, the divisive legacy of the partitions, the impoverished peasantry and the general economic backwardness did not favour conditions wherein liberalism could flourish. During the spell of independence between the wars, the neighbouring states, with the brief notable exception of Masaryk's Czechoslovakia, hardly provided models to follow. Indeed, by comparison with the Germany and Russia of the thirties one could wax nostalgic over the conditions of relative freedom which did prevail.

One likes to think that the treatment of Jews provides a standard for gauging the moral temperature of a country. This may well be so, but one must not think of it as the only measure. Minorities, particularly if they are substantial, distinctive and competitive, do give rise to acute problems. The will, the wisdom and the means to solve or assuage them are precious commodities, in short supply, and the love of one's neighbour is, sadly, not a universal fact of life. Whether one sees it as a virtue or a fault, the fact is that the Jews of Poland, in their mass, *were* unassimilable — and in that sense remained "foreign." It is regrettable but not surprising that the ultimate advantage of diversity and the enrichment of the living fabric of a pluralistic society was not apparent to the Polish "nationalists" — as it is not even now to many other people the world over.

The Jews were subject to their historic condition of dispersion and foreignness, a condition which the Poles did not invent and did not know how to deal with. It is now idle to speculate how the problem would have developed without Hitler. It certainly was heading with increasing momentum towards the sharpest conflict. But that was still the time before the word "solution" was conceived as a synonym for extermination by poison and fire.

Jewish life in Poland moved in its own orbit. In the tightly knit, inward-looking urban community, the Jewish trader or artisan or worker went about his business almost exclusively among his coreligionists, with only a sporadic and superficial contact with the local population, separated from it by force of reciprocal prejudice, suspicion and profound ignorance of what the man across the street was really like. The Jews lived, in the main, in tenement houses, where — as likely as not — the only non-Jewish occupant was the concierge in the basement. Even the intelligentsia of the middle classes, where contacts were more frequent, stayed effectively at double-arm's length, not ever seeing the inside of each other's homes, the doctors tending their Jewish patients, the lawyers their Jewish clients, the teachers teaching mainly in Jewish schools. The occasional Jewish civil servant, university professor or judge had the rarity value of a freak and made people wonder how surpassingly good, or well-connected, he had to be to have got there. Charitable, social and political organisations proliferated and displayed the community's diverse concerns, sometimes parallel to but seldom identical with those of the local population.

The pattern of such assimilation as there was in Poland followed the familiar general forms, but it also had its specificity. With their ears cocked to the stirrings of emancipation in the West, the rebels and innovators were given to their own visions. The Haskalah having effected the first breach from the inside, the magnet of the new passwords, "freedom for mankind — equality for the Jews," exercised a mighty pull. The Polish struggle against the foreign yoke and the fight for independence forged bonds of common understanding, of "our freedom and yours." The thrust was reinforced by growing revulsion against the old Jewish milieu, its claustrophobia and separatism and its antiquated forms — religious and social. By comparison, the attractions of the greener grass on the other side of the hill appeared irresistible.

A new breed of Polish patriots sprang from the midst of the Jewish community. With the zeal of the novice they embraced the dominant culture, so exciting and so different from their own or their parents'. They felt genuine attachment to the land where their ancestors had dwelt for generations, with its language and literature. Within that schizophrenic situation, the dilemmas of divided loyalties, the pull and recoil of the old and the new which always attends the process of assimilation, there were those who remained with a foot in both camps; those who fell between the two proverbial stools and also some who achieved, particularly among the left-wing groupings and intelligentsia, a degree of acceptance as genuine and complete as anywhere in Europe.

There were, of course, also those who for quite unsentimental reasons joined the stream because it offered better career prospects and, as they saw it, a more attractive future. Some of them went the whole hog and got baptised — the Church welcomed converts and the act often revealed a road to social and professional advancement otherwise inaccessible. Their numbers do not seem to have been significant. The atavistic odium which stigmatised a convert remained potent even among those whose links with the Jewish religion had atrophied or were consciously rejected. Excepting the case of a genuine religious conversion, which is as rare as it is mysterious — apostasy for self-advancement carried the penalty of the contempt of the old side and the suspicion of the new. When the end of that era was being acted out in wartime ghettoes, in the depth of misery, this group was the most wretched — alienated from its origins, not at ease among the Jews, uncomprehending why it should be joined with them in death — they suffered the ultimate isolation without the comfort of fellowship.

Despite the fact that entry into the surrounding element was being made increasingly more prickly, assimilation would have continued to grow in scope and numbers but for the emergence of Zionism, which aimed at the physical and moral rehabilitation of Jewry, offered new ideals and hope for the future, and successfully contested the leadership of Jewish life in Poland. Though fragmented into parties of every possible hue in conflict with each other, it was united in blocking the road to assimilation. On the other side, the Bund, whilst fiercely opposing Zionism, proved, among the working class, an influential centre of its own distinct group consciousness.

Whilst the input from the Jewish side into the various aspects of Polish cultural life has been considerable, one need not distort it by exaggeration. The contribution to Polish writings is not comparable, for example, with its German counterpart. Apart from Julian Tuwim, who was in a class apart and undoubtedly the greatest Polish poet of our time, one could list perhaps no more than a dozen names of above-average importance — Slonimski, Lesmian and Wazyk among the poets, Wittlin, Rudnicki, Schulz and Brandys among the novelists, Klaczko, Feldman and Kleiner among the critics, Askenazy and Handelsman among the historians.

It is also interesting to note that in some of the finest examples of Polish literature, in the works of Mickiewicz, Lenartowicz or Norwid, Orzeszkowa or Konopnicka, the figure of the Jew is portrayed with sympathy and compassion.

A potent process of osmosis, of mutual influences transcending the conscious will of the protagonists, was incessantly at work.

The time has come to face the obstinate fact that the stage for the extermination of the Jews proved to be conveniently chosen. It is clear that the genocide could not have been carried out with the same implacable thoroughness and efficiency, down to the last child, if it had not been correctly assumed that the victims would be considered strangers in their own land, with whose fate their co-citizens would not identify. The searching out, the assembly, the transport, the poisoning and the burning would not have been possible if the local population had felt that this was being done to their own flesh and blood. They would not have looked on, indifferently, or perhaps with a pious sigh, month after month, on the passing cattle trains and on the rising smoke of the ovens — but at whatever cost and risk would have disrupted the process. Moreover, the Germans, moving in an element foreign to them, could not distinguish, on sight, who was and who was not a Jew; the Poles were unfailingly sensitive to every Jewish peculiarity. They could tell by a twist in the hair, by the colouring, by a mannerism, by voice inflection, by word usage, by a look in the eye. Above all, if the victims had known that they would find a hiding place among their fellow citizens, that they would meet enough compassion and solidarity against their common enemy, countless numbers would have saved themselves, aided or unaided, over the vast tracts of the country. But the opposite was known to be desperately true — that the Poles in their overwhelming majority would not hide or help, but would seek out, denounce and deliver.

Why this should be so is, like so many "whys" which cry to heaven, an unanswerable question, of the same order of mystery as why a nation with the proudest cultural tradition and achievement suddenly and quickly sank to the lowest depth of depravity. Beyond the partial answers of politics, economics and psychology one has to look for further (partial) answers into the unplumbed darkness of the human soul.

Louder than the volumes which have and will be written on the subject speaks a brief Yiddish poem by Mordechai Gebirtig, *"S'tut Vey!"* (It Hurts!). Gebirtig, a poor carpenter in Cracow, the centenary of whose birth, like Korczak's, ought to be fittingly commemorated this year (1977), was a true folk singer and poet, whose simple words and melodies circulated among the people. His life and work epitomise the character, the spirit and the ways of a whole generation. He became the troubadour of the ghetto, where his few songs written before he was murdered with his wife and two daughters in 1942, although unbearably poignant, brought solace to those who heard them, the way only true poetry can. *"S'tut Vey!"* speaks of young Poles making fun of the blows and humiliation inflicted on the Jews by the common enemy and the pain and puzzlement which this causes. To Gebirtig's sensibility the injury is greater than the one due to the outright German beatings. You do not expect compassion from a beast, you do from a fellow sufferer... It is significant that in some of the most evocative Polish writing about that time, in the works of, say, Andrzejewski, Rudnicki, Wygodzki, Grynberg, this motive of the hostility of the Poles and the danger which they presented to the hunted Jew is also seen as causing the greater anguish.

Now, it must not be forgotten that active efforts to help and to save, as the screw tightened, often incurred mortal risks and called for qualities of character bordering on the heroic — rare in any circumstances and especially so in an environment of shattered values and rampant evil. In no other occupied country was the crime of aiding a Jew punishable by death. In spite of that, there were many hundreds of well-attested cases of surpassing goodness, self-sacrifice and nobility in the name of friendship and common humanity. And, no doubt, thousands more deeds of kindness, unsung and unrecorded, other than in the memory of those who received them, if they but lived to tell the tale. But it is quite beyond question which was the rule and which the exception.

Hitler brought the history of the Jews in Poland to an end. And with whatever degree of abhorrence and pity the Polish population watched — or turned their heads away from — the process of extermination, the vast majority, it must be admitted, were not displeased with the outcome. They would not and could not have done it themselves. As it turned out, the deed was done and cannot be undone and Hitler is to blame.

The lesson he gave was not lost. With the Germans gone, with the country liberated, the Jews who emerged from the bunkers and from the forests into the sunlight were often hunted and murdered. Remember Kielce, where 200 survivors tried to reestablish a semblance of a community. In July 1946 a group of Polish "nationalists" staged a pogrom and slaughtered 42 people.

The ironical twist of history is that Poland, having got rid of its Jews, has its "Jewish" past clinging like Deianira's tunic. Poland's modern history is often seen in the West through the prism of the discrimination against the Jews, as if that were the predominant and distinguishing mark and as if nothing else mattered. The world remembers it as the scene of the extermination of the Jews by their millions, and the unhinging dimensions of the drama have largely obscured Poland's own position. Mention, for instance, the Warsaw Uprising and, as likely as not, the reference will be widely understood to be the rising in the ghetto and not Poland's own heroic insurrection. Poland's destruction and sacrifices, loss of life and territory are found to pale into insignificance by comparison with what is thought the larger tragedy. She commands no great store of sympathy and goodwill and her voice carries little moral authority.

The future will pass its verdict upon what, in the historical balance sheet, is Poland's profit and loss on this account. It is permissible to surmise that the excision of the Jewish genetic pool from the grain of national life, the severance of the creative strain, the stimulant and the catalyst must lead to an impoverishment rather than enrichment of the national fabric.

But for the Jews, let there be no mistake, the loss of Poland is incalculable. For despite the chequered fortunes, despite the vicissitudes, or perhaps because of them, the Jews in Poland through generations formed the most energetic, resilient and productive, the most "Jewish" part of the Diaspora. Deep roots were struck and they nourished abundant growth.

One must not idealise the picture or view it through a haze of nostalgia. There was squalor aplenty, material and spiritual — often ruthlessly castigated and ridiculed by Jewish writers in the midst of it. There were features of character and mentality which mark a society in a distressed condition.

But the total scene was not, as is sometimes assumed, bleak and forlorn. In the unique historical and social situation of the Jews in Poland the inner strength which vouchsafed survival came from many sources. There was the religious life of intense spirituality, centred around local leaders. There was the family life of great warmth and cohesion. There was the total absence of serious crime. There was a feeling of responsibility for all members of the community, which resulted in a widely cast net of private charity and communal institutions. There was a reservoir of human material, talented and dynamic, on offer to every progressive movement.

This was the heartland of the Yiddish language, a potent unifying force, which gave rise to a flourishing literature. Indeed, there was a living culture — rich and many-faceted, one which drew on its own ancient tradition but was also sensitive to the surrounding influences; a culture which produced Nahum Sokolov and the Gaon of Vilna, Isaac Leib Peretz and Scholem Asch, I.M. Weissenberg and the brothers Singer, and a great many of the major Yiddish writers who emigrated to the United States and laid the foundation for the American Yiddish literature that developed there (also, for that matter, Julian Tuwim, who wanted to be known as a Jew *doloris causa*.) But the loss goes beyond the list of illustrious names, however long. It concerns a social organism, a dense, complex and fertile human mixture of sharply distinctive character and spirit. The ingredients and the chemistry which gave rise to that amalgam can never be repeated and the world will remain the poorer for its passing.

It is hard to know what the current grass-roots Polish perception of the Jew is, what new image is formed in the common psyche. It is an eerie thought that a generation has now grown up in Poland which has never come across a living specimen of the ancient race. The new vestigial Marranos have now fully merged with their surroundings, while those who openly cling to their roots and faith live out their days in a muted, twilight existence. The clerics have lost their target — and a good deal of their power. The anti-Russian sentiments which unify the nation can no longer be focused and vented on the Jews in the Communist Party. On the contrary, some of the bitter recriminations which flared up after the 1967 Israeli-Arab war were due to the fact that part of the population openly cheered the Israeli feat of arms, acclaiming it as a victory of "our Jews" over "their allies." One suspects that in that unseemly joy, which incurred the government's wrath, there was more of a *Schadenfreude*, tinged with envy, over the humbling of the big bully than a genuine affection for the victors. All the same, a new picture, a Jew no longer pushed around and trampled upon, but defiant and victorious in his own war, has emerged, and the word "*żydek*," a partly contemptuous, partly endearing diminutive, has lost its place in the vocabulary.

What contemporary scribes and authors of schoolbooks are allowed or instructed to say in the matter is another story. Orwellian "newspeak" and rewriting of history to serve the latest twist of policy is common practice and affects not only the Jewish aspects but also the relationship with Russia, which calls for massive "reinterpretation" of traditional and well-established Polish views. How effective and longlasting such made-to-measure agit-prop can be, remains to be seen.

The spectre of Korczak holds up a mirror to the rulers of present-day Poland — and the reflection is grim. Whilst they are keen to take credit and bask in his posthumous fame, not a word must be breathed in public that he was a Jew. The obsession with the Jew haunts them beyond the grave: it has survived Hitler; it survives the absence of Jews.

Published in *The Jewish Quarterly*, Summer Issue 1977

Warsaw ghetto

When the German army entered Warsaw on 20th September 1939, nearly 400,000 Jews were living in the city, roughly a third of the population. Immediately they became the target of mounting repression — subjected to forced labour, prohibited from using railways and other public transport, made to wear the Star of David, stripped of their possessions. Virtually without protection of the law, they fell to the mercy of hooligans, sadists, and robbers, of whom there was no shortage. The daily food ration for Warsaw's Jews became 184 calories compared with 669 for a Pole and 2,613 for a German.

On 2nd October 1940 the Germans established an area into which all Warsaw Jews — roughly 138,000 people — along with persons of Jewish origin and Jewish refugees from the provinces were herded; some 113,000 "Aryans" living in that area had to leave. The Germans then declared the district a "plague-infested" zone, and the Jews were required to build a wall around it.

The Germans did not like the word "ghetto" and forbade its use; they referred to it as the "Jewish residential district" (*Wohnbezirk*). Indeed, the comparison with a medieval ghetto is totally inappropriate, as it implies a degree of normalcy, where people were born, pursued their interests, died in their beds. In that "district," surrounded by a ten-foot-high wall and a parapet of barbed wire, in a space of approximately 1,000 acres, a population of about 500,000 had to sustain itself, thirteen persons to a room, and many thousands without a roof over their heads. Nearly sixty percent of the population was left without a means of making a living.

In Warsaw, as in other occupied towns, the Germans designated a Judenrat (Jewish council) as the body responsible — with their own lives — for the enforcement of orders in the Jewish community. After the establishment of the ghettos, the Judenrat was given control of the police, economic management, and all matters of food supply, housing, and education. Although this seemed to be giving Jews a great deal of managerial autonomy, in reality the Germans created the Judenrat solely for their own convenience. Judenrat members had no option whatsoever but to respond to every command or caprice of their masters. They were often charged with collecting punitive contributions, one method of reducing the Jewish population to penury. As might be expected — and this indeed was part of the German plan — the Judenrat often attracted the fierce hostility and hatred of the Jewish population, deflecting these emotions from the real executioners. The role of the Judenrat remains a subject of controversy in the study of the behaviour of Jews under German occupation.

The Germans appointed Adam Czerniakow as head of the Warsaw Judenrat — it mattered little to them who would act as their puppet. Czerniakow kept a diary in which he noted his daily dealings with various German officials — a diary that remains a most important source of knowledge of that period. It shows Czerniakow, much maligned by his contemporaries, as an almost heroic figure, pleading and arguing with his implacable masters with great courage and dignity, wringing from them small concessions here and there, trying to persuade himself and those around him, in the face of mounting evidence to the contrary, that the worst would not happen. When it became clear, even to him, that "resettlement" was a euphemism for murder, he refused to put his signature to a directive ordering the deportation of children, and took his own life. He was condemned by many as a coward, and his contemporaries comment bitterly in their diaries: he should have warned the ghetto, he should have issued a call for resistance. Later judgements are kinder to him. This points to the agonising moral dilemmas that often faced people in those apocalyptic times, dilemmas to which there was and is no answer.

The Warsaw ghetto was a vast concentration camp with a simple ultimate purpose — to exterminate the Jews through hunger, through cold, through disease. As time went on, it became common to see corpses on the street. Bands of children roamed the alleyways searching for food scraps. Even though the gates were guarded and the penalty for leaving the ghetto without permission was death, the residents tried to survive by smuggling food from the outside. Risking their lives, children proved the most effective smugglers and supporters of their families.

The German governor, Hans Frank, stated in a report, "It is not necessary to dwell on the fact that we are sentencing the Jews to death. If the Jews do not die of starvation, it will be necessary to step up anti-Jewish measures, and let us hope that, too, will come to pass." Frank's vision soon materialised in the fulfilment of the Wannsee Conference decision on the "Final Solution." In July 1942, under the pretext of "resettlement," a mass deportation to the death camps began and continued, with short pauses, until mid-September. During those seven weeks some 265,000 Jews were transported to Treblinka and murdered in the gas chambers. Some of the victims, lured by the promise of food, presented themselves voluntarily at the *Umschlagplatz* — the railway siding from which the human cargo was packed into cattle trucks and dispatched to the death camps. The deportation drastically reduced the ghetto population; 35,000 inhabitants were permitted to stay — mainly workers employed in

German workshops and their families. In addition, some 25,000 Jews were hiding in the ghetto illegally.

Under such conditions, as a defiant gesture and in a quixotic attempt "to die as human beings," Jews organised resistance. A few hundred desperate people, gathered from the whole spectrum of Jewish society, formed battle units, arming themselves with a few pistols, submachine guns, and Molotov cocktails. In all, their defense amounted to very little. On 19th April 1943, when German troops entered the ghetto finally to liquidate the last remnants of the population, they met with armed resistance. To their surprise and shock, the Jewish fighters inflicted losses on them and forced them to retreat. The outcome of the battle was, of course, never in doubt for a moment. General Juergen Stroop crushed the uprising with tanks, heavy artillery, and flamethrowers. Avoiding open street combat, he systematically burned the houses, block by block. German bombs and hand grenades killed the fighters huddled in bunkers and sewers. In spite of that, the battle continued sporadically until 8th May 1943. As a final, triumphant act in the war against the Jews, General Stroop blew up the Great Synagogue in Warsaw and wrote in his report: "The Jewish residential district is no more."

The Warsaw Ghetto Uprising had an enormous effect on the morale of the Jews and non-Jews around the world. The longest battle against the Germans in occupied Europe before April 1943, the Ghetto Uprising story has become a legend.

We owe a great deal of our knowledge of that period to the effort and initiative of one man, Emanuel Ringelblum (1900–1944). A teacher, historian and social worker, he is one of the unsung heroes of our time. From the initial outbreak of war, he became one of the chief organisers of Warsaw self-help and mutual assistance committees. He kept a chronicle of events and, at his inspiration, in the autumn of 1940, a group with the cryptonym "*Oneg Shabbat*" (The Joy of the Sabbath) started writing bulletins describing and documenting the situation. Under his guidance, Oneg Shabbat developed a network of reporters all over the country who collected information in response to a prepared questionnaire. They thought, rightly, that every scrap of paper relating to Jewish life would be of inestimable historical value. Thus they collected official posters, public announcements, diaries, letters, advertisements, packaging, copies of the monitored foreign radio broadcasts and, above all, newspapers and news sheets of the many underground groupings. They commissioned special reports on various aspects of life and fed news items to the Polish underground press.

The Germans took little interest at first in what the Jews were doing among themselves. Jews could write, talk, curse, and gossip almost openly. They could discuss in the streets and cafes the illegal news sheets that circulated freely in the ghetto. Semi-official and clandestine committees sustained the fabric of communal life on all levels, alleviating hunger, providing education, organising cultural events, setting up projects for medical research, generally keeping up the spirits and the morale of the population. Behind the facades of the tenement houses, around the large, typical Warsaw courtyards, cultural and religious life took on new forms adapted to the unprecedented, immediate needs.

The network of Oneg Shabbat was the first to obtain eyewitness reports of the mass murders by gas in Chelmno, the first to raise the alarm in the Polish underground press and, finally, abroad. On 26th June 1942, the BBC broadcast news of the extermination of Polish Jews, based on reports sent by Ringelblum. He noted: "By alerting the world to our fate we fulfilled a great, historic mission. Maybe this will save some hundreds of thousands of Polish Jews. The near future will show. I don't know which one of our group will remain alive, whom fate will choose to make use of our archives, but of one thing we are certain — that our sacrifices, the risks taken, the tension of constant danger, our toil and suffering, have not been in vain."

As the noose tightened, the danger of losing the archives caused serious concern. A few months before the liquidation of the ghetto, all materials were assembled, packed into sealed milk churns and metal containers and buried in a cellar deep under the ghetto buildings. After the war, in 1946 and 1950, two parts of the treasure were found under the mountain of rubble which was all that remained of the ghetto. The third part must be considered beyond retrieval, and the sense of its loss is haunting.

The recovered collection consists of some forty thousand pages, mostly still awaiting analysis and publication. The largest and the most important archive of the era, it remains a priceless source of what we currently know and may yet know about the life and death of the Warsaw Ghetto and the destruction of Polish Jews.

Ringelblum gave of himself unstintingly to the last. In March 1943 he was persuaded to leave the ghetto and find shelter on the "Aryan side." On 18th April, the day before the last deportation and the eve of the Ghetto Uprising, he reentered the ghetto, wishing to spend Passover with the last survivors. He was caught in a roundup and sent to a concentration camp near Lublin. When his location became known, a team smuggled him out of the camp and brought him back to his Warsaw hiding place, reuniting him with his wife and son. He continued writing; amazingly, without access to books and sources, he wrote one of his key studies, *The Relations Between Poles and Jews in the Second World War*.

In March 1944 the Gestapo discovered Ringelblum's hiding place which reputedly housed sixty people. All of the Jews and the Polish family who sheltered them were taken to Pawiak Prison and shot — within a stone's throw of the ghetto.

In one respect, at least, the Germans were unlucky in their choice of victims. The Jewish people were determined to leave a trace of their fate, at whatever cost. Feeling abandoned by God and man, they were haunted by the thought that the world would not know how they lived and died. Writing made dying easier. The last entry in Chaim Kaplan's diary before his deportation to Treblinka was his anguished cry: "If I die — what will happen to my diary?"

Primo Levi, in *The Drowned and the Saved*, imagines members of the SS taunting their victims: "However this war may end, we have won the war against you, none of you will be left to bear witness, and even if someone were to survive, the world would not believe him. There will perhaps be suspicions, discussions, research by historians, but there will be no certainties, because we will destroy the evidence together with you. And even if some proof should remain and some of you survive, people will say that the events you describe are too monstrous to be believed; they will say that they are exaggerations of Allied propaganda and will believe us, who will deny everything, and not you."

Because of these writers and scribblers, the truth has been recorded, has become known to the world, and no one but a maniac or pervert will deny it. These testimonies give us a picture of consummately hideous times. They show us the depth to which humans can descend, and they document how hatred can bring hell on this earth.

The photographs were handed to me by Willy Georg, a former soldier in the German army, to whose doorstep I was led by friends who knew of my consuming interest in this field. Willy Georg is now over eighty years old — of a generation of Germans with whom I am not at ease without further probing. I am satisfied that he is not suspect: a man of good education and a fairly prosperous background, a professional photographer; at the age of thirty, when these photographs were taken, he still held the humble rank of *Funke* — a radio operator. This does not point to someone who was favoured by or benefitted from membership in the Nazi Party.

How did these photographs come to be taken? Willy Georg has a clear recollection. He was stationed with his unit in Warsaw (in a district called Mokotow, he thinks). Known to his colleagues and superiors as a professional photographer, he was earning extra money to send home by taking snapshots of his fellow soldiers. One day, in summer of 1941, his officer called him and said, lightheartedly: "There are some curious goings-on behind that wall. I am issuing you with a pass to enter the enclosed area through one of the gates. Take your Leica, and food for the day, and bring back some photos of what you find."

He did as he was told. He entered the ghetto, walked around, snapped what he saw on four rolls of film, loaded the fifth. Toward evening a German police

134

detachment entered the ghetto, spotted him, and told him to hand over the camera. They opened the back and removed the film; Georg said nothing about the four rolls in his pocket. His credentials verified, he was led outside the gates. He developed the film himself in a photo laboratory in Warsaw. He is proud of his professionalism: after half-a-century, the film looks as crisp as new. He sent the film home, to his wife in Munster. He gave it little thought in the intervening years, until lately, when he felt the time was approaching to make his final dispositions.

He felt shocked to the core, he says, when he saw these photos anew and recalled those times. It would have been tempting to ask him how he felt then, fifty years ago, when he came, unprepared, upon that horrific scene, unlike anything he could have encountered before. But there would have been no point in this: all he would have said is what he thinks of it now, or, rather, what he thinks would be appropriate to say to me now. He remembers how polite these people were to him. Although he might not have known it, they had to be polite: a Jew encountering a German was obliged by order to doff his cap and step off the pavement.

This photographic record is not unprecedented. Other photographs still exist that were taken in the ghetto by the Germans around that time and later. (The most famous image — of a small boy in a peaked cap, with his hands raised — stems from one such source.) A team from the German Propaganda Ministry assembled a collection that is now in the official German archives in Koblenz. These photographs were made with the explicit purpose of showing the degradation of that subhuman race, of their indifference to the suffering of their brethren (look how they pass the corpses lying on the street without batting an eyelid!), of people allegedly enjoying themselves playing cards in coffeehouses. These photographers and their masters were clearly unaware of the reverse effect of their work — ultimately, the images degrade not the victims but those who created them.

Willy Georg's snapshots, on the other hand, were totally spontaneous; they simply record the passing scene. The people caught in these photographs — busy, feverish, emaciated, oppressed, but still living a life of sorts — are unaware of the unthinkably cruel end that awaits them shortly. Virtually none will escape a horrible death. One's instinct is to shout a word of warning — run! hide! — but it is too late. At that stage nothing, but nothing, they could have done or left undone would have had the slightest effect on their fate.

To many of us who grew up within or next to that human landscape and who remember it lovingly, these people — shameful to confess — did not at that time look attractive. These misty eyes, beards, sidelocks, crooked noses — one looked away, embarrassed by what a non-Jewish onlooker might feel or say. It now seems clear that these faces, etched with worry and wisdom, lit with inner light, otherworldly, Rembrandtesque, were inexpressibly beautiful. Set against that rogue's gallery, the flower of the "master race" — Goebbels, Goering, Streicher, Frank, and Hitler himself — little more need be said.

These photographs give a last glimpse of a people about to be murdered, leaving the world forever and irreparably the poorer for it. The lessons of their lives become more valuable as the time approaches when there will be no living witnesses, and future generations might find such things beyond belief.

Introduction to photograph album
In the Warsaw Ghetto — Summer 1941, Aperture, New York 1993

Witnesses

T he extermination of the Jews by the Germans during the Second World War has given rise to an explosion of writing in all branches of literature.

There is a categorical imperative to continue to record, to relive, to analyse, to understand, to transmit. Every book, every journal, memoir or poem, every case history, every document, every scrap of testimony is a gift to the future — and it is all that will remain after us. The direct testimony of eyewitnesses is self-evidently of supreme importance. The time is approaching when there will be none of them left to speak to us. This book is one of the last of its kind.

On 6th September 1939 the German army entered Cracow and, for the 60,000 Jews who lived there, some with roots extending over many generations, the world which they knew collapsed, overnight, never to recover. Even though their ultimate and not-far-distant fate was not yet apprehended, the pattern of persecution leading inexorably to their physical destruction emerged from the start. *Bekanntmachungen*, edicts of increasing severity, pasted on the walls, marked the stages.

First, the separation from the rest of the population — all Jews had to wear armbands with the Star of David. Then, the destruction of the economy. Shops had to be clearly marked — an invitation, smartly taken up, to robbery and looting. Money, except for a pittance, had to be surrendered; anything of value was confiscated, and not to be destitute became illegal. Personal freedom was restricted — every Jew had to register, was forbidden to change his address, was not allowed to use the railways.

These edicts were brutally enforced and were accompanied by continuous harassment, raids, manhunts, searches, beatings. Jews found themselves outside the law, a free prey to brutes and scoundrels — of whom there was no shortage.

The next stage came when the Jewish population was locked in ghettos, where the conditions were very harsh and degrading. Escape from the ghetto was punishable by death. Slave labour detachments taken from the ghetto and put to work beyond human strength led to a rapidly rising death rate. Special work camps, like the one on the periphery of Cracow, in Plaszow, were only thinly veiled instruments of slow destruction.

The pace quickened when the way led through a KZ, a concentration camp proper, where calculated cruelty was the norm and where the inmates were often reduced to walking corpses. And so to the final stage, the extermination camp pure and simple, death factories which had no other purpose than to gas and burn human cargoes as quickly and efficiently as the state of the art — Zyklon B and the crematoria — permitted.

It calls for a painful mental effort to envisage this apocalyptic world, for which there is no analogy in history. There have been wars, foreign occupation, oppression, persecution and murder on a massive scale; such horrors continue to abound, but it is totally without precedent that a whole people, without exception, should be separated from its surroundings and condemned to death, and that this verdict should be carried out with the utmost efficiency, over-riding war aims and — in view of the magnitude of the task — involving tens of thousands of Germans operating the various stages of the gruesome mechanism of extermination. This is the background against which the story of our authors unfolds. Historical events take on flesh and become more real when seen through the prism of individual lives of people who we think are like us.

Miriam was born and brought up on her father's small holding, not far from Cracow, from which the family eked out a modest livelihood. Lack of means prevented her from continuing her studies at Cracow University, but she kept her links with the socialist youth organisations, and at the outbreak of war this gave her entry to the underground resistance movement and contacts which she was able to put to good use. As contemporary photographs testify, she was a woman of arresting presence — a dubious asset in the circumstances, but, providentially, she was totally free of Jewish features, and there hangs the whole tale.

Mordecai, born in Tarnow, an autodidact, a man of great sensitivity and intelligence, clearheaded and self-assured, had no hesitation in deciding what he must do when darkness fell.

These two, separately and at first unknown to each other, but clearly of similar cast of mind, which made them later into ideal partners, assumed roles which, as will transpire, were nothing short of heroic. They themselves remained unaware of this dimension: ordinary people, you might say, who had greatness thrust upon them and took it in their stride, not fearlessly, but by overcoming fear and in full knowledge of the consequences — with the comforting feel of the phial of cyanide in their pocket, since no one knows the limits of endurance under torture. It would have been easy for them to slide into relative safety and merge with the surroundings — with their "good looks" and impeccable speech, their chances of survival were reasonable.

Instead, whilst being vulnerable in the extreme, particularly the man, they courted constant danger. They plied their errands of mercy in places the prudent would shun like the plague: in railway stations, assisting people on their journeys; in crowded shops which were used to deposit and pick up printed

138

matter for distribution and where they could be recognised by former acquaintances or friends (even those with the best intentions could, unwittingly, be
dangerous); in offices, seeking rubber-stamping of fake documents.

Having secured for their wards "good papers" — an identity card, a birth
certificate, a confirmation of employment in the right firm — there was always
the problem of finding a hiding place: for some it was a cellar, a loft, a dark room
at the end of the corridor; for others a place in a convent or orphanage. There
followed frequent visits — to pay "rent," or to deliver the money allowance
or a message from the family. Few of these hiding places remained permanent —
a careless word, a suspicious noise, a disturbance in the neighbourhood, made
it imperative to move, and quickly. All this took place under the prying eyes of
a suspicious and jumpy population, the Gestapo, the police and hordes of inform-
ers and blackmailers. Even reading about it, fifty years on, one's heart misses
many a beat and one is challenged to think whether in similar circumstances
one would have found the inner resources to act as they did.

In the eyes of the ghetto-dwellers the world outside the wall, on the "Aryan
side," was normal. Although it was far from that in any accepted sense of the
word, its dangers were of a different order, and it offered a possibility of survival at least to those few who had the necessary equipment, that is, the looks, the
language and the physical and mental stamina to withstand the terrible stress
of the situation, of pretending to be someone else, of never lowering one's
guard, of living every minute of day and night in mortal dread of discovery.

One could have the appearance of an angel, yet the telltale details which
could give one away were legion; the eyes could be cornflower-blue but their
uncontrollable sadness was hard to disguise — dark glasses in themselves were
highly suspect. Men, of course, carried their death sentence with them, ready
for inspection.

As important as the physical mimicry was the mastery of characteristic Polish
forms of speech and behaviour, particularly in religious settings — how were
Jews or Jewesses to know when to cross themselves, when to kneel down or
get up during Mass — a moment's hesitation could mean that the game was
up. The learning of prayers and the minutiae of ritual was imperative.

The masking of one's feelings in public was a further ordeal, testing
endurance to the breaking point, particularly after the details of the death camps
became known. How to hold back the "tears by which a Jew is known," how
to react when the topic of the murder of the Jews was raised in conversation
with the Poles, as happened all too often — to feign indifference, to condemn?
Miriam speaks at one point of how, risking all, she simply could not hold her
tongue. Mordecai mentions how hard it was to keep up the pretence when a Jew
whom he was helping and whom he tried to console, would burst out, bitterly,
"It is easy for you to talk…"

In many cases the strain proved too much. Having taken the enormous risk and trouble of getting themselves established on the "Aryan side," some of these wretches returned voluntarily to the ghetto to live and die with their own people. And how can one come to terms with the situation where a mother and her child, having been given shelter and hospitality by Polish friends, cannot endure the thought that her presence so greatly endangers her hosts that, one day, she simply leaves, never to be heard of again? What were the feelings of these people then?

In their understandable resentment of the misfortunes that engulfed them, Jews were often not sufficiently sensitive to the Polish situation and the agonising choices facing their neighbours. Only by comparison with the terminal tragedy of the Jews does the fate of the Polish people appear tolerable. By any other standards their sacrifices, their suffering and their losses during the war mark them out as the great victims of their history — and geography.

The extent and nature of the support given by Poles to Jews in their pathetic efforts to survive outside the ghetto walls has been and remains the prickliest issue in the post-mortem analysis of Polish–Jewish relations. It is the Jewish perception that, on the whole, the Poles have not emerged from the infernal trial with credit. They are accused, at best, of indifference and, at worst, of abetting the Germans in their murderous design — the notable exceptions being those few thousand celebrated in Jerusalem as "The Just Among The Nations" and, surely, the many unrecorded who did not live to tell the tale. It is revealing, in view of the indictment, that the indifference and hostility came as no surprise; it was what the Jews had been led to expect through the many years of uneasy cohabitation — the sowing of hatred would not yield a harvest of compassion.

The Poles counter, with justice, that effective aid on a massive scale was simply not possible, in view of the power and the utter ruthlessness of the Nazi forces, to whom the extermination of the Jews became an overriding war aim. Giving aid in individual cases was perilous in the extreme and called for readiness to risk one's life and that of one's family — the Decree of 10th December 1942 issued by the Governor General set the death penalty not only for the Jews caught outside the ghetto but also for all who gave them shelter or aid of any kind. This was no mere threat and many paid the ultimate penalty.

Despite that, in 1942, an organisation was set up by the Polish underground in Warsaw and Cracow, under the name "Zegota," with a network thinly spread over the whole of the Generalgouvernement, for the specific purpose of helping the Jews on the "Aryan side." The aid took the form of finding accommodation, supplying false documents, distributing money, protecting them against blackmail, reclaiming them by bribes or cunning from the hands of the police or the Gestapo. The activity of Miriam and Mordecai Peleg was carried out under the aegis and within the framework of Zegota, and as we know from the evidence available to us, many people owed their lives to this organisation.

In the controversy which bedevils Polish–Jewish relations to the present day, objective evidence is hard to come by. Here the testimony of Miriam and Mordecai is of singular value. Their integrity and trustworthiness are beyond question. Their daily engagement with both Poles and Jews gives them a unique viewpoint from which as true a picture can be drawn as is humanly possible. No study of that period and problem can disregard this case history.

The purpose of *Witnesses*, as Miriam Marianska sees it, is to try "to express in human language things which are not human." One cannot know how this will strike the reader, remote from that time and those events. Sensitivity differs and man has shown a great capacity to endure the suffering of others. But one thing will surely come through: it is people like Miriam and Mordecai, living in those consummately hideous times, who allow us to hold on to the belief that goodness has a chance in the eternal contest with evil.

Introduction to *Witnesses — Life in Occupied Kraków*
by Miriam Peleg-Marianska and Mordecai Peleg
Routledge, London and New York 1991

Saints or madmen?

A meditation on Ephraim Oshry's *Responsa from the Holocaust*

T his is one of the most extraordinary documents of our time, of any time. A large claim this — let us consider the evidence.

Ephraim Oshry was a young rabbi in Slobodka, a suburb of Kovno in Lithuania, at the time when the German armies occupied that territory in the last war. That part of the world was famed for its yeshivahs, founded early in the nineteenth century — Slobodka, Mir, Volozhin, Ponieviezh — presided over by great sages and scholars, attracting students from all over the world. For those who believed that the study of the Torah was the highest of human pursuits, that territory was hallowed ground, "the second *Eretz Yisroel*," and Vilna was named "the Jerusalem of Lithuania."

Rabbi Oshry was an eyewitness to the entry of the German army into Kovno on 25th June 1941, a date which marked the beginning of the end of Lithuanian Jewry. The Lithuanian "fifth column," the fascist grouping which comprised a substantial portion of the population, went instantly on a murderous rampage against their Jewish neighbours. Armed with guns and axes they broke into house after house, killing whole families. Rav Zalman Ossovsky, the Rabbi of Slobodka, was bent over a folio of the Talmud when the mob forced the door; he was tied to his chair and decapitated. The head was put into the window for passers-by to see. That day many hundreds were put to death, among them a large number of yeshiva students.

With varying degrees of intensity the murder and plunder continued for two months. However, that proved merely to have been a prologue, a pogrom following historic precedents, an idyll by comparison with what was in store — the systematic programme of total extermination. As elsewhere, the process began by forcible transfer of the Jewish population into the confines of the work camps and ghettoes, in the course of which thousands were left homeless and died of exhaustion. It was an intermediary stage prior to despatch to the sites of mass execution and death camps.

In the crowded ghetto behind the barbed wire, with just about enough space to turn around, life, of sorts, went on. The physical hardship and psychological oppression created conditions in which human beings tend to lose their humanity — which was the additional purpose of the enterprise. The space was constantly shrinking, as the population became decimated by disease, hunger, daily murder and finally "resettlement."

In this purgatory the young Rabbi Oshry carried on his ministry. He proved himself to be a man of great authority, courage and faith, a veritable tower of strength. He was brought face to face with human and theological problems of agonising complexity. People came to him with questions because — he says — "they were not always sure what the Torah required of them." He noted the questions and wrote down his brief rulings on paper torn from cement sacks. For some time he had access to the sources which he had to consult: there was in the ghetto a large store of sacred books — the Germans collected them in order to exhibit them later as "artefacts of an extinct race" — and Oshry, providentially, was put in charge of those stores. Oshry packed the notes he made into cans and buried them in the ground. He vowed that if he survived he would expand his notes into full-length responsa. Happily, he did survive and on the day of the liberation of the ghetto he recovered his notes.

Rabbi Ephraim Oshry lived for some years after the war in Rome, where he founded the Yeshiva Me'or Hagola for survivors. He now lives in New York where he occupies the pulpit of Beth Hamedrash Hagadol and is the president of an organisation of rabbis who survived the camps. As promised, he elaborated and expanded his original responsa and published them under the title *Sheilos Utshuvos Mima'amakim* in five volumes. The book under review is a short selection, containing 112 responsa, translated into English (published by Judaica Press, New York). On the face of it, it is a traditional item of rabbinical literature in the customary form but, because of the time and place when it was started and the nature of the problems it tackled, it is unlike anything else ever written. The background and context of the questions that are raised — quite apart from the answers — provide a record, detailed, authentic and immediate, of life in circumstances which numb the imagination. Everybody's daily existence hangs on a thread, depending on the whim of the commander, the guard, the distant masters in Berlin, on an additional piece of bread or a spoonful of soup; life around is brutish and dangerous in the extreme; there is a systematic and seemingly irreversible destruction of all one holds dear; parents look on helplessly at the suffering of their children. And people come to the rabbi to ask what to do.

The scene is the classroom where Oshry teaches his students Talmud. A woman bursts in, screaming that the Germans have just shot dead her husband and three children. Her father-in-law, Reb Zalman Sher, dies of a heart attack on hearing the news. The question put to the rabbi is: since it is impossible to know if the Germans will allow them to make arrangements for the funeral, is it permissible to make the *tahara* — the preparation of a corpse for burial — *in advance* rather than *as close to* the funeral as possible? (Oshry permitted immediate *tahara*.)

On 4th Elul 5701 — 27th August 1941 — the Germans captured stray dogs and cats and brought them into a house of study in the ghetto in Slobodka, where they shot them. They then forced a number of those present to rip apart a Torah scroll and use the sheets of parchment to cover the carcasses of the shot animals. The participants and the witnesses of this desecration later asked the rabbi to prescribe a programme of penitence. Oshry ruled that all those who saw the scroll being torn were to rend their garments. Those who were forced to tear the Torah scroll with their own hands were obliged to fast; if they could not fast because of debility they were excused. Those who were not present but only heard of it from others were to make a contribution to charity.

In September 1941 the Kovno ghetto contained some 30,000 souls, among them 10,000 labourers. The Germans ordered the Judenrat to distribute among them 5,000 permits (called "*Jordan Schein*" from the name of the German commander) which would entitle them to stay in the ghetto with their families; the implication for the rest was clear. The labourers besieged the office of the Judenrat and fearful scuffles began, with many trying to grab the permits by force. The question was put to Oshry; was the Judenrat permitted to obey Jordan's order and distribute such permits? On what basis could they determine whose life was more significant than another person's? A further question was asked: is it permissible for anyone to grab a permit to save his life? For by grabbing a *Jordan Schein* for oneself, one was condemning another man and his family to death.

A similar event took place several months later in Kovno (and countless other places). The Kovno Rabbi, Rav Avrohom Dov Ber Kahana-Shapira, in a responsum to the Judenrat on whether to obey the German order to gather the whole of the ghetto population without exception in the central square (to co-operate in the process of extermination), rules: "If a decree is issued that a Jewish community be destroyed and a possibility exists to save some part of the community, the leaders of the community must gird themselves to take every possible measure to save *as many as can be saved*." Oshry's responsum was similarly phrased. As to the second question of grabbing a permit by force, he says that, initially, no Jew is ever allowed to do anything that places another Jew's life in danger. Nevertheless, according to the principle that one must save whoever can be saved, it seemed that each labourer was entitled to do whatever he could to save his life and that of his family.

On 6th Cheshvan 5702 — 27th October 1941 — forty-eight hours before the Black Day of the Kovno ghetto, when some 10,000 men, women and children were taken away to slaughter and the German purpose of total extermination was made apparent to everybody inside, one member of the community came to Rabbi Oshry with the following problem. Since it is known from former practice that women and children are shot in front of the men, the petitioner cannot endure the thought that he will witness such a scene. He asks, therefore, whether he is permitted to take his own life. This would have the additional advantage that he would be buried in the Jewish cemetery in the ghetto. Responding, Oshry denies him the permission to commit suicide. It would mean surrendering to the enemy, who welcomed such confusion and despondency among the Jewish captives. It also showed a lack of trust in God's ability to save the Jews from the hands of their oppressors. Oshry notes with pride that he knows of only three instances of suicide in the Kovno ghetto.

Standing in the central square in Kovno (Demokratiaplatz no less) with the whole of the ghetto population, some 30,000 souls, awaiting the final "selection," Oshry is approached by a man with the following query: what is the precise formula of the blessing which a martyred Jew should utter as he dies to fulfil his very last *mitzvah*? He wished to tell this to as many people as possible so that when their turn came they should use the right words. Oshry offers him the formula which he, Oshry, himself intended to utter: *asher kideshonu bemitzvosov vetzivonu lekadeish shemo berabim.*

In the winter of 1942, several months before Passover, many Jews in the ghetto began to think about how to secure some matzah. Most basic foods were not available, let alone white flour from which matzah is baked. Moshe Goldkorn, who worked in an outside brigade, came into contact with Lithuanians who were ready to barter goods for flour. In the course of time he managed to smuggle into the ghetto, bit by bit, each crossing of the gate fraught with danger, enough flour to bake matzah for nearly a hundred Jews, each of whom would receive one olive-sized piece, enough to fulfil the commandment on Passover Eve. After preparing the oven according to the Halachah the matzah was baked in one of the bakery workshops.

Two days before Passover, Goldkorn was stopped at the gate and searched — a small bag of flour was found on him. He was beaten black and blue and had all his teeth knocked out. He came to Oshry with the following problem: "With my knocked-out teeth how can I fulfil the commandment of eating an olive-sized piece of matzah? I come from a Hassidic family whose custom is never to eat matzah that is 'soaked' on Pesach. I cannot break that custom and yet I cannot bite anything which is not softened." Oshry ruled that he be allowed to soak the matzah in water even though he is descended from Hassidim whose custom is not to do so, in order that he may fulfil the *mitzvah* for which he had risked his life. However, he must obtain from a *beit din* an annulment of the implicit vow of the tradition of his forebears not to eat soaked matzah on Pesach.

There was an absolute prohibition by the Germans on bringing food into the ghetto from the outside — the meagre ration of those working outside had to be consumed so that it was not shared with one's children and family. Oshry notes a case of a man who saved a piece of bread and hid it between his thighs, hoping to sneak it past the guard. He was caught, beaten and kicked, so that his testicles were crushed. He came to Oshry with the following: "I am prohibited from living with my wife (Deuteronomy 23:2) and I can have no children. Since I am a *kohein* I have always been 'called up' to read the portion of the Torah as the 'first reader.' Now I am blemished and therefore forbidden to read as the 'first reader.' Is there any way I can still be treated as a reader and a *kohein*?" Oshry is unable to rule against Deuteronomy 23:2, which forbids a man who has had his testicles crushed to live with his wife. But as for his status as a *kohein* Oshry is ready to interpret the Law entirely in his favour.

On 20th Iyar 5703 — 7th May 1942 — the Germans decreed that any woman found pregnant would be killed. Oshry was asked whether, in the circumstances, contraception is permitted. The answer was — yes. He also ruled that in view of the threat to the woman's life abortion was permitted.

A question was put whether a person could be permitted to buy a baptismal certificate which, if he could subsequently escape to the forest, would enable him to join the partisans. Oshry opines that there is no way that this may be permitted, even if one expected to owe one's life to such a transaction.

These are some cases chosen at random, out of hundreds, thousands. Each one a glimpse of hell, reflecting dilemmas which no man should be asked to face, showing sentient beings at the extreme of the human condition. Each one a text for meditation.

There is another series of cases put to Oshry after the liberation but arising from circumstances of the war. For instance: is a Jew allowed to enter church premises to search for Jewish children hidden and protected there by the priests in order to get them returned to the fold? (Yes, he is.) The children saved by the gentiles now had to be "saved" from the gentiles. Oshry was himself involved, often at risk to his life, in the searches and "recovery" — and this is a story apart. The process took time and some of the boys found were six or seven years old. The question arose: is anaesthetic permitted in circumcision? One boy refused to be circumcised unless he was promised that he would suffer no pain. Oshry permits the use of an anaesthetic (even though to feel the same pain as our forefather Abraham felt is a merit) on the grounds that, since that particular boy had already lived among gentiles, if we caused him pain he might rebel against other commandments of the Torah and leave the fold. Immediately after the liberation there was a severe shortage of tefillin. Many sets were found in gentile homes. Was it permissible to use such a set immediately without waiting for an inspection to check whether they were kosher or not? Oshry records that when he ruled in favour of immediate use people cried for joy.

There was a case of the *mamzer* rabbi, born in a union which, in retrospect, was deemed unlawful. The story goes back to October 1941 when a rumour spread in the ghetto that all husbandless women would be put to death. By that time, as experience taught, nothing was past belief, and the rumour caused panic among single women who scurried round for husbands at all costs. One woman, whose husband had been taken away by the Germans and disappeared without trace, assumed that he was dead. She found herself a new partner and married him. The couple escaped from the ghetto, survived and, after the war, moved to another country. Here they had a son who, in the fullness of time, studied in a yeshiva and became the rabbi of a community. One day, out of the blue, a man turned up declaring, and proving, that he was the first husband of the rabbi's mother, wrongly presumed dead. It had taken him a long time to come upon the trace of his wife but when he discovered that she had married another and had borne him a son, he felt outraged by his wife's "betrayal." He was determined to track her down, force her to divorce her second husband and publicly reveal her shame. However, by that time the woman was no longer alive and his wrath turned upon her son, the product of that bigamous marriage; the man would spare no efforts to have the rabbi cast out from the Jewish community.

Rabbi Oshry tried to persuade the vengeful man to remain silent — publicising such an issue constitutes in itself *chilul Hashem*, a desecration of God. The young rabbi's life was in ruins anyway. Oshry ruled that he should resign his office, for although according to the Law a *mamzer* is not disqualified from being a rabbi, "people will not listen to him." He also made the necessary arrangements for him to divorce his wife, for it is forbidden for a *mamzer* to be married to a Jewish-born woman unless she herself was similarly begotten.

What is one to make of these people?

In the context of the Holocaust, where other people despaired and lost direction, they maintained their unshakeable faith — despite daily evidence to the contrary — in God's ultimate loving purpose. Where other people felt helpless and rudderless, they searched for answers and knew where to look for them. Risking torture and death for defying the German order forbidding communal prayers and teaching, they studied the Torah and observed the *mitzvoth*, convinced that "Jewishness" had to be preserved and only thus could it be preserved. They refused to be dehumanised and maintained a feeling of infinite superiority over their oppressors. This was spiritual resistance of a high order. It was undoubtedly a source of enormous inner strength in the fight for survival. On the other hand, at a time when every flicker of energy had to be summoned to want to live another day, it was an awesome hindrance if one insisted on fasting on Yom Kippur, strove to observe *kashruth* and had to ask the rabbi whether it was permissible, if there was no other way of getting a meal, to cook on Sabbath and — a further question — whether it was permitted to eat what another Jew thus cooked. And if a piece of paper like a certificate of baptism, which could prove to be a lifesaver, had to be refused.

What is this phenomenon? Is it human, perchance superhuman? Where is its place in the sum of things? To the lay, secular, rational mind the questions and the responsa might appear absurd, grotesque, eerie, not to say insane. But one would have to be quite devoid of feeling not to perceive that we witness here a dimension of spirituality which is transcendental. One may not be able to comprehend it or even remotely empathise with it but it is impossible to shrug it off. Whether one is inclined to shake one's head in disbelief or weep with compassion, one cannot but stand in awe in the face of this degree of devotion and trust in God.

Must we not try to form a balanced view of the mental landscape of these, our brethren, even though, to them, our own is meaningless and unworthy and we ourselves are apostates and scoffers who will burn in hell? In fact, if hell, by the best definition, is separation from God, for all we know we are there already.

The Jewish Quarterly, No. 128, 1987

All our yesterdays…

On the album by Roman Vishniac

R oman Vishniac's album of photographs* taken between 1934 and 1939 in Poland, Czechoslovakia, Rumania, Carpathian Ruthenia, Hungary and Lithuania, entitled *A Vanished World*, is a work of genius. It is a document of enduring value: potent, evocative and inexpressibly sad. Those who remember and those who want to imagine what these people and these places were like, having seen these photographs, will be thinking in his images.

In all weathers, sunshine or dusk, in the street or in basement hovels, with an unerring eye for subject and composition and artistry which conceals art, time and again Vishniac captures these astonishing images which bring to mind the great Dutch Masters. A passing moment is caught in a blinding flash of insight and now fixed for as long as books are printed.

We have known of Vishniac from former exhibitions and publications (*Polish Jews*, Schocken Books, New York 1947; *Life of the Six Million*, 1969) and the appearance of some of his photographs in other albums (*Image Before My Eyes*, Schocken Books and YIVO, New York 1977; Franz Hubmann's *The Jewish Family Album*, Routledge and Kegan Paul, London 1975), but this album is the long-awaited selection — 200 of the best.

Roman Vishniac, now 86 and living in New York, where he has just been made an honorary citizen, is a truly remarkable man, and the story of how these photographs were taken could be the subject of a picaresque novel.

Vishniac was born in Russia and studied medicine and zoology at Moscow University. After the Revolution he moved to Berlin where he became an eminent specialist in microphotography.

After the access of Hitler to power he was possessed by a sombre premonition that the threats uttered in *Mein Kampf* would be fulfilled. As if guided by an inner voice he embarked on this improbable venture: armed with a Rolleiflex and a Leica camera he made his way through Eastern Europe, through town and village, casting a compassionate eye upon the Jewish scene. He operated without flashlight, and mostly with a camera hidden from view. This he thought advisable because Orthodox Jews often refuse to be photographed, but also a stranger wandering through the countryside with a camera in that part of Europe in those days (as now) was courting trouble. In fact, Vishniac was taking grave risks;

* *A Vanished World* by Roman Vishniac, Allen Lane, 1983.

repeatedly he was manhandled and pushed over frontiers — only to reenter at another point. He was arrested eleven times, spent time in various prisons, his negatives were often confiscated. He covered enormous distances and took over 16,000 photographs — of which he managed to smuggle out 2,000 negatives which were hidden throughout the war by his father in Vichy France. He himself landed in a concentration camp in Clichy from which he escaped early in 1941, across Spain and Portugal to America. It did not take him long to reestablish himself as an outstanding scientific photographer in New York. All in all, one might think, a good Jewish life.

Turning the pages of the album... that dreamy, downy-cheeked boy with eyes like saucers pulls at the heartstrings; like those other boys in the *cheder*, so innocent and yet knowing, one wants to embrace them; like that other boy in the oversize peaked cap and arms raised, in that famous photograph from the Warsaw ghetto (taken by a Nazi for a souvenir), which has become a Jewish icon.

Those three Hassidim in full regalia, kaftan, tallith, shtreimel — caught in a graceful movement like a ballet group, leaving the synagogue after morning service, still in full flight of argument, a telling point made with a characteristic gesture.

A bleak, snow-swept street corner, the nameplate reads "Street of Isaac," in the heart of Kazimierz in Jewish Cracow — where else would streets be named after Patriarchs? — an old wall bruised and bespattered, ghostly figures in emptiness, strangely moving...

By way of contrast — a bustling courtyard in Nalewki on a warm day, every one of the hundred windows in the tenement open to air the tiny rooms which also serve as offices, shops, workshops; a motley crowd streaming in all directions; signs offering ribbons, corsets, underwear, sewing thread, aprons, trunks, umbrellas. A little segment of what, multiplied a thousandfold, formed the greatest concentration of Jewish life on earth...

One is startled by the singular beauty of these people. If one could, for a hundredth of a second, forget what happened to them a few years or months after the Vishniac snapshot, one could simply be enchanted. But one knows the imminence of massacre, one knows that the whole scene is an anteroom to hell — one smothers the impulse to shout a warning. This is still not graspable: that within four years this thousand-year-old civilisation had vanished without trace, smashed, stamped out, annulled, burnt... Nothing of it remains — only by some miracle would a single soul captured in these pages have remained alive. How is one to adjust to this eternal absence?

Vishniac has earned our admiration and gratitude. His work will not be supplanted or amplified (other than by himself from hitherto unpublished stock) — it will become, in fact already is, a classic of its kind. It is therefore important not to let pass the inaccuracies and the bias which permeate the notes and captions. The notes which precede the photographs and can be read virtually as a continuous narrative are often ill-informed and misleading. They were written by Vishniac recently, in old age, many decades after the events. With all due respect, memory plays him false or his emotions get the better of him, which is understandable — but the notes distort the perspective and blemish the book as a source of information. The Polish government and population, to take the example of that country alone, have enough to answer for without being accused of things they did not do and could not help.

For example: on page 20, an Orthodox Jew in his *bekeshe* (kaftan) and round peaked cap is said to have been dismissed, under pressure of the boycott committee, after twenty years' service — it is fanciful to imagine that a man like him would have worked for a non-Jewish Polish firm or institution in the first place.

A note to pages 27–28 says: "After the boycott transporting freight by handcraft or on their back was the only occupation permitted to Jews of Warsaw" — the assertion is quite absurd and should not have got past the editors. A note to page 65 speaks of rules of employment for Jewish office girls as opposed to their non-Jewish counterparts — there were no such discriminatory rules as those described. A note to page 66 says about a "bagel seller": "On Jewish streets nobody had money to buy anything but ordinary bread" — no, no; some had little, some had more, some had plenty; "bagels" were within the means of most. Note and caption to photo No. 178 — a face of a Jew through a small window in an iron gate — allegedly the "Endeks," the *pogromschschiki* are coming to beat him up. Would they but try! They knew better than to trespass on this territory at risk to life and limb.

Vishniac repeatedly refers to the boycott — as if this was the main reason for Jewish poverty. This was not so. Poverty preceded the boycott and had deeper causes. The boycott was villainous but its effects were probably marginal; it made some Jewish traders a bit poorer and no Polish trader any richer. A great many Jewish shopkeepers and artisans never saw a non-Jewish customer anyway. It was possible, in the larger towns, for a Jew to live totally within his milieu, only in very marginal contact with the surrounding local population. The shopkeepers who served gentile customers were proverbially cheaper than the less experienced and less industrious competitor. The buyers would mutter under their breath but would not be ready to pay more elsewhere; and big business, as is its nature, did what it found profitable, regardless.

Vishniac focuses on Jewish poverty — the ragged shopkeepers with their bare shelves, the beggars, the pedlars, the artisans in their sunless hovels, which were also their kitchens and bedrooms, often with one bed for the whole family. Indeed poverty was dire and widespread. But it was not a specifically Jewish poverty which contrasted with non-Jewish well-being. On the contrary, urban squalor knew no boundaries and the gentile unemployed workman suffered the same, if not worse, hardship and degradation. The countryside could be harsher still: the small holder or landless peasant led, in a bad year, a pitiful existence. Vishniac concentrates almost entirely on the poor and the Orthodox — as a photographer he found them the more picturesque and as a man he felt the greater affinity with them — it is his prerogative. But the result is a very partial and one-sided view.

The idea that Jewish existence in Poland was always one of unredeemed gloom and oppression is ill-founded. There were lights as well as shadows; the manifold fabric of Jewish life was woven of many strands and some of its brightest and most life-enhancing manifestations have taken place on Polish soil.

World War I brought Poland political independence, after nearly 150 years of being partitioned between Russia, Prussia and Austria. The socio-economic problems of unifying the country, its respective parts differing in structure, law and traditions, were formidable. The minorities — Byelorussian, Ukrainian, German and Lithuanian with their separatist tendencies and conflicting demands — also the perennial Russian threat under a new guise, made for conditions which were a breeding ground of injustice. Rising Polish nationalism, the chronic economic depression and unemployment led to predictable effects. The Jews represented a ten-percent minority, predominantly urban, distinguishable and competitive. Between the age-old Russian anti-Semitism and the lethal influences from Germany, the Poles would have to have been saints for their own brand of anti-Semitism, religious, political and economic, not to have come to the fore — and saints, decidedly, they were not.

In the middle thirties, anti-Jewish discrimination, as it had always been the core of "Endecja" and other right-wing parties, gained government support, and whilst the Constitution continued to guarantee equal rights, discriminatory measures were enforced. The then-Prime Minister General Slawoj-Skladkowski uttered his infamous "*Owszem*" ("why yes, by all means") in support of an economic boycott of Jewish enterprises. (Ironically, the said general lived in Palestine during the war and died in Israel in 1952.) Riots at the universities and picketing of Jewish shops were defined as "natural instincts of cultural self-defence and the tendency for self-sufficiency."

But against this background of menace and uncertainty Jewish life was throbbing — tumultuous and irrepressible. A degree of oppression was accepted as natural, this was after all the Diaspora-*Galuth*, another chapter of an old story, what else would you expect?

It is important to remember that there existed a considerable area where the division between the Polish and the Jewish world was blurred and the long co-habitation had resulted in mutual acceptance, tolerance and harmony. This had produced a cross-fertilisation with an untold enrichment of both cultures. As in that nursery rhyme about the girl with the curl in the middle of her forehead — a Pole, when he is good, he is very, very good... There is a native specimen marked by noble spirit, romantic dash, contempt for danger, idealism, which any society would be proud of.

Antoni Slonimski, one of the finest Polish poets and the grandson of Hayyim Selig Slonimski, the founder and editor of the Hebrew newspaper *Hatsefira*, has a poem about "the two unhappiest nations on earth." Their paths have parted forever.

When the Polish Jews perished, a part of Poland perished with them. But the Poles have hardly shed a tear over this loss. There was a momentary unease — and a pretence that, somehow, the Jews had never been. There was a widespread relief that the intractable "Jewish problem" in Poland had been solved in a way for which the Poles could not be blamed. What would have happened if at the end of the war millions of Jews had surfaced to claim their position and property does not bear thinking about. Indeed, the welcome accorded to the pitiful remnant that emerged from their hideouts, from the camps, the bunkers, the forests, gives an inkling of the nightmare that would have followed.

When the Jews and their children were murdered and their environment annihilated, "one of the roots from which history grows" — as George Steiner puts it — was torn up; the genetic pool from which this specific tradition arose has been blotted out. "The absence from our present needs, our evolutionary hopes" — to use his own words — "of the strains of moral, psychological, cerebral quality extinguished at Belsen and Treblinka constitutes... the slow, sad vengeance of the unremembered dead."

The Jewish Quarterly, No. 113, 1983/84

Reflections on the unspeakable

It is well-nigh impossible to sustain a rational discourse about Auschwitz. The very word lacerates a raw nerve. It means many things. It is not only a physical place in Poland, where there is a museum, visited through the years by millions of people of all nationalities, religions and ages, wanting, for their own diverse reasons, to see the site where not long ago was enacted one of the most horrific events in human history. It is also an abstract notion which fills us with awe and profound unease. It is a symbol — holding different meanings to different people.

To Jews, Auschwitz is the symbol of the Holocaust. They are surprised and outraged at any attempt to invest it with a different meaning. But, for Poles, Auschwitz is not, primarily, a "Jewish" camp, but a symbol of the German rape of their country and the persecution of their nation — and they have their very good reasons for perceiving it thus.

It is salutary to bear certain data in mind, for sometimes we talk and act as if we did not want to be confused by the facts. (Auschwitz, by the way, is the name the Germans imposed on the very ordinary town of Oswiecim, and one should really try to revert to the original name. But like the word "Holocaust" — which is wrong, misleading, inappropriate, an alien import — it has gained such a firm grip in all languages that the battle against it must be considered lost.)

Auschwitz was opened in June 1940 as a concentration camp for Polish political prisoners. The Hitler-Stalin "Boundary and Friendship Treaty" contained secret provisions for the "elimination" of the potential opponents of both regimes. In April and May of 1940 the Soviets murdered about 15,000 Polish POWs, 45 percent of the prewar Polish officer corps, in the Katyn Forest and other locations. At the same time, the Germans, honourably keeping their side of the bargain, sent 20,000 Poles to concentration camps. It was the beginning of their grand design to destroy the spiritual and political elite of the nation.

Auschwitz was situated in territory incorporated into the Reich from which most Poles were removed to create a no-man's land. On 14th June 1940 the first transport of Polish prisoners arrived in Auschwitz, and for the next twenty-one months the Poles were the only inmates of that camp. (The first Jewish prisoners, women from Slovakia, arrived in Auschwitz towards the end of March 1942.) Referred to as the *Stammlager* or main camp, Auschwitz I, where Poles always formed the majority, was a slave-labour camp, the hub of over forty

154

subcamps in the vicinity. Many thousands of inmates perished there from hunger, overwork, disease, sporadic executions. But there were also many survivors.

In October 1941 the Germans started building a subcamp, Birkenau (Brze-zinka), about two miles away from the base. This became known as Auschwitz II: the gas chambers and the crematoria were sited there.

From May 1942 the majority of the Jews arriving in Auschwitz-Birkenau were sent straight from the railway ramp to the gas chambers. The precise figure cannot be established but most recent research sets the number of Jews gassed and burnt there at one-and-a-half million.

Of the six death camps — Belzec, Chelmno, Sobibor, Majdanek, Treblinka and Auschwitz — this last is the only one where most of the physical fabric has survived — the Germans, having dynamited the installations in an attempt to cover up the traces of their crime, left the camp in haste, escaping from the Russian advance.

The former administration buildings, the barracks, the watchtowers, the pylons with the barbed wire, the ruins of the gas chambers and crematoria and the fields themselves form the structure of the museum which the Polish government established shortly after the end of the war. The purpose of the museum was to show Polish martyrdom and the danger of fascism. In accordance with the official historiography, the victims were "people" distinguished by their nationalities, twenty-eight of them, listed in alphabetical order: Jews, with the letter J, between Italians and Letts. There was no mention that virtually all of them, of whatever nationality, were Jews, murdered there for no other reason. To the communist "historian" this was an irrelevance. Various nationalities were given their own section in which to tell their own story — the Bulgarian, for instance, illustrated the glorious achievements of their Communist Party. But a Jewish exhibition section was only opened in 1978, and to this day, despite some improvements introduced since, it is totally inadequate in form and substance.

With the sweeping changes in Poland and elsewhere, there is a call for the falsification of history to be corrected, and not only in this respect. The Polish authorities responsible for the Museum show an open-minded and far-reaching willingness to listen to and, if possible, implement the advice of the "Jewish side." There is, of course, no single authoritative Jewish voice in this matter and no agreed view on what to tell and how to tell it. (Some years ago, at a World Conference of Polish Jews in Jerusalem, I heard Prime Minister Shamir addressing the audience with the following words: "If Jews in Europe had followed Jabotinsky's warnings and come to Palestine in their masses, there would have been no Shoah." Recently I heard General Barak, the head of the Israeli army, deliver a moving speech to a group of soldiers and schoolchildren from Israel in front of the "Jewish barrack" in Auschwitz. "We came here fifty years too late… Only a strong Jewish state and a strong Jewish army are a guarantee that this will not happen to Jews again.")

An International Auschwitz Council, with a strong Jewish representation, was recently called into being by the Polish authorities. The Organisation of Camp Survivors, with their headquarters in Belgium, guards, understandably, their claim to have their voice heard. Yad Vashem has undoubtedly the greatest expertise and moral authority to offer guidance. Various American institutions bring their influence (and money) to bear in these matters.

An independent group of writers and scholars from nine countries came together at Yarnton Manor in England in May 1990, under the aegis of the Oxford Centre for Hebrew Studies and in the presence of specially appointed representatives of the Polish government. They formulated a set of recommendations and desiderata concerning the policy and the practical arrangements on the site of the Auschwitz camp.

A similar group was reconvened recently in Cracow and Auschwitz to monitor progress since the "Yarnton Declaration" and to reinforce and update a further set of proposals. Since it is solely the Polish authority which has power — and by the same token the duty — to preserve and present Auschwitz, it is imperative that the guidance offered be practical, well thought out, based on exact knowledge of local conditions, and directed, with due delicacy, through channels which are sympathetic and effective. In this respect the "Yarnton-Cracow" group has good credentials and a significant role to play.

The questions which arise are many and complex. Leaving aside the philosophical issues, which are in a category of their own, and touching only on practical problems: which "history" is the Museum to show and through which texts, images, captions, exhibits, artefacts? Having acknowledged and shown the predominantly Jewish victims of Auschwitz, how should due weight be given to the very large numbers of non-Jewish victims? How is the dignity and the integrity of the site to be preserved in view of the nature of mass tourism? How is the vulgarisation of the place to be prevented, with thousands of people of all cultures and ages milling around, in need of occasional relief and refreshment, looking for "souvenirs" to take away? How is orderly and thoughtful behaviour to be ensured? How are people to be prevented — the terrain is vast and cannot be strictly supervised — from placing in various spots, no doubt with the purest intention, their own signs, plaques or symbols? This is an enormously sensitive issue. As I have said elsewhere, to Christians the Cross is a sign of love and hope: how are they to be made to understand that to most Jews it symbolises oppression, persecution, the Church's triumphalism, the intention to convert "the stray brothers"? Can they see that the Cross, in what is perceived as a Jewish cemetery, offends the deepest Jewish sensibilities? How are the guides, who every day of their working life have to relate the gruesome story in accurate detail, to be educated? How are they to retain their freshness and sincerity, and not get numb or even blasé? Standing on the site of the gas chamber, one must, to preserve one's sanity, use all one's strength to repel the imagery which assaults the senses. How and where is the viewer, the pilgrim, given an overview of Jewish society and culture — what these millions of murdered people believed in and created and stood for and what was lost to the world with them?

Now consider the problems of the physical preservation and restoration of the site and its contents. Through the ravages of time and weather the fabric of the camp is threatened; it disintegrates, rots and crumbles. How is one to deal with it? The watchtowers around the camp, for instance, the most well-known feature of that bleakest of landscapes, have been completely rebuilt, with new materials — thus losing their "authenticity." Was this wrong? They would have otherwise disappeared... Is this a precedent to be followed or avoided? The barbed wire around the perimeter of the camp has rusted and soon there will be no trace of it: replace it with new? preserve it at all costs? let it go? What about the most telling and poignant exhibits in their showcases: the human hair, the mound of shoes, the suitcases with their names: they change colour, mould, rot. What is to be done?

What is to be done with the piles of bricks which are the ruins of the gas chambers and crematoria, dynamited by the Germans? Rebuild them in their original shape? Conserve them as they are at the moment? Let nature take its course? Half of an original wooden barrack at Birkenau has been removed and taken to the National Holocaust Museum in Washington. It would have disintegrated if left on site — so the argument runs — and the Holocaust Museum needs genuine relics; they have a better home now. Is this an act of piety or cultural vandalism? Battered and confused by all these perplexing dilemmas, one may well ask: DOES ALL THIS MATTER?

The "Yarnton-Cracow" group came up with many constructive suggestions. To implement them, even some of them, will cost money, a lot of it. The Polish government will give some but, for reasons all too obvious, not much can be expected from that source. It has been suggested that funds should be sought from UNESCO; Auschwitz-Birkenau is listed as part of the Common Heritage of Mankind, but it is only one of many competing causes. However, millions of dollars are spent on the Holocaust museums in the United States, new ones are planned all the time. Would not a moment's rational thought make clear where such funds should go in the first place?

The Jewish Quarterly, No. 146, Summer Issue 1992

A peculiar people

Contemplating the massive contribution to contemporary European culture which is, by some reckoning, attributable to Jews or people of Jewish origin, one would want to know what were the sources of such creativity, what kind of people were those who gave rise to it, what was the soil and the climate in which this phenomenon grew?

To try to convey this in a few pages is like an attempt to pour the ocean into a hole in the ground, but at least a little of the story can be told, and let it begin thus:

Once upon a time, in the basins of the Rivers Oder, Vistula, Niemen, Dniepr and Dniester, there lived a people like no other, the Jews. They arrived in that part of the world gradually, over centuries, by diverse routes — some from Spain and Portugal, some from the West, some from Asia and Africa. They spread over a vast territory and their characteristics differed. But they had important things in common. They were all exiles, their ancestors were driven away from their erstwhile homeland, the Holy Land, and they were destined to live dispersed among other peoples who claimed a better title to the land and who, most of the time, treated them as unwelcome intruders.

Other groups in history, exposed to similar conditions, have long disappeared, intermingling with other races and nations — the Jews, mysteriously, survived. Some want to see in this very fact proof of the existence of God, but in terms of rational discourse, other reasons will have to be found. One of them was that Jews shared a singular religion which kept them apart, a faith in One God, based on a Book, which they called the Torah, the Bible, which not only is the greatest work of literature ever written, but also prescribes, in minute detail, the way they should live and worship. The Book assures them that they are God's Chosen People — and if that means being chosen to suffer, then so be it. The Book also contains a promise of redemption, at the end of days, when the Messiah comes. The Book told them also "to be fruitful and multiply" and this they did, prodigiously.

They cared little for manmade borders; whether the destination was named Bukovina or Bessarabia, Volhynia or Podolia, Galicia or Lithuania — when oppression increased they moved to join their brethren in another place where life was, for the time, more bearable. They often gained an autonomy of sorts, developed their own institutions, judiciary, tax collections, schools. They established famous yeshivahs — *sui generis* academies of Talmudic learning, wherein they maintained the age-old tradition of intensive, day and night study to which they attracted students from far and wide, even from the Western Hemisphere.

There was a cult of learning, although for most of them study was confined to the Bible, the legal codes and commentaries and the rabbinical writings. Illiteracy was unknown; all children were taught to read on their father's knee. The social standing of a man was tied to his learning, following the saying that "the learned man takes precedence over the high priest." This developed the sharpness of intellect which proved so effective when it had a chance to spill over to other spheres — in philosophy, in science, literature, art or business.

A predominant and distinguishing feature of the internal landscape of those people was a high degree of spirituality — a conviction that "not by bread alone," that no matter how humble or oppressed, man must aspire to some higher ideal, however defined. There was an underlying belief in the ultimate rightness and justice of the world. One might think that this belief would have been extinguished by the all-too-tangible evidence to the contrary.

If spirituality was one hallmark, internal dissent was another. Throughout history (and to the present day) Jews have not been at peace with each other. Communities were often shaken to their foundations by fratricidal strife due to depth of conviction (some call it fanaticism) and the lack of tolerance which tends to afflict people who claim to hear voices from on high. Sadducees against Pharisees, Hassidim against Mitnagdim, Zionists against Bundists, Orthodox against Reform, Lubavitch against Satmar, traditionalists against assimilationists, peaceniks against settlers. Jews have been turbulent people, people "who do not sleep themselves and keep others awake."

One of their most important cultural achievements is the development of their own language, Yiddish, which formed a strong bond, across borders, between the diverse offshoots of the people. It was estimated that on the eve of World War II there were eleven million speakers of that language worldwide, from Ukraine to Holland and in America.

Yiddish is a curious mixture of German, Hebrew, Polish and a small component derived from the language spoken by the surrounding population. To the unaccustomed ear it sounds unattractive, and many considered it to be a jargon, not worthy to be called "language." It was lively, adaptable, colourful, witty. Its grammar was flexible to the point where it was hardly possible to commit a grammatical error (would that other languages had this gift!). It flourished not only as a means of oral communication but also as a medium of literary expression. There were thousands of newspapers, magazines and pamphlets printed and published in Yiddish — printing was one of the crafts, like shoemaking, tailoring and watch-repairing, which became a Jewish speciality.

YIVO, the Institute for Jewish Research, founded in 1925, with headquarters then in Wilno, and now in New York, has in its archives hundreds of thousands of books, manuscripts, theatrical collections, letters, photographs and sundry items recovered from the Nazis after the war.

Yiddish literature was an influential and inseparable feature of Jewish life. Jewish theatre gave scope to playwrights like Goldfaden and Anski, whose play *Dybbuk* achieved widespread fame. Actors like Abraham Morewski, the Turkow brothers and Esther Rachel Kaminska performed the classic repertoire in their own theatres or on tour and had a wide following. Great writers arose, of whom the literature of any nation would have been proud — I.L. Peretz, Shalom Aleichem, Mendele, the Singer brothers, of whom the younger, Isaac Bashevis, won the Nobel Prize and brought prestige to the language in which he wrote. During the war Itzhak Katzenelson wrote in Yiddish, in the Warsaw ghetto, an elegy on the destruction of the Jews, which is amongst the most moving documents of our time.

The Founding Fathers of Zionism, with the exception of Theodor Herzl — Weizman, Sokolov, Jabotinsky, Borochov, Ben Gurion, Achad Ha'am — all coming from the same East European background and undoubtedly Yiddish speakers and orators themselves, perceived that the future Jewish nation for the creation of which they strove should have a language not associated with the miseries of the Diaspora, but one going back to their source in Palestine. It was a near-impossible task to raise Hebrew from the dead and set it, as a matter of principle, against Yiddish, which was very much alive and kicking. The fact that in that battle, Hebrew, "the holy tongue," prevailed over Yiddish, "the mother's tongue" (*mame-loshen*), and is now a sign of Israeli identity, the natural language of people born there, the sabras, used for all daily needs, for scientific pursuits, as well as for worship, as of old, is one of the miracles associated with the rebirth of the Jewish nation in its old land.

The fences which separated the Jewish communities from their neighbours were strong and tall, for they were erected and kept in good repair by both sides. The indigenous population was, on the whole, quite ignorant of what the Jew was really like. They held on to a stereotyped image of something dark and sinister. The Jewish communities were inward-looking, sufficient unto themselves, other than on the margin where the need to earn a living made them enter the outside world. They felt, and for good reasons, threatened and at the not-so-tender mercies of the native population. The contempt shown to them they reciprocated; they had an idea of their own value ("When the natives were still in the trees — Jews already had diabetes!"), and the humblest of them would not want to swap places with the princes of that hostile world.

In the second half of the eighteenth century, in the aftermath of the Chmielnicki massacres and the upheavals brought about by the false messianic and kabbalistic movements of Sabbatai Tzvi and Jacob Frank, there arose in the southeast of the Polish-Lithuanian Commonwealth a new religious movement,

Hassidism. Jews are good conductors of ideas and Hassidism swept over the eastern part of Europe like a bushfire. It was meant to revitalise Judaism by leading people back to the traditional tenets of Judaism in a spirit of love and joy. By 1900 there were more than a million Hassidim in the world, including almost a third of prewar Polish Jewry. In the course of two hundred years Hassidism has produced some fifteen hundred teacher/leaders, outstanding practitioners of the movement, attracting devoted followers to this or that *tzaddik* and his court.

At the time when Jews in that part of the world had little to rejoice about, Hassidism preached joy in simply being a Jew and in the performance of everyday drudgery. Against the traditional view that learning was supreme, Hassidism accorded every Jew, however humble and unlearned, equal rank in communion with God, in a mystic bond and ecstatic prayer, induced by violent body motions, shouting and singing.

The founder of this revolutionary movement, the Baal Shem-Tov, preached that the essence of religion is in feeling, not reason; ceremonial details are unimportant; it is necessary to live and serve God in a cheerful and happy mood. The life of the Russo-Polish Jew became thus brighter at heart but darker in intellect. The telling of stories of the great, miraculous deeds of the *tzaddikim* was a continuous, life-enhancing activity, stimulating the imagination, a sort of worship in itself. Martin Buber, an inspiring writer, thinker and spiritual leader, collected and wrote down the Hassidic stories, a literary genre *sui generis*. Hassidism — although nothing was further from what Hassidism thought — created a climate which was favourable to the development of art.

By a curious linguistic coincidence, in the Jewish encyclopedias the word "Hassidism" is preceded by "Haskalah" (which means, roughly, enlightenment). This is most appropriate not only in linguistic but also in historical terms. Towards the end of the eighteenth century, a new movement under that name sprang up and spread among the Jews of Eastern Europe. To start with, it meant to substitute the study of the Talmud with modern subjects, stressing the poetical and critical works of Hebrew literature. It meant, further, to fight obscurantism, superstition and Hassidism, to encourage Jews to adopt agriculture and handicrafts, abandon their exclusiveness and acquire the knowledge, manners and aspirations of the nations among whom they dwelt. Moses Mendelssohn, the German philosopher and man of letters who was "the Father of the Haskalah," directed Jews towards "the broad highway of human culture."

The Vilna Gaon, one of the greatest spiritual leaders of his day and the fiercest opponent of Hassidism, was also an opponent of the Haskalah. He foresaw, correctly, that the first step on the path of so-called progress would set many Jews on the slippery slope of assimilation and, perish the thought, conversion (a suspicion which Mendelssohn shared).

Jews were ready to welcome and take advantage of the Enlightenment and the Emancipation which dawned in Europe. With the new spirit spreading, and with Jews, at least formally, obtaining equal rights of citizenship in most countries, they began to spill out from their ghettoes onto the world scene. That process of contradictory pulls, challenges and conflicts often tore the guts out of Jewish communities, but the release of talents impacted on every walk of life, for all the world to see. If some latter-day Goebbels arose and wanted to separate the "Jewish" contribution to culture from the rest, he would have little joy. Modern culture is unthinkable without that particular input; without the eternal rebel, the outsider, the dissident, the Jew.

One could preen oneself and bask in the reflected glory of the great many artists and men of letters who have immeasurably enriched the human heritage — from Antokolski to Zadkine and from Babel to Zamenhof — all of them had their roots in or around Odessa and Czernowitz and Vitesbsk and Warsaw.

Chaim Nachman Bialik, the greatest of modern Hebrew poets (born in Zhitomir, died in Tel Aviv) is known to have bemoaned the fact that so much Jewish talent goes to the "goyim's" credit. He need not have worried, should not have begrudged it, there is enough to go round. Such is the blessed chemistry of art — nobody gets poorer, all get richer.

It is worth mentioning that among the consumers of art, among those who create interest and demand, without which the supply would wither, among those who buy, spread and propagate art, who read books, go to theatres and concerts, there has always been an inordinately high proportion of Jews. That also is no mean contribution.

*   *
*

...And then there arose in the West a mighty leader, Hitler, who became the head of the German nation. He preached a gospel of hate against the Jews and vowed to destroy them. His armies overran and conquered the lands where most of them lived and Jews were murdered by the millions. In the course of a few years the world of European Jewry, a thousand-year-old civilisation, was destroyed and is no more. One utters these words but their full meaning cannot be grasped.

We who are in a state of perpetual mourning for that vanished world seek solace in dwelling on the matchless heritage left to us, and to humanity, for all times.

Published in *Europa-Europa* — catalogue of the exhibition
Das Jahrhundert des Avantgarde in Mittel- und Osteuropa
Bonn, May 1994 (in German)

Beloved Teacher

Yitzhak Katzenelson, the author of the elegy in Yiddish, "The Song of the Murdered Jewish People" — which was written in the Warsaw Ghetto and is probably the most moving document of that time, wrote the following in a tribute to his father:

"When did he learn the Bible by heart?
The Commentaries of Onkelos and Martin Luther?
The Talmud, Codes, Midrash, Shakespeare and Heine?
When did he read Gogol, Thucydides and Plutarch?
When did he study the Holy Zohar?
When did he sleep?"

The immeasurable and ungraspable loss lies in this: that the human type which Katzenelson described here has perished and will not recur. Those who constituted the civilisation of the Jews of Eastern Europe and who were the main victims of the Shoah are no longer a part of the human landscape.

The *shtetl* was full of them: amateur scholars, perhaps not so well versed in secular literature as Katzenelson's father, but totally at home in Jewish religious writings, masters of vast and complex texts. And yet for most of them — excepting the rabbi in office and the son-in-law of some magnate — studying could have been only a partial pursuit, a hobby, as it were, for their waking hours were mainly consumed in laboriously earning a living. Providing for the family was seen as the overriding duty of the father.

A Polish poet, Antoni Slonimski (the grandson, incidentally, of Selig Slonimski, the founder and editor of the first Hebrew journal in Poland, *Hatsefira*), describes the *shtetl* in one of his poems as "a place where the cobbler was a poet, the watchmaker a philosopher and the barber a troubadour."

I knew many such souls, but one particularly remains in my memory. Benzion Rapaport, a simple teacher, my teacher in the Hebrew school in Cracow, where Hebrew subjects — the Bible, Jewish history and literature — were taught concurrently with the Polish curriculum. Benzion Rapaport was one of a number of Hebrew teachers in that school.

Biblical studies were his speciality and it was commonly known, although he himself never made much of it, that he was immensely learned not only in this, but in a variety of secular subjects. His position was not easy — to deviate from the traditional Orthodox teaching would endanger his job, and yet he wanted at all costs to implant in us the spirit of free, far-ranging, open-minded enquiry. More important than the formal lessons during which he usually had his nose stuck in a book — almost literally, for he was very shortsighted — whilst we were left to our own, noisy devices — were the discussions we had with him after the bell had rung for the break. Then he felt freer to speak his mind and we soon learned to take advantage of it. "You do not have to believe, literally, in every word of the Scriptures to remain a good and observant Jew" — he used to say (when have we heard that, in different places, since?).

I remember one occasion, before Pesach, we were re-reading the Haggadah, and he explained the miracle of "the parting of the seas" — *Yam suf.* What we call the Red Sea, he told us, is clearly a "sea of reeds," the waters thickly overgrown with bulrushes, papyrus. Jews could cross it, light of foot, even though laden with the riches they carried. The Egyptians in pursuit, in heavy chariots, sank.

One of us, innocently, must have repeated this at home.

An irate parent came to complain that Rapaport was teaching us to disbelieve in miracles. He had to defend himself:

"Is the Exodus less of a miracle because of that explanation? Is Moses less of a prophet and leader because he did not, literally, split the sea but knew the best way to go?"

In one of those discussions with him, I remember pronouncing with the self-assurance of a teenage know-all:

"There is nothing easier than the facile acceptance of faith, as a package, just like that, on somebody's say-so."

He shook his head indulgently.

"There is one thing easier still — a facile rejection. You can be an unbeliever, an iconoclast, an agnostic if you wish. But, please, not a shallow one. In both cases it is the shallowness which is unworthy."

On another occasion I remember asking him the following:

"To accord a learned man high praise, they say sometimes: 'he knows *Shas*,' the whole of the six books of the Mishnah, by heart — in my own family they say this about my grandfather. Surely this is hyperbole and cannot be taken literally? No human brain could retain millions of words and recall them at will, and they are not like an orderly sequence of an actor's part, but often quite random. Surely, this is not possible?"

Rapaport took a deep breath:

"I understand your scepticism but I want to assure you that it is possible. It requires, of course, not only a talent and love for the matter, but above all constant application, *yomam v'layla*, day and night study, poring over the texts in the conviction that they interpret the word of God. There are people who have done it and" — here he smiled shyly — "I have very nearly done it myself."

I was overcome by admiration and embraced him and he uttered a blessing.

Rapaport was the one who was preparing me for my *bar mitzvah*. I used to go to his home — a room and a kitchen, full of books stacked on the floor — to be taught how to put on the tefillin, how to read the portion of the Torah, what prayers to say in the morning. He also wrote the *drasha* for me, the address which I learned by heart and delivered to the congregation. It was composed in beautiful Hebrew. (I remember it to this day, and it is my "party piece" during our school reunions in Israel.)

Next morning after the ceremony in the synagogue, before going to school, I applied myself to *shacharit*, the full, adult morning prayers. These, as we know, are quite long and take time. I took the tefillin from the embroidered bag, put them on as he had taught me, opened the prayer book and set out to read the text, under my breath; verse after verse, page after page. For the first time in my life I came to school late. And so the next day and the day after that — as my mother watched with increasing impatience and anxiety. She certainly did not want to be the one who stopped me from praying. But, on the other hand, to make me get up earlier, she feared, would also not do me any good and probably arouse my resentment against the whole procedure. What should she do? She went to consult Rapaport.

He took me aside and what he told me I have never forgotten.

"Dear boy" — he said — "remember that going to school, learning, is also a form of worship, equally — or, perhaps, even more pleasing to God than prayer, and coming late to school is an affront to Him. I know that *shacharit*, the morning prayer, is long — maybe too long for youngsters like you, who knows? We have to shorten it to enable you to get to school on time. We have to extract from it the essence, what is most important in it. The most important thing is the question man has to put to himself when he raises his eyes to heaven: *Ma chovato b'olamo* — 'what is my duty in this world?' Every morning, before you begin your day, ask yourself this question — but seriously, not just casually. Every day afresh — and think about it a minute. Do not try to answer it — there is no short answer to it, it will not come to you quickly, maybe it will never come to you — it matters not. The thing is to realise that the question is important, that you have a duty to perform and have to search for it. Give it a thought — that's all. Then go to school — on time."

It is true that since that day I have never put on tefillin again, and in that sense one could argue that Rapaport led me astray. But I like to think that, on the contrary, he gave me a complete lesson in morality. And if sometimes, often, I do not live up to it, at least I feel that I know it and am conscious of my failing.

There is another reason why I shall never forget Rapaport. It was June 1945. The war had just ended and its conclusion found me in the British army, in Norway. I was a sergeant in the Intelligence Corps, charged with the task of interrogating members of the German occupation forces and weeding out the criminal elements among them before their repatriation to the Fatherland. News reached me, via London, that my mother was alive, having miraculously survived the war. Almost instantly I was on a plane to Germany, to British Army Headquarters on the Rhine, where I picked up a staff car and a driver (this took some doing, but there was no stopping me) and started on my journey to Cracow, via Warsaw. We drove through the Ruhr in Germany and, I confess, my heart leapt for joy when I saw the destruction wrought on that territory by the Allied Air Force. But coming to Warsaw — or rather to what was supposed to have been Warsaw on the map — a pile of rubble stretching for miles, a landscape riven with moon-like craters, I realised that the bombing of the Ruhr had been a picnic by comparison.

One of the few buildings in the centre of Warsaw still standing with its roof on was the Hotel Polonia, where the British Embassy was located, and I pulled up in front of that building to report my presence (and draw coupons for petrol for my further journey).

In the hotel lobby a crowd of people were milling around, hustling and shoving, transacting business. In that crowd — a heart-stopping moment this — I spot a familiar face, a former schoolmate of mine! We shake hands, embrace, it appears that he has just arrived from Palestine, in search of survivors.

As we talk, feverishly, exchanging information about mutual friends, a Polish peasant who, I notice, has been observing us for a while, comes up to us. "You are Jews?" he asks. "Indeed we are," we reply.

He takes out from his breast-pocket a bundle of papers, pages from an exercise book, covered in Hebrew handwriting, in fading ink. With it a scrap of paper, scrawled in Polish. "Pious soul," the message reads, "this is a man's life work. Give it into good hands."

We look at the Hebrew manuscript, we can hardly believe our eyes. It appears that this is the writing of Benzion Rapaport, which he threw out of the window of the train taking him to the death camp in Belzec, on to an open Polish field. A man, the one who now stands in front of us, finds it, deciphers the Polish message, safeguards the manuscript. When the war ends, he travels to Warsaw to look for Jews to hand it over to. They are hard to find, but in the crowded lobby of the Hotel Polonia he spots two Jews — two former pupils of Benzion Rapaport.

We saw to it, of course, that the manuscript was published in Israel. The book carries the title *Teva v'ruach* (Nature and Spirit). It is a collection of essays on the glories of German philosophy, on Hegel, Kant, Schopenhauer, and Rapaport's own thoughts on religion, on ethics, on the method of scientific enquiry.

The pity, the horror and the irony of it all…

Judaism Today, No. 1, Spring 1995

Booksearch! From Przemysl to the British Library

My father's family hails from Oswiecim, Oshpitzin in Yiddish, a *shtetl* which the Germans renamed Auschwitz and gave cause for it to be one of the most sinister sounds in any language. My father was one of fifteen children, so it will be clear that there were at one time hundreds of Scharfs in Oswiecim, from the patriarch Elias to the four-year-old Chanele.

There were many rabbis among them, which added lustre to the family name, and also, as was natural, some "no-goodniks" which detracted from it. But the figure of whom one spoke with awe and pride belonged to a previous generation — Rabbi Moshe Yaacov Jekel Scharf, born in 1784, died in 1869, the "official" Rabbi of Oswiecim for fifty years. To be one of his descendants, in direct line, was a *yichus*, a distinction one had to try to live up to, as my father never tired of telling me.

Rabbis were often known not by their family name but by the title of the book which they had written, like *Megale Amukot* or *Chofetz Chaim*.

The books of Moshe Yaacov stood, of course, on the bookshelves in our drawing room, among the other *seforim* — the large volumes of religious books, bound in their characteristic mottled yellow-brown covers. I remember in particular one slim volume, with a red flash and gold embossing — my father would look at it lovingly and occasionally stroke its spine in passing. Not that he would have understood a great deal of the text, that was not the point. He knew that the book, those books, belonged to another realm and formed a spiritual resource which made life meaningful.

And so I always remembered where the book stood, the spine and the binding, but — I confess — I had forgotten the title and therefore could not, on those occasions which called for it, bask in his glory. This caused me some distress through the years — since my memory is, on the whole, reasonable and I have total recall of a myriad trivial details of that time. Yet I had forgotten the title of my great-grandfather's book — shame on me.

There was, of course, a way of finding out, but I was too ignorant to think of it. Bernard Friedberg (1876–1961), a fellow Cracovian (yes, you find them everywhere), published, among other important works on Hebrew printing, the bibliographical lexicon *Beit Eked Sefarim* in four volumes, which is the standard, indispensable work and — as I now know — Moshe Yaacov Scharf's books (note the plural) feature in it.

However, the spirit moves in mysterious ways, and the other day a little book fell into my hands, entitled: *From Oswiecim to Auschwitz — Poland*

Revisited by Rabbi Moshe Weiss (Mosaic Press, P. O. Box 1032, Oakville, Ontario, Canada). Rabbi Weiss, who now lives in Canada but was born in Oswiecim, travels to Poland at frequent intervals, visiting various places in search of traces of Jewish life and the remaining Jews, to whom he brings aid and comfort. Describing his recent visit to Oswiecim, he mentions that Moshe Yaacov Scharf, a disciple of the *Sanzer Tzaddik,* was Rabbi there for fifty years and, bless him, he mentions the title of the book: *DARKEI YOSHER!*

To see it suddenly, in black and white, was for me like a shaft of light across a darkened sky. *Darkei Yosher,* of course! How could I have forgotten? *Darkei Yosher* — "The Ways of the Just."

Since this happened on a Monday, the day on which I attend Rabbi Louis Jacobs' Talmud lesson, I told him of my great joy at this rediscovery. Next morning he phoned me to say that the book indeed appears in Friedberg's bibliography, that it contains 192 pages and had been printed in Przemysl, near Cracow, in the year 1872. He thought that a copy might be found in the British Library.

I confess I had thought this highly improbable: a little Hebrew book, published more than 120 years ago, in Przemysl, in an edition of — what would it have been? — 200, 300 copies, how could it be expected to have found its way to the shelves of the British Library?

To go there, I dug up my old Reader's Ticket to the Reading Room in the British Museum — and there hangs another tale.

I came to London from Cracow shortly before the outbreak of war, and I have this vivid recollection how, the very day after arrival, I stood on the steps of the British Museum and pinched myself to prove that I was not dreaming, that I was in England, in London, at the gateway to this glorious temple.

I went to the office and applied, there and then, for a reader's ticket, to which I proved my title: I was a working journalist, a foreign correspondent for my paper in Cracow and had been admitted as a postgraduate student at the London School of Economics, intent on completing my thesis begun at the Jagiellonian University in Cracow. I entered the Reading Room — I thought I was in Paradise. I thought I should happily spend the rest of my life there.

World events intervened, there was little time for such cosy dreams, life took a different course, years went by in other pursuits. But thirty-and-some years later, at "retirement," I felt this nostalgic tug at the heart as I stood, once again, in the office of the Museum, filling in an application form for a Reader's Ticket. The last item on the application form read:

"Have you had a ticket before?"

"Yes," I said jokingly to the man behind the counter, "I have had a ticket before, before the war" — and I waved in front of him the old, faded card, which I had retained as a souvenir.

"You don't require a new ticket, you want a renewal," said the man, apparently in all seriousness.

"It was a long time ago," I stuttered.

"Not long for a museum," he said, took the ticket from my hand, and in the space provided, after former renewals which read "10 July 1940," "31 January 1941," he put a stamp "14 December 1972."

I keep this as a rare document, a museum specimen of sorts. I find this somehow enormously endearing and reassuring. Thirty years on, thirty miles of bookshelves later, with World War II in between, empires risen and fallen and the world changed beyond recognition, the man said: "It is not long for a museum."

And so, armed with that renewed ticket, I went on to the British Library — the Hebrew books are no longer housed in Bloomsbury, but in Orbit House near Blackfriars Bridge. I presented my request to the librarian, Ms. Ilana Tahan. A few buttons pressed on the computer — a breathtaking moment this — yes, the book is catalogued and available. In a few moments it appears in front of me on my desk.

I handled the book tenderly, overcome by a strange feeling. There it was, as if flown from my old home, a fragment of life that is no more. Bookshelves of *seforim*, religious books, stood in thousands of Jewish homes — not only the Orthodox where they sometimes occupied half the living space, but in many ordinary homes, where no member of the household would open them any more, a sort of natural backdrop, without which the room felt cold and empty. If you add to this the books in the synagogues and yeshivahs and *shtiblech*, through the land, one is clearly talking about vast numbers, millions of books. It is a measure of the destruction, of the uprooting of a civilisation, that one does not find any religious Hebrew books in Poland, other than by accident, some tattered copies among the bric-a-brac in a flea market.

After all this excitement, you may well be curious about the content of the book. All I am able to say, for the moment, is that the text is extremely difficult to follow, even for somebody not entirely ignorant in these matters.

The front page says that this book is a collection of "innovations and wonderful explications of most of the chapters of the Mishnah, both in the casuistic (*pilpul*) and in the straightforward manner"; brought to the printing house by Rabbi David Scharf, the son of Moshe Yaacov; printed by Zupnik and Partners, in Przemysl, in 1872.

The inside page carries the "imprimatur" and fulsome commendation of the great Rabbis Chaim Halbersztam of Sanz and Josef Natanson of Lwow and Galicia. It is printed, as was customary for works of that kind, in the "square" Rashi alphabet, without vowels, of course, or punctuation. And if that was not enough of a trial, virtually every line of text contains one or more of the *rashe tevot*, the shorthand, where single letters stand for words or phrases. (When I

see the *lamed-kof*, denoting that the question under discussion is easy to answer
— *lo kashe*, I am inclined to cry out for mercy — it is difficult! Very difficult!)

When one tries to follow the argument and breaks through the many
qualifying clauses, one finds innumerable references to other passages in the
Scriptures and the Talmud — in fact the whole strength of the argument seems
to be derived from these scattered quotations.

How these passages were recalled by the authors and marshalled at will,
without the aid of lexicons or concordances or a card index, boggles the mind
(and how infinitely easier is the work of modern scholars, when a "search"
button will instantly bring to the screen every mention of a word in the whole
text).

To ask why those Rabbis, with such prodigious minds and creative talents
which make one's own endowment look so puny, devoted their entire lives to
the study of problems which, for thousands of years, had absolutely no rele-
vance to any contemporary issue, would show a misunderstanding of what such
writing is. For those Rabbis and their disciples and followers, the preoccupation
with these problems and the treatment of them was simply (well, perhaps not so
simply) a form of worship, a labour of love of God. How could one think that
this was not enough, that there was something better, more practical to do?

Finally, can one guess or explain how such a book found its way from
Przemysl to the British Library? One must know whom to ask, and in this case
it was obvious to me that the person who knows everything there is to be known
in these matters is Professor Chimen Abramsky, not only a leading scholar on
Jewish subjects but, in one of his previous careers, a bookseller of Jewish
books. Indeed, as it transpires, he knows of Zupnik, the nineteenth-century
printer in Przemysl in Galicia, at that time in the Austro-Hungarian Empire.
Zupnik, like other printers, and there were many of them, circulated their
"catalogues" or loose sheets of books they printed, to the Jewish booksellers,
wherever they found them. One such, the best known in England, was Yaacov
Lifschitz, who — according to Abramsky — supplied the Museum, in the course
of years, with many hundreds of Jewish books. It is almost certain that it was he
who spotted *Darkei Yosher* on Zupnik's list, thought it worthy of purchase and
persuaded the librarian to acquire it for the collection — wouldn't Moshe
Yaacov be surprised.

End of story — but not quite. The computer tells me that the book was
reprinted in Baltimore in 1969, by Y.S. Gotteher — and I confess that I find the
whole thing utterly amazing.

Judaism Today, No. 2, Autumn 1995

RAFAEL F. SCHARF

CO MNIE I TOBIE POLSKO...
Eseje bez uprzedzeń

Spis treści

Rodzinie i przyjaciołom — z wdzięcznością

Felek

Przedmowa

Któż to dzisiaj, idąc krakowską ulicą Dietla, potrafi jeszcze odnalcźć w pamięci przynajmniej jedno, dwa nazwiska spośród przedwojennych lokatorów? Lokatorów, którzy wszyscy niemal zginęli, bo „planty Dietlowskie" były najszacowniejszą ulicą dzielnicy żydowskiej... Potrafi to tylko Rafael Scharf, wychowanek krakowskiego hebrajskiego gimnazjum, zajadły w młodości syjonista, który jednak z Polski do Izraela nie dojechał, bo po drodze zatrzymało go w Londynie najpierw małżeństwo, a potem wojna... I tak przyjął jakby na siebie rolę strażnika żydowskiej i krakowskiej pamięci: rolę ostatniego świadka, który pragnie uchować żydowską i krakowską szczególność. Jak Gebirtig w pieśni, tak Scharf pozostanie w pisanej pamięci Krakowa, przynosi nam bowiem żywe świadectwo miasta i, przede wszystkim, społeczności ludzkiej. Ostatniego pokolenia, które w Krakowie tłumnie mieszkało i lepiej czy gorzej, ale przecież jakoś współżyło z Polakami!

A przecież nic Scharfa do tej roli nie zdawało się przeznaczać! Pochodzi z rodziny średniozamożnego przedsiębiorcy, który — urodzony w Oświęcimiu — dorobił się dopiero w Krakowie. Otoczenie i rodzina przestrzegały — jak znaczna większość — przepisów wiary i obyczajów. Idolem jego młodości był radykalny syjonista, Żabotyński, co mogło go zaprowadzić nie tylko do Izraela, ale nawet do terroryzmu. „Niewiele brakowało, abym bomby rzucał" — mówi dziś pół żartem: uchroniły go Londyn, zdrowy rozsądek i chyba także wrodzona życzliwość do ludzi... Jednak także w Londynie zadowolił się Scharf jakby tylko częścią swej istoty: trudnił się dalej żydowskim dziennikarstwem i sprawami tak Izraela, jak diaspory... Zwłaszcza tej najbardziej opuszczonej, polskiej. Był też wśród pierwszych, którzy — gdy tylko stało się to politycznie możliwe — zatroskali się zarówno o żydowską przeszłość Krakowa, jak o budowanie zrozumienia — bo jeśli nie porozumienia, to przynajmniej wspólnego języka — między Żydami a Polakami.

Co ta krakowska pamięć wnosi szczególnego? Przecież żydowskich sprawozdań i pamiętników napisano tysiące... Choć trudno to ocenić, myślę, że żydowska społeczność Krakowa zaszła — stosunkowo — najdalej w procesie nie asymilacji, ale akulturacji do polskości. Choć w ogromnej większości zachowała obyczaj, nie mówiąc już o religii, to była też chyba bardziej otwarta a nawet włączona w życie miasta, szczególniej zaś — kulturalne. Jakąś rolę grać w tym musiała pamięć historyczna, pamięć o Esterze i Kazimierzu, królu i mieście. Ale też — o austriackiej (cesarsko-królewskiej) umiejętności przedkładania interesu państwa nad interesem rozlicznych narodów, co osłabiało etniczne napięcia.

Może też działała inna jeszcze analogia. Dociekania religijnej prawdy, szerzej zaś czy później, wszelkie intelektualne dociekanie cieszyło się w żydowskiej tradycji szczególnym szacunkiem. Uczonego w piśmie ceniono nie niżej, ale wyżej niż kapłana, który był jeszcze w istocie przywódcą, działaczem. „Ten etos — pisze Scharf — w szczątkowej formie przetrwał". Ale i polski Kraków, wydrwiwany za centusiowe ubóstwo i ciasnotę zmieszaną z historycznymi pretensjami... także stawiał wyżej profesora czy artystę niż człowieka sukcesu, a już zwłaszcza interesu. Czyż przez długie lata nie rządzili nim — przynajmniej moralnie — arystokraci, kler i profesorowie? Tak więc, jak przypomina Scharf, „krakowianie przywykli do tego, że państwowym obchodom przewodziła trójca: arcybiskup Sapieha pomiędzy Kapellnerem-Kaplickim i Mondem", czyli prezydentem miasta i jedynym chyba w Polsce generałem żydowskiego pochodzenia. Zapewne więc duch miasta nie był szczególnie antysemicki.

Czy to znaczy, że Żyda się nie zauważało, nie odróżniało, że włączał się spontanicznie w polskie życie, zaś różnica wyznaniowa nie wpływała na ludzkie zachowania? Nie, tak nie było, co Scharf doskonale pokazuje, a nawet podkreśla. Polacy żyli swoim życiem, Żydzi swoim. Rodzina Scharfa-ojca nie miała żadnych niegospodarczych kontaktów z Polakami. Podobnie na całej ulicy Dietla z okolicami... Jeszcze bardziej zamknięta w swym kręgu była oczywiście żydowska biedota, wszyscy tak liczni rzemieślnicy, przekupnie, pośrednicy i pomocnicy wszelkiego rodzaju. Ale nawet do nich z każdym rokiem wyraźniej docierał wpływ polskiego otoczenia. Podobnie jak z każdym rokiem zaostrzały się spory i niechęci...

Zrozumieć to można, jak postępowała akulturacja, nasilały się ambicje i także — wzajemne pretensje. Ale przeżyć je trudno, a w sobie samym jeszcze trudniej uzgodnić. Stąd także różnice — choć nie — sprzeczności — we wspomnieniach Scharfa. Przeżywa on niezwykle silnie literaturę, kulturę polską, przejmuje, jak tylu innych, wzory myśli i zachowań, także politycznych (czyż Żabotyński nie podziwiał Piłsudskiego?). Ale jednocześnie czuje się odtrącony, boleśnie odczuwa, kiedy między nim a Polakami rośnie mur. Nie może pojąć obojętności, tym zaś bardziej, poczucia wyższości, którego pełno u polskich rozmówców. Czuje, że zbliża się moment wielkich zmian, katastrof może? Decyduje się wreszcie na wyjazd do Palestyny. Ale wcale się tam nie spieszy, bo nie może oderwać się od rodziców, od Krakowa, Europy... Stąd w tych wspomnieniach blisko od sentymentu do pretensji: im bardziej Scharf Kraków i Polskę kocha, tym trudniej mu zrozumieć, czemu rośnie niechęć do Żydów, dlaczego strach przed przyszłością (odczuwany także przez Polaków) wyraża się rosnącym antysemityzmem? Ale i jego osobisty los jest nieustającym paradoksem: ten człowiek, który „nigdy nie był w polskim domu czy mieszkaniu", mówi, że „gdybym się (...) mej polskości pozbył (...) pozostałbym okaleczony".

Bo też „na przekór zwiększającej się pauperyzacji i rosnącej fali antysemityz-mu, lata międzywojenne można uważać za swego rodzaju złoty wiek żydostwa polskiego”.

Jaka to ciekawa, niecodzienna opinia! Zazwyczaj inaczej oceniają te lata Żydzi i nie-Żydzi! Ale Scharf patrzy dalej, głębiej niż polityk czy ekonomista. Za „dominującą cechę” międzywojennej społeczności żydowskiej uważa „pew-nego rodzaju uduchowienie”, świadomość, „że w tym życiu chodzi o coś wię-cej niż o spożywanie chleba”, przekonanie, że „człowiek musi — bez względu na warunki materialne (...) zdążać i przyczyniać się do realizacji jakiegoś ideału, (...) przeświadczenie, że codzienne, godziwe życia, religijna praktyka (...) obcowanie ze słowem bożym (...) przyspieszy przyjście Mesjasza i zapo-czątkuje erę powszechnej sprawiedliwości”. Piękne — ale i osobliwe — słowa... Rozumiem je tak: w tych latach — zapewne za sprawą syjonizmu — ogarnęło wielu polskich Żydów pragnienie wielkiej odnowy, polepszenia i usprawiedliwienia własnego życia; pragnienie, które wyraziło się w dziedzi-nie religijnej, kulturalnej, politycznej... i odnowiło żydowską tożsamość[1]. A wszystko to dokonywało się raczej w sercach niż w praktycznym życiu, nie było więc skażone egoizmem i interesem...

Takie są wspomnienia — i marzenia — Rafaela Scharfa. Jaka szkoda, że nie umieliśmy dostrzec czy wysłuchać takich głosów i tęsknot wtedy, kiedy po-wstawały! Było raczej przeciwnie: przecież w tych właśnie latach antysemicki obłęd ogarniał coraz liczniejsze umysły. Zaś drogi Żydów i Polaków roz-chodziły się coraz boleśniej, coraz okrutniej... Scharf prosi tylko o jedno: o przyznanie, że nie była to wina polskich Żydów. Ta skromna formuła poru-szyła mnie głęboko, kiedy wypowiadał ją przed kilkunastu laty. Ale też ona w istocie wystarcza, aby móc wspólnie zrozumieć i przeżyć te krakowskie lata, jakie podtrzymuje w istnieniu opowieść Rafaela Scharfa.

Jan Błoński

---

[1] Może łatwiej byłoby taki nastrój zrozumieć przez analogię, pamiętając o klimacie przeło-mu lat siedemdziesiątych i osiemdziesiątych w Polsce?

Co mnie i tobie, Polsko...

M uszę wyjaśnić osobliwą formę tej książki. Była ona pisana na przemian, to po polsku, to po angielsku. Odzwierciedla więc trafnie indywidualność autora, tę dwutorowość losu, poplątanie korzeni. W trakcie pisania czułem, że język polski służy mi lepiej do traktowania pewnych okresów czy tematów, angielski — do innych. Potem — to, co było wpierw pisane po polsku, przetłumaczyłem na angielski i *vice versa*. Nie są to zawsze dosłowne przekłady, kiedy mi się wydawało, że tak będzie składniej, pozwalałem sobie odbiegać od oryginału, najczęściej tam, gdzie w wersji polskiej są jakieś cytaty czy echa polskiej poezji niezrozumiałe albo mało znaczące dla czytelnika angielskiego, albo gdzie inny styl wypowiedzi wydawał mi się bardziej odpowiadający duchowi języka.

Ten zbiorek nie jest pomyślany jako książka z początkiem, środkiem czy końcem, do czytania jednym ciągiem. Nie była ona pisana jednym ciągiem, są to fragmenty pisane przy różnych okazjach — glosy marginesowe, refleksje, *pensées*, w zamierzeniu bezpretensjonalne, materiał do dyskusji.

Nie mam obrazu hipotetycznego czytelnika. Większość tych, którzy byli mi znani, poszli z dymem, z tych, co kataklizm przeżyli, wielu już opuściło nas, umierając tą nienaturalną dla Żyda w naszej epoce śmiercią we własnym łóżku i pozostaję w trwałej po nich żałobie. Lata minęły, jak to jest w ich zwyczaju, szybko i niespostrzeżenie, byle szkrab jest po sześćdziesiątce, byle dzierlatka — jeśli się jej poszczęściło — babką.

W żydowskim folklorze jest gadka, że kiedy Anioł Śmierci przychodzi po kogoś i widzi, że ten ktoś jest czymś bardzo zajęty, np. pisze książkę, zostawia go na razie w spokoju i wypełnia kontyngent kimś, kto mu się wydaje gnuśny — stąd rabini zawsze udają, że są bardzo zajęci. (Może, podświadomie, i ja się takim motywem kieruję).

Gdy byłem mały, miałem zwyczaj, w obecności dorosłych, wyrywać się z uwagami jak Filip z konopi (widać zostało mi coś z tego po dziś dzień). Matka studziła mój zapał: nie otwieraj ust, póki nie pomyślisz, co powiedzieć. Odpowiadałem jej z tą nieodpartą dziecięcą logiką: przecież nie wiem, co myślę, dopóki nie powiem. Taka kartezjańska teza: mówię, więc myślę — *loquor ergo cogito*.

Nadałem tej rozprawce tytuł „Co mnie i tobie, Polsko..." Jest to echo Ewangelii św. Jana (2.4), gdzie Jezus strofuje Matkę Boską za to, że go przynagla do sprawienia cudu. (Zawsze ten zwrot brzmiał w mych uszach nienaturalnie — tak arogancko żydowski chłopak nie zwykł był mówić do matki. Istotnie, porównując różne przekłady, okazuje się, że ten passus τι ἐμοι και σοι γύναι nastręczał tłumaczom trudności i może być rozumiany łagodniej aniżeli w utartych wersjach: „Co mnie i Tobie, kobieto..." albo „Co ja mam z Tobą, niewiasto...").

Chcę samemu sobie wyjaśnić raz na zawsze (nie, nie raz na zawsze, a tylko do następnego, głębszego przemyślenia) jakim ja jestem Polakiem, co mnie naprawdę z Polską łączy, jak patrzę na polskie sprawy, dawne i obecne, z perspektywy emigranta-Żyda? Co mnie jeszcze w tym kompleksie spraw podnieca, na co stałem się obojętny? Mówię „ja", ale oczywiście nie o mnie tylko chodzi — gdyby to była wyłącznie moja indywidualna sprawa, nie zdobyłbym się na to, by przyłożyć pióro do papieru.

Mówię o ludziach specyficznej formacji. Jest nas wielu, rozsypanych po świecie, ale niełatwo nas opisać. Spektrum Żydów-Polaków, czy też Żydów polskiego pochodzenia jest rozległe i niewyraźnie zdefiniowane — od skrajnej ortodoksji do skrajnej asymilacji. Są tacy, którzy nici z krajem, w którym się urodzili, całkowicie zerwali, związek z polskością negują, nie chcą o tym słyszeć. Są tacy, dla których definicje i etykietki mało znaczą, weszli w otaczające ich środowisko, nie widzą potrzeby introspekcji czy jakichś abstrakcyjnych ustaleń. Są wreszcie tacy, którzy do pewnych aspektów polskości żywią prawdziwe uczucie. Każda z tych grup, w swych różnych odcieniach, ma świadome i podświadome powody, dla których tak właśnie a nie inaczej na te sprawy patrzy. Fakt, że mam potrzebę wypowiedzenia się na ten temat świadczy o tym, że znajduję się (czy też odnajduję się) bliżej tej ostatniej grupy, aniżeli tych poprzednich. Jak blisko — wyniknie to, mam nadzieję, w toku tych rozważań.

Uważam — i ufam, że nie brzmi to nieskromnie — iż mam do takich rozważań specjalne kwalifikacje. Byłem naocznym świadkiem krytycznego okresu w historii Żydów i Polaków, jednym z ostatnich: potem przyjdzie inny rodzaj przekazu, niejako z drugiej ręki. Przyjdzie też „późny wnuk", w którym rozbudzi się zainteresowanie przeszłością, przyjdzie historyk, który się pożali, żeśmy mu poskąpili świadectwa. Mówimy o rzeczach coraz bardziej odległych, dystans zmienia perspektywę, temperatura doznań opada — o wielu rzeczach mogę powiedzieć za Lechoniem, że „wiem już obojętnie, com wiedział z goryczą..." Mogę mówić na te tematy szczerze i swobodnie, bez żadnych ubocznych motywów. Nie bronię niczyich interesów, nie zależy mi nawet na tym, by kogoś przekonać, mogę się zdobyć na to, by zrewidować wiele przekonań, którym hołdowałem przez lata.

W tym rozdzierającym lamencie żałobnym, jaki Tuwim napisał na wygnaniu, gdy go doszły wieści o zagładzie Żydów w Polsce, zatytułowanym *My, Żydzi polscy*, jest sformułowanie: „Jestem Polakiem bo mi się tak podoba". Zastanawiam się, czy jakiś wariant tej deklaracji nie nadałby się na tytuł moich wynurzeń, na przykład: „Jestem Polakiem, choć mi się to nie podoba", albo

„Jestem Polakiem, choć im się to nie podoba", albo „Jestem Polakiem, bo nie wiem, jak nim przestać być".

Te warianty już same wskazują, jaki to skomplikowany problem: tożsamość Żyda polskiego pochodzenia. W moim wypadku, oczywiście nie tak dramatycznym jak u Tuwima, komplikacja jest potrójna — Polacy mnie zawsze uważali i uważają za Żyda, Żydzi za Anglika, Anglicy za Polaka. Ja z kolei mógłbym powiedzieć, że Izrael uważam za kochankę, Anglię za żonę, Polskę za macochę.

Piszę to półżartem, aby zilustrować głębię tych problemów, ale w istocie ja sam nie mam z tym trudności, nie mam żadnego rozdwojenia jaźni, wiem doskonale i bezspornie, kim jestem, niezależnie od tego, za kogo mnie inni uważają. Jestem Żydem *tout court*, całkowicie, jawnie, naturalnie, oczywiście. W przeciwstawieniu do tego moja polskość wymaga dowodów — i jakieś dowody to ja mam, choć nie przechwalam się nimi i na pewno nie chcę się nikomu narzucać. Pisze gdzieś Kisielewski, że Polska „jest katolicka nie tylko z wiary i tradycji. Polak jest katolikiem z temperamentu, z upodobania i — co najważniejsze, z typu swojego światopoglądu". To wszystko jest mi oczywiście całkowicie niedostępne i obce, dzieli mnie od tego ogromna przepaść.

Czy można się z polskości „wychrzcić"? Świadomie, aktem woli, na zawsze się jej pozbyć? Myślę, że można — szczególnie jeśli się mieszka za granicą, jeśli się ma żal o to, jak wielu Polaków Żydów traktowało, jeśli się przeżywa to, co się z Żydami na polskiej ziemi stało — można się od tego odwrócić, przestać poczuwać się do jakiejkolwiek z tym krajem wspólnoty. Wielu ludzi w moim środowisku to zrobiło, nie widzę w tym nic niegodnego czy fałszywego, wymagam od nich tylko, by wykazali podobną tolerancję wobec mojego stanowiska. Ja mieszkam od ponad półwieku poza krajem, nikt w mojej rodzinie nie mówi po polsku, ni żona, ni dzieci, ni wnuki, nie brałem udziału w życiu emigracji, nie mam żadnego wkładu w dorobek narodowy, materialny czy duchowy — ale „wychrzcić" się z polskości nie chcę. Chociaż czasami różne myśli o Polsce doprowadzają mnie do pasji, chociaż wiele rzeczy, które widzę i które pamiętam, Polskę mi obrzydzają — po prostu nie chcę.

Zastanawiam się, co by ze mnie zostało, gdyby jakimś nakazem ludzkim czy boskim ogołocić mnie ze wszystkiego, co polskie. Więc przede wszystkim z języka, który choć zardzewiały i zaniedbany półwieczem nieużywania został częścią wewnętrznego inwentarza, bez którego wnętrze jest puste. Z tych wierszy co mnie utulają do snu — Asnyka, Konopnickiej, Ujejskiego, Mickiewicza, Słowackiego, Leśmiana, Tuwima, Lechonia, a także — aby było śmieszniej — Boya-Żeleńskiego. Z widoku i zapachu krajobrazu młodych lat (Janusz Korczak podczas swego pobytu w Palestynie żalił się, że eukaliptus nie mówi do niego tym samym językiem co sosna) — więc Wisły i przełomu Dunajca, „kominów" w Strążyskiej i Giewontu, tego podwórka Gomulickiego, gdzie „pościel się wietrzyła... a w kącie dwie akacje marły na suchoty". Bogaty angielski drzewostan to nie to samo co smreki na połoninie i chyba tylko w Polsce lipa (koniecznie rosochata) „rozwija złocisty swój puch".

Gdyby wyzuć się ze wspomnień dzieciństwa i młodości, która wiąże się z tamtym krajobrazem, z pamięci wspólnej przeszłości, dobrej i złej, i wreszcie z tej części osobowości, w której Żydzi upodobnili się do Polaków (i Polacy do Żydów — bo wbrew pozorom to wieloobjawowe podobieństwo doprasza się osobnego studium); gdybym miał wymazać to wszystko — pozostałbym zubożały, jałowy, osierocony, okaleczony. Ta polskość, czy jej resztki — nie wiadomo jak ocenić to czy zważyć — przydaje życiu dodatkowego wymiaru. Kto z nas jest tak bogato wyposażony, by odrzucić ten spadek?

Wydało mi się zrazu, że moje wspomnienia są zbyt fragmentaryczne, że wszystko to działo się bardzo dawno temu, przed potopem, z tamtej strony koszmaru. Ale w pamięci nic nie ginie, nawet to, co zepchnęliśmy do lamusa podświadomości i radzi bylibyśmy zapomnieć. Trzeba tylko odpowiedniego bodźca — dla mnie na przykład spaceru krakowskimi uliczkami — a już „coś się kłębi jak w malignie", „szumią wichry, cieką głębie", jedno wspomnienie zazębia się o drugie, lecą ciurkiem.

Ale postaram się mówić tylko o rzeczach, które, wydaje mi się, rzucają jakieś światło ogólne na pewien ten okres historii, na życie Żydów, ich rysy i obyczaje, zasię wspomnienia tyczące się tylko rodziny i przyjaciół odłożę na inny czas, chyba *ad calendas Graecas*.

Był za moich czasów w Krakowie rabin o nazwisku Szmelkes, nauczał religii żydowskiej uczniów gimnazjów państwowych. Kursowała o nim gadka, że jak go angażowano, by wygłosił jakieś przemówienie okolicznościowe na czyimś ślubie albo innej uroczystości, zwykł był mawiać: „Nu, ja mam takie przemówienie za 150 złotych, mam takie za 100 złotych, mam też takie za 50 złotych. To za 50 złotych, to ja Państwu nie radzę..." Ponosi mnie ambicja, by skonstruować coś może za 100 złotych.

Zaimek osobowy jest najbardziej podejrzaną częścią mowy. Nasz stosunek do słowa „ja" decyduje o naszej osobowości. Czuję się z tym zaimkiem nieswojo i chętnie bym go z tych wynurzeń wyeliminował, ale on tkwi w samym założeniu tematu i nie ma od niego ucieczki. Co mnie ośmiela, by pisać w pierwszej osobie to fakt, że przy czytaniu tego rodzaju memuarów często nasuwała mi się myśl, iż nie ma w nich nic niezwykłego, a jednak ktoś — poza autorem — uznał, że z takich czy innych względów zasługiwały na wydanie. Więc może i to, co ja powiem...

W stylu angielskich wypowiedzi dostrzega się często nutę samopomniejszania — taka jest w Anglii maniera. Nie przyjęła się ona snadź w Ameryce. Przed jednym z moich wykładów na konferencji w Nowym Jorku przyjaciel, który zna moje zwyczaje, ostrzegał mnie, że jeśli w Ameryce mówisz słuchaczom, iż nie jesteś największym znawcą danego przedmiotu, albo masz wątpliwości co do tego, czy twoja wypowiedź jest ostatecznym zdaniem w tej materii

— będą się dziwili po coś przyszedł im zawracać głowę, skoro sam twierdzisz, że jesteś tylko małym pionkiem.

Przypomina się żydowska anegdota, jak to w Sądny Dzień, utartym zwyczajem, przed Arkę Przymierza w synagodze (gdzie spoczywają rodały Tory) wychodzi rabin, bije się w piersi i mówi: „Boże, wybacz mi moje winy, ja jestem tylko prochem i niczym..." W ślad za nim lokalny bogacz bije się w piersi i mówi: „Boże, wybacz mi moje winy, ja jestem tylko prochem i niczym..." Potem wpycha się na to honorowe miejsce najbiedniejszy członek kongregacji i mówi: „Boże, wybacz mi moje winy, ja jestem tylko prochem i niczym..." Na to bogacz poszturchuje rabina: „Popatrz, co za chucpa, co on sobie wyobraża, że on też jest prochem i niczym!"

Mój Kraków to zamierzchłe czasy... Pozostały z nich nazwy ulic na Kazimierzu: Brzozowa, Podbrzezie, Bocheńska, Miodowa, Szeroka, Wolnica, Meiselsa, Plac Bawół...

Zapuszczam się w te zaułki... Zieją pustką, choć mam przed oczyma tę ludzką ciżbę, setki twarzy, które znałem osobiście albo z widzenia, ludzki krajobraz mego dzieciństwa i młodości. „Pełno ich — nigdzie" — mówi Ficowski w wierszu o Korczaku. To poczucie straty nigdy mnie nie opuszcza, ale w Krakowie jest bardziej dotkliwe i namacalne.

Społeczeństwo żydowskie w Krakowie było zróżnicowane i — jak to bywa — skłócone ze sobą. Tylko napór z zewnątrz trzymał to jakoś w kupie. Co miał wspólnego sklepikarz, który sprzedawał na Szerokiej „szwarc, mydło i powidło", z bogaczem, mieszkającym w willi z kortem tenisowym na Zwierzyńcu? Albo mełamed z chederu na Wolnicy z profesorem prawa rzymskiego na UJ? Albo stolarz z Berka Joselewicza z sędzią Sądu Okręgowego, właścicielem pięknego mieszkania przy ulicy Pijarskiej? Tyle chyba, że i jedni, i drudzy byli przedmiotem takich samych ataków ze strony antysemitów. (Dygresja: w poszukiwaniu definicji „kto jest Żydem?" wielki premier państwa Izrael, Ben Gurion, orzekł, że Żydem jest ten, kto się za takiego uważa, albowiem tylko ktoś niepoczytalny podawałby się za Żyda, gdyby nim nie był. Ale ja hołduję prostszej definicji: czy Hitler by cię za to zabił? Jeśli tak, to jesteś Żydem).

Ortodoksi, zgrupowani w partii Aguda, żyli własnym życiem, popierali rząd i nawzajem korzystali z poparcia rządu — jako stronnictwo polityczne byli władzom wygodni. Bund, odmiennie jak w Łodzi i Warszawie, był w Krakowie słaby; potencjalny narybek ze sfer robotniczych i rzemieślniczych ciążył ku lewicowym ugrupowaniom syjonistycznym. Drobnomieszczaństwo było w przygniatającej większości rozparcelowane przez syjonistów — od Haszomer Hacair, poprzez Gordonię, Akibę, Ogólnych Syjonistów („A" i „B"!), rewizjonistów spod znaku Żabotyńskiego. Były nawet korporacje — Kadima, Emuna, El-Al — na modłę korporacji studentów niemieckich (i polskich), małpujące ich rytuał z „komersami", „deklami" i — trudno uwierzyć, ale to fakt — pojedynkami na szpady. Zacietrzewienie partyjne pośród samych syjonistów było ogromne — dochodziło do bójek ulicznych. Rewizjonistyczny Betar nosił, od święta i na parady oraz demonstracje w dzielnicy żydowskiej, mundury domowego wyrobu — ciemnobrunatne koszulki z niebiesko-białymi wyłogami — niefortunny kolor, kojarzący się z hitlerowskimi SA. Żabotyński tłumaczył, że to inny odcień, kolor ziemi palestyńskiej, ale odium przylgnęło. Podczas procesu o zabójstwo członka Agencji Żydowskiej Arlosoroffa, który się toczył w Palestynie, a szczególnie po wyroku skazującym rzekomego zabójcę, Stawskiego, na śmierć, na ulicy żydowskiej aż kipiało.

Moim językiem ojczystym jest polski. W domu Ojciec zwracał się do Matki w jidysz. Matka odpowiadała mu po niemiecku, który znała lepiej niż jidysz. Do mojego brata i mnie Ojciec mówił po polsku — z żydowskim akcentem, Matka — najczystszą polszczyzną, my z bratem między sobą tylko po polsku, podobnie jak z jego i moimi kolegami.

* * *

Kiedyś jidysz nie zasługiwał nawet na miano języka, bowiem w oczach, a raczej w uszach, Polaków i tak zwanych zasymilowanych Żydów był to żargon, szwargot, którym posługiwali się ci czarni, brodaci i pejsaci Żydzi, niewątpliwie knujący coś złowieszczego lub rzucający uroki swym chrapliwym i gardłowym głosem, gestykulując przy tym bez opamiętania.

W rzeczywistości jidysz jest językiem stworzonym i rozwiniętym przez Żydów aszkenazyjskich („aszkenaz" w hebrajskim oznacza Niemcy), pochodzących z terenów Nadrenii, z miast takich jak Moguncja, Wormacja czy Ratyzbona nad Dunajem. Żydzi aszkenazyjscy osiedlili się w centralnej i wschodniej Europie, gdzie wzbogacili swój język słownictwem lokalnych społeczności.

Słownik *Der groyser Verterbuch fun der yidischer Sprach* zawiera 180 000 haseł. Większość z nich wywodzi się z rozmaitych dialektów niemieckich, pod wpływem jidysz zmieniła się jednak ich wymowa i struktura gramatyczna. Część ma swe źródło w języku hebrajskim, np. Starym Testamencie, liturgii i literaturze średniowiecznej. Jest też wiele słów zaczerpniętych z języków krajów zamieszkałych przez Żydów, głównie z polskiego, rosyjskiego, ukraińskiego i białoruskiego. Jidysz stał się swoistą *lingua franca* Żydów Europy, od Holandii poprzez Polskę, Rumunię, Węgry aż po kraje bałkańskie, a potem został wywieziony w bagażu emigrantów za Ocean do Ameryki Północnej i Południowej. Szacuje się, że w przededniu wybuchu drugiej wojny światowej językiem jidysz posługiwało się 11 milionów ludzi. Liczba ta zmniejszyła się dramatycznie w wyniku eksterminacji Żydów i poprzez zmiany kulturowe.

Z nastaniem ruchu syjonistycznego i osadnictwa w Palestynie zaczęto uważać nie bez racji, że jidysz zagraża odrodzeniu języka hebrajskiego. Renesans hebrajskiego miał z założenia towarzyszyć odrodzeniu narodu wybranego na jego własnej ziemi, zdobyciu pustyni, zerwaniu z tradycją diaspory.

W tym konflikcie siły były nierówne. Niemal wszyscy posługiwali się jidysz — było to takie proste. Bardzo niewielu natomiast mówiło po hebrajsku, gdyż było to trudne. Przez dwa tysiące lat hebrajski był językiem martwym; już w czasach Chrystusa nie hebrajskim, lecz aramejskim posługiwano się codziennie w Palestynie. To, że z batalii o język mimo wszelkich przeciwności zwycięsko wyszedł hebrajski, jest swoistym cudem czasów współczesnych i żywym dowodem wytrwałości i uporu Żydów. W pionierskim okresie w Palestynie człowiek, który odważył się mówić w jidysz, wzbudzał pogardę. Nie publikowano niczego w tym języku. Gdy w 1927 roku usiłowano wprowadzić jidysz jako przedmiot na uniwersytecie, podniósł się donośny krzyk, że „do Świątyni ściąga się pogańskich bogów" i projekt ten został zaniechany. Dopiero w 1951 roku, gdy już trzecie pokolenie uważało hebrajski za swój język ojczysty, jidysz został oficjalnie uznany za przedmiot uniwersytecki. Cieszył się teraz powszechnym szacunkiem i prestiżem, które zawdzięczał nostalgii za przeszłością, idealizowaną i bezpowrotnie straconą; odkryciu piękna i wartości literatury w tym języku autorstwa Jehudy Lejb Pereca, Szaloma Alejchema, Mendele Mojcher Sforima, Szaloma Asza, braci Singer i innych; świadomości, że język ten stanowił integralną część narodowego dziedzictwa, i że to on był na ustach ludzi, którzy zginęli.

Isaac Bashevis Singer przyjmując Nagrodę Nobla w dziedzinie literatury powiedział, że zaszczyt, którego dostąpił, jest w rzeczywistości dowodem uznania dla języka jidysz — „języka bez kraju, bez granic, nie będącego na utrzymaniu żadnego rządu ani władców lub możnych tego świata, języka, który jest środkiem wyrazu tysiącletnich doświadczeń Żydów".

Jidysz jest językiem zwięzłym, barwnym, ekspresyjnym, przyziemnym, a jednocześnie jest pełen poetyki, charakterystycznych zwrotów, metafor, przysłów i dowcipu. Odzwierciedla ducha społeczeństwa, które się nim posługiwało — jego charakter, usposobienie, sposób myślenia i poczucie humoru. Jest ciepły, używa wielu form zdrobniałych. Martin Buber zauważa, że gdy Żyd zwraca się do Boga słowem „Gotteniu", oznacza to tak zażyły związek z Bogiem, jaki tylko jest możliwy do osiągnięcia przez człowieka.

Warto zauważyć, że największy komplement, wyróżnienie, hołd złożony drugiej osobie w języku jidysz brzmi: „Er iz a mensch" — on jest człowiekiem, istotą jaką powinno się być, na której można polegać w każdej sytuacji.

W pewnym sensie jidysz jest językiem unikatowym. A mianowicie, niemożliwe jest w nim popełnienie błędu gramatycznego. Jakkolwiek coś zostanie powiedziane, pod warunkiem, że jest jasno wyrażone, nawet za pomocą towarzyszącego temu gestu, to będzie to przyjęte bez krytycznego komentarza. Jeśli chcemy, żeby przedmiot był rodzaju żeńskiego, choć powszechnie uważany jest za rodzaj męski — „zoll zajn", niech tak będzie. Gdy chcemy zmienić szyk wyrazów w zdaniu lub wprowadzić neologizm naszego autorstwa — to proszę bardzo, nie jest to koniec świata (a koniec świata w jidysz też nie jest końcem świata!), nikt z tego powodu nie uzna nas za ignorantów czy prostaków. Nie będzie to „klasyczny" jidysz, ale nie każdy ma ambicję, by zostać Perecem czy Singerem. Jeśli weźmiemy pod uwagę, ile wysiłku, a nieraz i cierpienia kosztowało ludzi poprawne opanowanie w innych językach rodzajników, deklinacji i przypadków, z jaką pogardą spogląda się na tych, którzy popełniają błędy gramatyczne lub mają niewłaściwy akcent, to zrozumiemy jaki wspaniały to język, z jego niezależnością, wolnością i tolerancją, które mogą być przedmiotem zazdrości, ale nigdy nie będą przedmiotem naśladownictwa.

* * *

Mieszkaliśmy w trzypokojowym mieszkaniu z balkonem, na trzecim piętrze, w czynszowej kamienicy na rogu ulicy Sebastiana i Berka Joselewicza. Jak we wszystkich domach w tej dzielnicy, poza stróżem, który ze swą rodziną mieszkał w suterenach, lokatorami byli omal wyłącznie Żydzi — ci zamożniejsi od frontu, ubożsi w oficynach, mikrokosmos żydowskiego społeczeństwa. Na każdym piętrze jakiś mały światek, jakaś balzakowska ludzka komedia, jakaś miłość, jakaś kłótnia, intryga i plotka, od których życie kipiało.

Gdy mowa o tych zamożnych i tych uboższych, trzeba mieć na uwadze żydowskie przysłowie, które w jidysz brzmi *men kenisz szetzen a yidisze kiszke*, co znaczy, że trzeba być ostrożnym w szacowaniu żydowskiej kiesy. Istotnie, podczas gdy było powszechnie wiadomo, co się gotuje w cudzym garnku (nawet jeśli się nic nie gotowało), to utrzymywał się zwyczaj, by prawdziwy stan majątkowy trzymać w tajemnicy, głównie przed Urzędem Skarbowym, a także przed zazdrosnym sąsiadem — ostentacyjne szastanie pieniędzmi uchodziło za prostactwo i głupotę. Wielu Żydów lokowało kapitał w nieruchomościach (stąd nieproporcjonalnie wysoki procent kamienic w żydowskich rękach), także za granicą — w Berlinie i Wiedniu.

Dla ilustracji mała dygresja: tercjanem w Szkole Hebrajskiej przy ulicy Brzozowej był niejaki Hamer. Miał na parterze sklepik z ciastkami i słodyczami, otwarty w czasie pauz i zajęć popołudniowych — kompensowało mu to głodową pensję. Syn Hamera, nie orzeł, ot, jak mówiono na takich, „dupek dzwoncy", po maturze w tej szkole dostał się na wydział lekarski na Uniwersytecie Jagiellońskim. Było jasne, że mogło się to stać tylko za daniem pokaźnej łapówki komuś w administracji wydziału lekarskiego. Istotnie, taki łapówkarski skandal wyszedł na jaw w dochodzeniu policyjnym — i to nikogo nie dziwiło. Dziwiło ludzi tylko — skąd Hamera było na to stać.

„Protekcja", łapówki były integralną częścią systemu, uważano je za rzecz normalną, łagodziły w pewnym sensie rygor prawa. (Inicjały PKP — Polskie Koleje Państwowe — były odczytywane: Płać Konduktorowi Połowę). Wiadomo było, że wszystko da się za pieniądze załatwić, trzeba tylko znać „taryfę" i właściwą drogę. Pani Lustig wiedziała, komu dać w łapę w magistracie, pan Buchholz — na policji, pan Bader w sądzie. Pamiętam, jak jeden z takich pośredników relacjonował mojemu Ojcu rozmowę z urzędnikiem podatkowym: „Stanęliśmy przed tą narożną kamienicą Koernerów (róg Starowiślnej i Dietla), powiedziałem mu — niech pan sobie ten dom obejrzy, on może być pański, jeśli pan tę sprawę dobrze załatwi. Wyobraźcie sobie — tutaj w głosie było zdumienie i oburzenie — on odmówił! Ein solcher Hund — taki pies! Teraz muszę iść do kogoś innego, będzie kosztowało więcej..."

Pieniądze się liczyły jak zawsze, jak wszędzie (liczyły się też później, do pewnego czasu, w getcie), jak to mówi Kochanowski „kto ma pieniądze, ten ma wszystko w ręku..." Ale jest stara tradycja żydowska, która się wyraża talmudycznym zdaniem, że człowiek uczony w piśmie ma pierwszeństwo przed Naczelnym Kapłanem. Ten etos, w szczątkowej formie, przetrwał. Prawdziwym respektem cieszyli się Ozjasz Thon, rabin Kornitzer, dr Chaim Hilfstein — nie zaś Wasserberger, właściciel łuszczarni ryżu w Gdyni, czy pan Lachs z fabryki czekolady Sucharda.

Na parterze w oficynie mojej kamienicy był cheder, przychodzili do niego chłopcy z okolicznych ulic, przyprowadzał ich belfer (pomocnik mełameda), często na siłę. Przez cały dzień, przez niedomknięte okna rozchodził się z podwórza śpiewny, monotonny rytm, jakim dzieci powtarzały za mełamedem wersety Pisma Świętego. Od czasu do czasu słychać krzyk, płacz — to mełamed bije chłopaka pasem lub kańczugiem, tradycyjna metoda wychowawcza.

Byłem w chederze jeden raz, Ojciec uważał, że to należy do moich (a raczej jego) obowiązków, choć Mama się sprzeciwiała. Nie podobało mi się, więcej nie poszedłem. Tych parę modlitw na co dzień Ojciec nauczył mnie „w try miga" — wystarczyły na długo (ale nie na całe życie).

Gorzej, że w podobny sposób zakończyłem — po jednej próbie — lekcje fortepianu. Nauczyciel mi się nie spodobał, groził mi, półgłówek, do dziś mu tego nie wybaczyłem, że jak nie będę ćwiczył, będzie mnie bił po łapach — znowu metoda wychowawcza w moim wypadku najmniej skuteczna. Od takich drobiazgów nieraz zależy cały bieg życia — co ja bym później dał za to, by móc, jak mój brat, zasiąść do fortepianu i zagrać etiudę Szopena. Mam za złe rodzicom, że mi pod tym względem folgowali, wyszłoby na lepsze, gdyby byli czasami surowsi. Snadź nie widzieli potrzeby, w szkole byłem zawsze prymusem, przychodziło mi to łatwo, zbyt łatwo. „Mój Feluś — przechwalała się moja Mama przed sąsiadami — ma »wytrwałe« (to był stopień za pilność), »chwalebne« (to był stopień za zachowanie) i z góry do dołu »bardzo«".

Na parterze mieszkał pan Einhorn z żoną i dwoma synami. Oskar był w wieku mojego brata, Bruno w moim. Pan Einhorn przyjechał do Krakowa z zagranicy, zdaje się z Czechosłowacji, mówił po polsku troszkę śmiesznie, chociaż to samo w sobie nie miało znaczenia, wielu Żydów, jeśli w ogóle mówiło po polsku, mówiło troszkę śmiesznie. Imiona synów — Oskar, Bruno — brzmiały bardziej „postępowo" niż te biblijne, które były w zwyczaju. Wiele można było z imion wyczytać. Mój brat, starszy ode mnie o cztery lata, miał w metryce „Jechiel Kalman 2-ga imion", dziedzicząc je, jak nakazywała tradycja, po jednym z dziadków. Ja już miałem w metryce „Rafael" — o ile mi wiadomo po nikim konkretnym, ot, Mama sobie uroiła, że to brzmi po europejsku, a nie odbiega od tradycji żydowskich — bądź co bądź to Archanioł. Wprawdzie jeden z czterech i to ten, który strzeże „od tyłu" — co brat lubił mi przypominać — ale można się z nim na świecie pokazać. To, że wkrótce i na zawsze Rafael przeobraził się w Felka, zawdzięczam tendencji polskiego języka do zdrobnień (angielski tego nie ma, a szkoda; stół, stolik, stoliczek — całą tę pieszczotliwą gradację trzeba w angielskim tłumaczyć: *table, little table, sweet little table*). Nie można na dziecko wołać: Rafael, więc robi się Rafaelek, stąd już niedaleko do zwyczajnego Felek. Między tym „Jechielem Kalmanem 2-ga imion" (zresztą też szybko przeobrażonym w Kazimierza, Kazika) a Rafaelem mieszczą się cztery lata nieustępliwej walki, krok po kroku, kobiety postępowej, światłej, oczytanej, walki z tradycją rodzinnego domu mojego Ojca. Ojciec tu i ówdzie protestował, dla formy, półgębkiem — w głębi serca przyznawał jej rację i sam się stopniowo emancypował.

Musiało coś być wiadome o przeszłości pana Einhorna, bo moja Mama nie była zachwycona, gdy chadzałem do ich mieszkania bawić się z chłopcami. Mieli duże pudło *Steinbaukasten*, kamyczków budowlanych, z których wznosiliśmy twierdze i mury obronne dla armii ołowianych żołnierzyków — przynosiłem do tych batalii własnych. Chodziła fama, że pan Einhorn przepuścił fortunę grając w karty i musiał z Pragi uciekać, bo za takie nieuiszczone długi honorowe groziły poważne konsekwencje pozaprawne.

Byli i w Krakowie utracjusze, o których wiedziało się, że zaniedbywali rodziny, dni i noce grywali w karty, przepuszczali fortuny (nigdyśmy nie słyszeli o tych, co wygrywali, a jeśli ktoś przegrywał, ktoś inny przecież musiał wygrywać). Jednym z miejsc, gdzie hazard uprawiano, była kawiarnia w hotelu „City" niedaleko Wawelu. Gdy przechodziłem tamtędy z Mamą, kazała mi odwracać głowę, bym nawet okiem nie rzucił na to miejsce występku, co miało skutek odwrotny.

Przekonanie, że karty są diabelskim wynalazkiem sprawiało, że u nas w domu nie było talii kart, nawet do niewinnych gier chłopięcych, i po dzień dzisiejszy nie rozróżniam pików od trefli i kierów od kara. Potem, gdy do Krakowa trafił brydż i wziął go szturmem, moja wczesna awersja przeszkodziła mi w opanowaniu tej wspaniałej gry i pozbawiła na zawsze towarzyskiego atutu. Została mi natomiast niegasnąca pasja do szachów. Gdyby nie purytański nawyk myślowy, że posuwanie figurek po szachownicy, jakkolwiek wyrafinowane, jest koniec końców stratą czasu, mógłbym większość uwagi poświęcić szachom. Dziś to uchodzi za działalność zasługującą na respekt jak każde inne zajęcie, można tym zarobić na utrzymanie, a niekiedy nawet się wzbogacić; wówczas nie było gry mniej popłatnej, wielcy mistrze grywali po kawiarniach o grosze.

Purytanizm dominujący w rodzinie rozciągał się także na alkohol. W domu była zawsze butelka wódki, którą Ojciec częstował gościa-goja, gdy załatwiał z nim jakąś sprawę. Sam nalewał sobie kieliszek z drugiej, identycznie wyglądającej butelki, w której była woda. Może to nietypowe, w tradycji żydowskiej alkohol traktowany jest tolerancyjnie — chasydzi wprowadzając się w stan ekstazy nie gardzili śliwowicą. W Biblii są różne aluzje do konsumpcji wina, zupełna abstynencja jest uważana za odwrót od cywilizacji, w Księdze Przypowieści są zawarte przestrogi, ale i zachęta. Talmud mówi żartobliwie, że w święto Purim należy się tak upić, aby nie rozróżnić między „błogosławieństwem dla Mordechaja, a przekleństwem dla Hamana". Pijaństwo było Żydom obce. Było omal nie do pomyślenia, aby w szynku, nawet w żydowskiej dzielnicy, znalazł się klient Żyd. Był karczmarzem, ale sam rzadko wódki tykał. Była to może reakcja na rozpowszechnione i wulgarne pijaństwo dookoła. Żydowska piosenka brzmi: *sziker iz a goj — szikier iz er — trinken miz er — weil er iz a goj* (goj to jest pijak — pić musi — bo jest goj).

Wracam do kamienicy. Na pierwszym piętrze, po prawej stronie, mieszkali Zuckermanowie. Ojciec miał skład drzewa w Podgórzu, a także tartak i wyrąb lasu na Podkarpaciu. Był u nich w mieszkaniu duży aparat radiowy, rzekomo do odbioru zagranicznych ceduł giełdowych. Mieli czworo dzieci, wszystkie chodziły do hebrajskiej szkoły za rogiem, najstarszy, Baruch, do jednej klasy z moim bratem. Był członkiem partii komunistycznej. Któregoś dnia pod dom, ku wielkiemu poruszeniu przechodniów i mieszkańców, zajechała karetka policji, wysiedli dwaj agenci tzw. Defy w cywilu, zapukali do mieszkania Zuckermanów, przeprowadzili rewizję, tzn. przewrócili mieszkanie do góry nogami w poszukiwaniu „bibuły". Zaaresztowali Barucha, zabrali go do więzienia śledczego „Pod Michałem", którego zakratowane okna wychodziły na Planty. Chodziliśmy go „odwiedzać", staliśmy grupką na trawniku, machaliśmy rękami. Widzieliśmy go w okienku, dawał nam znak zaciśniętą pięścią. To, że rodziców przyprawiał o udar serca, było dla niego mniej ważne niż światowa rewolucja. Wkrótce potem odbył się proces (bo w tej niby dyktatorskiej Polsce nie wolno było trzymać kogoś w więzieniu bez wyroku, a na procesie można się było bronić i robić propagandę). Sprawa pod nazwą „Henner i towarzysze" objęła kilku studentów z Uniwersytetu i kilku gimnazjalistów. Oskarżał prokurator Szypuła, biadał nad zdeprawowaniem młodzieży, podkreślał żydowskie pochodzenie oskarżonych. Bronił ich adwokat Bross, wymownie, ale bezskutecznie. Oberwało się im wszystkim po parę lat, normalna taryfa. Wojna otworzyła bramy więzień. Zuckermana spotkałem po wojnie w Polsce, był jakimś wysokim dygnitarzem — i słusznie, kto miał być, przedwojenny wyrok za „agitację wywrotową" to była bezsporna zasługa.

Na tej samej kondygnacji mieszkała liczna rodzina Apfelbaumów, bardzo ortodoksyjna, trzy pokolenia, brodaci mężczyźni w chałatach, kobiety w perukach, wyrostki w kaszkietach, z pejsami po barki. Nie wiem, z czego oni żyli, uderzało, że wszyscy byli bardzo schludni, można powiedzieć, że na swoją modłę — eleganccy. Nie zamieniłem z żadnym z nich ani słowa, choć grasowałem po tej klatce schodowej bez przerwy i ocierałem się o nich wielokrotnie, ale z jakimś poczuciem zakłopotania, niepewny jak się mam do nich odnieść. Oni, pogrążeni we własnych myślach, jakby mnie, nas, w ogóle nie dostrzegali. Pamiętam jak jednego dnia przeszedłem koło ich mieszkania i zza drzwi doszły mnie wybuchy śmiechu. Jakoś ciarki mnie przeszły, to oni umieją się śmiać? Z czego oni się śmieją?

O piętro wyżej mieszkał pan Danziger z żoną i synem. Pan Danziger był korpulentny, w cwikierze, z pomadowanym, w górę podkręconym wąsikiem. Podczas pierwszej wojny był feldfeblem w armii austriackiej, w gablotce na kredensie w pokoju jadalnym stała jego fotografia w mundurze i *Eiserner Kreuz*. Z zawodu był nauczycielem w szkole na Miodowej. Jego syn Zygmunt, przystojny młodzieniaszek, chodził do gimnazjum św. Jacka na ulicy Siennej. O Zygmuncie nasza służąca Emilia wyrażała się z przekąsem, mówiła o nim, że jest „zepsuty", przypuszczalnie próbował się do niej dobierać, ale bezskutecznie — ona była jak mniszka, i faktycznie, mimo perswazji mojej Mamy, poszła od nas do klasztoru.

Zygmunt miał więcej powodzenia z własną służącą, urodziwą Wandzią. Pani Danziger nie robiła z tego sekretu, tłumaczyła — za Panią Dulską — że przyjęła ją po to, by Zygmunt nie musiał się szwendać po mieście. Gdy Wandzia zaszła w ciążę, pani D. obruszała się, że dziewczyna ją oszukała, gdyż przed wynajęciem wypytywana o swe życie płciowe zapewniała, że jest „bezpieczna", bo już miała trzy skrobanki, a rajfurka potwierdzała, że „na wydeptanej ziemi trawa nie rośnie". Za to dostawała miesięczne wynagrodzenie odpowiednio wyższe od przyjętej stawki — a teraz, patrz... Pani Danzigerowa odprawiła ją oczywiście. Co się z takimi dziewczynami potem zwykle działo, nie wiem — podobne wypadki nie należały do rzadkości. Albo wracały do swej wsi rodzić lub poronić, albo gdy się tego bały, szły do baby w bocznej uliczce, gdzie w oknie wisiała kartka: „Stawia się bańki i pijawki" — procedery uprawiane równolegle z tym głównym.

Z Wandzią był jednak ciąg dalszy. Pamiętam jak jakiegoś dnia zjawiła się przed drzwiami mieszkania Danzigerów, owinięta w chustę, z niemowlęciem przy piersi, waliła w drzwi pięściami i darła się wniebogłosy: „Weźcie sobie tego bękarta!" Drzwi się nie otwarły, Wandzia ochrypła, usiadła na stopniu w sieni tarasując bramę, nikt się nie odważył forsować wyjścia. Nie było jej tam następnego ranka — przypuszczam, że Danzigerowie zapłacili jakiś grubszy okup. Zygmunt, jak mi potem opowiadał, groził rodzicom, że się z nią ożeni.

Na tym samym piętrze, po drugiej stronie korytarza, mieszkali Bertramowie. Panią domu była Salcia Bertram — gorseciarka. To był wówczas ważny i trudny zawód, mówimy nie o takich przewiewnych opaskach i biustonoszach jak dziś, kupowanych w sklepie, ale o kunsztownych pancerzach, robionych na miarę, ze stalówkami, fiszbinami, sprzączkami, tasiemkami do ściskania talii. Taka część garderoby to było nie byle co, wymagała wielkiego mistrzostwa, jak to zrobić, by pasowało tu i tam, jak się w to ubrać (nie mówiąc już o rozebraniu). Pani Bertram miała mały sklepik-pracownię na ulicy Szewskiej, pod szyldem „Gracja" i miała wyszukaną klientelę, nie każdą panią z towarzystwa stać było na gorset od Bertramowej. W tym samym maleńkim lokalu miał warsztat jej mąż, pan Bertram, który był zegarmistrzem. Zawód ten uprawiał między przymiarkami — gdy wchodziła klientka, pan Bertram usuwał się za parawan i starał się nie oddychać.

Młodsza córka państwa Bertram, Olga, była najpiękniejszą dziewczyną w tej okolicy — to nie podlegało dyskusji (a może i w całym Krakowie, co już było sporne, bo konkurencja była ogromna). Olga dobrze podpatrzyła kunszt swojej matki i miała snadź w tym kierunku zdolności — ten talent okazał się zbawczy. W Oldze zakochał się mój przyjaciel, Janek E., z ulicy Brzozowej 13. Na rok przed wojną Janek wyjechał do Ameryki, uzyskał tzw. „pierwsze dokumenty", które go uprawniały do powrotu i w sierpniu 1939 przyjechał do Krakowa, by zabrać Olgę, „jako żonę swą" — jak w piosence — „hen do pałacu bram". Wybuch wojny pokrzyżował te plany, ale po wędrówce przez Rosję, przez Japonię, po kilkunastu miesiącach tułaczki i nieprawdopodobnych zbiegów okoliczności, młoda para wylądowała w Ameryce, w Kalifornii. Potem przychodzi historia jak z amerykańskiej bajki. Olga zrobiła nowy model biustonosza, Janek zaoferował go jednemu z największych domów towarowych — „Bloomingdale" czy „Macy's", dostał duże zamówienie. Trzeba umieć z takich sposobności skorzystać, wybudował fabryczkę, potem większą, założył firmę (oczywiście pod nazwą „Olga"), rzucił jej akcje na giełdę, wzbogacił się. Każdy artykuł, jaki firma produkowała — gorsety, opaski, biustniki („nadupniki" jak zwykł był mawiać) miał etykietkę z fotografią Olgi i slogan: *Behind every Olga garment, there is a real Olga* — czyli że za każdym produktem stoi prawdziwa Olga — ta z ulicy Sebastiana w Krakowie.

Janek pochodził z przeciętnie ortodoksyjnej rodziny — sklep z konfekcją damską na Grodzkiej był oczywiście zamknięty w sobotę, ojciec pokazywał się w synagodze w ważniejsze święta, kuchnia była koszerna, Janek zdawał maturę w hebrajskiej szkole.

W pierwszym liście pisanym zaraz po przyjeździe do Ameryki, liście, który przyjąłem z nieopisaną radością, że on i Olga się uratowali, Janek napomknął, że przystąpił do Kościoła (Episkopalnego? Kongregacjonistów? kto się w tym wyznaje?). Byłem zaskoczony, ale rozumowałem, że ma po temu widocznie swoje utylitarne powody. Tylko takich przechrztów znałem, i choć wzbudzało to we mnie niesmak, przechodziłem nad tym do porządku dziennego. Ale okazało się z dalszej korespondencji, a potem podczas osobistych spotkań, że mamy tu do czynienia z innym fenomenem. Janek — twierdził — przechrzcił się z przekonania (i to nie z takiego przekonania, o jakim mówił jeden z profesorów Uniwersytetu Jagiellońskiego gdy go pytano, czy się przechrzcił z przekonania. „Owszem — odpowiedział — z najgłębszego przekonania, że lepiej zostać profesorem Uniwersytetu w Krakowie, aniżeli nauczycielem Talmudu w Mszanie Dolnej").

Janek twierdził, że objawiła mu się nowa, wielka, olśniewająca Prawda. Nie wiem, dlaczego tak mi trudno było i jest przyjąć to za dobrą monetę, przecież przez wieki miliony ludzi nawraca się na jakąś wiarę i byłoby arogancją powątpiewać w szczerość ich motywów. Ale u Janka, cóż, nie uwierzyłem w jakieś autentyczne, wewnętrzne objawienie, są to zjawiska, do których odnoszę się sceptycznie. Tym bardziej, że — jak się to często zdarza — poszło to w parze z agresywnym potępieniem judaizmu. Od tego czasu nasza wymiana zdań, w słowie i piśmie, przeradzała się wyłącznie w teologiczne dyskusje, w trakcie których on starał się mnie nawracać. W efekcie miało to skutek odwrotny, w poszukiwaniu argumentów zagłębiałem się w praktykę i dogmaty judaizmu, które wydały mi się jakoś bliskie i łagodziły mój bezkompromisowy agnostycyzm. Gdy prosiłem Janka, aby zaprzestał ćwiczenia na mnie swoich misjonarskich talentów, mawiał: „Nie żądaj tego ode mnie, robię to z przyjaźni i szacunku dla ciebie. Ja ujrzałem prawdę — ty pozostajesz na nią ślepy. Mam wewnętrzną potrzebę i wręcz obowiązek starać się otworzyć ci oczy".

Nie ukrywam faktu, że przez te różnice poglądów na podstawowe sprawy oddaliliśmy się od siebie nieco, co mnie smuciło, albowiem mam ogromny sentyment do przyjaciół i przyjaciółek (-ółek nawet bardziej), z którymi chodziłem, jak z Jankiem, do szkoły, na Uniwersytet, i dzieliłem szmat szczęśliwej przeszłości w Krakowie. Uratowało się z nich niewielu, kilku zmarło nienaturalną żydowską śmiercią w łóżku, każdy z nich jest mi drogi.

Wracam do kamienicy. Na drugim piętrze w oficynie było małe mieszkanko, zajęte przez mężczyznę z bródką, w średnim wieku. Był nim Iciu Mann, kantor w bóżnicy. Miał piękny, potężny głos. Z jego mieszkania dochodziły nas często dźwięki arii *Śmiej się, pajacu* i *La donna e mobile*. Pewnego dnia Mann się ulotnił i doszły nas słuchy, że śpiewa w operze w Nowym Jorku. Na Kazimierzu kursowała piosenka: „Czy pamiętasz ty, Iciu, — Te chwile w twym życiu — Gdyś śpiewał w bóżnicy — Na Kupa ulicy".

Trzecie piętro — Scharfowie, Fischer, Rehman. Fischer, szewc, gnieździł się ze swą liczną rodziną — żoną, sześcioma synami i córeczką w maleńkim mieszkanku, jeden pokoik z kuchenką („nie ma ciasnoty w domu matki" — cytował werset z Talmudu). Rehman, jedyny nie-Żyd (poza stróżem) w tej kamienicy, był kominiarzem. Jego matka (jędza nie z tej ziemi), z którą dzielił mieszkanie, miała koncesję, tzw. „rewir", na czyszczenie kominów w określonej dzielnicy, co przynosiło skromny, ale regularny dochód. Młody Rehman uczył się tego zawodu w jakiejś szkole w Austrii. Przy tej okazji nauczył się doskonale niemieckiego (a przez ustawiczne obcowanie z Żydami — jidysz). Rosły młodzieniec, wesoły, inteligentny, oczytany, w wolnych chwilach przesiadywał na ganku, rozwiązywał krzyżówki, które zaczęły się wtedy ukazywać w gazetach. Z moimi rodzicami i z resztą lokatorów był w najlepszej komitywie, a jeśli wierzyć plotce — szczególnie zażyłej z panią Glass z sąsiedztwa — kiedy u Glassów urodził się syn, doszukiwano się podobieństwa. Pamiętam Franka Rehmana w pełnym stroju kominiarskim, na czarno, z czapeczką, z szuflą na jednym ramieniu, na drugim zwój drutów zakończony miotełką i dużą żelazną kulą — jak na starych forografiach (spotkanie z kominiarzem uchodziło za dobry omen). Widywałem go, jak się wspinał na dachy okolicznych kamienic, wpuszczał żelazną kulę do komina, w ślad za nią, rozwijając drut, pchał miotłę. Wracał do domu całkowicie umorusany, twarz, ręce i ubiór pokryty sadzą — tylko łypał białkami oczu.

Kiedy moja Matka, gdy przyszedł nakaz pójścia do getta, opuszczała Kraków i wyjeżdżała do Warszawy, gdzie było się łatwiej ukryć, powierzyła wszystko, co miała wartościowego w mieszkaniu, zwłaszcza liczne obrazy, pieczy Rehmana, jednego z bardzo niewielu znanych jej nie-Żydów. Miał on jej adres w Warszawie i od czasu do czasu, na żądanie Matki, spieniężał jakiś obraz i przesyłał jej pieniądze. Jemu samemu nie było łatwo — z niemieckim nazwiskiem i znajomością języka mógł uchodzić za folksdojcza. Istotnie wywierano na niego presję, by „podpisał listę", ale skutecznie się temu opierał, bez względu na konsekwencje. Po wojnie wszystko, co zostało, oddał — co może nie zasługiwałoby na wzmiankę, gdyby nie to, że w większości analogicznych wypadków było, niestety, odwrotnie. Nieszczęśników, którzy zgłaszali się po odbiór przechowywanych rzeczy, często wyrzucano za drzwi. Rehman należał do rzadkości.

Ot jedna, zwyczajna kamienica — jedno pasemko w tkaninie, kamyk w mozaice. Nic, nic się z tego nie ostało.

Panny na wydaniu dzieliły się w pierwszym rzędzie na te, o których wiadomo było, że miały posag i te, które go nie miały. Były też oczywiście małżeństwa z miłości, ale panowało nagminne przekonanie, że panna ma mieć posag, i to w odwrotnej proporcji do urody. Stanowiło to niewyczerpany temat rozmów i plotek przy stolikach kawiarnianych, domyślano się ile, gdzie, w jakiej walucie, w postaci jakiej kamienicy. Pan F., na przykład, dał swej córce w posagu kamienicę czynszową przy ulicy Berka Joselewicza, w której rzekomo dawno temu (ale krakowianie takich rzeczy nie zapominali) mieścił się dom publiczny. Wzbudziło to w Krakowie chichot (może z zazdrości — rzeczona córka była bardzo urodziwa i znalazłaby, gdyby jej pozwolono, niejednego amanta) — mówiono, że Frydzia dostała w posagu bajzel, a że mężowi dostał się róg obfitości, a także obfitość rogów. Wiedziano też, kto był łowcą posagów; panowie z tytułami — lekarze, adwokaci, inżynierowie — mieli „taryfę". Liczył się także „yichus", tj. swoista arystokracja, dobre imię rodziny, wynikające bądź to z pochodzenia rabinackiego, bądź ze starego majątku. Ojcowie za główny cel i obowiązek swego życia uważali dorabianie się majątku gwoli wyposażenia córek.

Gdy moi rodzice się pobierali, „partia" oczywiście była swatana. W rodzinie kursowała gadka, że mój Ojciec domagał się zapewnienia — i poszedł sam sprawdzić z oddali — że przyszła oblubienica nie jest rudowłosa. Wiedziano, że dziewczyny z domu Loewi, przyrodnie siostry mojej Matki, były rude.

W tamtym społeczeństwie swat to była instytucja nieodzowna. Jakżeby inaczej panna „z dobrego domu" miała znaleźć męża? Sposobności do poznania z osobą płci męskiej, rozmawiania, zaprzyjaźnienia się — nie mówiąc już o czym innym — poza kręgiem rodzinnym nie było. Panny dorastały w owym czasie (mówię o schyłku XIX wieku, potem postęp — czy też regres — potoczył się szybko) — nie tylko w dziewictwie, ale często w nieświadomości spraw seksualnych. Nieraz dopiero w ostatniej chwili któraś z mądrych ciotek uświadamiała pannę młodą, czego ma się spodziewać w noc poślubną. Czy narzeczonego też trzeba było uświadamiać, nie wiem — przypuszczam, że współżycie w grupie, w chederze, w jeszybocie, dawało wiele sposobności do obgadania tych spraw, ba, podejrzewam, że poza analizą świętych tekstów były one głównym tematem rozmów. Co się w takich warunkach w noce poślubne pod pierzyną rozgrywało, trudno sobie dziś wyobrazić — myślę, że nie było to źródłem obopólnej ekstazy.

Swat kojarzył pary, które — wedle jego znajomości natury ludzkiej i spraw finansowych — rokowały dobre współżycie. A więc brał pod uwagę pochodzenie, wygląd, wykształcenie, stan majątkowy i pośredniczył w delikatnych rokowaniach tyczących się posagu. Oczywiste, że podstawą takiej transakcji nie była miłość — to pojęcie z innej planety — ale przyjęcie obowiązującej konwencji. Staropanieństwo uchodziło za najgorszy los, jaki może kobietę spotkać. Groźbę „urośnie ci, panno, siwy warkocz" traktowano poważnie. Społeczeństwo czuło się odpowiedzialne za wydanie za mąż dziewcząt, które nie miały nikogo, kto by się o nie zatroszczył. Na czyją łaskę zostawały one potem zdane, nietrudno sobie wyobrazić, ale i to było lepsze niż nic.

Mąż miał być w pierwszym rzędzie tym, który zarabia i utrzymuje rodzinę — żona tą, która troszczy się o dom, przygotowuje posiłki, rodzi dzieci i je wychowuje. To był podstawowy podział ról — życie oczywiście tworzyło różne warianty. Często się zdarzało, że ciężar zarobkowania spadał także na żonę.

W rodzinach ortodoksyjnych, zamożnych, była jeszcze inna konwencja. Ojciec córek objeżdżał jeszyboty, robił lustrację zdolnych studentów w odpowiednim wieku i spośród nich wybierał zięcia. Taki wybraniec zostawał całe życie „na garnuszku", tzw. *kest* u teścia. Nie miał innych obowiązków jak ślęczeć nad księgami i płodzić dzieci.

Rozwody należały do rzadkości. Nie były w zwyczaju, nadzieja na szczęście w małżeństwie była mała, mężowie z reguły nie pili, ani żon nie bili, sposobności do stosunków pozamałżeńskich było niewiele, sąsiedzka kontrola była surowa, troska o los dzieci głęboka. Nade wszystko — gdzie się rozwódka miała podziać, jaki los ją czekał? Wszystko to przyczyniało się do stabilności związku. Wedle żydowskiego prawa rozwodowego mąż jest tym, który daje rozwód żonie, jeśli ma takie życzenie (wiemy jak Praojciec Abraham bezceremonialnie wystawił za drzwi swą żonę, Hagar, z małym Ismaelem — nienawiść Arabów do Izraela ma starożytne korzenie!) — i odmawia rozwodu, jeśli go nie chce — w ortodoksyjnych sferach żydowskich do dziś te przepisy prowadzą czasem do tragicznych dla kobiet sytuacji i są przedmiotem ostrych dyskusji, jak to prawo interpretować.

W tym systemie kobieta nader często wychodziła za mąż poniżej swego stanu, nie mogła wiele przebierać, presja na nią była nieodparta. Tak i moja Matka, która miała macochę, nie mogła sobie pozwolić na kaprysy. Przyjęła swój los z dobrą miną. Zdawała sobie sprawę z różnicy poziomu kultury: ona pochodziła ze średniozamożnego domu, jej ojciec był handlarzem wina sprowadzanego z Węgier — miała „kindersztubę", maniery, przeszła przez dobrą niemiecką szkołę, była oczytana w niemieckiej literaturze (co się w pewnej chwili okazało zbawcze), także — nieco mniej — w polskiej. Wywierała cywilizujący wpływ na dom i na Ojca. Miała, trzeba przyznać, więcej od niego czasu. W domu zawsze była służąca, nadzorowanie skromnego gospodarstwa nie pochłaniało zbyt wiele czasu. Zostawało go dość na czytanie książek z wypożyczalni Gumplowicza, na pracę charytatywną — w Domu Sierot, w szkolnym Komitecie Rodzicielskim. Matka brała też udział w zbiórkach ulicznych na cele dobroczynne, przygotowywała posiłki dla starych, samotnych ludzi w okolicznych domach. Popołudnia często spędzała w kawiarniach, plotkując z kumami.

Było też o czym.

— Co powiecie na to, że wczoraj pani N. wpadła jak bomba do „Secesji", gdzie jej mąż grał w karty i zrobiła mu taką awanturę, że się biedak nie może pokazać na ulicy, zrujnowała mu życie… Panu K., który dzień i noc wysiaduje przy stoliku kawiarnianym, coś takiego by się nie mogło przydarzyć, ha, on by takiej kości połamał… — Wiecie, kogo swatają tej brzydkiej córce Nattlów? Doktora S. z Przemyśla, mówią, że on dostanie katedrę na UJ. Nasza Stasia, która się przyjaźni z Maryną od Nattlów, mówiła, że on był u nich wczoraj na uroczystej kolacji, oblewali zaręczyny, na odchodne wsunął Marynie w rękę suty napiwek i przy tym uszczypnął ją w tyłek, że aż gwiazdy zobaczyła… — Pan B. z Grodzkiej, żona mu niedawno umarła, jeszcze ciało ciepłe, on się dostawia do tej aktoreczki z teatru Słowackiego, co była u nich sublokatorką, mógłby być jej ojcem, wstyd... — Czytaliście, było we wszystkich gazetach, adwokat G. zadał się z jakąś kurwą i ona, tak w „Kurierku" stoi, ugryzła go w język? Krasomówcą już nie będzie, a taki miał cięty ozór. — Wiecie, ten nauczyciel łaciny z hebrajskiego gimnazjum, Bronstein, uczniowie go uwielbiają, ale dr Hilfstein, który tam rządzi, wymówił mu posadę, rzekomo jest podejrzany o komunizm, z tym nazwiskiem to chyba jakiś krewny Trockiego. — Patrzcie, Jasia B. sąd zwolnił w tej sprawie o zabójstwo M., on się tłumaczył, że to był pojedynek, jaki tam pojedynek... Musieli grubą łapówkę za ten wyrok zapłacić, stać ich na to... — Syn Lustigowej, tej przekupki ze Starowiślnej, dostał się na medycynę, wiadomo, ona wszystko potrafi... Tak się to dobrodusznie suchej nitki na nikim nie zostawiło — przy jednej kawie z pianką.

Ojciec był surowy, nie było z nim dyskusji, uważał za prawo natury, że ma pierwsze i ostatnie słowo w każdej sprawie. Nie do pomyślenia, aby przewinął pieluchy albo wziął dziecko na rękę, gdy płakało, aby pchał wózek albo nosił torbę z zakupami. Do kuchni nigdy nie zaglądał, przed pójściem spać uchylał drzwi i wstawiał tam swe buty do czyszczenia, rano stały wypucowane przed drzwiami do kuchni. Wracał na obiad z biura, które było niedaleko (w Krakowie nic nie było daleko), przed powrotem do pracy ucinał drzemkę popołudniową — chodziliśmy wtedy na palcach, mówiliśmy szeptem.

Koncentrował się całkowicie na pracy zarobkowej, na zdobywaniu lepszej pozycji materialnej — co mu się, w skromnym zakresie, udawało. Był wpierw subiektem w handlu skór, potem, jak to bywało z żydowskimi subiektami, otworzył własny skład w tej branży, konkurując z byłym szefem. Nieco później awansował na przemysłowca — firma pod nazwą Wiedeńska Fabryka Pasów Transmisyjnych wyrabiała prymitywnymi środkami ten właśnie produkt; Wiedeń znalazł się na szyldzie tylko dlatego, że sugerował wysoką jakość.

O jego byłym szefie, który uchodził za spryciarza, różne chodziły gadki. Mówiono, że w biurze na chwilę nie spuszcza z oka swoich urzędników, a kiedy któryś z nich idzie do toalety, patrzy na zegarek jak długo trwa załatwienie tego interesu. Ci, którzy wracają do biura truchcikiem, zapinając rozporek, widać wiedzą, że czas to (szefa) pieniądz i zasługują na podwyżkę przed swoimi, mniej rączymi kolegami. Mój ojciec snadź należał do tych, którym się nie spieszyło i, w efekcie, nie zagrzał tam miejsca.

Pieniądze na utrzymanie domu i gospodarstwo Ojciec wydzielał Matce skromnymi dawkami, nigdy nie stracił poczucia niepokoju, że nie będzie dosyć, że przyjdzie czarna godzina. W latach trzydziestych słowem, które się najczęściej przez rozmowę przewijało, był „kryzys"; obiektem, który wzbudzał w nas respekt i trwogę był „weksel", których Ojciec miał stos na biurku. Często gęsto taki weksel, gwarancja zapłaty, nie był przez dłużnika honorowany i wtedy szedł w obieg, „do protestu", tj. do pierwszego na liście żyranta — potem, wzbogacony o odcinek papieru z pieczątką, do następnego i tak dalej, aż znalazł się na liście ktoś, kto dług uiścił, albo i nie. Czasami taki protestowany weksel był długi na metry, pamiętam te wstęgi papieru jako symbol kryzysu. Bankructwa osób, upadłości firm były na porządku dziennym — prawdziwe i oszukańcze — prowokując reakcję łańcuchową. „Scharf nie bankrutuje" — mawiał Ojciec z dumą, jakby sam fakt, że — w odróżnieniu od otoczenia — zaciągnięte długi się płaciło, należał do rzadkości.

Nawet w maleńkim Krakowie, gdzie dzielnica żydowska, Kazimierz, stykała się i przeplatała z nieżydowską, a wiele rodzin żydowskich mieszkało w dzielnicach nieżydowskich, w centrum lub na peryferiach — było to życie osobne. Można było normalnie egzystować, tj. dorastać na łonie rodziny, uczyć się, szkolić w zawodzie, uprawiać handel i rzemiosło, na swój sposób używać życia, nie wychodząc poza krąg żydowskiej społeczności. Poważny jej odłam, od Nalewek w Warszawie do Kazimierza w Krakowie, poprzez dziesiątki miasteczek, poza sporadycznym kontaktem z polskim dostawcą czy klientem, tak właśnie żył — nie wspólnie, a obok, na liniach równoległych, w akceptowanej, naturalnej izolacji.

Przez całe moje życie w Krakowie, aż do wyjazdu tuż przed wojną, nie byłem nigdy w polskim domu, którego zapach pochwycony przelotnie, przez uchylone drzwi, był jakiś dziwnie inny, obcy. Nie brakowało mi tego, uważałem to za rzecz naturalną. Nie pamiętam też, by w naszym domu, często pełnym gości, przejezdnych, interesantów, kolegów moich i mojego starszego brata, kiedykolwiek postała noga „goja" — poza jednym sąsiadem i stróżem, który przychodził inkasować za „szperę" i, oczywiście, służącą mieszkającą w kuchni.

Kuchnia była przestronna, ciekawsza niż salon, spędzałem w niej dużo czasu — uczyłem się wielu rzeczy od tej czy innej służącej — niektóre z nich służyły u nas po parę lat, czasem do zamążpójścia. Były to dziewczyny ze wsi, dla których brakło miejsca w rodzinnej chałupie — służba przy mieszczańskiej żydowskiej rodzinie oznaczała dla nich awans społeczny i schron przed niebezpieczeństwami miejskiego bruku. Uczyły się manier, mówienia „po miejsku". Pracowały ciężko — sprzątały, szorowały podłogi, wiórowały parkiety, trzepały dywany na stojaku w podworcu, nosiły węgiel z piwnicy (u nas — na trzecie piętro), paliły w dużych, kaflowych piecach, wynosiły z nich popiół. Gdy dochodząca praczka prała bieliznę w balii, nosiły w koszu mokrą bieliznę na strych, potem do magla, potem prasowały. Wstawały wcześnie — niejeden raz słyszałem jak moja Mama, skądinąd uosobienie dobroci, mawiała: „Nie leniłam się posłać Kasię po świeże pieczywo o 6 rano". Szły spać, gdy wszyscy inni członkowie rodziny pogasili światła — pozostawiwszy w kuchni buty do wypucowania.

W niedzielę miały wychodne — Kasia, Wandzia czy Zocha szły do kościoła, skąd przynosiły dewocjonalne gazetki („Dzwon Niedzielny", „Rycerz Niepokalanej") — pełne paskudnych karykatur i antyżydowskiego jadu, chyba celowe *antidotum* na kontakt z Żydami, których obserwowały z bliska i widziały, że nie tacy straszni jak ich malują. Szła Kasia potem na spacer na Planty albo pod Wawel, pod pachę z kawalerem, przeważnie żołnierzem (Kraków był miastem garnizonowym). Pod wieczór przyprowadzała go do domu, gdzie wysiadywali do późna na schodach w oficynie, dokąd mu wynosiła ze spiżarki specjały, jakich w koszarach nie dostawał — sukcesy, chyba nie jedyne, jego zalotów.

Gdy byłem małym chłopcem, moja Matka zabierała mnie czasami na zakupy w sercu Kazimierza, na Placu Nowym, czyli jak nazywaliśmy go Fiszplacu, z jatkami i sklepikami w okrągłym, ceglanym budynku. Pamiętam ten proceder — wpierw, po targu, kupno żywej kury albo gęsi, nie w jatce, a od przekupki pod gołym niebem (było snadź o grosik taniej). Potem ubój — ptakowi, który głośno, ale bezskutecznie protestował, rzezak czekający obok podrzynał gardło wedle przepisanego rytuału, tj. jednym cięciem wyszlifowanego noża — nóż nie może mieć nawet mikroskopijnej szczerby — strumień krwi spływał do ścieku. Stamtąd do stoiska skubaczek. Kilka kobiet z chustami na głowach siedząc na zydlach skubało ptaka, piórka fruwały aż w oczach się dwoiło — trwało to parę minut, zapłatą zdaje się był ten puch i pióra, dla dużych handlarzy artykuł eksportowy. Nagie, białoróżowe, odrażające zwłoki owinięte w gazetę szły do przepaścistej torby, by na stole kuchennym poddać się dalszej operacji.

Wiele wspomnień łączy się z boiskiem sportowym „Makkabi", u wylotu ulicy Koletek i Dietla, sceną meczów piłki nożnej w lecie („bez względu na pogodę" — jak głosiły afisze), a ślizgawki w zimie. Grać w pierwszej drużynie piłki nożnej było ambicją każdego żydowskiego wyrostka, nazwiska tych futbolistów były wszystkim znane, pamiętam je do dziś. (Wychodził przez jakiś czas w Krakowie tygodnik „Karykatury", głównie zajmował się sportem, pamiętam stamtąd taki kuplet: „Czy mróz czy upał, pogoda czy burza / Kopie Synowiec, Przeworski, Kałuża / Dziecko co za pierś jeszcze trzyma mamkę / Już chce pod bramkę..." — wymienieni to gracze „Cracovii"). Był jeszcze drugi klub żydowski, „Jutrzenka", z boiskiem na Błoniach, grali w koszulkach w pasy czarno-białe („Makkabi" oczywiście miała pasy biało-niebieskie), ale to był klub robotniczy, nie syjonistyczny, więc nie cieszył się naszym fanatycznym poparciem.

Parkan otaczający boisko „Makkabi" miał szpary i dziury, przez które widać było część boiska. Podczas meczów parkan był zawsze gęsto obstawiony („odsuń się ty taki owaki — to jest moja dziura!"). Z okien paru okolicznych domów, godnych zazdrości, widać było jedną bramkę. Miałem dostęp do takiego okna na pierwszym piętrze domu od strony ulicy Koletek, w mieszkaniu rodziny Simanowicz. Ojciec rodziny, uczony w piśmie, był częściowo sparaliżowany. Na krótko przed wybuchem wojny młody Simanowicz otrzymał za sprawą swego brata, który już był w Palestynie, „certyfikat" dla siebie i matki. Nie sposób było jednak zostawić ojca samego. Pewnego dnia ojciec dowlókł się do okna i „wypadł" na bruk, by uwolnić ich od ciężaru.

Szkoła — „Szkoła Powszechna i Gimnazjum Hebrajskie" przy ul. Brzozowej 5 by wymienić oficjalną nazwę — to był zakład wychowawczy z przepisanym przez Ministerstwo Oświaty świeckim programem w języku polskim, co po maturze dawało automatyczny wstęp na większość wydziałów Uniwersytetu. Równolegle z nauką przedmiotów świeckich biegł program nauki w języku hebrajskim — Biblii, historii Żydów i żydowskiej literatury, łącznie 10 godzin tygodniowo — wedle modelu szkolnictwa hebrajskiego rozwiniętego w Polsce. Od założenia szkoły aż do wybuchu wojny przeszło przez nią ponad 2000 wychowanków, którzy żywili dla niej prawdziwy kult. Po dziś dzień wspominamy te bezgrzeszne lata, spędzone pod opieką niezapomnianego grona nauczycieli — z których nikt prawie nie przeżył. Była to niejako oaza, w której można się było cieszyć złudnym przeświadczeniem, że świat jest i pozostanie życzliwy.

Nie wszyscy moi koledzy-Żydzi chodzili do Hebrajskiego Gimnazjum przy ul. Brzozowej — dla wielu to było za daleko — za wielki dystans fizyczny i kulturowy. Państwowych gimnazjów było w Krakowie wiele, dziewięć mówiąc ściśle, odróżniających się typem programu: klasycznym, humanistycznym czy matematyczno-przyrodniczym, i kolorem opaski na uczniowskiej czapce — od czerwonej Nowodworskiego–św. Anny do brązowej Jaworskiego. (My, zgadliście, mieliśmy niebiesko-białą). O gimnazjum Jaworskiego jakiś jego wychowanek powinien szerzej napisać. To był niejako azyl dla uczniów wyrzuconych za różne przekroczenia z innych gimnazjów. Łagodziło to, krakowskim zwyczajem, rygor prawa i dawało ponowną szansę zdania matury tym, którzy w innych miastach, w analogicznych wypadkach, dostaliby tzw. „wilczy bilet", czyli zakaz nauki w gimnazjum, co zamykało drogę do studiów uniwersyteckich. W efekcie u Jaworskiego gromadziła się banda zawadiaków, którą trudno było utrzymać w ryzach, nie mówiąc już o nauce — ale jeśliby ktoś chciał sobie zadać trud, znalazłby pośród nich wiele ciekawych i utalentowanych indywidualności.

Między innymi znalazł się tam, w 6 klasie, mój przyjaciel Maks Boruchowicz (alias Michał Borwicz). Ktoś doniósł dyrektorowi naszej szkoły, że Maks przemawiał na jakimś wiecu politycznym. Dyrektor nie miał wyboru, musiał wyciągnąć z tego konsekwencje. Nasza szkoła miała prawa szkoły publicznej i była pod baczną obserwacją Kuratorium. Podejrzenie, że toleruje się wśród wychowanków jakieś lewicowe ciągoty, było niebezpieczne. Dyrektor przywołał do siebie matkę Boruchowicza i kazał jej zabrać Maksa ze szkoły. Poszedł naturalnie wprost do „Jaworka", gdzie zaprzyjaźnił się z wyrzutkiem z innego gimnazjum — Józkiem Cyrankiewiczem. Stali się nierozłączni, ich wspólna działalność w PPS, w różnych kółkach na Uniwersytecie Jagiellońskim, gdzie organizowali najrozmaitsze wieczory dyskusyjne, polityczne i literackie, wywierały piętno na życiu Krakowa. Ich drogi się rozeszły, gdy po wojnie Cyrankiewicz dał *placet* na tzw. „fuzję" PPS z PPR — wiemy, co to za „fuzja" była, wilka z jagniątkiem. Boruchowicz uważał to za zdradę. Cyrankiewicz został premierem, Boruchowicz musiał z Polski uciekać. Osiadł w Paryżu, gdzie go do końca jego życia odwiedzałem i gdzie prowadziliśmy rozhowory o naszej młodości i o starym Krakowie, jak już niewielu potrafi.

Trójkątny plac między ulicami Berka Joselewicza, Brzozową i Sebastiana był od rana do nocy sceną gier i zabaw wyrostków. Tu miejscowe urwisy grały w palestrę (gra gdzie indziej zwana kiczką), w zbója i żandarma, w szmaciankę — o prawdziwej piłce nożnej, takiej z gumowym „szlauchem" i skórzanym „mantlem" oczywiście nie można było marzyć. Szmacianka — pończocha upchana na twardo łachami, opleciona sznurkiem w kształt kuli — zrobić taką, by się nadawała do kopania w kurzu i błocie, to był specjalny kunszt. Królował tutaj we wszystkich grach syn naszego stróża z ulicy Sebastiana 33, obdarty, bosy i rachityczny, ale zręczny jak małpa. Często popisywał się na chodniku przed domem chodzeniem na rękach — podziwiałem go i zazdrościłem mu tej sztuki; o tym, żeby się z nim wspólnie bawić, mowy być nie mogło.

W suterenach kamienic, w norach od podworca, dokąd promień słońca nigdy nie docierał, gnieździła się biedota. Wieloosobowe rodziny, bose, suchotnicze, rachityczne dzieci były częścią ulicznego krajobrazu. Tylko raz w życiu odbyłem „wizję lokalną" w takich mieszkaniach — podczas spisu ludności studenci jak ja działali jako urzędnicy wypełniający formularze. Kto z nas wtedy po tym doświadczeniu nie chciał zostać rewolucjonistą i obalić system, który to tolerował? Mówiono, że najlepszym materiałem propagandowym na rzecz komunizmu była oficjalna publikacja *Mały Rocznik Statystyczny*, ukazujący się w czerwonych okładkach.

Wracam do tego, że chciałbym się przedstawić jako dziecko Kazimierza.

„Mój" Kraków (używam tego zaimka bez oporu i wahania) to nie był *sensu stricto* Kazimierz, a w każdym razie nie tylko Kazimierz. Chodziłem po nim od czasu do czasu — odwiedzałem kolegę, szedłem na przedstawienie do żydowskiego teatru na Bocheńskiej, albo na zebranie protestacyjne na podwórzu kamienicy Sussera na Krakowskiej. Ale codzienna trasa po szkole, która mieściła się na rogu Brzozowej i Podbrzezia, prowadziła z kamienicy przy ulicy Dietla, trzeci dom od rogu Starowiślnej (rodzice przeprowadzili się tam z ul. Sebastiana nr 33, gdy miałem 14 lat), w stronę Śródmieścia, wzdłuż Starowiślnej, Sienną, do Rynku, na przestrzał Sukiennic, ulicą Szewską, na Planty, pod Uniwersytet i ulicą Wolską na Błonia, albo wprost Karmelicką do pływalni w Parku Krakowskim. Pamiętam, że idąc obok kościoła Karmelitów, gdzie na rogu Garbarskiej we wnęce wiszą trzy ogromne, ukrzyżowane figury, przechodziłem na drugą stronę ulicy, by na to nie patrzeć.

Mogłoby się komuś wydawać z tej litanii ulic, że to jakiś ogromny obszar — w rzeczywistości to wszystko było małe, do obejścia na piechotę, nie dało się tam zgubić. Czasami, gdy wieczorem wracałem do domu po jakiejś schadzce na peryferiach, mój Ojciec już wiedział z kim mnie widziano i gotowa awantura. Można się było zaszyć w czeluści kina — taktowny operator w kinie „Promień" dawał sygnał dzwonkiem, że seans dobiega końca. Kin było wiele — „Uciecha" i „Nowości" na Starowiślnej, „Wanda" na Gertrudy, „Lubicz" na Lubicz, „Sztuka" na Tomasza, „Apollo" tam gdzie teraz, „Warszawa" na Stradomiu. Oglądało się wczesne filmy amerykańskie z Jackie Cooganem i Charlie Chaplinem, Haroldem Lloydem, *Tarzana* z Johnny Weismüllerem, kowbojów jak Tom Mix, Gretę Garbo. Potem niemieckie z Martą Eggert-Kiepura, Emilem Janningsem, Franciscą Gaal, Lilianą Harvey, Marleną Dietrich, francuskie z Maurice Chevalierem, Charlesem Boyer, Danielle Darieux. No, i jeśli ktoś chciał — polskie ze Smosarską, Eugeniuszem Bodo, Junoszą Stępowskim, Brodziszem. (Słonimski w odpowiedzi na ankietę „Wiadomości Literackich" *Jaki film zagraniczny i jaki film polski uważasz za najlepszy* napisał: „Za najlepszy film zagraniczny uważam *Vive la Liberté* René Claire'a, na polskie nie chodzę").

Filmy były jedną formą rozrywki, drugą równie częstą był Teatr Słowackiego. Nie pamiętam, abym kiedy kupił bilet wstępu — mieliśmy „zblatowanego" portiera, który za parędziesiąt groszy wpuszczał nas na „jaskółkę". Dyrektorami teatru byli w owych czasach Teofil Trzciński, potem Zygmunt Nowakowski (którego miałem sposobność w czasie wojny spotkać w Londynie jako redaktora „Wiadomości" Grydzewskiego), potem Osterwa. Repertuar był urozmaicony, przeważał oczywiście lekki. Pamiętam wodewile *Krakowiacy i Górale*, *Krowoderskie Zuchy*, sztukę amerykańską *Artyści* z Jaraczem i uwielbianą przez nas Jaroszewską, węgierskie komedie Molnara i Bus-Fekete (Słonimski pisał, że dowcipuszki węgierskiego Busa go nie bawią). Grano Szekspira, Bernarda Shawa — wiele jego sztuk, w tłumaczeniu Sobieniowskiego, miało swoje prapremiery w Polsce, nim jeszcze ukazały się na deskach teatrów Anglii. (Ciekawostka: Król Magnus w sztuce *Applecart*[1] do dziś w wielu inscenizacjach jest przedstawiany w kołpaku z piórem, tak jak Matejko malował Stefana Batorego). No i oczywiście pełny wachlarz klasycznego repertuaru polskiego — Słowacki, Mickiewicz, Wyspiański, Zapolska, Fredro, którego pomnik stoi przed frontem, i Bałucki, którego pomnik stoi od tyłu teatru. Znakomici aktorzy: Solski, Adwentowicz, Zelwerowicz, Junosza-Stępowski, Nowakowski, Osterwa — kultura teatralna w Polsce nie ustępowała w niczym teatrowi na Zachodzie.

Z teatru — do kawiarni. Był „Feniks" na Rynku, „Bisanz" przy Plantach, „Secesja" na św. Anny, „Esplanada" na rogu Podwala, gdzie grywał „jazz-band" Golda i Petersburskiego, „Cyganeria" na Szpitalnej (to tu, w roku 1940, bojówka żydowska, paru wyrostków, których zresztą znałem, rzuciło bombę do sali,

---

[1] Sztuka Bernarda Shawa *The Applecart* (*Wielki kram*) była w repertuarze Teatru Słowackiego (przyp. aut.).

gdzie zwykli zabawiać się niemieccy oficerowie). W „Cyganerii" było parę metrów kwadratowych froterowanej podłogi i codziennie o piątej potańcówka — tzw. fajf — pary „w zachwyceniu słodkim trą się" — jak mówił Tuwim i oddają się sobie „sercem całym — całym ciałem" — jak mówił Włast.

Paroletni okres studiów na Uniwersytecie Jagiellońskim to były szczęśliwe lata. To nie zasługa Uniwersytetu, choć ma on zasług wiele, ale jeśli między 19. a 23. rokiem życia młody człowiek, który ma dobry dom rodzinny, dobrych przyjaciół i przyjaciółki, jest zdrowy i ma apetyt na życie, nie czuje się szczęśliwy — to jest z nim źle. Wybrałem studia prawnicze, to była moja naturalna inklinacja, z perspektywą na uprawianie tzw. „wolnego zawodu".

Trzeba powiedzieć, że w tej przedwojennej Polsce każdy uczeń gimnazjalny, który zdał maturę, miał automatyczny wstęp na uniwersytet (z wyjątkiem studiów medycznych) — nie wiem, gdzie jeszcze tak jest, czy było. Prawda, że na wydziale lekarskim był stosowany tzw. *numerus clausus*, o co robiliśmy dużo hałasu. Gdyby nie było ograniczeń dla studentów-Żydów i przyjęcie zależałoby wyłącznie od uzyskanych stopni, to istniała możliwość, że uniwersytety kształciłyby w przygniatającej większości lekarzy-Żydów, co w ówczesnych warunkach — i trudno się temu dziwić — nie było do przyjęcia. Jeśli dodać do tego, że dla synów i córek lekarzy dostęp na wydział lekarski był nieograniczony, norma *numerus clausus* nie wydaje się tak bardzo monstrualna.

Wydział Prawa miał za owych czasów wielu znakomitych wykładowców. Wróblewski i Taubenschlag od prawa rzymskiego, Krzyżanowski i Zweig od ekonomii, Kutrzeba, Vetulani, Gwiazdomorski, Zoll — było się u kogo uczyć. Było kilku profesorów Żydów, albo żydowskiego pochodzenia.

Po czteroletnich studiach wyszedłem z tytułem *magister iuris*. Miałem zamiar pisać pracę doktorską, nawet wtedy, gdy dojrzał mój plan wyjazdu do Anglii. Omawiałem wybór tematu z profesorem Langrodem, zasugerował, ażebym pisał w Anglii pracę na temat zarządzania koloniami, to będzie użyteczne i aktualne! W tej Polsce „mocarstwowej" mówiono poważnie, że na międzynarodowym forum winniśmy się domagać kolonii w Afryce. Istniała organizacja działająca w całym kraju, Liga Morska i Kolonialna — zdolna przygotować grunt i objąć ster, gdy się te plany zrealizują. Może prof. Langrod widział we mnie przyszłego gubernatora Kamerunu albo Zanzibaru? Plany, jak wiemy, nie ziściły się, i tej pracy nigdy nie napisałem, inne wydarzenia zaprzątnęły mą uwagę. Gdy miewam wykłady w Niemczech czy Ameryce, tytułują mnie zawsze profesorem i doktorem, nie sposób to wiecznie prostować. Zostałem przy skromnym tytule magistra i tylko raz tego żałowałem. Kilka lat temu byłem obecny w Auli Uniwersytetu Jagiellońskiego przy ceremonii odnowienia doktoratu profesorowi Altschulerowi z Jerozolimy. Było to akurat 50 lat po moim egzaminie i gdybym był wtedy osiągnął doktorat, również byłbym „odnowiony" w takiej todze i birecie, w którym, myślę, byłoby mi do twarzy.

Zawsze byłem namiętnym czytelnikiem gazet. Nie brakowało ich w Krakowie. Był stateczny, konserwatywny „Czas", socjalistyczny „Naprzód", endecki „Głos Narodu" i wszędobylski, prorządowy, popularny „Ilustrowany Kurier Codzienny", czyli Ikac. Właścicielem „Kuriera" i jego bratnich organów, jak „Światowid", „Tajny Detektyw", „Wróble na dachu" był Marian Dąbrowski, poseł na Sejm, o którym Tuwim pisał: „... ty co mieszkasz dziś w Pałacu / A srać chodziłeś pod chałupę / Ty wypasiony na Ikacu..."[1] Zważywszy, do jakich nizin stacza się prasa brukowa nawet w Anglii, nie był ten Kurierek jeszcze taki zły. W jakimś procesie o zniesławienie, na poparcie twierdzenia, że „Kurier" był pismem stręczącym do nierządu, cytowano ogłoszenie, które się tam ukazało i które wzbogaciło język: „Stuprocentowa dziewica poszukuje absztyfikanta".

Daleko od Pałacu Prasy, siedziby „Kuriera" i innych pism Dąbrowskiego, na Orzeszkowej 7, mieścił się „Nowy Dziennik", gazeta żydowska w języku polskim (w Warszawie był „Nasz Przegląd", we Lwowie „Chwila"). Dla żydostwa krakowskiego było to główne źródło informacji o wydarzeniach na świecie, w Polsce, w Palestynie. Wstępne artykuły pisywał tam często dr Ozjasz Thon, poseł na Sejm i prezes koła żydowskiego tamże, rabin w postępowej synagodze „Tempel", teoretyk syjonizmu. „Nowy Dziennik" to instytucja, bez której życie krakowskich Żydów byłoby trudne do wyobrażenia. Zacząłem tam moją dziennikarską karierę i wyjeżdżając do Londynu w 1938 roku zostałem uzbrojony w kartę dziennikarską jako zagraniczny korespondent tej gazety.

Dygresja: podczas mojego ostatniego pobytu w Krakowie zaszedłem do lektorium Biblioteki Jagiellońskiej i — tknięty jakimś impulsem — poprosiłem o tom „Nowego Dziennika" z roku 1938. Chciałem rzucić okiem na te szpalty, na te artykuły, które pisywałem wtedy — ku uciesze mojego Ojca i może innych czytelników. Wkrótce na moim stole pojawił się oprawiony rocznik. Otworzyłem drżącą ręką, zacząłem wertować nadwątlone stroniczki, ogarnęła mnie fala wspomnień, „każda karta słodkim wspomnieniem rani". Każdy nagłówek, każde nazwisko, reklama („Kolektura Braci Safir — Co Drugi Los Wygrywa"), drobny inserat („Angielskim będziesz władał jak rodowity Anglik — Karmel Koletek 3") przywołują na pamięć twarze, wydarzenia, sceny, rozmowy... Pogrążyłem się całkowicie w tym świecie sprzed półwiecza, żal mi było to odwracanie kart przyspieszyć — nie dotarłem do moich artykułów przed zamknięciem biblioteki. Zatrzymałem się zbyt długo nad notatką ze stycznia 1938 roku, która brzmiała: „We środę, w lokalu organizacji Massada (której byłem wtedy prezesem) przy ulicy Halickiej 4, o godzinie 8-mej, Felek Scharf wygłosi referat na temat *Jak wyrzucić Anglików z Palestyny*".

---

[1] Wiersz kursował z ust do ust, tekst drukowany w *Jarmarku rymów* (przyp. aut.).

Może przy innej okazji dotrę jeszcze do tych moich artykułów „od własnego korespondenta" z Londynu. Jeden szczególnie pamiętam, mój ostatni, pisany w sierpniu 1939, w którym był passus, że „stawiam moją dziennikarską reputację (sic) na przepowiednię, że nie będzie wojny". W chwili gdy ten artykuł dotarł na biurko redaktora, w Krakowie już byli Niemcy.

W retrospekcji to wygląda, że byłem ślepy i naiwny — co było prawdą, ale znajdowałem się w dobrym towarzystwie. Wielu proroków, m.in. „The Daily Express", organ lorda Beaverbrooka, aż do ostatniego dnia pojawiał się pod sztandarowym nagłówkiem *There will be no war* — nie będzie wojny. Myśli się teraz, że wszyscy wiedzieli, że to było dla każdego oczywiste, że wojna była nieunikniona. Nie tak to wyglądało, szczególnie w oczach obserwatora nowoprzybyłego do Anglii, olśnionego bogactwem i pozorną potęgą, tym Imperium, które miało posiadłości na całym globie, w którym słońce nigdy nie zachodziło. Ja to widziałem — czyżby Hitler tego nie widział, on się nie odważy...

Gdy we wrześniu 1939 r. Niemcy zbliżali się do Krakowa, Ojciec wręczył Matce klucze do biura i do fabryki, pożegnał się z nią, mówiąc: „Kobiety będą bezpieczne" i włączył się w strumień uciekinierów zdążających na wschód, podobnie jak mój brat Kazio z żoną (ale osobno; moja bratowa nie wybaczyła nigdy Ojcu, że małżeństwu się sprzeciwiał). Brat i jego żona byli pośród tych, których Niemcy w końcu dogonili i zabili — natknąłem się po wojnie na naocznego świadka, znał dokładnie miejsce, datę i okoliczności, ale nie potrafiłem tego wysłuchać.

Ojciec znalazł się we Lwowie. Pewnej nocy funkcjonariusze NKWD zabrali go z grupą mężczyzn, którzy, będąc bez rodzin, zostali oskarżeni o szpiegostwo. Ojca zesłano na daleką północ do Karelii, by rąbał drzewo w tundrze. Tam zmarł — czy można tu użyć wyrażenia „naturalną śmiercią"?

Miałem szczęśliwe dzieciństwo — dobrze mi było w domu i w szkole. Byłem otoczony bezgraniczną miłością Matki, to starczyło na całe życie. W ostatnich latach życia Matki, w moim domu w Anglii, gdy rozpamiętywaliśmy dawne czasy, dobre i złe, głównie jej losy pod okupacją, pytałem, skąd brała siły wewnętrzne, które pozwoliły przetrwać te nieludzkie warunki. Odpowiadała z melancholijnym uśmiechem: „Wiedziałam, że ty jesteś gdzieś daleko, bezpieczny, i że któregoś dnia wojna się skończy i że do mnie, po mnie, przyjedziesz i że cię jeszcze zobaczę. To i tylko to trzymało mnie przy życiu".

To, że danym mi było jej życzenie spełnić, uważam za największe szczęście, jakiego mi los użyczył.

Los, nie całkiem ślepy, który zrządził, że prawie cały „wiek męski" upłynął mi w Anglii, uważam za łaskawy. Anglia jest krajem dla przybysza (szczególnie o białej skórze) stosunkowo gościnnym, z tym cywilizowanym brakiem ciekawości prywatnego życia sąsiada, nie zaglądaniem w cudze garnki (ani spodnie). Dawniej było tu powszechne poczucie wyższości wobec cudzoziemców.

Kontakty z ludźmi innych narodowości i ich masowy napływ, częste podróże zagraniczne, a także oczywisty brak sukcesów w skali światowej, pozbawiły Anglików przesadnie dobrego samopoczucia. Wahadło pobiegło w przeciwnym kierunku. Anglicy stali się bardzo samokrytyczni. Są przez to bardziej ludzcy i sympatyczniejsi.

Byłoby niewdzięcznością wobec losu niedocenianie tego przywileju, jakim było znalezienie się na tej ziemi, co umożliwiło włączenie w orbitę anglosaskiej cywilizacji i uzyskanie bezpośredniego dostępu do skarbów angielskiego języka, kultury i literatury, które należą do największych osiągnięć ludzkiego ducha.

Kiedyś dałbym sobie wyciąć jakąś część ciała, aby mówić po angielsku bez akcentu; aby się upodobnić do otoczenia i nie być, w chwili gdy otwieram usta, rozpoznawalny jako cudzoziemiec. Minęło mi to i patrzę na ówczesne pragnienia z politowaniem. Wyleczyłem się z tego kompleksu niższości widząc, że obiekt mojego podziwu nie był w istocie lepszy ode mnie, a tylko nieco inny. Dostrzegłem, że kolorowa rozmaitość jest wartościowsza od szarej jednolitości. Dziś, może na złość samemu sobie, gdy już ten akcent prawie zatraciłem, staram się jego szczątki utrzymać, aby bodaj tym wyróżnić się od otoczenia.

Na rok przed wybuchem wojny wyjechałem z Krakowa — „dobrowolnie" (o tym cudzysłowie można by wiele napisać). Byłem świadomy, że jest to decyzja nieodwracalna, która zaważy na całym toku życia. Dojrzewała ona powoli, przez wiele bezsennych i przegadanych nocy. Było to rozstanie się z przytulnym, bezpiecznym domem rodzinnym, do którego, szczególnie do Matki, byłem bardzo przywiązany. Wyjeżdżając miałem poczucie winy, widziałem to jako pewnego rodzaju ucieczkę z placu boju, zrzucenie odpowiedzialności za wspólny los. Miałem krąg przyjaciół i przyjaciółek, takich jak już nigdy potem — ciężko się było z nimi rozstać.

Z drugiej strony życie w Polsce coraz mniej mi się podobało. Antysemityzm przenikał atmosferę jak eter. Perspektywy zawodowe dla absolwenta Wydziału Prawa — wpierw 5 lat aplikantury, potem praktyka w przeludnionym zawodzie były mało obiecujące. Pewnego dnia wróciłem z rozprawy w sądzie, gdzie zastępowałem klienta o złym wyglądzie, ale którego roszczenie było ponad wszelką wątpliwość słuszne, nawet w takich jak moje niedoświadczonych rękach. Sprawę przegrałem, było jasne, że mój klient się po prostu sędziemu nie podobał. Że ze strony władz było się narażonym na dyskryminację, do tego człowiek przywykł, ale wymiar sprawiedliwości? To oznaczało kwalitatywną zmianę.

Wróciłem do kancelarii długą, okrężną drogą. Oddałem patronowi akta, powiedziałem, że więcej do pracy nie przyjdę. Obruszył się: „Niechże się pan kolega tym nie przejmuje, pójdziemy do apelacji i sprawę wygramy. To jest przykre, ale trzeba się zaadaptować do realiów". Niech on się adaptuje, pomyślałem, ja nie. To był koniec mej kariery prawniczej. Incydent na pozór błahy, ale fakt, że pamiętam to po tylu latach, świadczy jak głęboko się wówczas zarył w świadomość i zaważył na decyzjach.

Staram się, o ile to możliwe, odtworzyć ówczesny bieg myśli, odkryć jawne i ukryte motywy, ale sedno sprawy było w tym, że zrobiło mi się ciasno i chciałem w świat.

Główną ideą, która zaprzątała umysły i serca grupy ludzi w moim środowisku, był syjonizm. Za czasów studenckich byłem aktywnym działaczem — z łamów prasy i trybuny propagowałem wyjazd do Palestyny na jej pionierski podbój (przypomina się tu stara definicja syjonisty — że był to Żyd, który za pieniądze drugiego Żyda posyłał trzeciego Żyda do Palestyny). Ja brałem to poważnie, poważniej niż wszystko inne. Miałem najszczerszy zamiar tam wkrótce jechać, ale podobnie jak święty Augustyn, który prosił Boga, aby go zrobił czystym i cnotliwym „ale jeszcze nie teraz", tak i ja nie byłem w pełni gotów poświęcić się całkowicie tej Wielkiej Sprawie, nim jeszcze czegoś nie zobaczę, nie zaznam i czegoś się nie nauczę. Moje usługi, tak sobie to tłumaczyłem, będą potem tym cenniejsze. I tak się odwlekło i uciekło. Przyszła wojna, miłość, małżeństwo, rodzina, odpowiedzialność nie tylko za własny los. Ta okrężna droga do Ziemi Świętej tudzież (za bardzo) Obiecanej, do której nie dotarłem, prowadziła przez Anglię.

Dlaczego wybór padł na Anglię? Chciałem otrzaskać się z cywilizowanym światem. Anglia cieszyła się wówczas dobrą opinią. Zainwestowałem już poprzednio w naukę języka, zdawało mi się, że już coś niecoś umiem, choć okazało się, że mój ówczesny nauczyciel wyprzedzał mnie tylko o parę stron podręcznika. Czytywałem namiętnie angielskie powieści (w polskich przekładach) — Sagę rodu Forsytów znałem na wylot, Kiplinga wszystko co było, Stalky i Spółka to jedna z moich ulubionych lektur, ach, taka „public school", to było życie. Thomas Hardy, Somerset Maugham, nade wszystko Aldous Huxley — to wyrafinowane, intelektualne środowisko, ten powiew szerokiego świata, te dyskusje pozornie głębokich idei — to formowało moje wyobrażenie o kraju, do którego zmierzałem.

Był rok 1938 — dostać się wówczas do Anglii nie było łatwo. Pretekst, dla pewności, miałem podwójny. Pracowałem wówczas w „Nowym Dzienniku" i zostałem delegowany na „zagranicznego korespondenta". Istotnie, zaraz po przyjeździe zacząłem pisywać tygodniowe felietony z Londynu, ciekawostki z życia codziennego, literackiego — ta angielska egzotyka była wdzięcznym tematem. Nie wiem, czy to bawiło czytelników, ale — co było dla mnie ważniejsze — bawiło mojego Ojca, który był dumny z tego, że widział moje nazwisko w gazecie, przyjmował gratulacje od znajomych w bóżnicy i w kawiarni (częściej w kawiarni) i łatwiej mu się było rozstać z miesięcznym zasiłkiem dla mnie (wynagrodzenie z gazety nigdy nie przyszło). Waluta angielska stała wysoko, tych parę funtów, wystarczających na bardzo skromne utrzymanie, w przeliczeniu na złotówki to było, w jego ocenie, dużo pieniędzy (nie wiedział, że matka wspierała mnie po cichu, z pieniędzy zaoszczędzonych na gospodarstwie).

Po długiej podróży pociągiem i statkiem przybyłem na Liverpool Street Station, jedną z mniej atrakcyjnych stacji kolejowych w Londynie. Byłem obciążony jak juczny muł — waliza, która zawierała mą starannie zaplanowaną wyprawę: garnitury robione na miarę z angielskiej wełny, wedle ostatniej krakowskiej mody (która, jak się okazało, jeszcze nie była dotarła do Londynu), w tym oczywiście, smoking (na te przyjęcia w *high society*, od których się nie będę mógł opędzić), pumpy czyli spięte pod kolanami bufiaste spodnie, takie jakie nosił książę Walii na fotografii w jakimś magazynie. Dźwigałem dumnie maszynę do pisania — niech ludzie wiedzą, że jedzie dziennikarz — marki „Underwood" z polskimi czcionkami, ważyła 10,5 kilo (miałem wrażenie, że ten przecinek dziesiętny po drodze wypadł). Mały plecak wypełniony ciastkami wyrobu mojej Matki — skonsumowałem to wszystko, kontemplując przyszłość na żelaznych schodkach bocznego peronu, spowity dymem lokomotywy — ostatni posmak domu. Nic już w życiu potem tak niebiańsko nie smakowało. Byłem nieco wystraszony, a równocześnie podniecony — Anglio, jestem! Gotuj się na mój podbój!

Pojechałem kolejką podziemną do East-Endu, to była wonczas żydowska dzielnica ze słynną arterią Whitechapel. Noc przespałem w schronisku Armii Zbawienia, rankiem poszedłem na poszukiwanie dachu nad głową. Była gęsta, żółta mgła, jaką znałem z opisu, osiadała w gardle i nozdrzach, bielizna była wkrótce czarna od zawiesiny sadzy. Słońce starało się bezskutecznie przedrzeć przez tę zasłonę. Poszwendałem się nieco po zaułkach, ze zdumieniem odcyfrowywałem szyldy sklepów malowane hebrajskim alfabetem. Ale krajobraz ludzki nie był mi obcy — to byli Żydzi z Polski, z Rosji, uprawiający swój handel i rzemiosło przeważnie między sobą, szwargocąc w swym nowym narzeczu Anglo-jidysz.

Znalazłem pokoik przy rodzinie, ciemny i ciasny, zgoła niepodobny do tego, który opuściłem w domu rodzinnym — odległy o lata świetlne od Forsyte'ów, Kiplinga i Huxleya (choć blisko Zangwilla). Jak się okazało, pokoik miał swoje kompensaty — gospodyni, rodem z Chrzanowa, troszczyła się, by zaspokoić jeden mój apetyt, a urodziwa córka — drugi.

Za rogiem domu, w którym zamieszkałem, przy Ridley Road, często w godzinach popołudniowych odbywał się rodzaj wiecu — mówca na drewnianej skrzynce przemawiał do parudziesięciu osób, które mu przyklaskiwały. Aha, pomyślałem, żywy przykład angielskiej demokracji. Jednego dnia podszedłem bliżej, aby pochwycić tenor przemowy. Nosiłem wówczas koszulę czarnego koloru, modną i praktyczną. Wtem z sąsiedniego zaułka wypadła gromada żydowskich wyrostków i zaatakowała przemawiającego i jego słuchaczy, przepędzając ich na cztery wiatry. Pamiętam to, bo i mnie się przy tym oberwało

209

(stałem blisko mówcy). Okazało się, że był nim Oswald Mosley, założyciel i przywódca angielskich faszystów, których mundurem były czarne koszule, a wiecyk *blackshirts* na żydowskiej ulicy był regularną prowokacją, Ridley Road była z tego znana. Podpatrując angielską demokrację, wziąłem guza za faszystę.

Wspomniałem, że miałem drugi argument na wypadek, gdyby urzędnik imigracyjny robił mi trudności przy wjeździe. Chodziło o podyplomowe studia nad administracją kolonialną (pisałem o tym wcześniej). Zapisałem się na odpowiedni kurs w London School of Economics, uczęszczałem na wykłady i seminarium, przygotowywałem pracę doktorską, której w końcu nie napisałem; można powiedzieć, że jest to jedna z konsekwencji wybuchu drugiej wojny światowej.

Życie tak się potoczyło, że Anglia, która miała być tymczasową przystanią, stała się domem, gdzie spędziłem cały dojrzały wiek, założyłem rodzinę, doczekałem trojga dzieci, pięciorga wnucząt — dobrych, zdrowych, normalnych, istny ogród boży. W trakcie tej długiej drogi (długiej wedle kalendarza, w rzeczywistości przeleciało jak z bicza trzasnął) nie stałem się, nawet pozornie, Anglikiem. Ustrzegła mnie od tego nieustanna świadomość, że jestem bez reszty Żydem z Polski, a więc innym stworem. Żywię do Anglii głęboką, choć nie bezkrytyczną sympatię, jestem losowi wdzięczny, że mnie tu a nie gdzie indziej rzucił, ale na przekór więzom rodzinnym, szczerym przyjaźniom, ukochaniu języka i krajobrazu, pozostaję tu obcy. Nie dolega mi to, powiedziałbym może nawet, że wręcz przeciwnie, że mi ten stan alienacji, ta pozycja na marginesie odpowiada.

Ta „obcość" odnosi się, w pewnym sensie, także do stosunków w moim własnym domu, z moją własną rodziną, z ludźmi, których kocham i którzy są mi najbliżsi na świecie. Nie dzielę z nimi mego „wewnętrznego krajobrazu"; sprawy, które mnie najbardziej zaprzątają, te żydowskie, te izraelskie, są dla nich marginesowe. Nie przekazałem im prawie nic ze swej przeszłości, a więc z siebie. Nie wiedziałem, jak się to robi i kiedy, może myślałem, że jest to jakiś ciężar, którym ich nie należy obarczać.

Myślę czasami, że gdybym się znalazł w latach trzydziestych — czterdziestych w Palestynie, byłbym tam bardziej użyteczny, bez względu na to, co bym robił — był czas, że sama żydowska obecność była tam potrzebna. Był to też czas — nie trwało to długo, może nie mogło trwać długo — kiedy to małe skupisko Żydów w Palestynie, składające się z idealistów natchnionych wizją fizycznego i duchowego odrodzenia narodu żydowskiego na własnej ziemi, przedstawiało godny podziwu model ludzkiego współżycia.

Ale myślę, że gdybym się tam wtedy znalazł, byłbym niezawodnie — z uwagi na moje poprzednie więzy z organizacją Syjonistów-Rewizjonistów w Polsce — w grupie bojowników Etzel, blisko Begina, ze wszystkimi konsekwencjami, które z tego wynikały. Nawet gdyby metody ich walki były sprzeczne z moimi zapatrywaniami na to, do jakiego stopnia cel uświęca środki, lojalność wobec starych przyjaciół, towarzyszy, kolegów byłaby, przypuszczam, mocniejsza aniżeli inne zasady. Łacno mogłoby się było zdarzyć, że zostałbym, w tamtych warunkach, terrorystą — ale złym, *malgré-moi.*

Okres okupacji w Polsce rzuca głęboki cień na wszystko, co zdarzyło się przedtem i potem. Od chwili gdy doszły do Londynu pierwsze wiadomości o obozach zagłady, byłem blisko źródeł informacji. Współpracowałem wtedy z dr Ignacem Schwarzbartem, który był, aż do przyjazdu Szmula Zygielbojma, jedynym żydowskim reprezentantem w Polskiej Radzie Narodowej przy Rządzie Emigracyjnym w Londynie i byłem świadkiem, gdy po otrzymaniu telegramu polskiego podziemia, bliski obłędu, napisał drżącą ręką w swym dzienniku: TO JEST NIEMOŻLIWE. Byłem z nim także, gdy wiadomości zaczęły się ponad wszelką wątpliwość potwierdzać i gdy napisał w dzienniku: A JEDNAK PRAWDA. Może ktoś powiedzieć, że to było dawno, ale w moim życiu nie minął dzień, abym w jakiś sposób nie wracał myślą do tych wydarzeń.

Moja Matka przeżyła wojnę na „aryjskich papierach", cudem — bez cudów nikt nie przeżył. Miała tzw. „dobry wygląd", co jak wiadomo, w tym kontekście nie znaczy, że była piękna (choć w moich oczach była), lecz że nie posiadała semickich rysów twarzy. Mówiła nieskazitelną polszczyzną, a także po niemiecku jak Niemka (w papierach miała podany zawód nauczycielki języka niemieckiego, co było korzystne). Przesłuchiwana przez gestapo, dokąd ją odprowadził szantażysta, któremu odmówiła okupu wiedząc, że nie byłoby temu końca, zanim jeszcze padło pierwsze pytanie Mama zarecytowała wierszyk Goethego: „Edel sei der Mensch — hilfreich und gut — denn das allein unterscheidet ihn — von allen Wesen die wir können" — humanistyczne *credo,* które przeczyło wszystkiemu, co się dookoła działo. Szansa, że te słowa obudzą jakąś iskierkę ludzkości w kanalii za biurkiem była znikoma, ale gambit okazał się skuteczny. Gestapowiec orzekł, że Żydówka tak nie mówi i tak się nie zachowuje — może na jego opinię wpłynął również fakt, że w czasie indagacji Matka bawiła się złotą obrączką, którą upuściła na dywan i nie schyliła się, by ją podnieść. Dodatkowym ryzykiem było, że Matka cytując Goethego, w mniemaniu, że ją to maskuje, wręcz zdradzała swe pochodzenie — byłoby niezwykłe, gdyby nie-Żydówka w Polsce wykazała taką znajomość języka i literatury niemieckiej.

W kwietniu 1943 roku, gdy getto się paliło, Matka podnajmowała pokoik nieopodal, dokąd dochodził swąd spalenizny. Jej gospodarze, u których wieczorami odbywały się konspiracyjne zebrania Podziemia, patrzyli na to bez emocji, rzucali od czasu do czasu uwagi, od których krew się ścinała w żyłach. Jak Matka to znosiła, skąd brała ten hart ducha, by się nie zdradzić gestem, skurczem twarzy, łzą; skąd się u niej brała ta spostrzegawczość, która pozwalała jej podczas świątecznych posiłków lub wizyty w kościele naśladować spod oka obserwowane obyczaje — klękanie, żegnanie się, zdrowaśki...

Pieniądze na czynsz i wikt Matka uzyskiwała ze stopniowego wyzbywania się biżuterii — paru pierścionków, broszek, kolczyków, naszyjnika pereł, ot, prezentów od Ojca na urodziny czy na rocznicę ślubu, jak to było w zwyczaju w średniozamożnej rodzinie mieszczańskiej. Każda sprzedaż przybliżała ostateczną katastrofę. Od czasu do czasu dostawała, nie wiem jaką drogą, drobną sumę pieniędzy z Krakowa. To nasz były sąsiad wysprzedawał obrazy pozostawione jego pieczy, gdy przyszło opuszczać mieszkanie. Były tam Kossaki — Wojciech i Jerzy, był Fałat (polowanie z wyżłem), Wyczółkowski (akwarela: Morskie Oko), Malczewski (portret żony z faunem), Wodzinowski (wesele chłopskie), Vlastimil Hoffman (dziewczę z martwym ptakiem w dłoni), Rychter-Janowska (wnętrze w dworku), Markowicz (chasydzi grający w szachy — ten się oczywiście nie nadawał do sprzedaży, aż dopiero po wojnie). W owych czasach modne było wieszanie w „salonie" obrazów — zdaje się, że głównymi odbiorcami współczesnej sztuki byli Żydzi.

Aby się nie zdradzić przed gospodarzami, że ma „dochód", Matka miała duży kłąb włóczki, z której robiła sweter na drutach albo szydełkiem. Gdy sweter był gotowy, Matka wychodziła na miasto, pod pozorem sprzedaży. Wracała z tym samym swetrem ukrytym w torbie, a w nocy moja najdroższa Penelopa pruła go, by nazajutrz dziać od nowa.

Ci, którzy przeżyli i opisali życie „na aryjskich papierach", przekazują obraz koszmarnej egzystencji, sytuacji bez precedensu w historii. To, że żyło się we wrogim żywiole, gdzie fałszywy ruch czy słowo oznaczały śmierć, gdzie jedna ludzka hiena mogła sprowadzić nieszczęście na głowy tych, którzy ewentualnie gotowi byli pomóc sprawiało, że wielu Żydów, którzy kosztem ogromnego wysiłku i ryzyka znaleźli się na „aryjskiej stronie", nie mogło wytrzymać tego ustawicznego strachu i nerwowego napięcia i wracało do getta, by przymierać głodem i zginąć w płomieniach, ale wśród swoich.

Wiem, że ja bym tam nie przeżył. Opcje były ograniczone. Ucieczka przed Niemcami na wschód — wielu ludzi, jak wiemy, uszło z życiem, nawet przez sowieckie gułagi, posiołki, potem zbawcze wyjście z Andersem. Nie uratował się tą drogą mój brat z żoną, których Niemcy dogonili. Nie uratował się mój Ojciec, którego Rosjanie zesłali ze Lwowa do tundry w Karelii, by rąbał drzewo — praca, do której nie przywykł i której nie podołał, jedna z milionów ofiar wielkiej socjalistycznej zasady „kto nie rabotajet — nie kuszajet". Wiem, że w owym czasie nie opuściłbym Krakowa bez Matki, która do takiej wędrówki, wydawało się, nie była zdolna.

Życie na „aryjskich papierach" nie dawałoby mi szans — nie miałem przyjaciół po tamtej stronie i mój wygląd, choć nie rzucający się w oczy semickimi rysami, był dostatecznie kompromitujący, by mnie zdradzić, nie tylko w oczach Niemców, którzy nie byli na to dostatecznie wyczuleni, ile przed pierwszym gorszym Polakiem. Nasza służąca, chłopka ze wsi, która była gotowa pójść za nas w ogień i która ukrywała przez jakiś czas Matkę, nie byłaby w stanie i mnie ukrywać — z mężczyzną było nieporównanie trudniej.

Wypadłoby więc iść, jak większość, do getta czy obozu i dzielić ich los do końca. Prawda, że i pośród nich była mała garstka, która przeżyła, ale to wymagało nadludzkiej wytrzymałości i szczęścia (jeśli można to tak nazwać), a nade wszystko żelaznej woli przetrwania, której, wiem na pewno, bym nie miał, patrząc na to, co się dookoła działo. Z tym zastrzeżeniem, że człowiek sam nie wie, do czego jest zdolny w okolicznościach, które przerastają wszelką wyobraźnię.

Gdy wojna się skończyła, Matka natychmiast wróciła do Krakowa, do mieszkania w jednej z kamienic, których formalnie była właścicielką i czekała. I oto istotnie — jak w bajce, niebawem zapukałem do drzwi. Tych wzruszeń i tej wdzięczności wobec losu nie potrafię i nie będę próbował opisać.

Moja Matka żyła i mieszkała z nami jeszcze dziesięć lat, nauczyła się języka, prowadziła gospodarstwo, doczekała wnucząt. Zdawałoby się na pozór, że wróciła do równowagi, że stała się normalnym człowiekiem, że koszmar, z którego się przebudziła, zasnuła mgiełka niepamięci. Do ostatniej chwili, gdy podczas kolacji dzwonił dzwonek przy drzwiach i wstawałem, by otworzyć, Matka bladła, łapała mnie za rękaw, szeptała „nie idź" — potem kiwała smutnie głową. Całymi latami długie wieczory przesiadywałem przy jej łóżku, wysłuchiwałem w nieskończoność jej przygód i przeżyć. Dla niej była to terapia, dla mnie poznanie tamtego świata przez przekaz naocznego świadka. Od tego czasu wiele na ten temat przeczytałem, i nawet napisałem; nic mi się tak nie zaryło w pamięci jak opowiadania mojej Matki o tych nieskończenie ohydnych latach.

Największą męką na jaką człowiek może być wystawiony w życiu jest ból matki, ojca, patrzących na cierpienie swego dziecka i nie mogących ulżyć mu czy pomóc. Pomyśl, ilu było w owym czasie rodziców patrzących bezsilnie, jak ich dziecko powoli dogorywa z głodu, jak odrywają je od nich przy „selekcji", jak jest zatrzaśnięte z nimi w komorze gazowej.

Gdy myślę o tym, co moja Matka przeszła w owym czasie — myśli, które nauczyłem się odpędzać, ale które mnie nawiedzają w bezsenne noce — chciałbym podpalić świat. A to „tylko" Matka, nie dziecko…

W różny sposób mógł Żyd zginąć w Polsce podczas wojny: z głodu, z choroby, podczas „akcji" od kuli — ponieważ któremuś z Niemców przyszła ochota go zastrzelić; mógł popełnić samobójstwo, gdy życie stało się nie do zniesienia; mógł być zaharowany do ostatniego tchu w obozie pracy, albo storturowany na śmierć w obozie koncentracyjnym. W końcu mógł zginąć, jak większość, w komorze gazowej, od wyziewów gazu cyklon B (Niemcy mieli też cyklon C — gaz trujący, który działał szybciej, ale był droższy w produkcji, niech się Żydy pomęczą troszkę dłużej...). Mógł też, zawieruszony pośród Polaków, zginąć jako Polak.

Tropiąc losy mojej rodziny odkryłem, że w każdej z tych kategorii był któryś z Scharfów. Jak przywyknąć, jak się zaadaptować do normalnego życia, gdy ma się świadomość, że wszyscy nieomal ludzie, których się dawniej znało — rodzina, przyjaciele, nauczyciele, sąsiedzi, sklepikarze, żebracy — wszyscy zginęli jakąś straszną śmiercią, i że własne życie zawdzięcza człowiek tylko jakiemuś osobliwemu splotowi okoliczności? Kiedykolwiek chcę przywołać pamięcią jakąś twarz z tamtych czasów, objawia mi się ona zniekształcona spazmem bólu, łapiąca oddech w masie skręconych ciał...

Jak ta świadomość wpływa na stosunek do świata, do historii, religii, moralności, na naszą wiedzę o człowieku?

Generacja Żydów po holokauście, ci ocaleli w najszerszym tego słowa znaczeniu, są ludźmi specyficznymi. Obciążeni tą pamięcią, porażeni, w odwiecznej żałobie. Zdaje się, że nikt „z zewnątrz" nie jest w stanie tego pojąć.

Polacy-Żydzi pod okupacją ... W tym kontekście chcę zanotować następującą historię. Na jednej z kolonii wakacyjnych ŻAKMK-u (Żydowskie Akademickie Koło Miłośników Krajoznawstwa) w Kuźnicy nad Bałtykiem zaprzyjaźniłem się ze Staszkiem K. z Warszawy. Był, jak i ja, namiętnym taternikiem, jeździliśmy latem i zimą do Zakopanego, na Halę, na Kasprowy, do „Trzaski" lub „Morskiego Oka", na podbój gór i kobiet (w obu dziedzinach więcej było gadania niż osiągnięć). Staszek był chłopem na schwał — wysportowany, niebieskooki blondyn. Po maturze wstąpił na Wyższe Studium Wychowania Fizycznego. Opowiadał mi często, że wśród jego rówieśników była grupa endeków czy ONR-owców, którzy mu dokuczali, wymyślali od Żydów-parchów, kazali wynosić się do Palestyny. Ironią losu było to, że Staszek pochodził z bardzo zasymilowanej rodziny, ojciec był adwokatem, matka znawczynią sewrskiej porcelany — jego więź z żydostwem była w zaniku i tylko te endeckie ataki na niego nie pozwalały mu zapomnieć, że jest Żydem i przemieniły go w końcu w żydowskiego nacjonalistę. Szczególnie pewien Ślązak o nazwisku Jurczyga posuwał się do fizycznych zaczepek, a że Staszek nie był z tych, co sobie pozwalali dmuchać w kaszę, więc kończyło się często bójką, wybitym zębem, podbitym okiem — ot, normalne przejawy ówczesnego życia akademickiego.

Gdy powstało getto w Warszawie, Staszkowi ani przez głowę nie przeszło, by dać się w nim zamknąć. Przewidywał słusznie, że czułby się tam całkowicie wyobcowany — jest faktem, że w tym kotle poniżenia jakim było getto, na samym dnie znaleźli się asymilanci i przechrzty, którzy nie mieli poczucia wspólnoty z otaczającą ich ciżbą i czuli do niej niechęć a nawet odrazę serdecznie odwzajemnianą.

Staszek pożegnał się (jak się okazało — na zawsze) z rodzicami, kupił metrykę chrztu (szczęśliwym trafem na imię i nazwisko o tych samych inicjałach S.K., nie musiał niszczyć haftowanych monogramów na bieliźnie) i wyjechał do Zakopanego — gdzieżby indziej. Zamieszkał na Kościeliskiej u gazdy znanego mu z naszych przedwojennych eskapad. Nabył dwa duże wilczury, częściowo dla towarzystwa, częściowo dla jeszcze skuteczniejszej mimikry — tego barczystego blondyna z wilczurami na smyczy, który umiał intruza zrugać gwarą góralską nikt nie mógł wziąć za Żyda — czuł się pod tym względem całkiem bezpieczny i odsuwał od siebie tę natrętną myśl, co będzie, gdy się pieniądze skończą, gdy przyjdzie pozbyć się złotej papierośnicy, sygnetu, wiecznego pióra Watermana, zegarka Omega — i na jak długo to wystarczy...

Jednego dnia wyszedł, jak zwykle, na spacer po Krupówkach. Nagle, jak w zmorze nocnej, wychodzi mu naprzeciw jego prześladowca, ten Ślązak z Wychowania Fizycznego. Przerażenie, panika, za późno by uniknąć zderzenia — stoją twarzą w twarz, Staszek myśli — to koniec.

Jurczyga robi jeszcze jeden krok — rzuca mu się na szyję. „Stasiu — woła — Ty się mnie boisz? Na miły Bóg, za kogo ty mnie masz? Ja życie za Ciebie oddam! Masz tu pieniądze, bierz, bierz wszystko, tu jest mój adres, kiedykolwiek będziesz czego potrzebował, w dzień czy w noc, o każdej porze, zadzwoń, zapukaj do drzwi, wszystko dla Ciebie zrobię...”

Później, gdy wskutek donosu Staszek uciekał przed gestapo — Jurczyga uratował mu życie, narażając własne.

W każdej dyskusji na tematy okupacyjne trzeba mieć na uwadze, że mowa o apokaliptycznych czasach, że okoliczności, w których ludzie żyli i działali nie miały precedensów, a decyzje, jakie musieli podejmować, były często tak przerażające, że nasz sąd o nich winien być niesłychanie ostrożny. Matka stojąca wobec wyboru, które z dwojga dzieci ratować, gdy jest szansa na uratowanie tylko jednego — sama myśl o tym ścina krew w żyłach i obezwładnia. A taka i podobne decyzje były na porządku dziennym. Kto zdoła wyobrazić siebie w takiej sytuacji i potrafi racjonalnie na ten temat dyskutować?

Przez długie lata po wojnie, w kręgu krakowskich przyjaciół wypływało w rozmowach imię Artka Loefflera. Był to mój kolega z ławy szkolnej, a potem z czasów uniwersyteckich, bardzo mi bliski. Grał na kornecie w orkiestrze szkolnej, na koloniach wakacyjnych dzień się zaczynał od hejnału mariackiego w wykonaniu Artka. Po maturze wykorzystał talent muzyczny jako źródło zarobku, grywał w jazz-bandzie na potańcówkach, na dancingach. Nie był wielkim orłem, nie wyróżniał się intelektem, zwyczajny, dobry „chłop z wiary”.

Pod okupacją niemiecką w Krakowie Artek został zwerbowany do OD — żydowskiej policji. Problem werbunku, dobrowolnego (w ogromnym cudzysłowie) i przymusowego został szeroko opisany; było jasne, że żydowska policja jest po to, żeby się Niemcom wysługiwać i robić za nich brudną robotę — nikt nie oczekiwał, że ktoś wyjdzie z tej służby z czystymi rękami. Tym niemniej było wiele wypadków, kiedy żydowscy policjanci potrafili złagodzić okrucieństwo niemieckich akcji.

Wiemy od naocznych świadków, że Artek w trakcie służby zachowywał się źle, a nade wszystko, że tropił i odprowadzał na gestapo ludzi, których rozpoznawał jako Żydów, między innymi swoich kolegów szkolnych. W rozmowach o nim padało uporczywe pytanie — jak on mógł, jak on mógł...

Pytanie — jak on mógł — odnosi się oczywiście nie tylko do Artka Loefflera, ale do tysięcy wypadków, w których decyzje wtedy podjęte wydają się nam niezrozumiałe i godne potępienia. Nie można takich czynów usprawiedliwiać — są granice moralności, których w żadnej sytuacji nie wolno przekroczyć — ale trzeba pamiętać, do jakiej psychicznej i fizycznej presji niemiecki potwór gotów się był posunąć, by swoją wolę wymusić. I gdy ktoś pyta „jak on mógł", jak mógł odprowadzić na gestapo Waechtera czy Schenkera, trzeba wziąć pod uwagę, że nim jego przełożony wysłał go na miasto, by wypełnił swój kontyngent ofiar, groził mu, że jeśli wróci z pustymi rękami, ofiarą padnie jego ojciec, matka, brat czy siostra... Kto chce, niech wyda o tym moralny osąd.

W modlitwie Szema — kluczowym tekście liturgii żydowskiej — zawarty jest nakaz, by nieustannie pouczać młode pokolenie o esencji judaizmu. W Hagadzie, tekście upamiętniającym wyjście z niewoli egipskiej, który czyta się w święto Paschy, podana jest metoda przekazywania pamięci — tym dzieciom, które pragną się dowiedzieć, i tym, które nie chcą o tym słyszeć, tym, którym jest to obojętne i tym, które nie wiedzą nawet jak o te rzeczy pytać.

Zagłada Żydów w Europie w czasie ostatniej wojny jest i pozostanie najtragiczniejszym wydarzeniem w długiej martyrologii narodu żydowskiego. Pamięć o tym dominuje moje życie wewnętrzne — wszystko, co myślę, czynię, mój pogląd na świat jest determinowany przez tę świadomość. Ale na przekór tradycji niewiele przekazałem moim dzieciom z tej wiedzy i tej świadomości.

Motywy tej wstrzemięźliwości były różne, nie zawsze mi jasne. Wiedzą oczywiście, że jestem Żydem, podkreślałem to często i głośno, może czasem za głośno. Wiedzą o moim pochodzeniu, o moich powiązaniach z Izraelem, z Polską, taki był i jest klimat mojego domu. Ale o zagładzie Żydów, mojej rodziny, o tym, co to dla mnie znaczy — o tym prawie nie mówiłem. Myślałem może — są wolne od tej grozy, wyrastają wolne, normalne, wesołe — po co wpływać na ich usposobienie, rzucać cień na to wszystko, cień, w którym ja całe życie spędzam.

Innym jeszcze powodem było chyba to, że rozmowa na te tematy przychodziła mi z niesłychanym trudem, nie znajdywałem adekwatnego języka. Teraz czuję się z tego powodu nieco winny. Nie doceniłem może, że ta przeszłość to nie tylko ciężar, ale także dziedzictwo i że chroniąc dzieci przed tym bolesnym brzemieniem, pozbawiałem je także części ojcowizny, zubożałem. Pokolenie, które nie zna swych korzeni, które nie prowadzi dialogu ze swą przeszłością, jest w pewnym sensie ułomne. A jeśli świadomość tej przeszłości jest bolesna, to jest to cena, którą godzi się zapłacić.

Jak to przekazać? Są od tego zawodowcy — większość z nas to amatorzy, którzy muszą sobie radzić jak potrafią (ale pocieszam się myślą, że budowniczy Arki był amatorem, a budowniczy Titanica zawodowcem). Główna trudność leży w tym, jak przedstawić bezgraniczną grozę wydarzeń, które nie mają analogii w dziejach, a jednocześnie nie podważyć wiary w sens istnienia, w ludzkie wartości, w sprawiedliwość.

Indywidualne relacje, a jest ich mnóstwo, często trafiają do świadomości głębiej aniżeli abstrakcyjne cyfry. Jest wiele źródeł, do których warto zajrzeć i z których można czerpać informacje, ale trzeba baczyć, jak dozować dawki.

Jedna z moich znajomych, pisarka, która straciła podczas okupacji całą rodzinę, opowiadała mi, że wiele lat temu była na wakacjach w Hiszpanii, ze swoim 10-letnim synem. Na tym letnisku była w owym czasie istna plaga much, które im uprzykrzały życie. Pewnego dnia zamknęła szczelnie wszystkie okna i drzwi mieszkania i gruntownie wydezynfekowała wszystkie kąty mieszkania środkiem owadobójczym. Gdy po paru godzinach wróciła do mieszkania sprawdzić skutki zabiegu — podłoga była całkowicie pokryta owadami, martwymi lub otumanionymi, wlokącymi się jeszcze w ostatnich podrygach.

Na ten widok syn ją zapytał: „Mamo, czy tak Żydów zatruto? Czy tak Żydzi umierali w komorach gazowych?"

Co ona mu kiedyś opowiedziała, jaki obraz zarył się w tej główce, że coś takiego z niego wyszło? Jak to zaważyło na jego przyszłym życiu? Czy wolno jej było coś takiego przekazać? Czy wolno było nie przekazać? Myślę, że chociaż świadomie nie podjąłem kroków, aby dzieciom tę moją, a zatem ich przeszłość w ten czy inny sposób udostępnić, nauka udziela się nie tylko przez słowa, ale przez samą obecność, przez codzienne zachowanie, przez pojedyncze uwagi, przez gesty. Ponieważ jestem tą przeszłością do szpiku kości przesiąknięty, nie mogło to ujść uwagi moich domowników i może więcej im się z tego udzieliło, niż przypuszczam.

Przeczytałem gdzieś aforyzm, który mnie ubawił: „Miłość to jest funkcja fizjologiczna, która zrobiła karierę". Analogicznie: antysemityzm to jest prymitywna idea, która zrobiła karierę — ponad swe najśmielsze oczekiwania. Elementy sukcesu były w niej od początku. Przedmiotem nienawiści byli Żydzi, którzy mają ten tajemniczy (boski) dar, że prowokują zazdrość i jednocześnie pogardę. Są słabi (choć jest mit o ich potędze) i rozproszeni, więc łatwo ich atakować. Antysemityzm jest zjawiskiem niezwykle trwałym — przetrwał zagładę milionów Żydów. Jak się okazuje, może istnieć nawet gdy Żydów nie ma. Polacy mają chyba patent na ten ostatni wariant, choć antysemityzmu nie wymyślili — jest to zjawisko odwieczne, o podłożu religijnym, społecznym, politycznym.

W różnych esejach zawartych w tym tomiku, w dyskusji z Andrzejem Szczypiorskim na łamach paryskiej „Kultury", w moich wypowiedziach na konferencjach w Oksfordzie, w Jerozolimie, dałem wyraz moim myślom na temat stosunków polsko-żydowskich. W pewnym sensie wszystko, co mówię i piszę obraca się dookoła tego tematu. Dodam tu parę luźnych obserwacji, nie nowych, niestety, albowiem wydaje mi się, że mimo upływu lat, w ciągu których wyrosło w Polsce nowe pokolenie, niewiele się w poglądach na te sprawy zmieniło. Nadal trzeba się przebijać przez gąszcz przesądów, stereotypów, ignorancji i złej woli. Nadal gdzieś w świadomości wielu Polaków kołacze się demonizacja Żyda, myśl, że „jest coś z prawdy" w oskarżeniu, że Żydzi biorą krew na macę; że Żydzi jako rasa, naród, społeczność, noszą w sobie jakiś pierwiastek zła.

Jak głębokie muszą być korzenie tej polskiej obsesji antyżydowskiej, jeśli po tym wszystkim, co się w ciągu naszego życia rozegrało na polskiej ziemi, i mimo że żyje tam najwyżej 20 000 Żydów — topniejące w oczach resztki 3,5 milionowej społeczności — wielu Polaków kultywuje swoje do nich urazy i gotowych jest do aktywnej wobec nich wrogości. Zdanie, które się zaraz po wojnie często w Polsce słyszało, że „za jedną rzecz trzeba Hitlerowi dziękować — uwolnił Polskę od Żydów", jest najhaniebniejszą wypowiedzią do jakiej ludzki język jest zdolny. Jeśli ten typ myślenia miałby być dla Polski charakterystyczny, to niziny moralne, o jakich świadczy, są tragiczną prognozą dla przyszłości tego kraju.

Co Żydzi zrobili, jakie niewybaczalne grzechy popełnili, że tak się zaryli w świadomości i podświadomości wielu Polaków? Czy jest to tylko przejaw zwyczajnej, pospolitej nienawiści do tego „obcego", „innego", połączonej z tradycyjną chrześcijańską doktryną bogobójstwa — czy też jest w tym coś więcej, coś specyficznie polskiego, czego przyczyn trzeba szukać nie w charakterze Żydów, ale w psychice Polaków?

Jakiekolwiek są tego przyczyny, wynik jest zjawiskiem psychopatycznym, neurozą schorzałego organizmu, która przesłania obraz prawdziwego świata i prawdziwych problemów. Gdybym był „prawdziwym" Polakiem (w definicji Lecha Wałęsy), bolałbym głęboko nad tą narodową obsesją, nie z troski o Żydów, których to już właściwie nie tyczy i którzy na te uczucia są obojętni, ale z troski o mój naród. Martwiłoby mnie nie tylko marnotrawstwo energii i emocji i idąca z tym w parze głupota, ale także pytanie — po czyjej stronie znajdujesz się w tej sprawie? Po stronie Hitlera?

EKSKURS

W języku polskim, w praktyce, nie ma słowa na określenie Żyda, które brzmiałoby neutralnie. *Żyd* w ustach i uszach Polaka jest słowem specyficznie zabarwionym, brzmi pogardliwie, ma wydźwięk pejoratywny, którego trudno uniknąć. Prowadziło to dawniej do używania takich eufemizmów, jak „staro-zakonny" albo „Izraelita". Wyrażeniem, będącym jeszcze dziś w użyciu, jest zdrobniałe „Żydek". Słowo to może być użyte pogardliwie, ale na ogół jest używane w dobrej intencji, aby złagodzić brutalne — jak się mówcom wydaje — określenie *Żyd*. Paradoksem jest, że w żydowskich uszach *Żyd* nie brzmi obraźliwie (oczywiście, można temu nadać obraźliwy wydźwięk przez odpo-wiedni akcent, przez niejako wyplucie tego wyrazu — jak zawsze *c'est le ton qui fait la musique*). „Żydek" natomiast zawsze brzmi obraźliwie, bez względu na to, jak pieszczotliwie byłoby pomyślane i wypowiedziane. W pewnych sfe-rach w powszechnym użyciu było słowo „parch" i „Żyd-parch", ale to jest inna kategoria. Poświęcam tej sprawie parę słów, albowiem uważam, że to wyjaśnia dosyć pospolite nieporozumienie.

Nie czas tu i miejsce na szczegółowy wykład historii Żydów w Polsce, ale trzeba uprzytomnić moim rozmówcom, często tego po prostu nieświadomym, że w latach międzywojennych, a więc w tym krótkim, ale doniosłym okresie, gdy Polacy byli za swój los i losy mniejszości narodowych odpowiedzialni, Ży-dzi nie mogli mieć wątpliwości, że nie są uważani za równych „prawdziwym" Polakom, że nie mają tych samych praw — to było jednym z podstawowych znamion ich egzystencji w diasporze. Z formalnym, konstytucyjnym równo-uprawnieniem, na piśmie, było nieźle, ale nawet ten najbardziej zasymilowany Żyd, zewnętrznie już niczym nie różniący się od nie-Żyda, w głębi serca wie-dział, że jest tu gościem, a nie gospodarzem. Gdy się przez chwilę łudził, że jest inaczej — przypominano mu faktyczny stan rzeczy w każdej sferze i na każdym kroku — w szkole, na ulicy, w prasie, w życiu sąsiedzkim, zawodo-wym, politycznym.

Gdyby tak skomponować antologię wypowiedzi gazetowych i różnych pu-blikacji o Żydach w okresie międzywojennym (nie wyłączając „Małego Dzien-nika" i „Rycerza Niepokalanej" świętego Ojca Kolbego), zilustrowaną karyka-turami, jakich nie powstydziłby się „Der Stürmer" Streichera, mogłoby to słu-żyć za *antidotum* na sentyment, oblekający pamięć w „złote malowidła".

W obrazie Polski utrwalonym w świadomości Żydów figurują też wydarze-nia powojenne — pogrom w Krakowie, pogrom w Kielcach, nagonka mocza-rowska, która spowodowała *exodus* lat sześćdziesiątych. Co by było, gdyby po wojnie Żydzi, wielu Żydów, wróciło do swych miejsc urodzenia, do swych do-mów, mieszkań, warsztatów, sklepów, przedsiębiorstw, i domagało się zwrotu swego dobytku? Przyjęcie, jakie ludność lokalna, przywykła już do żydowskiej nieobecności i do nowego stanu posiadania, zgotowała powracającym niedo-bitkom w wielu miejscach w Polsce, smutnie świadczy o naturze ludzkiej, o tym *homo*, który aspiruje do miana *sapiens*.

Z drugiej strony prawdą jest, że wielu Żydów po doświadczeniach, jakie ich naród dotknęły, uważa, że cały świat jest im wrogi i nie widzi powodów, by z tego wyłączyć Polaków.

Jest to pogląd jednostronny i niesprawiedliwy. Trzeba bowiem pamiętać, że ten polski antysemityzm, nawet w swych najbardziej obrzydliwych i brutalnych przejawach, był fenomenem innej natury aniżeli doktryna i praktyka nazistowska. To, co Niemcy zrobili, było poza kategoriami ludzkiego myślenia i wyobraźnią nawet najbardziej zajadłego antysemity.

Wczuwam się w położenie młodego człowieka z okresu niepodległości, deklarującego się jako antysemita, i staram się zrozumieć jego stanowisko. Znajduje się on nareszcie w swoim własnym, wolnym, niepodległym kraju, po prawie stu pięćdziesięciu latach niewoli. Można za Wordsworthem powtórzyć: „Jakież to było szczęście żyć, gdy wschodził ów dzień — a młodym być wtedy, znaczyło żyć w niebie" (tłum. Jerzego Pietrkiewicza).

I oto w tym kraju widzi liczną społeczność, która jest mu w przygniatającej większości obca, wygląda w jego oczach brzydko, wyznaje inną religię (o której ksiądz w kościele źle mówi), nie dzieli — wydaje mu się — jego entuzjazmu do odzyskanej wolności i która, co więcej, ostro konkuruje w handlu i przemyśle, a także w wolnych zawodach. Wara im — myśli, nie chcę ich widzieć ani słyszeć, niechby sobie poszli (bodaj, jak wielu pośród nich mówi, do Palestyny). Trzeba ich tą myślą, mniej albo bardziej energicznie, natchnąć.

Nie aprobuję oczywiście tego punktu widzenia, ale się nie dziwię, że był wielce rozpowszechniony. Chcę wierzyć, że gdybym był w owym czasie Polakiem, nie dałbym się porwać temu nurtowi, służyłbym innym, bardziej humanitarnym a nie mniej patriotycznym ideałom, że widziałbym, do czego szowinizm i nienawiść mogą prowadzić. Rad jestem, że nie byłem wystawiony na taką próbę.

Nasuwa się też inne pytanie. Jeśli Polacy (niektórzy, wielu) są Żydom wrodzy i ich nienawidzą, i ta nienawiść jest tak głęboka i długotrwała — czemu to przypisać? Może mają ku temu powody — a jeśli one są, może by dało się je usunąć?

Wydaje mi się, że takie postawienie sprawy jest w podstawowej przesłance fałszywe. Przyjmuje ono model: Żydzi są znienawidzeni, ponieważ Żydzi mają takie i takie wady — usuń te wady, Żydzi nie będą więcej znienawidzeni. Nie wierzę, że model ten odpowiada rzeczywistości. Tam, gdzie Żydzi są znienawidzeni, są znienawidzeni za to, że są, że istnieją — i jedyną receptą byłoby przestać istnieć (czasami, jak się okazało i to nie pomogło). Ich wielką, główną wadą (a mają ich, jak wszyscy inni, sporo) jest ich żydostwo. Któż by sobie nie życzył — oni sami najbardziej — aby byli lepsi, pole do poprawy jest ogromne (choć nie zawsze jest jasne, co poprawę stanowi i jak ją osiągnąć), ale nie wydaje mi się, aby poprawa odniosła jakikolwiek skutek. To iluzja, że gdyby byli inni, ominęłoby ich najgorsze. Inni? To znaczy, gdyby przestali być sobą.

* * *

Gdy człowiek żyje w oderwaniu od macierzystego języka — wydarzenie w naszych czasach nader codzienne — hamuje to jego rozwój i kaleczy osobowość. Trudno o pełny rozwój jaźni, kiedy zostało uszkodzone najbardziej istotne ogniwo łączące z przeszłością.

Przejście w nowy język może się odbyć sprawnie i nawet dać szczęśliwe wyniki; nowy język może stworzyć gładką powierzchnię, po której się człowiek swobodnie porusza. Ale taka biegłość ma swe źródło w mózgu, a nie w trzewiach i brak jej tych świadomych połączeń, tych wielobarwnych warstw asocjacji, z których słowa czerpią pełnię znaczenia i bogactwo odcieni. Tylko w języku wyssanym z mlekiem matki potok słów bucha z podświadomości, domaga się ujścia w trakcie tego — tworzy. W języku nabytym człowiek szuka odpowiednich słów i owszem, znajduje je i buduje zdania jak z klocków. Tak też one u mnie wyglądają — poprawne i, wydaje mi się, bezduszne. Czy ja się skarżę?

Ot, masz Czytelniku przykład: piszę słowo „skarga" — i ciarki przechodzą: widzę księdza Piotra Skargę na obrazie Matejki i równocześnie te inne obrazy, *Hołd Pruski, Rejtan, Sobieski pod Wiedniem*, szczęk husarii. Równocześnie słyszę chorał Ujejskiego: „My już bez skargi nie znamy śpiewu / Wieniec cierniowy wrósł w naszą skroń...", a także Lechonia „Wznieśmy w górę kielichy i pijmy na stypie / Bo żal nasz byłby śmieszny, a skarga daremna..." A więc, gdy mi się to słowo ciśnie pod pióro, to jest ono poparte takim nawałem i siłą asocjacji, że aż kipi. Ale gdy chcę użyć tego słowa po angielsku, przyciskam guzik, na powierzchnię wyłania się grzecznie i sprawnie: *plaint, complaint, grievance* — koniec, myśl się urywa, *thank you very much*.

Wypada mi coś powiedzieć o naturze emigranta, jako że ten status był znamienną cząstką naszego bytu i egzystencji.

Niewielu emigrantów, osiadłych na tym brzegu już w wieku poszkolnym, uzupełniło swą wiedzę tysiącem tych szczegółów historii, geografii, folkloru, poezji, jakie są naturalnym inwentarzem dziecka, tu wychowanego. Pozostają wyrwy w wykształceniu, których jakoś nigdy człek nie miał czasu ani sposobności nadrobić — braki, z którymi trzeba się ukrywać (najlepiej przez milczenie), aby nie narażać się na towarzyską dyskwalifikację.

Imigranta często znamionuje z jednej strony obojętność na losy kraju zamieszkania, z drugiej — dystans do wydarzeń w kraju pochodzenia. Życie, w materialnym sensie, jest tutaj prawdopodobnie lepsze, bezpieczniejsze, ale bardziej puste. Choćby myśl o „powrocie" przestała być realna — cała egzystencja jest niejako „prowizoryczna", tymczasowa (francuskie powiedzonko: *rien ne dure que la provisoire* zostało jakby wynalezione do opisu takiej sytuacji).

Trzonem osobowości jest pamięć. To, co pamiętamy i jak się odnosimy do własnej przeszłości, robi nas tym, kim jesteśmy. Przerwanie ciągłości egzystencji — to jedna z definicji losu emigranta. Język macierzysty staje się mniej żywy, płynny, sprawny — to część (wielka) ceny, którą się płaci, część nieuniknionego zubożenia swojej indywidualności. Do jakiego stopnia człowiek potrafił to zubożenie skompensować nową wiedzą, nowym językiem, nowymi zainteresowaniami jest, może główną, miarą sukcesu lub porażki życiowej.

Jedna z reguł życia społecznego głosi, że emigrant jest przez ludność tubylczą niemile widziany — tak się manifestuje wrodzony instynkt trzody. Ta niechęć, paradoksalnie, często bywa najmocniejsza w środowisku, które „tubylcze" jest od niedawna, i które czuje się tym nowym napływem zagrożone. Żydzi, osiedleni w Wielkiej Brytanii od dawna, przybrali już barwy ochronne i często patrzyli niechętnie na Żydów napływających z Rosji, czy potem z Niemiec. Wstydzili się ich nieco, obawiali się odpowiedzialności za nich.

We wczesnych latach pobytu w Anglii nasz stosunek do „tubylców" odznaczał się nieszczerością — nie mieliśmy odwagi powiedzieć im, a nawet wyznać przed sobą, co o nich naprawdę myślimy. A myśleliśmy — co jest naturalne — rozmaicie. Zazdrościliśmy im normalnej, ustabilizowanej egzystencji, podziwialiśmy ich niektóre rysy charakteru i zachowania, pragnęliśmy się włączyć w pewnym momencie w nurt, w tkankę ich życia, chcieliśmy, aby mieli dobre o nas mniemanie, schlebialiśmy im.

Z drugiej strony byliśmy wobec nich krytyczni, wydawali się nam dziwaczni, stwarzaliśmy sobie obraz nie bardzo przypadający nam do gustu — nie zdając sobie jasno sprawy z podstawowego, oczywistego faktu, że — jak we wszystkich innych narodach i społeczeństwach — są pośród nich najróżniejsi: ciepli i zimni, sztywni i przystępni, mądrzy i głupi, dobrzy i źli.

Gdy przyjechaliśmy — Anglia panowała na pokaźną częścią globu. Teraz jest małym państwem, uginającym się pod ciężarem problemów ekonomicznych i społecznych, wyspą niepewną swej roli w świecie. Wydaje się, paradoksalnie a może i nie, że Anglicy jako naród, Anglicy jako ludzie, zmienili się w świetle tych zmian na lepsze. Można by powiedzieć, że wahadło poleciało w przeciwną stronę. Od dominującego dawniej typu (stereotypu?) wyspiarza nieco aroganckiego, świadomego swej pozycji w świecie i swej naturalnej wyższości, do aż nadto często spotykanych teraz Anglików surowo i krzywdząco samokrytycznych.

Stosunkowo wcześnie i szybko uzmysłowiłem sobie, że nie muszę się do Anglika upodabniać, że nie muszę go naśladować ani się na nim wzorować — że w pewnym, tym najgłębszym, sensie jestem mu równy, chociaż on się tu urodził i jego rodzice, i to jest jego kraj — a mnie rzucił tu los.

W ciągu lat, przy różnych okazjach, wypływało pytanie: jak by się Anglicy zachowali, gdyby Anglia została okupowana przez Hitlera (bądź co bądź wiele nie brakowało). Jak by się zachowali wobec Niemców i jak — co mnie głównie interesowało — wobec Żydów? Podobnie do Polaków, czy do Francuzów, czy do Włochów, czy jeszcze inaczej? To jest bolesne rozważanie, na szczęście hipotetyczne. Gdybym był zmuszony wyrazić na to pogląd, oparty na mojej znajomości tego kraju, a także zrozumieniu natury ludzkiej — musiałbym wyrazić przekonanie, że nie wyszliby z takiej szatańskiej próby moralnej bardziej obronną ręką niż inne narody (mała lekcja poglądowa z okupowanych Wysp Normandzkich nie napawa optymizmem). Nie ma wątpliwości, że znalazłby się natychmiast jakiś Quisling czy Pétain — spośród Mosleyów, Halifaxów czy Ravensdale'ów, którzy przez kolaborację „ratowaliby" Anglię i wydawali w ręce Hitlera może najpierw tych „obcych", imigrantów niedawno przybyłych z Niemiec i innych krajów, a potem „własnych", tzn. tych, którzy przybyli nieco wcześniej.

Myślę jednak — i jest to wyraz szacunku dla mego przybranego kraju — że co by się tyczyło udzielania osobistej pomocy, ukrywania, ratowania pojedynczych osób czy małych grup, liczba osób zaangażowanych w taką humanitarną działalność byłaby procentowo większa niż w innych krajach, może znacząco większa. (Takie twierdzenie jest oczywiście gołosłowne i rzuca światło nie na Anglików, a tylko na mój o nich pogląd).

Żyd, jakiegokolwiek pochodzenia, jest innym emigrantem aniżeli Polak. Polak traktował emigrację jako prowizorium, nie przyszło mu do głowy, że ten stan może się przedłużyć do drugiego, do trzeciego pokolenia, do wieczności... Nie myślał o zapuszczaniu korzeni, o asymilacji, o upodobnianiu się — do kogo i po co? Żyd patrzył na to „przemieszczenie" inaczej. Nie myślał o powrocie, przyjmował natychmiast, że imigracja to jest nowy początek, niejako naturalny bieg rzeczy w żydowskiej historii i że ten nowy kraj może być dla niego, a już na pewno dla jego dzieci, lepszy niż ten, który opuścił. Często też miał jakieś zaplecze, bliższych albo dalszych krewnych z poprzednich fal imigrantów. Ale i bez krewnych w ścisłym tego słowa znaczeniu było „tubylcze" społeczeństwo żydowskie, do którego się ciążyło w optymistycznym przekonaniu, że Żyd Żydowi poda pomocną rękę. („Żydzi trzymają ze sobą" — mówiło się w Polsce w formie zarzutu. Atoli jest to zaleta i nie byle jaka). Chociaż i Polakom w historii emigracja nie była obca, Żydzi niejako genetycznie są do niej lepiej przygotowani. Przecież do niedawna jeszcze diaspora, stan rozproszenia, brak własnej ojczyzny był stanem naturalnym. Stąd też wynika, że imigranci-Żydzi nader szybko wnoszą wkład w kulturę swego nowego kraju, podczas gdy Polacy taki wkład mają rzadko, ich siły twórcze wyrażają się dorobkiem we własnym języku, we własnej problematyce i we własnej kulturze.

Gdybym ostatnich paręnaście lat przeżył w jakimś wellsowskim wehikule czasu, w innym wymiarze, nieświadom tego, co się na tej ziemi działo — i nagle, wypuszczony stamtąd znalazłbym się w Polsce, rozejrzałbym się dookoła i ku mojemu nieopisanemu zdumieniu uświadomiłbym sobie, że jestem w kraju wolnym i niepodległym, nie zagrożonym przez żadnego z sąsiadów, ani ze Wschodu, ani z Zachodu. Co więcej, że warunki geopolityczne tak się zmieniły, że takie zagrożenie można wyeliminować z prognozy historycznej (byłbym skłonny powiedzieć „na zawsze", ale jestem świadom tego, że „na zawsze" to bardzo, bardzo długo, a na tej ziemi — jak się okazuje — niewyobrażalne zmiany zachodzą czasem szybko i nagle). Obecne granice Polski uznałbym zaś za fizycznie i politycznie korzystniejsze aniżeli kiedykolwiek w historii. Zobaczyłbym też, że Polska jest krajem etnicznie i religijnie jednolitym, bez związanych z mniejszościami narodowymi problemów, które ją w przeszłości rujnowały i z którymi, tak jak wiele innych krajów, nie umiała sobie poradzić.

Nigdy w przeszłości, wydawałoby się, nie było równie sprzyjających warunków, w których ten kraj mógłby żyć własnym życiem, kierować własnym losem, decydować o własnej przyszłości.

Gdybym był Polakiem, upewniwszy się, że to nie sen a jawa, padłbym w ekstazie na kolana. Dlaczego nie widzę Polaków skaczących z radości? Czy to możliwe, że w ich świadomości kołacze myśl, że ta etniczna i religijna jednolitość to nie zdobycz, a strata, niezastąpiona, niepowetowana, która się wyrazi duchowym, kulturowym zubożeniem?

Praktykuję czasem zabieg konwersacyjny, który, przekonałem się, ożywia rozmowę i daje do myślenia: czy i kiedy, pytam, zdarzyło się wam spotkać kogoś, kto sprawiał wrażenie, że jest osobą niezwykłą, jakościowo inną niż my, przerastającą otoczenie, innymi słowy — wielką. Rzadko się zdarza, by któryś z rozmówców odpowiedział twierdząco. Co wskazuje na oczywisty fakt, że niezwykłych ludzi jest mało, i że sposobność, by pospolici zjadacze chleba jak my znaleźli się blisko nich, jest rzadka. Ja natomiast mogę na to pytanie bez wahania odpowiedzieć: znalazłem się, parokrotnie, w najbliższym otoczeniu Włodzimierza Żabotyńskiego i miałem wtedy świadomość, że jestem w orbicie jakiegoś niecodziennego zjawiska, w polu magnetycznym potężnej indywidualności, która wzbudza mój podziw, respekt i uczucie, że gotów byłbym iść za nią w ogień.

Było to, częściowo, rezultatem swoistego „prania mózgu", jakiemu zostałem poddany. Żabotyński był założycielem i przywódcą partii Syjonistów-Rewizjonistów, której młodzieżowym odpowiednikiem była organizacja Brit Trumpeldor, czyli Betar. Od wczesnych lat należałem do ugrupowania studentów w ramach tej partii, pod nazwą Massada. Agresywny, wojowniczy program i retoryka Żabotyńskiego, propagujące „państwo żydowskie po obu brzegach Jordanu", przemawiały do mojego patriotycznego ferworu bardziej aniżeli lewicująca i — jak mi się wydawało — zbyt ugodowa polityka Chaima Weizmanna, Nahuma Sokołowa, czy potem Ben Guriona, Czertoka, Arlossorowa. Śpiewaliśmy z zapałem *Hymn Betaru* pióra Żabotyńskiego, mówiący o wielkim pokoleniu Żydów, które wznieci bunt i przeleje krew, ale zdobędzie Ojczyznę — byliśmy urzeczeni i wierzyliśmy w każde jego słowo. Przez pewien okres, w latach trzydziestych, Żabotyński pisywał tygodniowe artykuły do żydowskiej prasy w Warszawie, najpierw do dziennika „Hajnt", potem, na tle różnic politycznych, do dziennika „Moment". Odgrywały one ogromną rolę w formowaniu opinii w społeczeństwie żydowskim — to było dziennikarstwo *in excelsis*, przekonywało bystrością analizy, proroczą wizją. W późnych latach trzydziestych wychodził w Krakowie tygodnik „Trybuna Narodowa — Organ Partii Syjonistów-Rewizjonistów". Pracowałem wówczas w redakcji i do moich funkcji należało tłumaczenie artykułów Żabotyńskiego, nadsyłanych nam z jego biura na Rue de la Boëtie w Paryżu.

Jednym z naszych smutnej sławy wyczynów był dodatek specjalny krakowskiego dziennika konserwatywnego „Czas", do którego dostarczaliśmy materiały. Na całej pierwszej stronie był artykuł wstępny Żabotyńskiego (w moim tłumaczeniu) pt. *Sprzyjająca Burza*, w którym autor analizował beznadziejność sytuacji Żydów w diasporze i sugerował jedyne, jego zdaniem, rozwiązanie: masowy *exodus* Żydów z Polski i krajów diaspory do Palestyny. (Jak się to praktycznie miało odbyć, jak zmusić Anglików do otwarcia bram Palestyny — tę kwestię na razie zostawiał na boku). Taka teza była oczywiście wodą na młyn polskich endeków i nacjonalistów, którzy chcieli się pozbyć Żydów z Polski i tym hasłem szermowali. Pozyskali oni nagle w Żabotyńskim sprzymierzeńca, na którego się entuzjastycznie powoływali. Głoszenie przez niego takiej tezy w owym czasie i fakt, że nie przewidział albo nie liczył się z tym, jak i przez kogo jego nazwisko będzie w tym kontekście nadużyte, było aktem skrajnej nieodpowiedzialności. Ale jego przepowiednia, że Żydom zagraża bezprzykładna, historyczna katastrofa, że grozi im fizyczna zagłada, sprawdziła się co do joty.

Żabotyński zjawiał się od czasu do czasu w Krakowie i wygłaszał czterogodzinne przemówienia w sali Starego Teatru. Jako orator nie miał sobie równego, był natchniony, a zarazem wyrachowany, wizjoner i demagog na wzór autentycznych trybunów ludu. Z Krakowa wyjeżdżał na objazd innych ośrodków, w ten sposób odbywała się agitacja syjonistyczna — mówcy odwiedzali swe organizacje w miasteczkach, przemawiali na wiecach (sam byłem jednym z nich). Ale wizyta Żabotyńskiego to było wydarzenie, o którym mówiło się długo przedtem i długo potem. Często się zdarzało, że gdy na dworcu kolejowym wsiadał do dorożki, jego sympatycy wyprzęgali konia i sami ciągnęli pojazd do hotelu, ku uciesze gawiedzi. Żabotyńskiego otaczał kult, jakiego żaden inny przywódca żydowski nie doznawał.

Jeden z moich przyjaciół, który przeżył wojnę na wygnaniu w głębi Rosji, opisał mi incydent rzucający światło na to, czym Żabotyński był dla niektórych ludzi. W półmroku syberyjskim ciągnie pochód zesłańców. W oddali, na horyzoncie, zarysowuje się podobny pochód, idą sobie naprzeciw. Gdy są już tak blisko siebie, że dochodził głos, słychać ochrypłe zawołanie: „Żabotyński lebt?" W tej śnieżnej pustyni, na dnie ludzkiej egzystencji, ktoś pyta o jedno —

czy Żabotyński żyje. Jeśli tak, to jest nadzieja, że świat ocaleje i warto próbować przetrwać.

W owym czasie, był to chyba rok 1941, ci nieszczęśliwcy nie mogli wiedzieć, że Żabotyński już nie żyje. Zmarł w Ameryce w roku 1940, w wieku 60 lat.

Jego miejsce w historii pozostaje sporne. Był samowolny, nie umiał pracować w zespole, folgował własnym pomysłom. W roku 1935 wyrządził ogromną szkodę sprawie, której chciał służyć — wystąpił z oficjalnej Światowej Organizacji Syjonistycznej, założył własną, spowodował ogromny upust energii na wewnętrzne, bratobójcze swary. Zacietrzewienie w społeczeństwie żydowskim było ogromne — objawiło się to nawet w najtragiczniejszym momencie — w powstaniu w getcie warszawskim. „Rewizjoniści" nie poddali się komendzie ŻOB-u, której przywódcą był Mordechaj Anielewicz z Haszomer Hacair. Walczyli osobno, na własnym odcinku. Wszyscy zginęli, prawie nic o nich nie wiemy.

Wzajemna nienawiść nie ostygła w Palestynie, ani po stworzeniu Państwa Izrael. Zaciekła walka między stronnictwami nigdy nie ustała, toczy się po dziś dzień. Skłaniałem się do poglądu, że tylko Żydzi mogą się tak wzajemnie nienawidzić, ale pomyślałem o Irlandczykach. Także o Polakach.

Do czego mnie ta rozprawa czy medytacja prowadzi? Do tego, że moja ojczyzna jest nieterytorialna. Nie jest związana ani zależna od tego czy innego skrawka ziemi, od żadnej rubieży, godła czy chorągwi. Nie jest nią Polska, ani Kraków, gdzie się urodziłem, gdzie była wypisana moja metryka, gdzie spędziłem dzieciństwo i wczesną młodość. Nie jest nią Anglia czy Londyn, gdzie spędziłem całe dojrzałe życie, gdzie wystawiono mi dokumenty naturalizacji, gdzie czuję się mniej więcej w domu. Nie jest nią Izrael i Jerozolima, którą kocham i do której się łaszę, ale w której jestem tylko przygodnym gościem nie zasługującym na żadne względy. Ktoś mógłby wyciągnąć z tego wniosek, że jestem „kosmopolitą bez korzeni" — przydomek, który w pewnym czasie i w pewnych krajach uchodził za głęboko szkalujący i był wręcz niebezpieczny. Był to po prostu kryptonim zastępujący słowo „Żyd" w czasie, gdy oficjalna doktryna negowała antysemityzm, a system w praktyce był głęboko antysemicki. Jestem gotów ten epitet rehabilitować. Kosmopolityzm stawiam wysoko na skali ludzkich wartości, w krańcowym przeciwstawieniu do szowinizmu, którego nienawidzę — w Polsce, w Anglii, w Izraelu. Jest to ideał, do którego godzi się zmierzać — nie jest to łatwe, trzeba się po drodze wyzbyć balastu wielu uprzedzeń i nawyków. Klimat jest po temu na razie nieprzyjazny. Po ciemnej nocy komunizmu, w wielu krajach wybucha jakby w termosie zachowany wrzątek nacjonalizmu, który w przeszłości był i znowu stać się może przekleństwem Europy.

Co się zaś tyczy przydomka „bez korzeni", to odpowiadam za Georgem Steinerem, że drzewo ma korzenie i stoi nieruchomo w jednym miejscu, ale ludzie mają nogi i mogą chodzić swobodnie po ziemi gdzie dusza zapragnie (i straż graniczna przepuści, może dodać cynik, ale to inna sprawa). Soki żywotne trzeba czerpać ze skarbca uniwersalnych, wszechludzkich idei. Nade wszystko chciałbym powiedzieć za Lamartinem: *Ma patrie c'est la verité*. Dystans, dzielący mnie od możliwości powtórzenia tego stwierdzenia jest, w moich oczach, miarą sukcesu lub klęski życiowej.

Lżej mi na sercu, że sobie pewne rzeczy wyjaśniłem. Nie wiem, co komu z tego przyjdzie i komu to było potrzebne? Mnie było potrzebne.

Co powiemy Miriam?

Nadałem tej opowiastce tytuł, który może się wydać nieco dziwny: *Co powiemy Miriam?* Zakładam bowiem, że wszędzie, gdzie postała noga Żydów, tzn. omal wszędzie na świecie, jest gdzieś Miriam, Sara czy Debora, jakiś Samuel czy Szymon, czy Daniel, którzy już teraz albo niebawem zaczną swoim rodzicom albo dziadkom zadawać pytania o sprawy, które dotychczas wydawały im się obojętne: jak naprawdę wyglądało życie w tym kraju, z którego pochodzicie, w tej zamierzchłej przeszłości przed drugą, ba, przed pierwszą wojną światową? Co to byli za ludzie, ci nasi dziadowie i pradziadowie, jak żyli, czym się zajmowali, o czym myśleli; jak tam wyglądało, czym pachniało? Pytania takie są częścią naturalnego, cyklicznego procesu — wpierw obojętność, potem ciekawość.

Wydaje mi się, że warto zadać sobie trud, by im na te pytania odpowiedzieć — któż to zrobi, jeśli nie my, z tego ostatniego już pokolenia naocznych świadków. Oczywiście, najprościej byłoby ciekawych skierować do biblioteki. Literatura na ten temat we wszystkich językach jest obfita, szczególnie w języku hebrajskim i jidysz — żeby wspomnieć tylko Szaloma Alejchema, Pereca, Szaloma Asza, laureatów Nobla Samuela Agnona i Bashevisa Singera. W polskiej literaturze są skarby informacji o tym środowisku, u Konopnickiej, Gomulickiego, Orzeszkowej, Klemensa Junoszy, potem u Stryjkowskiego i innych.

Nie każdy chce się zagłębiać w książki. Chciałbym się tu uciec do innej metody — uprzystępnić ten obraz na przykładzie własnej rodziny.

Waham się nieco czy wprowadzić wątek autobiograficzny — zaimek osobowy jest najbardziej podejrzaną częścią mowy — ale w tym wypadku jest to może usprawiedliwione, albowiem historia mej rodziny, w swym głównym nurcie i rozgałęzieniach, jest typową ilustracją wielu aspektów żydowskiego życia w „zachodniej Galicji", tj. w Krakowie i okolicy, pod koniec XIX i w pierwszych dekadach XX wieku.

Wywodzę się po mieczu (jeśli w tym kontekście wyrażenie to nie zabrzmi groteskowo) z długiej linii rabinów — może mniej snobistycznie godziłoby się ich określić jako „mełamedów", ludzi uczonych w piśmie, którzy gdyby widzieli na co mi przyszło, przewróciliby się w grobie.

Mój ojciec był jednym z piętnaściorga dzieci — rzecz jasna nie z tej samej matki i nie wszystkie z nich wyrosły ponad dzieciństwo. Już z tego dużo da się wywnioskować — osnowa jest rozległa. Mój dziadek, patriarcha z długą białą brodą, z zawodu karczmarz (jak Tag Stryjkowskiego), za swych młodych lat, opowiadają, rosły jak dąb, z dowodami swej męskości widocznymi gołym okiem, w mojej pamięci zachował się już tylko jako cień dawnej świetności, zgięty w kabłąk, bezzębny, sterany wiecznym trudem, troską i ciosami losu. Umarł dźwigając ździebełko ponad szósty krzyżyk — na owe czasy podeszły wiek — w jidysz słowa pociechy brzmiały: „oby nigdy młodszy niż on nie umarł".

Jak to sobie łatwo wyliczyć — w tej części kraju od Scharfów się roiło po wioskach, mieścinach, miasteczkach jak Chrzanów (kwatera główna!), Kalwaria, Alwernia, Żywiec, Bielsko, Bochnia, okolice Krakowa — dziw, że było dosyć miejsca dla innych. (Ciekawostka statystyczna: przeważająca większość ludności żydowskiej zamieszkiwała miasta liczące mniej niż 20 000 mieszkańców). Ten liczny szczep aż kipiał energią i zdawał się być w stanie ustawicznego ruchu — taszcząc się ze skrzyniami, walizkami, pakunkami, pociągiem czy furmanką, w gorączkowej gonitwie za interesami lub w drodze na spotkania z rodziną, na śluby, pogrzeby. Pamiętam tę kolorową, hałaśliwą ciżbę, przesuwającą się przez nasz dom w Krakowie, w przelocie do następnego postoju, aby zaczerpnąć oddechu, zasięgnąć rady u mojej Matki lub pożyczki u Ojca i odświeżyć się szklaneczką herbaty — to wszystko. Kuchnia mojej Matki była im podejrzana — nie bez kozery. Aczkolwiek mięso pochodziło z uboju rytualnego i szynki się w domu nie jadło, to na obiad po pieczonej gęsi, wbrew przepisom rytualnym, bywały na deser poziomki ze śmietaną.

Rozpiętość religijnych przekonań, w sferze wiary i praktyki, była wielka. Mój najstarszy stryj Motl, niemal o 40 lat starszy od mojego Ojca, postać ascetyczna i posępna, był do obłędu zwolennikiem cadyka z Bełza — i w związku z tym odciął się całkowicie od swego młodszego brata Saula, który z kolei był związany — jak to zrozumieć i wybaczyć! — z innym cadykiem, o wiele mniej świętym. Jako chłopiec odmawiałem stanowczo wizyt u niego, od czasu kiedy mnie tak uszczypnął w policzek, że bolało przez tygodnie. Był to pozornie znak czułości, ale dobrze wiedziałem, iż to kara za to, że — jak odkrył z niesmakiem — nie nosiłem *tsitsit*, tej koszulki ze „sznurkami", którą rytuał nakazuje nosić.

Był kuzyn Herszele, marzyciel i fantasta, z głową w obłokach, pełen projektów, które gdyby zostały uwieńczone powodzeniem, postawiłyby całą rodzinę na nogi, ale tymczasem wymagały ustawicznych zastrzyków kapitału — wykapany sobowtór Menachema Mendla z powieści Szaloma Alejchema.

Była ciotka Rachela, wcześnie owdowiała, pobłogosławiona tyloma dziećmi, ile lat trwało jej szczęśliwe małżeństwo, trudniąca się zawodem, który tradycyjnie był męską domeną — swataniem małżeństw, czyli tzw. „partii". Zawód ten wymagał ustawicznych podróży w celu poszukiwania informacji, umacniania koneksji, łagodzenia konfliktów i nadzorowania tzw. „oględzin" (do których przyszła para była proceduralnie upoważniona) — subtelna i delikatna rola. Ciotka Rachela była także rodzinnym aniołem-stróżem, pielęgniarką chorych, gdziekolwiek się na nich natknęła (a było ich pełno), przy czym stosowała swoją rozległą wiedzę aplikowania babskich leków i domowych specyfików oraz instynktowną znajomość ludzkiej psychologii. Na długo przed zaistnieniem pojęcia choroby psychosomatycznej rozumiała te stany psychiczne i miała na to nazwę, która w przekładzie z jidysz brzmiałaby mniej więcej „wmawianie sobie dziecka w brzuch".

Ukryta gdzieś głęboko w świadomości tego klanu, kołatała pamięć o pięknej, rzekomo, ciotce Rózi — jej pożółkła fotografia schowana była w szufladzie ze świecidełkami mojej Matki, bezpieczna, ale nie przed moimi wszędobylskimi palcami. Ciocia Rózia — sklecam te historie z urywkowych rozmów i sekretnych aluzji — uciekła z domu z „austriackim oficerem" i potem, gdy ten ją porzucił (co było do przewidzenia), stoczyła się do rynsztoka. Nie ma żadnych dowodów, że tak właśnie było, ale w ogólnym przekonaniu utrwaliła się myśl, że inaczej być nie mogło. Jej rodzice oczywiście wyrzekli się jej i odbyli rytuał „pokuty po umarłych". Do końca życia dźwigali stygmat żałoby i wstydu.

Ten motyw i jego warianty powtarzają się w żydowskiej literaturze — a także polskiej — aż stwarza się stereotyp, od Chave Szaloma Alejchema w powieści *Tewje Mleczarz* (prototyp *Skrzypka na dachu*) do Cheremian u Stryjkowskiego. Dowodzi to, że sytuacje takie były plagą niejednej rodziny, wyrywały trzewia żydowskiej społeczności; gorszej rzeczy nie można sobie było wyobrazić. Atoli w tym marginesowym współdziałaniu z otaczającym światem, zagrażającym a jednocześnie ponętnym, sporadyczne przekraczanie granic było nieuniknione. Ale odstępca pozostawał w oczach społeczności pogardzaną i odstręczającą postacią. Żaden Żyd nie wierzył, że zmiana wiary wynikała z prawdziwego przekonania — podejrzenie, które niezawodnie podzielała i druga strona. Powszechnie panował pogląd, że apostata, zobojętniały wobec własnej religii i symulujący przywiązanie do tej nowej, wdawał się w tę sprawę gwoli osobistej korzyści, takiej czy innej natury.

Wypadek mniej dramatyczny niż ciotki Róży, lecz prawdopodobnie nie mniej typowy, tyczył się mojego stryja Jozuy. Jego i mojej Matki macocha uznała, że nie było dla niego miejsca w rodzinnym domu — spakowała mu manatki i wysłała go w drogę do Ameryki, tak po prostu. Jak wiemy, nie była to w owych czasach rzadka praktyka — emigracja okazała się największym dobrodziejstwem. Ale Jozua w owym czasie — ile mógł mieć wtedy lat, 14, 15 — nie myślał o tym, że jest cząstką historycznego procesu, zaprzątał go jedynie własny los zagubionego chłopca. Jaki był mechanizm tych podróży — zakładam, że zaopatrzono go w *Schiffskarte* i że podróż miał zacząć w Liverpoolu; jak miał dotrzeć do tego portu — nie wiem. W każdym razie — niedaleko zajechał. Po drodze natknął się wśród towarzyszy podróży na ludzi, którzy znali rodzinę i którzy byli oburzeni, że chłopca się tak wysyła w świat, pozbawiając go jego cząstki dziedzictwa (o którym mieli niezawodnie wygórowane wyobrażenie). Chłopiec zrobił w tył zwrot, ale w drodze powrotnej wpadł w ręce jakiegoś towarzystwa misjonarzy, w których przekonaniu (moim zdaniem błędnym) nawrócenie Żydów musi poprzedzić przyjście Mesjasza — i w związku z tym zadecydowali, że przeznaczeniem Jozuy jest to przyjście przyspieszyć. Ciepły posiłek i parę dobrych słów, wtedy jak i teraz, działają cuda. Po dziś dzień udziela mi się dreszcz grozy, z jakim moja Matka opowiadała tę historię — pół wieku po wydarzeniu! — jak sąsiedzi i przyjaciele wpadli do domu, zgorszeni do szpiku kości, by donieść ojcu, macosze i reszcie rodzeństwa, że Jozue stoi na rynku i sprzedaje misjonarskie pisma! Był szok, wyrzuty sumienia, obawa skandalu. Koniec końcem — łapówką, perswazją albo siłą — chłopca ponownie wyprawiono w drogę, tym razem skutecznie, by dotarł do owej Ziemi Obiecanej. Słuch o nim zaginął — aż do chwili, gdy na krótko przed wybuchem drugiej wojny niektórzy członkowie rodziny dokopali się jego adresu i zaczęli pisać alarmujące listy z prośbą o *affidavit*. Było za późno.

Mój Ojciec był wczesnym buntownikiem. Dusząc się w atmosferze małego miasteczka, zademonstrował swój sprzeciw przez obcięcie swego surduta „na krótko" i zmianę kapelusza — czarnego, aksamitnego, który był częścią ortodoksyjnego ubioru — na modniejszy, jaśniejszego koloru. Ten protest wymagał zapewne większej odwagi cywilnej niż sobie wyobrażamy. Przyjechał do Krakowa w poszukiwaniu żony i fortuny — i wkrótce uwieńczył pierwszą część planu sukcesem ponad swoje najśmielsze oczekiwania; druga stała się jakoś mniej ważna.

Zachował oczywiście pełne przywiązanie do judaizmu, nie znał niczego innego, nie odczuwał najmniejszej potrzeby czego innego. Widzę go, jak w sobotę po południu zdejmuje z półki foliał Talmudu i ze sposobu z jakim się z nim obchodzi, z szacunkiem a pieszczotliwie, widać, że to księga święta. Zgięty nad foliałem powoli przewraca kartki, jakby kuszony tym nadmiarem bogactw i w końcu, z westchnieniem ukontentowania, skupia się nad jakimś znanym mu fragmentem. Nie był „uczonym w piśmie", miał za sobą tych parę przepisowych lat nauki w chederze i nie posiadał odpowiedniego przygotowania, by samodzielnie przebijać się przez te bite złomy tekstu, obrośnięte gąszczem komentarzy i przysypane maczkiem glos. Lecz to nie miało znaczenia — nie szukał tam rozwiązań problemów ani prawnych orzeczeń, ale chciał obmyć się z trywialności kłopotów codziennego życia w strumieniu odwieczności. Wierzył po prostu, że ta księga zawierała prawdę, i że dobrze było jej dotknąć.

Pragnął, bym i ja dzielił ten pogląd, ale myśmy nie umieli ze sobą rozmawiać i on zdawał sobie sprawę z tego, że dyskusja z przemądrzałym młokosem do niczego nie prowadzi. Raz jedyny, pamiętam, wybuchł niepohamowanym gniewem, gdy go zapytałem: „komu to potrzebne, po co to wszystko?" „Po co to wszystko, głupcze? Całe życie jest właśnie po to!"

Widział się w roli żywiciela rodziny, ale chociaż wszystko, co robił — święcie w to wierzył — było dla naszego dobra, wychowanie dzieci nie nale-

231

żało do niego. Ta doza sukcesu, którą osiągnął jako drobny fabrykant i kupiec, była rezultatem nieustannej gonitwy i wysiłku bez reszty. Do niego należała troska, jak zaspokoić wszystkie nasze potrzeby — ale on też był wyłącznym arbitrem, co za potrzebę uchodzi.

Zakup książek, owszem, był aprobowany, nie bez fochów i oporu. Powieści były w jego oczach błazeństwem, dziecinadą. Jak poważny człowiek mógł zaprzątać sobie uwagę zmyślonymi perypetiami nieistniejących ludzi! Ja zaś twierdziłem, że podsycają one uczucie i wyobraźnię, dają dostęp do doświadczeń poza zakresem osobistych przeżyć i rzucają światło na różne aspekty rzeczywistości. Jakże inaczej zdobyć wiedzę o świecie? Czy te skandaliczne przygody p. G. z przeciwka nie stawały się bardziej zrozumiałe po przeczytaniu *Pani Bovary*?

Ojciec rozumiał z tych spraw może więcej, niż gotów był przyznać. On i ja utrzymywaliśmy chwiejne zawieszenie broni, aż do czasu, gdy na krótko przed wybuchem wojny opuściłem domowe ognisko i wyjechałem w świat. Nigdy go więcej nie widziałem — zmarł w 1942 roku, rąbiąc drzewo w rosyjskiej tundrze.

Przed wojną niektórzy członkowie rodziny przystawali do partii komunistycznej. To była poważna sprawa, niebezpieczna, która mogła się źle skończyć i często miała smutne następstwa. Rewizje w domu, ku rozpaczy rodziców, areszty, wyroki, więzienia. Na przekór temu, a może właśnie dlatego, idea ta przyciągała wybrany element. Była przecież niesłychanie atrakcyjna — obiecywała nie tylko rozwiązanie tzw. kwestii żydowskiej, która wydawała się w tym kontekście stosunkowo drobna, ale też rozwiązanie wszystkich innych problemów społecznej niesprawiedliwości i wyzysku, w wyniku historycznie nieuniknionego zwycięstwa proletariatu. Braterstwo ludów spełni się niejako automatycznie, naturalnym biegiem rzeczy, jako jego produkt uboczny. Idea ta zasługiwała na to, by się jej poświęcić — i poświęceń było wiele, włączając te ostateczne i masowe pod murem egzekucyjnym Stalina. Mój ulubiony kuzyn Mojsie, potem Misza, genialny poliglota i szachista, poszedł tą drogą.

Inni znów krewni związali się z ruchem Bundu, ale większość dała się ponieść fali syjonizmu, w jego wszystkich odcieniach — Haszomer Hacair, Gordonia, Akiba, Betar. Można powiedzieć, że w późnych latach dwudziestych i wczesnych trzydziestych „sztetł" — miasteczko — odbiegło w przeszłość i większość członków rodziny wyemigrowała do większych miast, przeważnie do Krakowa, gdzie się zmieszali, spokrewnili, spowinowacili z innymi podobnymi rodzinami, do tego stopnia, że wszyscy w końcu byli w bliższy czy dalszy sposób powiązani gałęziami swych genealogii. Czarnobrodzi Schwarzbartowie i rudobrodzi Rotbartowie, wszędobylscy Landauowie, Grossy i Kleiny, Schusterowie i Schneidrowie, Wolfy i Schafy, Sperlingi i Spatze, Spirowie i Szapirowie, Kohny, Kahany, Koheny (tu także należą Löwy), Sontagi, Montagi, Freitagi, Sonnabendy, Zuckery i Pfeffery, Gruny, Brauny, Goldy i Silbery, Nussbaumy, Grunbaumy, Rosenbaumy, wszystkie inne -baumy, a także Aszkenasy i Gumplowicze. Wymieniłem tylko nazwiska powiązane z rodziną Scharfów.

Była to urozmaicona społeczność, o skomplikowanym charakterze. Dobrze przedstawia ją anegdota: ktoś pojechał do Krakowa i po powrocie zdaje przyjacielowi sprawę z pobytu. „Żydzi w Krakowie — mówi — to jacyś dziwni ludzie. Spotkałem tam Żyda, który dzień i noc ślęczy nad Talmudem. Spotkałem Żyda, któremu się po nocach marzy rewolucja, a w dzień planuje, jak ją urzeczywistnić. Spotkałem Żyda, który ustawicznie ugania za kieckami. Spotkałem Żyda, który stroni od płci żeńskiej. Spotkałem Żyda, który jest całkowicie zaprzątnięty myślami, jak się szybko wzbogacić". Ten drugi mu odpowiada: „Nie wiem, czemu się dziwisz. Kraków to wielkie miasto, mieszka tam wielu Żydów, są wśród nich najrozmaitsi". „Nie — mówi ten pierwszy — to był ten sam Żyd".

Ale chciałbym nakreślić jeszcze inny wizerunek Żyda z tamtych czasów. Zaczerpnąłem go z krótkiego wiersza zatytułowanego *Mój Ojciec*, pióra Icchaka Kacenelsona, autora elegii *Pieśń o zamordowanym żydowskim narodzie*, może najbardziej wstrząsającego poematu napisanego w czasie Zagłady. Pisze on:

„Kiedy mój Ojciec nauczył się na pamięć Biblii? Komentarzy Onkelosa i Marcina Lutra? Talmudu, Kodeksów, Midraszu, Heinego i Szekspira? Kiedy przeczytał Gogola, Tucydydesa i Plutarcha? Kiedy studiował Świętą Księgę Zoharu? Kiedy on spał?!"

W obliczu tego człowiek czuje się mały. Takich ludzi dziś się nie spotyka. W tamtych czasach nie należeli do rzadkości. Co więcej, trzeba pamiętać, że nie jest tu mowa o jakimś „zawodowym" uczonym, który na gromadzenie wiedzy mógł poświęcić całe życie, ale o kimś, kto zarabiał w pocie czoła na kęs chleba, i który te księgi pożerał po nocach, przy świecy lub płomyku naftowej lampy.

Gdyby wszyscy ci ludzie nie zginęli w apokaliptycznych czasach, wielu z tej ciżby włączyłoby się w inne nurty, rozproszyłoby się po mapie, i swoimi rozmaitymi talentami, energią i dynamizmem wzbogaciłoby świat. A stało się tak, że na przykład z mojej rodziny (a ta, jak wspomniałem, liczyła setki osób) nie przeżył nikt, z wyjątkiem, szczęśliwie, mojej Matki.

Kiedy mowa o Żydach w Polsce przed wojną światową, tą pierwszą i drugą, trzeba ostrożnie żeglować między mgiełką nostalgii a trzeźwym odtwarzaniem realiów. Można tej przeszłości żałować, lecz nie należy przystrajać jej „w złote malowidła". Literatura owego czasu, jedyne autentyczne świadectwo, w języku jidysz i hebrajskim, jest surowo i bezlitośnie krytyczna, choć krytykę tę przenika troska i współczucie, w tradycji biblijnych proroków. Mendełe[1], Szolem

---

[1] Mendełe (właśc. Abramowicz Szalom Jakow, 1836–1917), powieściopisarz żydowski, jeden z twórców literackiego języka jidysz, w swych utworach zawarł krytyczny obraz życia społeczności żydowskiej (przyp. wyd.).

Alejchem[1], Perec[2], Opatoszu[3] opisują te opłakane warunki życia, ubóstwo, niemoc, ucisk, obskurantyzm — i buntują się przeciw temu; taka jest rola, czy też misja literatury.

Gdy chcesz się dowiedzieć, na przykład, jaka była pozycja kobiet w tym społeczeństwie, powie to — lepiej niż dziesiątki uczonych rozpraw — krótki passus z książki *Debora* napisanej przez Esterę Kreitman, siostrę Jozuy i Bashevisa Singerów, obdarzoną podobnym do nich talentem.

Jednego dnia — pisze Estera — podsłuchała, jak ich ojciec mówił z dumą o jednym z synów: „On w przyszłości zasłynie jako znakomity znawca Talmudu". Na co ona podeszła do ojca i zapytała: „Powiedz mi tato, czym ja będę w przyszłości?" Ojciec spojrzał na nią jak gdyby nie rozumiał pytania: „Czym ty będziesz w przyszłości? Niczym, oczywiście". Obraz jest wymowny, niewiele można dodać.

Prawda, że ubóstwo było nagminne. Ale nie należy przyjmować, że to było specyficzne żydowskie ubóstwo, w przeciwieństwie do ogólnego nie-żydowskiego dobrobytu. Wręcz przeciwnie — nędza nie zna granic, nie-żydowski bezrobotny cierpiał ten sam, jeśli nie gorszy niedostatek. Na wsi los był często jeszcze surowszy — drobny rolnik wiódł, w złym roku, godną pożałowania egzystencję. Z drugiej strony wyobrażenie, że życie Żydów w Polsce przedstawiało niezmiennie szary i smutny obraz, jest fałszywe. Były zarówno światła jak cienie, a urozmaiconą kanwę bytowania tkało wiele nici. Niektóre z najznakomitszych osiągnięć nacji żydowskiej miały miejsce na polskiej ziemi. Jeśli pełny obraz, który się z tego wszystkiego wyłania, wyda się komuś ponury — można zadać pytanie: skoro było tak źle, dlaczego było tak dobrze?

Struktura tej społeczności, którą ktoś nazwał „żydowskim narodem w Polsce" była różnorodna. Składał się na nią miejski proletariat złożony z robotników fabrycznych i rzemieślników (przeważnie krawców i szewców); „Luftmenschów" bez określonego źródła dochodów; licznej klasy średniej — sklepikarzy i kupców najrozmaitszego autoramentu; wolnych zawodów — lekarzy, adwokatów, inżynierów, architektów; a także plutokracji — fabrykantów, bankierów, wielkich przemysłowców.

Zarząd gminą religijną leżał w rękach kahału, instytucji o znacznym stopniu autonomii i szerokich kompetencjach. Istniała sieć szkół żydowskich, jeszybo-

---

[1] Szolem Alejchem (właśc. Szolem Rabinowicz, 1859–1916), klasyk literatury żydowskiej. Pisał w jęz. jidysz i hebrajskim. Powieściopisarz, nowelista, dramaturg, w swych dziełach zawarł panoramę życia Żydów w Europie na przełomie XIX/XX w., sięgał też do podań żydowskich (przyp. wyd.).

[2] Perec Icchak Lejb (1852–1915), pisarz, tworzył w języku jidysz. Autor opowiadań i sztuk teatralnych (przyp. wyd.).

[3] Opatoszu (właśc. Opatowski Josef, 1887–1954), pisarz żydowski, autor powieści i opowiadań w jęz. jidysz, w których m.in. opisywał udział Żydów w walkach o wolność Polski. Od 1907 r. przebywał w USA (przyp. wyd.).

tów, gimnazjów, instytutów naukowych — między innymi słynny Instytut YIVO we Wilnie i Wyższa Szkoła Studiów Judaistycznych w Warszawie, mająca status uniwersytecki. Kwitła prasa żydowska w języku jidysz, hebrajskim i polskim (w roku 1939 było w Polsce 30 żydowskich gazet codziennych i 130 periodyków najrozmaitszego rodzaju). Były niezliczone związki i stowarzyszenia handlowe i zawodowe — pisarzy, dziennikarzy, prawników, kupców, właścicieli realności (w latach trzydziestych 40% posiadłości miejskich w Warszawie było w żydowskich rękach). Była gęsta sieć instytucji charytatywnych, szpitali, sierocińców, kas pożyczkowych, obozów letnich dla ludzi mniej majętnych. Były kluby sportowe. Nade wszystko — były partie polityczne, każda ze swoją organizacją młodzieży, z wizją lepszej przyszłości. W Sejmie i Senacie zasiadali wybrani przedstawiciele żydostwa, reprezentujący całą jego polityczną różnorodność.

Społeczeństwo to było pełne wewnętrznych waśni, antagonizmów i konfliktów. Ale ponad różnicami społecznymi i politycznymi łączyło je przekonanie o wspólnym losie wszystkich Żydów. Istniało też, nawet w sferach odległych od religii, omal powszechne, instynktowne przywiązanie i respekt dla duchowych wartości, pojmowanych jako esencja żydowskiej etyki; głęboko zakorzeniona wiara, że człowiek ma się wspinać ponad codzienność ku rzeczom wyższym, jakkolwiek by je definiować.

Godzi się pamiętać, że była też szeroka strefa, w której podział na świat polski i świat żydowski zacierał się i długie współżycie niosło wzajemną tolerancję i harmonię. Na tym styku działała swojego rodzaju osmoza, z dobroczynnymi skutkami dla obu kultur. Na polskiej ziemi kwitła żydowska cywilizacja, ze swoistą tradycją, językiem, folklorem, literaturą, muzyką, o korzeniach głębszych i starszych niż cywilizacja polska.

Czy któremuś z Polaków przyszło na myśl, że w sąsiednim mieście, ba, na tej samej ulicy, działo się coś, co zasługiwało na uwagę? Że istniała tu specyficzna cywilizacja? Trzeba przyznać, że — z małymi wyjątkami — taka myśl się w umyśle Polaka nie rodziła. Ludność żydowska była nagminnie uważana za „czarny ląd", prymitywny i zacofany, wywołujący uczucie niechęci i odrazy. Polak automatycznie uważał się za istotę stojącą nieporównanie wyżej — każdy Polak wyżej od każdego Żyda — od rabina, od pisarza, od kupca, od szewca. Żydzi reagowali na to wzruszeniem ramion: czego się można „po nich" spodziewać? Jakoś nie pasowaliśmy do siebie. Ale jak tu oczekiwać, że mniejszość liczna, widoczna, konkurencyjna, świadoma swej odrębności i swych własnych narodowych aspiracji, ma równocześnie „pasować" do otoczenia — na to pytanie jeszcze nikt nie odpowiedział, na to wręcz nie ma odpowiedzi; o czym wszyscy aż nadto dobrze wiemy...

Migawka z pamięci: wracając do Krakowa pierwszy raz po wojnie, unikałem ulicy, gdzie mieściło się nasze dawne mieszkanie. Ale z czasem zdawało się, że rany się zabliźniły i podczas jednej z mych późniejszych wizyt w kraju ogarnęło mnie nieodparte pragnienie, by rzucić okiem na dom kiedyś rodzinny — czy zachowały się stare meble, ta szafa z książkami, ten bohomaz Jerzego Kossaka *Odwrót Napoleona spod Moskwy* co wisiał nad biurkiem? Dom stał w dzielnicy, która wtedy uchodziła za średniozamożną, obecnie — jeśli sądzić po obłupanych fasadach — zaniedbana, podupadła, bezpańska.

Wszedłem do znajomej bramy. W kącie ta sama czy łudząco podobna kupka gruzów co przed laty. Przy świetle zapałki odczytałem z listy lokatorów nazwisko rodziny w mieszkaniu numer 4. Gdy zbierałem się na odwagę, aby wspiąć się na schody i układałem w myśli, jak tu przeprosić za moją upiorną wizytę — otworzyły się drzwi w mieszkaniu na parterze. Wyszedł jakiś mężczyzna, zachmurzony, zły — jak to jest w zwyczaju. „Zgubiliście tu co? Czego tu szukacie? Niczego tu dla was nie ma!" Istotnie — pomyślałem. Jak on to trafnie wyraził... Czego ja tu szukam? Niczego tu dla mnie nie ma.

W filmie Lanzmana *Shoah* jest scena, w której chłopi, opisując Żydów, mówią, że Żydzi cuchnęli. Odpowiadając na pytanie, co to był za zapach, mówią, że był to zapach skóry. Istotnie, Żydzi ci pracowali w garbarni i trudno wymagać, by roztaczali zapach róż. Tę woń skóry mam po dziś dzień w nozdrzach, wielu członków mej rodziny pracowało w branży skórzanej.

W latach trzydziestych odnotowano następujący wypadek: jakiś polski arystokrata opuścił przedział kolejowy, gdy wszedł do niego Żyd. „Nie mam nic przeciwko Żydom — powiedział — po prostu nie znoszę zapachu czosnku". Incydent ten był opisany w prasie i zdaje się o nim mówi fragment wiersza Tuwima:

> ...i ty, fortuny skurwysynu,
> gówniarzu uperfumowany,
> co splendor oraz spleen Londynu
> nosisz na gębie zakazanej...itd.[1]

Prawda, że na żydowskiej ulicy unosił się specyficzny zapach — potu, stęchłych mieszkań, niewietrzonej pościeli, pikantnych przypraw (jak mówi Gomulicki: „... z kuchni woń ryb smażonych płynęła niemiła"), kwaśny zapach ubóstwa, to, co Niemcy nazywają *Armeleutegeruch*. Nie był to zapach tylko żydowski, ale ten drugi, w odróżnieniu, miał też w sobie mocny dodatek wódki. Przypomina się słynna fraszka Paczkowskiego:

> Są dwa poważne powody,
> Dla których Polska mi zbrzydła:
> Za dużo święconej wody,
> Za mało zwykłego mydła.

---

[1] Z tomiku *Jarmark rymów* (przyp. aut.).

Dla uzupełnienia obrazu — jeszcze parę migawek, które rzucają światło na sytuację Żyda urodzonego i dorastającego w kraju, gdzie katolicyzm dominował i był wszechobecny w atmosferze jak powietrze.

Jednego razu, dawno, dawno temu, nasza — jak się wtedy mówiło — „służąca", a dziś chyba „gosposia" — powodowana rzetelną troską o moją duszę, zaprowadziła mnie do kościoła i kazała mi podnieść oczy na tę ogromną postać rozpiętą na krzyżu, przybitą gwoździami, z krwią sączącą się z ran. Pochylona nade mną szeptała gorączkowo: „To jest Bóg-Jezus Chrystus, i On cię kocha, choć jesteś Żydem i twoi przodkowie Go ukrzyżowali — i zaklinam cię, ani słowa o tym twojej Mamie". Byłem jakby omdlały ze strachu, brakło mi tchu. Gdy wróciłem do domu, zanosiłem się od płaczu, ale nie sposób było ze mnie wydobyć przyczynę. (Może z tego doświadczenia wywodzi się moje długotrwałe zainteresowanie kwestiami teologii. Po wielu latach i wielu uczonych książkach, gdy licznik coraz szybciej bije, pozostaję zatwardziałym agnostykiem, dzięki Bogu. To mi dobrze służy za dnia, choć nie tak dobrze w bezsenne noce).

Przypominam sobie z dzieciństwa, że gdy jakiś urwis z sąsiedztwa chciał mi dokuczyć albo mnie przegonić, robił to nie kijem czy kamieniem (choć czasami i w ten sposób), lecz metodą, którą uznał za bardziej wyrafinowaną: ustawiał palce wskazujące obu rąk w znak krzyża i pchał mi je pod oczy — oczekiwał, że się żachnę i będę zmykał — w czym się nie mylił.

Wydaje mi się, że ta ilustracja *Ecclesiae Militans* daje temat do rozważań, jak się potoczyły — nie, jak musiały się potoczyć — losy tych dwóch chłopców: tego, który robił znak krzyża i tego, co zasłaniał przed nim oczy.

Na koniec — scenka z mojego niedawnego pobytu w Krakowie. Mam zwyczaj, gdy zmrok zapada, opuszczać mą ulubioną kanapkę u Noworolskiego i iść po przekątnej Rynku do kościoła Mariackiego. Kontempluję ołtarz Wita Stwosza i przysłuchuję się wieczornemu nabożeństwu.

Podczas ostatniej wizyty moim sąsiadem na ławie był młody mężczyzna o uduchowionej twarzy, który modlił się w wielkim skupieniu. Gdyśmy razem wychodzili z kościoła, wdaliśmy się w rozmowę, z wzrastającą sympatią i zainteresowaniem — dwaj autentyczni krakowianie kolejnych pokoleń. Wyrażał się jasno i precyzyjnie. Jedno zdanie szczególnie utkwiło mi w pamięci: „Ja jestem, jak pan widzi, wierzącym i praktykującym katolikiem. Jestem także znawcą historii chrześcijaństwa. Wiem doskonale — i nie mam z tym większych trudności — że Jezus, nasz Zbawiciel, był Żydem. Czego jakoś w żaden sposób nie mogę emocjonalnie zaakceptować, to faktu, że Matka Boska, Święta Maryja, Królowa Korony Polskiej, była Żydówką".

Nie wiedziałem, co mu powiedzieć. Zrozumienie tych dylematów w sposób nietrywialny, głęboki, sprawiedliwy, obiektywny, przerasta moje zdolności, i, wydaje mi się, zdolności większości z nas.

Chciałbym zakończyć te wspominki dwoma cytatami. Jeden, ze zbioru wierszy mego przyjaciela Jerzego Ficowskiego, którego *Odczytanie popiołów* uważam za najbardziej wymowny i wzruszający głos Polaka na temat zagłady Żydów:

> ...
> przez podlasia zarzecza
> przez jesień zgarbionych lichtarzy
> przez komory gazowe
> kirkuty powietrzne
> szli do Jeruszalaim
> i martwi i żywi
> w swoje powrotne ongiś
>
> i aż tam przemycili
> garstkę wierzbowych gruszek
> i na pamiątkę
> ze śledzia
> do dziś kłującą ość

I drugi cytat, z opowiadania *Kometa* Brunona Schulza, gdzie opisuje on kres jednego ze światów:

> Tak jest, tak jak stał, niegotowy i niewykończony, w przypadkowym punkcie czasu i przestrzeni, bez zamknięcia rachunków, nie dobiegłszy do żadnej mety, w połowie zdania niejako, bez kropki i wykrzyknika, bez sądu...

Prorocze epitafium dla świata, którego już nie ma.

The Jews in Poland
Jagiellonian University, Cracow 1992

Kraków błogosławionej pamięci

By o Krakowie dumać na londyńskim bruku, wystarczy drobny bodziec — jakieś słowo dawno nie słyszane, czyjeś imię, strzępek melodii, smak biszkopta domowego wypieku — niczym u Prousta. Fotografie Markowskiego otwierają na oścież zawory pamięci. „Coś się kłębi i jak w malignie..." Ale nie ponosi mnie ochota, by dać temu upust, wręcz przeciwnie, piętrzy się opór, instynktowny odruch, by zejść temu z drogi. To wszystko było dawno, przed potopem, z tamtej strony koszmaru. Nie ma poczucia ciągłości, tam się wszystko nagle, gwałtownie przerwało. Ludzie, z którymi tę przeszłość dzieliłem, są rozproszeni po świecie (przeważnie tamtym). Chcę uciekać — ale coś mnie trzyma... Byłem naocznym świadkiem owego okresu historii i ten czas jest w mej pamięci wytatuowany. Do przezwyciężenia oporu, by dać temu wyraz, ośmiela mnie przekonanie, że każde autentyczne świadectwo jest ważne — nie ma tego wiele, a jest to wszystko, co po nas zostanie.

Dla mnie Polska owych czasów to wyłącznie Kraków. Nie tylko, że nie byłem w „Kutnie lub Sieradzu", ale nie byłem w Warszawie, bo po co? Na wakacjach niedaleko, w Zakopanem, Zawoi czy Rabce — powrót do Krakowa był radosnym wydarzeniem. Przypuszczam, że mieszkańcy Lwowa, Łodzi czy Warszawy mieli podobny patriotyzm lokalny, ale trudno mi to sobie wyobrazić. Miało to miasto jakiś swoisty czar, który zapadł w serce, skoro prawdziwi krakowianie, gdziekolwiek człek się na nich natknie (rzadko w samym Krakowie), tak ciepło go wspominają (nawet ci, którzy do reszty kraju nie mają żadnego sentymentu).

Był mały i piękny. Mały — to coraz wyżej ceniona zaleta. Najdłuższy chyba spacer (tj. nie wybiegając do Lasku Wolskiego, na Wolę Justowską czy Sikornik) był z Cichego Kącika, przez Błonia, koło Parku Jordana i boiska „Cracovii", przez Wolską, pod Uniwersytetem, Szewską, Rynkiem, Sienną, Starowiślną, przez „3 Most", do Podgórza, pod bramę domu dziewczyny — niemal codzienny spacer, nie dość długi, by zdążyć wszystko sobie powiedzieć.

Jakiś czas temu spotkałem w Londynie starszego pana, którego zawierucha wojenna przywiała do Meksyku. Okazało się, że to z pochodzenia krakowianin, więc wiadomo, od pierwszego wejrzenia nawiązuje się komitywa i nić sympatii (jakby samo to pochodzenie gwarantowało jakość). Jakoś nie natknęliśmy się na siebie przed wojną. Gdzie mieszkałeś? Na Sebastiana. Co za zbieg okoliczności, ja też. Pod którym numerem? Pod 33. Ach, ja mieszkałem pod 6. To było daleko, nic dziwnego, że nie znaliśmy się...

Był piękny. Okalał go pierścień Plant, gdzie wiosną kwitły jaśminy i bez (ten biały i ten bzowy), gdzie były urocze zakątki: „Pod Łabędziami", pod pomnikiem Grażyny, Grottgera albo Michała Bałuckiego, przy wejściu „od kuchni" do Teatru Słowackiego. Był Wawel z Dzwonem Zygmunta, Katedrą, Smoczą Jamą, pomnikiem Kościuszki, widokiem na zakręt Wisły. Gdy stałeś pod arkadami Sukiennic i obejmowałeś wzrokiem Rynek, kościółek św. Wojciecha, pomnik Mickiewicza, kościół Mariacki, roztaczała się przed tobą panorama, jaka nie ma sobie równej. (Przyłapuję się na tym, że piszę o tym w czasie przeszłym, a to wszystko przecież dziś na szczęście stoi jak stało, nie zmienione, a tylko dla mnie jest to czas bardzo przeszły).

Przejdź ulicą Grodzką i Stradom, gdzie jest kino „Warszawa", pamiętne jako scena wieców politycznych — tu przemawiał Włodzimierz Żabotyński po wyroku za zabójstwo Arlosoroffa w Palestynie. Przekroczysz ulicę Dietla, tę szeroką arterię biegnącą od Grzegórzek po Wisłę, i już jesteś w sercu byłego żydowskiego Kazimierza. Tu była restauracja Thorna, tu kamienica Süssera, która mogła służyć za model do tego wiersza Gomulickiego, gdzie „na krużgankach balkonów pościel się wietrzyła, z kuchni woń ryb smażonych płynęła niemiła, a w kącie dwie akacje marły na suchoty". Na podwórze tej kamienicy wylegały tłumy na zebrania protestacyjne (pretekstów nie brakowało). Nie było mikrofonów, mówcy wydzierali sobie płuca, stojąc na ganku — przeciw ograniczeniom emigracji do Palestyny, przeciw ustawie Prystorowej mającej na celu zniesienie uboju rytualnego, przeciw pogromowi w Przytyku, przeciw awanturze Doboszyńskiego w Myślenicach...

Zapuść się w ten labirynt uliczek, zaułków noszących imiona ze Starego Testamentu — Jakuba, Józefa, Izaaka, Estery. Tu na ulicy Szerokiej była „tandeta" — można ją nazwać „matką wszystkich tandet". Tu słynna bóżnica Remu, nazwana na cześć wielkiego krakowskiego rabina i uczonego, Mojżesza Isserlesa, i wielka Stara Bożnica „Alterschul".

Na rogu ulic Brzozowej i Podbrzezia (nie zalatywało tu wonią drzew, ale aromatem świeżego pieczywa z piekarni p. Beigla) stała szkoła, Szkoła Powszechna i Gimnazjum Hebrajskie, by dać jej pełny tytuł. Parę lat temu przypadło mi w udziale odsłonić na fasadzie tych budynków tablice pamiątkowe, w języku polskim i hebrajskim, przypominające przechodniom, że tu było coś żydowskiego.

Był to zakład wychowawczy ze świeckim programem obowiązującym w gimnazjach państwowych. Dodatkowo była nauka przedmiotów judaistycznych — Biblii, historii literatury w języku hebrajskim. Uczniowie ciągnęli do szkoły z daleka — z Dębnik, z Prądnika, z Krowodrzy, nawet z Wieliczki. Opłaty były skromne, większość miała zniżki lub zwolnienie, nikt nie był odesłany z kwitkiem. Wychowankowie, którzy w ciągu lat przeszli przez wrota tej szkoły, żywili do niej prawdziwą miłość. Była to oaza, w której można się było wyżyć, a także czegoś się nauczyć, w złudnym przeświadczeniu, że świat był i pozostanie życzliwy.

Na ulicy Miodowej był tzw. Tempel, synagoga postępowa, w której kaznodzieją był szacowny Dr Ozjasz Thon, poseł na Sejm, przewodniczący Koła Posłów Żydowskich w Sejmie, syjonistyczny przywódca. Niedaleko stamtąd były inne bóżnice, Poppera, Kupa, Ajzyka, Wysoka. Na ulicy Orzeszkowej pod nr 7 była redakcja i drukarnia „Nowego Dziennika", który (jak „Chwila" we Lwowie i „Nasz Przegląd" w Warszawie) był żydowską gazetą codzienną w języku polskim — dla większości czytelników główne i niezastąpione źródło informacji o tym, co działo się w Polsce, w Palestynie, na świecie. Nakład wzrastał, gdy działo się coś, co społeczność specjalnie poruszało. W roku 1924/1925 toczył się we Lwowie proces Steigera, Żyda oskarżonego o zamach na życie prezydenta Wojciechowskiego. Bronili go znakomici reprezentanci palestry, między innymi Natan Loewenstein i Leib Landau (a także nie-Żydzi, jak Grek i Szurley). Ich wywody i przemówienia przez całe tygodnie trzymały czytelników w napięciu. Na przekór oczywistej manipulacji władz, które proces ukartowały, Steiger został uniewinniony — ku wielkiej uldze żydowskiego społeczeństwa, czującego się tą sprawą spotwarzone i zagrożone.

Na ulicy Bocheńskiej był teatr żydowski — zespoły aktorów, w tym słynna „Trupa Wileńska" z Jonaszem Turkowem, grały sztuki autorów żydowskich — Pereca, Szaloma Alejchema, Goldfadena, Anskiego. Za rogiem na Skawińskiej mieścił się kahał — zarząd gminy żydowskiej, a także Żydowskie Towarzystwo Gimnastyczne.

Jednym z ośrodków życia żydowskiego było boisko sportowe „Makkabi", gdzie w lecie odbywały się mecze piłki nożnej, a w zimie ślizgawka. Klub „Makkabi", z sekcją piłkarską (drużyna ta wygrała raz z „Cracovią" 1 : 0; raz tylko i dawno temu, ale o „roku ów! Kto cię widział w naszym kraju...!"). Były sekcje wszystkich dziedzin sportu, lekkoatletki miały chlubne wyniki, a sekcja piłki wodnej miała mistrzostwo Polski. W święta państwowe i żydowskie święto Lag Be'Omer (w osiemnastym dniu miesiąca Iyar) orkiestra hebrajskiego gimnazjum (mój starszy brat, Kazio, był jej pierwszym „tamburmajorem"), poprzedzona biało-niebieskim sztandarem, szła pochodem na boisko, gdzie odbywały się popisy gimnastyczne i zawody sportowe uczniów i uczennic. Niedaleko stamtąd był lokal Haszomer Hacair — organizacji młodzieży skrajnej lewicy, na granicy komunizmu, granicy ledwo widocznej. W różnych lokalach na Kazimierzu gnieździły się rozmaite organizacje młodzieży robotniczej, studenckiej — Haszachar, Akiba, Gordonia, Massada, Betar.

Podczas gdy część młodzieży kształciła się i wyżywała ideologicznie, inna wysiadywała w kawiarniach (ja byłem i tu, i tam) — w „Feniksie", u „Bisanza", w „Esplanadzie", w „Cyganerii" (wsławionej podczas okupacji atakiem żydowskiej organizacji podziemnej na oficerów niemieckich). Moją ulubioną kawiarnią była „Jama Michalika", siedziba w swoim czasie kabaretu Zielony

Balonik, po którym zostały nieocenione *Słówka* Boya. Niejedną tam godzinę przesiedziałem na pluszowej kanapce, wydaje mi się, że jest zroszona łzami tej dziewczyny, z którą wtedy, jak się to mówiło, „chodziłem" (nie byłem dla niej dobry, żałuję tego).

Wypada wspomnieć ulicę Szpitalną, wprawdzie poza obszarem Kazimierza, ale była to w pewnym sensie ulica żydowska. Nie tylko dlatego, że istniała tam bóżnica, ale z powodu licznych antykwariatów książek, należących do Taffetów, Seidenów — handel starymi książkami, podobnie jak cholewkarstwo czy zegarmistrzostwo, to była prawie wyłącznie żydowska domena. Z początkiem każdego roku szkolnego odbywał się tam istny karnawał — tłumy uczniów, studentów przewalały się przez chodnik i jezdnię sprzedając, kupując i wymieniając krakowskim targiem zeszłoroczne książki na „nowe", setnie się przy tym bawiąc.

Ulica Dietla, po obu stronach tych „gorszych" Plant, miała ponad sto kamienic — od Wisły aż po wiadukt kolejowy. Tutaj gnieździło się parę tysięcy żydowskich rodzin (w pewnym okresie i moja). Kiedy przechodzę tą ulicą, wydaje mi się, że pamiętam tych wszystkich ludzi z twarzy i imienia — Einhornów, Johanesów, Luftglasów, Lipschützów, Bloederów, Sonntagów, Fallmanów, Ohrensteinów, Rakowerów, Weisbrodów, Holzerów — aż po Schneidrów, tych od „Makkabi" i wody sodowej, wszystkich tych, których — jak mówi Ficowski — „przyłapano na gorącym uczynku życia".

Mieszkanie rodzinne mieściło się w pewnym okresie w domu narożnym przy ulicy św. Sebastiana i Berka Joselewicza, tak blisko szkoły, że gdy słyszałem dzwonek, przyśpieszałem kroku i wbiegałem do klasy jeszcze przed nauczycielem. Ulicę Berka Joselewicza upamiętnił Boy w *Słówkach*, pisząc, że ulica ta „posiadała w Krakowie swoje osobliwe przeznaczenie" i że Wilhelm Feldman, z którego pochodzenia i akcentu Boy dobrotliwie podrwiwa, też może doczeka się ulicy, po której „będziem jeździć do hetery" (historyk obyczajów mógłby wnioskować z tego, że nie było wiele domów rozpusty w Krakowie, skoro panowie musieli jechać po to fiakrem aż na Kazimierz).

Dla mnie ulica Berka wiązała się z czymś całkiem innym. Pod numerem 5, w oficynie, mieszkał Mordechaj Gebirtig, stolarz. Pamiętam jego drobną niepozorną postać, mało kto zwracał na niego uwagę, on sam nie wierzyłby, gdyby mu ktoś przepowiedział pośmiertną sławę. Gebirtig był autentycznym pieśniarzem ludowym, bardem ulicy żydowskiej — komponował melodie i teksty w jidysz, które przekazywano sobie z ust do ust. Jedną z najpopularniejszych jego pieśni jest napisana w 1936 roku, po pogromie w Przytyku, *Dos sztetł brent (Miasteczko gore)*, wzywająca do czynu, często potem śpiewana w getcie. W jednym z wierszy Gebirtig żegna się z Krakowem, przed wywózką do obozu: „Krakowie, bądź mi pozdrowiony / przed domem czeka zaprzężony wóz / jak psa mnie gnają stąd / ostatni raz cię widzę może / miejsce tak bliskie i znajome / na grobie matki wypłakałem serce / ostatnią łzą zwilżyłem kamień ojca /

święta ta ziemia…" W innym wierszu, pisanym w lutym 1940, zatytułowanym *S'tut wej*! (*To boli*) Gebirtig skarży się na tych „synów i córy polskie, których się Polska kiedyś powstydzi", którzy drwią z cierpień zadawanych Żydom przez wspólnego wroga. Anna Kamieńska napisała piękną balladę o „stolarzu i poecie żydowskim z Krakowa".

Gebirtig miał dwie urodziwe córki. O jednej z nich napisał piosenkę — jak to na chodniku przed domem stoi chłopiec, który gwiżdżąc wzywa ją na schadzkę. Matka ostrzega, nie idź, to jakiś nieżydowski urwis, żydowscy chłopcy tak się nie zachowują. Myliła się — tym urwisem łacno mogłem być ja. Niejeden raz stałem naprzeciw bramy tego domu, czekając, by, jak w piosence, Rejzełe zbiegła do mnie po schodach.

Gebirtiga, razem z córkami, zamordowali Niemcy w 1942 roku. Po wojnie jego pieśni zostały wydane w zbiorach, zostały nagrane, są w repertuarach koncertów — część żydowskiej, krakowskiej spuścizny.

Naszym sąsiadem był szewc Fischer. Miał warsztat na parterze, od ulicy, gdzie go widać było do późnej nocy pochylonego nad kopytem. Mieszkał w jednym pokoiku z kuchnią, w oficynie, z dojściem spiralnymi, żelaznymi schodami. Zadeklarował, że będzie płodzić dzieci, aż mu się urodzi córka, więc wpierw był Jankiel, Hesiek, Josek, Szmulik, Mojsie — aż położyły temu kres narodziny Sabci.

Ocalał jedynie zaradny Szmulik — mój rówieśnik. Opisał mi swą metodę, gdy się natknąłem na niego w Krakowie zaraz po wyzwoleniu. Grał na harmonii na stopniach kościoła św. Katarzyny, nucąc cichutko chasydzkie melodie — jedyne, jakie znał. Był w łachmanach, miał umorusaną twarz i przymykał oczy — ciemne okulary były jedynie rekwizytem — udawał niewidomego, ale to, co widział, wypełniłoby tomy. Sypiał w jakiejś piwnicy, w tekturowym pudle wypchanym gazetami, gdzie go gryzły szczury. Przez lata nie zamienił z nikim słowa. Ludzie dawali mu grosik, kromkę chleba, dożywiał się odpadkami ze śmietników, gdy mógł, kradł jakieś ochłapy. Przy pierwszej okazji wyjechał do Palestyny. Padł od egipskiej kuli w wojnie 1948 roku. Ot, dziecko naszych czasów, żydowskie dziecko naszych czasów.

Pamiętam, w maju 1935, ostatni etap pogrzebu Piłsudskiego — lawetę jadącą przez miasto na Wawel. Pochód obserwowałem z okna Kolektury Losów Loterii Państwowej Braci Safer (dużego przedsiębiorstwa pod hasłem „Szukasz szczęścia — wstąp na chwilę").

W pochodzie za trumną, pośród dygnitarzy z całej Europy, zwracał uwagę kapiący medalami marszałek *Luftwaffe* Hermann Göring. Szli też w czołówce prezydent miasta, były legionista (co miało z urzędem związek przyczynowy) Kapellner-Kaplicki, oraz komendant garnizonu generał Bernard Mond (jedyny w Polsce Żyd w tej randze). Krakowianie przywykli byli do tego, że państwowym obchodom przewodziła trójca: Arcybiskup Sapieha pomiędzy Kapellnerem-Kaplickim i Mondem.

Kraj okryła żałoba — szczera lub udana. Nie było bezpiecznie bagatelizować tę narodową tragedię i nie okazywać żalu. Hołdy i panegiryki w prasie i z mównicy publicznej nie znały miary. Był też prawdziwy żal, poczucie osierocenia — „Dziadek", ten mityczny, był kochany i uważano, że los narodu spoczywa w jego opiekuńczych rękach.

Pamiętam, że mój ojciec, zasklepiony całkowicie w swym światku codziennych kłopotów, na wiadomość o śmierci Marszałka nie mógł się powstrzymać od łez, co mnie zdumiało i wzruszyło, nieczęsto widziałem go poruszonego do głębi publiczną sprawą. Podzielał widać rozpowszechnione w społeczności żydowskiej przekonanie, że Piłsudski, wróg Dmowskiego, był niejako tarczą przed programem i wybrykami endecji i że z zakończeniem jego epoki nadejdzie gorszy, groźny czas. Wypadki aż nazbyt szybko wykazały, jak jasnowidząca i trafna była ta opinia.

Krakowianie byli dumni ze swego miasta, z jego tradycji kulturalnych, puszyli się. Warszawiacy, Łodzianie, Lwowiacy patrzyli na nich z pobłażaniem jako na prowincjonalnych dusigroszów. Prawdą było, że przed godziną 10 wieczorem miasto pustoszało, ludzie gnali w te pędy do domu, by zdążyć, nim stróż zamknie bramę i trzeba będzie zapłacić mu 20 groszy za „szperę". Mówiono, że typowym krakowskim zaproszeniem była formuła: „Przyjdźcie do nas po kolacji, będzie herbata świeżo dziś rano zaparzona..."

W społeczeństwie, zarówno polskim, jak żydowskim, była ostra gradacja pozycji na socjalnej drabinie, wiadomo było „kto miał przodek wszędy", aspiracje ponad stan źle widziano.

Przypominam sobie taką scenę. Na rogu ulic Starowiślnej i Dietla siedział żebrak. Mówię siedział, ale to przesada. Był bez nóg, miał kikuty owinięte szmatami, posuwał się po chodniku, przenosząc tułów metr po metrze, wspierając się rękami, w których trzymał jakieś drewniane uchwyty. Trudno opisać ten środek lokomocji. Gdy było błoto, a było często (jakości już dzisiaj rzadko spotykanej), szmaty chlapały i zostawiały za sobą smugę brudu. Widok zaiste przerażający, ale spowszedniały; przechodziło się koło tego nieszczęśnika bez dreszczu, rzucając mu grosik do garnuszka zawieszonego na szyi.

Pewnego dnia dowiedziałem się, że biedak ma potomstwo — byłem wstrząśnięty, jak on to robi? Syn tego żebraka został uczniem w naszej szkole. Fakt ten stał się kiedyś przedmiotem ostrej dyskusji w naszej rodzinie. Mój ojciec uważał takie aspiracje nędzarza za arogancję, za wygórowaną ambicję, podczas gdy my, ja i mój brat, twierdziliśmy, że on ma te same uprawnienia co my, ba, lepsze. „Lepsze?!" — mój ojciec był bliski apopleksji, przerażony faktem, że spłodził półgłówków.

„Pełno ich — nigdzie" — mówi Ficowski. Ta wieczna tłumna nieobecność jest tutaj dla mnie bardziej namacalna niż gdziekolwiek indziej na świecie. Jak żyć, skoro wiesz, że wszyscy ludzie, których wtedy znałeś — rodzina, przyjaciele, sąsiedzi, nauczyciele, sklepikarze, żebracy — zginęli: z głodu, od kuli, od gazu, w mękach; i że ty sam, tylko przez jakiś przypadkowy zbieg okoliczności, nie zginąłeś wraz z nimi? Nie umiem tego wyrazić słowami, myślę, że takie słowa nie istnieją.

Ten ludzki krajobraz, który Markowski utrwala na fotografii, nie wydawał się nam wówczas atrakcyjny. Wręcz przeciwnie — wyznaję to z poczuciem wstydu — wielu z nas patrzyło na to z zażenowaniem. Te brody, pejsy, krzywe nosy, zamglone oczy — co myślą o tym nasi nieżydowscy współobywatele?...

Teraz jest jasne, że te twarze przeorane troską i mądrością, uduchowione, żarzące się jakimś wewnętrznym światłem, jakby z portretów Rembrandta, były wręcz piękne. Trzeba było kataklizmu, by to docenić. Pozostaje nam odmawiać za nich modlitwę ogromnym milczeniem.

Wstęp do albumu: Stanisław Markowski, *Krakowski Kazimierz 1870–1988*, Wydawnictwo Arka, Kraków 1992

Cum ira et studio

Jak wynika z raportów w prasie, z listów, z rozmów, konferencja w Oksfordzie spotkała się z aprobatą tych, którzy brali w niej udział i tych, do których dotarły jej pogłosy. Zgodnie z zamierzeniami organizatorów, dano sposobność do wymiany poglądów, dociekania, jak to istotnie z tymi Żydami w Polsce było. Być może był to zaczyn, który będzie fermentował, a także będzie miał znaczenie terapeutyczne.

Temat jest obszerny, skomplikowany i w większości aspektów niemiły; obie strony podejmują go z ciężkim sercem. Wydaje mi się, że Polacy, którzy chcą o tych rzeczach myśleć i mówić (być może jest ich tylko garstka), czują się w tej materii nieswojo, jak gdyby się spodziewali, że wypłynie na powierzchnię coś, z czym będzie się trudno uporać. Nikt nie lubi zarzutów pod swoim adresem, tych urojonych ani tym bardziej tych prawdziwych.

Pośród Żydów też jest wielu takich, którzy nie chcą do tego tematu wracać, nie chcą rozdrapywać ran; chcą o przeszłości w Polsce zapomnieć, odwrócić się od tego na zawsze. Konferencje, sympozja, dialogi poświęcone tym sprawom uważają za luksus pięknoduchów, pytają, co komu z tego.

Zagłada Żydów w Polsce (unikam słowa *holocaust*, bo jest ono zgoła niefortunne i znieczulające, nawet w językach, w których się przez częsty użytek zadomowiło — a na pewno już całkiem sztuczne w polskim) pozostawiła w psychice ocalałych urazy tak krwawe i głębokie, że ich reakcje nie zawsze są wyważone. Trzeba ostrzec: nie będziemy mówili na ten temat „obiektywnie" — obiektywizm, tj. dystans, spokój, równowaga, byłby tu sztuczną pozą.

Tkanka współżycia Polaków i Żydów na ziemi polskiej została bezpowrotnie zniszczona. Tych parę tysięcy pozostałych w Polsce Żydów, którzy się za takich otwarcie uważają i którzy niejako przepraszają, że żyją — bez szkół, bez rabina, bez synagog, bez kontaktu z Izraelem, bez kierownictwa, bez przyszłości — są fizycznie i duchowo społecznością w zaniku, nikt nie ma co do tego złudzeń. Trzeba przyznać — może to niegodziwe, ale Żydzi na świecie przestali się o nich troszczyć, odpisali ich niejako na straty, więc ze strony żydowskiej nie mówimy o sprawach aktualnych, a wyłącznie o historii.

Natomiast dla Polaków jest to, wydaje mi się, tematyka żywotna i pierwszorzędnej wagi. Tysiącletnia obecność Żydów na ziemiach polskich i ta nagła i ostateczna nieobecność to są fakty, bez których nie można zrozumieć własnej przeszłości, a zatem i teraźniejszości. Historia Polski — w wersji nauczanej i udostępnianej — jest zakłamana nie tylko na tym odcinku, jak wszędzie, gdzie ma monopol oficjalna wersja przykrojona do bieżącego dogmatu i gdzie badacz jest skrępowany brakiem dostępu do źródeł i cenzorem. Moralna regeneracja wymaga autentycznego dialogu z przeszłością. Własne odbicie w cudzych oczach jest niezbędną korekturą wizerunku w zwierciadle. W tym procesie samopoznania Żydzi występują już nie jako strona, ale jako świadek, którego trzeba uważnie wysłuchać, a także, owszem, przesłuchać.

Jeśli znalazła się sposobność, aby Polacy spotkali się z Żydami na neutralnym gruncie, to ważne jest, aby sobie powiedzieć wzajemnie to, co najbardziej dręczy — nie gwoli rekryminacji i retoryki, ale aby zbliżyć się do prawdy. Był czas, że Polak mógł powiedzieć publicznie o Żydzie co mu się żywnie podobało (najczęściej się nie podobało), a Żydzi musieli to połykać albo uciekać się do szyfru czy eufemizmów — co za ulga, kiedy można rzeczy nazywać po imieniu. Wiadomo też, że z reguły Polacy prywatnie między sobą mówią o Żydach inaczej (szczególnie, że na razie antysemityzm uchodzi jeszcze ciągle za coś, z czym szanujący się człowiek nie afiszuje się), a Żydzi między sobą o Polakach inaczej — warto by się z tej dwulicowości wyzwolić i wreszcie zerwać ze stereotypami.

Po izraelskiej wojnie „sześciodniowej" zmienił się radykalnie stereotyp Żyda w oczach Polaka (i natychmiast narodził się nowy, równie błędny). Żydzi zaś aż nadto często takie mają wyobrażenie o Polakach, że domagają się ustawicznych zapewnień i dowodów, że ten czy inny Polak nie jest antysemitą — uważają takiego za wyjątek.

Wszystko to stanowi niełatwy punkt wyjścia do rzetelnej i szczerej dyskusji. Trzeba by zacząć od uzgodnienia historycznych faktów, ale zgoda na to, co stanowi fakt, też nie jest automatyczna.

Weźmy ten obszerny, choć nieco już przesłonięty mgłą temat stosunków polsko-żydowskich w Polsce Dwudziestolecia. Jeśliby zadać pytanie, czy Polska była wówczas krajem, w którym szerzył się i panoszył antysemityzm, dla każdego Żyda, naocznego świadka, odpowiedź jest tak oczywista i jednoznaczna, że na samą myśl o takim pytaniu „śmiech zbiera pusty, a potem litość i trwoga..."

Ledwie minął pierwszy powiew odzyskanej niepodległości, już się zarysowały zręby antyżydowskiego ruchu, który wzbierał na sile i stał się dla nas zjawiskiem wszechobecnym, wypełniającym atmosferę jak eter. To, że Polacy nie byli i nie są tego świadomi — przynajmniej wielu tak twierdzi — jest dla nas zagadką. Albo zapomnieli, albo patrzyli na to zgoła inaczej — a tym młodszym już nic nie powiedziano i nie mieli się skąd dowiedzieć.

Czy to przesadna żydowska wrażliwość skłania, że pamięta się endecję, chadecję, ONR — stronnictwa polityczne, których głównym programem była mniej czy więcej brutalna walka ze współobywatelami-Żydami? Czy to nasz wymysł, że był oficjalnie aprobowany bojkot gospodarczy, dyskryminacja na wszystkich szczeblach służby państwowej, *numerus clausus* na uniwersytetach, bojówki z żyletkami, getto ławkowe („doroczny wstyd", nazywała to Maria Dąbrowska — to się jej też pamięta!), codzienne judzenie w prasie, programowy i prymitywny antyjudaizm Kościoła, tu i ówdzie pogromy z ofiarami w mieniu i ludziach.

Pod koniec lat trzydziestych dominującą partią był Ozon, który licytował się w antysemityzmie z innymi wymienionymi partiami i jest wielce prawdopodobne, że gdyby nie wybuch wojny, na wokandę sejmową trafiłby jakiś wariant ustaw norymberskich (projekt był gotowy). To były realia polityczne Dwudziestolecia, można powiedzieć: jakaś obsesja antyżydowska, która odciągała uwagę od problemów stokrotnie ważniejszych.

Trzeba jednakowoż opowiedzieć także i o drugiej stronie medalu. Ktoś słusznie zapytał: jeśli było tak źle, to dlaczego było tak dobrze? Albowiem na przekór temu, że klimat był surowy (a może dzięki temu, kto to wie?) kwitło na tych ziemiach pełne, bujne, urozmaicone, twórcze życie żydowskie. Istniała całkowita swoboda kultu, autonomia w sprawach religijnych, z rabinami wszelkiego autoramentu, od ultraortodoksyjnych do tzw. postępowych (jak i dziś, w nieustannej ze sobą waśni!), było szereg „cadyków" ze swymi dworami wiernych, były szkoły z językiem wykładowym hebrajskim i jeszyboty dla studiów Talmudu, była prasa w języku polskim, jidysz i hebrajskim (wedle studium Mariana Fuchsa z Żydowskiego Instytutu Historycznego, w 1939 roku było w Polsce żydowskich 30 gazet codziennych i 130 periodyków wszelkiego rodzaju), wydawnictwa książek religijnych i świeckich, były partie polityczne — syjonistyczne, religijne, robotnicze, asymilatorskie, byli posłowie i senatorzy, literaci i pisarze, były teatry, towarzystwa dobroczynności, kółka oświatowe, kluby sportowe — słowem kwitła specyficzna cywilizacja.

Musimy teraz, choć to dla obu stron niesłychanie trudne, mówić o czasie okupacji. Tutaj jest źródło najboleśniejszego zadrażnienia w stosunkach polsko-żydowskich — nie jestem pewien, czy kiedykolwiek da się coś w tym aspekcie zrobić. Co sprawę zaogniło do cna, to fakt, że od pierwszej chwili po wojnie — i, można rzec, dotychczas — nie zezwolono na ten temat naprawdę szczerze i otwarcie mówić i pisać. Do tematu zagłady Żydów wracało się rzadko i półgębkiem i tylko w myśl oficjalnej tezy: że w swej ogromnej większości społeczeństwo polskie z Żydami współczuło, że gdzie mogło Żydom pomagało i ich ratowało, że sporadyczne wypadki (o które teraz tyle wrzasku) szantażu, donosów i wydawania Żydów to była działalność jednostek, „szumowin z marginesu społecznego", których podziemie karało śmiercią; że w sumie społeczeństwo polskie wyszło z tej okrutnej próby moralnej nadspodziewanie korzystnie i z niesplamionym honorem.

Rozumiem dobrze, że Polacy chcą, że muszą w to wierzyć. Władysław Bartoszewski, naoczny świadek i jeden z organizatorów pomocy Żydom, więc jak mało kto upoważniony do wyrażenia poglądu w tej sprawie, wierzy w to. Ja sam wiele bym dał, by móc w to uwierzyć.

Niestety — i to jest absolutne sedno tej całej sprawy czy rozprawy — opinia Żydów, tj. tych, którzy to wiedzą najlepiej, tych, którzy to przeżyli i tych, którym przekazane zostało świadectwo z pierwszej ręki, w swej przygniatającej większości głosi, że ta teza jest sprzeczna z ich doświadczeniem: że Polacy, z nielicznymi wyjątkami, którym tym większa, wieczna chwała, nie okazywali współczucia, nie pomagali, nie ratowali, że Żyd ukrywający się czy maskujący żył w trwodze nie przed Niemcem, lecz przed sąsiadem i przechodniem, z ich wyostrzoną polską wrażliwością na żydowskie rysy, wymowę czy strach w oczach; że gdyby ów Żyd mógł był liczyć już nie na aktywną pomoc, która wymagała bohaterstwa, ale na neutralność, na to, by Polak patrzył w inną stronę — szanse przeżycia zwiększyłyby się stokrotnie. A gdyby wiadomo było, że można przystać do partyzantki — iluż by się uratowało (wielu myślących, że to była szansa, przypłaciło to życiem).

Chcę zwrócić uwagę na niezwykle znamienny dokument — raport Jana Karskiego, śmiałka i bohatera, który wszedł do historii jako naoczny świadek eksterminacji Żydów w obozie śmierci w Bełżcu i który pierwszy przyniósł na Zachód autentyczne świadectwo o komorach gazowych i krematoriach. Wcześniej tenże Karski był jednym z pierwszych kurierów z okupowanego Kraju i zawitał już w lutym 1940 roku do Angers we Francji, ówczesnej siedziby rządu na emigracji.

Karski był, jak się okazuje, doskonale rozeznany we wszystkich aspektach sytuacji w kraju. Minister Stanisław Kot, żądny najdrobniejszych szczegółów wszystkiego, co się w kraju działo, zlecił Karskiemu m.in. napisanie raportu o sytuacji Żydów. (Oryginały dokumentów znajdują się w Hoover Institution Archives, Stanford, Ca: „Kolekcja Dokumentów Rządu Polskiego", zbiór 921, Akta Informacji i Dokumentacji N/55 — Żydzi, oraz — drugi egzemplarz — Akta Stanisława Mikołajczyka, teczka „Żydzi w okupowanej Polsce". Informacje te zawdzięczam badaniom Dawida Engla).

Elaborat Karskiego jest przenikliwym i dalekowzrocznym sprawozdaniem, pełnym trafnych spostrzeżeń i bezcennych informacji. Konstatuje w nim, że wielu Polaków okazuje Żydom jawną wrogość i w zasadzie sympatyzuje z dążeniem Niemców do „rozwiązania" kwestii żydowskiej na ziemiach okupowanych. Podaję parę cytatów (w tłumaczeniu z dostępnego mi tekstu angielskiego):

„Rozwiązanie kwestii żydowskiej" przez Niemców — stwierdzam to w pełnym poczuciu odpowiedzialności za to, co mówię — jest poważnym i bardzo niebezpiecznym narzędziem w rękach Niemców, prowadzącym do „moralnego rozbrojenia" szerokich sfer polskiego społeczeństwa ... Aczkolwiek naród ich (Niemców) do gruntu nienawidzi, ta kwestia stwarza niejako pomost, po którym Niemcy dochodzą do zgody z wielką częścią społeczeństwa polskiego ... Co więcej, sytuacja ta grozi demoralizacją szerokich sfer ludności i to z kolei może stworzyć poważne problemy dla przyszłych władz, które będą odbudowywały Polskę ... „nauka nie idzie w las" ... Czy nie zaistniałaby możliwość, aby do pewnego stopnia, skoro istnieje trzech przeciwników (jeśli, oczywiście, można w obecnej sytuacji uważać Żydów za przeciwników), starać się stworzyć coś w rodzaju wspólnego frontu dwóch słabszych partnerów przeciwko trzeciemu mocniejszemu i śmiertelnemu wrogowi, a zostawić rozrachunki między tymi dwoma na później? ... Zmontowanie jakiegoś szerszego wspólnego frontu napotka na ogromne trudności z punktu widzenia szerokich sfer polskiej ludności, pośród której antysemityzm bynajmniej się nie zmniejszył...

Jest tego więcej. To nie są już żydowskie wymysły i potwarze — to jest raport Karskiego.

I teraz pointa. Członkowie Rządu (wynika z odręcznych adnotacji, że raport zatrzymano w ścisłym gronie) — Mikołajczyk, Stroński, Kot — zdali sobie sprawę, że jest to dynamit: że opis antyżydowskich nastrojów, ich zasięgu i charakteru mógł, gdyby wyszedł na jaw, zdyskredytować sprawę polską w oczach aliantów. Nie wolno było przedstawić Polaków jako sprzyjających w jakiejkolwiek mierze nazistowskim celom. Cóż robić? Zredagowano drugą wersję raportu, w której cała polska ludność przedstawiona jest jako bez wyjątku zjednoczona w swym potępieniu antyżydowskiej działalności Niemców! Kto tę drugą wersję zredagował, nie wiadomo, może sam Karski. W każdym razie wiedział o niej, albowiem na oryginałach obu wersji są jego własnoręczne adnotacje wskazujące na ustępy różniące się w tekstach. *Sapienti sat.*

Parę lat temu w dyskusji z Andrzejem Szczypiorskim na łamach „Kultury" pisałem, że gdy trwał proces palenia w krematoriach, gdy pociągi do Chełmna, Sobiboru, Bełżca, Treblinki, Majdanka i Oświęcimia szły dzień i noc, i miesiącami buchał dym z kominów — gdyby wtedy wiadomo było, że to nie „Żydki się palą", tylko rodzimi polscy ojcowie, mężowie, matki, żony i dzieci, wybuch gniewu i zemsty narodu byłby nie do opanowania, choćby nawet — użyłem wtedy zwrotu — „szyny przyszło zębami zrywać".

Szczypiorski surowo się wtedy ze mną rozprawił za te „szyny", podkreślając bezsilność społeczeństwa wobec takich akcji jak pacyfikacja Zamojszczyzny, jak łapanki, wywózki do kacetów, publiczne egzekucje, jak systematyczne mordowanie polskiej elity umysłowej, jak późniejsze zmiażdżenie Warszawy, gdy ofiary to była krew z krwi i kość z kości polskiej, i wskazuje, że i wtedy nikt nie rwał szyn zębami... A zatem moje pretensje w tym względzie były nieuzasadnione i krzywdzące.

Wiele od tego czasu na ten temat myślałem — tak jak zawsze, codziennie, o tych rzeczach myślę. Smutno mi, że nie mogę zdania zmienić. To, że proces gazowania i palenia Żydów, który trwał latami, nie został zakłócony ani jednym incydentem z zewnątrz, utrwala mnie w przekonaniu, że społeczeństwo polskie, choć może patrzyło na to ze współczuciem — kamień by się wzruszył! — nie czuło się dostatecznie osobiście dotknięte i wzburzone, by indywidualnie czy zbiorowo interweniować, „wyrywać szyny" czy cokolwiek, bez względu na konsekwencje. To, co Niemcy zrobili w obozach śmierci, można było zrobić tylko Żydom.

Prawdą jest, że w swej goryczy Żydzi często byli i są nieczuli na niedolę i trudności Polaków, nie pamiętają, że za próbę pomocy Żydowi groziła śmierć, myślą, że nic innego się nie liczy tylko stosunek do Żydów, widzą tylko te ciemne strony, „bo się krzywda w głazie ryje, a dobrodziejstwo na piasku…" Ale dopóki polska apologetyka trwa przy swej oficjalnej wersji i uważa opinię żydowską w tym względzie za paszkwil, dopóty będziemy zaangażowani w „dialog głuchych". Tragedią Polaków jest, że pośród okrutnych dopustów losu zostali wystawieni na bezprzykładną, szatańską próbę moralną. Z próby tej nie wyszli zwycięsko. Można twierdzić, że nikt inny z takiej próby nie wyszedłby lepiej — ale dla Żydów mała w tym pociecha.

Parę słów o roli Kościoła. Bartoszewski jakoś zbyt łatwo rozgrzesza polski Kościół — to tak w rzetelnym bilansie nie zostanie. Jeśli Kościół będzie kiedyś miał odwagę (i potrzebę) zrobienia rachunku sumienia, zobaczy z przerażeniem i skruchą, jak wielką rolę w zagładzie żydostwa odegrał jego odwieczny i nieubłagany antysemityzm — *in capite et in membris*. Kościół polski ma w stosunku do Żydów swą własną niechlubną kartę — posiew nienawiści nie obrodził żniwem miłosierdzia. Michał Borwicz omówił stanowisko kleru w związku z pogromami i mordowaniem Żydów po wojnie. Jedno zdanie z wypowiedzi kardynała Wyszyńskiego prześladuje mnie i podważa wiarę w skuteczność dialogu: „Na procesie Bejlisa zebrano dużo dawnych i współczesnych ksiąg żydowskich, lecz kwestia używania przez Żydów krwi nie została decydująco rozwiązana"[1]. Jeśli dla późniejszego kardynała Wyszyńskiego nie było całkiem jasne, czy Żydzi biorą krew na macę, to w co wierzą jego księża i w co pasterska trzoda? A jeśli tak — to z kim i na jaki temat prowadzić dialog?

I taki jeszcze ironiczny splot: najnowszy polski święty, ojciec Kolbe, był w teorii i praktyce zagorzałym antysemitą, i choć jego bohaterska męczeńska śmierć wzbudza podziw i respekt, nie może to zmienić oceny jego wieloletniej, żydożerczej działalności, która, mówiąc łagodnie, do świętości się nie kwalifikowała.

W swym rozdzierającym lamencie *My, Żydzi polscy…*, który Julian Tuwim napisał w Ameryce, gdy doszły go wieści o zagładzie, jest taki passus:

… Na opaskach, jakie nosiliście w ghetcie, wymalowana była gwiazda Dawida. Wierzę w taką przyszłą Polskę, w której ta gwiazda, ta z opasek, stanie się jednym z najwyższych odznaczeń, udzielanych najwaleczniejszym żołnierzom i oficerom polskim. Będą ją z dumą nosili na piersi obok dawnego Virtuti Militari. Będzie i Krzyż Ghetta — nazwa głęboko symboliczna. Będzie Order Żółtej Łaty — zaszczytniejszy niż niejedno

---

[1] Po pogromie w Kielcach (4 czerwca 1946), którego ofiarą padło 42 zabitych i wielu rannych, delegacja organizacji żydowskich została przyjęta na audiencji u Stefana Wyszyńskiego, wówczas biskupa Lublina. W tekście jego wypowiedzi, że wrogość wobec Żydów jest spowodowana „aktywnym udziałem Żydów w politycznym życiu Kraju", znajduje się również powyższy passus o procesie Bejlisa. Cyt. za artykułem Michała Borwicza w publikacji *The Jews in Poland*, Basil Blackwell Ltd., London 1986 (przyp. aut.).

dotychczasowe świecidło ... Z dumą, z żałobną dumą nosić będziemy tę rangę, wszystkie inne zaćmiewającą — rangę Żyda Polskiego — my, cudem i przypadkiem pozostali przy życiu...

Sancta simplicitas. Naiwny, zagubiony, genialny Tuwim (którego opuścił geniusz w powojennej Polsce) dożył, by na własne oczy zobaczyć, że żółta łata pozostała żółtą łatą. Nad wszystkim, co żydowskie postanowiono przejść do porządku dziennego, jak gdyby nic się nie stało. Na tę straszliwą wyrwę w organizmie społeczeństwa narzucono całun zapomnienia. Starano się po prostu nie zauważyć owej ogromnej nieobecności (choć dobrze zauważono i skrzętnie zapamiętano tych, co uchodzili za Żydów w Urzędzie Bezpieczeństwa). Nawet w Oświęcimiu, latami całymi, Żydów jakby pomijano milczeniem — trzeba się było dopytywać o pawilon żydowski i szukać kluczy, by go otworzono, w myśl zasady, że chociaż tylko Żydzi byli gazowani i paleni i zginęło ich tysiąckrotnie więcej niż wszystkich razem wziętych, nie należy wśród ofiar wyróżniać narodowości.

Było wśród Polaków powszechne omal uczucie ulgi, że „problem żydowski" został „rozwiązany" w sposób, za który Polacy nie mogą być obwinieni, że zaczyna się Polskę budować od nowa, bez Żydów — i tak lepiej. Niedobitki Żydów, które wyszły z obozów, z kryjówek, nierzadko spotykały się ze zdaniem, że co jak co, ale Hitler z Żydami dobrą robotę zrobił. Nauka, ta rodzima i ta świeżo zaszczepiona, istotnie — jak przewidział Karski — nie poszła w las.

Tych niewielu, którzy się uratowali na „aryjskich papierach", w większości uznało, że w tym klimacie bezpieczniej jest maskaradę kontynuować i często nie zdradzało swej prawdziwej tożsamości nawet własnym dzieciom. Ci, którzy wrócili z Rosji też się szybko zorientowali w klimacie i przybrali, jeśli mieli po temu dane, barwy ochronne. Zdawało się, że ci „marrani" już się jakoś, acz z wiecznym niepokojem w duszy, przepchają, aleć okazało się, że brzydkie pochodzenie było gdzieś w kartotekach, gwoli przyszłości, skrzętnie odnotowane — a przyszłość, jak było do przewidzenia, nie dała na siebie długo czekać. W tym ponurym okresie od roku 1967 i w następnych latach, gdy władze rozpętały znowu falę antysemityzmu (ufając, że to zawsze mile widziane), poprzednie nazwiska, ku zdumieniu ich posiadaczy, zostały z fanfarą przypomniane jako coś, co samo w sobie automatycznie dyskwalifikuje (ot, Tuwimie, ta „ranga wszystkie inne zaćmiewająca"...). Ten haniebny okres wymaga specjalnego omówienia, ale jakkolwiek się go interpretuje, dla Żydów był to ostateczny sygnał, że nie mieli i nie mają czego w Polsce szukać.

W świadomości Żydów, którzy rozproszyli się z Polski po świecie, wryło się głębokie poczucie krzywdy za tę przeszłość — przedwojenną, okupacyjną, powojenną. Niech Polak, który się skarży, że Żydzi psują Polsce reputację w świecie, zada sobie pytanie, czy taka przeszłość, ta bliższa i dalsza, była szkołą dla ambasadorów dobrej woli.

I w końcu ten uraz zawiedzionej miłości. Wielu Żydów, w tej generacji na odchodnym, nie może wymazać z serca tego Kraju, gdzie się „urodzili, wzrośli, wychowali, nauczyli", gdzie się — jak Tuwim — „po polsku spowiadali z niepokojów pierwszej miłości i po polsku bełkotali o jej szczęściu i burzach"; gdzie kochali ten krajobraz, mowę, poezję; gdzie gotowi byli się za Polskę wykrwawić i być jej nieodrodnymi synami. Że to wszystko było nie dosyć — tego im żal.

W różnych zakątkach są jeszcze ci, którzy, jak mówi Jerzy Ficowski, „…szli do Jeruszalaim … i tam przemycili / garstkę wierzbowych gruszek / i na pamiątkę / ze śledzia / do dziś kłującą ość…" I jak ten Słonimskiego stary Żyd koło jafskiej bramy pytają „czy ogród Saski jest jeszcze? Ciągle taki samy?"

Rozeszły się bezpowrotnie drogi „dwu najsmutniejszych narodów na ziemi". Nie wiem, czy Polacy świadomi są tego, że z Żydami została także zgładzona autentyczna część ich Polski. Ciśnie się na usta pytanie: czy lepsza, bogatsza w dobra duchowe i materialne, będzie kiedyś ta Polska bez Żydów?

Wypowiedź na Konferencji w Oksfordzie poświęconej stosunkom polsko-żydowskim, wrzesień 1984. Pierwodruk w kwartalniku „Puls" Nr 24, Londyn, luty 1985

Z kim i o czym

Jestem ograniczony czasem, tolerancją przewodniczącego i — co najważniejsze — cierpliwością słuchaczy[1]; to są ciasne granice. Przygotowałem wobec tego tylko luźne kartki, które łatwo przetasować i gdy trzeba — opuścić. Poruszę parę zagadnień, które mi się wydają zasadnicze — na wyrywki. Może te nieskoordynowane fragmenty połączą się przy okazji w bardziej spoistą całość.

Gdy myślałem, jak zatytułować moje wystąpienie, różne tytuły przychodziły mi do głowy. Myślałem zrazu o tytule „Do Przyjaciół-Polaków", ale to echo Mickiewiczowskie wydawało mi się w moich ustach pretensjonalne. Myślałem o tytule „Na rozstaju dróg" — w naśladownictwie słynnego *Al Parashat Drahim* Achad-Haama[2], to jest znakomity, uniwersalny tytuł, zawsze aktualny — my zawsze, wszyscy, wiecznie jesteśmy na jakimś „rozstaju dróg". Odrzuciłem go jako zbyt ogólny. Myślałem o haśle „Bardzo trudne porachunki" — to oddaje ducha rozprawy, ale ja chcę właśnie od „porachunków" odbiec. Zmieniłem więc na „Nie wszystko czarno-białe" — co określa bliżej moje stanowisko. Ale ostatecznie sprowadzam to do samej esencji, do najprostszego: „Z kim i o czym". I ażeby nie brzmiało tak twardo i sucho, dodaję motto z Kochanowskiego: „Macamy, gdzie miękcej w rzeczy, a ono wszędy ciśnie..."

A więc Z KIM? Jeśli ma być dialog, to trzeba mieć wyraźny obraz rozmówcy. Przyjmuję tu model „elitarny" — chcę zasiąść do stołu z tym, co najlepsze, nie z tym, co najgorsze. Nie z tymi, którzy Żydów nienawidzili przed wojną, wydawali Niemcom w czasie wojny albo wypędzili z Polski po wojnie. Nie z Polską „Grunwaldu", Moczarów, nie z tymi, którzy w kościele przy ulicy Zagórnej w Warszawie sprzedają egzemplarze *Protokołów Mędrców Syjonu*, nie z tymi, którzy przy każdej sposobności wypisują jadowite bzdury o Izraelu, lub piszą, że Korczak znęcał się nad chrześcijańskimi dziećmi (jak notują „Nowiny-Kurier" nr 17); nie z tymi, którzy — jak ten publicysta w piśmie „Ład" w Warszawie — przewidują, że jeśli Żydzi się nie poprawią to — cytuję — „przyjdzie czas, że znowu trzeba ich będzie chować po piwnicach" (łatwo

---

[1] Publikowany tu tekst jest wypowiedzią w panelu „Problemy etyczne Holocaustu w Polsce" podczas Międzynarodowej Konferencji Historii i Kultury Żydów Polskich (Jerozolima, 31 stycznia — 5 lutego 1988).

[2] Achad Haam (właśc. Asher Ginzberg, 1856–1927), pisarz, filozof, jeden z teoretyków syjonizmu. *Al Parashat Drahim* to tytuł zbioru jego esejów (t. I–IV, Berlin 1895). Przyp. aut.

zgadnąć, ilu ten by przechował), ani nie z tymi, od których często słyszę w Londynie, że — cytuję — „cokolwiek powiemy, Żydzi nas i tak przekrzyczą". Od kołtunów się roi — niestety u nas także.

Rozumiem, że Polak nie może prowadzić dialogu z ludźmi, którzy twierdzą, że każdy Polak to antysemita, którzy nic w Polsce poza antysemityzmem nie widzieli i nie widzą, którzy twierdzą, że obozy zagłady były w Polsce, bo Niemcy mogli byli liczyć na obojętność Polaków, i że to wyczerpuje temat.

Chcę mówić z Polakami o Polsce, która zrodziła Kochanowskiego, Mickiewicza i Norwida, Konopnicką, Prusa, Orzeszkową, Gomulickiego, Dąbrowską, Nałkowską, a także Turowicza, Błońskiego, Bartoszewskiego, Kołakowskiego, Szczypiorskiego, Annę Kamieńską, Wisławę Szymborską, Miłosza, Ficowskiego; o Polsce, gdzie kwitła — i gdzie zginęła — jedyna w swoim rodzaju i niepowtarzalna cywilizacja żydowska. W jednej z moich poprzednich wypowiedzi skarżyłem się na to, że ta cywilizacja kwitnąca w najbliższym sąsiedztwie, ba, pośrodku społeczeństwa polskiego, pozostała mu całkowicie obca, nieznana, nieciekawa. Polacy nieświadomi jej istnienia byliby zdumieni, gdyby usłyszeli, że działo się tu coś, co zasługiwało na miano cywilizacji.

Warto się w tym miejscu zastanowić, JAK Polacy na ogół widzieli swych współobywateli-Żydów, bo to przecież kształtowało ich opinię i stosunek. A więc przede wszystkim widzieli brodaczy, chałaciarzy, z pejsami, w bekieszach, kaftanach, jarmułkach, kaszkietach; na jarmarkach, po miasteczkach, szwargocących, hałaśliwych, śmiesznych, ubogich — ale jakimś innym ubóstwem niż polskie ubóstwo. Widzieli pachciarzy, sklepikarzy, u których często zaciągali kredyt i którzy na przekór hasłu „Swój do swego po swoje" i próbom oficjalnie aprobowanego bojkotu, konkurowali tym skuteczniej, że Polacy często uważali handel za coś poniżej swej godności. Widzieli rzemieślników — zegarmistrzów, szewców, krawców — niedoścignionych w swej specjalności. Widzieli też klasę średnią, miejską, która ubiorem i zachowaniem mało różniła się od polskiego otoczenia, aczkolwiek jej styl życia był nieco inny. Widzieli „kamieniczników"; prawdą jest, że stan posiadania realności — tradycyjna u Żydów lokata kapitału — był nieproporcjonalnie wielki. Widzieli w szkołach, gimnazjach uczniów, studentów, którzy jeśli się czymkolwiek wyróżniali, to pilnością i zdolnościami. Widzieli na uniwersytetach kolegów, którzy często (powiedzmy to — nie zawsze i nie wszędzie) — byli zmuszeni siedzieć w „getcie ławkowym". Widzieli te „zażydzone" klasy profesjonalne: lekarzy i adwokatów, pośród nich bez wątpienia tych najlepszych. Widzieli paru — choć im się to często dwoiło w oczach — Żydów na wysokich stanowiskach, zapewne chrzczonych. Widzieli jeszcze w życiu literackim chluby polskiej literatury, gwiazdy dotąd nie zaćmione: Leśmiana, Tuwima, Słonimskiego, Wittlina, i to często na łamach „Wiadomości Literackich" Grycendlera-Grydzewskiego (i Bormana). Ale to był już objaw osmozy na styku społeczeństwa, odłam żydostwa zasymilowanego, tak narodowo polskiego jak tylko za Piłsudskiego można było być. Proces asymilacji był coraz trudniejszy i niewdzięczniejszy, co zresztą było po myśli, instynktownej i programowej, przygniatającej większości społeczeństwa żydowskiego. Ta większość była od społeczeństwa polskiego odgrodzona tym skuteczniej, że obie strony w tym procesie współdziałały. Dla drobnej, ale znamiennej ilustracji wspomnę np., że gdy żyłem w Polsce w okresie międzywojennym, nigdy nie byłem w polskim domu czy mieszkaniu, chyba że się liczy chłopska chata wynajęta na wakacje w Zakopanem czy Zawoi. Co więcej, nie brakowało mi tego, uważałem to za najnaturalniejszą rzecz w świecie. Miałem wielu kolegów na uniwersytecie, mieliśmy też wielu klientów w kancelarii adwokackiej, ale stosunki towarzyskie z reguły nie istniały. Różne były po temu przyczyny, ale jedną z głównych była ta, że Polacy nie uważali Żydów za równych sobie ludzi, patrzyli na nich z pozycji naturalnej wyższości; bez względu na pozycję socjalną Polak z reguły, z natury, z definicji czuł się stworem lepszym, wyższym niż Żyd. Ten brak poczucia wspólnoty, ukształtowany obiektywnymi warunkami, najlepiej tłumaczy fakt, że większość społeczeństwa polskiego nie była wyczulona na los Żydów pod okupacją. Abstrahując od „szumowin z marginesu społecznego" (jak się to w Polsce nazywa) i tej części politycznego środowiska, które wyniszczenie Żydów obcymi rękami witało z zadowoleniem; zakładając również, że musiało być bardzo wielu dobrych, zwyczajnych ludzi do głębi wstrząśniętych tym potwornym spektaklem i szczerze współczujących ofiarom — prawdą jest, że większość społeczeństwa pozostała obojętna. Wiadomo, że aktywna pomoc była ryzykowna i wymagała odwagi i poświęcenia — trudno było oczekiwać, aby ogólne nastawienie formowane przez pokolenia zmieniło się przez noc.

Teresa Prekerowa opierając się na dostępnych jej źródłach ocenia, że około 1–2,5% ludności brało aktywny udział w akcji pomocy Żydom (w tym znaczny ułamek za pieniądze, ale to drobiazg). Można się spierać o statystykę, tu i ówdzie ułamek procentu zaokrąglić. Sedno jest w tym, że bez statystyk, bez dokumentacji (nie pomniejszam doniosłości tych prac, wręcz przeciwnie, wysoko je cenię) **Żydzi po prostu wiedzą, jak to było.** Polacy na ogół tego nie wiedzą, nie mogą wiedzieć, a także chyba nie chcą wiedzieć. O to, **jak** było, Żydzi mają żal, który czasem wyrażają, nawet hałaśliwie — to ich prawo, już jedyne. Mają żal, ale trudno twierdzić, że było to dla nich niespodzianką, i to samo w sobie ma swą głęboką, tragiczną wymowę. Żal — nie tylko zresztą do Polaków; do świata, w którym taka rzecz była możliwa i tolerowana; w ostatecznej instancji — żal do Pana Boga (ale to nie mój temat).

Nasuwa się w związku z tym pytanie: Czy etyka, moralność stanowią absolutny probierz, wobec którego osądzamy ludzkie zachowanie, czy odkładamy tę miarę do składu jakichś utopijnych, nieosiągalnych ideałów, zaś na co dzień przyjmujemy trzeźwo i pragmatycznie, by nie powiedzieć cynicznie, prymat i dominację tych ciemnych ludzkich cech i prymitywnych instynktów, które człowieka robią zdolnym do okrucieństw i podłości? Ta myśl kojarzy się

256

z następnym dylematem: Czy, jeśli w naszej słabości czy też zrozumiałej trosce o życie własne i swoich bliskich nie postępujemy etycznie i nie realizujemy zasad moralności, które są nam znane z religii i filozofii i które, w teorii, aprobujemy i podziwiamy — czy w takiej sytuacji uważamy nasze zachowanie za całkowicie usprawiedliwione racjonalnymi wymogami, czy też pozostaje w nas poczucie wstydu, żeśmy czemuś nie sprostali, wstydu wzmożonego świadomością, że kto inny — może niewielu, ale ktoś — tej sytuacji jednak sprostał? Poddaję tę myśl pod rozwagę tym, którzy śpią spokojnie, „bo nic nie można było zrobić".

Przykład Błońskiego, moralny ton jego wypowiedzi, daje mi asumpt, by starać się wznieść ponad „porachunki", rekryminacje, słowne utarczki i retoryczne zwycięstwa. To było potrzebne, powiedziałbym nieuchronne — trzeba było mówić bez obwijania w bawełnę, powiedzieć, co leży na sercu i żołądku, inaczej te niestrawne kęsy będą nas wiecznie zatruwać. Ja sam brałem w tej fazie udział. Pisząc o najbardziej drażliwym i bolesnym elemencie w tym kompleksie uraz, wyraziłem pogląd, że w czasie, gdy jechały pociągi do Oświęcimia, Treblinki, Majdanka, Sobiboru i Bełżca i gdy dzień i noc buchał z kominów dym roznosząc po polach swąd palonych ciał, gdyby wtedy wiadomo było, że to nie „Żydki się smażą", tylko giną rodzimi polscy mężowie, matki, żony i dzieci, wybuch zemsty i gniewu narodu byłby nie do opanowania, choćby — użyłem wtedy zwrotu — „szyny przyszło zębami rwać…" Oberwało mi się za te szyny i ten zwrot do dziś w polemikach pokutuje. W gruncie rzeczy nie zmieniłem w tej sprawie zdania, ale dziś myślę, że temperatura dyskusji opadła i że można mówić także innym językiem. Zbliżamy się do czasu, gdy nie będzie naocznych świadków, ludzi, którzy sami przez to piekło przeszli. Nie będzie tych, którzy przeżyli obozy, tych, którzy przeżyli w bunkrach, tych z „aryjskich papierów" i tych, których uratowała zsyłka na Sybir. Nie będzie „5. kolumny Gomułki" i tych „Żydów z Bezpieki" i tych wygnańców z '68 r., i tych, którzy się nigdy nie wyleczyli ze swej miłości do Polski, nie będzie Wygodzkich i Brandysów, nie będzie tych, którym „Tamiza wiślaną połyskuje falą" i tych, którzy — jak ja sam, wybaczcie, jeśli to brzmi patetycznie — po 50 latach z dala od Polski recytują sobie do snu *Sonety Krymskie* czy *Grób Agamemnona*. Wydaje mi się, że wtedy zmieni się historyczna perspektywa i parametry naszych dyskusji. Z dystansu stanie się jasne, że to nie tylko o nas chodzi. Że te nasze waśnie, urazy i porachunki, to jest rzecz uboczna; że tu toczyła się wielka, wspólna ludzka sprawa o uniwersalnym zasięgu; że zagłada Żydów na ziemiach polskich to było kluczowe i przełomowe wydarzenie w historii, które sygnalizuje kryzys chrześcijaństwa i kryzys naszej cywilizacji (niektórzy uważają te pojęcia za identyczne, ale tak, na szczęście, nie jest). Wydarzenia tego nie można zapomnieć ni pominąć, będzie ono ciążyło nad przyszłymi pokoleniami po wsze czasy. Jaką lekcję człowiek wyniesie z tego wydarzenia; jak się z tym upora, świadom otchłani zła, do której jest zdolen się stoczyć; jak odnowi wiarę w podstawowe moralne wartości — w świecie, w którym istnieje instrument zagłady, wobec którego bledną nawet komory gazowe — od odpowiedzi na te pytania zależy przyszłość gatunku.

Wracam do tytułu: **O czym mamy mówić**. Zapyta ktoś, co tu nowego można powiedzieć. Odpowiem na to cytatem z Hagady, księgi, którą się czyta w święto Pesach; w wolnym przekładzie brzmi on, że chociaż zjedliśmy wszystkie mądrości i jesteśmy uczeni w wielu pismach, jest nam nakazane, aby na ten temat mówić. Wiem, nie każdy się z tym zgodzi — *mejleh*... (cały kunszt tłumacza nie wystarcza, by znaleźć polski odpowiednik tego słówka. Chyba „gest" — też nie polski...).

Mam tutaj, a także w Anglii, wielu przyjaciół, którzy mówią: czym ty sobie (i nam) zawracasz głowę, co to kogo obchodzi. Wszystko, co się łączy z tamtymi czasami, jest niesłychanie smutne i bolesne, po co to odgrzebywać. Rozumiem, o co im chodzi, ale mnie to nie przekonuje. Myślę, że to jest zubożenie, że tym, których **to** nie obchodzi, wiele innych rzeczy również nie obchodzi — myślę, że im więcej spraw nas obchodzi, tym lepiej.

Jest o czym mówić: o historii, tej wspólnej i osobnej, jedynej w swoim rodzaju; i tym, jak to naprawdę było, z daleka, i z bliska; o klimacie, którym oddychaliśmy, o warunkach, które nas kształtowały; o wzajemnych wpływach, złych i dobrych; o wspólnocie i obcości, o zbliżeniu i wrogości; o krzywdzie i dobrodziejstwach, o tym, co nas dzieliło i łączyło — o tym wszystkim, byle poważnie, niepowierzchownie, bez demagogii, byle w trosce o prawdę. Co nie znaczy, że ujrzymy tę prawdę tak samo, bo ta prawda jest skomplikowana i wielowymiarowa — jesteśmy wyczuleni na niektóre jej aspekty, ślepi na inne; każdemu z nas jest, w najlepszym razie, dostępny tylko jakiś jej wycinek. Świadomość, że tak właśnie jest, stanowi już krok we właściwym kierunku.

Co do nas, to przecież wszystko, co się tych spraw tyczy, tej blisko tysiącletniej obecności Żydów na ziemiach polskich, to jest część spuścizny, którą musimy zapamiętać, kultywować, przekazać. Każda cegiełka, każdy kamień węgielny czy cmentarny, każdy dokument, skrawek papieru, każdy ślad, każde wspomnienie jest bezcenne dla narodu, którego korzenie są sensem jego historii i którego pamięć przeszłości gwarantowała ciągłość istnienia. Historia Żydów nie zaczęła się w 1948 r. z powstaniem państwa Izrael. Wielka część historii rozgrywała się właśnie na ziemiach polskich. Więc jakże to — odwrócić się od tego, zapomnieć, przeorać? Nie, moi drodzy, przeciwnie.

Dowiaduję się z prasy i od przyjaciół w Polsce, że jest, przeważnie wśród młodzieży, żywe i szerokie zainteresowanie sprawami żydowskimi: historią, literaturą, zabytkami, szczątkami. Pisze mi jeden z nich: „Dziwny my naród, Polacy... Przez czterdzieści lat leży nad tym całun zapomnienia, jakby programowe tabu, wstydliwe przemilczanie, jak gdyby Żydów nigdy w Polsce nie było, a tu nagle jakby spontaniczny wybuch zainteresowania, ciekawość, żądza wiedzy. Czy to zdrowe, do czego to prowadzi?" — pyta. Cóż mu mam powiedzieć: lepiej późno niż nigdy? Jeśli takie zainteresowanie się obudziło (ktoś powie: poniewczasie) i jest rzetelne, a nie jakieś psychopatyczne, to temu przyklaskuję i myślę, że w tej nauce możemy być pomocni. Nie obawiam się, jak mój korespondent, ewentualnych konsekwencji, że w tym zmiennym, niespokojnym klimacie wahadło znów poleci w przeciwnym kierunku — nam się już z tej strony nic złego nie może stać. Wydaje mi się, że gdy ten „późny wnuk" zapozna się z tą częścią swej historii, odkryje, jak tam z Żydami w Polsce było i co to była za społeczność — że będzie to dla niego proces nie tylko poznawczy, ale terapeutyczny. Wypadnie mu się nad tą przeszłością zadumać i jakoś się z nią rozliczyć. Chcę wierzyć, że wyrasta w Polsce pokolenie nie zatrute wirusem antysemityzmu i antyjudaizmu. To jest ich sprawa raczej niż nasza, bo jako społeczność my się już nigdy nie znajdziemy, fizycznie, w sąsiedztwie. Błoński wskazał drogę i zrobił początek — w tym jego ogromna zasługa.

Gdym czytał po raz pierwszy, z wypiekami na twarzy, artykuł Błońskiego, przyznaję, że mnie aż dreszcz przeszedł, gdy natknąłem się na aluzję do jednego z mówców na konferencji w Oksfordzie, którego słowa, między innymi, natchnęły Błońskiego do tych rozważań. Z cytatów przez niego przytoczonych wynika, że tym mówcą byłem ja. Byłem wzruszony, a także zaskoczony tym przykładem, jak jedno słowo, zdanie, myśl może się zaryć w świadomości innego człowieka, tam kiełkować i owocować ponad spodziewanie. Mówiłem wtedy — tak to przynajmniej Błoński odebrał — o tym, że my, Żydzi, już niczego od Polaków nie oczekujemy, jak tylko by uderzyli się w piersi. Istotnie, przez całe lata nastawialiśmy ciekawie ucha, by usłyszeć głos z Polski — nikt nie wołał. Myślałem, że się nie doczekamy. Okazuje się, żeśmy się doczekali.

Wielu ludzi w Polsce mówi, że Błoński to „ptak, co własne gniazdo kala", że nawet jeśli to, co mówi, jest prawdą, nie powinien tego wywlekać na publiczne forum i swą krytyką przychodzić w sukurs „wrogom" Polski. To jest stary argument — *do not rock the boat* mówi się po angielsku, nie wstrząsaj szalupą. Znamy to szczególnie dobrze w Izraelu, gdzie jest nagminna surowa i bezlitosna samokrytyka, ale też ogromna troska, by to pozostało w rodzinie — śliska droga.

Mija bez mała rok, odkąd rozległ się głos Błońskiego. Chcę zapewnić tych wszystkich, którzy się obawiali, że to podziała na szkodę Polski, że wręcz przeciwnie, że to samo w sobie jest pewną rehabilitacją. Ja sam w wielu sytuacjach, gdy paradoksalnie i niezasłużenie znajduję się w roli *advocatus Poloniae*, odwołuję się do tego artykułu i do tych, które po nim nastąpiły. Nie można więcej, twierdzę, mówić o opinii Polaków na ten temat, bez brania pod uwagę tych nowych głosów, które reputację Polski ratują.

Z tą reputacją jest prawdziwy kłopot. Odbija się to na każdym Polaku za granicą, szczególnie w Ameryce, gdzie na obcym forum musi ciągle wyjaśniać — i nie zawsze wie jak — że nie każdy Polak był i jest antysemitą. To „obce forum", rzecz jasna, też najczęściej nie jest o sprawie dobrze poinformowane, ale tyle zawsze wie i to wystarcza: że w Polsce Żydom było źle. Polacy się często skarżą, że to Żydzi psują im opinię, co znaczy chyba, że, w ich mniemaniu, opowiadają o Polsce niestworzone rzeczy, wyolbrzymiają swe urazy, zapominają o doznanych dobrodziejstwach, niesłusznie ją oczerniają. Jeśliby tak było w istocie, to nasuwałoby się pytanie: dlaczego ci Żydzi (mówię o tych, do których takie zarzuty są kierowane) mieliby Polskę szkalować? Z czystej złośliwości, bo to już tacy ludzie? Czy to brzmi prawdopodobnie? Czy też może, jeśli taka jest ich percepcja, to jest ona wynikiem przeżyć, doświadczeń, poczucia krzywdy? Stawiam to w ten sposób, by zilustrować, jak szybko i schematycznie możemy się znaleźć na znajomym terytorium, które nosi nazwę: oni swoje, my swoje. Tym bardziej mi się wydaje, że ten publiczny rachunek sumienia Błońskiego oferuje inny model i wzywa do stworzenia nowego poziomu i klimatu stosunków. Godzi się nam pamiętać, że Polacy antysemityzmu nie wymyślili, że jest to odwieczne zjawisko socjologiczne, teologiczne, polityczne, które nam w większym lub mniejszym stopniu towarzyszy, które nas określa i bez którego (co nam zresztą nie grozi) czulibyśmy się nieswojo, a na pewno bylibyśmy innym narodem, inną społecznością, innymi ludźmi. Nie jest pewne, czy lepszymi. Nie znaczy to, że trzeba antysemityzm pasywnie przyjmować, nadstawiać ewangelicznie drugi policzek. Wręcz przeciwnie, trzeba z nim walczyć wszelkimi możliwymi środkami — myślę, że nasze spotkanie tutaj, w Jerozolimie, w stolicy żydowskiego państwa, jest znamiennym aktem tej walki.

Natchnieniem Błońskiego do jego wypowiedzi były wiersze Miłosza. Rozumiem to. Poezja sięga do źródeł jestestwa, myśli i uczuć, które są inną drogą nieosiągalne, i wznieca w nas siły, których jesteśmy czasem sami nieświadomi. Josif Brodski, w swej mowie z okazji przyjęcia nagrody Nobla, powiedział: „Człowieka, który czyta poezję, jest trudniej złamać niż tego, który jej nie czyta". Nieodżałowanej pamięci Maks Boruchowicz (Michał Borwicz), którego niestety już pośród nas brak, brak jak nikogo innego, ten który się „nie spłonił na widok powroza", w swej książce *Literatura w obozie* pisze, jak to okruchy zachowanej w pamięci poezji były niejako pasem ratunkowym, który w najpotworniejszych warunkach ludzkiego poniżenia pomagał przetrwać. Myślę o tej scenie w obozie janowskim, gdzie odbywa się „selekcja", gdzie jego towarzysz, u kresu sił, prosi go wzrokiem o jakieś słowo pociechy i jak mu Borwicz cytuje, jak sam to nazywa, banalny wiersz: „...Na łzę w mym oku nie czekaj daremnie, / Nie okupię się śmierci ani skurczem twarzy..." i jak te słowa utrzymują jakoś tego towarzysza przy życiu. Nie mnie się mierzyć z Błońskim mą polszczyzną sprzed pół wieku. Ale aby pozostać z nim bodaj w stylistycznej harmonii, uciekam się do cudzych słów i chcę tę wypowiedź zakończyć wierszem:

Podszedł pies do mnie wczoraj — i patrzył
pytał jakby czy nienawidzę
sierści mokrej, nawilgłego nosa —
i odszedł niepogłaskany
wzrokiem, co się zaplątał
przy bucie w prętach ławki.
Dawniej (kilka sumień temu) pytały oczy ludzkie
o to samo.
Nienawiścią opięci jak mundurem
Nazarejczyka wypędzaliśmy razem z kramem
ale nas spotkał przy prętach luf, pod murem
tym samym.

Jerzy Pietrkiewicz

Myśl Polska, 1950

Sen o powrocie

Niejeden z Państwa się zdziwi, że mnie właśnie przypada zaszczyt, aby przy tej uroczystej okazji parę słów powiedzieć — ja sam się dziwię. Przyznaję, że uważam to za nie lada wyróżnienie i że mnie to wzrusza. Spotyka mnie ten honor nie za żadne zasługi, których nie mam, ale przez przypadek urodzenia, który sprawia, że w tym kontekście jestem niejako rekwizytem muzealnym: autentycznym, przedwojennym *homo Cracoviensis* i — na dobitkę — Żydem, krakowskim Żydem, który gotów jest na każde zawołanie do tego Krakowa przez góry i lasy przypędzić.

Śniło mi się jednej nocy, niedawno, że widziałem na ekranie telewizji premiera Izraela Itzhaka Rabina, który ściskał rękę Yassera Arafata i robili do siebie grymasy, które miały uchodzić za uśmiech. Działo się to, zdaje się, na stopniach Białego Domu w Waszyngtonie i, jak to bywa w snach, przewijały się tam jakieś znajome twarze, prezydent Carter, prezydent Bush, prezydent Clinton, Kissinger... Dochodziły mnie głosy z różnych stron, że zaświtała nowa era, że będzie pokój na Bliskim Wschodzie, w Izraelu... Szkoda się z takiego snu obudzić.

Innej nocy znowu śniło mi się, że w Krakowie powstał na Kazimierzu jakiś piękny dom i że to się nazywa Centrum Kultury Żydowskiej, i że mnie przypada przywilej otwarcia tej Instytucji, i że stoję przed mikrofonem, w obliczu licznego i dostojnego audytorium i — co mi się nieczęsto zdarza — nie wiem, co powiedzieć. Z tego snu także szkoda mi się obudzić.

Wydaje mi się, że ta ceremonia oznacza dla mnie kres jakiejś dalekiej, okrężnej drogi. Opuściłem ten mój Kraków, rodzinę i przyjaciół, ponad 50 lat temu, a zatem przed wybuchem wojny. Dlaczego ten Kraków opuściłem — na ten temat można by napisać traktat o stosunkach polsko-żydowskich w latach trzydziestych — nie czas teraz o tym rozprawiać. Ale byłoby nieszczerością i nie w duchu, w jakim chcemy, aby to Centrum działało, nie nazywać rzeczy po imieniu. Wystarczy powiedzieć, że ja, jak wielu ludzi mojego pokroju, nie mogliśmy sobie znaleźć w ówczesnej Polsce miejsca. (W moich papierach znalazłem nie bardzo zręczną, ale znamienną „Fraszkę pożegnalną", w której był taki passus: „Chciałem ją pokochać — nie dali; Chciałem się bić za nią — skopali; Mam ci ja swoją dumę — Z drogi im się usunę; Będą jeszcze palce po mnie lizali..."). Obraziłem się, odwróciłem, postanowiłem zapomnieć, z polskości się „przechrzcić". Ale, jak to mówił Hemar — „nie przyjęło się". Zdałem sobie sprawę z tego, że jeśli bym się w jakiś sposób mej polskości pozbył, gdyby mnie z niej odarto — pozostałbym okaleczony, zubożały, niepełny. Co więcej, często myślę o tamtych czasach i zadaję sobie pytanie: Jeśli było tak źle — dlaczego było tak dobrze?

Więc wracam, „zmęczony burz szaleństwem", by rzucić okiem na ten krajobraz dzieciństwa i wczesnej młodości, gdzie każdy kamień „słodkim wspomnieniem rani". Przejść się znowu tymi ulicami, gdzie się nasze losy splatały, gdzie ulica Bożego Ciała krzyżuje się z ulicą Rabina Meiselsa, a św. Sebastiana z Berka Joselewicza; ulicami Estery, Jakuba, Izaaka — gdzie to jeszcze w diasporze były ulice nazwane imionami ze Starego Testamentu? Przejść ulicą Koletek pod boisko „Makkabi", ulicą Orzeszkowej pod „Nowy Dziennik", Miodową pod Tempel, Brzozową pod Żydowskie Gimnazjum? Zatrzymać się pod bóżnicami Poppera, Wysoką, Kupa, Starą, Remu — pomyślałby ktoś z tej liczby synagog, że żydostwo krakowskie było wyjątkowo bogobojne — owszem, było; ale byli i tacy, którzy — jak pisze Izaak Deutscher, słynny biograf Lenina, Stalina i Trockiego, syn drukarza z Krakowa — w post Sądnego Dnia szli na grób Rabina Isserlesa i jedli kanapkę z szynką — jemu i rodzicom swym na złość.

Można powiedzieć, że Kraków był pięknie „zażydzony". Była to społeczność, pośród której żyli i działali dr Ozjasz Thon, kaznodzieja w Templu i poseł na Sejm, dr Ignacy Schwarzbart, przywódca syjonistyczny (w czasie wojny członek Rady Narodowej przy Rządzie Emigracyjnym w Londynie), dr Chaim Hilfstein, którego imię nosiło Żydowskie Gimnazjum; grono tegoż gimnazjum: Scherer, Haber, Mifelew, Rapaport, Katz, Szmulewicz, Feldhorn, Stendig, Waldman, Metalman, Goldwasserowa i wielu innych; członkowie palestry — Süsskind, Hoffman, Feldblum, Goldblatt, Bader, Schechter; Rabin Kornitzer — głowa odłamu ortodoksyjnego, zasymilowany dr Rafał Landau — prezes Gminy; Wilhelm Berkelhammer, Mojżesz Kanfer, Dawid Lazer z „Nowego Dziennika", Rywek Wolf z Domu Akademickiego, Róża Rockowa z Domu Sierot. Tu działały organizacje młodzieży — Przedświt — Haszachar, Haszomer Hacair, Gordonia, Akiba, Betar, Massada; kluby sportowe „Makkabi" i „Jutrzenka". Żyły tu zacne, drobnomieszczańskie rodziny żydowskie — Tigner, Einhorn, Fallman, Lipschütz, Leser, Selinger, Rosthal, Stoeger, Freiwald, Herzig, Aleksandrowicz, Karmel, Freilich, Monderer, Ehrlich...

To brzmi jak szary spis lokatorów, to jest spis lokatorów, ale dla mnie nie szary, wręcz przeciwnie — widzę każdą z tych sylwetek z niesłychaną wyrazistością, każdy ich gest, uśmiech, grymas, jakby to było wczoraj. Myślę o nich tkliwie, znalazłbym po tylu latach drogę do ich mieszkań na ślepo, po omacku — dotykając dla pewności wyżłobienia na framudze drzwi, gdzie dawniej była mezuza.

Ten ludzki krajobraz jest zaryty w mym sercu, duszy i pamięci. Na chwilę nie mogę zapomnieć, że większość tych ludzi, przyjaciół, rodziny, znajomych — nikt z nich nie był mi obcy — zginęła zaszczuta w gettach, w obozach pracy, w kacetach, w fabrykach śmierci, w komorach gazowych. Przywykliśmy o tym mówić, pisać słowami zaczerpniętymi z powszedniego, ludzkiego języka, ale ogromu i znaczenia tej straty nikt nie jest w stanie ogarnąć.

Kocham tę żydowską Polskę, która była i zginęła. Kocham ją miłością inną niż ta, którą żywię do Izraela. Wiem, że to uczucie destyluje się przez filtr wspomnień dzieciństwa i młodości i jest po części smakowaniem proustowskiego „zaginionego czasu". Ale to coś więcej. Mam to przeświadczenie, że był to świat, w którym działo się coś autentycznie, unikalnie żydowskiego — w sensie, w jakim nie dzieje się to w normalnym kraju jak Izrael. Syjonizm, który to państwo stworzył, był w swym założeniu protestem przeciw warunkom życia w diasporze i trzeba dziękować jego twórcom, że ich dzieło ziściło się w chwili największego poniżenia i rozpaczy narodu żydowskiego, który tylko dzięki temu ostał się i odrodził. Ale rezultatem tych historycznych wydarzeń, ich efektów zamierzonych i przypadkowych, jest także bezpowrotna utrata tych form i wartości, które stanowiły esencję życia żydostwa w diasporze, których jednym ze znaków rozpoznawczych było powszechne przekonanie, że człowiek musi — bez względu na warunki materialne i zmagania dnia powszedniego — zdążać i przyczyniać się do realizacji jakiegoś ideału, jakkolwiek by go zdefiniować. Było głęboko zakorzenione przeświadczenie, że codzienne, godziwe życie, religijna praktyka, przestrzeganie etycznych nakazów, obcowanie ze słowem Bożym objawionym w świętych księgach, przyśpieszy przyjście Mesjasza i zapoczątkuje erę powszechnej sprawiedliwości.

Dzieje się dziś jakaś zdumiewająca rzecz. Oto w sercu starego Kazimierza, jak Feniks z popiołów, w roku Pańskim 1993, a żydowskim 5754, powstaje budynek, który się mieni Centrum Kultury Żydowskiej. Fakt, że coś takiego może w Krakowie zaistnieć, w czasie gdy ten kraj zmaga się z trudnościami, od których bieleje włos, zakrawa na jakieś wydarzenie nadnaturalne.

Jak wszystkie cuda, nie dzieje się to bez pomocy ludzkiej, lecz dzięki wizji, zapałowi i ciężkiej pracy kilku osób, których nie chcę wymieniać po imieniu, ale wszyscy wtajemniczeni wiedzą, że chodzi tu głównie (żeby nie powiedzieć wyłącznie) o naszego oddanego przyjaciela z Waszyngtonu, Marka Talismana, o profesora Gierowskiego i o Joachima Russka, którym gratuluję urzeczywistnienia ich marzeń i którym w imieniu nas wszystkich składam dzięki.

Widzę w tym jakiś nowy początek, którego konsekwencji nie możemy jeszcze przewidzieć. Może się okaże — przyszły historyk to oceni — że to tu właśnie jest punkt zwrotny naszego pojednania i przymierza. Że Polska wychodzi obronną ręką z tej choroby antysemityzmu, która ją ogłupiała, że nareszcie zaczęliśmy dostrzegać w sobie nawzajem to, co najlepsze, a nie to, co najgorsze, że dawne rany się zabliźniają, że wyrasta nowe pokolenie wolne od przesądów i uprzedzeń, że Polska i Państwo Izrael, to państwo, w które właśnie Żydzi z Polski mają tak ogromny wkład, że te nasze państwa będą ze sobą w najlepszych stosunkach i będą może na międzynarodowym forum przykładem cywilizowanych obyczajów. Jest w języku jidysz powiedzenie, które się nasuwa, gdy człowiek wyraża jakieś pobożne życzenie — *fun dein mojl — ins Gott's ojren* — „oby to dotarło z Twoich ust do uszu Pana Boga".

Jest w powstaniu tego Centrum głęboki symbol. Ale nie byłoby to po naszej myśli, ani nie warte by to było ogromnego wysiłku i kosztów związanych z realizacją takiego zamysłu, gdyby miało ono zostać jedynie symbolem. Symbol swoją drogą, a solidna, codzienna praca swoją. Mury, dach nad głową, to jest konkret, to jest rama, skorupa, która wypełni się bogatą, żywotną treścią. To jest adres, którego dotąd nie było — adres, do którego przybysz z daleka i z bliska skieruje swe kroki, gdy zawita do Krakowa, gdzie napotka życzliwą twarz za biurkiem, gdzie znajdzie książki i informacje, których szuka, gdzie odpocznie i się zaduma, gdzie spotka się z ludźmi podobnego pokroju, gdzie poczuje się w domu.

To tutaj, w tym miejscu, będziemy zachowywać i kultywować pamięć o Żydach polskich. Będziemy głosili prawdę o ich życiu. W tym skłóconym świecie bratobójczych wojen, w Jugosławii, w Irlandii, na terenie Rosji, w Południowej Afryce, możemy wskazać, że tu, przez wieki, istniał — na przekór wszystkiemu — model współżycia, symbiotycznej egzystencji, wzajemnych wpływów dwóch cywilizacji z ogromnym pożytkiem i wzbogaceniem obu.

Jest zwrot w języku hebrajskim *Ir wa'em be'Israel* — „miasto i matka w Izraelu". Niewiele miejsc na świecie się tym przydomkiem obdarza — Kraków, nasz Kraków błogosławionej pamięci jest jednym z tych miejsc. To, co się dzisiaj tu dzieje, utrwali jego miejsce w historii i naszych sercach. Zakończę słowami modlitwy dziękczynnej: *Sze'hechejanu w'kimanu we'higianu la zman haze*. „Dziękujemy Bogu, że dożyliśmy tej chwili".

Przemówienie wygłoszone podczas otwarcia Centrum Kultury Żydowskiej na krakowskim Kazimierzu, 14 listopada 1993 r.

Z otchłani

S zukaliśmy tytułu na dzisiejszy wieczór poezji pisanej w getcie i w obozach — takiego, aby nikogo nie zwiódł, aby wiadomo było, o czym będzie mowa, a z drugiej strony — aby nie odstraszył. Wiadomo, większość ludzi — trudno się dziwić — od tych smutnych spraw ucieka. Jedni pytają po co to, dla innych stało się to wszystko bardzo odległe, jak grecka mitologia, ale dla niektórych jest to zaledwie wszechobecne wczoraj.

Tytuł, który mi się wpierw nasunął brzmiał: *Z otchłani* — albowiem pod tym tytułem ukazał się, w Warszawie w roku 1944, zbiór wierszy pisanych w getcie i w obozach. Uważam to wydarzenie za całkowicie unikalne w historii literatury.

Wiersze zawarte w tym tomiku zostały przedrukowane i historia ich powstania została opowiedziana po raz pierwszy po wojnie w antologii pod tytułem *Pieśń ujdzie cało...*, zredagowanej w roku 1947 w Krakowie przez Michała Borwicza, który był moim kolegą z ławy szkolnej w Hebrajskim Gimnazjum w Krakowie; jego prawdziwe nazwisko brzmi Maks Boruchowicz.

Boruchowicz znalazł się w czasie wojny w getcie na Janowskiej we Lwowie. Został stamtąd wyprowadzony przez przyjaciół z PPS-u i przetrwał wojnę jako dowódca partyzantki w Mieleckiem. Nie uchroniło go to od losu emigranta, wkrótce po wojnie musiał Polskę opuścić i w latach osiemdziesiątych zmarł w Paryżu.

Czytając te wiersze człowiek naraża się na to, że jego wrażliwość literacka tępieje pod ich obuchem. W porównaniu z nimi tradycyjne tworzywo poetyckie wydaje się sztuczne i trywialne. Kochanowski w *Trenach* opłakujący swą Urszulę; Słowacki w *Ojcu zadżumionych* opisujący śmierć swej rodziny, Ugolino w *Piekle* Dantego wżerający się w czaszkę swego syna; Jeremiasz biadający nad upadkiem Jerozolimy; Hiob, mąż boleści, wystawiony na szatańską próbę wiary — to są wspaniałe dzieła literatury, ale czymże one są w porównaniu ze stopniową zagładą narodu i prawdziwym cierpieniem na skalę, która jest nie do ogarnięcia?

Gdy prawdziwa dola człowiecza objawia się w gettach, w obozach, w fabrykach śmierci, w komorach gazowych — czy literatura, kunsztowne metafory, „przędza myśli i uczuć kwiaty" jak mówił Mickiewicz, literatura która przynosi *katharsis* i pociechę nie zakrawa na jakieś okrutne urągowisko? I sam fakt pisania, który jest wyrazem wiary w człowieka, nie przeczy sam sobie? To zapewne miał na myśli Adorno, gdy wypowiedział słynne zdanie, że „pisanie poezji po Oświęcimiu jest barbarzyństwem".

266

Wiersze pisane w getcie trzeba widzieć w tym kontekście. Osąd oparty o normalne kryteria, estetyczne normy, systemy krytyczne nie wchodzi tutaj w grę. Mierząc je przyjętymi kategoriami wiele z tych wierszy wypadałoby uznać za prymitywne, niedojrzałe, niektóre wręcz złe.

Banalna fraza, że to były wiersze „pisane krwią", nabiera tu świeżego, dosłownego znaczenia. Były one pisane przez ludzi stojących na krawędzi otwartego, masowego grobu, w pośpiechu, nim padnie strzał. One są jak przekaz wydrapany paznokciami na ścianie celi śmierci. Rozpacz dyktuje zdania, które są okrutne, oskarżenia, które są niesprawiedliwe, przekleństwa na oprawców, na widzów, na świat.

Są to głosy mężczyzn i kobiet poza obrębem prawa — ludzkiego i boskiego. One mówią o cierpieniu, o nadziei i jej utracie, o bezsile i samotności, o samym dnie egzystencji. One świadczą o odwadze, woli życia w warunkach agonii, o śmierci — własnej, swoich najbliższych, tych wszystkich, których się kochało.

Były one także wyrazem walki i oporu. Były dowodem człowieczeństwa, na przekór wysiłkom Niemców, by Żydów zredukować do stanu podludzi. Parę ludzkich słów — napisać, albo bodaj ich wysłuchać — to był łyk świeżego powietrza, chwilowa ucieczka od rzeczywistości. To był rodzaj zaklęcia, magii co uzdrawia.

Borwicz opisuje moment, gdy w obozie na Janowskiej, który był jednym z bardziej wyrafinowanych miejsc kaźni, jeden z jego towarzyszy na *Apelplatzu* jest u kresu wytrzymałości, gotów wyzionąć ducha, i jak on, Borwicz, szepce mu parę linijek wiersza, który mu przyszedł do głowy. Ów towarzysz jakoś odżywa, wraca mu chęć i siła przetrwania. Jest takich przykładów wiele. Josif Brodski mówi, że trudniej jest złamać człowieka, który czytuje poezję niż takiego, który na nią jest nieczuły.

Drobną ilustrację jak takie wiersze powstawały czerpię znowu ze wspomnień Borwicza. Trzeba pamiętać, że za przekroczenie zakazu pisania w obozie groziła śmierć — a pisało się między jednym biciem a drugim, jedną egzekucją a następną.

Lodowaty styczeń 1943 — pisze Borwicz. — Szesnaście godzin (bez przerwy) na dobę na siarczystym mrozie. Człowiek zamienia się w takich warunkach w sopel lodu. Rąbanie lodu i usuwanie śniegu we Lwowie, tym razem na ul. Zamarstynowskiej. Podczas tego zajęcia zaczynają gnębić mnie coraz wyraźniej słowa tworzonego odruchowo wiersza. Uświadomiwszy sobie tę (zrazu instynktowną) czynność, zaczynam — nie przerywając pracy — uściślać i precyzować w myśli poszczególne linie wierszowe. Gdy pierwsza zwrotka była gotowa, pomyślałem o zanotowaniu jej. Odwożąc wózek z lodem do kanału, znalazłem na ulicznej stercie śmiecia kartkę brudnego papieru. Zdobyłem ołówek, za czym — zastępując biurko śmieciarskim wózkiem — zgrabiałą od zimna ręką zanotowałem, w stosownej chwili, gotową zwrotkę. Papier i ołówek powędrowały do kieszeni. Zaczęło się budowanie w myśli następnej strofy.

Gdzie tu jest jakieś porównanie z procesem „pisania" w normalnym tego słowa znaczeniu?

Pod jednym względem Niemcy nie mieli szczęścia w wyborze ofiary. „Naród Księgi" umiał się obchodzić z piórem i wierzył w słowo pisane. Potrzeba utrwalenia wydarzeń na piśmie, pozostawienie śladu po sobie, była przemożna. Obawa, że te wydarzenia, których Żydzi byli świadkami i ofiarą, pozostaną nieznane, albo będą niewiarygodne, była większa aniżeli troska o własne życie. Chaim Kaplan, w pamiętniku pisanym w getcie, który jest jednym z najbardziej przejmujących dokumentów naszych czasów, pisze w przededniu deportacji do Treblinki: „Jeśli ja zginę, co się stanie z moim dziennikiem?"

W warszawskim getcie od czerwca 1940 do lipca 1942 ukazało się 56 różnych publikacji — 26 w jidysz, 20 w języku polskim, 10 w hebrajskim. To, co się z tego zachowało, dzięki graniczącym z cudem splotom okoliczności, to jest zaledwie szczyt góry lodowej — ale już to czyni okres zagłady Żydów najgruntowniej udokumentowanym okresem w historii. Dlatego sądzę, że poglądy tzw. „rewizjonistów", którzy usiłują zaprzeczać temu, co się stało, są irytujące, ale nie są niebezpieczne i prawdzie nie zagrażają.

Jednym z najbardziej ponurych i serce rozdzierających obrazów, jakie sobie można wyobrazić, był widok getta po „akcji" — puste mieszkania, z których wywleczono lokatorów, pierze fruwające z poduszek i pierzyn rozprutych w poszukiwaniu skarbów, porzucona odzież, zabawki, łachy, zwłoki tych, którzy nie dotrzymali kroku i papiery — pojedyncze kartki albo zeszyty, na klatkach schodowych, na bruku, unoszone wiatrem — pismo, myśli, idee, uczucia stłamszone w pół słowa...

Niewątpliwie najbardziej popularnym poetą piszącym w getcie warszawskim w języku polskim był Władysław Szlengiel, którego nazwiska większość z Państwa na pewno nigdy nie słyszała. Urodzony w 1914, zginął w bunkrze w roku 1943, w czasie powstania w getcie. Przed wojną był to początkujący pisarz, autor piosenek, „szlagierów" w stylu Tuwima, Hemara, Własta, Jurandota czy Refrena (*Jadziem panie Zielonka, Dziś panna Andzia ma wychodne* — kto to pamięta?), satyrycznych tekstów, drukowanych od czasu do czasu w „Naszym Przeglądzie", żydowskiej gazecie warszawskiej w języku polskim, albo — co nadawało specjalną rangę — w „Szpilkach".

Szlengiel był zamknięty w getcie od jego utworzenia do zniszczenia i tam wyrósł na jego głównego piewcę. Życie w getcie jest nam dobrze znane. Szalał głód, tyfus dziesiątkował ludność tak szybko, że nie nadążano z uprzątaniem zwłok z rynsztoków. Nikt nie wiedział, kiedy go wyrwie ze snu zgiełk „akcji", czy będzie wywleczony z łóżka, czy wyszedłszy z domu wróci cało.

Co wieczór Szlengiel ukazywał się na scenie w *sui generis* kabarecie, w kawiarni „Sztuka" na Lesznie. On był organizatorem wieczorów, konferansjerem, głównym autorem tekstów. W tych tekstach odbija się historia getta w jego wszystkich aspektach — od nostalgii za utraconym rajem przedwojennej Warszawy, poprzez upokorzenia życia codziennego, ustawiczny lęk, okrucieństwa okupanta, obcowanie ze śmiercią, pragnienie zemsty, bunt. Gdyby nie było innych świadków, innego opisu, moglibyśmy odtworzyć sobie z tych wierszy pełny obraz życia w owych niewiarygodnych warunkach. Wiersze Szlengla wypełnią dzisiejszy wieczór.

Częstym tematem wierszy pisanych w getcie i obozach jest kłótnia z Panem Bogiem. Jest to w tradycji żydowskiej dysputy talmudycznej, gdzie argumenty *pro* i *contra* są uświęconym instrumentem dociekania prawdy. Opowiada się, że w getcie w Wilnie *quorum* rabinów urządziło sąd nad Panem Bogiem i w świetle oczywistej niesprawiedliwości, krzywdy, cierpienia i okrucieństw, które On toleruje, orzekli, że Bóg jest winny. Po czym spostrzegli, że zbliżył się czas wieczornej modlitwy i poszli zmówić modły.

Izabella Gelbard-Czajka ma tu *Pieśń o kupcu żelaza Abramie Gepnerze*, zastępcy prezesa Czerniakowa w warszawskim Judenracie, człowieku nieskazitelnego charakteru, który widzi, że ten rachunek sprawiedliwości boskiej szwankuje, „saldo wciąż się nie zgadza — bilans nieuczciwy". Czajka dochodzi do wniosku: „Nie było Boga w getcie — chyba go teraz za to dławi wstyd".

Józef Bau, w wierszu zatytułowanym *Głód*, modli się:

> ...chleba mojego powszedniego
> choćby na kredyt
> — użycz mi, Panie!
> Boże, byłeś Ty głodny kiedy?[1]

Stefania Ney opowiada o małym chłopcu, Herszku, który prosi Boga, by mu zezwolił na bezpieczny powrót z jednej z jego szmuglerskich wypraw: „O Boże, żebym jeszcze dziś wrócił z tej drogi!" — modli się Herszek.

> Ale Bóg w czasie wojny ma ważniejsze sprawy
> I ciężko porozumieć się z getta do nieba.
> Więc kiedyś Herszek poszedł i więcej nie wrócił,
> Bo żandarm zabił Herszka, jak niósł kilo chleba.

Henryka Łazowertówna podejmuje temat dzieci-szmuglerów:

> ...Przez mury, przez dziury, przez cegły
> Po nocy, o świcie i w dzień
> Zgłodniały, zuchwały, przebiegły
> Przesuwam się cicho jak cień.
>
> A jeśli dłoń losu znienacka
> Dosięgnie mnie kiedyś w tej grze,
> To zwykła jest życia zasadzka,
> Ty, mamo, nie czekaj już mnie.

---

[1] Ten i następne cytaty pochodzą z antologii *Pieśń ujdzie cało...*, opr. M. Borwicz, wyd. Centralna Żydowska Komisja Historyczna, Kraków 1947 (przyp. aut.).

Nie wrócę już do Ciebie,
Nie dotrze z dala głos.
Uliczny pył pogrzebie
stracony dziecka los.
I tylko jedną troską
Na wargach grymas skrzepł,
Kto Tobie, moja mamo,
przyniesie jutro chleb?

Nie sposób w ramach krótkiej prelekcji nawet wymienić wszystkich nazwisk autorów, których „pieśń uszła cało..." Halina Nelken, Natan Gross, Henryk Vogler, Henka i Ilona Karmel — jest tu materiału na niejeden taki wieczór.

Godzi się także wspomnieć tych, którzy pisali w owym czasie poza gettem, w ukryciu, na tzw. „aryjskich papierach". Zuzanna Ginczanka, piękna, czarująca dziewczyna, o wybitnie semickich rysach, ukrywająca się wpierw we Lwowie, potem w Krakowie, zadenuncjowana, rozstrzelana zimą 1944.

Krzysztof Kamil Baczyński, który walczył w szeregach AK i stał się jednym z czołowych poetów podziemia — po wojnie ciążyła na nim ta akowska przeszłość, a żydowskie pochodzenie było całkowicie przemilczane, choć niektóre z jego najlepszych wierszy można rozszyfrować tylko rozumiejąc ukryte aluzje do losu Żydów.

Stanisław Jerzy Lec (ten od *Myśli nieuczesanych*) w swych wierszach pisanych w ukryciu pisze o wiecznym strachu, że może być zdradzony przez nieopatrzne słowo, przez gest, przez towarzysza czy sąsiada, przez własne oczy, na których tęczówce wypalony jest obraz zagłady Żydów.

Mieczysław Jastrun, nazwisko rodzinne Agatstein, urodzony w roku 1903, uznany już przed wojną za wybitnego poetę, w wierszach pisanych w ukryciu — *Godzina strzeżona* i *Tu także jak w Jeruzalem* daje wyraz swemu osamotnieniu, uczuciu, że wciąż umiera „obcy i sam".

Sytuacja ludzi na „aryjskich papierach" miała swoją tragiczną specyfikę (moja Matka się tak uchowała). Wielu tych, którzy ryzykowali życie i wszystko co mieli, by wydostać się z getta, nie potrafiło znieść tego strachu ściganej zwierzyny i wracało do getta, by dzielić do końca los swego ludu.

U poetów piszących w tych warunkach powtarza się nuta goryczy i wyrzutu wobec wrogości czy obojętności otoczenia. Baczyński mówi o „winie przez zaniedbanie". Ginczanka, w parafrazie Słowackiego, tak kończy swój wiersz *Non omnis moriar*:

...Niech przyjaciele moi siądą przy pucharze
I zapiją mój pogrzeb i własne bogactwo:
Kilimy i makaty, półmiski, lichtarze —
Niechaj piją noc całą, a o świcie brzasku
Niech zaczną szukać cennych kamieni i złota
W kanapach, materacach, kołdrach i dywanach,

O, jak będzie się palić w rękach im robota,
Kłęby włosia końskiego i morskiego siana,
Chmury prutych poduszek i obłoki pierzyn
Do rąk im przylgną, w skrzydła zmienią ręce obie;
To krew moja pakuły z puchem zlepi świeżym
I uskrzydlonych nagle w aniołów przerobi.

Jastrun wypomina:

...nie rzucił nikt dobrej ziemi
na ten masowy grób —
milczeniem pozdrowieni
wolni od zdrady słów!

Gdyście ustami jak rany
pragnący wołali wody
Z pociągów odrutowanych
Nikt wody nie podał...

Ale najbardziej przejmujący głos na temat samotności umierania i porachunku z własnym sumieniem pochodzi od Miłosza, wpierw w słynnym *Campo di Fiori* pisanym podczas wojny i opublikowanym, w pierwszej wersji, w tomiku *Z otchłani*, o którym wspominałem, a wiele lat później we wstrząsającym wierszu *Biedny chrześcijanin patrzy na getto*. W nietypowym dla niego, surrealistycznym opisie, od którego ciarki przechodzą, Miłosz przedstawia scenę pod ziemią zburzonego, spalonego getta, gdzie tajemniczy strażnik-kret przedziera się przez zwały trupów:

...Powoli, drążąc tunel, posuwa się strażnik-kret
Z małą czerwoną latarką przypiętą na czole.
Dotyka ciał pogrzebanych, liczy, przedziera się dalej,
Rozróżnia ludzki popiół, po tęczującym oparze,
Popiół każdego człowieka po innej barwie tęczy.
[...]
Boję się, tak się boję strażnika-kreta.
Jego powieka obrzmiała jak u patriarchy
Który siadywał długo w blasku świec.
Czytając wielką księgę gatunku.

Cóż powiem mu ja, Żyd Nowego Testamentu,
Czekający od dwóch tysięcy lat na powrót Jezusa?
Moje rozbite ciało wyda mnie jego spojrzeniu
I policzy mnie między pomocników śmierci:
Nieobrzezanych.

Miłosz porusza tu bolesny i skomplikowany problem, którego nie można przeoczyć i nie wolno przemilczać, problem polsko-żydowskich stosunków przed wojną i po wojnie, ale nade wszystko w czasie wojny. Trzeba o tych sprawach mówić, z wzajemnym respektem; trzeba mówić prawdę, tak jak ją widzimy — choć ją często widzimy nie tak samo. Nie godzi się nam licytować w cierpieniu, ale trzeba pamiętać, że losy Polaków i Żydów pod okupacją były nieporównywalne. Musimy widzieć w sobie nawzajem to, co najlepsze, a nie to, co najgorsze. Musimy wierzyć, że wyrasta nowe pokolenie wolne od wzajemnych uprzedzeń i przesądów. Wydaje mi się, że takie spotkanie jak dzisiaj stanowi dobry omen.

Proszę Państwa, mam dla Was dobrą wiadomość — zbliżam się do końca. Ograniczyłem się do powierzchownego omówienia kilku utworów powstałych w getcie i obozach, to wszystko, na co zezwala czas. Temat zagłady Żydów zajmuje poczesne miejsce w literaturze polskiej. Tuwim, Wittlin, Słonimski, Wierzyński, Broniewski, Borowski, Nałkowska, Kamieńska, Szymborska, Ficowski, Rudnicki, Wojdowski, Wygodzki, Grynberg — ich utwory zostawiają niezatarty ślad w świadomości współczesnych czytelników i będą pożywką dla czytelników w przyszłości. Nasuwa się pytanie, czy to piśmiennictwo, które ilustruje głębie, do których człowiek zdolny jest się stoczyć, a także, choć rzadziej, wyżyny, do jakich może się wznieść — czy to piśmiennictwo podtrzyma w ludzkości promyk nadziei, czy tylko pogłębi jej cynizm i rozpacz — pytanie, na które nikt z nas nie ma odpowiedzi.

Chciałbym zakończyć paru prostymi słowami — nie moimi. Są to słowa dzieci, pochwyconc przez kogoś, potem utrwalone na papierze:

„Tato — mówi żydowski chłopiec — jak ja podrosnę, ja chcę być Niemcem".

Głos dziecka, zasłyszany w obozie śmierci w Bełżcu:

„Mamusiu, ja przecież byłem grzeczny... Ciemno, ciemno..."

W dzień wyzwolcnia, po wyjściu z kryjówki: „Mamo, czy wolno już płakać?"

I inny jeszcze głos dziecka: „Mamusiu, czy jak nas zabiją, to będzie bolało?" „Nie, kochanie, tylko chwileczkę..."

To trwało tylko chwileczkę, ale wystarczy, by spędzać nam sen z powiek po wsze czasy.

Wprowadzenie do wieczoru poświęconego poezji w getcie, który odbył się w Polskim Ośrodku Społeczno-Kulturalnym w Londynie 1 marca 1994 r.

Lekcja Oświęcimia

C zuję się onieśmielony — nikt się temu nie zdziwi — zadaniem, jakim mnie obarczono: powiedzieć parę słów na ten bolesny temat, w chwili, gdy w różnych częściach świata, w domach modlitwy i salach recepcyjnych gromadzą się ludzie pogrążeni w żałobie po tych, co zginęli, by zadumać się nad znaczeniem Oświęcimia, w pięćdziesiątą rocznicę oswobodzenia obozu. Jest to szczególnie wstrząsające dla nas, którzy znajdujemy się niejako w sąsiedztwie Oświęcimia, w jego złowieszczym cieniu.

Muszę wyjaśnić, dlaczego ten obowiązek spada na mnie, aczkolwiek ja nie jestem „ocalałym" w ścisłym tego słowa znaczeniu, a tylko jednym z milionów porażonych, którzy potracili swoich bliskich i przyjaciół w czasie zagłady.

Rodzina mojego Ojca wywodzi się z niewinnego miasteczka, które się zwało Oświęcim, którego imię zgwałcono i które zdobyło pośmiertną niesławę jako Auschwitz — ten najbardziej złowrogi dźwięk w ludzkiej mowie. Mój Ojciec był jednym z piętnaściorga dzieci, więc można przyjąć, że w Oświęcimiu żyły, dosłownie, dziesiątki Scharfów, najrozmaitszego autoramentu, od patriarchy rodu, 90-letniego Eliasza, do 4-letniej Racheli. Nikt z nich nie ocalał. Nie było im daleko iść.

Ale mam jeszcze inny tytuł, by tu przemawiać. W sercu Kazimierza, tej do niedawna jeszcze żydowskiej dzielnicy Krakowa, miasta, w którym się urodziłem, dzięki czemu jestem bezspornie autentycznym krakowianinem; oraz miasta, które kocham, dzięki czemu jestem nim jeszcze bardziej. Znam tu każdą uliczkę, każdy dom, każdy zaułek; w bramach straszą zjawy, okna szczerzą na mnie puste oczodoły. Jak Jeremiasz nad zgliszczami Jeruzalem, chcę wołać: „Jakże odludne stoi to miasto, które kipiało życiem; jako wdowa stało się ono, miasto, które słynęło między narodami…"

Kraków, a w nim Kazimierz (*ir va'em be'yisrael* — miasto i matka w Izraelu) był miejscem, gdzie przez pokolenia kwitło żydowskie życie i rozwijała się żydowska kultura. To prawdziwe żydowskie życie i kultura, które spotkał nagły, gwałtowny kres i które się już nigdy i nigdzie nie powtórzą. Kraków można wziąć za symbol życia, które było. Gdy myślimy o tej oszałamiającej statystyce Oświęcimia, Kraków niejako przywraca ludzką twarz anonimowym cyfrom, skłania nas do myślenia, co to było, po czym dziś nosimy żałobę.

Paradoksalnie, lata międzywojenne, na przekór zwiększającej się pauperyzacji i rosnącej fali antysemityzmu, można uważać za pewnego rodzaju „złoty wiek" żydostwa polskiego. Żydzi rodzili się, podrastali, zakładali rodziny, uczyli się, uprawiali handel, rzemiosło czy wolne zawody, utrzymywali chedery i jeszyboty, organizacje charytatywne i kluby sportowe, gazety i periodyki, świeckie szkoły i instytuty wyższych studiów, budowali synagogi i teatry. Bawili się, tańczyli i używali życia, kultywowali swoje najrozmaitsze zainteresowania i — nade wszystko (dlatego nazywam to „złotym wiekiem") — umierali we własnych łóżkach i byli grzebani na zwyczajnych cmentarzach.

Żyli tu, w jakiej takiej zgodzie, pośród swych polskich sąsiadów, razem, choć osobno i wnosili ogromny wkład do polskiego przemysłu i handlu, polskiej literatury i kultury. Narody, pośród których Żydzi zamieszkiwali, zawsze wynosiły z tego ogromną korzyść.

Gdyby mi przyszło wymienić jedną, dominującą cechę, która charakteryzowała to społeczeństwo, powiedziałbym, że było to pewnego rodzaju uduchowienie. Bez względu na stan społeczny czy majątkowy, Żydzi, ci biedni i ci zamożni, w przeważającej większości byli świadomi tego, że w tym życiu chodzi o coś więcej niż o spożywanie chleba, że trzeba wznieść oczy ponad powszedniość i dążyć do realizacji jakiegoś ideału, jakkolwiek by go zdefiniować.

Jest nieomal rzeczą niemożliwą prowadzić racjonalną dyskusję o Oświęcimiu. Każde słowo drażni obnażony nerw. Ten termin jest wieloznaczny. Określa on nie tylko konkretną miejscowość na polskiej ziemi. Jest to także pojęcie abstrakcyjne, które przejmuje nas lękiem i napawa grozą. Jest symbolem różnie pojmowanym przez różnych ludzi.

Dla Żydów Oświęcim jest symbolem Holocaustu. Żydzi są zdziwieni i oburzeni, jeśli ktoś pojmuje ten symbol inaczej. Ale Polacy widzą w tym symbol niemieckiego gwałtu dokonanego na ich kraju i prześladowań polskiego narodu — mają dobre powody, by tak na to patrzeć.

Podobnie dla chrześcijan: krzyż jest znakiem miłości i nadziei. Trudno im pojąć, że dla większości Żydów krzyż jest symbolem uciemiężenia, prześladowań, triumfalizmu Kościoła, nawracania „błądzących braci". Jak ich przekonać, że krzyż w miejscu, które uchodzi za największy żydowski cmentarz w historii, obraża najgłębsze żydowskie uczucia?

Zamierzam powiedzieć coś, co może urazić moich nieżydowskich przyjaciół, ale dziś nie czas na głaskanie. Nasunęła mi się ta myśl po mojej pierwszej wizycie w Oświęcimiu. Wstyd mi wyznać, ale przez długie lata nie mogłem się jakoś zdobyć na taką wizytę. Jakiś czas temu brałem udział w międzynarodowej konferencji w Krakowie o sprawach z tym związanych i wizyta w obozie była nieunikniona. Gdyśmy wrócili i długo siedzieli razem, pogrążeni w myślach, pozwoliłem sobie wyrazić pogląd, że Żyd odbiera i reaguje na Oświęcim inaczej aniżeli nie-Żyd, choćby ten był jak najbardziej wrażliwy, współczujący i życzliwy.

Jeden z moich polskich przyjaciół, człowiek, dla którego mam głęboki szacunek, powiedział mi potem, że czuje się tą moją uwagą urażony. „Czy mój puls bije innym rytmem niż twój? — zapytał. — Moje uczucia, moje impulsy, mój rozum są inne od twoich, jakoś mniej ludzkie? Czy ja jestem mniej zdolny niż ty objąć ogrom i uniwersalne znaczenie tej tragedii?" Nie, nie chciałem nikogo urazić. Wręcz przeciwnie, myślę, że przez nasze myśli i zaangażowanie stajemy się sobie bliżsi i w obliczu Oświęcimia jesteśmy wszyscy — w najgłębszym znaczeniu tego słowa — równi. Ale Żydzi zostali od innych odgrodzeni, napiętnowani, wyznaczeni na śmierć — i miliony ich tę śmierć poniosło. Inni, koniec końców, przejdą nad tym do porządku. Żydzi nie przeszli i nie przejdą, poczucie straty i ból nigdy ich nie opuszczą. W moich podróżach po świecie nie natknąłem się na jedną bodaj żydowską rodzinę, w której bliższy albo dalszy krewny nie był ofiarą zagłady. Każdy żydowski refleks, indywidualny, społeczny czy narodowy, jest uwarunkowany pamięcią Oświęcimia. Czy to iluzja z mej strony, jeśli twierdzę, że Oświęcim znaczy dla Żydów co innego i coś więcej, aniżeli dla nie-Żydów?

Gdy chcemy mówić o Oświęcimiu, stajemy przed nierozwiązywalnym dylematem. Człowiek jest zdolny zrozumieć i opisać świat tylko przez słowa, przez język. Ale w tym przypadku czujemy, że słowa nie są adekwatne. Cokolwiek mówimy na ten temat, brzmi trywialnie. Słynne *dictum* Adorno, że „po Auschwitz pisanie poezji jest barbarzyństwem", znaczy chyba, że czym Oświęcim był i co on znaczy, nie powinno w żadnym przypadku służyć jako tworzywo dla literatury. Jeśli prawda jest taka, że dola człowiecza objawia się w gettach, w obozach, w fabrykach śmierci — czyż w obliczu tego literatura, która przynosi *katharsis*, pociechę, nie jest okrutnym urągowiskiem? A piśmiennictwo, które jest aktem wiary, czyż to nie jest, w tych okolicznościach, niedopuszczalna dywersja?

Ale taki pogląd zakreśla ciasne granice i nakłada ryzy na nasze najgłębsze potrzeby — podzielić się uczuciem i doświadczeniem, pouczyć, przestrzec, przekazać. Stąd ten dylemat: gdy mówimy o tym — trywializujemy, a zatem popełniamy fałsz; gdy milczymy — nie spełniamy obowiązku, popełniamy zdradę.

Nie popadliśmy w milczenie. Powstała ogromna literatura — pamiętniki, wspomnienia, relacje, świadectwa, dokumenty, opowiadania, traktaty naukowe — każdy aspekt, każdy szczegół został opisany, zanalizowany i nie ma temu końca. (Dlatego tych „wypocin" tzw. rewizjonistów, którzy chcą podać w wątpliwość rzeczywistość Holocaustu, nie uważam za niebezpieczne, a tylko absurdalne.)

A jednak, mimo tej ogromnej literatury i dokumentacji, problemy z tym związane są tak zagadkowe, skomplikowane i bez precedensu, że nadal nie sposób ich zrozumieć.

Jak to się stało, że na pozór cywilizowany naród, w XX wieku, w sercu Europy, dał się uwieść szajce degeneratów i stoczył się do stanu barbarzyństwa?

Jak to było możliwe — powziąć i realizować plan budowania komór gazowych i krematoriów, celem wytrucia i spopielenia milionów ludzkich istot?

W ten proces musiało być aktywnie zaangażowanych wiele tysięcy „zwyczajnych" ludzi i jeszcze więcej takich, którzy to świadomie tolerowali.

Jak to się stało, że stara, wielka cywilizacja została w przeciągu czterech lat wymazana z powierzchni ziemi, tak że z trudem doszukujemy się jej śladów w kraju, w którym kwitła?

I wreszcie, jak my, niedobitki polskiego żydostwa, mamy dawać sobie radę z tym naszym życiem, obciążeni pamięcią tego, co się stało i jak się to stało?

Jak wypełnić obowiązek wobec nowego pokolenia, wobec świata? Co mamy przekazać i w jaki sposób?

Czy my naszych doświadczeń dosyć przekazujemy naszym dzieciom i wnukom? We właściwym czasie? Kiedy jest ten właściwy czas?

Niezawodnie, są lekcje, których nas Oświęcim uczy. Wiemy już, jak cienki jest fornir cywilizacji, jak łatwo ten *homo*-zwany-*sapiens* ulega zepsuciu. W pięćdziesiąt lat po Oświęcimiu, w chwili, gdy to mówię — sto rozmaitych wojen toczy się na świecie, niektóre w odległych krajach, o których mało wiemy, niektóre w bliższych, o których wiedzieć nie chcemy. Jedna lekcja wynikająca z Oświęcimia, wydaje mi się, jest najbardziej wymowna — że następnym razem będzie łatwiej...

Trzeba się wysilić, by nie popaść w rozpacz. Ortodoksyjny etos żydowski nie pochwala okazywania przesadnego żalu (mogłoby to oznaczać, że żałobnik jest zdolny do większego współczucia niż Wszechmocny). Życie musi biec swoim torem (i w pewnym sensie pobiegło tak, jak gdyby się nic nie stało). Duchowe zasoby nie są wyczerpane, jest nowe pokolenie, wyzwanie, jakie stawia przyszłość. Nade wszystko dla nas jest państwo Izrael, spełnienie marzeń, źródło dumy i siły.

Musimy kurczowo trzymać się wiary, że wbrew wszystkiemu, w ostatecznej instancji, istnieje na tym padole sprawiedliwość (choć nie zawsze dostrzegalna gołym okiem), że nasze filozoficzne, racjonalistyczne, teologiczne założenia nie są bez podstaw.

Holocaust ukazał dno, do którego człowiek może się stoczyć, a także wyżyny, na jakie duch ludzki może się wznieść. Nieomal zawsze jest wybór między tym dobrym a tym złym, i może być chwila, kiedy trzeba się na ten wybór zdecydować, może z wielkim dla siebie ryzykiem. Godzi się pamiętać, że „aby zło zapanowało, wystarczy, aby ludzie dobrej woli wstrzymali się od czynu".

Dobre obyczaje nakazują, aby taką wypowiedź jak moja kończyć jakąś optymistyczną nutą. Mnie to przychodzi trudno — ta przeszłość mnie przytłacza, dominuje mój wewnętrzny krajobraz. Tym niemniej, tym niemniej — Nadzieja Umiera Ostatnia.

Przemówienie wygłoszone w Centrum Kultury Żydowskiej na krakowskim Kazimierzu w r. 1995, w 50. rocznicę oswobodzenia obozu oświęcimskiego

Na 50. rocznicę powstania w Getcie Warszawskim

Nie ukrywam zadowolenia z faktu, że w środowisku polskim w Londynie zrodziła się inicjatywa uczczenia rocznicy powstania w getcie warszawskim i choć nie wiem, dlaczego mnie właśnie wybrano, abym przy tej sposobności parę słów powiedział — przyznaję, że czuję się tym zaszczycony.

Może mój tytuł do mówienia na ten temat — jeśliby ktoś o to pytał — polega na tym, że większość mojej rodziny po mieczu wywodziła się z Oświęcimia, miasteczka, które weszło do historii i okryło się przesmutną sławą. W miasteczku tym większość ludności stanowili Żydzi, a pośród nich klan rodziny Scharfów, tak liczny, że się od nich czerniło. Nikt z nich nie przeżył. Nie mieli daleko...

Emigracja miała zawsze to do siebie, że Żydzi i Polacy mogli ze sobą rozmawiać jak równi z równymi. Możemy się nawzajem wysłuchać, przekonywać, możemy się wykłócać o byle co, a także nie o byle co. Możemy sobie mówić prawdę — tak jak ją widzimy. Nasze poglądy na żydowską egzystencję w Polsce przed wojną, a przede wszystkim pod okupacją, są odmienne. Dialog polsko-żydowski toczy się jakoś półgębkiem, nie jest otwarty i szczery. Odnosi się wrażenie, że Polacy między sobą, prywatnie, często mówią o Żydach inaczej niż publicznie, i — dla symetrii — Żydzi o Polakach tak samo (walczę z tym — na obu frontach).

Często, gdy Polacy mówią na tematy żydowskie, te wojenne, okupacyjne, jest w tym jakiś niepokój — jakby się obawiali, że lada chwila wypłynie na powierzchnię coś, co będzie dla nich niemiłe, postawi ich w defensywie, będzie trudne do wytłumaczenia. Jest w tym często nie zła wola, lecz po prostu nieznajomość przedmiotu. Mało Polaków naprawdę znało życie żydowskie, piśmiennictwo, wewnętrzną politykę czy poglądy społeczności żydowskiej — nie było to dla nich dostatecznie ciekawe.

Rocznica, którą obchodzimy, służy za dobrą ilustrację. Gdy Żydzi mówią „powstanie", mają na myśli powstanie w getcie warszawskim; gdy Polacy mówią „powstanie", myślą oczywiście o powstaniu warszawskim — o tym pamiętnym i tragicznym epizodzie w historii polskiej.

Rocznica powstania w getcie była w PRL obchodzona w okrągłe rocznice. Niejednokrotnie brałem w tych obchodach udział. Zawsze miałem uczucie, że organizatorom nie chodzi o jakieś szczere uczczenie pamięci czy też złożenie hołdu bohaterom, ale że jest w tym jakiś ukryty motyw, jakaś oficjalna teza, którą trzeba przy tej sposobności wykazać. Chodziło np. o to, ażeby zademonstrować przed światem, jaki ten reżym jest sprawiedliwy, jak się troszczy o Żydów, jakim fałszem jest oskarżanie go o antysemityzm, którego w Polsce nie ma. Innym razem cały nacisk był położony na ogromną pomoc, jaką w czasie powstania niosła ludności żydowskiej Armia Ludowa; był opis dostarczanej broni, do ostatniej kuli (nie było tego wiele nawet wedle ich własnej rachuby). Innym razem była znowu okazja, by perorować z trybuny o spisku niemiecko- -syjonistycznym zagrażającym niepodległości Polski, której jedynym gwarantem jest Rosja Sowiecka.

Powstanie w getcie było szaleńczym, beznadziejnym, samobójczym zrywem, gdzie jedynym zwycięstwem mogła być śmierć z bronią w ręku. Z motyką na słońce, a raczej z pukawką na tanki i armaty, „do krwi ostatniej kropli z żył", „jak kamienie przez Boga rzucane na szaniec", taki — nie waham się użyć tego przymiotnika — prawdziwie polski zryw (bo Polacy i Żydzi, na pozór odmienni, w gruncie rzeczy są pod wielu względami do siebie podobni — szczególnie w swej tendencji do wewnętrznych waśni). W dziejach ruchu oporu jest to wydarzenie wyjątkowe. Urosło do rozmiarów symbolu w skali światowej.

Powstanie w getcie jest często widziane jako częściowa bodaj rehabilitacja społeczeństwa żydowskiego, które się oskarża o pasywizm, o pójście na rzeź bez oporu. Nie godzę się z tym poglądem. Całkowita dysproporcja sił — ludzie wycieńczeni chorobą i głodem, sterroryzowani i bezbronni — przeciw potężnej, zwycięskiej armii i aparatowi państwa policyjnego. W Oświęcimiu znalazło się np. 13 000 rosyjskich jeńców wojennych, młodych, mocnych, zdyscyplinowanych; gdy Oświęcim oswobodzono — było ich przy życiu 92. Jeśli oni nie mogli się zdobyć na zbrojny opór, czego oczekiwać od reszty?

Nadto Niemcy prowadzili akcję eksterminacyjną z niesłychaną perfidią i chytrością, więźniowie byli w izolacji od świata zewnętrznego, nieświadomi jaki ich los czeka, a więc z ognikiem nadziei na przeżycie. Najmniejszy odruch oporu był natychmiast krwawo i brutalnie tłumiony dziesięciokrotną wspólną odpowiedzialnością. Mimo to były próby zbrojnego oporu w getcie w Częstochowie, w Białymstoku, w obozach zagłady w Treblince i Sobiborze.

Co więcej — opór to nie tylko desperacki strzał z pistoletu, ręczny granat czy butelka z benzyną. Opór to także podziemne nauczanie dzieci i dorosłych, opór to siatka charytatywnej pomocy, opór to „Archiwum Ringelbluma" — kolekcjonowanie raportów i dokumentów, nasze główne dziś źródło wiedzy o tym, co się tam działo; opór to działalność artystyczna, koncerty, piosenki satyryczne, wiersze pisane i kolportowane na skrawkach papieru; opór to prasa podziemna, rozpowszechnianie biuletynów, informacji zasłyszanych w radio. Opór to Janusz Korczak, model ludzkiej godności, idący z dziećmi na śmierć. Opór, nade wszystko, to każdy dobry uczynek, który przywraca wiarę w człowieka, znak, że w tej powodzi barbarzyństwa nie wszystko bezpowrotnie stracone.

W retrospekcji nikt poza tymi, którzy w ten czy ów sposób walczyli w getcie, nie wychodzi z tego wydarzenia z honorem. Rządy alianckie pozostały głuche na rozdzierające apele z getta, m.in. na osobisty apel śmiałka i bohatera Jana Karskiego, czy na samobójstwo Szmula Zygielbojma[1]. Tezą Roosevelta było, że „klęska Niemiec przyniesie wyzwolenie ludności żydowskiej". Ludność żydowska klęski Niemiec nie doczekała.

Nie wychodzi z honorem polskie „podziemie". Armia Krajowa, która była odbiciem społeczeństwa, była — z nielicznymi wyjątkami — na los Żydów obojętna, a w wielu wypadkach wręcz im wroga. Główny dowódca, gen. Grot-Rowecki, w radiogramie z 2 stycznia 1943 do rządu w Londynie donosi: „Różne grupy żydowskie, włączając komunistów, zwracają się do nas ostatnio o dostarczenie im broni, tak jak gdybyśmy mieli pełne składy. Jako eksperyment dostarczyłem im parę rewolwerów. Nie ma pewności, że zrobią z nich użytek. Nie dostarczę im więcej broni, wiecie że sami jej wiele nie mamy..."

Nie wolno mi pominąć milczeniem roli tzw. Narodowych Sił Zbrojnych. Nie wiem, jak ta rola jest oceniana przez współczesnych historyków, ale jest niezaprzeczalnym faktem, że w porozumieniu z Niemcami i zgodnie ze swym programem Narodowe Siły Zbrojne wymordowały tysiące Żydów.

W czasie powstania rząd na emigracji, nagle zaskoczony sprawą Katynia i zerwaniem stosunków z Rosją — był tym całkowicie zaprzątnięty.

Nie wyszli też z honorem działacze i prowodyrzy żydowscy w Ameryce. Przywódcy powstania wzywali ich, by się położyli pokotem na stopniach Białego Domu i nie ruszyli się, dopóki rząd amerykański nie podejmie jakiejś akcji ratunkowej czy odwetowej. Może Nahum Goldmann[2] czy Stephen Wise[3] chadzali do Roosevelta tylnymi schodami — nikt niczego nie zdziałał. Mieszkańcy getta — i to było najboleśniejszym aspektem ich tragicznej egzystencji — czuli się opuszczeni przez Boga i ludzi.

Zakres i możliwości pomocy różniły się oczywiście ogromnie — co innego leżało w możliwościach Roosevelta, co innego Churchilla, co innego w rękach Grota-Roweckiego, co innego w rękach Nahuma Goldmanna. Nikt, nikt nie wyszedł z tego z honorem. Honor wynieśli tylko bojownicy getta.

Ktokolwiek chce sobie wyrobić pogląd na te sprawy, musi pamiętać, że mówimy o apokaliptycznych czasach, bez precedensu w historii, gdzie podstawowe

---

[1] Szmul Zygielbojm (1895–1943), jeden z przywódców Bundu w Polsce, radny miasta Warszawy i Łodzi. W czasie wojny członek Rady Narodowej przy rządzie polskim na emigracji. Po upadku powstania w getcie warszawskim, na znak protestu przeciw obojętności, jaką świat okazywał wobec tragedii Żydów pod okupacją, Zygielbojm popełnił samobójstwo.

[2] Goldmann Nahum (1874–1982), działacz żydowski w Niemczech, Ameryce, Izraelu, założyciel i długoletni prezydent Światowego Kongresu Żydowskiego, jedna z czołowych postaci żydostwa w XX wieku (przyp. aut.).

[3] Stephen Wise (1874–1949), liberalny rabin, jeden z najbardziej wpływowych przywódców żydowskich w Ameryce (przyp. aut.).

pojęcia, nawyki myślowe, normalne refleksy przestały funkcjonować. Były sytuacje tak potworne, tak — w dosłownym tego słowa znaczeniu — nieludzkie, że osądzanie ich, *ex post*, sprawdzianami urobionymi na codzienną ludzką miarę nie ma sensu. Jak rozdzielasz swą rację chleba pomiędzy członków rodziny, jeśli ona nie wystarcza dla wszystkich? Jak matka dokonuje wyboru, które z dwojga dzieci uratować, gdy jest szansa na uratowanie jednego tylko? Jak reagujesz na Żyda pukającego do twych drzwi w ucieczce przed gestapo, gdy danie mu schronienia może grozić śmiercią tobie i twojej rodzinie? Słyszeliście może o Adinie Szwajgier, która zmarła onegdaj w Łodzi — jej nekrologi ukazały się w „Timesie" i „Independent"; była lekarką w szpitalu dziecięcym w getcie. Podczas opróżniania szpitala, do transportu do Treblinki, Adina Szwajgier, aby zaoszczędzić dzieciom tej koszmarnej podróży do gazu, szła od łóżeczka do łóżeczka i dawała dzieciom śmiertelny zastrzyk morfiny. Jakimi kategoriami oceniać taką decyzję? Dotarł do mnie następujący cytat z pamiętnika pisanego w getcie przez niejakiego Jana Mawulta:

Pomyślcie: garść ludzi postanawia się bronić. Broni nie mają, umocnień nie mogą wznosić, amunicji nie mogą gromadzić, każdy rewolwer muszą — z wielkim trudem — kupić, szmuglować. Postanowili umrzeć, paść jeden za drugim? Dobrze. Ale co zrobić ze starcami, z matkami i ojcami? Co z dziećmi? Żony będą walczyć razem, ramię przy ramieniu, ale co z tamtymi zrobić? Zostawić ich losowi? Ich los to prawdopodobnie spalenie żywcem, obecnie już nawet nie komory gazowe. Więc temu losowi ich zostawić? Niepodobna. Więc co zrobić? Chyba samemu ich zabić. Ale to niełatwe; te kilka kul, które są, to cenna rzecz, nie można ich trwonić, każdej trzeba strzec, każda musi przypaść Niemcowi. Więc chyba otruć, ale czym? Gazu już nie ma. Chyba cyjankiem potasu — ale skąd wziąć to w dostatecznej ilości? I kiedy, w którym momencie to zrobić?

Powstanie w getcie to bezapelacyjnie ostatni rozdział egzystencji Żydów na ziemiach polskich. Getto warszawskie zostało zrównane z ziemią i stało się nie tylko grobem tej ostatniej garstki bojowników, ale też symbolicznym kamieniem cmentarnym żydowskiej cywilizacji we Wschodniej Europie. To tutaj na polskiej ziemi, w surowym często klimacie, kwitła najbardziej twórcza, życiodajna, prężna gałąź narodu żydowskiego w diasporze.

Jedna trzecia narodu żydowskiego została zgładzona, wytruta, obrócona w popiół. Ilu w tych popiołach było przyszłych Einsteinów i Freudów, Henryków Heine, Mendelsohnów, Gotliebów i Chagallów, Leśmianów, Słonimskich, Tuwimów, Korczaków — ludzi obciążonych tym dziedzictwem, z którego się rodzi geniusz.

Blisko tysiąc lat cywilizacji Żydów w Polsce, tej osobnej i tej wspólnej, symbiotycznej, zostało zniszczone w ciągu czterech lat teutońskiego barbarzyństwa — jest to fakt nie do ogarnięcia, przed którym się myśl wzdraga. Naród żydowski wyszedł z tej wojny nie tylko fizycznie okaleczony, ale uszkodzony psychicznie w tym sensie, że każde inne zło na świecie wydaje się nam w porównaniu z tym, co się stało — trywialne, nasza wrażliwość na cudze cierpienie jest umniejszona.

Jest w zwyczaju, że przy okazjach takich, jak ta, prelegent kończy na jakąś podniosłą nutę, jakimś akcentem nadziei i optymizmu, że na przekór i tak dalej... Proszę mi wybaczyć, mnie na to nie stać. Stoję w obliczu tego bezradny, osierocony, obciążony poczuciem ogromnej krzywdy. Nie mija dzień w moim życiu, bym o tym nie myślał. Nie mogę o tym zapomnieć, nie wolno mi zapomnieć, nie chcę zapomnieć. Chciałbym, aby świat nigdy o tym nie zapomniał.

Wygłoszone w Polskim Ośrodku Społeczno-Kulturalnym w Londynie 19 kwietnia 1993 r.

Rola Rumkowskiego

Nim przystąpiłem do opracowania tematu, prowadziłem ze sobą przysłowiowy żydowski pojedynek, tj. „biłem się z myślami", czy ograniczyć się ściśle do meritum sprawy, czy też pozwolić sobie na parę ogólnych uwag. Wybrałem tę drugą możliwość, albowiem wydaje mi się, że byłoby z mojej strony przeoczeniem, zaniedbaniem okazji, wręcz nieszczerością, gdybym przebywając w Łodzi, tej ongiś wielonarodowej, która stała się za naszych czasów sceną żydobójstwa — gdybym tu ograniczył się wyłącznie do przeszłości, a nie pisał o tym, co naprawdę najbardziej leży mi na sercu. Muszę to zrobić w wielkim skrócie — nie jestem pewien, czy się to uda.

Wiem, że jest to w pewnym sensie historyczny moment, że mamy tę możliwość może po raz ostatni. Gdy mówię „my", mam na myśli pokolenie uczestników, ofiar i naocznych świadków zagłady i męczeństwa Żydów w Polsce. Mija bez mała pół wieku od chwili, gdy nad ugorem Oświęcimia, Treblinki, Majdanka, Sobiboru, Chełmna i Bełżca unosił się swąd palonych ciał. Ta garstka ludzi, którzy jakimś cudem przeżyli getta i obozy, jest już przetrzebiona naturalnym biegiem rzeczy. Niezadługo nie będzie nikogo, kto tam był i kto to widział — i wejdziemy w sferę innej formy przekazu, w literaturę, dziejopisarstwo, relacje z drugiej ręki, to jest w inną kategorię wiarygodności.

Nie należę do tych, którzy obawiają się, że sam fakt tych nieprawdopodobnych potworności, jakich Niemcy bezkarnie w Polsce dokonali, zostanie z czasem zaprzeczony. Prawdą jest, że i mnie uderza krew do głowy, gdy słyszę albo czytam, że komory gazowe i krematoria to były pralnie albo stacje dezynfekcyjne i kusi mnie, aby zapytać, co się stało z moją rodziną liczącą setki osób (mój ojciec był jednym z piętnaściorga dzieci), z której nikt nie przeżył. Ale takie „tezy" są albo świadomym kłamstwem, albo zjawiskiem patologicznym, nie ma ani celu, ani sensu wdawać się z tym w dyskusję.

Epoka ta jest najszerzej i najgruntowniej udokumentowaną epoką w historii. Podnoszą się czasem głosy, że jest tego za dużo, że czas się od tej obsesji uwolnić i patrzeć w przyszłość. Nie podzielam tego zdania — owszem, to jest obsesja, ale nieunikniona i potrzebna. Co w tym kontekście znaczy „za dużo", co znaczy „dosyć"? Jeśli bibliografia przedmiotu obejmuje 5000 poważnych pozycji — czy to jest dosyć? 10 000 — czy to jest dosyć? Nie, każda wypowiedź, każde świadectwo, każdy skrawek wspomnień będzie się liczył na wagę złota — tylko to po nas zostanie.

Jest nas niewielu, może parędziesiąt osób na obu kontynentach, które się poczuwają do obowiązku, aby podtrzymywać polsko-żydowski dialog, aby w tym skłóconym świecie budować jakieś mosty, aby w zgiełku oskarżeń i rekryminacji utrzymać prymat zdrowego rozsądku, dobrej woli i obiektywnych prawd. Przygniatająca większość, po obu stronach, patrzy na te prace obojętnie albo wrogo. Warchołów nigdzie nie brak i nie wiadomo, czy jest na to rada. Na przekór temu, w chwilach optymizmu (bez poważnej jego dawki nikt by się w tę sprawę nie angażował) sądzę, że niezdrowy klimat, w jakim się od wielu lat ta dyskusja toczyła — złagodniał; że język — którym się w tej sferze operuje i który odzwierciedla atmosferę i nastroje — zmienił się, i to radykalnie, na lepsze. Jest to bez wątpienia postęp, który mamy do zawdzięczenia paru konferencjom — w Bostonie, w Oksfordzie, w Tyńcu, w Krakowie, w Jerozolimie — teraz dodamy do tego Łódź; periodykom, jak: „Znak", „Więź", „Tygodnik Powszechny", londyński „Aneks", oksfordzki „Polin", artykułom Błońskiego, Turowicza, wierszom Ficowskiego, Miłosza. Dowodzi to siły pisanego i mówionego słowa — w sytuacji, w której, niestety, już tylko o słowa chodzi. Ileż to może zdziałać szczerze powiedziane jedno słowo: „przepraszam" albo „wybacz"…

Jest postęp — ale jakiż on kruchy… Byle incydent — żeby tylko wspomnieć ten nieszczęsny klasztor Karmelitanek w Oświęcimiu — byle jakaś nieprzemyślana wypowiedź tego czy innego dygnitarza — już znowu na siebie z pazurami, już znowu trzeba niejako zaczynać od początku, aż ręce opadają w zwątpieniu, czy to do czegoś prowadzi. Te wybuchy są tylko symptomem tego, jak tuż pod powierzchnią kipią emocje i jak głęboko są zakorzenione wzajemne uprzedzenia i przesądy.

Trzeba przyjąć, że między Polakami a Żydami jest jakieś wiekowe, fundamentalne nieporozumienie. Nie wiem, jak temu zaradzić inaczej, jeśli właśnie nie poprzez otwartą i szczerą ze sobą rozmowę. I myślę, że w tej wymianie postaw winniśmy pamiętać słynną przestrogę Olivera Cromwella: *I beseech you on the bowels of Christ, think it possible you may be mistaken* (Zaklinam cię na trzewia Chrystusa, przyjm tę możliwość, że jesteś w błędzie).

Mogę tylko mówić o tym, jak tę sprawę widzą Żydzi (niektórzy Żydzi) — i jestem zawsze gotów wysłuchać z uwagą, jak to widzą Polacy (niektórzy Polacy). Mówię w obu wypadkach o ludziach światłych, życzliwych, świadomych swych ułomności. W tej wymianie myśli (celowo unikam słów takich jak spór czy dysputa, ażeby zneutralizować akcenty konfrontacyjne — mówię raczej o wspólnym wysiłku dociekania prawdy), zgodzimy się, jestem pewny, że Żydzi są tą stroną pokrzywdzoną. Spotykam się czasami z argumentem, że tzw. „antypolonizm" Żydów, szczególnie w Ameryce, niejako równoważy antysemityzm, że jest w tych zjawiskach jakaś symetria i że nikomu się z tego nie należy reszta. Nie widzę tu symetrii, tzw. „antypolonizm" jest nieprzyjemnym zjawiskiem, godnym potępienia, ale nie ma tego elementu demonizacji, utożsamiania przeciwnika ze wszelkim złem, które jest u podstaw antysemityzmu. Analizowałem to zjawisko na jednej z konferencji. Zapytywałem, czemu je przypisać, zapytywałem, czy tacy ci Żydzi z natury są perwersyjni i złośliwi, że szkalują tę Polskę dla czystej frajdy, zmyślają zarzuty, robią z igły widły, odpłacają czarną niewdzięcznością za doznane dobrodziejstwa. Czy też nie jest bardziej prawdopodobne, że ich stanowisko i wypowiedzi są po prostu wyrazem poczucia doznanej krzywdy?

W tym jest sedno sprawy — dopóki tego nie zrozumiemy, nie wyjaśnimy i w jakiś sposób nie załagodzimy, rana będzie jątrzyć i wysiłek zdążający do zbliżenia pójdzie na marne. Lista roszczeń jest długa — nie będę jej tu powtarzał, bo niemiło tego słuchać (i jeszcze niemilej recytować).

U podstaw leży odwieczny, pogardliwy i triumfalistyczny stosunek Kościoła do religii żydowskiej, do judaizmu, z którego się Kościół wywodzi. Powiedział ktoś, że antysemityzm to jest chrześcijańska choroba, na którą Żydzi umierają. Kościół w Polsce był w tej dziedzinie wysoko wyspecjalizowany, *in capite et in membris*, od kazań proboszcza w wiejskim kościele do listów pasterskich najwyższych dostojników. Nauka ta, przez całe pokolenia, wyryła głębokie piętno na świadomości narodu, określała jego stosunek do Żydów. Jaki on był wiemy, posiew nienawiści nie wschodził żniwem miłosierdzia. Nie wiem, czy po dziś dzień kler w Polsce zrozumiał i przyswoił sobie encyklikę *Nostra Aetate* i posoborowe interpretacje i poprawki. Nie jestem pewny, czy się tu coś radykalnie zmieniło — na szczęście nie ma to dla Żydów praktycznie większego znaczenia. Wydaje mi się, że ma to ogromne znaczenie dla Kościoła — ale to już nie moja sprawa i nie mnie się na ten temat wypowiadać.

Na liście roszczeń największy żal i rozgoryczenie budzi rozpamiętywanie okresu zagłady. W żydowskiej percepcji powszechnie dominuje pogląd — celowo formułuję to najłagodniej jak umiem — że poza nielicznymi wyjątkami, zachowanie się Polaków wobec swych współobywateli i bliźnich w tych niewypowiedzianie tragicznych czasach było niemoralne. Trzeba przyznać, że Polacy byli wystawieni na iście szatańską próbę, na podejmowanie decyzji, jakich w normalnym życiu człowiek nie spotyka — ale z tej próby nie wyszli obronną ręką. Można się tylko zastanawiać, czy ktokolwiek inny wyszedłby z takiej próby chwalebniej — ale dla Żydów mała w tym pociecha.

Często w takich chwilach podnoszą się wśród Polaków głosy: „Im, Żydom, wydaje się, że tylko oni cierpieli!" Prawdą jest, że cierpienie własne nie wyczula, jakbyśmy to chcieli, na cierpienie bliźniego, nie przerabia zwyczajnych zjadaczy chleba w aniołów; niestety, wręcz przeciwnie — zasklepia, zaślepia, dzieli. Nikt nie przeczy, że Polacy byli również zagrożeni, prześladowani, że przechodzili własną gehennę. Ale te sytuacje były niewspółmierne i nieporównywalne. Tylko Żydzi byli całkowicie skazani na zagładę, mężczyźni, kobiety, dzieci i starcy, bez wyjątku i bez apelacji, wyłącznie za to, że byli Żydami; tylko Żydzi (i Cyganie) ginęli w komorach gazowych — milionami, a także setkami tysięcy po obozach i gettach, jak w Wilnie, Warszawie i Łodzi, i pod kulami *Einsatzkommandos*, jak w Babim Jarze.

Nie należy się dziwić, gdy się ocenia współczesną sytuację, że społeczeństwa żydowskie, gdziekolwiek one są, to organizmy okaleczone, fizycznie i psychicznie. Takie rany nie mogą się zabliźnić w ciągu jednego pokolenia — kto wie, czy kiedykolwiek. Nie należy oczekiwać od nich spokojnych, obiektywnych, wyważonych sądów. Każda reakcja, każdy odruch ma swe źródło w dniu wczorajszym, w lęku, że jeśli taka rzecz była możliwa, może być powtarzalna. Wszystko, co się dzieje w państwie Izrael, jest uwarunkowane tą świadomością (i co ważniejsze — podświadomością), bo, paradoksalnie, tam jest największe zagrożenie, aktualne i potencjalne.

Najdłuższa nawet droga zaczyna się od pierwszego kroku, a pierwszym krokiem jest starać się wiele trudnych rzeczy zrozumieć. Na przekór francuskiemu powiedzonku — zrozumieć, to niekoniecznie wybaczyć, już sam rzetelny wysiłek w tym kierunku ma znaczenie terapeutyczne. Trapi mnie bardzo, jeśli czegoś w tym kompleksie nie mogę zrozumieć. Nie mogę na przykład zrozumieć osobliwego, chyba specyficznie polskiego fenomenu: antysemityzmu bez Żydów. Większość Polaków przecież — chyba, że im się dwoi w oczach — prawdziwego Żyda już dawno nie widziała. Już ich on nie drażni kędzierzawą brodą i pejsami, jarmułką i chałatem, charkotliwą mową. Już nie konkuruje na straganie czy w sklepiku za rogiem, gdzie szwarc, mydło i powidło jest o grosik tańsze. Już nie ssie krwi robotnika jako fabrykant, kamienicznik i lichwiarz, już nie knuje przeciw władzy jako komunista, już nie bierze krwi dzieci na macę. Już się nie domaga zwrotu mienia, już się nie pcha, gdzie go nie szukają, już się nie płaszczy, już się nie wywyższa — JUŻ GO NIE MA. A jednak... pokutuje tu jakieś widmo.

Jak to nazwać, czemu przypisać tę dalekosiężną, pozagrobową nienawiść? Jak głęboko tkwi ten uraz, zakażenie, z którego sączy się jad? Co się tu stało między tymi narodami w trakcie wielowiekowego współżycia, że pozostaje po tym taki osad? Nie umiem na to odpowiedzieć, choć nie przestaję o tym myśleć.

Doceniam trudności, jakie napotyka Polak, gdy chce te problemy zgłębić. W pierwszym rzędzie, gdy pada słowo „Żyd" — czy jest mu jasne o kim mowa? Czy zdaje sobie sprawę, jakie to zawiłe pojęcie? Czy jest w stanie stworzyć sobie jakiś autentyczny model, dookoła którego będzie snuł swe rozważania? Wydaje mi się także, że będzie mu stał na przeszkodzie po prostu brak prawdziwych informacji, danych, do których przez dziesięciolecia nie było w Polsce dostępu. Do niedawna współczesna historia Żydów w Polsce, czas okupacji i zagłady, z różnych psychologicznych i politycznych względów były traktowane jak *sui generis* pornografia, wstydliwie, półgębkiem, najchętniej wcale. Zagłada Żydów miała być pojmowana jako część wielkiej, wspólnej tragedii Polaków, ludzkości — to, że w komorach gazowych ginęli wyłącznie Żydzi, było podrzędnym szczegółem. Związane to było częściowo z nieczystym sumieniem, częściowo z faktem, że oficjalna teza jakoś nie przystawała do ogromu zjawiska — stąd te warstwy zakłamania, spod których tylko tu i ówdzie coś się przedzierało. Trzeba skonstatować z radością, że już od jakiegoś czasu wraz z wielu innymi zmianami i to się zmieniło, trudno mi nawet nadążyć za wszystkim, co się publikuje na te tematy w Polsce.

Społeczeństwo, naród, by przetrwać, musi bezustannie, intymnie obcować ze swą przeszłością — tylko tak naród żydowski przetrwał Rozproszenie. Gdy Polak zechce się w swą przeszłość wsłuchać i, niejako, się z niej „rozliczyć", uderzy go ta wyrwa w krajobrazie, ta ogromna, nieodwołalna nieobecność Żydów. Sposób, w jaki on tę część swej historii rozumie, napisze, przekaże — to określi oblicze przyszłego pokolenia i zaważy na jego losie bardziej może, niż wszystkie rozrachunki z bankierami i Międzynarodowym Funduszem Walutowym.

Proces poznawczy nie może się odbyć bez koronnego świadka, tego narodu, który — jak ktoś powiedział — „sam nie śpi i innym spać nie daje". Jakkolwiek się nasze losy potoczą — a toczą się szybko i gwałtownie odrębnymi już nurtami — w naszych rękach spoczywa historyczne świadectwo wspólnego bytu i rozstania. Cokolwiek przyszłość ma w zanadrzu dla narodu żydowskiego — to jego historyczną misją jest pozostawienie świadectwa po wsze czasy i o tym, czego Żydzi doznali z rąk niemieckich na tej ziemi, „na oczach świata".

Wracam jednak do tematu artykułu.

Chaim Mordechaj Rumkowski był jedną z tych skomplikowanych, groteskowych, tragikomicznych postaci zasługujących na pióro Dostojewskiego lub Balzaka, postaci, która mogła zaistnieć tylko w obłędnych okolicznościach owego czasu.

Z początku był on zwyczajnym „Lodzermenschem", o nader skromnej edukacji, ale wielkiej wrodzonej inteligencji i żelaznej woli, który w swoim czasie zbił majątek i potem go stracił — ot, normalne wzloty i upadki tego typu ludzi w tej „Ziemi Obiecanej", jaką była Łódź u schyłku ubiegłego wieku. Był także społecznikiem, filantropem. W okresie międzywojennym wybudował, z funduszów przez siebie zebranych, wielki sierociniec w Helenówku, który zdobył przydomek „małej Palestyny", albowiem wychowanków uczono rolnictwa, przygotowując ich do pionierstwa w Ziemi Świętej. Gdy Niemcy zajęli Łódź, zwołali żydowskich ławników, by mianować *Judenrat*. Rumkowskiego ustanowili prezesem, Starszym Rady (*der Aelteste des Judenrates*) nie wiadomo dlaczego, przypuszczalnie dzięki temu, że był wysoki i miał bujną białą czuprynę — ostatecznie im było wszystko jedno, kto ma wykonywać ich rozkazy, robaczek przekazujący zlecenia innym robaczkom.

Niemcy nie mogli przewidzieć, jaki to był dla nich szczęśliwy wybór. W Rumkowskim znaleźli wiernego funkcjonariusza o demonicznej energii i genialnym zmyśle organizacyjnym. Wyglądało na to, jakby on tylko czekał, aby w rozkwicie swych sześćdziesięciu lat móc wykazać pełną wartość i stać się — ku uciesze swych panów — „królem getta".

Za kolczastym drutem, na Bałutach, w natłoku sześciu osób na pokój, bez kanalizacji, Rumkowski stworzył samorządne terytorium, państewko, z własnym aparatem administracyjnym, sądami, walutą — i, oczywiście, policją i więzieniami. Racje chleba, żywności, były dostateczną sankcją i namacalnym instrumentem absolutnej władzy. Rumkowski zorganizował fabryki, warsztaty, szpitale, garkuchnie, szkoły — był to czas, gdy ludzie jeszcze myśleli o wychowaniu dzieci. Ze swojego gabinetu kierował całym systemem przedsiębiorstw. On był jedynym łącznikiem z Niemcami, jedyną wykładnią ich rozkazów.

Jasne jest, patrząc wstecz, że nie był to zły człowiek, jak ci Żydzi, którzy współpracowali z Niemcami dla własnych korzyści i którzy robili ich brudną robotę, by ratować własną skórę. Rumkowski był bez wątpienia człowiekiem czystych intencji i szczerze przekonanym, że działał w interesie społeczności. Otoczył się wielu zdolnymi ludźmi, których ręce pozostały czyste. Miał jedną myśl, która mu przyświecała jak gwiazda przewodnia: że jeśli Żydzi okażą się Niemcom „użyteczni", jeśli będą pracować, pracować, pracować, aż zedrą ręce do kości — usprawiedliwią swoją egzystencję i przetrwają. Łatwo dziś powiedzieć, jak bezdennie głupia była taka filozofia. Ani Rumkowski, ani nikt inny nie mógł wtedy wiedzieć, ani przewidzieć w najgorszych snach, że Niemcy mieli w planie totalną zagładę Żydów i że ten plan miał prymat nad wszystkimi innymi ich zamierzeniami, że nic, absolutnie nic, co Rumkowski zrobił lub omieszkał zrobić nie mogło mieć najmniejszego wpływu na los Żydów.

Będąc zwyczajną marionetką w rękach Niemców, Rumkowski jakoś popadł w manię wielkości. Mawiał „moje fabryki, moje szpitale, moi lekarze, moi Żydzi", zwracał się nieustannie do tej „swojej" ludności, przeważnie wrzeszcząc, w stylu krasomówstwa Goebbelsa. W zamian za to domagał się i dostawał pochlebstwa: „Nasz wielki prezes, nasz mądry prezes..." Jak mało miał prawdziwej władzy i jak Niemcy nawet nie udawali, że mu cokolwiek są winni za jego wspaniałe usługi, wskazuje fakt, że gdy jednego dnia odważnie poszedł do gestapo, by interweniować w sprawie aresztowanego kolegi z *Judenratu*, pobito go i wyrzucono za drzwi jak pierwszego lepszego Żyda.

Czy Rumkowski sam siebie oszukiwał, czy też pozował na użytek swego otoczenia, trudno dociec. Nabrał manier absolutnego władcy i despoty i te pozory władzy, jak to było do przewidzenia, przewróciły mu w głowie.

Czerniakow, prezes *Judenratu* w Warszawie, który w podobnie tragicznych okolicznościach również odgrywał dwuznaczną rolę spełniając niemieckie rozkazy, gdy przyszło do podpisania zarządzenia o przesiedleniu, kiedy wiadomo mu już było, że to chodzi o „przesiedlenie" do obozu zagłady, odmówił podpisu popełniając samobójstwo. Ten fakt oczywiście w niczym nie zmienił losu Żydów, ale Czerniakow tym aktem zrehabilitował się przed sądem historii. Rumkowski inaczej — do ostatniej chwili sygnował rozkazy, aż do dnia, kiedy on sam, ze swą młodą żoną (którą poślubił w gettcie), ze swym adoptowanym synem i resztą członków rodziny został wyprawiony do Oświęcimia. Twierdzą, że prawdziwy władca getta, kupiec z Bremy, Hans Biebow, dla którego Rumkowski bezustannie gromadził fortunę, 23 sierpnia 1944 r. wyprawił Rumkowskiego do Oświęcimia nie, jak innych, bydlęcym wagonem, ale pierwszą klasą.

Czy Rumkowski to był potwór, dobroczyńca, dureń, przywódca? Nie sposób dojść tu do jakiejś obiektywnej konkluzji. Warto przytoczyć jego przemówienie do ludności z 4 września 1942 r., po otrzymaniu od Niemców nakazu dostarczenia na „przesiedlenie" 20 000 osób spośród dzieci i starców:

Na getto spadł ogromny smutek. Żądają od nas, byśmy oddali co mamy najdroższego: dzieci i ludzi starych. Ja nie miałem tego szczęścia, aby mieć własne dzieci, dlatego poświęciłem najlepsze lata mego życia dzieciom cudzym. Nigdy nie przypuszczałem, że to moje ręce będą składały taką ofiarę na ołtarzu. Przypadło mi w losie, że muszę dziś wyciągnąć do was ramiona i błagać: bracia i siostry, ojcowie i matki — wydajcie mi swoje dzieci... [tłumem wstrząsa ogromny szloch].

Miałem przeczucie, że nam coś zagraża, oczekiwałem jakiegoś ciosu i stałem dzień i noc na straży, by mu zapobiec. Nie udało mi się to, nie wiedziałem, z której strony on padnie, nie wiedziałem, co nas czeka. Nie przewidywałem tego, że wyniosą naszych chorych ze szpitali, macie najlepszy dowód, że moi najbliżsi i najdrożsi byli pośród nich i nic dla nich zrobić nie mogłem. Myślałem, że na tym będzie koniec, że nas potem zostawią w spokoju. Okazuje się, że się wyłoniła nowa groźba. Taki jest żydowski los — coraz to nowe i sroższe cierpienia.

Wczoraj po południu dostaliśmy rozkaz, aby deportować 20 000 ludzi z getta. Jeśli nie — powiedziano nam — „zrobimy to sami". Stanęliśmy przed dylematem: czy zrobimy to my, czy zostawimy to im. Z myślą o tym — nie ilu zginie, ale ilu potrafimy uratować, ja i moi najbliżsi współpracownicy doszliśmy do wniosku, że jakkolwiek jest to dla nas straszne, musimy wziąć na siebie odpowiedzialność za wypełnienie tego dekretu. Ja muszę przeprowadzać tę krwawą operację. Ja muszę amputować członki, aby ratować ciało. Ja muszę odebrać wam dzieci, bo inaczej inni zginą wraz z nimi. Nie przyszedłem, by was pocieszać, nie przyszedłem, by wam ulżyć na sercu — jestem tu, by dzielić ogrom waszej żałoby. Przyszedłem jak złodziej, by ukraść, co macie najdroższego. Nie szczędziłem sił, by ten dekret unieważnić. Gdy to okazało się niemożliwe, starałem się go złagodzić. Kazałem zrobić rejestr dzieci dziewięcioletnich i starszych, który je wyjmie spod dekretu. Nie chcieli na to przystać. Jedyna rzecz tylko mi się udała — dzieci od lat dziesięciu wzwyż nie podlegają dekretowi. Niech to nam będzie jakąś pociechą.

Mamy w getcie wielką ilość zakażonych na gruźlicę, którym pozostaje tylko parę dni, może tygodni życia. Nie wiem, może ten plan jest diabelski, muszę zwrócić się do was z zawołaniem: wydajcie tych chorych, aby na ich miejsce ratować zdrowych. Ja wiem, jak każda rodzina troszczy się o swych chorych. Ale w obliczu takiej groźby musimy rozważyć i zadecydować: kto może, kto winien być uratowany? Zdrowy rozsądek dyktuje, aby ratować tych, których się da, którzy mają szansę przeżycia, a nie tych, którzy umrą tak czy owak. Żyjemy w warunkach, gdzie nie ma dosyć środków żywności dla zdrowych, nie mówiąc już o chorych. Każdy z nas utrzymuje chorego przy życiu kosztem własnego zdrowia, dajemy choremu naszą rację chleba, naszą kostkę cukru, nasz kęs mięsa — w rezultacie jego to nie ratuje, a my sami zapadamy na zdrowiu. Rozumiem, takie ofiary są szlachetne. Ale gdy stoi przede mną wybór, czy ratować chorych, czy zdrowych, nie mogę się długo wahać. Nakazałem lekarzom, aby wydali wszystkich nieuleczalnie chorych, aby w ich miejsce uratować tych, którzy chcą i mogą żyć [pośród zgromadzonych płacz, jęki i biadanie].

Ja was rozumiem, matki, widzę wasze łzy. Czuję smutek waszego serca, ojcowie, którzy jutro, gdy wam wasze dzieci zabiorą, pójdziecie jak codziennie do pracy. Wiem to wszystko i serce mi pęka. Od 4-tej godziny wczoraj po południu, gdy mi obwieszczono ten dekret, jestem złamany, dzielę wasz ból, nie wiem skąd wziąć resztki sił, by to przeżyć. Jedną rzecz wam powiem — żądanie było na 24 000 ofiar, 3000 dziennie przez osiem dni, ale udało mi się wytargować tę cyfrę do 20 000, a może i nieco mniej, ale tylko pod warunkiem, że pójdą wszystkie dzieci do dziesiątego roku życia. Ponieważ dzieci i starców jest tylko 13 000, musimy dopełnić kwoty wydając ludzi chorych. Trudno mi mówić, siły mnie opuszczają. Zwracam się do was z apelem: pomóżcie mi wykonać tę akcję. Drżę na myśl, że broń Boże, inne ręce tę akcję przeprowadzą.

Widzicie przed sobą ruinę człowieka. To jest najtrudniejszy moment mojego życia. Wyciągam do was ramiona i błagam was: oddajcie w me ręce te ofiary, chroniąc nas od większych ofiar, chroniąc społeczność stu tysięcy Żydów...

Wydaje mi się, że nikt, kto tam nie był, nie ma prawa do wydania sądu o Rumkowskim i o tych, którzy znaleźli się w podobnej jak on sytuacji. Jehoszua Sobol, izraelski dramaturg, napisał sztukę o getcie w Wilnie (graną obecnie w Teatrze Narodowym w Londynie), w której jedną z głównych postaci jest Jakub Gens, szef żydowskiej policji, a potem — jak Rumkowski — prezes *Judenratu*. Gens stoi w obliczu tych samych dylematów — „wysługuje się" Niemcom, dostarcza ludzi do pracy, sporządza listy skazanych na transport do obozów śmierci — zawsze z myślą o tym, że uda mu się jednakowoż kogoś uratować.

Sobol wkłada w usta Gensa następujący *passus*:

Wielu z was uważa mnie za zdrajcę. I dziwi się, że egzystuję tu jeszcze pośród was, niewinnych, czystych, nieskalanych. Ja, Jakub Gens, który demaskuje wasze kryjówki i wydaje was Niemcom. Ten sam Jakub Gens, który dzień i noc knuje, jak ratować życie Żydów. Ja ważę na szali żydowską krew, nie żydowską godność. Gdy domagają się ode mnie tysiąca Żydów, ja znajduję dla nich tysiąc Żydów. Inaczej oni sami przyjdą po nich i zabiorą nie jeden, a dziesięć tysięcy. Wy, z waszą moralnością! Gdzie jest podłość, plugastwo — wy odwracacie oczy. Jeśli któryś z was przeżyje — pokaże swe ręce czyste. Podczas gdy moje kapią od szlamu, po łokcie we krwi. Ja stanę przed żydowskim sądem, poddam się wyrokowi. Powiem im — cokolwiek zrobiłem, zrobiłem, by ratować Żydów, ilu się da, by wyprowadzić ich na wolność. Aby tego dokonać musiałem niektórych prowadzić na śmierć — tak, własnymi rękami. Abyście wy mogli zachować czyste sumienie — jak się pogrążyłem w brudzie. Mnie nie stać było na luksus czystego sumienia...

Nie wiem, czy ma sens jeszcze coś po tym mówić. Co tu można dodać? Ile ludzka wrażliwość może znieść, a rozum pojąć? Przyznaję, że choć większość mojego życia spędziłem myśląc o tych rzeczach, nie jestem bliżej zrozumienia, jak się to mogło stać, nie jestem bliżej ogarnięcia wymiarów tego kataklizmu ani zasięgu jego konsekwencji. Może, w samoobronie, umysł się wzbrania działać — i chyba dobrze, że tak jest, lepiej na samo dno nie patrzeć.

289

Ale z jednego sobie zdaję sprawę: że zagłada Żydów na ziemi polskiej to jest krytyczne wydarzenie w historii, tyczące się nie tylko Niemców, Polaków i Żydów, ale całej ludzkości: że oznacza ono kryzys chrześcijaństwa i kryzys naszej cywilizacji (są tacy, którzy chcieliby te pojęcia uważać za synonimy, ale na szczęście tak nie jest).

Jaką lekcję ludzkość wyciągnie z tego wydarzenia; jak sobie poradzi z tą świadomością bezgranicznego zła, do jakiego człowiek okazał się zdolny; jak odnowi wiarę w podstawowe moralne wartości — w świecie, który rozporządza środkami zniszczenia, wobec których bledną nawet komory gazowe — od odpowiedzi na te pytania zależy przyszłość ludzkiego gatunku.

Wypowiedź na Konferencji w Łodzi w roku 1990. Druk w zbiorze
Dzieje Żydów w Łodzi 1820–1940, Wydawnictwo Uniwersytetu Łódzkiego, 1991

Janusz Korczak i jego czasy

Pamięć ludzka funkcjonuje w zadziwiający sposób. Z niezliczonych wydarzeń, słów i obrazów, które pozostawiają ślad w świadomości, wybiera i zatrzymuje jakiś szczególnie wymowny wizerunek albo postać lub nawet zestaw słów, tworzących symbol danej epoki. Tysiące ofiar zginęło na stosach inkwizycji walcząc o wolność myśli, ale to Giordano Bruno spalony na Campo di Fiori symbolizuje tamte czasy. Złożona w samoofierze pochodnia Jana Palacha świeci nad Pragą. *Babi Jar* Jewtuszenki posiada większą moc niż wszystkie wysiłki podjęte, aby pozbawić go znaczenia. *Szema* rabbiego Akiby rozbrzmiewa głosami żydowskich świętych. Spośród tysięcy fotografii przedstawiających hitlerowską przemoc widzimy w bezsenne noce tę z chłopcem z warszawskiego getta, w zbyt dużej czapce, ze wzniesionymi ramionami i wielkimi oczami, które patrzą prosto na nas i wiedzą za wiele…

Janusz Korczak też stał się legendą naszych czasów. Jego historia jest prosta, ale tkwi w samym sednie holokaustu i może bardziej niż inne wydarzenia ilustruje horror i litość tamtych lat. 6 sierpnia 1942 roku Niemcy rozpoczynając likwidację warszawskiego getta zarządzili wywóz dzieci z sierocińca Korczaka na śmierć do Treblinki. Korczak ustawił swoich 200 podopiecznych w równych szeregach i spokojnie poprowadził ich na *Umschlagplatz*, u zbiegu ulic Stawki i Dzikiej, gdzie — on i oni — zostali załadowani i wysłani do pieców.

Ten marsz przez ulice getta, obserwowany jedynie przez kilkaset osób, miał się odbić donośnym echem. Niewielka postać Korczaka w jego drodze na Kalwarię, nieświadomego własnego heroizmu, zrozpaczonego, wykonującego rzecz dla niego naturalną — zawładnęła ludzką wyobraźnią. Wiadomość o tym akcie odwagi rozeszła się błyskawicznie, przekazywano ją sobie uzupełniając szczegółami. Jak to Korczak niósł w ramionach dwoje maluchów — mało prawdopodobne, gdyż był tak chory, że sam poruszał się z trudem; jak — w wyniku interwencji *Judenratu* — kolumnę dogonił posłaniec z uzyskanym od Niemców poleceniem uwolnienia Korczaka, a on wysłannika z pogardą odepchnął; jak rzekomo strażnik wagonu tuż przed zapieczętowaniem drzwi zaproponował Korczakowi, że go pominie i jak Korczak wspiął się na schodki, ani razu nie patrząc za siebie. Jak, by oszczędzić dzieciom niepokoju i zdenerwowania, powiedział im, że jadą na wycieczkę za miasto, i jak ufnie podążyły za nim bez łez i lęku. Samo to wydarzenie, przedstawione najprościej, nie potrzebuje upiększeń i nie trzeba nic dodawać, by bardziej było przejmujące. To, co różni ducha od siły, lub — jeśli wolicie — Żyda od nazisty, zostało tu precyzyjnie ukazane. Wykształcony, bezinteresowny, opiekuńczy człowiek wobec bezmyślnego i nienawidzącego barbarzyńcy uosabiającego szatańskie zło.

Wśród miliona anonimowych ofiar śmierć Korczaka miała szczególne znaczenie. Krążąca po obozach i gettach wiadomość o niej pokrzepiała ducha wtedy, gdy największą pomocą w przetrwaniu była uparta wiara, na przekór faktom, że ludzka godność doczeka swego triumfu.

Zarówno podziemna literatura obozowa, jak i ta „po drugiej stronie", są świadectwem pocieszenia i dumy, jakie przyniosła jego współczesnym najwspanialsza godzina życia Korczaka. Od tego czasu jego sława i kult stale rosły; świat nie omieszkał dostrzec moralnego symbolu Korczaka. Napisano o nim artykuły, książki i sztuki, wydano znaczki, wzniesiono pomniki, wielu instytucjom i nagrodom nadano jego imię.

Należy wiedzieć, że sposób, w jaki umarł, nie przyćmiewa jego życia. Henryk Goldszmit, chociaż raz użyjmy jego prawdziwego nazwiska (Janusz Korczak jest pseudonimem zaczerpniętym z powieści Kraszewskiego), urodził się w r. 1878 (lub 1879) w zamożnej rodzinie w Warszawie. Jego ojciec był wziętym prawnikiem, a dziadek lekarzem, co świadczy o wysokim stopniu zasymilowania tej rodziny. Miał bezpieczne dzieciństwo, dorastał prawie nieświadomy swego żydowskiego pochodzenia ani tego, co by to miało oznaczać. Gdy chodził do szkoły, umarł jego ojciec, cierpiący na chorobę umysłową. Po tej śmierci rodzina z dobrobytu stoczyła się do całkowitej nędzy. Wkrótce Henryk wziął na siebie utrzymanie matki i siostry. Nieobce mu były lata głodu i walki z przeciwnościami. Studiował medycynę. Dopiero gdy został lekarzem, los zaczął się do niego uśmiechać, rosła jego popularność jako pisarza — i właśnie wtedy, pod jakimś wewnętrznym przymusem podjął w pełni świadome kroki, które zmieniły bieg jego życia.

Od momentu gdy w wieku 34 lat porzucił praktykę lekarską i zamieszkał w Domu Sierot, który odtąd do końca pozostał związany z jego nazwiskiem, był opętany jedną ideą — chciał spędzić życie w służbie dzieciom. Nie był rozmarzonym idealistą, lecz człowiekiem obdarzonym niezwykłą empatią w stosunku do dzieci i ogarniętym głęboką troską o ich prawa w świecie rządzonym przez dorosłych. Nie miał zaufania do tego świata, lecz jak każdy prawdziwy reformator wierzył, że lepiej jest zapalić świecę niż ubolewać z powodu ciemności. Nie przemawiały przez niego względy sentymentalne, swoje przekonania oparł na stałej obserwacji klinicznej oraz pedantycznym zbieraniu i uzupełnianiu danych. Był mądry, kochający i absolutnie uczciwy, obojętny na takie potrzeby zwykłych śmiertelników, jak pieniądze, sława, dom czy rodzina.

Sierociniec, zbudowany i utrzymywany w całości ze środków prywatnych, służył najbardziej potrzebującym — dzieciom z najbiedniejszych dzielnic Warszawy. Zbiórka pieniędzy na dobry cel ma w sobie coś żenującego, co drażni tych, którzy są od niej zależni. Korczak kręcił nosem na „koszt woskowania podłogi przed tańcami na balu charytatywnym" i żałował czasu spędzonego na oprowadzaniu gości po Domu. Jednak dzięki sile osobowości wzbudzał głęboki szacunek dla swej pracy wśród ofiarodawców, którzy udzielenie mu poparcia poczytywali sobie za przywilej.

Był oryginalnym i pragmatycznym myślicielem w dziedzinie psychologii dziecięcej i pedagogiki, wprowadził pojęcia, które stały się modelowymi. Pracował nad udoskonaleniem systemu opartego na zrozumieniu najgłębszych potrzeb dziecka. Korczak wpływał na wychowanków nie tylko przez stałą obecność w Domu, lecz również pisząc do wewnętrznej gazety, która była redagowana dla dzieci i przez dzieci, a wspólne jej czytanie należało do najważniejszych wydarzeń tygodnia. Podobno w ciągu 30 lat niestrudzonej działalności Korczak nigdy nie zapomniał o dostarczeniu cotygodniowego tekstu. Częścią systemu samorządowego było wymierzanie sprawiedliwości według kodeksu, który zawierał budzący lęk paragraf 1000: usunięcie z Domu jako sankcję ostateczną. Każde dziecko z jakąś skargą miało prawo pozwać każdego przed sąd rówieśników — sam Korczak musiał się stawić na wezwanie i poddać ocenie. Wieczorem, po obejściu wszystkich sypialni Korczak udawał się do małego pokoju na poddaszu, jedynego „domu", jaki miał w całym swym dorosłym życiu, by uzupełnić notatki i pisać książki.

Pisał wiele z dziedziny swojej specjalności zawodowej, ale przede wszystkim był płodnym autorem opowieści dla dzieci i o dzieciach. Pozornie proste w formie i treści, z domieszką melancholii i humoru, odzwierciedlające jego własne usposobienie, często satyrycznie ukazujące społeczeństwo, ale zawsze serdeczne i pełne trafnych spostrzeżeń — książki te pozostawiały niezatarty ślad w pamięci młodych i starych czytelników.

W połowie lat trzydziestych Korczak dwukrotnie odwiedził Palestynę, zatrzymując się w kibucu Ein Harod. Czuł się odnowiony duchowo i poruszony tym, co zobaczył. Nakłaniany i zachęcany przez wielu przyjaciół i byłych uczniów zaczął poważnie myśleć o przeniesieniu się do Palestyny na stałe. Ale widział tu również wiele przeszkód. Ogromnie martwiło go, że nie mógł znaleźć odpowiedniego następcy, który kontynuowałby jego pracę w Warszawie. Myśl o wyrwaniu korzeni z ziemi rodzinnej była nie do zniesienia. W listach do przyjaciół, tłumacząc opóźnianie swojego przyjazdu wzruszająco pisze o „mojej Wiśle", „mojej ukochanej Warszawie", z którymi rozstanie byłoby dlań bardzo bolesne. Obawiał się również, że będąc bez grosza stanie się dla kogoś ciężarem.

Wzrastająca fala antysemityzmu w Polsce odsunęła na bok wszelkie wątpliwości i Korczak nie mógł już dłużej znieść takiej sytuacji. Został wyrzucony z radia, musiał zrezygnować z nieżydowskiego sierocińca. Był rok 1939. Postanowił spakować się i wyjechać.

Stefa Wilczyńska, kobieta wielkiego serca i niezwykłej odwagi, przez lata bliska koleżanka Korczaka i podpora jego przedsięwzięć, wyjechała do Palestyny rok lub dwa wcześniej. Znając bezradność Korczaka w sprawach materialnych wróciła, aby pomóc mu zakończyć działalność i wyruszyć w podróż. Wybuch wojny złapał ją w potrzask. Naturalnie ponownie zajęła swoje miejsce w sierocińcu u boku Korczaka.

Kiedy Niemcy umieścili warszawskich Żydów w getcie, sierociniec stracił swój dom przy ulicy Krochmalnej, która znalazła się po stronie „aryjskiej", i musiał przenieść się do zastępczych pomieszczeń w obrębie murów getta. Już wtedy Korczak widział znacznie wyraźniej niż większość ludzi, że śruba będzie stale bezlitośnie dokręcana, aż zginie całe życie wewnątrz murów. Nie miał jednak zamiaru rezygnować ze swego niezbywalnego prawa do niesienia ulgi w cierpieniu. Sam zrozpaczony i schorowany, zebrał wszystkie siły, by dzień po dniu zdobywać niezbędne zapasy jedzenia i lekarstw. Był niestrudzony w swoich prośbach o żywność i pieniądze, chociaż zdarzało się, że były one daremne. Nie odczuwał zażenowania apelując, żebrząc i zawstydzając ludzi, aby poparli tę najlepszą ze wszystkich spraw. W ostateczności przedstawiał swą prośbę szefom żydowskiego gangu przemytników i szantażystów.

Mimo coraz większego głodu i szerzących się chorób usiłował stworzyć w przytułku atmosferę normalności — odbywało się nauczanie, były gry i zabawy. Nierzadko do już maksymalnie przepełnionych pomieszczeń przyprowadzał nowe dziecko, które zabierał z ulicy, i dla którego znalezienie się w ostatnich dniach życia pod skrzydłami Korczaka stanowiło jedyną radość.

Korczak jest dowodem na to, czego człowiek może dokonać z miłości w warunkach w normalnym czasie niewyobrażalnych.

Jego życie można nazwać przykładowym; w tej kruchej postaci w fartuchu dozorcy (tak go zapamiętała większość ludzi) dostrzec można kwintesencję całego pokolenia. A jego wielkość polegająca na załatwianiu spraw przyziemnych, którymi mógłby przecież zająć się każdy człowiek, i nawet jego dramatyczna śmierć były czymś zwyczajnym w miejscu, gdzie męczeństwo było rzeczą codzienną. Trudno znaleźć postać uosabiającą trafniej niż Korczak to, co najistotniejsze dla jego czasów i miejsca, w stopniu, w jakim los jednego człowieka może symbolizować prawdziwy wymiar historii w jej szczególnie dramatycznym momencie.

Korczak dorastał czując się w pełni Polakiem. Był ogromnie przywiązany do polskiej ziemi, historii, literatury i języka. Pod tym względem był typowym przedstawicielem polskiego społeczeństwa zakochanego w idei „polskości". Jednak stopniowo i boleśnie, w pogarszającej się sytuacji ideowej i politycznej w kraju, musiał wreszcie przyznać, że była to miłość nieodwzajemniona, i że bez względu na to, jak szczere i głębokie było jego oddanie, on i tak zostanie odtrącony, jedynie z powodu swego pochodzenia. To odrzucenie na zawsze pozostało bolesną raną, która nigdy nie miała się zagoić.

Aby Korczaka w pełni zrozumieć, należy zastanowić się nad życiem Żydów w Polsce jako nad światem, który należy już do przeszłości.

Słusznie zauważono, że Polska była zawsze krajem o wielkiej historii, ale niefortunnej „geografii". Nieustannie najeżdżana, długo okupowana i rządzona przez zachłannych sąsiadów, miała niewiele szans, by rozwinąć się w niezależny i stabilny organizm. Ciężka i wszechobecna ręka Kościoła katolickiego, podziały etniczne, różnicująca kraj spuścizna zaborów, zubożałe chłopstwo i ogólne zacofanie ekonomiczne — nie stwarzały warunków, w których mógłby rozkwitać liberalizm. W krótkim okresie niepodległości międzywojennej państwa ościenne, z wyjątkiem Czechosłowacji Masaryka, nie dostarczały przykładów godnych naśladowania. Porównanie z Niemcami czy Rosją lat trzydziestych może uświadomić rozmiar swobód i wolności, panujących wtedy w Polsce.

Kuszące jest twierdzenie, że sposób traktowania Żydów był miernikiem politycznej i społecznej moralności kraju. Być może, ale nie wolno przyjmować tego za jedyne kryterium. Mniejszości, zwłaszcza te znaczące, wyróżniające się i konkurencyjne, stwarzały poważne problemy. Wola i umiejętność ich łagodzenia są cennym darem, acz nie występują w nadmiarze, a miłość do sąsiada nie jest niestety cechą uniwersalną. Czy postrzegamy to jako zaletę czy wadę — pozostaje faktem, że Żydzi w Polsce, jako grupa, nie poddawali się asymilacji, i w tym sensie pozostawali „obcy". Godne to ubolewania, ale nie zaskakujące, że polscy nacjonaliści nie dostrzegli zalet wynikających z różnorodności wzbogacającej pluralistyczne społeczeństwo. Podobnie dzieje się obecnie w wielu innych krajach na świecie.

Historia skazała Żydów na diasporę i wyobcowanie — rzeczywistość, której Polacy sami nie doświadczyli i dlatego nie potrafili sobie z nią poradzić. Daremne jest teraz dociekanie, jak rozwijałoby się współistnienie Polaków i Żydów, gdyby nie Hitler. Z pewnością wyraźnie zmierzało do ostrego konfliktu. Wszystko to jednak działo się przed „ostatecznym rozwiązaniem" — synonimem eksterminacji za pomocą gazu i ognia.

Życie Żydów w Polsce biegło po własnej orbicie. W zżytej, zapatrzonej w siebie społeczności miejskiej, żydowski handlarz, rzemieślnik czy robotnik załatwiał swoje interesy niemal wyłącznie wśród współwyznawców. Z ludnością nieżydowską miał jedynie sporadyczne i powierzchowne kontakty. Ta izolacja spowodowana była wzajemnymi uprzedzeniami, obustronną podejrzliwością i kompletną nieznajomością ludzi „z drugiej strony ulicy". Żydzi mieszkali głównie w kamienicach, gdzie najczęściej jedynym nie-Żydem był stróż w suterynie. Nawet inteligencja, której kontakty były znacznie szersze, skutecznie zachowywała odpowiedni dystans, nie odwiedzając polskich domów. Lekarze leczyli żydowskich pacjentów, prawnicy mieli żydowskich klientów, nauczyciele uczyli głównie w żydowskich szkołach. Urzędnik państwowy, profesor uniwersytetu lub sędzia zdarzali się rzadko i dostarczali tematu do plotek o ich nieprzeciętnych umiejętnościach czy też koneksjach, które umożliwiły im zdobycie takich stanowisk. Liczne organizacje charytatywne, społeczne i polityczne wyrażały zainteresowania żydowskiego środowiska, często podobne, ale rzadko identyczne z tymi, które pasjonowały społeczność nieżydowską.

Asymilacja Żydów w Polsce, mimo że przebiegała podobnie jak gdzie indziej, charakteryzowała się pewnymi specyficznymi cechami. Żydowscy buntownicy i nowatorzy, wyczuleni na wszelkie przejawy emancypacji na Zachodzie, posiadali swoje własne wizje. Haskala[1], będąca jakby pierwszym wyłomem w szeregach ortodoksji, i atrakcyjność hasła „wolność dla ludzkości — równość dla Żydów" miały wielką siłę oddziaływania. Walka Polaków z obcym jarzmem, ich dążenie do odzyskania niepodległości spowodowały, że ideę walki „za naszą i waszą wolność" oba narody rozumiały podobnie. Tę tendencję umacniała rosnąca niechęć do konserwatywnego środowiska żydowskiego, do jego klaustrofobii i separatyzmu, do przestarzałych form religijnych i społecznych.

Ze społeczności żydowskiej wyłonił się nowy rodzaj polskich patriotów. Z zapałem nowicjuszy skwapliwie przyjęli panującą kulturę, tak ekscytującą i jakże różną od kultury ich rodziców. Czuli autentyczne przywiązanie do ziemi, na której ich przodkowie żyli od pokoleń, do jej języka i literatury. Z tej schizofrenicznej sytuacji wynikały dylematy podzielonej lojalności, nowe i stare zarówno pociągało, jak i odstręczało — jak to zwykle bywa w procesie asymilacji. Niektórzy stali każdą nogą w innym obozie, niektórzy przysłowiowo usiłowali siedzieć na dwóch stołkach, jeszcze inni, zwłaszcza spośród ugrupowań lewicowych i inteligencji, zostali w pełni zaakceptowani, podobnie jak to miało miejsce w Europie Zachodniej.

Oczywiście byli i tacy, którzy dążyli do asymilacji z pobudek bynajmniej nie sentymentalnych, ale licząc na lepszą perspektywę zrobienia kariery czy po prostu bardziej atrakcyjną przyszłość. Niektórzy „poszli na całego" i przyjęli chrzest — Kościół z zadowoleniem witał nawróconych, a posunięcie to często otwierało drogę do awansu społecznego i zawodowego, niemożliwego do zdobycia w inny sposób. Takich było jednak niezbyt wielu. Atawistyczne odium piętnujące odstępcę tkwiło bowiem w świadomości nawet tych, których związki z religią żydowską zanikły lub zostały celowo odrzucone. Pomijając przypadki autentycznego nawrócenia religijnego, zjawiska równie rzadkiego co i tajemniczego, odstępstwo od wiary pociągało za sobą karę w postaci pogardy dawnych współwyznawców i podejrzliwości nowych. Właśnie ta grupa była najbardziej nieszczęśliwa w okupacyjnych gettach. Odcięci od swych korzeni, nie czujący się swobodnie wśród Żydów, nie rozumieli, dlaczego śmierć miała być też ich udziałem i cierpieli w poczuciu ostatecznego osamotnienia, nie znajdując otuchy we wspólnocie.

---

[1] Haskala — hebr. 'oświecenie', ruch zdążający do emancypacji Żydów przez upowszechnienie europejskiej wiedzy świeckiej (przyp. aut.).

Mimo że wtopienie się w otaczające środowisko stawało się coraz trudniejsze, proces asymilacji rozwijałby się nadal, gdyby na jego drodze nie stanął syjonizm, dążący do fizycznej i moralnej rehabilitacji Żydów. Oferując nowe ideały i nadzieje, syjonizm jednocześnie skutecznie sprzeciwiał się ówczesnemu przywództwu środowiska żydowskiego w Polsce. Był rozbity na skłócone partie o różnych odcieniach, lecz w blokowaniu drogi do asymilacji okazał się jednomyślny. Z drugiej strony Bund, ostry przeciwnik syjonizmu, wywierał wpływ na świadomość klasową robotników.

Udział Żydów w różnych dziedzinach polskiego życia kulturalnego niewątpliwie był znaczący, jednak nie należy popadać w przesadę. Ich wkładu w polską literaturę nie można porównywać na przykład z udziałem w literaturze niemieckiej. Poza Julianem Tuwimem, który zaliczał się do osobnej kategorii i niewątpliwie był największym polskim poetą naszych czasów, można by jeszcze wymienić nie więcej niż tuzin nazwisk o ponadprzeciętnym znaczeniu. Będą to poeci — Słonimski, Leśmian, Ważyk; pisarze — Wittlin, Rudnicki, Schulz, Brandys; krytycy — Klaczko, Feldman, Kleiner; historycy — Askenazy, Handelsman.

Interesujące, że w utworach najlepszej polskiej literatury, w dziełach Mickiewicza, Norwida, Lenartowicza, Orzeszkowej czy Konopnickiej postać Żyda jest przedstawiana z sympatią i współczuciem.

Zjawisko przenikania i wzajemne wpływy, niezależne od świadomej woli Żydów i Polaków, występowały nieustannie.

Czas zająć się kłopotliwym faktem wyboru miejsca na eksterminację Żydów. Jasne jest, że ludobójstwo nie zostałoby tak dokładnie i skutecznie przeprowadzone, gdyby nie słuszne założenie, że ofiary na własnym terenie uważane były za obcych, z których losem współmieszkańcy nie identyfikowali się. Wyszukiwanie, gromadzenie, transport, gazowanie i palenie nie byłyby możliwe, gdyby miejscowi uważali, że dokonuje się tego na ich własnym organizmie. Nie przyglądaliby się obojętnie lub tylko z pobożnym westchnieniem, jak miesiącami przejeżdżają wagony bydlęce, a potem unosi się dym z pieców, lecz bez względu na koszt i ryzyko przerwaliby ten proceder. Tym bardziej, że Niemcy poruszali się po obcym terenie i nie potrafili rozróżnić z wyglądu kto jest, a kto nie jest Żydem; to Polaków nie zawodziło wyczulenie na wszelkie cechy żydowskie. Zauważali skręt włosów, karnację, sposób bycia, modulację głosu, dobór słów, wyraz oczu. A co najważniejsze, gdyby ofiary wiedziały, że mogą liczyć na schronienie u innych mieszkańców, że spotkają się ze współczuciem i solidarnością w obliczu wspólnego wroga, to ogromna w skali kraju ich liczba uratowałaby się, niezależnie od udzielonej im pomocy. Wiadome było natomiast coś tragicznie przeciwnego — że Polacy w przeważającej większości nie ukryją i nie pomogą.

Pytanie dlaczego tak było (podobnie jak wiele innych „dlaczego", kierujących do nieba pytania bez odpowiedzi), dotyczy takiej samej tajemnicy, jak pytanie dlaczego Niemcy, kraj dumny ze swej kulturalnej tradycji i osiągnięć, nagle gwałtownie spadły na najniższy poziom zdeprawowania. Oprócz odpowiedzi szukających częściowych wyjaśnień w sferze polityki, ekonomii i psychologii, należy poszukiwać innych (również częściowych) przyczyn w niezgłębionych ciemnościach duszy ludzkiej.

Krótki wiersz w jidysz Mordechaja Gebirtiga pod tytułem *S'tut Vey!* (To boli!) jest bardziej wymowny niż wszystkie tomy, jakie zostały i będą napisane na ten temat. Gebirtig, ubogi stolarz z Krakowa, był prawdziwym ludowym śpiewakiem i poetą, a jego proste melodie i słowa krążyły wśród ludzi. Jego życie i praca są odbiciem charakteru, ducha i sposobu bycia całego pokolenia. Stał się trubadurem getta, gdzie — zanim został w 1942 roku zamordowany wraz z żoną i dwiema córkami — jego nieliczne piosenki, mimo że nieznośnie wzruszające, przynosiły ukojenie słuchaczom niczym prawdziwa poezja. *S'tut Vey!* mówi o młodych Polakach wyśmiewających się z ciosów i poniżenia, jakie spotkały Żydów z rąk wspólnego wroga, o zaskoczeniu i bólu wywołanych tą sytuacją. Gebirtig w swej wrażliwości uważał ten rodzaj bólu za znacznie dokuczliwszy niż ból zadany przez Niemców. Człowiek nie spodziewa się litości po wrogach, oczekuje jej od współmieszkańców. Charakterystyczne, że we wspomnieniach z tego okresu, na przykład u Andrzejewskiego, Rudnickiego, Wygodzkiego czy u Grynberga ten motyw wrogości Polaków i niebezpieczeństwa, jakie mogli oni stanowić dla ściganego Żyda, jest również postrzegany jako źródło największej udręki.

Nie wolno też zapominać, że aktywne próby pomocy i ratowania Żydów narażone były na śmiertelne niebezpieczeństwo i wymagały cech charakteru graniczących z heroizmem — rzadkim w każdych okolicznościach, a zwłaszcza w czasach upadku wartości i szerzącego się zła. W żadnym innym kraju poza Polską pomaganie Żydom nie było karane śmiercią. Mimo to istnieje wiele setek poświadczonych przypadków niezrównanej dobroci, poświęcenia i szlachetności okazanych w imię przyjaźni i zwykłego człowieczeństwa. I niewątpliwie były jeszcze tysiące życzliwych uczynków nigdzie nie zarejestrowanych, znanych tylko tym, którzy ich doświadczyli, ale już niczego nie opowiedzą. Poza dyskusją jednak pozostaje, jaka postawa była regułą, a jaka należała do wyjątków.

Hitler zakończył historię Żydów w Polsce. I niezależnie od tego, z jaką odrazą i litością Polacy eksterminację obserwowali — lub odwracali się od niej — to trzeba przyznać, że znaczna ich część nie była niezadowolona z jej wyniku. Nie dokonaliby tego sami. Czyn się dopełnił i się nie odstanie — i winowajcą jest Hitler.

Jego nauka nie poszła w las. Nie było już Niemców, kraj został wyzwolony, a Żydów, którzy wyszli na światło dzienne z piwnic i lasów, często ścigano i mordowano. Wystarczy przypomnieć Kielce, gdzie 200 pozostałych przy życiu usiłowało odtworzyć swoją gminę. W lipcu 1946 roku grupa polskich „nacjonalistów" urządziła pogrom i wymordowała 42 osoby.

Ironicznym grymasem historii jest, że mimo iż Polska pozbyła się Żydów, jej „żydowska" przeszłość pozostaje jej przypisana niczym szata Dejaniry. Polską historię nowożytną często postrzega się na Zachodzie poprzez pryzmat dyskryminacji Żydów, jak gdyby był to jej znak dominujący i rozpoznawczy, a nic innego nie miało znaczenia. Świat kojarzy Polskę z miejscem zagłady milionów Żydów, a szaleńcze rozmiary tego dramatu w dużej mierze przysłoniły los samego kraju. Na przykład wzmianka o powstaniu w Warszawie nasunie raczej skojarzenie z powstaniem w getcie, a nie z bohaterską polską insurekcją. Wyniszczenie Polski i jej ofiary, straty w ludziach i terytorium tracą na znaczeniu w porównaniu z tym, co uważa się za większą tragedię. Polska nie wzbudza wielkiej sympatii i nie wywołuje aktów dobrej woli, a jej głos ma niewielki moralny autorytet.

Przyszłość wyda werdykt, co w bilansie historii okaże się zyskiem dla Polski a co stratą. Można przypuszczać, że wyrwanie żydowskiego potencjału genetycznego z życia kraju, pozbawienie go żydowskiego twórczego wysiłku i stymulatora muszą prowadzić raczej do zubożenia niż wzbogacenia narodowego gmachu.

Nie ma najmniejszych wątpliwości, że dla Żydów utrata Polski jest trudna do oszacowania. Bo mimo burzliwych losów, mimo zmiennych warunków, a może właśnie dzięki nim, całe pokolenia Żydów w Polsce stworzyły najbardziej energiczną, prężną i produktywną, najbardziej „żydowską" część diaspory. Głęboko wrosłe korzenie dostarczały pożywienia dla bujnego rozwoju.

Nie wolno nam idealizować tego obrazu ani patrzeć przez mgiełkę nostalgii. Istniała przecież widoczna nędza materialna i duchowa, często zresztą bezlitośnie wytykana i ośmieszana przez żydowskich pisarzy. Istniały też cechy charakteru i mentalności typowe w warunkach niedoli.

Obraz ten nie był jednak tak smutny i beznadziejny, jak to się czasami uważa. Żydzi w Polsce posiadali wewnętrzną siłę, która pozwalała im przetrwać. Miała ona różne źródła. Rozkwitało życie religijne, mocno uduchowione i skupione wokół lokalnych przywódców. Życie rodzinne charakteryzowało się wielkim ciepłem i spójnością. Nie zdarzały się poważne przestępstwa. Panowało poczucie odpowiedzialności za wszystkich członków gminy, stąd gęsta sieć prywatnych i komunalnych instytucji dobroczynnych. Był to bogaty potencjał ludzki, utalentowany i dynamiczny, do zdobycia przez każdy postępowy ruch.

Była to również kolebka języka jidysz, o wielkiej jednoczącej mocy, w którym powstała wspaniała literatura. W ogóle rozwijała się kultura, bogata i wszechstronna. Czerpała ze swojej starożytnej tradycji, ale była też wyczulona na wpływy z zewnątrz. Uformowała ludzi tej miary co Nahum Sokołow[1], Gaon z Wilna[2], Icchak Lejb Perec[3] i Szalom Asz[4], I. M. Weissenberg[5], bracia Singer i wielu znaczących pisarzy, którzy wyemigrowali do Stanów Zjednoczonych i dali początek amerykańskiej literaturze w jidysz. Szczególne miejsce zajmuje Julian Tuwim, który chciał uchodzić za Żyda *doloris causa*.

Składniki i chemia, które stworzyły tę formację ludzką nigdy się już nie powtórzą, świat pozostanie uboższy.

Trudno powiedzieć, jakie są obecnie podstawy polskiego postrzegania Żydów, jaki nowy obraz formuje się w powszechnej psychice. Niesamowita wydaje się natomiast świadomość, że w Polsce dorosło całe pokolenie, które nigdy nie spotkało przedstawiciela tej starożytnej rasy. Nader nieliczni nowi marrani w pełni wtopili się w otoczenie, a ci, którzy otwarcie trwają przy swoich korzeniach i wierze, dożywają swych dni w samotności. Duchowni stracili swój cel — i niemałą część znaczenia. Antyrosyjskie resentymenty jednoczące naród nie mogą się już skupiać i wyładowywać na Żydach w komunistycznej partii. Wręcz przeciwnie: ostre wzajemne oskarżenia, które pojawiły się po wojnie izraelsko-arabskiej w 1967 roku, były spowodowane otwartym uznaniem części społeczeństwa dla bohaterskiego wyczynu Izraela, przyjętego jako zwycięstwo „naszych Żydów" nad „ich sojusznikami". Można podejrzewać, że w tej niestosownej radości, która ściągnęła gniew rządu, było więcej *Schadenfreude* zabarwionej zazdrością o upokorzenie wielkiego tyrana, niż autentycznej sympatii dla zwycięzców. Abstrahując od tego, wyłonił się nowy obraz Żyda, już nie popychanego i zdeptanego, lecz zbuntowanego i zwycięskiego, a określenie „Żydek", trochę pogardliwe, trochę pieszczotliwie zdrobniałe, straciło swoje miejsce w słowniku.

Przedmiotem odrębnej dyskusji jest to, co mogą i powinni pisać autorzy podręczników szkolnych. Orwellowska nowomowa i przedstawianie historii w sposób wygodny dla aktualnych trendów polityki jest praktyką powszechną i nie dotyczy tylko aspektów żydowskich, lecz również stosunków z Rosją, które wymagają gruntownej reinterpretacji tradycyjnego i mocno zakorzenionego polskiego punktu widzenia.

---

[1] Sokołow Nahum (1859–1936), pisarz, pionier odrodzenia jęz. hebrajskiego, teoretyk i działacz syjonistyczny, prezydent Światowej Organizacji Syjonistycznej, jedna z czołowych postaci żydowskich naszych czasów (przyp. aut.).

[2] Gaon — honorowy tytuł nadawany w XVIII i XIX wieku wybitnym uczonym talmudystom. Tu chodzi o Eliasza ben Salomona (1720–1797). Prócz studiów talmudycznych uprawiał matematykę i astronomię, zajmował się także anatomią i historią. Przeciwnik chasydyzmu, największy autorytet religijny swoich czasów (przyp. aut.).

[3] Perec I. L., zob. przyp. na str. 233.

[4] Asz Szalom (1880–1957), wybitny pisarz, jeden z klasyków literatury jidysz. Autor licznych powieści i sztuk teatralnych poświęconych życiu społeczeństwa żydowskiego. W r. 1914 osiedlił się w USA, pod koniec życia mieszkał w Izraelu (przyp. aut.).

[5] Weissenberg Izaak Meir (1881–1938), popularny pisarz i dramaturg w języku jidysz (przyp. aut.).

Duch Korczaka dzierży lustro, w którym przeglądają się dzisiejsi władcy Polski — i odbicie jest ponure. W czasie, gdy chętnie przypisują sobie zasługi i pławią się w jego pośmiertnej sławie, rzadko się mówi o jego żydowskim pochodzeniu. Obsesja na punkcie Żydów straszy ich nawet zza grobu; przeżyła Hitlera i przetrwa nieobecność Żydów.

Tłum. *M. Lohman*

„Jewish Quarterly", lato 1977

Warszawskie getto

Gdy 20 września 1939 roku armia niemiecka wkroczyła do Warszawy, żyło tam około 400 000 Żydów, co stanowiło mniej więcej jedną trzecią mieszkańców miasta. Żydzi natychmiast zostali poddani surowym represjom; obowiązywał ich nakaz pracy, nakaz noszenia Gwiazdy Dawida, zakaz korzystania z wszelkiego transportu publicznego; pozbawiono ich także nieruchomości. Nie chroniło ich prawo, więc wkrótce padli ofiarą chuliganów, sadystów i rabusiów, których w mieście nie brakowało. Dzienna racja żywnościowa dla warszawskiego Żyda to 184 kalorie, 669 kalorii dla Polaka, a dla Niemca 2613.

2 października 1940 r. Niemcy wyznaczyli teren, na którym stłoczono wszystkich warszawskich Żydów oraz ludzi żydowskiego pochodzenia i żydowskich uchodźców z prowincji. 113 000 „aryjskich" mieszkańców musiało opuścić ten teren. Niemcy uznali tę dzielnicę za „zadżumioną" i kazali Żydom odgrodzić się murem.

Niemcom nie podobało się słowo „getto" i zabronili używania go, zastępując określeniem „żydowska dzielnica mieszkaniowa" (*Wohnbezirk*). Rzeczywiście porównanie ze średniowiecznym gettem jest tutaj całkowicie niewłaściwe, gdyż sugeruje pewien stopień normalności, miejsce, gdzie ludzie przychodzili na świat, wykonywali swoje zawody, umierali we własnych łóżkach. Natomiast w tej „dzielnicy", otoczonej trzymetrowym murem ze zwojami drutu kolczastego, na przestrzeni około 4 km^2 musiało żyć 500 000 ludzi. Część z nich mieszkała w pokojach, na które przypadało po 13 osób, a wiele tysięcy nie miało nawet dachu nad głową. Prawie 60 procent populacji getta zostało pozostawione bez żadnych środków do życia.

W Warszawie, podobnie jak w innych okupowanych miastach, Niemcy powołali *Judenrat* (Radę Żydowską), jako ciało odpowiedzialne — własnym życiem — za realizację rozkazów dotyczących społeczności żydowskiej. *Judenrat* kontrolował w getcie policję, gospodarkę, dostawy żywności, zakwaterowanie i szkolnictwo. Sprawiało to wrażenie autonomii w dziedzinie zarządzania, jednak w rzeczywistości *Judenrat* istniał wyłącznie dla wygody Niemców, którym Rada musiała być całkowicie posłuszna. Do jej obowiązków należało między innymi pobieranie karnych kontrybucji, co było jedną z metod doprowadzenia Żydów do nędzy. Jak można się było spodziewać — zgodnie z planem Niemców *Judenrat* stał się obiektem wrogości i nienawiści ze strony mieszkańców getta, ściągając na siebie emocje przeznaczone dla prawdziwych oprawców.

Rola *Judenratu* pozostaje wciąż przedmiotem kontrowersji w studiach nad zachowaniem się Żydów pod niemiecką okupacją.

Na szefa warszawskiego *Judenratu* Niemcy wyznaczyli Adama Czerniakowa, który miał być marionetką w ich rękach. Czerniakow prowadził dziennik, gdzie zapisywał swoje codzienne kontakty z różnymi urzędnikami niemieckimi. Dziennik ten pozostaje najważniejszym źródłem wiedzy o getcie. Jednocześnie ukazuje autora, mocno oczernianego przez współczesnych, jako postać niemal heroiczną w zabiegach i pertraktacjach z nieprzejednanymi zwierzchnikami, osobę o wielkiej odwadze i godności, której udawało się od czasu do czasu wydrzeć Niemcom jakieś małe ustępstwa, i która na przekór faktom usiłowała przekonać siebie i otoczenie, że najgorsze nie nastąpi. Kiedy nawet dla niego stało się oczywiste, że „rozśrodkowanie"[1] jest eufemizmem morderstwa, odmówił złożenia podpisu pod zarządzeniem nakazującym deportację dzieci i odebrał sobie życie. Wielu potępiło go jako tchórza, w ich dziennikach pozostały gorzkie komentarze, że powinien ostrzec getto i wezwać do stworzenia ruchu oporu. Późniejsze sądy są bardziej mu przychylne. To świadczy o rozdzierających dylematach ludzi w tych apokaliptycznych czasach, dylematach, na które nie było i ciągle nie ma odpowiedzi.

Warszawskie getto to wielki obóz koncentracyjny, którego celem ostatecznym była eksterminacja Żydów za pomocą głodu, zimna i chorób. Z czasem widok zwłok na ulicach stał się rzeczą powszechną. Bandy dzieciaków włóczyły się w poszukiwaniu resztek jedzenia. Mimo że bramy getta były strzeżone a karą za wyjście bez pozwolenia była śmierć, mieszkańcy, by przeżyć, szmuglowali żywność z zewnątrz. Ryzykujące życiem dzieci okazały się najlepszymi przemytnikami i żywicielami rodzin.

Niemiecki gubernator Hans Frank napisał w raporcie: „Nie jest konieczne rozwodzenie się nad tym, że skazujemy Żydów na śmierć. Natomiast jeżeli Żydzi nie umrą z głodu, konieczne będzie przedsięwzięcie anty-żydowskich środków, które miejmy nadzieję spełnią swoje zadanie". Wizja Franka wkrótce zmaterializowała się jako realizacja postanowienia konferencji w Wannsee na temat „ostatecznego rozwiązania". W lipcu 1942 roku pod pretekstem „przemieszczenia" rozpoczęły się masowe deportacje do obozów śmierci, trwające z niewielkimi przerwami aż do połowy września. W ciągu tych siedmiu tygodni blisko 265 000 Żydów zostało przewiezionych do Treblinki i zamordowanych w komorach gazowych. Niektóre z ofiar, zwabione obietnicą jedzenia, dobrowolnie zgłosiły się na *Umschlagplatz* — bocznicę kolejową, na której ludzki towar załadowywano do bydlęcych wagonów i wysyłano do obozów śmierci. Deportacje drastycznie zmniejszyły populację w getcie; pozwolono zostać 35 000 mieszkańców, głównie robotnikom zatrudnionym w niemieckich war-

---

[1] Tak Niemcy nazywali wysyłki mieszkańców getta do obozów zagłady (przyp. aut.).

sztatach i ich rodzinom. Poza tym w getcie ukrywało się nielegalnie około 25 000 Żydów.

W takich okolicznościach, w geście buntu a zarazem w szlachetnym i beznadziejnym pragnieniu „by umrzeć jak istota ludzka", Żydzi zorganizowali ruch oporu. Kilkuset zdesperowanych ludzi z różnych środowisk stworzyło oddziały bojowe uzbrojone w kilka pistoletów, karabiny i koktaile Mołotowa. Było to bardzo marne uzbrojenie. Gdy 19 kwietnia 1943 r. wojsko niemieckie weszło do getta, aby ostatecznie rozprawić się z pozostałymi mieszkańcami, napotkało zbrojny opór. Ku zaskoczeniu hitlerowców żydowscy bojownicy zadali im straty i zmusili do odwrotu. Oczywiście ani przez moment nikt nie miał wątpliwości co do końcowego wyniku tej walki. Generał Jürgen Stroop stłumił powstanie za pomocą czołgów, ciężkiej artylerii i miotaczy ognia. By uniknąć otwartej walki ulicznej, systematycznie palił domy. Niemieckie bomby i granaty ręczne dosięgły bojowników stłoczonych w piwnicach i kanałach. A mimo to walki trwały sporadycznie aż do 8 maja 1943 r. W geście ostatecznego triumfu w wojnie przeciw Żydom generał Stroop wysadził w powietrze Wielką Sy-nagogę w Warszawie, a w swoim raporcie zapisał: „Nie ma już żydowskiej dzielnicy mieszkaniowej".

Powstanie w getcie warszawskim wywarło wielkie wrażenie na Żydach (i nie tylko) na całym świecie. Była to najdłuższa do tego czasu bitwa z Niemcami w okupowanej Europie, a historia powstania stała się legendą.

Naszą wiedzę na temat tego okresu zawdzięczamy w dużej mierze wysiłkowi i inicjatywie jednego człowieka, Emanuela Ringelbluma (1900–1944). Ten nauczyciel, historyk i społecznik jest jednym z nie opiewanych bohaterów naszych czasów. Od początku wojny był organizatorem komitetów samopomocy w Warszawie. Pisał kronikę wydarzeń i z jego inicjatywy jesienią 1940 roku grupa pod kryptonimem *Oneg Shabbat* (Radość Szabatu) zaczęła redagować biuletyn opisujący i dokumentujący ówczesną sytuację. Pod kierownictwem Ringelbluma *Oneg Shabbat* zorganizował w całym kraju sieć reporterów, którzy zbierali informacje w formie odpowiedzi na kwestionariusz. Uważali, że najmniejszy skrawek papieru relacjonujący sytuację Żydów będzie posiadał bezcenną wartość historyczną. Kolekcjonowali więc oficjalne afisze, ogłoszenia publiczne, dzienniki, listy, opakowania, teksty zagranicznych audycji radiowych, a przede wszystkim gazety i biuletyny wydawane przez rozmaite ugrupowania podziemne. Przygotowywali również specjalne raporty na temat różnych aspektów życia, które potem wypełniały serwis informacyjny polskiej prasy podziemnej.

Niemcy początkowo nie wykazywali żadnego zainteresowania działalnością Żydów. Żydzi mogli niemal swobodnie pisać, dyskutować, plotkować i przeklinać. Na ulicach i w kawiarniach rozmawiali o nielegalnych gazetkach krążących po getcie. Półoficjalne i tajne komitety organizowały życie gminy we wszystkich dziedzinach: walcząc z głodem, krzewiąc oświatę, przygotowując imprezy kulturalne, opracowując projekty badań medycznych i generalnie podtrzymując ducha wśród mieszkańców. Za fasadami kamienic, wokół dużych, typowo warszawskich podwórek życie kulturalne i religijne przybrało nowe formy na użytek owych bezprecedensowych czasów.

Sieć *Oneg Shabbat* jako pierwsza zdobyła zeznania naocznego świadka masowych mordów za pomocą gazu w Chełmnie i pierwsza podniosła alarm w polskiej prasie podziemnej, a potem za granicą. 26 czerwca 1942 roku BBC podała wiadomości o eksterminacji polskich Żydów, oparte na raporcie wysłanym przez Ringelbluma. Pisał on: „Zwracając uwagę świata na nasz los spełniamy wielką historyczną misję. Może w ten sposób uratuje się kilkuset spośród tysięcy polskich Żydów. Niedaleka przyszłość to pokaże. Nie wiem, która z naszych grup pozostanie przy życiu, którą los wybierze, aby zrobiła użytek z naszego archiwum, ale jestem pewien jednego — nasze poświęcenie, ryzyko i niebezpieczeństwo, na które jesteśmy nieustannie narażeni, nasze zmagania i cierpienia nie idą na marne".

W miarę zaciskania się pętli niebezpieczeństwo utraty archiwum stawało się coraz większym problemem. Kilka miesięcy przed likwidacją getta zgromadzono wszystkie materiały, które następnie zapakowano do zapieczętowanych baniek na mleko i metalowych pojemników i zakopano głęboko pod budynkami getta. Po wojnie, w roku 1946 i 1950 dwie części tego skarbu zostały znalezione pod górami gruzu, który był wszystkim, co pozostało z getta. Trzecią część należy uznać za zaginioną.

Odzyskany zbiór składa się z około czterdziestu tysięcy stron, w większości nadal nie poddanych analizie i nie opublikowanych. To największe i najważniejsze archiwum tamtej epoki pozostaje bezcennym źródłem naszej wiedzy na temat życia i śmierci warszawskiego getta i eksterminacji polskich Żydów.

Ringelblum do końca dawał z siebie wszystko. W marcu 1943 roku namówiono go do opuszczenia getta i znalezienia ukrycia po „aryjskiej stronie". 18 kwietnia, na dzień przed ostatnią wywózką i w przededniu powstania, Ringelblum powrócił do getta, aby wspólnie z ostatnimi mieszkańcami spędzić Paschę. Został złapany w łapance i wywieziony do obozu koncentracyjnego koło Lublina. Po ustaleniu miejsca jego pobytu koledzy przeszmuglowali go z obozu i zawieźli ponownie do kryjówki w Warszawie, gdzie dołączył do żony i syna. Nadal pisał. Bez dostępu do książek i materiałów źródłowych napisał jedno ze swoich kluczowych opracowań: *Stosunki pomiędzy Polakami i Żydami w czasie drugiej wojny światowej.*

W marcu 1944 roku Gestapo odkryło kryjówkę Ringelbluma, którą zasiedlało jeszcze 60 osób. Zarówno Żydzi, jak i polska rodzina, która ich ukrywała, zostali zabrani na Pawiak i rozstrzelani.

Żydzi, czując się opuszczeni przez Boga i ludzi, pragnęli za wszelką cenę pozostawić po sobie ślad. Prześladowała ich myśl, że świat nie dowie się, jak żyli i umarli. Pisanie sprawiało, że śmierć stawała się łatwiejsza. Ostatni zapis w dzienniku Chaima Kaplana przed wywozem do Treblinki był krzykiem rozpaczy: „Jeżeli umrę — co stanie się z moim dziennikiem?"

Primo Levi[1] w *The Drowned and the Saved* wyobraża sobie członków SS szydzących ze swoich ofiar:

> Bez względu na to jak ta wojna się skończy, my wygraliśmy wojnę z wami. Nikt z was nie pozostanie, więc nie będzie świadków, a nawet gdyby ktoś przeżył, świat mu nie uwierzy. Pewnie będą jakieś podejrzenia, dyskusje, badania prowadzone przez historyków, ale zabraknie pewników, ponieważ my zniszczymy nie tylko was, ale i wszelkie dowody. A nawet jeśli jakiś dowód pozostanie i niektórzy z was przeżyją, ludzie powiedzą, że wydarzenia, które opisujecie są zbyt okropne by w nie uwierzyć, powiedzą, że to aliancka propaganda przesadza i uwierzą nam, a my wszystkiemu zaprzeczymy.

Dzięki tym pisarzom i kronikarzom prawda została zarejestrowana, poznał ją świat, i chyba tylko ktoś szalony mógłby jej zaprzeczyć. Te świadectwa przekazują obraz niewyobrażalnie koszmarnych czasów. Ukazują dno, na jakie może się stoczyć istota ludzka i dokumentują piekło zgotowane przez nienawiść.

Przygotowując ten tom starałem się ograniczyć wybór materiałów do tych, które powstały w getcie. Kilkakrotnie włączyłem jednak wyjątki z zapisków dokonanych poza murami getta wkrótce po ucieczce ich autorów „na aryjską stronę".

Wybór tych fragmentów okazał się udręką; w obliczu takiego koszmaru ludzka wrażliwość w końcu staje się odrętwiała. Mimo że świadectwa te dotyczą wydarzeń sprzed pół wieku, ich groza pozostaje w człowieku na całe życie. Tak to odczuwam.

Fotografie dostarczył mi Willy Georg, były żołnierz armii niemieckiej, do którego zaprowadzili mnie przyjaciele, świadomi moich zainteresowań. Ponad osiemdziesięcioletni Willy Georg należy do pokolenia Niemców, z którymi nigdy nie czuję się swobodnie, zanim nie poznam ich lepiej. Cieszę się, że jest poza podejrzeniami; to wykształcony człowiek z zamożnego środowiska, zawodowy fotografik, który w wieku trzydziestu lat, gdy robił te zdjęcia, posiadał skromną rangę *Funke* — radiotelegrafisty. To zbyt niska funkcja, aby być faworyzowanym lub czerpać jakieś profity z racji członkostwa w partii nazistowskiej.

Jak doszło do powstania tych fotografii? Willy Georg dobrze to pamięta. Stacjonował wraz ze swoim oddziałem w Warszawie, prawdopodobnie na Mokotowie. Zarabiał dodatkowe pieniądze, które potem wysyłał do domu, robiąc

---

[1] Primo Levi (1919–1987), włoski pisarz urodzony w Turynie, więzień Oświęcimia. Opisał swoje życie w obozie zagłady w książce *Se questo é un uomò* (1947). Książka ta, jak i jego następne, przetłumaczone na wiele języków, uchodzą za arcydzieła literatury i przyniosły mu światową sławę. Dręczony wspomnieniami przeszłości Primo Levi popełnił samobójstwo w roku 1987 (przyp. aut.).

zdjęcia swoim kolegom-żołnierzom i przełożonym. Pewnego dnia, latem 1941 roku, jeden z oficerów zwrócił się do niego niefrasobliwie mówiąc: „Jakieś dziwne rzeczy dzieją się za tym murem. Daję ci przepustkę do tego zamkniętego terenu. Weź leikę, jedzenie na cały dzień i wróć ze zdjęciami tego, co tam zobaczysz".

Tak też zrobił. Po przekroczeniu bram getta Georg spacerując zużył cztery rolki filmu, piątą miał w aparacie, gdy zatrzymała go niemiecka policja i zażądała leiki. Niemcy wyciągnęli film, ale Georg nie wspomniał ani słowem o pozostałych czterech, które miał w kieszeni. Po sprawdzeniu dokumentów pozwolono mu opuścić getto. Sam wywołał filmy w warszawskim laboratorium. Jest dumny ze swojego profesjonalizmu; pół wieku później film wygląda jak nowy. Po wywołaniu wysłał zdjęcia żonie do domu. Nie myślał o nich aż do niedawna, gdy poczuł, że nadszedł czas, by wydać ostatnie dyspozycje.

Doznał szoku, gdy zobaczył te zdjęcia ponownie po latach i przypomniał sobie tamte czasy. Chciałoby się zapytać, jak czuł się pięćdziesiąt lat temu, kiedy zupełnie nie przygotowany wkroczył na scenę horroru, jakiego nigdy wcześniej nie doświadczył. Ale nie ma to sensu, bo zapewne starannie dobierając słowa, aby mnie nie zranić, opowiedziałby mi, jakie są jego odczucia teraz. Pamięta, jak uprzejmi byli dla niego ludzie za murem. Pewnie nie wiedział wtedy, że musieli być uprzejmi; spotkawszy Niemca Żyd miał obowiązek zdjąć czapkę i zejść z chodnika.

Nie jest to jedyny dokument fotograficzny. Istnieją inne zdjęcia wykonane w getcie przez Niemców w tym okresie i później. Najbardziej znane — przedstawiające chłopca w kaszkiecie, ze wzniesionymi ramionami — pochodzi właśnie z takiego źródła. Zespół z niemieckiego Ministerstwa Propagandy zgromadził kolekcję zdjęć, która znajduje się teraz w państwowych archiwach niemieckich w Koblencji. Zdjęcia te służyły wyraźnemu celowi: aby pokazać degradację tej podludzkiej rasy, obojętność Żydów na cierpienia swych braci (spójrzcie, jak przechodzą obok zwłok leżących na ulicach, nie mrugnąwszy nawet okiem!), wesołe spędzanie czasu na grze w karty w kawiarniach. Fotograficy i ich przełożeni nie byli świadomi odwrotnego efektu swojej pracy — ostatecznie obrazy te nie degradują ofiar, lecz oprawców.

Zdjęcia Willego Georga były całkowicie spontaniczne, po prostu rejestrowały kolejne sceny. Ludzie na nich uchwyceni — zajęci, zabiegani, wyniszczeni, zgnębieni, ale ciągle prowadzący jakieś życie — byli nieświadomi niewyobrażalnie okrutnego końca, który miał niebawem nastąpić. Nikomu nie uda się uciec przed straszną śmiercią. Człowiek chciałby instynktownie krzyknąć: uciekajcie, kryjcie się! — ale jest już za późno. Cokolwiek by zrobili lub pozostawili nie zrobione, nie miałoby już najmniejszego wpływu na ich los.

Dla wielu z nas, którzy dorastali w tym środowisku, i którzy wspominają je z czułością, Żydzi — wstyd to przyznać — nie przedstawiali się atrakcyjnie. Zażenowany tym, co nieżydowski widz może czuć lub powiedzieć, niejeden współrodak odwracał się od widoku zamglonego spojrzenia, bród, pejsów i haczykowatych nosów. Teraz wydaje się oczywiste, że te twarze wyrzeźbione troską i mądrością, rozjaśnione wewnętrznym światłem, innymi słowy rembrandtowskie, były niewypowiedzianie piękne. Zwłaszcza gdy zestawi się je z albumem przestępców, z kwiatem „rasy panów": Goebbelsem, Göringiem, Streicherem, Frankiem i samym Hitlerem.

Na tych fotografiach po raz ostatni zostali uchwyceni ludzie, którzy mieli zostać zamordowani, pozostawiając świat nieodwracalnie uboższy. Ich lekcja życia staje się coraz bardziej cenna, gdyż nadchodzi czas, kiedy zabraknie świadków ich losu, a przyszłe pokolenia mogą nie dać mu wiary.

Tłum. *M. Lohman*

Posłowie do: *In the Warsaw Ghetto. Summer 1941.* Photographs by Willy Georg; with passages from Warsaw Ghetto Diaries. Compiled and with an afterword by Rafael F. Scharf. Aperture, New York 1993

Świadectwo

Pokłosiem eksterminacji Żydów w czasie II wojny światowej był gwałtowny rozwój wszelkiego rodzaju działalności literackiej, poświęconej tej największej zbrodni w historii ludzkości. Istnieje kategoryczny imperatyw, żeby dokumentować, przeżywać wszystko na nowo, analizować, próbować ogarnąć umysłem i przekazywać innym. Każda książka, każde czasopismo, pamiętnik czy wiersz, każda historia indywidualna, każdy dokument, każdy najmniejszy fragment historycznego świadectwa jest darem dla przyszłości — bo tylko to po nas pozostanie. Bezpośrednie świadectwo naocznych świadków ma tu oczywiście wartość największą. Nadchodzi przecież nowa epoka: niedługo nie pozostanie już żaden z nich. Książka, o której piszę, jest więc jedną z ostatnich w swoim rodzaju.

6 września 1939 roku armia niemiecka wkroczyła do Krakowa: dla 60 tysięcy Żydów, zamieszkałych tam niekiedy od wielu pokoleń, świat nagle, z dnia na dzień, się zawalił. I chociaż nie rozumieli jeszcze swojego ostatecznego i niedalekiego losu, droga prześladowań, które doprowadziły do ich zagłady, objawiła się już na samym początku. Złowieszcze *Bekanntmachungen*, przyklejane na murach obwieszczenia o coraz surowszej wymowie, wyznaczały kolejne stadia tej drogi.

Najpierw odróżniono ich od reszty ludności: wszyscy Żydzi musieli nosić na ramieniu opaski z gwiazdą Dawida. Następnie zniszczono źródła ich utrzymania: sklepy żydowskie musiały być w sposób z daleka widoczny oznaczone; było to oczywiście grubymi nićmi szytą zachętą do grabieży i rabunków, z której skwapliwie korzystano. Wszelkie pieniądze, z wyjątkiem żebraczego grosza na osobę, musiały zostać oddane, a wszelkie przedmioty wartościowe konfiskowano. Nędza stała się obowiązkiem wobec prawa. Wreszcie ograniczono wolność osobistą Żydów: każdy z nich musiał się zarejestrować, nie wolno im było zmieniać miejsca zamieszkania, nie wolno im było jeździć koleją.

Te nakazy były egzekwowane z całą surowością, a towarzyszyło temu ciągłe nękanie, najazdy policji, pościgi za ludźmi, rewizje, fizyczne znęcanie się. Żydzi znaleźli się poza prawem i stali się łatwym łupem dla wszelkiego rodzaju łotrów i bandytów, których bynajmniej nie brakowało.

W następnym etapie zamknięto ludność żydowską w gettach, gdzie panowały urągające godności ludzkiej warunki. Ucieczkę z getta karano śmiercią, a przy niewolniczej, przekraczającej ludzkie siły pracy poza gettem śmierć zbierała coraz większe żniwo. Specjalne obozy pracy, takie jak obóz w podkrakowskim Płaszowie, były niemal niczym nie zawoalowanymi instrumentami powolnego wyniszczania Żydów.

Proces ten uległ przyspieszeniu, gdy Żydzi znaleźli się w obozach koncentracyjnych, gdzie zimne okrucieństwo było obowiązującym sposobem życia i gdzie więźniowie szybko zamieniali się w chodzące szkielety. Był to więc ostatni etap, precyzyjna fabryka śmierci, która nie miała celu innego niż ten, żeby zagazowywać i spalać ludzkie „ładunki" tak szybko, jak tylko pozwalała na to najnowsza technologia — cyklon B i krematoria.

Wspomnienie tego apokaliptycznego świata, bez precedensu w historii, nadal rodzi ból. Ludzkość przeżywała już wojny, okupacje, terror, prześladowania i ludobójstwo na masową skalę i zdarza się to wszystko nadal, ale nigdy jeszcze nie skazano całego narodu, bez wyjątku, na oddzielenie od innych narodów i na śmierć. Nigdy też nie wykonywano takiego wyroku z zapałem i poświęceniem, które przewyższały w hierarchii ważności wysiłek wojenny i które, z uwagi na ogrom przedsięwzięcia, wymagały w sumie, na różnych etapach ponurej machiny zniszczenia, udziału dziesiątków tysięcy Niemców. To jest tło historyczne opowiadania naszych autorów. Wydarzenia historyczne stają się bliższe i bardziej realne, gdy patrzy się na nie przez pryzmat indywidualnych przeżyć ludzi.

Miriam urodziła się i wychowała w małym podkrakowskim gospodarstwie, z którego jej rodzina czerpała środki na skromne utrzymanie. Brak funduszy uniemożliwił jej kontynuowanie studiów na Uniwersytecie Jagiellońskim, nawiązała natomiast kontakty z lewicowymi organizacjami młodzieżowymi, co po wybuchu wojny dało jej wstęp do podziemnego ruchu oporu i otwarło przed nią możliwości, które zdołała skutecznie wykorzystać. Jak świadczą fotografie z tego czasu, była osobą o wyróżniającej się urodzie (co było raczej wątpliwą zaletą w tamtych okolicznościach), ale niemal całkowicie pozbawiona fizycznych cech semickich — i temu zawdzięcza swój los.

Mordechaj urodził się w Tarnowie, był samoukiem, człowiekiem o ogromnej wrażliwości i inteligencji, posiadającym dar jasnego myślenia i pewności siebie. Kiedy nadeszła chwila próby, nie wahał się przed podjęciem decyzji.

Tych dwoje, nie znając się początkowo, ale mając podobne charaktery (co później stworzyło z nich idealną parę partnerów), każde na własny rachunek wcieliło się w role, które, jak zobaczymy, w pełni zasługiwały na miano heroicznych. Oni sami nie mieli świadomości tego wymiaru swojego życia: to byli zwykli ludzie, którym los narzucił wielkość, a oni przyjęli ją jako rzecz zupełnie naturalną, nie bez obaw, ale przezwyciężając je, z pełną świadomością konsekwencji swojej decyzji (jedyną gwarancją była dla nich noszona zawsze w kieszeni fiolka cyjanku — nikt przecież nie zna granic swojej wytrzymałości na tortury).

Ze swoim wyglądem i akcentem bez zarzutu mogli się z łatwością wtopić w otoczenie i żyć stosunkowo bezpiecznie, a ich szanse na przetrwanie byłyby spore. Zamiast tego, mimo ogromnego osobistego zagrożenia (zwłaszcza Mordechaja), nieustannie igrali z losem. Regularnie udawali się z misjami pomocy do miejsc, których ludzie ostrożniejsi unikaliby jak ognia: na stacje kolejowe, pomagając innym w podróży; do zatłoczonych sklepów, których używano jako miejsc kontaktowych do kolportażu różnych druków, gdzie mogli ich rozpoznać dawni znajomi i przyjaciele (a niebezpieczni mogli być nawet ci życzliwi); do biur, w poszukiwaniu pieczątek na fałszywe dokumenty.

Po zdobyciu dla swoich podopiecznych „mocnych papierów" — dowodu tożsamości, metryki urodzenia i świadectwa zatrudnienia we właściwej firmie — stawali zawsze przed problemem odpowiedniej dla nich kryjówki: dla niektórych znajdowała się jakaś piwnica, strych, ciemny pokój na końcu korytarza, dla innych miejsce w klasztorze lub sierocińcu. Wiązała się z tym konieczność częstych tam odwiedzin: by zapłacić „komorne", by dostarczyć zasiłek czy wiadomość od rodziny. W większości kryjówki te były tylko tymczasowe: jedno nieostrożne słowo, podejrzany hałas, jakiś ruch w okolicy zmuszały do przeprowadzki i to natychmiastowej. Wszystko to działo się pod czujnym okiem podejrzliwych i nerwowych sąsiadów, gestapo, policji i całych hord konfidentów i szantażystów. Nawet czytanie o tym, po pięćdziesięciu latach, nadal przyprawia o szybsze bicie serca i mimo woli nachodzą człowieka myśli, czy w podobnych okolicznościach znalazłby dość wewnętrznej siły, żeby zachować się tak jak tych dwoje.

W oczach mieszkańców getta świat poza murami, „po stronie aryjskiej", był normalny. Chociaż daleko było do tego, nawet w bardzo szerokim znaczeniu, niebezpieczeństwa tam grożące miały jakby inny wymiar, dawały możliwość przetrwania przynajmniej tym nielicznym, którzy zostali właściwie przez naturę wyposażeni, tzn. mieli odpowiedni wygląd, mówili odpowiednim językiem i mieli siłę fizyczną i psychiczną, pozwalającą przetrzymać potworny stres tego położenia: udawania, że jest się kimś innym, stałego zachowywania ostrożności, nieustannego życia w śmiertelnym strachu przed zdemaskowaniem.

Można było mieć wygląd anioła, ale istniała wielka ilość zdradliwych szczegółów: oczy mogły być intensywnie niebieskie, ale ich charakterystyczny smutek był trudny do ukrycia, a czarne okulary już same w sobie budziły podejrzenia. Mężczyźni oczywiście nosili swój wyrok śmierci stale ze sobą, w każdej chwili gotowy ich wydać.

Równie ważne jak fizyczne upodobnienie się do otoczenia było opanowanie typowych polskich form mówienia i zachowania, szczególnie w kościele — skąd Żyd lub Żydówka mogli wiedzieć, kiedy się przeżegnać albo uklęknąć w czasie mszy — a moment zawahania mógł kosztować wiele. Nauka modlitw i szczegółów nabożeństw była więc życiową koniecznością.

Ciężką próbą było ukrywanie uczuć w miejscach publicznych, co na dłuższą metę stawało się niemal nie do wytrzymania, zwłaszcza w okresie, gdy wyszły na jaw szczegóły dotyczące obozów śmierci. Jak powstrzymać „łzy, po których poznać Żyda", jak reagować, gdy w rozmowie z Polakami (zdarzało się to aż nadto często) poruszano temat mordowania Żydów — udawać obojętność, potępiać? Miriam opowiada, że w pewnym momencie, ryzykując wszystko, nie zdołała utrzymać języka za zębami. Mordechaj wspomina, jak trudno było zachować pozory, kiedy na przykład pewnemu Żydowi, któremu pomagał i próbował pocieszyć, nagle wyrwały się gorzkie słowa „tobie to łatwo mówić..."

W wielu przypadkach napięcie okazywało się zbyt wielkie. Po podjęciu ogromnego wysiłku i ryzyka, by urządzić się jakoś „po aryjskiej stronie", niektórzy z uciekinierów z własnej woli wracali do getta, aby żyć i umrzeć ze swoimi. Ale czy można zrozumieć matkę, która razem z dzieckiem znalazła schronienie w gościnnym domu polskich przyjaciół i nie mogąc już wytrzymać myśli, że jej obecność wystawia gospodarzy na tak wielkie niebezpieczeństwo, pewnego dnia po prostu wychodzi i znika bez śladu? Jak mogli się czuć ci ludzie?

W swoim zrozumiałym proteście wobec nieszczęść, jakie na nich spadły, Żydzi często nie byli wystarczająco wrażliwi na położenie Polaków i nie dostrzegali rozpaczliwych wyborów, przed jakimi stawali ich sąsiedzi. Los narodu polskiego wydaje się łagodny jedynie w porównaniu z ostateczną tragedią Żydów. Według wszelkich innych norm, ich poświęcenie, ich cierpienia i straty poniesione w czasie wojny czynią z Polaków naród najbardziej doświadczony przez własną historię — i geografię.

Stopień i istota pomocy okazywanej przez Polaków Żydom, podejmującym heroiczne wysiłki, aby przeżyć poza murami getta, stanowiła i nadal stanowi jedną z najbardziej spornych kwestii w powojennych stosunkach polsko-żydowskich. W odczuciu Żydów Polacy, generalnie, nie wyszli z tej próby zwycięsko. Oskarżani są przynajmniej o obojętność, jeśli nie o sprzyjanie Niemcom w realizacji ich morderczych planów, a wyjątkiem jest jedynie tych kilka tysięcy szlachetnych, którym oddaje się należny szacunek w Jerozolimie jako „Sprawiedliwym wśród narodów świata", oraz niewątpliwie wielu innych, którzy nie doczekali możliwości opowiedzenia swojej historii. Według tego oskarżenia charakterystyczne jest, że obojętność i wrogość nie były niespodzianką; po latach niełatwego współistnienia Żydzi mogli się tego spodziewać — przecież siew nienawiści nie mógł zrodzić plonu współczucia.

Polacy bronią się twierdząc nie bez racji, że skuteczna pomoc na masową skalę po prostu nie była możliwa w obliczu potęgi i całkowitej bezwzględności Niemców, dla których eksterminacja Żydów stała się celem strategicznym. Udzielanie pomocy w indywidualnych przypadkach niosło ze sobą ogromne niebezpieczeństwo i było równoznaczne z ryzykowaniem życia własnego i swojej rodziny, bowiem 10 grudnia 1942 roku niemiecki gubernator wydał dekret, wyznaczający karę śmierci nie tylko dla Żydów złapanych poza gettem, ale także dla wszystkich, którzy daliby im schronienie czy udzielili jakiejkolwiek pomocy. Nie była to pusta groźba i za pomoc wielu zapłaciło ostateczną cenę.

Mimo to, w roku 1942 polskie państwo podziemne powołało w Warszawie i Krakowie organizację, mającą na celu właśnie pomoc Żydom znajdującym się „po stronie aryjskiej". Organizacja ta, o nazwie „Żegota", objęła swoim zasięgiem cały obszar Generalnego Gubernatorstwa. Formy pomocy obejmowały znajdowanie mieszkania, dostarczanie fałszywych dokumentów, zaopatrywanie w pieniądze, ochronę przed szantażem, wykupywanie, za pomocą różnych przemyślnych forteli lub łapówek, z rąk policji czy gestapo. Działalność Miriam Mariańskiej i Mordechaja Pelega była prowadzona właśnie pod egidą i w ramach organizacyjnych „Żegoty", a jak wiadomo z wiarygodnych źródeł, organizacji tej zawdzięczało życie bardzo wielu ludzi.

W spornych sprawach, które do dziś ciążą nad stosunkami polsko-żydowskimi, bardzo trudno o obiektywne ustalenie faktów. Dlatego świadectwo Miriam i Mordechaja ma szczególną wartość. Ich prawość i wiarygodność są niewątpliwe. Dzięki swoim codziennym kontaktom zarówno z Polakami, jak i z Żydami patrzyli na sprawy z perspektywy jedynej w swoim rodzaju. Temu zawdzięczamy możliwość poznania autentycznej do ostateczności prawdy o tych czasach. Żadne badania tego okresu i jego problemów nie mogą pominąć świadectwa tej pary.

Celem tej książki, jak określiła to Miriam Mariańska, jest próba „wyrażenia ludzkim językiem rzeczy, które do ludzkich nie należą". Trudno przewidzieć reakcję czytelnika, spoglądającego na tamte czasy i tamte wydarzenia z dalekiej perspektywy. Wrażliwość ludzka jest różna, a człowiek wykazuje wielką łatwość przechodzenia do porządku nad cierpieniem innych ludzi. Ale jedna rzecz na pewno będzie jasna: to właśnie ludzie pokroju Miriam i Mordechaja, którzy żyli w tych potwornych czasach, pozwalają nam nadal wierzyć, że dobro w swojej odwiecznej walce z potęgą zła ma jednak jakąś szansę.

Tłum. *Wł. Chłopicki*

Wstęp do angielskiego wydania książki Miriam Mariańskiej *Witnesses —*
Life in Occupied Kraków, Routledge, London–New York 1991. Polskie
wydanie ukazało się nakładem Wydawnictwa Literackiego w Krakowie
pt. *Wśród przyjaciół i wrogów — Poza murami getta w okupowanym Krakowie*

Święci czy szaleńcy?
Refleksja nad książką Efraima Oszry'ego
Responsa from the Holocaust

J est to jeden z najniezwyklejszych dokumentów naszego czasu i chyba jakiegokolwiek czasu. To bardzo śmiałe stwierdzenie, ale rozważmy przemawiające za nim fakty.

Efraim Oszry to młody rabin, który w czasie, gdy armia niemiecka zajmowała Litwę, mieszkał na jednym z przedmieść Kowna, w Słobodce. Północne kresy były znane, nie tylko w środowisku żydowskim, ze swoich akademii talmudycznych, zwanych jeszybotami (hebr. *jesziwa*), które powstały tam (w Słobodce, Mirze, Wołożynie, Poniewieżu) na początku XIX wieku i działały pod egidą wielkich mędrców i uczonych, ściągając studentów z całego świata. Dla tych, którzy wierzyli, że studium Tory jest najwspanialszym z ludzkich powołań, rejon ten był ziemią świętą, „drugim Eretz Yisroel", Wilno zaś uchodziło za „litewską Jerozolimę".

25 czerwca 1941 roku rabin Oszry był naocznym świadkiem wkroczenia armii niemieckiej do Kowna, co było początkiem końca litewskich Żydów. Litewska „piąta kolumna", ugrupowania faszystowskie skupiające znaczny procent ludności kraju, natychmiast rozpoczęły mordercze napady na swoich żydowskich sąsiadów. Uzbrojeni w karabiny i siekiery, włamywali się do ich domów zabijając całe rodziny. Rabin Słobodki, Zalman Ossowski, właśnie pochylony był nad jakimś foliałem Talmudu, gdy do jego pracowni wtargnął tłum; przywiązano go do krzesła i ścięto, a głowę wystawiono w oknie, aby mogli ją zobaczyć przechodnie. Tego dnia zginęły setki Żydów, w tym wielu studentów jeszybotu.

Rabunki i morderstwa trwały ze zmiennym nasileniem przez dwa miesiące. Okazały się one jednak tylko prologiem, naśladującym historyczne wzory pogromem, który, w porównaniu z mającą nastąpić całkowitą eksterminacją, wydaje się niemal idyllą. Tak jak gdzie indziej, cały proces rozpoczął się od przymusowego przesiedlenia ludności żydowskiej do gett i obozów pracy, w trakcie którego tysiące osób zostało bez dachu nad głową lub zmarło z wycieńczenia. Był to etap przejściowy, który poprzedził wysyłkę Żydów do miejsc masowych egzekucji i do obozów śmierci.

W zatłoczonym getcie, za drutami kolczastymi, gdzie ciasnota bardzo ograniczała ludzką aktywność, życie, a raczej jego namiastka, toczyło się nadal. Trudności bytowe i prześladowania tworzyły warunki, w których ludzie łatwo tracą swoje ludzkie cechy, co było dodatkowym celem niemieckiego działania.

314

Przestrzeń życiowa nieustannie się kurczyła, a ludność dziesiątkowały choroby, głód, codzienne egzekucje i wreszcie ostateczne „przesiedlenie".

W tym piekle sprawował swoją posługę młody rabin Oszry. Okazał się człowiekiem o wielkim autorytecie, odwadze i sile wiary, prawdziwym oparciem dla swoich współwyznawców. Stanął jednak przed problemami teologicznymi i ludzkimi o przerażającej skali złożoności. Ludzie przychodzili do niego z pytaniami, ponieważ, jak mówił, „nie zawsze byli pewni, czego wymagała od nich Tora". Te pytania i swoje krótkie odpowiedzi zapisywał na kawałkach worków z cementu. Przez pewien czas miał dostęp do potrzebnych mu źródeł: w getcie znajdował się duży zbiór świętych ksiąg, które Niemcy zgromadzili, aby potem urządzić wystawę „wyrobów wymarłej rasy", a na kustosza, za wyraźnym podszeptem Opatrzności, mianowali właśnie rabina Oszry. Swoje notatki rabin pakował do puszek i zakopywał w ziemi. Ślubował sobie, że jeśli przeżyje, rozwinie swoje myśli szerzej i spisze je jako pełne wyjaśnienia. Szczęśliwym trafem rzeczywiście przeżył i w dniu wyzwolenia getta wydobył swoje notatki.

Przez kilka lat po wojnie rabin Efraim Oszry mieszkał w Rzymie, gdzie dla ocalonych z zagłady założył jeszybot *Me'or Hagola*. Obecnie mieszka w Nowym Jorku, jest rabinem w *Beth Hamedrash Hagadol*[1], przewodniczy także organizacji rabinów, którzy przeżyli hitlerowskie obozy. Tak jak obiecał, rozwinął i rozszerzył swoje oryginalne „responsa" i opublikował je w pięciu tomach pod nazwą *Sheilos Utshuvos Mima'amakim*. Książka, której dotyczy niniejsza recenzja, jest krótkim wyborem zawierającym 112 przetłumaczonych na język angielski odpowiedzi rabina[2]. Na pierwszy rzut oka jest to typowy przykład tradycyjnego piśmiennictwa rabinicznego, ale z uwagi na czas i miejsce swojego powstania oraz treść poruszanych kwestii jest dziełem jedynym w swoim rodzaju. Tło i kontekst stawianych pytań to autentyczne, bezpośrednie i szczegółowe świadectwo egzystencji w okolicznościach, których dramatyzm przechodzi wyobraźnię. Życie każdej osoby wisiało na włosku i było zależne od kaprysu niemieckiego komendanta, strażników czy dalekich władców z Berlina, od dodatkowego kawałka chleba czy jeszcze jednej łyżki zupy. Życie wokół było w najwyższym stopniu brutalne i niebezpieczne, następowało systematyczne i wyraźnie nieodwracalne niszczenie wszystkiego, co dla serca Żyda było najdroższe, rodzice musieli bezradnie patrzeć na cierpienie swoich dzieci. I ludzie przychodzili do rabina, żeby zapytać, co w takich sytuacjach robić.

Oto na przykład scena, która rozegrała się w klasie, gdzie Oszry uczył swoich studentów Talmudu. Pewna kobieta wpada do sali krzycząc, że Niemcy właśnie zastrzelili jej męża i trójkę dzieci, a na wieść o tym jej teść, Reb Zalman Szer, umarł na atak serca. Pytanie do rabina brzmi: ponieważ nie można

---

[1] Wielki Dom Modlitwy (przyp. aut.).
[2] Zbiór wydany przez nowojorską oficynę Judaica Press, 1985 (przyp. aut.).

przewidzieć, kiedy Niemcy pozwolą na przygotowanie pogrzebu, czy można przygotować ciało do pochówku (tzw. *tahara*) z wyprzedzeniem zamiast, jak to jest przyjęte, tuż przed pogrzebem? (Oszry zgodził się na natychmiastową *taharę*).

Czwartego dnia miesiąca Elul 5701 roku wg kalendarza żydowskiego (czyli 27 sierpnia 1941) Niemcy wyłapali bezpańskie psy i koty, przyprowadzili je do budynku szkolnego w słobodzkim getcie, a następnie wystrzelali. Potem zmusili szereg obecnych przy tym osób do podarcia zwojów Tory i użycia płacht pergaminu do owinięcia ciał martwych zwierząt. Uczestnicy i świadkowie tego zbezczeszczenia poprosili później rabina o zadanie im odpowiedniej pokuty za ten niegodny czyn. Oszry zawyrokował, że wszystkie osoby, które widziały jak zwoje Tory były rozdzierane, mają rozedrzeć swoje ubrania. Ci, którzy zostali zmuszeni do własnoręcznego darcia zwojów mieli podjąć post; mógł on być im darowany, jeśli nie mogli pościć z powodu wycieńczenia. Osoby, które nie były obecne przy tym wydarzeniu, a jedynie słyszały o nim od innych, miały z kolei dać jałmużnę na rzecz biednych.

We wrześniu 1941 roku w kowieńskim getcie mieszkało około 30 tysięcy osób, z których 10 tysięcy było zatrudnionych. Niemcy nakazali starszyźnie żydowskiej, tzw. *Judenratowi*, rozdać wśród tych ostatnich 5 tysięcy uprawnień (zwanych *Jordan Schein*, od nazwiska komendanta getta) do pozostania w getcie wraz z rodzinami. Los pozostałych był raczej jasny. Robotnicy oblegli więc biuro *Judenratu*, gdzie rozgrywały się dantejskie sceny, a wielu próbowało zdobyć pozwolenia siłą. Pytanie zadane rabinowi brzmiało: czy *Judenrat* mógł podporządkować się rozkazowi Jordana i rozdawać pozwolenia? Jakimi zasadami mieli się kierować decydując czy życie danej osoby jest ważniejsze od życia innej? Było jeszcze drugie pytanie: czy wolno komukolwiek siłą zabrać zezwolenie, żeby ratować swoje życie? Ponieważ zabierając je dla siebie skazywało się drugą osobę wraz z rodziną na śmierć.

Podobne zdarzenie miało miejsce kilka miesięcy później w Kownie (i licznych innych miejscach). Kowieński rabin, Raw Awrohom Dow Ber Kahana--Szapira, w odpowiedzi na pytanie *Judenratu*, czy wolno poddać się zarządzeniu niemieckiemu, by zgromadzić całą bez wyjątku ludność getta na głównym jego placu (i w ten sposób współdziałać w procesie eksterminacji) zawyrokował: „Jeżeli wydano dekret głoszący, że społeczność żydowska ma zostać zlikwidowana, a istnieje możliwość uratowania jakiejś części tej społeczności, jej starszyzna ma obowiązek przedsięwziąć wszelkie możliwe środki, aby ocalić *jak największą liczbę osób*". Odpowiedź rabina Oszry'ego brzmiała podobnie. Co do drugiego pytania, dotyczącego wydzierania zezwoleń siłą stwierdził, że w zasadzie żadnemu Żydowi nie wolno uczynić niczego, co postawiłoby życie innego Żyda w niebezpieczeństwie, jednak zgodnie z zasadą, że trzeba ratować jak największą liczbę osób, wydaje się, że każdy robotnik ma prawo zrobić wszystko, by ratować życie swoje i rodziny.

6 dnia miesiąca Cheszwan (27 października 1941), na 48 godzin przed czarnym dniem kowieńskiego getta, kiedy to około 10 tysięcy mężczyzn, kobiet i dzieci wywieziono na egzekucję i morderczy cel niemieckich działań stał się jasny dla wszystkich mieszkańców getta, pewien Żyd przyszedł do rabina Oszry z pytaniem: ponieważ wiadomo, że Niemcy rozstrzeliwują kobiety i dzieci na oczach mężczyzn, a on nie może znieść myśli, że mógłby być świadkiem takiej sceny, czy ma prawo sam odebrać sobie życie? Miałoby to ten dodatkowy atut, że byłby wtedy pochowany na cmentarzu żydowskim w getcie. W odpowiedzi Oszry odmawia mu prawa do samobójstwa twierdząc, że oznaczałoby to poddanie się wobec wroga, który dążył do tego, by wśród więzionych Żydów wywołać dezorientację i poczucie beznadziejności. Wykazałoby to również brak wiary w zdolność Boga do wybawienia Żydów z rąk prześladowców. Oszry zauważa z dumą, że zna tylko trzy przypadki samobójstwa w kowieńskim getcie.

Na centralnym placu getta w Kownie (przezwanym *Democratiaplatz*), gdzie Oszry, wraz z wszystkimi mieszkańcami getta, ok. 30 tysiącami dusz, oczekiwał na ostateczną selekcję, podszedł do rabina pewien mężczyzna pytając, jak dokładnie brzmi formuła błogosławieństwa, którą Żyd powinien wygłosić w chwili śmierci, aby wypełnić swój ostatni dobry uczynek (czyli *micwa*)? Chciał to przekazać jak największej liczbie osób, aby, kiedy przyjdzie ich kolej, mogli użyć właściwych słów. Oszry podał mu formułę, której sam zamierzał użyć: *aszer kideszonu bemicwosow weciwonu lekadeisz szemo berabim*[1].

W zimie roku 1942, na kilka miesięcy przed świętem Paschy, wielu Żydów w getcie zaczęło przemyślać nad sposobem zdobycia skądś macy. Wiele produktów żywnościowych było niedostępnych, nie mówiąc już o białej mące, z której wyrabia się mace. Mosze Goldkorn, pracujący w brygadzie roboczej poza gettem, wszedł w kontakt z Litwinami, którzy byli gotowi przyjąć inne towary w zamian za mąkę. Mimo że każde przekroczenie bramy getta stało się dla niego bardzo niebezpieczne, zdołał stopniowo przeszmuglować wystarczającą ilość mąki, żeby upiec macę dla stu Żydów, z których każdy miał otrzymać kawałek wielkości oliwki, wystarczający by dopełnić rytuału wigilii święta Paschy. Po przygotowaniu pieca zgodnie z tradycją mace wypieczono w jednej z sal miejscowej piekarni.

Na dwa dni przed Paschą Goldkorna zatrzymano przy bramie i poddano rewizji, w czasie której znaleziono przy nim małą torebkę z mąką. Został bardzo mocno pobity i wybito mu wszystkie zęby. Przyszedł więc do Oszry'ego z następującym pytaniem: „Skoro mam wybite zęby, jak mogę wypełnić przykazanie i zjeść kawałek macy wielkości oliwki? Pochodzę z rodziny chasydzkiej, w której przestrzegano zwyczaju, że w święto Paschy nie je się macy 'moczonej'. Nie mogę złamać tej tradycji, a jednocześnie nie jestem w stanie

---

[1] „On, który nakazał nam robić dobre uczynki i uświęcać Jego imię pośród ludzi" (przyp. aut.).

ugryźć niczego, co nie byłoby zmiękczone". Oszry zezwolił, aby zamoczono dla niego macę w wodzie, mimo że jest potomkiem chasydów, tak aby mógł dopełnić dobrego uczynku (*micwa*), dla którego ryzykował życiem. Nakazał mu jednak uzyskanie od *beit-din* zgody na anulowanie tradycyjnego ślubu jego przodków dotyczącego niejadania w Paschę zmiękczonej macy.

Niemcy bezwzględnie zakazali wnoszenia na teren getta produktów żywnościowych z zewnątrz — robotnicy pracujący na zewnątrz getta musieli zjeść swoje mizerne racje sami, nie wolno im było dzielić się nimi z dziećmi i rodziną. Oszry wspomina przypadek mężczyzny, który oszczędził kawałek chleba i ukrył go między nogami, mając nadzieję, że strażnicy tego nie zauważą. Został złapany, pobity i skopany, tak że zgnieciono mu jądra. Przyszedł do rabina Oszry'ego z zapytaniem: „Nie wolno mi współżyć z żoną (zgodnie z nakazem Księgi Powtórzonego Prawa) i nie mogę mieć już dzieci. Ponieważ jestem z plemienia kapłanów (*kohein*), zawsze byłem wzywany do czytania fragmentu Tory jako pierwszy lektor. Teraz jestem skażony i nie mogę już czytać jako pierwszy lektor. Czy jest jakiś sposób, abym mógł nadal być traktowany jako lektor i 'kohein'?" Oszry zinterpretował prawo całkowicie na korzyść nieszczęśnika.

20 dnia miesiąca Ijjar roku 5703 (7 maja 1942) Niemcy zarządzili, że każda kobieta, która zajdzie w ciążę, zostanie rozstrzelana. Do rabina zwrócono się więc z pytaniem, czy w tych okolicznościach dozwolone jest stosowanie środków antykoncepcyjnych. Odpowiedź była twierdząca. Ogłosił on także, że w obliczu zagrożenia życia kobiety możliwe jest przerwanie ciąży.

Zapytano go również, czy wolno kupić świadectwo chrztu, które jeśliby ktoś zdołał uciec do lasu, umożliwiłoby przyłączenie się do partyzantów. W tym przypadku Oszry uznał, że nie ma prawa udzielania takich zezwoleń, nawet gdyby miało to uratować komuś życie.

Kilka przypadków wybranych z setek czy nawet tysięcy. Każdy daje możliwość wglądu w wycinek tego piekła na ziemi i pogląd na temat dylematów, jakich nikomu nie powinno się stawiać, a przed jakimi stanęli ci zwykli przecież, postawieni w warunkach ekstremalnych ludzie. Każdy może jednocześnie służyć jako tekst do medytacji.

Po wyzwoleniu Oszry spotkał się z inną serią przypadków, wynikających z okoliczności wojennych. Na przykład, czy Żyd może wchodzić na teren kościoła, aby szukać dzieci żydowskich ukrywanych tam i chronionych przez księży, tak aby umożliwić im powrót do narodu? (Tak, może.) Dzieci ocalone przez nie-Żydów teraz musiały być „ocalone" przed nimi. Sam Oszry angażował się, nawet ryzykując życie, w ich poszukiwanie i „odzyskiwanie", co stanowi osobną historię. Trwało to długo i w momencie odnalezienia niektórzy chłopcy mieli już po sześć i więcej lat. Pojawiło się tedy pytanie: czy przy obrzezaniu wolno używać środków znieczulających? Jeden z chłopców zgodził się poddać obrzezaniu jedynie w przypadku gdyby mu obiecano, że nie odczuje bólu. Oszry zgodził się na zastosowanie znieczulenia (chociaż odczucie tego samego bólu, jaki odczuwał nasz praojciec Abraham, powinno się uważać za zasługę), uzasadniając to tym, że ten chłopiec żył już wcześniej wśród nie-Żydów i zadanie mu bólu mogłoby skłonić go do buntu przeciw pozostałym przykazaniom Tory i do sprzeniewierzenia się wierze.

Po wyzwoleniu nieraz brakowało filakterii (*tefilin*), często natomiast znajdowały się one w domach nie-Żydów. Czy można skorzystać z pary takich filakterii, nie czekając aż rabin obejrzy je i stwierdzi, czy spełniają wymóg koszerności? Oszry wspomina, że jego zgoda w tej materii wywołała u wielu łzy radości.

Była też sprawa rabina bękarta (hebr. *mamzer*) urodzonego ze związku, który okazał się potem związkiem nieprawym. Historia zaczyna się w październiku 1941 roku, kiedy to w getcie rozeszła się pogłoska, że wszystkie niezamężne kobiety będą zgładzone. W tym czasie doświadczenie mieszkańców getta wskazywało, że wszystko tam jest możliwe, więc plotka ta spowodowała panikę wśród niezamężnych kobiet, które zaczęły za wszelką cenę poszukiwać mężów. Pewna kobieta, której mąż został zabrany przez Niemców i zniknął bez śladu, myślała, że ten nie żyje, więc znalazła sobie nowego męża i wyszła za niego. Para ta uciekła z getta, przeżyła wojnę, a po wojnie przeprowadziła się za granicę. Mieli tam syna, który w swoim czasie skończył studia w jeszybocie i został rabinem. Pewnego dnia, ni stąd ni zowąd, zjawił się pewien mężczyzna, który stwierdził i przedstawił dowody na to, że był pierwszym mężem matki rabina i niezgodnie z prawdą został uznany za nieżyjącego. Minęło bardzo wiele lat zanim natrafił na jakikolwiek ślad po swojej żonie, ale kiedy dowiedział się, że wyszła za innego i urodziła syna, poczuł się oburzony „zdradą", jakiej się dopuściła. Był zdecydowany ją wytropić, zmusić do rozwodu z drugim mężem i publicznie ujawnić jej hańbiący uczynek. W tym czasie jednak kobieta ta już nie żyła, więc gniew mężczyzny skupił się na jej synu, owocu tego bigamicznego związku; dołożył wszelkich starań, aby usunąć tego rabina ze społeczności żydowskiej.

Rabin Oszry usiłował przekonać mściwego męża, aby zachował milczenie, publiczne ujawnianie takich informacji stanowi samo w sobie świętokradztwo (*chilul haszem*). Życie młodego rabina i tak już zostało zrujnowane. Oszry zarządził, że rabin powinien zrezygnować ze swojego stanowiska, bo „ludzie nie będą go słuchać". Poczynił również wszelkie starania, aby mógł on rozwieść się z żoną, gdyż prawo zabrania, aby bękart miał za żonę Żydówkę, chyba że i ona ma podobne pochodzenie.

Co można sądzić o postawach tych ludzi?

W kontekście zagłady Żydów, kiedy inni ludzie rozpaczali lub stracili cel w życiu, ci utrzymali niewzruszoną wiarę w ostateczną dobroć Boga, mimo codziennie pojawiających się nowych dowodów świadczących przeciw temu. Tam, gdzie inni ludzie czuli się bezradni i opuszczeni, oni szukali odpowiedzi i, co może ważniejsze, wiedzieli, gdzie ich szukać. Ryzykując tortury i śmierć za przekraczanie niemieckiego zakazu zbiorowych modlitw i prowadzenia szkoły, studiowali Torę i przestrzegali *micwot*[1], przekonani, że „żydowskość" trzeba chronić i że ochronić ją można jedynie w ten sposób. Nie pozwolili się odhumanizować i kultywowali w sobie uczucie nieskończonej wyższości wobec swoich prześladowców. Był to z ich strony potężny opór duchowy, który niewątpliwie był dla nich źródłem ogromnej siły wewnętrznej w walce o przetrwanie.

Z drugiej strony, w czasie gdy każdy przejaw energii niezbędny był do przeżycia do następnego dnia, upieranie się przy poście w święto Jom Kippur czy przy przestrzeganiu prawa *kaszrut*[2], albo pytanie rabina czy, jeżeli nie ma innej możliwości przygotowania pożywienia, wolno gotować w szabat, względnie czy wolno jeść to, co zostało w ten sposób przygotowane przez innego Żyda, kolosalnie utrudniało życie. A jeżeli kawałek papieru taki jak świadectwo chrztu mógł uratować życie — jakże można było taką możliwość odrzucać?

Czym było to zjawisko? Czy było ono ludzkie, czy może ponadludzkie? Gdzie znajduje się jego miejsce w porządku rzeczy? Dla świeckiego, racjonalnego umysłu zarówno pytania, jak i odpowiedzi na nie wydać się mogą absurdalne, groteskowe, nie z tej ziemi, może nawet obłędne. Ale trzeba być całkowicie pozbawionym uczucia, by nie dostrzegać w tym świadectwa pewnego transcendentalnego wymiaru duchowości. Można tego nie rozumieć, ani nie czuć żadnej sympatii dla postaw tych ludzi, ale nie można tak po prostu wzruszyć ramionami. Czy będzie się z niedowierzaniem kręcić głową czy też płakać ze wzruszenia lub współczucia, nie można chyba nie podziwiać ich bezgranicznego oddania i zaufania Bogu.

Czy wolno nam tworzyć sobie wyważony obraz duchowości tych naszych braci w sytuacji, gdy dla nich nasza duchowość byłaby pozbawiona wartości i znaczenia, a my bylibyśmy odstępcami i szydercami, których miejsce jest w piekle? Jeżeli piekło, jak twierdzi najbardziej przekonywająca jego definicja, jest oddzieleniem od Boga, wszystko wskazuje na to, że już tam dawno jesteśmy.

Tłum. *Wł. Chłopicki*

„Jewish Quarterly", Nr 4 (128), 1987

---

[1] *micwot* (hebr.) — l. m. od *micwa* — nakaz, dobry uczynek (przyp. aut.).
[2] *kaszrut* (hebr.) — przepisy rytualne tyczące się pożywienia (przyp. aut.).

Nasze dni wczorajsze ...

Nad albumem Romana Wiszniaka

Album fotografii Romana Wiszniaka, wykonanych w latach 1934–39
w Polsce, Czechosłowacji, Rumunii, na Rusi Karpackiej, Węgrzech
i Litwie, wydany pod tytułem *Zaginiony świat* (*A Vanished World*,
Allen Lane, Londyn 1983), nosi cechy dzieła prawdziwego geniuszu. Jest to
dokument o trwałej wartości i wymowie silnej a zarazem niezmiernie przygnę-
biającej. Ci, którzy pamiętają i ci, którzy pragną zyskać wyobrażenie o tym, jak
ci ludzie i tamte miejsca wyglądały, zobaczywszy ten album będą już myśleć
jego obrazami.

Zdjęcia robione przez Wiszniaka przy każdej pogodzie, w słońcu i o zmro-
ku, na ulicy i w podziemnych norach, z niezwykłym wyczuciem tematu i kom-
pozycji, które zdradza artystę, utrwaliły obrazy w sposób tak niezwykły, że
fotografie te przypominają dzieła wielkich mistrzów holenderskich. Czas za-
trzymał się jedynie na oślepiający błysk flesza, a zawarta w zdjęciu treść
zostaje na tak długo, dopóki będą istnieć książki.

Wiszniak znany jest ze swoich wcześniejszych wystaw i publikacji[1] oraz ze
zdjęć publikowanych w innych albumach[2], ale ten album stanowi długo ocze-
kiwany wybór 200 jego najlepszych zdjęć.

Artysta, który obecnie ma 86 lat i mieszka w Nowym Jorku, gdzie właśnie
otrzymał honorowe obywatelstwo miasta, jest człowiekiem niezwykłym, a historia powstania tych zdjęć mogłaby posłużyć za temat do jakiejś powieści z gatunku łotrzykowskich.

Urodził się w Rosji i studiował medycynę i socjologię na uniwersytecie
w Moskwie. Po rewolucji przeniósł się do Berlina, gdzie stał się wybitnym
specjalistą od mikrofotografii.

Po dojściu Hitlera do władzy prześladowało go ponure przeczucie, że zawarte w *Mein Kampf* groźby zostaną zrealizowane. Jakby prowadzony przez
jakiś wewnętrzny głos rozpoczął to nieprawdopodobne przedsięwzięcie: uzbrojony w rolleiflexa i leikę przemierzał wioski i miasta wschodniej Europy, współ-
czująco obserwując życie społeczności żydowskiej. Zdjęcia robił przeważnie
z ukrytej kamery. Stosował ten środek ostrożności, gdyż ortodoksyjni Żydzi

---

[1] *Polish Jews* [*Żydzi polscy*], Schocken Books, Nowy Jork 1947; *Life of the Six Million*
[*Życie sześciu milionów*], 1969 (przyp. tłum.).
[2] *Image Before My Eyes* [*Obraz przed mymi oczyma*], Schocken Books oraz YIVO, Nowy
Jork 1977, a także *The Jewish Family Album* [*Album rodziny żydowskiej*], Routledge and
Kegan Paul, Londyn 1975 (przyp. tłum.).

często odmawiali zgody na fotografowanie, a poza tym w tamtych czasach cudzoziemiec wędrujący przez kraje tej części Europy z aparatem fotograficznym w ręku mógł mieć kłopoty. Wiszniak autentycznie narażał się na niebezpieczeństwa: był wielokrotnie napadany i usuwany za granice państw, po czym ponownie wkraczał do nich w innym miejscu; jedenaście razy aresztowany, spędził sporo czasu w więzieniu, a jego negatywy były wielokrotnie konfiskowane. Przemierzył ogromne dystanse i wykonał przeszło 16 tysięcy fotografii, z których 2 tysiące negatywów zdołał wywieźć i ukryć je na czas wojny u swojego ojca w rządzonej przez reżim Vichy Francji. Sam znalazł się w obozie koncentracyjnym w Clichy, z którego uciekł na początku roku 1941 i przez Hiszpanię i Portugalię dotarł do Ameryki. Niedługo po przyjeździe do Nowego Jorku znów stał się znanym zawodowym fotografem. Ogólnie można by powiedzieć, że ma porządny żydowski życiorys.

Obracam kartki albumu... Ten rozmarzony chłopiec z zapadniętymi policzkami, z oczyma jak spodeczki chwyta za serce; jest jak inni chłopcy z chederu, tacy niewinni a jednocześnie rozumiejący, że aż chce się ich uściskać, albo jak ten chłopiec w zbyt dużej czapce z daszkiem i rękami wzniesionymi do góry ze słynnej fotografii z warszawskiego getta (zrobionej na pamiątkę przez jakiegoś hitlerowca), który stał się niejako żydowską ikoną.

Trzech chasydów w pełnej krasie, w chałatach, *tallitach, sztreimelach*[1] — uchwyconych we wdzięcznej pozie, jak grupa baletowa, gdy wychodzą z synagogi po rannym nabożeństwie, nadal pogrążeni w dyskusji, wzmacniający swoje racje charakterystycznym gestem.

Posępny, owiany śniegiem róg ulicy, na tabliczce słowa „ulica Izaaka", to samo serce żydowskiego Kazimierza w Krakowie (gdzież indziej ulice mogły być nazwane imionami patriarchów); stary obity, obdrapany mur, kilka postaci poruszających się jak duchy, dziwnymi ruchami we wszechogarniającej pustce...

Kontrastuje z tym widok tętniącej życiem ulicy Nalewki, gdzie w ciepły dzień każde z setek okien otwiera się, by przewietrzyć maleńkie pomieszczenia, które jednocześnie służą za biura, sklepy, warsztaty; różnokolorowy tłum płynie we wszystkich kierunkach na raz, tablice reklamują tasiemki, gorsety, bieliznę, nici, fartuchy, kufry, parasole. To maleńki wycinek, który pomnożony przez tysiąc dałby w całości największe skupisko żydostwa na ziemi.

Żydowskie twarze uchwycone są ze współczuciem niemal rembrandtowskim, stroskane, melancholijne, palimpsesty cierpienia. Ich cechą wspólną nie są haczykowate nosy czy obfity zarost i pejsy, ale oczy, o niezbadanej głębi, ciężkie od znajomości świata, pamięci i przeczuć... Kiedy zjawili się Niemcy,

---

[1] *tallit* — szal modlitewny, chusta w pasy, zarzucana na ramiona w czasie modłów; *sztreimel* — lisia czapa, należąca do stroju ortodoksyjnych Żydów (przyp. aut.).

te oczy były głównym, bardzo wymownym i niemożliwym do ukrycia znakiem rozpoznawczym, który wydawał próbującego ocalić swe życie Żyda.

Uderza osobliwe piękno tych ludzi. Jeżeli choć na jedną setną sekundy zapomnieć o tym, co się stało w kilka lat czy miesięcy po zrobieniu przez Wiszniaka zdjęcia, można by być oczarowanym. Ale w obliczu nieuchronności nadchodzącej rzezi wiadomo, że cała ta scena jest przedsionkiem piekła i aż trudno się powstrzymać, by nie wykrzyczeć słów ostrzeżenia... Przecież nadal trudno to pojąć: w przeciągu czterech lat ta tysiącletnia cywilizacja zniknęła bez śladu, rozbita, zdeptana, spalona, wykreślona z rejestru... Nic z niej nie zostało i tylko cud mógł sprawić, że jakaś pojedyncza postać z utrwalonych na tych stronicach uszła z życiem. Jak można się przyzwyczaić do tego stanu wiecznej nieobecności?

Wiszniak zasłużył na nasz podziw i wdzięczność. Jego dzieła nie można ani niczym zastąpić, ani go uzupełnić (chyba że o jego własne dotychczas nie publikowane fotografie), tak więc stanie się on, a nawet już się stał, klasykiem tego rodzaju twórczości. Ważne jest więc, aby zauważyć i sprostować szereg niedokładności w podpisach pod zdjęciami wykazujących brak znajomości rzeczy. Notatki, które poprzedzają zdjęcia i które można czytać praktycznie jak jedno opowiadanie, są często mylące i niezgodne z prawdą. Zostały one spisane przez Wiszniaka niedawno, w podeszłym już wieku, wiele dziesiątek lat po utrwalonych na kliszach wydarzeniach. Z całym szacunkiem dla artysty trzeba podkreślić, że pamięć go zawodzi i górę biorą emocje; jest to zrozumiałe, ale notatki zamazują właściwą perspektywę i negatywnie wpływają na ocenę książki jako źródła informacji. Polski rząd i naród, żeby posłużyć się przykładem tylko jednego kraju, mają dosyć własnych prawdziwych przewinień i nie muszą być oskarżane o rzeczy, których nie zrobili albo na które nie mieli żadnego wpływu.

Na przykład na stronie 20 ortodoksyjny Żyd w swoim chałacie (*bekesze*) i okrągłej czapce z daszkiem jest opisany jako zwolniony po dwudziestu latach pracy pod presją „komisji d/s bojkotu"[1] — trudno sobie wyobrazić, żeby taki człowiek jak on w ogóle kiedyś pracował w polskiej, nieżydowskiej firmie czy instytucji.

Notatka dotycząca stron 27–28 stwierdza: „Po ogłoszeniu bojkotu, przewożenie towarów na ręcznie ciągniętych wózkach lub na własnych plecach było jedynym zajęciem, na które zezwalano warszawskim Żydom" — to stwierdzenie jest zupełnie absurdalne i nie powinno było ujść uwadze redakcji. Notatka na str. 65 opisuje zasady przyjmowania do pracy w biurach dziewcząt żydowskich, które przeciwstawione są zasadom przyjmowania dziewcząt nieżydowskich — takie dyskryminujące zasady w ogóle nie istniały. Notatka na str. 66

---

[1] Nie było takiej komisji. Była presja prawicowych partii i aprobata bojkotu przez rząd gen. Składkowskiego, ale nie był to ruch zorganizowany i jego efekt był niewielki (przyp. aut.).

tak mówi o sprzedawcy bajgli: „Na żydowskich ulicach nikt nie miał pieniędzy, żeby kupić cokolwiek poza zwykłym chlebem" — nie, nieprawda: niektórzy mieli mało, inni więcej, a jeszcze inni bardzo dużo pieniędzy, a na bajgle stać było prawie wszystkich. Notatka i podpis pod fotografią na str. 178 (twarz Żyda w niewielkim okienku w żelaznej bramie) — rzekomo właśnie nadchodzą endecy (*pogromczycy*), żeby go bić. Niechby tylko spróbowali! Wiedzieli, że nie mogą wkraczać na ten teren, gdyż ryzykowaliby zdrowiem, a nawet życiem.

Wiszniak wielokrotnie powraca do tematu bojkotu, jakby to był główny powód żydowskiej biedy. Tak bynajmniej nie było. Bieda istniała przed bojkotem i miała znacznie głębsze przyczyny. Bojkot był akcją wrogą, ale jego skutki były prawdopodobnie zupełnie marginalne: uczynił on niektórych żydowskich kupców nieco biedniejszymi, ale nie zyskał na nim żaden polski kupiec. Ogromna większość żydowskich sklepikarzy i rzemieślników nie miała i tak żadnych polskich klientów. W wielkich miastach Żyd mógł żyć całkowicie we własnym środowisku, a jego kontakty z otaczającą ludnością miejscową mogły być jedynie okazjonalne. Sklepikarze, którzy obsługiwali nieżydowskich klientów sprzedawali przysłowiowo już niemal taniej od mniej doświadczonych i mniej pracowitych swoich konkurentów. Kupujący mogli sobie mruczeć pod nosem, ale nie kwapili się iść gdzie indziej i wydać więcej pieniędzy. A wielki biznes, zgodnie ze swoją naturą, zawsze kierował się jedynie możliwością zysku.

Wiszniak koncentruje się na żydowskiej biedzie — sklepikarze w podartych łachach, puste półki sklepowe, żebracy, uliczni handlarze, rzemieślnicy w swoich ciemnych norach, które były także ich kuchniami i sypialniami, a cała rodzina miała tam zwykle tylko jedno łóżko. Bieda była rzeczywiście wielka i wszechobecna. Ale nie była to bieda szczególnie żydowska, która kontrastowałaby z zamożnością nie-Żydów. Przeciwnie — panująca w miastach nędza nie znała granic i nieżydowscy bezrobotni cierpieli ten sam, jeśli nie gorszy, niedostatek i degradację. Na wsi zdarzała się sytuacja jeszcze gorsza: jeśli nadszedł zły rok, egzystencja małorolnego lub bezrolnego chłopa była bardzo mizerna.

Wiszniak zajmuje się niemal wyłącznie Żydami biednymi i ortodoksyjnymi — jako fotograf uznał ich za najbardziej malownicze obiekty, a jako człowiek czuł do nich największą sympatię — to jego prawo. Ale wynikiem takiego podejścia jest obraz bardzo jednostronny i nieobiektywny.

Twierdzenie, że życie Żydów w Polsce było zawsze pełne bezbrzeżnego smutku i prześladowań jest niezgodne z prawdą. Ich egzystencja miała tak blaski, jak i cienie. Złożone dzieje Żydów składały się z wielu aspektów; niektóre z ich najjaśniejszych i najbardziej optymistycznych stron zapisane zostały właśnie na ziemi polskiej.

Pierwsza wojna światowa przyniosła Polsce niepodległość polityczną po niemal 150 latach rozbiorów i podziału między Rosję, Austrię i Prusy. Problemy socjoekonomiczne, jakie stanęły na drodze do zjednoczenia trzech części kraju, różniących się podziałem administracyjnym, systemem prawnym i tradycjami, były ogromne. Mniejszości narodowe — białoruska, ukraińska, niemiecka i litewska — z których każda miała tendencje separatystyczne i wysuwała sprzeczne żądania, a także nieustanne zagrożenie ze strony Rosji, tym razem w kształcie sowieckim, stworzyły korzystne warunki dla rodzenia się niesprawiedliwości. Rozwój polskiego nacjonalizmu, chroniczny stan zapaści gospodarczej i bezrobocie doprowadziły do przewidywalnych skutków. Żydzi stanowili ok. 10 procent ludności kraju, mieszkali głównie w miastach, byli mniejszością wyróżniającą się wśród innych i stwarzającą konkurencję. Wciśnięci między stary jak świat antysemityzm rosyjski i groźne wpływy niemieckie, Polacy musieliby być świętymi, żeby nie pozwolić rozwinąć skrzydeł politycznemu, religijnemu czy ekonomicznemu antysemityzmowi własnego chowu — a świętymi z całą pewnością nie byli.

W połowie lat trzydziestych dążenie do wprowadzenia dyskryminacji Żydów, od dawna wpisane w programy endecji i innych partii prawicowych, zyskało poparcie prorządowego ruchu politycznego OZON i niektórych przedstawicieli władz państwowych. Ówczesny premier, generał Sławoj-Składkowski, wypowiedział swoje niesławne „owszem" w odpowiedzi na propozycję wprowadzenia bojkotu żydowskich przedsiębiorstw (jak na ironię, ów generał mieszkał w czasie wojny i po niej w Palestynie). Zamieszki na uniwersytetach i pikiety przed żydowskimi sklepami określano jako „naturalne, instynktowne reakcje obronne naszej kultury i samowystarczalności (ekonomicznej)".

Ale na tym tle gróźb i niepewności, życie Żydów toczyło się wartkim i swobodnym nurtem. Pewien stopień dyskryminacji traktowali jako rzecz zupełnie naturalną — przecież w końcu żyli w diasporze, był to następny rozdział prastarej historii, czego innego można by się spodziewać?

Należy przy tym pamiętać, że istniała znaczna strefa, gdzie podział między polskością i żydowskością był zatarty, a owocem długich wieków wzajemnego współżycia obojga narodów była wzajemna akceptacja, tolerancja i harmonia. Okazało się to bardzo płodne i przyniosło niezwykłe ubogacenie obydwu kulturom. Jak w pewnym angielskim wierszyku, Polak jeśli jest dobry, jest bardzo, bardzo dobry... (ale jeśli jest zły, to biada...). Jest u Polaków wiele szlachetnego ducha, romantycznego szaleństwa, pogardy dla niebezpieczeństw, idealizmu, z których to cech dumny byłby każdy naród.

Jeden z najznakomitszych polskich poetów Antoni Słonimski, wnuk założyciela i redaktora hebrajskiej gazety „Hazefira", Haima Seliga Słonimskiego, napisał poemat o „dwóch najnieszczęśliwszych narodach na ziemi". Ich drogi rozeszły się już na zawsze.

Kiedy zginęli polscy Żydzi, część Polski zginęła wraz z nimi. Ale Polacy nie bardzo przejęli się tą stratą. Poczuli chwilowy niepokój — i zaraz udali, że Żydów jakby nigdy nie było. Wielu doznało uczucia ulgi, że nierozwiązywalny dotąd „problem żydowski" w Polsce został rozwiązany w sposób, za który Polacy nie mogli ponosić winy. Co by się stało, gdyby po zakończeniu wojny miliony Żydów pojawiły się z żądaniem zwrócenia im dawnej własności, nawet trudno sobie wyobrazić. Zapowiedzią tego koszmaru, który mógłby nastąpić, było powitanie zgotowane (np. w Kielcach) żałosnym resztkom Żydów, którzy wyszli ze swoich kryjówek, wrócili z obozów, z bunkrów, z lasu.

Kiedy Żydzi i ich dzieci zostali wymordowani, a społeczna struktura ich życia zniszczona, wyrwano „jeden z korzeni, z których wyrasta historia", jak to ujął George Steiner. Zniszczono genetyczne źródło, z którego się ich tradycja wywodzi.

Tłum. *Wł. Chłopicki*

„Jewish Quarterly", Nr 113, 1983/84

O Oświęcimiu — raz jeszcze

U trzymanie obiektywizmu w dyskusji o Oświęcimiu jest niemalże niemożliwe. Już samo słowo trafia w czułą strunę. Oznacza ono wiele rzeczy. To nie tylko nazwa polskiego miasta, gdzie znajduje się muzeum, które na przestrzeni lat odwiedziły miliony osób, młodych i starszych, wszystkich narodowości i religii, pragnąc, z różnorakich powodów, zobaczyć miejsce, gdzie nie tak dawno dokonano jednej z największych zbrodni w historii ludzkości. Jest to także pojęcie abstrakcyjne, które napełnia nas obawą i głębokim niepokojem. Jest to symbol, który dla różnych ludzi znaczy różne rzeczy.

Dla Żydów Oświęcim jest symbolem zagłady [dla jej określenia używa się najczęściej słowa „holocaust" (dosł. „całopalenie"), które jest niewłaściwe, nieodpowiednie, mylące, obce — ale przyjęło się już na tyle, że walka z nim wydaje się z góry skazana na porażkę]. Dziwią ich i oburzają wysiłki nadania mu jakichś innych znaczeń. Ale dla Polaków Oświęcim nie jest tylko obozem „żydowskim", lecz symbolem niemieckich gwałtów dokonanych na ich kraju i prześladowania ich narodu — i mają wiele powodów, by tak go właśnie postrzegać.

Mówiąc o tych sprawach, dobrze jest znać pewne fakty, gdyż czasem nasze słowa i czyny zdają się tym faktom zaprzeczać. Obóz w Oświęcimiu powstał w czerwcu 1940 roku jako obóz koncentracyjny dla polskich więźniów politycznych. Traktat o granicy i przyjaźni pomiędzy Hitlerem a Stalinem (z września 1939 roku) zawierał tajną klauzulę dotyczącą eliminacji potencjalnych przeciwników obydwu reżimów. W kwietniu i maju 1940 roku Sowieci zamordowali około 15 tysięcy polskich jeńców wojennych, w tym 45% przedwojennego korpusu oficerskiego, w lesie katyńskim i innych miejscach. W tym samym czasie Niemcy, lojalnie dotrzymując zawartej umowy, wysłali do obozów 20 tysięcy Polaków. Był to początek wielkiego planu zniszczenia intelektualnej i politycznej elity narodu polskiego.

Oświęcim, położony na terenie wcielonym do Rzeszy, z którego usunięto większość Polaków, aby stworzyć tam pas ziemi niczyjej, miał być jednym z ośrodków realizacji tego programu. 14 czerwca 1940 roku do Oświęcimia dotarł pierwszy transport polskich więźniów. Przez następne 21 miesięcy Polacy byli jedynymi więźniami tego obozu, a pierwszy transport ludności żydowskiej (były to Żydówki ze Słowacji) przybył tu pod koniec marca 1942 roku. Obóz macierzysty, Auschwitz I (niem. *Stammlager*), gdzie Polacy zawsze stanowili większość więźniów, był obozem niewolniczej pracy, wokół którego rozciągała się sieć ponad 40 podobozów. Tysiące więźniów zginęło tu z głodu, przepracowania, chorób, w wyniku egzekucji. Ale wielu z nich ocalało.

W październiku 1941 roku Niemcy rozpoczęli budowę podobozu w Brzezince (Birkenau), w odległości ok. 3 km od obozu macierzystego. Zaczęto go później nazywać Auschwitz II. Krematoria i komory gazowe znajdowały się właśnie tutaj.

Od maja 1942 roku większość Żydów przyjeżdżających do Brzezinki wysyłano do komór gazowych bezpośrednio z rampy kolejowej. Dokładna ich liczba trudna jest do ustalenia, ale większość ostatnich badań wskazuje, że cyfra zagazowanych i spalonych tam Żydów wyniosła 1,5 miliona.

Spośród sześciu obozów zagłady — były to Bełżec, Chełmno, Sobibór, Majdanek, Treblinka i Oświęcim — tylko w tym ostatnim ocalała większość zabudowań obozowych. Niemcy bowiem, chcąc zatrzeć ślady zbrodni, zdążyli wysadzić w powietrze instalacje tej fabryki śmierci, ale w obliczu szybkiej ofensywy rosyjskiej musieli zaraz potem opuścić obóz.

Dawne budynki administracyjne, baraki, wieże strażnicze, ogrodzenia z drutów kolczastych, ruiny komór gazowych i krematoriów i sam teren obozu stanowią muzeum, które zaraz po wojnie utworzono na polecenie rządu polskiego. Celem tego muzeum było ukazanie męczeństwa narodu polskiego i groźby ze strony faszyzmu. Według oficjalnej historiografii ofiarami obozu byli ludzie 28 różnych narodowości: na tej liście Żydów (ang. *Jews*) umieszczono w angielskim porządku alfabetycznym (pomiędzy Włochami (*Italians*) a Łotyszami (*Letts*)). Nigdzie nie wspomniano, że praktycznie wszyscy oni, niezależnie od obywatelstwa, byli Żydami, których mordowano tu właśnie z tego powodu. Dla komunistycznych „historyków" był to fakt bez znaczenia. Różnym narodowościom przydzielono własne baraki, które miały opowiadać ich historię — Bułgarzy, na przykład, w swoim baraku urządzili ekspozycję wspaniałych osiągnięć bułgarskiej organizacji komunistycznej. Barak żydowski utworzono dopiero w roku 1978 i do dnia dzisiejszego[1], pomimo wprowadzonych z czasem ulepszeń, zupełnie nie oddaje on prawdy ani swoją formą, ani treścią.

Wraz z ogromnymi zmianami politycznymi w Polsce i gdzie indziej, pojawia się konieczność wyprostowania historycznych zafałszowań i to nie tylko w tym zakresie. Polska dyrekcja muzeum w Oświęcimiu-Brzezince wykazuje wielką otwartość i daleko idącą gotowość do współpracy i tam, gdzie to możliwe, wprowadzenia w życie rad udzielanych przez „stronę żydowską". Oczywiście nie istnieje żaden oficjalny autorytatywny głos Żydów, nie ma też między nimi zgody na to, co i w jaki sposób należy mówić[2]. Niedawno polskie

---

[1] Pisane w r. 1992 (przyp. aut.).

[2] Kilka lat temu, na międzynarodowej konferencji Żydów polskich w Jerozolimie, słyszałem, jak premier Szamir zwrócił się do słuchaczy następującymi słowami: „Jeśliby Żydzi europejscy posłuchali ostrzeżeń Żabotyńskiego i masowo przenieśli się do Jerozolimy, zagłady można było uniknąć". Niedawno natomiast słyszałem jak gen. Barak, dowódca armii

władze powołały Międzynarodowy Komitet Oświęcimski, gdzie Żydzi mają silną reprezentację. Organizacja ocalonych więźniów obozów koncentracyjnych, która ma swą siedzibę w Belgii, także strzeże, co jest zrozumiałe, swojego prawa do publicznego zabierania głosu. Jerozolimski Instytut Yad Vashem dysponuje bez wątpienia największą wiedzą i autorytetem moralnym, które uprawniają go do udzielania rad w tej sprawie. Ponadto różne amerykańskie instytucje używają swoich wpływów (i pieniędzy), aby wywierać naciski na bieg spraw.

W maju 1990 roku niezależna grupa pisarzy i naukowców z dziewięciu krajów zjechała się do angielskiej miejscowości Yarnton Manor, gdzie, pod egidą oskfordzkiego ośrodka studiów hebraistycznych i w obecności przedstawicieli rządu polskiego, sformułowała zbiór wymagań i zaleceń, które obejmują ogólne zasady i praktyczne wskazówki dotyczące spraw obozu w Oświęcimiu.

Podobne forum zebrało się ostatnio w Krakowie i Oświęcimiu, aby skontrolować sposób wykonania „Deklaracji z Yarnton", jak również wprowadzić w życie i uaktualnić następny zestaw propozycji. Ponieważ prawo, a jednocześnie obowiązek utrzymywania muzeum w Oświęcimiu mają wyłącznie polskie władze, jest sprawą niezwykle istotną, aby udzielane przez stronę żydowską wskazówki były praktyczne, dobrze przemyślane, wykazywały dokładną znajomość warunków lokalnych oraz były kierowane z należytą delikatnością tam, gdzie mogą spotkać się z życzliwością i okazać się skuteczne. Pod tymi względami grupa z Yarnton i Krakowa posiada duże możliwości i ważną rolę do odegrania.

Pytania, które się tu pojawiają, są liczne i skomplikowane. Pozostawiając na boku kwestie filozoficzne, które stanowią kategorię samą w sobie, i poruszając jedynie sprawy polityczne należy zapytać: jaką historię ma przedstawiać muzeum i za pomocą jakich tekstów, obrazów, napisów, eksponatów ma to czynić? Pokazawszy, że więźniami Oświęcimia byli głównie Żydzi, w jaki sposób należy podkreślić rolę bardzo wielkiej liczby więźniów nieżydowskich? W jaki sposób zachować godność i powagę tego miejsca, znając charakter masowej turystyki? Jak przeciwdziałać trywializacji terenu, gdzie przybywają tysiące turystów z wszystkich krajów świata, którzy przecież chcą zjeść, odpocząć i szukają pamiątek, aby je zabrać ze sobą do domu? Jak zapewnić porządek i zadbać o odpowiednią postawę zwiedzających? Jak powstrzymać ludzi przed umieszczaniem w różnych miejscach tego ogromnego i trudnego do skontrolowania terenu własnych znaków, tabliczek czy symboli (niewątpliwie w najczystszych intencjach)? Jest to sprawa niezmiernie drażliwa. Dla chrześcijan

---

izraelskiej, wygłosił przed „barakiem żydowskim" w Oświęcimiu wzruszającą przemowę do grupy żołnierzy i dzieci szkolnych z Izraela: „Przyjechaliśmy tu 50 lat za późno... Jedynie silne państwo żydowskie i silna armia żydowska są w stanie zagwarantować, że nie zdarzy się to Żydom ponownie" (przyp. aut.).

krzyż jest znakiem miłości i nadziei: jak sprawić, by zrozumieli, że dla większości Żydów symbolizuje on tyranię, prześladowanie, triumfalizm Kościoła, zamiary nawrócenia „braci odłączonych"? Czy będą oni w stanie dostrzec, że umieszczanie znaku krzyża na tym uważanym przez Żydów za cmentarz miejscu uderza w najczulszą strunę żydowskiej duszy? W jaki sposób kształcić przewodników, którzy muszą codziennie, ze wszystkimi szczegółami opowiadać ponurą historię tego miejsca? Jak mogą oni zachować świeżość i szczerość spojrzenia i uniknąć znieczulenia czy obojętności? Stojąc tam, gdzie znajdowały się komory gazowe i chcąc zostać przy zdrowych zmysłach trzeba z całej siły powstrzymywać obrazy, które pchają się ze wszech stron. Czy i w jakiej formie widz lub pielgrzym otrzymuje informacje na temat kultury i społeczeństwa żydowskiego: w co wierzyły te miliony zamordowanych ludzi, kim oni byli, co stworzyli i co świat utracił wraz z ich zniknięciem?

Wreszcie rozważmy problemy związane z zachowaniem i renowacją samego obozu i znajdujących się tam obiektów. Przez lata ulegały one powoli zniszczeniu, rozpadały się, gniły, znikały z powierzchni. Jak sobie z tym radzić? Wieże strażnicze na przykład, najbardziej charakterystyczna cecha ponurego krajobrazu obozowego, zostały w całości odbudowane przy pomocy nowych materiałów i w ten sposób straciły swoją autentyczność. Czy była to niewłaściwa decyzja? Przecież inaczej rozsypałyby się całkowicie... Czy jest to precedensowy przypadek, który należy naśladować czy też unikać? Druty kolczaste otaczające cały obwód obozu przerdzewiały i wkrótce nie będzie po nich śladu. Zastąpić je nowymi czy może za wszelką cenę zachować w obecnym kształcie? A co z najbardziej wymownymi i bolesnymi eksponatami, które znajdują się w oszklonych gablotach: ludzkie włosy, stosy butów, walizek z nazwiskami zmieniają kolor, pleśnieją, gniją. Co można z nimi zrobić?

A co zrobić ze stosami cegieł, które stanowią ruiny komór gazowych i krematoriów, wysadzonych przez Niemców? Odbudować je w oryginalnym kształcie? Zakonserwować je tak, aby pozostały w dzisiejszym stanie? A może pozostawić sprawy naturalnemu biegowi rzeczy? Połowa jednego z oryginalnych drewnianych baraków z Brzezinki została zabrana i przewieziona do Narodowego Muzeum Zagłady Żydów w Waszyngtonie. Jeżeli zostawiono by barak na miejscu, zapewne uległby zniszczeniu — tak się argumentuje — a tam ma lepsze warunki. Czy jest to akt pobożności czy też wandalizmu kulturowego? Wobec całkowitego zamętu w obliczu tych trudnych dylematów ciśnie się na usta pytanie: czy to wszystko ma jakiekolwiek znaczenie?

Grupa z Yarnton i Krakowa wystąpiła z szeregiem konstruktywnych propozycji. Aby zrealizować choćby niektóre z nich potrzeba funduszy i to bardzo znacznych. Polski rząd obiecał przeznaczyć na to pewne pieniądze, ale z powodów aż nadto oczywistych nie można się zbyt wiele tutaj spodziewać. Padają sugestie, aby zwrócić się do UNESCO: przecież obóz w Oświęcimiu znajduje się na liście światowego dziedzictwa kultury, ale figuruje tam jako jedna z wielu konkurujących ze sobą instytucji. W Stanach Zjednoczonych wydaje się miliony dolarów na coraz to nowe Muzea Zagłady. Czy chwila racjonalnego myślenia nie wystarczy, aby zdać sobie sprawę, gdzie należy najpierw skierować takie fundusze?[1]

Tłum. *Wł. Chłopicki*

„Jewish Quarterly" Nr 146, lato 1992

---

[1] Holokaust jest najlepiej udokumentowanym wydarzeniem w historii, a dotyczące go dowody i źródła są niekontrowersyjne i dostępne w ogromnej ilości. Tych niewielu kłamców czy szaleńców, którzy nie chcą poznać prawdy i zaprzeczają jej, może irytować, ale nie są oni niebezpieczni, chyba że dla siebie samych. Wyleczyłaby ich jedna wizyta w Oświęcimiu, gdyby tylko ośmielili się tam pojechać (przyp. aut.).

Naród szczególny

Wiadomo, jak ogromny wkład we współczesną kulturę europejską przypisywany jest Żydom lub osobom pochodzenia żydowskiego. Warto więc zastanowić się, jakie były źródła bogactwa tej twórczości, kim byli ludzie, którzy przyczynili się do jej rozkwitu, na jakim gruncie i w jakim klimacie rosło to zjawisko.

Próba odpowiedzi na te pytania na kilku stronach tekstu przypomina próbę przelewania oceanu łyżką do herbaty, ale daje możliwość przekazania przynajmniej jakiejś maleńkiej części wiedzy o tym zagadnieniu. Zacznijmy więc tak:

W dawnych czasach w dorzeczach Odry, Wisły, Niemna, Dniepru i Dniestru mieszkał naród zupełnie różny od innych narodów — Żydzi. Przybywali do tej części świata stopniowo, przez wieki, bardzo różnymi drogami: niektórzy z Hiszpanii i Portugalii, niektórzy z Zachodu, niektórzy z Azji i Afryki. Rozeszli się po ogromnym obszarze i różniło ich od siebie wiele cech. Mieli też jednak szereg ważnych cech wspólnych: byli wszyscy uchodźcami, ich przodkowie zostali wygnani z dawnej swojej ojczyzny, Ziemi Świętej, los zmuszał ich do życia w rozproszeniu wśród innych narodów, które uważały, że mają większe prawo do swojej ziemi i przeważnie traktowały ich jak intruzów.

W historii ludzkości inne grupy etniczne narażone na podobne przejścia dawno zniknęły z mapy świata, mieszając się z innymi rasami i narodami, a Żydzi jakimś cudem przeżyli. Z samego już tego faktu niektórzy wyprowadzają wniosek, że Bóg istnieje, ale patrząc na to racjonalnie, trzeba poszukać innych przyczyn. Był nią m.in. fakt, że Żydów łączyła jedna religia, która wyróżniała ich od innych starożytnych narodów, wiara w Jedynego Boga, oparta na Księdze, którą nazywali Torą — na Biblii, która nie tylko jest największym dziełem literatury światowej, ale także zawiera bardzo szczegółowe nakazy dotyczące sposobu życia i czci Boga. Księga zapewnia Żydów, że są Bożym Ludem Wybranym — nawet jeżeli oznaczałoby to wybranie do cierpienia. Księga zawiera również obietnicę zbawienia, na końcu czasu, kiedy przyjdzie Mesjasz. Księga nakazała im także, aby byli „płodni i rozmnażali się", co czynili bardzo skutecznie.

Nie mieli zbyt wiele szacunku dla wytyczonych przez ludzi granic; niezależnie od tego jak nazywał się kraj ich osiedlenia — Bukowina czy Besarabia, Wołyń czy Podole, Galicja czy Litwa — gdy wzrastała tam siła prześladowań, przenosili się do miejsc, gdzie inni ich bracia mieszkali we względnym jeszcze spokoju. Często zyskiwali pewien rodzaj autonomii, tworzyli własne instytucje,

332

sądy, urzędy podatkowe, szkoły. Powstawały też słynne „jeszyboty", jedyne w swoim rodzaju akademie talmudyczne, gdzie podtrzymywano starodawną tradycję nieustannego prowadzenia nauczania w dzień i w nocy i gdzie zjeżdżali się studenci ze wszystkich stron, także z półkuli zachodniej.

Panował tam kult wiedzy, choć dla większości ograniczała się ona do znajomości Biblii, kodeksów prawa, komentarzy i pism rabinicznych. Analfabetyzm był zjawiskiem nieznanym, gdyż wszystkie dzieci żydowskie uczyły się czytać siedząc na kolanach swoich ojców. Status społeczny człowieka łączył się ściśle z jego wykształceniem, według zasady, że „mędrzec ma pierwszeństwo przed arcykapłanem". Przyczyniło się to bardzo do tak powszechnej wśród Żydów bystrości umysłu, nader przydatnej także w filozofii, nauce, literaturze, sztuce czy handlu.

Cechą dominującą i wyróżniającą mentalność tych ludzi był wysoki stopień uduchowienia — przekonanie, że „nie samym chlebem...", że niezależnie od warunków życiowych człowiek musi zawsze dążyć do jakiegoś wyższego ideału, jakkolwiek by go sobie określił. Wierzyli też w głębi duszy w ostateczną sprawiedliwość tego świata, które to przekonanie uległo chyba presji rzeczywistości, gdy ta w sposób aż nadto oczywisty okazała się zupełnie inna.

Jeśli duchowość można by uznać za jedną z ich cech charakterystycznych, to wzajemna niezgoda była z pewnością drugą. Przez całą swoją historię (aż do dnia dzisiejszego) Żydzi nie byli narodem zgodnym. Ich gminy często wstrząsały bratobójcze spory, wynikające z siły przekonań (niektórzy nazwaliby to fanatyzmem) i braku tolerancji, który często cechuje ludzi twierdzących, że słyszą głosy z nieba. Saduceusze zwalczali faryzeuszy, chasydzi — tzw. „mitnagdim"[1], syjoniści — bundowców, ortodoksi — reformistów, tradycjonaliści — zwolenników asymilacji, w Izraelu stronnictwo zdążające do porozumienia z Arabami jest w konflikcie ze stronnictwem, które w taki pokój nie wierzy. Żydzi nie byli narodem spokojnym: „nie spali sami i nie dawali spać innym".

Jednym z ich największych osiągnięć jest stworzenie własnego języka, jidysz, który mimo podziałów i granic państwowych umożliwił utrzymanie wspólnej tożsamości różnym odłamom narodu żydowskiego. Ocenia się, że w przededniu II wojny światowej językiem tym mówiło około 11 milionów ludzi na obszarze od Ukrainy po Holandię oraz w Stanach Zjednoczonych.

Jidysz jest dziwną mieszaniną języka niemieckiego, hebrajskiego, polskiego oraz, w pewnej niewielkiej części, języków innych narodów, wśród których Żydzi żyli. Dla nie przyzwyczajonego ucha język ten brzmi mało atrakcyjnie, wielu uważa go za żargon, niegodny miana języka. Był on jednak żywy, barwny i dowcipny, łatwo się adaptował. Jego gramatyka jest tak elastyczna, że trudno popełnić gramatyczny błąd (żeby tak inne języki posiadały ten dar!).

---

[1] *mitnagdim* (hebr.) — przeciwnicy, tutaj przeciwnicy chasydyzmu (przyp. aut.).

Używany był nie tylko jako język komunikacji ustnej, ale także jako język literacki. W jidysz wychodziły tysiące gazet, czasopism i druków ulotnych: drukarstwo stało się jedną z żydowskich specjalności obok rzemiosł takich, jak szewstwo, krawiectwo czy naprawa zegarków.

YIVO, Instytut Studiów Żydowskich założony w roku 1925 w Wilnie (obecnie mieści się w Nowym Jorku), posiada w swoich archiwach setki tysięcy książek, rękopisów, zbiorów sztuk teatralnych, listów, zdjęć i różnych przedmiotów odzyskanych w Niemczech po wojnie.

Literatura w języku jidysz była bardzo ważną, nieodłączną wręcz cechą życia Żydów. Teatr żydowski dał pole do działania tak znanym dramatopisarzom, jak Abraham Goldfaden[1] czy Szymon An-ski[2], którego sztuka *Dybuk* osiągnęła szeroką sławę. Literatura ta szczyci się wielkimi pisarzami, z których twórczości dumna byłaby każda inna nacja, takimi jak I. L. Perec, Szolem Alejchem, Mendełe Mojcher-Sforim[3] czy bracia Singerowie, z których młodszy, Izaac Bashevis, otrzymał Nagrodę Nobla i w ten sposób podniósł prestiż języka swojej twórczości. W czasie wojny w getcie warszawskim Izaak Kacenelson napisał w języku jidysz elegię na temat zagłady Żydów, która należy do najbardziej poruszających dokumentów naszego czasu.

Wszyscy z wyjątkiem Teodora Herzla ojcowie — założyciele syjonizmu: Weizman, Sokołow, Żabotyński, Borochow, Ben Gurion, Achad Haam — pochodzili z Europy Wschodniej, mówili na co dzień i wygłaszali przemówienia w języku jidysz; uważali oni jednak, że przyszły naród żydowski, o którego powstanie walczyli, powinien mieć język, który nie kojarzyłby się z biedą diaspory, ale sięgałby początków historii tego narodu w Palestynie. Zadanie odrodzenia martwego już hebrajskiego i przeciwstawienie go żyjącemu i dynamicznie rozwijającemu się językowi jidysz było niemal niemożliwe do wykonania. Fakt, że „święty język" hebrajski odniósł w tej bitwie zwycięstwo nad „macierzystym językiem" (*Mame-loszen*) jidysz i stał się obecnie symbolem tożsamości mieszkańców Izraela, językiem ojczystym wszystkich rodzących się tam dzieci (*sabras*) i jak za czasów biblijnych używany jest w życiu codziennym, w nauce oraz jako język religii, stanowi jeden z cudów związanych z odrodzeniem się państwa żydowskiego w dawnej jego ojczyźnie.

Mury oddzielające wspólnoty żydowskie od sąsiadującej z nimi ludności były grube i wysokie, ponieważ obydwie strony dbały o ich staranne utrzymanie. Ludność miejscowa w większości zupełnie nie wiedziała, jak naprawdę wyglądali Żydzi i żywiła się stereotypowym wyobrażeniem o nich jako o ludziach złych i posępnych. Społeczności żydowskie były skierowane „do we-

---

[1] Abraham Goldfaden (1840–1908), uważany za twórcę nowoczesnego teatru żydowskiego (przyp. tłum.).

[2] właśc. Szlojme-Zajnwel Rapoport (1863–1920), pisarz żydowski (przyp. tłum.).

[3] Mendełe — zob. przyp. na s. 232.

wnątrz", samowystarczalne, z wyjątkiem marginesowych sytuacji, gdy konieczność zarobku zmuszała ich do pojawiania się w świecie zewnętrznym. Czuli się (i mieli do tego powody) zagrożeni i zdani na łaskę nie zawsze życzliwie nastawionej ludności, wśród której żyli. Pogardę, jaką im okazywano, oddawali z nawiązką, mieli przy tym poczucie własnej wartości („kiedy tubylcy byli jeszcze na drzewach, Żydzi już cierpieli na cukrzycę"), i nawet najskromniejsi z nich nie chcieli, nawet gdyby mogli, zamienić się miejscami z książętami wrogiego im świata.

W drugiej połowie XVIII wieku, pod wpływem rzezi hajdamackich i zamieszek wywołanych fałszywym mesjanizmem i ruchem kabalistycznym Sabbataja Cwi[1] i Jakuba Franka[2], na południowo-wschodnim pograniczu Rzeczpospolitej Obojga Narodów narodził się nowy ruch religijny nazwany chasydyzmem. Wśród Żydów idee rozchodzą się zwykle bardzo szybko, dlatego chasydyzm rozprzestrzenił się po Europie Wschodniej niemal z szybkością pożaru. Celem tego ruchu była odnowa judaizmu poprzez powrót do tradycyjnie żydowskich zasad miłości i radości życia. W roku 1900 na świecie było już ponad milion chasydów, w tym niemal jedna trzecia żydostwa polskiego. W trakcie dwustu lat swojej historii ruch chasydów zrodził 1500 charyzmatycznych przywódców-nauczycieli, wybitnych praktyków tego ruchu, tzw. cadyków, którzy przyciągali do swoich „dworów" oddanych im zwolenników.

W czasie gdy Żydzi w tej części świata mieli mało powodów do radości, chasydzi czerpali i głosili radość po prostu z bycia Żydem i z wykonywania codziennych obowiązków. W przeciwieństwie do tradycyjnego poglądu głoszącego wyższość wykształcenia, chasydzi dawali każdemu Żydowi, nawet najbardziej biednemu i niewykształconemu, równe prawa w zjednoczeniu z Bogiem, w mistycznej łączności i ekstatycznym transie modlitwy, w który wchodziło się przez gwałtowne ruchy ciała, krzyk i śpiew.

Założyciel tego rewolucyjnego ruchu Baal Szem Tow[3] głosił, że istota religii polega na uczuciu, nie na rozumie, że szczegóły ceremonii religijnych nie są istotne, że żyć i służyć Bogu należy w nastroju radości i szczęścia. Życie Żydów polskich i rosyjskich stało się więc radośniejsze, podupadło natomiast pod względem intelektualnym. Opowiadanie o wielkich, cudownych czynach cadyków stało się czynnością niemal nieustanną, wzmacniającą energię życiową, stymulującą wyobraźnię, właściwie rodzajem nabożeństwa. Martin Buber, natchniony pisarz, myśliciel i przywódca duchowy, zebrał i spisał opowieści

---

[1] Sabbataj Cwi (1625–1676), oryginalny myśliciel i kabalista żydowski żyjący w Palestynie, uznawany przez wielu za Mesjasza, pod groźbą śmierci przeszedł na islam (przyp. tłum.).

[2] Jakub Frank (Józef baron von Dobrucki) (1726–1791), założyciel żydowskiego ugrupowania religijnego frankistów, przyjechał w 1755 roku na Podole i ogłosił się Mesjaszem. Zwalczany przez ortodoksję żydowską, przyjął chrzest (przyp. tłum.).

[3] właśc. Izrael ben Eliezer, znany także jako Beszt (ok. 1700–1760), mistyk żydowski z Podola, cudotwórca i uzdrowiciel, założyciel ruchu chasydów (przyp. tłum.).

chasydów, które stanowią osobny gatunek literacki. Chasydyzm, choć taka intencja była jak najdalsza od zamiarów chasydów, stworzył więc klimat sprzyjający rozkwitowi sztuki.

Dziwnym językowym zbiegiem okoliczności, w encyklopediach żydowskich po słowie „chasydyzm" następuje zaraz słowo „haskala" (które oznacza mniej więcej to samo co „Oświecenie"). Jest to przypadek jak najbardziej odpowiedni nie tylko w sensie językowym, ale także historycznym. Pod koniec XVIII wieku nazwany tak nowy ruch powstał i rozpowszechnił się wśród Żydów wschodnioeuropejskich. Jego celem było, po pierwsze, zastąpienie studium Talmudu współczesnymi przedmiotami, ze szczególnym naciskiem na poezję hebrajską i krytykę literatury w języku hebrajskim. Po drugie, ruch ten wydał walkę obskurantyzmowi, zabobonom i chasydyzmowi, zachęcał Żydów do podejmowania pracy na roli i rzemiosła, do porzucenia izolacjonizmu, do poznawania wiedzy, obyczajów i aspiracji narodów, wśród których mieszkali. „Ojciec *haskali*", niemiecki filozof i pisarz Mojżesz Mendelssohn, kierował więc Żydów w stronę „szerokiego gościńca kultury ludzkości".

Gaon z Wilna[1], jeden z wielkich przywódców duchowych swoich czasów i zaciekły przeciwnik chasydyzmu, był także przeciwnikiem *haskali*. Słusznie przewidywał, że ten pierwszy krok na drodze tzw. postępu doprowadzi wielu Żydów do asymilacji, a nawet, o zgrozo, do przyjęcia chrztu (ta obawa nie była obca także Mendelssohnowi).

Żydzi byli gotowi, aby przyjąć korzystny dla siebie ruch Oświecenia i równouprawnienia narodów, który zaświtał nad Europą. Wraz z jego rozprzestrzenieniem się i przynajmniej formalnym zagwarantowaniem Żydom w większości krajów równych praw obywatelskich, zaczęli oni wychodzić z izolacji i wkroczyli na światową scenę. Ten proces sprzecznych często ze sobą pociągnięć, wyzwań i konfliktów prowadził do zaciekłych wewnętrznych sporów we wspólnotach żydowskich, ale wyzwolenie talentu i spętanej dotychczas energii przybyszów wkrótce wywarło potężny wpływ na każdą sferę życia całego świata. Jeśli pojawiłby się wtedy jakiś ówczesny Goebbels i chciałby oddzielić „żydowski" wkład do kultury od wkładu innych, nie miałby łatwego zadania. Trudno mówić o kulturze współczesnej bez tego właśnie wkładu: bez tego wiecznego buntownika, outsidera, dysydenta — Żyda właśnie.

Można by przeglądać się w blasku chwały bardzo wielu żydowskich artystów i ludzi kultury, którzy niezmiernie wzbogacili dorobek ludzkości; wszyscy — od Antokolskiego[2] do Zadkina[3] i od Babla do Zamenhofa — wywodzili się z okolic Odessy i Czerniowiec, Witebska i Warszawy.

---

[1] Gaon z Wilna — zob. przyp. na s. 233.
[2] Mark Antokolski (1843-1902), rzeźbiarz rosyjski (przyp. tłum.).
[3] Ossip Zadkine (1890-1967), ur. w Rosji francuski rzeźbiarz kubista (przyp. tłum.).

Chaim Nachman Bialik[1], największy ze współczesnych poetów hebrajskich, zwykł był narzekać, że tyle talentu żydowskiego przypisywanego jest „gojom". Nie musiał jednak się obawiać, nie powinien żałować — przecież wystarczy go dla wszystkich. Na tym polega błogosławieństwo sztuki — nikt przez nią nie ubożeje, a wszyscy się bogacą.

Warto także wspomnieć, że wśród odbiorców sztuki, wśród tych, którzy tworzyli klimat zainteresowania i popytu, bez których podaż nie miałaby sensu, wśród tych, którzy kupowali, propagowali i rozpowszechniali dzieła sztuki, czytali książki, chodzili do teatrów i na koncerty, zawsze była nieproporcjonalnie wysoka liczba Żydów. To także stanowi wkład trudny do przecenienia.

… i wtedy powstał na Zachodzie potężny przywódca, Hitler, który stał się głową narodu niemieckiego. Głosił ewangelię nienawiści wobec Żydów i ślubował ich zniszczenie. Jego armie najechały i zdobyły ziemie, gdzie żyła większość z nich i Żydzi ginęli całymi milionami. W ciągu kilku lat świat europejskich Żydów, cała ich tysiącletnia cywilizacja, zostały zniszczone i już nie istnieją. Te słowa wypowiedzieć łatwo, ale ich znaczenie trudne jest do rozumowego ogarnięcia.

My zaś, którzy pozostajemy w nieustannej żałobie po zaginionym świecie, szukamy pocieszenia w myśleniu i pisaniu o tym nieporównywalnym z niczym dziedzictwie, które dziś pozostało nam i całej ludzkości.

Tłum. *Wł. Chłopicki*

Referat wygłoszony w roku 1993 w Spiro Institute w Londynie

---

[1] Ur. w 1873 w Żytomierzu, zmarł w 1934 r. w Tel-Awiwie, poeta, eseista i tłumacz na język hebrajski (przyp. tłum.).

Nauczyciel

Cywilizację Żydów we wschodniej Europie tworzyli uczeni-amatorzy, znakomicie obyci z żydowskim piśmiennictwem religijnym, z tekstami obszernymi i skomplikowanymi. A jednak dla większości z nich, z wyjątkiem rabinów, studia mogły być tylko zajęciem marginalnym, rodzajem hobby, gdyż ich dzień skrzętnie wypełniało zarabianie na życie. Utrzymanie rodziny było nadrzędnym obowiązkiem każdego ojca.

Antoni Słonimski (wnuk Seliga Słonimskiego, założyciela i wydawcy pierwszego w Polsce czasopisma w języku hebrajskim „Hatsefira") w jednym ze swych wierszy opisuje *sztetł* jako „miejsce, gdzie szewc był poetą, zegarmistrz filozofem, a fryzjer trubadurem".

Znałem wiele takich postaci, ale jedna zajmuje szczególne miejsce w mojej pamięci. Bencjon Rappaport — nauczyciel, który uczył mnie w hebrajskiej szkole w Krakowie, gdzie przedmioty hebrajskie, takie jak Biblia, historia i literatura żydowska były prowadzone na równi z programem polskim. Bencjon Rappaport był jednym z kilku hebrajskich nauczycieli w tej szkole.

Jego specjalnością były studia biblijne, ale powszechnie wiedziano, choć on sam nie przywiązywał do tego wagi, że posiadał ogromną znajomość rozmaitych przedmiotów. Znajdował się w trudnej sytuacji, gdyż odstępstwo od tradycyjnego, ortodoksyjnego nauczania mogło zagrozić jego posadzie, a jednak za wszelką cenę chciał zaszczepić w nas ducha wolnej, śmiałej i pozbawionej uprzedzeń dociekliwości. Ważniejsze niż same lekcje, które prowadził dosłownie z nosem w książce (był krótkowidzem), podczas gdy my oddawaliśmy się hałaśliwym zajęciom, były dyskusje po dzwonku na przerwę. Wtedy mógł swobodniej wypowiadać swoje opinie, a my szybko nauczyliśmy się to wykorzystywać. „Nie musicie wierzyć dosłownie w każde słowo Pisma Świętego, aby stać się dobrymi i prawowiernymi Żydami" — mawiał do nas (kiedy słyszeliśmy te słowa później, w innych miejscach?).

Pamiętam, jak pewnego razu przed świętem Paschy czytaliśmy Hagadę, a Rappaport tłumaczył nam cud „rozstąpienia się mórz" — *Yam suf*. To, co nazywamy Morzem Czerwonym, mówił, jest oczywiście „morzem trzcin", wodami gęsto porośniętymi sitowiem i papirusem. Żydzi przeszli je łatwo nawet obciążeni bogactwem. Natomiast Egipcjanie, którzy użyli w pościgu ciężkich rydwanów, utonęli.

Któryś z nas musiał to widocznie powtórzyć w domu, bo wkrótce przyszedł zirytowany rodzic żalić się, że Rappaport uczy nas braku wiary w cuda. Nasz nauczyciel bronił się:

„Czy Exodus stanie się mniejszym cudem w wyniku takiego tłumaczenia? A czy Mojżesz będzie gorszym prorokiem, ponieważ nie rozdzielił dosłownie morza, ale znał najlepszy sposób by się przezeń przeprawić?"

Pamiętam, że podczas jednej z takich dyskusji powiedziałem z pewnością przemądrzałego nastolatka:

„Nie ma nic łatwiejszego niż zwyczajne zaakceptowanie wiary w całości, bo po prostu ktoś tak to przekazał".

Pokręcił wtedy pobłażliwie głową.

„Istnieje rzecz jeszcze łatwiejsza — łatwe odrzucenie. Możesz nie wierzyć, być obrazoburcą lub agnostykiem, jeśli chcesz. Ale nie płytkim, powierzchownym. W obu przypadkach to właśnie powierzchowność jest niegodziwa".

Pamiętam również, że zapytałem go kiedyś:

„Chwaląc uczonego człowieka mówi się czasami: on zna *Szas*, czyli wszystkie sześć ksiąg Miszny na pamięć. W mojej rodzinie mówi się tak o moim dziadku. Z pewnością to jest przenośnia i nie można traktować tego dosłownie? Żaden ludzki umysł nie byłby w stanie zapamiętać milionów słów i przywoływać je na żądanie, zwłaszcza że nie są one uporządkowaną sekwencją jak role aktora, lecz często są ułożone całkiem przypadkowo. Przecież to jest niemożliwe, prawda?"

Rappaport wziął głęboki oddech.

„Rozumiem twój sceptycyzm, ale chcę cię zapewnić, że jest to możliwe. Wymaga to oczywiście nie tylko talentu i zamiłowania, ale przede wszystkim studiowania, dzień i noc, ślęczenia nad tekstami w przekonaniu, że one interpretują słowo Boże. Są ludzie, którzy tego dokonali i — tu uśmiechnął się nieśmiało — ja sam już byłem blisko..."

Ogarnął mnie wielki podziw i uścisnąłem go, a on mnie pobłogosławił.

To Rappaport przygotowywał mnie do *bar micwy*[1]. Przychodziłem do niego do domu — pokoju z kuchnią, pełnych książek ustawionych na podłodze — by się nauczyć, jak założyć *tefilin*, jak czytać fragment Tory, które modlitwy odmówić rano. Napisał dla mnie również *drasha*, przemowę, której nauczyłem się na pamięć i wygłosiłem przed wiernymi. Była ułożona w pięknym języku hebrajskim. Pamiętam ją do dzisiaj i jest to mój popisowy numer podczas szkolnych zjazdów w Izraelu.

Następnego ranka po ceremonii w synagodze, przed pójściem do szkoły, przystąpiłem do odmawiania *szacharit*, porannej modlitwy dorosłych. Jest ona długa i zajmuje sporo czasu. Z haftowanej torby wyjąłem *tefilin*, który założyłem jak mnie uczono, otworzyłem modlitewnik i zacząłem czytać werset za wersetem, strona po stronie. Po raz pierwszy w życiu spóźniłem się do szkoły. Moja matka z rosnącą niecierpliwością i niepokojem zauważyła, że sytuacja ta

---

[1] *bar micwa* — w judaizmie obrzęd inicjacji 13-letnich chłopców przyjmujących wszystkie obowiązki dorosłych mężczyzn (przyp. wyd.).

powtarza się w następnych dniach. Nie chciała, żebym przestał się modlić. Z drugiej strony obawiała się, że wcześniejsza pobudka nie poprawi sprawy i prawdopodobnie zniechęci mnie do modlitw. Co miała więc robić? Poszła zasięgnąć rady u Rappaporta.

Wziął mnie na bok i powiedział mi coś, czego nigdy nie zapomniałem.

„Drogi chłopcze — rzekł — pamiętaj, że chodzenie do szkoły i nauka są również rodzajem czci, która w równym stopniu, a może nawet bardziej niż modlitwa cieszy Boga. Spóźnianie się do szkoły jest zniewagą Boga. Wiem, że *szacharit*, poranna modlitwa jest długa — może nawet za długa dla tak młodych ludzi, kto wie? Musimy ją skrócić, żebyś przychodził do szkoły punktualnie. Musimy wyciągnąć z niej samą istotę, to, co najważniejsze. A najważniejszą rzeczą jest pytanie, które człowiek zadaje sobie, kiedy wznosi oczy do nieba: *Ma chovato b'olamo* — jakie jest moje zadanie w tym świecie? Każdego ranka, zanim rozpoczniesz nowy dzień, zadaj sobie to pytanie, ale tak poważnie, nie od niechcenia. Ponawiaj pytanie każdego dnia i zastanów się nad nim przez minutę. Nie próbuj na nie odpowiadać — nie ma krótkiej odpowiedzi, nie nadejdzie ona szybko, może nawet nigdy, ale to nie ma znaczenia. Istotne jest, aby zdać sobie sprawę, że to ważne pytanie, że masz do wykonania jakieś zadanie i musisz je odszukać. Po prostu zastanów się nad tym. A potem idź do szkoły — punktualnie".

To prawda, że od tego dnia nigdy już nie założyłem *tefilin* i w pewnym sensie można mówić, że to Rappaport sprowadził mnie z właściwej drogi. Ale ja uważam wręcz przeciwnie, że otrzymałem pełną lekcję moralności. A jeżeli czasem, lub często, nie stosuję się do niej, to przynajmniej wiem, że ja znam i mam świadomość swoich zaniedbań.

Istnieje jeszcze inny powód, dlaczego nigdy nie zapomnę Rappaporta. To był czerwiec 1945. Koniec wojny zastał mnie w armii brytyjskiej w Norwegii. Byłem wtedy sierżantem w Korpusie Wywiadu, a do moich obowiązków należało przesłuchiwanie jeńców niemieckich w celu wyłapania przestępców wojennych zanim zostaliby repatriowani do ojczyzny. Tam dosięgła mnie wiadomość, że moja matka cudem przeżyła wojnę. Niemal natychmiast znalazłem się w samolocie do Niemiec, do głównej kwatery Brytyjskiej Armii Renu, gdzie zdobyłem służbowy samochód z kierowcą (wymagało to pewnych zabiegów, ale nic nie mogło mnie powstrzymać) i wyruszyłem w drogę przez Warszawę do Krakowa. Jechaliśmy przez Zagłębie Ruhry i muszę przyznać, że serce mi podskoczyło z radości na widok zniszczeń dokonanych na tym terenie przez alianckie lotnictwo. Ale gdy przyjechałem do Warszawy, a raczej do miejsca, które miało nią być, i zobaczyłem sterty gruzu ciągnącego się kilometrami i krajobraz rozorany dołami niczym księżycowe kratery, to zrozumiałem, że w porównaniu z tym zbombardowanie Ruhry było igraszką.

Jednym z budynków, które ocalały w centrum Warszawy, był hotel Polonia, gdzie ulokowała się ambasada brytyjska. Tam się zatrzymałem, aby się zameldować i przy okazji wziąć kartki na benzynę na dalszą podróż.

W holu hotelowym kręcił się tłum ludzi, którzy przepychając się i poszturchując załatwiali różne interesy. I nagle stanęło mi serce — dostrzegłem w tym tłumie znajomą twarz, mojego szkolnego kolegę! Gdy już się wyściskaliśmy — powiedział, że właśnie przyjechał z Palestyny w poszukiwaniu ocalałych.

Kiedy tak gorączkowo rozmawialiśmy wymieniając informacje o wspólnych przyjaciołach, podszedł do nas polski chłop, który przyglądał się nam od dłuższej chwili. „Jesteście Żydami?" — zapytał. „Tak, jesteśmy" — odparliśmy.

Wtedy wyjął z kieszeni na piersiach plik papierów, kartek z zeszytu zapisanych po hebrajsku atramentem, który zdążył już wyblaknąć. Do tego dołączony był skrawek papieru napisany po polsku: „Pobożna duszo, to jest dzieło życia człowieka. Złóż to w dobre ręce".

Spojrzawszy na hebrajski manuskrypt nie mogliśmy uwierzyć własnym oczom. Okazało się, że były to pisma Bencjona Rappaporta, które wyrzucił w szczere pole z okna pociągu wiozącego go do obozu śmierci w Bełżcu. Człowiek, który teraz stał przed nami, znalazł ten plik, odcyfrował polecenie napisane po polsku i pieczołowicie przechował cały manuskrypt. Po zakończeniu wojny przyjechał do Warszawy w poszukiwaniu Żydów, którym mógłby go przekazać. Nie było to łatwe zadanie, ale w końcu w zatłoczonym hotelu Polonia dostrzega dwóch Żydów — byłych uczniów Bencjona Rappaporta.

Oczywiście dopilnowaliśmy, żeby rękopis został opublikowany w Izraelu. Książka nosi tytuł *Teva v'ruach* (*Natura i duch*). Jest zbiorem esejów sławiących niemiecką filozofię, Hegla, Kanta, Schopenhauera i zawiera również rozważania Rappaporta na temat religii, etyki, metod naukowego dochodzenia.

Czyż to nie horror, litość i ironia razem wzięte…

Tłum. *M. Lohman*

„Judaism Today" Nr 1, wiosna 1995

Poszukiwanie książki
Od Przemyśla do British Library

Rodzina mojego Ojca pochodzi z Oświęcimia (*Oszpicyn* w języku jidysz), małego miasteczka przezwanego przez Niemców Auschwitz, którego nazwa stała się najbardziej ponurym słowem we wszystkich niemal językach. Mój ojciec był jednym z piętnaściorga dzieci, w Oświęcimiu żyły setki Scharfów, wśród nich wielu rabinów, co dodawało splendoru rodowemu nazwisku, a także, co naturalne, trochę łotrzyków, którzy temu nazwisku czci ujmowali. Ale postać, o której się mówiło z respektem i dumą, należała do poprzedniej generacji — był to rabin Mosze Jakow Jekel Scharf, urodzony w roku 1784, zmarły w 1869, „oficjalny" rabin Oświęcimia przez lat 50. Należenie do jego bezpośrednich następców było wyróżnieniem (*jichus*), jak powtarzał mi ciągle Ojciec, obowiązkiem, z którego trzeba się wywiązać.

Rabinów nazywano często nie nazwiskami, ale tytułem książki, jaką napisali, np. *Megale Amukot* czy *Chofec Chaim*.

Książki Mosze Jakowa stały oczywiście na półkach w naszym salonie, pośród innych wielkich dzieł religijnych (*seforim*), oprawnych w charakterystyczne nakrapiane, żółto-brązowe okładki. Pamiętam zwłaszcza jeden cienki tomik z jasnoczerwonymi i złotymi literami na okładce. Ojciec patrzył na niego z tkliwością i od czasu do czasu przechodząc gładził jego grzbiet. Nie żeby rozumiał wiele z tego tekstu, nie o to chodziło: wiedział, że ta książka i wszystkie pozostałe należały do innego świata i tworzyły wartości duchowe, dzięki którym życie nabierało sensu.

Tak więc pamiętałem zawsze, gdzie ta książka stała, jej grzbiet i oprawę, ale muszę się przyznać, że zapomniałem jej tytułu i nie mogłem, wtedy gdy przychodził czas po temu, się nią szczycić. Nękało mnie to przez lata, ponieważ moja pamięć nie jest generalnie poniżej przeciętnej i pamiętam dokładnie tysiące banalnych szczegółów z tamtego czasu. Ale zapomniałem tytułu dzieła mojego prapradziadka — wstyd!

Oczywiście istniał sposób na odnalezienie go, ale byłem zbyt wielkim ignorantem, żeby o nim pomyśleć. Bernard Friedberg (1876–1961), mój rodak z Krakowa (tak, tych można znaleźć wszędzie), opublikował, poza innymi ważnymi pracami dotyczącymi wydawnictw literatury hebrajskiej, leksykon bibliograficzny *Beit Eked Sefarim* w czterech tomach, który stanowi kompetentne i niezbędne dzieło z tej dziedziny i, jak dziś już wiem, omawia także książki (proszę zauważyć liczbę mnogą) Mosze Jakowa Scharfa.

Duch jednak działa w sposób tajemniczy i pewnego dnia wpadła mi w ręce mała książeczka zatytułowana *Od Oświęcimia do Auschwitz — jeszcze raz o Polsce* autorstwa rabina Mosze Weissa[1]. Rabin Weiss mieszka dziś w Kanadzie, ale urodził się w Oświęcimiu i często podróżuje do Polski, odwiedzając różne miejsca w poszukiwaniu śladów żydowskiego życia i pozostałych jeszcze Żydów, którym niesie pomoc i pocieszenie. Opisując swoją niedawną wizytę w Oświęcimiu wspomina, że Mosze Jakow Scharf, uczeń cadyka z Sącza (Sanzer Cadyk) był tam rabinem przez lat 50 i, jaka wspaniała niespodzianka, wspomina tytuł jego książki: *Darkei Jojscher*!

Zobaczywszy go tak nagle, czarno na białym, doznałem jakby olśnienia: tak, oczywiście *Darkei Jojscher*! Jak mogłem zapomnieć, *Darkei Jojscher* — „Drogi sprawiedliwych".

Ponieważ zdarzyło się to w poniedziałek, dzień, w którym chodzę na lekcje (*shi'ur*) Talmudu do rabina Louisa Jacobsa, powiedziałem mu o mojej wielkiej radości z dokonania ponownego odkrycia tego tytułu. Następnego dnia rano zadzwonił do mnie i powiedział mi, że książka ma 192 strony i że została wydana w Przemyślu w roku 1872. Dodał, że przypuszcza, iż egzemplarz tej książki może znajdować się w posiadaniu British Library w Londynie.

Przyznam, że uznałem to za wysoce nieprawdopodobne: jakim cudem mała hebrajska książeczka, wydana przed ponad 120 laty w Przemyślu w nakładzie 200, może 300 egzemplarzy, mogła się znaleźć na półkach British Library?

Chcąc tam pojechać, wygrzebałem moją starą kartę do czytelni British Museum — a z tym wiąże się następna historia. Przyjechałem do Londynu z Krakowa zaraz przed wybuchem II wojny światowej, i pamiętam bardzo wyraźnie jak pierwszego dnia po przyjeździe stanąłem na schodach prowadzących do British Museum i uszczypnąłem się, żeby się przekonać, czy przypadkiem nie śnię, że naprawdę jestem w Anglii, w Londynie, przy wejściu do tej wspaniałej świątyni wiedzy.

Poszedłem do biura i od razu złożyłem wniosek o kartę czytelnika, co uzasadniłem następująco: jestem dziennikarzem, korespondentem zagranicznym gazety w Krakowie, a także studentem w London School of Economics, gdzie miałem zamiar ukończyć rozpoczętą na Uniwersytecie Jagiellońskim pracę doktorską. Wszedłem do wielkiej, okrągłej sali czytelni i wydawało mi się, że znalazłem się w raju. Pomyślałem, że z przyjemnością spędziłbym tu resztę życia.

Przeszkodziły temu wydarzenia na światowej scenie politycznej — nie było tam miejsca na takie miłe marzenia. Moje życie obrało inną drogę i lata minęły mi na innych zajęciach. Ale trzydzieści kilka lat później, gdy po przejściu na emeryturę stanąłem znów w biurze muzeum wypełniając wniosek o wydanie

---

[1] *From Oświęcim to Auschwitz — Poland Revisited*, Mosaic Press, Oakville, Ontario, Kanada (przyp. aut.).

karty czytelnika, serce zabiło mi nostalgicznie. Ostatnie pytanie tego formularza brzmiało: „Czy miał Pan kiedykolwiek kartę czytelnika Biblioteki?"

„Tak", powiedziałem żartobliwie do pracownika stojącego za ladą. „Miałem już kiedyś kartę, przed wojną". I machnąłem swoją starą, wypłowiałą kartą, którą zachowałem jako pamiątkę.

„Wobec tego nie potrzebuje Pan nowej karty, wystarczy odnowić tę" — powiedział pracownik, zupełnie poważnie.

„To było bardzo dawno temu" — zająknąłem się.

„Dla muzeum to nie tak dawno" — powiedział, wziął ode mnie kartę i tam, gdzie było wolne miejsce, pod poprzednimi pieczątkami „10 lipca 1940" i „31 stycznia 1941", przybił pieczątkę „14 grudnia 1972".

Przechowuję tę kartę jak rzadki dokument, jakby eksponat muzealny. Wydaje mi się ona czymś ogromnie sympatycznym i pocieszającym. 30 lat później, 30 kilometrów półek dalej, w środku II wojna światowa, imperia powstały i upadły, świat zmienił się nie do poznania, a ten człowiek mówi: „Dla muzeum to nie tak dawno".

Tak więc ze swoją odnowioną kartą w ręce udałem się do czytelni. Książek hebrajskich nie przechowuje się już w głównym budynku w dzielnicy Bloomsbury, ale w Orbit House w pobliżu mostu Blackfriars. Poszedłem tam i wręczyłem swoją prośbę bibliotekarce, pani Ilanie Tahan. Ta przycisnęła kilka klawiszy w komputerze — chwila napięcia — tak, książka jest w katalogu i jest dostępna. Kilka minut potem pojawia się na stoliku przede mną.

Dotykałem jej z czułością, ogarnięty dziwnym uczuciem. Była przede mną, jakby przyleciała z mojego dawnego domu, wycinek życia, którego już nie ma. Półki z książkami religijnymi, *seforim*, stały w tysiącach żydowskich domów, nie tylko w mieszkaniach rodzin ortodoksyjnych, gdzie często zajmowały niemal połowę przestrzeni życiowej, ale w wielu zwykłych domach, gdzie nie były już otwierane, lecz stanowiły jakby naturalne tło, bez którego w pokoju było zimno i pusto. Jeżeli do tego dodać książki w synagogach, jeszybotach i *sztiblach*[1] w całym kraju, jasne jest, że mówimy o ogromnych liczbach, o milionach książek. Jest to miarą zniszczenia, wykorzenienia cywilizacji, jeśli nie można dziś w Polsce znaleźć żadnych hebrajskich książek religijnych, chyba że przypadkiem na jakiejś giełdzie staroci trafi się na pojedynczy potargany egzemplarz.

Ktoś może byłby ciekaw zawartości tej książki. Mogę jedynie powiedzieć, że tekst jest niezmiernie trudny do zrozumienia, nawet dla tego, kto nie jest zupełnym ignorantem w tych sprawach.

Na okładce można przeczytać, że książka ta jest zbiorem „innowacji i wspaniałych eksplikacji większości rozdziałów Miszny, zarówno na sposób kazuistyczny jak i prosty"; przygotowana została do druku przez syna Mosze Jakowa,

---

[1] *sztibel* — mały lokal, gdzie nabożni Żydzi studiują Księgi Święte (przyp. aut.).

rabina Dawida Scharfa, a opublikowało ją wydawnictwo Żupnik i spółka w Przemyślu w roku 1872.

Strona wewnętrzna okładki zawiera „imprimatur" i górnolotne słowa polecenia autorstwa wielkich rabinów Chaima Halbnersztama z Sącza i Józefa Natansona, rabina Lwowa i Galicji. Książka wydrukowana jest, jak to zwykle bywało z książkami tego rodzaju, kwadratowym pismem *Raszi*, oczywiście bez samogłosek ani interpunkcji. Jeżeli to jeszcze nie wystarczy, by uczynić z czytania próbę charakteru, niemal każda linijka zawiera jeden lub więcej znaków skrótów (*rashe tevot*), pojedynczych liter oznaczających słowa lub wyrażenia (kiedy np. widzę litery *lamed-kof*, oznaczające, że omawiana kwestia jest łatwa do rozwiązania — *lo kasze*, mam ochotę krzyczeć o zmiłowanie — to jest trudne! Bardzo trudne!).

Kiedy spróbujemy iść za argumentacją przedzierając się przez wiele kwalifikujących zdań podrzędnych, napotykamy na niezliczone odnośniki do fragmentów Pisma i Talmudu; co więcej, cała siła argumentacji wydaje się płynąć właśnie z tych rozproszonych cytatów. Sposób, w jaki te fragmenty stawały do dyspozycji autorów książek i w jaki były przez nich znajdywane, bez pomocy leksykonów czy konkordancji lub nawet zwykłego indeksu, przyprawia o zawrót głowy. Jakże nieskończenie łatwiej jest pracować współczesnym naukowcom, którzy chcąc odszukać dane słowo w tekście muszą jedynie wcisnąć klawisz „szukaj".

Pytanie, dlaczego rabini o tak zadziwiających umysłach i zdolnościach, przy których nasze własne wyglądają mniej niż miernie, poświęcali całe swoje życie studiowaniu kwestii, jakie przez tysiące lat nie miały żadnego związku z rzeczywistością, byłoby okazaniem niezrozumienia dla istoty takiego piśmiennictwa. Dla tych rabinów, ich uczniów i zwolenników bowiem zajmowanie się tymi problemami było po prostu (no, być może nie tak po prostu) formą oddawania czci Bogu, pracą wykonywaną dla miłości Boga. Jak można myśleć, że było coś lepszego, bardziej praktycznego do zrobienia?

Czy istnieje jakiś sposób odgadnięcia albo wytłumaczenia, jak taka książka odnalazła drogę z Przemyśla do British Library w Londynie? Trzeba wiedzieć kogo zapytać, a w tym przypadku było dla mnie zupełnie jasne, że jedyną osobą, która wie wszystko, co tylko można wiedzieć w tej dziedzinie, jest profesor Chimen Abramski, nie tylko czołowy badacz judaizmu, ale także niegdyś sprzedawca książek żydowskich. Rzeczywiście, okazało się, że słyszał o XIX-wiecznym wydawnictwie Żupnik z Przemyśla, który wtedy należał do państwa austro-węgierskiego. Żupnik, jak i inni wydawcy, a było ich wielu, rozpowszechniał swoje katalogi, czyli luźne arkusze drukarskie z książek, które drukował, wśród żydowskich księgarzy, gdzie tylko mógł ich znaleźć. Jednym z takich księgarzy, najbardziej znanym w Anglii, był Jakow Lifschitz, który, według Abramskiego, przez lata dostarczył do British Museum setki książek żydowskich. Jest niemal pewne, że to on zauważył *Darkei Jojscher* na liście

Żupnika, uznał książkę za wartą zakupu i przekonał dyrektora biblioteki do jej zamówienia — sam Mosze Jakow zapewne bardzo by się zdziwił...

To koniec tej historii, ale jeszcze nie całkowity. Według informacji z komputera bibliotecznego, książka została ponownie wydana w Baltimore w roku 1969 przez Y. Sh. Goettehera — wyznam szczerze, że cała ta wędrówka jest dla mnie zjawiskiem wręcz zdumiewającym.

Tłum. *Wł. Chłopicki*

„Judaism Today", Nr 2, 1995

Książkę tą, jak i inne nasze publikacje można nabyć lub zamówić
w Fundacji Judaica – Centrum Kultury Żydowskiej na Kazimierzu
w Krakowie, ul. Meiselsa 17, tel. (+48 12) 430 64 52, fax (+48 12) 430 64 97
e-mail: uwrussek@cyf-kr.edu.pl

This book and our other publications can be purchased or ordered
at the Judaica Foundation – Center for Jewish Culture in Kazimierz,
17, Meiselsa Street, tel. (+48 12) 430 64 52, fax (+48 12) 430 64 97
e-mail: uwrussek@cyf-kr.edu.pl